An Introduction to International Institutional Law

International organizations often have to compete with those very states that created them. This complicated relationship often leads to some uncertainty in the law relating to international organizations: the legal argument of an organization will often be counterpointed by an equally valid argument from a member state.

Professor Jan Klabbers is mindful of this complex relationship in his analysis of international institutional law. This second edition has been revised in the light of new developments and case-law. New sections are devoted to judicial review of Security Council acts and discussion of the ICJ's *Genocide* case (2007) and the *Behrami* judgment of the European Court of Human Rights (2007). Recent scholarly developments are also accommodated, such as the rise of constitutionalism and global administrative law, and the increased understanding that international organizations exercise public authority and therefore ought to be subject to some form of control.

Jan Klabbers is Professor of international organizations law at the University of Helsinki and Director of the Academy of Finland Centre of Excellence in Global Governance Research. He has served as visiting professor at Hofstra University (New York) in 2007 and at the Graduate Institute of International Studies and Development (Geneva) in 2008.

D1490003

An Introduction to International Institutional Law

Second edition

JAN KLABBERS

CAMBRIDGE UNIVERSITY PRESS

CAMBRIDGE UNIVERSITY PRESS

Cambridge, New York, Melbourne, Madrid, Cape Town, Singapore, São Paulo,
Delhi, Tokyo, Mexico City

Cambridge University Press
The Edinburgh Building, Cambridge CB2 8RU, UK

Published in the United States of America by Cambridge University Press, New York

www.cambridge.org
Information on this title: www.cambridge.org/9780521736169

© Jan Klabbers 2009

This publication is in copyright. Subject to statutory exception
and to the provisions of relevant collective licensing agreements,
no reproduction of any part may take place without
the written permission of Cambridge University Press.

First published 2002
Reprinted 2003, 2004, 2005, 2006, and 2007
Second edition 2009
5th printing 2011

Printed in the United Kingdom at the University Press, Cambridge

A catalogue record for this publication is available from the British Library

Library of Congress Cataloguing in Publication data
Klabbers, Jan.
An introduction to international institutional law / Jan Klabbers.
    p.   cm.
Includes bibliographical references and index.
ISBN 978-0-521-51620-4 (alk. paper)
1. International agencies.   I. Title.
KZ4850.K58   2009
341.2 – dc22   2009009340

ISBN 978-0-521-51620-4 Hardback
ISBN 978-0-521-73616-9 Paperback

Cambridge University Press has no responsibility for the persistence or
accuracy of URLs for external or third-party Internet websites referred to
in this publication, and does not guarantee that any content on such
websites is, or will remain, accurate or appropriate.

'You are my creator, but I am your master; obey!'
Mary Shelley

Contents

Colonization
Cold war
Bretton woods
vs

Legal personality

Preface to the First Edition

It was in the autumn of 1992, or perhaps the spring of 1993, when I received a phonecall from a former student of mine at the University of Amsterdam, now working for a solicitor's firm in London. After the usual expressions of surprise and politeness, he asked me what I knew about the responsibility of international organizations under international law.

The short answer was: nothing. Teaching international law in Amsterdam, one was not supposed to inquire into the law of international organizations beyond the merest basics (personality, the legal status of General Assembly resolutions, collective security, that sort of thing); after all, we had a separate department (or section, rather) to cover international institutional law.

The one thing I did remember from my student days was that the law of international organizations was taught to us as a seemingly endless enumeration of facts ('The Council of Europe was established in whenever'), numbers ('The European Parliament has umpteen members'), abbreviations ('IRO stands for whatever') and generally incomprehensible phrases ('Specialized agencies?' Specialized in what? Agencies of and for whom?').

Indeed, leafing through the textbooks I had to read as a student, it becomes clear that general legal issues relating to international organizations had no priority. One of our textbooks addressed such issues, but in the part that was not compulsory reading for our exams.[1] The other general textbook was more in the nature of a comparative review of internal provisions some organizations may have had in common, without emphasizing general legal issues.[2] In short, I had to tell my former student that on points of detail my knowledge displayed, er, a slight deficiency, but that I was sure the professor of international law at the London School of Economics at the time could be of more assistance to him.[3]

---

[1] This book was D. W. Bowett, *The Law of International Institutions* (4th edn, London, 1982). Recently, a new edition appeared: Philippe Sands and Pierre Klein, *Bowett's Law of International Institutions* (London, 2001). Unfortunately, I received it too late to be able to do much with it.

[2] This was the synoptic Dutch version of H. G. Schermers's famous *International Institutional Law*, condensed to some 300 pages under the title *Inleiding tot het internationale institutionele recht* (2nd edn, Alphen aan den Rijn, 1980).

[3] I did not know half how fortunate that suggestion was: Professor (now Judge) Rosalyn Higgins was at the time preparing a report for the Institut de Droit International on the very topic of the responsibility of international organizations and their member states.

Nonetheless, the episode got me thinking that there might be more to the law of international organizations than I had always been accustomed to, and when I started teaching EC law some years later (which involved, at the time, yet another department at the University of Amsterdam), I was forced to look a bit more closely into such notions as implied powers, *ultra vires*, legal personality, treaty-making by organizations, and judicial protection. So, when in 1996 I switched to the University of Helsinki and found out that there was no separate department for the law of international organizations, I readily volunteered to set up a course.

The one problem I encountered was that few of the textbooks available would address the issues I found to be important, with the exception of Amerasinghe's recent textbook.[4] Amerasinghe's excellent book, however, came with two drawbacks: not only was its retail price prohibitive, I also found myself often admiringly disagreeing, in particular when it came to the general outlook on international organizations.[5] While I could appreciate Amerasinghe's scholarship, I still felt that his textbook did not explain things in the way I would. And so, I figured, there was only one thing I could do, and that was to write my own textbook.

The famous (if controversial) philosopher Richard Rorty once wrote that education ought first to socialize people into the customs and ideas that make up the society they are a part of, after which at colleges and universities the happy few should be allowed and stimulated to question and debate all the things they have learned in the past: socialization first, followed by individualization.[6]

It is with both goals simultaneously in mind that the present book is written. All too often perhaps, textbooks and courses on the law of international organizations remain limited to socialization: introducing newcomers to the particular rites of international institutional lawyers. While that is a valuable goal in its own right (and indeed this book contains much socialization as well), my ultimate aims are to get people to think about the law of international organizations, and help the reader to understand how interesting it can be as long as one does not insist on approaching the topic as a mere gathering of numbers, dates, abbreviations and incomprehensible phrases. As my students have convinced me, it might actually be worth the effort of treating them not as mere receptacles for bits and pieces of information – useful only to impress tuition-fee-paying parents and for boosting their chances of victory at Trivial Pursuit – but as intelligent adults with critical faculties.

Admittedly, after reading this book, the reader may still not know how many seats the European Parliament has, or whether the IAEA is properly to be considered a Specialized agency, or in what year the Council of Europe

---

[4] C. F. Amerasinghe, *Principles of the Institutional Law of International Organizations* (Cambridge, 1996).

[5] I have set this out more broadly in a review of Amerasinghe's book (1997) 66 Nordic JIL, 553–55.

[6] Richard Rorty, 'Education as Socialization and as Individualization', reproduced in his *Philosophy and Social Hope* (London, 1999), 114–26.

was established, or what the name of the WTO's plenary body is. Instead, the reader will hopefully have come to an understanding of why seemingly simple legal questions (May organization X engage in activity Y? May state A become a member of organization B? May state F withhold its contribution from organization G?) usually seem to defy easy answers and become the stuff of politics.

Preface to the Second Edition

Authors of academic works don't usually get a second chance: once a book is published, it is published, and there is no opportunity left to make improvements. Unless, that is, when somehow a second edition seems opportune. Such a new edition seemed opportune in this case, for a lot has happened since the first edition was written. The EU has almost doubled in membership (from 15 to 27), it saw a Constitutional Treaty rejected by citizens in two of its member states, and a watered down version (the Lisbon Treaty) by the citizens of yet a third. The ECSC Treaty, moreover, died a natural death: it expired. NATO continued its activities out-of-area, which had started with the proverbial bang by bombing Belgrade. 9/11 happened, and arguably is the main factor behind the quasi-legislative role assumed by the UN Security Council and behind the willingness of the US to pay its membership contributions to the UN. But most of all, the discussion on the control of international organizations has really taken off. While the contours of that discussion have been visible since, say, the early 1990s, recent years have seen an explosion of activities somehow related to control: it is no coincidence that over the last couple of years many organizations have created the function of compliance officer, or have created or boosted organs dealing with issues of control and accountability. Organizations have, so to speak, become card-carrying members of 'the audit society'.

In Academia's ivory tower too, interesting things took place. Some important works were published (and one or two earlier ones belatedly discovered by me). Of greater structural importance, though, is that since 2004, international institutional lawyers have had their own forum: the *International Organizations Law Review* brings together practitioners and academics discussing the intricacies and relevance of institutional developments. As the footnotes to this edition testify, IOLR has already made a huge impact. The control discussion has in turn appeared in the form of dozens of studies on constitutionalism, judicial review, accountability and responsibility and the closely related phenomenon of global administrative law.

The structure of this edition has remained faithful to the first edition, as has the central argument that international institutional law owes much to the ambiguous relationship between the international organization and its member states. All chapters have been updated, incorporating new facts, new case-law, and new insights. Some chapters have been, to some degree, re-written and re-structured. This holds in particular for Chapter 8, on privileges and immunities, which contained a lengthy introduction that I was, in retrospect, not very happy with. Next, Chapter 10 on law-making has been improved in response to some observations in a published review of the first edition. The chapter on responsibility, Chapter 14, has been re-written so as to reflect predominantly the development of my own thinking on the topic, also due to having been exposed to the insights of political and moral theorists. In Chapter 7, on financing, I deleted most of the discussion on the US contribution, in light of the circumstance that the pre-9/11 financial crisis is not, at present, urgent. Some of the general points, of course, remain, and have been generalized. Finally, Chapter 16 has largely been re-written, precisely so as to reflect the discussion on control and accountability beyond the more specific confines of the responsibility discussion in Chapter 14.

Since the publication of the first edition, I have been teaching an entire course, or sizeable part of a course, on international institutional law, using my own book. This applies to Helsinki, of course, but also to Dresden. As a visiting professor at Hofstra Law School during the spring of 2007, exposure to a class of predominantly American students opened a few vistas that would otherwise have remained closed. In addition, I have taught parts of the course in Reykjavik, and conducted an advanced seminar on issues of control at the Graduate Institute of International Studies and Development. Many thanks to my hosts on those occasions: Sabine von Schorlemer, Jay Hickey, Thordis Ingadottir, and Andrea Bianchi. In addition, many, many thanks to James Fry, teaching assistant extraordinaire and an excellent scholar in his own right.

Over the years, the working atmosphere at the University of Helsinki within the Erik Castrén Institute of International Law and Human Rights and, since 2006, the interdisciplinary Centre of Excellence in Global Governance Research has proven to be challenging, stimulating and, quite simply, wonderful: many thanks to all those I work with on a daily basis. In addition, quite a few people have provided me with things to read, look into, or check up on. I have probably forgotten more of them than is socially acceptable, but those I remember having come with tangible suggestions include Niels Blokker, Armin von Bogdandy, Laurence Boisson de Chazournes, Richard Collins, Manfred Elsig, Toni Erskine, André de Hoogh, Antti Kivivuori, Riikka Koskenmäki, Pieter Jan Kuyper, Renato Matos, Anne Peters, Aleksandr Popov, Geir Ulfstein, Wouter Werner and Ramses Wessel. In addition, there has been close contact with the staff at the European Forest Institute and the Nordic Investment Bank, and conversations, debates and discussions with far too many people to mention. To all of them, my heartfelt thanks.

Finally, on the home front, I am hugely indebted to Marja-Leena and Johan for all the usual reasons and many more, and to the staff at CUP, especially Finola O'Sullivan and Sinéad Moloney, for their support, encouragement, and skilful handling of all sorts of problems.

Acknowledgements

A number of people have, directly or indirectly, contributed to this book. Much of what follows has benefited from discussions with Catherine Brölmann, Veijo Heiskanen, Martti Koskenniemi, Anja Lindroos, Inger Österdahl, Jarna Petman and Richard Wouters. Brief discussions with Martin Bjorklund, Balakrishnan Rajagopal and Chanaka Wickremasinghe helped convince me that the book might be of some interest.

Anja Lindroos and Jarna Petman have read and commented upon the entire manuscript, as have the anonymous referees for Cambridge University Press. Their comments have done much to improve the quality of the text.

I have also benefited enormously from being able to participate in an inter-disciplinary research project undertaken by the United Nations University, on the legitimacy of international organizations (directed by Veijo Heiskanen and Jean-Marc Coicaud: thanks, guys), in which some of the best minds of various disciplines participated. Without our free-flowing discussions at meetings in New York and Geneva, this book would have looked very different indeed.

My thanks go also to the organizations, both intergovernmental and non-governmental, that have over the years asked me to advise them on the law of international organizations. As is so often the case, the main benefit of acting as consultant accrues to the consultant: the insights gained from drafting a constituent document or an agreement on privileges and immunities, as well as from attending international meetings and being able to observe what goes on and how the process works, are invaluable.

As usual, however, the deepest professional gratitude is owed to my students, present and past, both in Helsinki and Amsterdam as well as (during a few visiting stints) in Addis Ababa. They have listened with patience, swallowed what they felt could be deemed plausible, and rejected some of the nonsense that made its way through to the classroom.

At home, thanks to Marja-Leena for her love, guidance, patience and support. Our son Johan feels he has an inherent power to monopolize his father's time and attention, and that any decision to the contrary is simply a decision *ultra vires*. He has a point, of course: it is difficult to imagine those concepts being put to better use.

Helsinki, June 2002

The publisher has used its best endeavours to ensure that the URLs for external websites referred to in this book are correct and active at the time of going to press. However, the publisher has no responsibility for the websites and can make no guarantee that a site will remain live or that the content is, or will remain, appropriate.

Table of cases

Permanent Court of International Justice

International Court of Justice

Court of Justice of the EC

Court of First Instance (EC)

Arbitration

Other international tribunals

Benelux Court of Justice

European Commission of Human Rights

Austria

Belgium

Canada

Denmark

Egypt

France

Madagascar

The Netherlands

Nigeria

Philippines

South Africa

Switzerland

United Kingdom

United States

A note on documentation

In writing this book, two compilations of source materials have proved immensely helpful. Many of the more current constitutional documents are brought together in Louis B. Sohn (ed.), *International Organisation and Integration: Student Edition* (Dordrecht, 1986); additional documents can be found in the tremendously useful eight-volume collection compiled by a number of Dutch scholars: P. J. G. Kapteyn *et al.* (eds.), *International Organization and Integration: Annotated Basic Documents and Descriptive Directory of International Organizations and Arrangements* (2nd rev. edn, The Hague, 1981–4).

More recent documents have sometimes been drawn from publications stemming from the relevant organization itself. Thus, the UN Charter has, since time immemorial, been published by the UN Department of Public Information in a small blue vest-pocket version. In a more updated version, many organizations have websites which invariably produce the organization's constituent document. The names of those sites generally follow the same pattern: the abbreviated name of the organization plus a dot and either the letters 'org' or 'int'. Thus, the Asian Development Bank can be found at www.adb.org; the OECD at www.oecd.org; the Council of Europe, at www.coe.int, and Interpol also has 'int' in its name: www.interpol.int. Sometimes there is a surprise, in that an abbreviation in a language other than English is chosen. Thus, the OAS can be found www.oea.org. A useful set of links to a number of organizations is maintained by the University of Bologna in Italy, at www.spfo.unibo.it/spolfo/INTORG.htm#oio.

For the text of the EC and EU treaties I have used the consolidated version published in (1998) 37 *ILM* 56, while more recent documents (the Treaty of Nice comes to mind) have been culled from the EU's official website, at europa.eu.int/eur-lex. Here one can also find decisions of the EC courts which have not been published in the European Court Reports just yet.

Finally, the UN maintains a number of important sites for information. One of these, very useful but, alas, accessible only at a fee, is the treaty collection, at untreaty.un.org/English/treaty.asp. When looking for Security Council and General Assembly materials, probably the quickest source nowadays is the UN's Documentation Service, at www.un.org/documents/ index.html.

My approach has been that constituent documents have not been repeatedly cited in footnotes, in light of their widespread and relatively easy availability. They can be found with the help of the few guidelines set out above. Other treaties have generally been listed with a place where they can be found.

Abbreviations

AD	*Annual Digest of Public International Law Cases*
AFDI	*Annuaire Français de Droit International*
AJIL	*American Journal of International Law*
AMF	Arab Monetary Fund
APEC	Asia Pacific Economic Co-operation Forum
ARIEL	*Austrian Review of International & European Law*
ASEAN	Association of South East Asian Nations
AU	African Union
Australian YIL	*Australian Yearbook of International Law*
BGBl	*Bundesgesetzblatt*
BIS	Bank for International Settlements
BISD	Basic Instruments and Selected Documents
BP	British Petroleum
Brooklyn JIL	*Brooklyn Journal of International Law*
BYIL	*British Yearbook of International Law*
Can YIL	*Canadian Yearbook of International Law*
CDE	*Cahiers de Droit Européen*
CFI	*Court of First Instance (of the EU)*
Chicago JIL	*Chicago Journal of International Law*
Chinese JIL	*Chinese Journal of International Law*
CMLRev	*Common Market Law Review*
Conn JIL	*Connecticut Journal of International Law*
COREPER	Comite des Représentants Permanents
Cornell ILJ	*Cornell International Law Journal*
CSCE	Conference on Security and Cooperation in Europe
CWC	Chemical Weapons Convention
EBRD	European Bank for Reconstruction and Development
EC	European Community
ECHR	European Convention on Human Rights
ECJ	European Court of Justice
ECOSOC	Economic and Social Council
ECOWAS	Economic Community of West African States
ECR	European Court Reports

ECSC	European Coal and Steel Community
ECtHR	European Court of Human Rights
EFI	European Forest Institute
EIB	European Investment Bank
EJIL	*European Journal of International Law*
ELR	*European Law Review*
EPO	European Patent Office
EU	European Union
FAO	Food and Agriculture Organization
FRG	Federal Republic of Germany
FYIL	*Finnish Yearbook of International Law*
GaJICL	*Georgia Journal of International & Comparative Law*
GATT	General Agreement on Tariffs and Trade
GDR	German Democratic Republic
GYIL	*German Yearbook of International Law*
Harvard ILJ	*Harvard International Law Journal*
IAEA	International Atomic Energy Agency
IATA	International Air Transport Association
IBRD	International Bank for Reconstruction and Development
ICAO	International Civil Aviation Organization
ICC	International Criminal Court
ICES	International Council for the Exploration of the Sea
ICJ	International Court of Justice
ICLQ	*International & Comparative Law Quarterly*
ICTY	International Criminal Tribunal for the former Yugoslavia
IDA	International Development Association
IFAD	International Fund for Agricultural Development
ILA	International Law Association
ILC	International Law Commission
ILDC	*International Law in Domestic Courts*
ILM	*International Legal Materials*
ILO	International Labour Organization
ILR	*International Law Reports*
IMCO	Intergovernmental Maritime Consultative Organization
IMF	International Monetary Fund
IMO	International Maritime Organization
IOLR	*International Organizations Law Review*
ITU	International Telecommunication Union
JCMS	*Journal of Common Market Studies*
JIEL	*Journal of International Economic Law*
JWT	*Journal of World Trade*
KEDO	Korean Peninsula Energy Development Organization
Leiden JIL	*Leiden Journal of International Law*
LIEI	*Legal Issues of European Integration*

Michigan JIL	*Michigan Journal of International Law*
NAFTA	North American Free Trade Area
NATO	North Atlantic Treaty Organization
NEAFC	North East Atlantic Fisheries Commission
Neth ILR	*Netherlands International Law Review*
Neth YIL	*Netherlands Yearbook of International Law*
NIB	Nordic Investment Bank
Nordic JIL	*Nordic Journal of International Law*
Nordisk TIR	*Nordisk Tidsskrift for International Ret*
OAPEC	Organization of Arab Petroleum Exporting Countries
OAS	Organization of American States
OAU	Organization of African Unity
OECD	Organization for Economic Co-operation and Development
OEEC	Organization for European Economic Co-operation
OJ	*Official Journal of the EC*
ONUC	Opération des Nations Unies au Congo
OPCW	Organization for the Prohibition of Chemical Weapons
OPEC	Organization of Petroleum Exporting Countries
OSCE	Organization for Security and Co-operation in Europe
ÖZöoR	*Österreichische Zeitschrift für öffentliches Recht*
ÖZöRV	*Österreichische Zeitschrift für öffentliches Recht und Völkerrecht*
PAU	Pan-American Union
PCIJ	Permanent Court of International Justice
PISA	Program on International Student Assessment
RBDI	*Revue Belge de Droit International*
RdC	*Recueil des Cours de l'Académie de Droit International*
RGDIP	*Revue Générale de Droit International Public*
RTDE	*Revue Trimestrielle de Droit Européen*
SWAPO	South West Africa People's Organization
TEC	Treaty establishing the European Community
TEU	Treaty on European Union
UN	United Nations
UNAT	United Nations Administrative Tribunal
UNCLOS	United Nations Convention on the Law of the Sea
UNCTAD	United Nations Conference on Trade and Development
UNDP	United Nations Development Programme
UNEF	United Nations Emergency Force
UNESCO	United Nations Educational, Scientific and Cultural Organization
UNHCR	United Nations High Commissioner for Refugees
UNICEF	United Nations Children's Fund
UNIDO	United Nations Industrial Development Organization

UNJY	*United Nations Juridical Yearbook*
UNMIK	United Nations Mission in Kosovo
UNRIAA	*United Nations Reports of International Arbitral Awards*
UNRRA	United Nations Relief and Rehabilitation Administration
UNRWA	United Nations Relief and Works Agency for Palestine Refugees in the Near East
UNWTO	World Tourism Organization
UPU	Universal Postal Union
VaJIL	*Virginia Journal of International Law*
Vanderbilt JTL	*Vanderbilt Journal of Transnational Law*
WEU	Western European Union
WHA	World Health Assembly
WHO	World Health Organization
WIPO	World Intellectual Property Organization
WMO	World Meteorological Organization
WTO	World Trade Organization
Yale JIL	*Yale Journal of International Law*
YbILC	*Yearbook of the International Law Commission*
YEL	*Yearbook of European Law*
ZaöRV	*Zeitschrift für ausländisches öffentliches Recht und Völkerrecht*
ZöR	*Zeitschrift für öffentliches Recht*

1

Introduction

Introduction

Whatever activity one wishes to engage in at the beginning of the twenty-first century, be it the sending of a postcard to a friend abroad or the purchase of a television set produced in a foreign country, it is more than likely that the activity is in one way or another regulated by the activities of an international governmental organization. Indeed, there are few, if any, activities these days which have an international element but which are not the subject of activities of at least one, and quite often more than one, international organization. International organizations have developed into a pervasive phenomenon, and according to most calculations, even outnumber states.[1]

Wherever human activity is organized, there will be rules of law, as expressed in the ancient adage *ubi societas, ibi jus*. Social organization without rules is, quite literally, unthinkable. Hence, the activities of international organizations are also subject to law, and give rise to law. Each and every international organization has a set of rules relating to its own functioning, however rudimentary such a set of rules may be. Moreover, as international organizations do not exist in a vacuum, their activities are also bound to exercise some influence on other legal systems, and absorb the influence of such systems. While it is by no means impossible for international organizations to be influenced by, and exert influence on, the law of individual nation-states (the law of the European Community is an excellent example), the more direct and influential links usually exist within the body of rules known as international law. Not surprisingly, therefore, international lawyers have attempted to describe and analyse these links and the resulting rules and legal concepts which make them possible to begin with.

---

[1] Brownlie's estimate of 170 organizations appears somewhat conservative. See Ian Brownlie, *Principles of Public International Law* (4th edn, Oxford, 1990), p. 680. Others, such as Peter Bekker, mention a figure of some 350. See his *The Legal Position of Intergovernmental Organizations: A Functional Necessity Analysis of their Legal Status and Immunities* (Dordrecht, 1994), p. 4. Possibly speaking from the top of his head, Jeremy Carver went so far as to suggest the figure of 7,000. See his intervention at the Taipei meeting of the International Law Association's Committee on Accountability of International Organisations, in ILA, *Report of the Sixty-eighth Conference* (London, 1998), p. 614.

This book will try to provide a comprehensive introduction to the law of international organizations, and aims to do so by concentrating on general legal issues. Thus, there will be little discussion of individual organizations, and fairly little presentation of decontextualized facts. Instead, the aim is to discuss legal problems relating to the creation, the functioning and the termination of international organizations.[2]

An introductory textbook on institutional law

The very fact that this textbook is intended to be introductory has several implications. The most obvious one will be a lack of detail, but existing works, such as the encyclopedic volume by Schermers and Blokker, offer more than adequate compensation.[3] In addition, there are numerous specialized works on various individual international organizations. In recent years, the United Nations has been the subject of various rich and detailed studies,[4] as have numerous other organizations.

This is a textbook about the law of international organizations, and that almost by definition entails that its focus will rest upon institutional law rather than on substantive law. After all, the most likely area for general rules and principles to develop is where international organizations have things in common. Generally speaking, they will have things in common when it comes to the way they are organized, rather than with respect to their substantive rules.[5]

Moreover, it would be absolutely impractical to devote attention to the substantive law of any organization, let alone the various substantive laws of a host of organizations. Indeed, with respect to some organizations, writers already divide their works into substantive and institutional studies.[6] Having said that, though, it should be pointed out that there is no firm line dividing the institutional from the substantive; references to substantive legal rules (legal philosopher H. L. A. Hart would speak of primary rules[7]) will be in abundance, but

---

[2] In its organization, this book owes much to C. F. Amerasinghe, *Principles of the Institutional Law of International Organizations* (Cambridge, 1996).

[3] H. G. Schermers and Niels Blokker, *International Institutional Law* (4th edn, The Hague, 2003).

[4] See, e.g., Bengt Broms, *United Nations* (Helsinki, 1990), or Benedetto Conforti, *The Law and Practice of the United Nations* (The Hague, 1997). Most insightful, without being 'legalistic', is Thomas M. Franck, *Nation Against Nation: What Happened to the UN Dream and What the US Can Do About It* (Oxford, 1985).

[5] Although here, too, comparative work may be beneficial. One can readily think of studies comparing the debate on free trade and environmental concerns in a multitude of organizations, such as the EU, the WTO, the OECD and the less well-known International Tropical Timber Organization.

[6] Thus, T. C. Hartley's *The Foundations of European Community Law* (3rd edn, Oxford, 1994) discusses mainly the EC's institutional and administrative law, whereas Derrick Wyatt and Alan Dashwood, without ignoring institutional matters, have their focus largely on substantive Community law: *The Substantive Law of the EEC* (3rd edn, London, 1993). Likewise, a first study of the institutional aspects of the WTO is Mary E. Footer, *An Institutional and Normative Analysis of the World Trade Organization* (Leiden, 2006).

[7] H. L. A. Hart, *The Concept of Law* (Oxford, 1961).

not as a goal in themselves. Rather, they will serve to explain and elucidate institutional issues.

Although meant as a textbook for university students, practitioners too may find this work of value, predominantly perhaps as a guide to understanding the often ambiguous legal precepts and in helping them to find further references.

For (it should scarcely warrant separate mention), a textbook's introductory character does not mean that further references and adequate footnoting can be dispensed with. Rather the opposite holds true: a proper introduction not only familiarizes the reader with the more important legal principles at stake, but also makes clear that few, if any, legal rules and principles are carved in stone. They are derived from precedent and research, so it stands to reason that precedent and research are referred to. Indeed, especially where a more or less critical mode of analysis is thought to be of great educational value, as in this book, any slackening of the requirements of reference would expose intellectual dishonesty.

Critical legal theory

As far as matters of theory go, the law of international organizations is still somewhat immature. We lack a convincing theory on the international legal personality of international organizations, to name just one thing. Moreover, if an international organization fails to meet its legal obligations, we are not at all sure as to whether and in what circumstances it can be held responsible, let alone whether its member states incur some responsibility as well. Furthermore, we are quick to point to the possibility that legal powers, while not explicitly granted to a given organization, may nonetheless be implied, but we are less certain as to the basis of such implied powers. In short, on numerous points, the law lacks certainty, and to the extent that certainty is apparent, it is usually the relatively indeterminate sort of certainty that 'problems are best solved by negotiations', or that 'an equitable solution is called for'.

Such problems stem, ultimately, from the lack of a convincing theoretical framework regarding international organizations,[8] and it is surprising to note that, while international organizations have been with us for roughly a century and a half, few attempts have been made at theorizing.[9] In particular, international legal doctrine has a hard time coming to terms with the

---

[8] See generally also Jan Klabbers, 'The Changing Image of International Organizations'. In Jean-Marc Coicaud and Veijo Heiskanen (eds.), *The Legitimacy of International Organizations* (Tokyo, 2001), pp. 221–55.

[9] An early example is A. Rapisardi-Mirabelli, 'Théorie générale des unions internationales' (1925/II) 7 *RdC*, 345–93. Amongst more recent attempts, see in particular David Kennedy, 'The Move to Institutions' (1987) 8 *Cardozo Law Review*, 841–988, and Deirdre Curtin and Ige F. Dekker, 'The EU as a "Layered" International Organization: Institutional Unity in Disguise'. In Paul Craig and Gráinne de Búrca (eds.), *The Evolution of EU Law* (Oxford, 1999), pp. 83–136.

relationship between an international organization and the very states which are its members.

While the optimist may hold that such uncertainties may decrease over time, as science progresses, recent theoretical work in the field of law generally, and international law in particular, suggests that such optimism may well be misguided. One of the core propositions of the critical legal studies movement is, rather, that law is doomed to go back and forth between two extremes. On the one hand (if we limit ourselves to international law), the law is supposed to respect the interests of individual states. As any introductory textbook on international law will make clear, international law is largely based on the consent of states; and they have given this consent as free and individual sovereign entities. Thus, the law must cater to their demands, or it runs the risk of losing the respect of precisely those whose behaviour it is supposed to regulate.

Yet, at the same time, the law must also take the interests of the international community into account, in two distinct but related ways. First, as those individual states are not isolated, but are in constant touch with one another, it may well be that the sovereign activities of one interfere with the sovereign prerogatives of the other. Perhaps the classic example is that of pollution caused in one state which wanders across the border into the other.[10] To a large extent, problems of extraterritorial jurisdiction have the same origin: a clash of sovereigns.

Secondly, and it is here in particular that international organizations come in, some interests override those of individual states. While arguably two states can agree on mutually limiting their respective industrial activities with an eye to each other's environment, such an agreement only acquires meaning if it is embedded in a wider normative framework. Put more simply, such an agreement will be deemed to bind both states by virtue of general international law. And to make matters a lot more concrete, it is easy to conceive of both their activities contributing to environmental degradation, while realizing that the consequences of such degradation will not remain limited to the two states of the example.

The two extremes sketched above have been the two poles that have dominated theories about (and of) international law such as they have developed, and it has long been a frustration that if a theory managed to explain a lot about sovereignty, it could not cope with considerations of community; and where it could cope with community, it was invariably at the expense of considerations of sovereignty.[11]

---

[10] Compare the classic *Trail Smelter* arbitration between the US and Canada, awards of 16 April 1938 and 11 March 1941, partly reproduced in 9 AD 315 and fully reported in III UNRIAA 1905.

[11] The very existence of such tension was explicitly noted in one of the seminal texts on the law of international organizations, Michel Virally's 'La notion de fonction dans la théorie de l'organisation internationale'. In Suzanne Bastid *et al.*, *Mélanges offerts à Charles Rousseau: La communauté internationale* (Paris, 1974), pp. 277–300, esp. p. 296.

It is the great merit of critical legal studies to have claimed that this tension between those two poles is, really, unsolvable, at least given our normative apparatus which does not allow us to make normative choices. Under the paradigm of liberalism, it is impossible to give priority to some values over other values. Indeed, the 'liberal' value *par excellence*, tolerance, is itself eminently empty. She who is tolerant of others is she who refuses to make normative choices.

Unavoidably, this affects international law. Following the critical legal tradition, international law is bound to swerve back and forth between the two poles of sovereignty and community, and never the twain shall meet. It is this tension which makes international legal rules often (if not always) ultimately uncertain, and it is this tension that will function as the red thread running through this book.

For, if the critical problem affects international law, and indeed affects other legal systems as well (the notion was first developed by American lawyers, with reference to US law[13]), it will also affect the law of international organizations. Indeed, above, I already mentioned, amongst other things, the tension between the implied powers doctrine on the one hand, and the principle that organizations and their organs can only act on the basis of powers conferred upon them (the so-called principle of attribution of powers, or principle of speciality) on the other hand. This tension can be seen as the tension between sovereignty and community in a different guise. Strict adherents to the notion of state sovereignty will not easily admit the existence of an implied power;[14] yet for the protection of community interests, an implied power may well be deemed desirable. Thus, the tension between the two strands of thinking is visible in some of the more general and central notions of the law of international organizations.

It is the great merit of critical legal studies to have illuminated the unsolvable nature of the tension between thinking in terms of state sovereignty and thinking in terms of the community interest. That is not to say, however, that the effects of the tension cannot be mitigated: they often can.[15] Critical legal studies is, after all is said and done, interested primarily in stating absolutes, and the way to do so is by juxtaposing extremes.[16] In practice, however, there may be some decent breathing room between the two extremes.

---

[12] Classic works are David Kennedy, *International Legal Structures* (Baden Baden, 1987) and Martti Koskenniemi, *From Apology to Utopia: The Structure of International Legal Argument* (Helsinki, 1989).

[13] See, e.g., Roberto Mangabeira Unger, *The Critical Legal Studies Movement* (Cambridge, MA, 1986).

[14] In a telling choice of words, implied powers have even been regarded as fundamental violations of national sovereignty. See Moshe Kaniel, *The Exclusive Treaty-making Power of the European Community up to the Period of the Single European Act* (The Hague, 1996), p. 101.

[15] Compare also Jan Klabbers, *The Concept of Treaty in International Law* (The Hague, 1996).

[16] This is why some authors are dismissive of critical legal studies, positing that the movement is too extreme. See, e.g., Andrew Altman, *Critical Legal Studies: A Liberal Critique* (Princeton,

Put differently, there is sufficient reason to believe that while critical theory may be right in the abstract, in everyday life the fact that no right answer is available does not immediately make legal analysis meaningless. Often, there is room for some form of compromise; often, there is room to discover some principle of more or less general application. Still, that takes nothing away from the usefulness of the critical method. Indeed, in contrast to more traditional approaches, it does not lure the reader into thinking that the law has any certainties to offer.[17]

Thus, the red thread running through this book will be a critical analysis of the law of international organizations, in order to show the problems involved in that area of international law. Nonetheless, that is where the theoretical focus will stop. My aim is not to provide a critical deconstruction of the law of international organizations;[18] rather, it is to provide an introductory look at international organizations from a critical perspective. Precisely because the main benefit of critical legal theory is its capacity to make visible the inherent tensions and contradictions which help shape the law, it can provide great services to an introductory textbook.[19]

Trying to define international organizations

Perhaps the most difficult question to answer is the one which is, in some ways, a preliminary question: what exactly is an international organization? What is that creature which will be central to this book? The short answer is, quite simply, that we do not know. We may, in most cases,[20] be able to recognize an international organization when we see one, but it has so far appeared impossible to actually define such organizations in a comprehensive way.[21]

What is only rarely realized is that it is indeed structurally impossible to define, in a comprehensive manner, something which is a social creation to begin with. International organizations are not creatures of nature, which lead a relatively intransmutable existence, so that all possible variations can be captured within

---

1990). The same argument (in nutshell version) can be found in Ronald Dworkin, *Law's Empire* (London, 1986), pp. 271–5.

[17] Incidentally, this type of analysis is not limited to critical lawyers only. See, e.g., the way in which Franck uses the notion of fairness as a means to reconcile the tensions noted above: Thomas M. Franck, *Fairness in International Law and Institutions* (Oxford, 1995), esp. Chapter 1.

[18] With respect to EC law, such an exercise has been undertaken by Ian Ward, *The Margins of European Law* (London, 1996).

[19] See, in a similar vein, Veijo Heiskanen, *International Legal Topics* (Helsinki, 1992).

[20] There have been some doubts recently about, e.g., the European Union and the OSCE; more traditionally, GATT's status as an international organization has been debated, which has led some scholars to the question-begging conclusion that if it was not a *de jure* organization, it was at least a *de facto* organization.

[21] Compare generally also Abdullah El-Erian, 'Preliminary Report on the Second Part of the Topic of Relations between States and International Organizations' (1977/II, pt 1), YbILC 139–55.

a single definition. Instead, they are social constructs,[22] created by people in order, presumably, to help them achieve some purpose, whatever that purpose may be.

It is important to realize, indeed, that international actors do not purposely set out to create an international organization following some eternally valid blueprint. Instead, their aim will be to create an entity that allows them to meet their ends, endow those entities with some of the characteristics they think those entities might need (certain organs, certain powers), and then hope that their creation can do what they set it up to do. They do not meet and decide to create, say, a 'functional open organization'. That may well be what their creation will eventually look like, but it will normally not be their intention. Labels such as 'functional open organization' are labels conceived by scholars, for the sole purpose of classifying organizations, in the hope that classification will contribute to our understanding. As far as the international actors themselves are concerned, they are probably not overly interested in such issues.

That said, it is common in the literature to delimit international organizations in at least some ways. One delimitation often made depends on the nature of the body of law governing the activities of the organization. If those activities are governed by international law, we speak of an international organization proper, or at least of an intergovernmental organization. If those activities are, however, governed by some domestic law, we usually say that the organization in question is a non-governmental organization; examples include such entities as Greenpeace or Amnesty International. While the activities of such entities may be international in character, and they may even have been given some tasks under international law,[23] they do not meet the usual understanding of what constitutes an international organization.

For the international lawyer, it goes without saying that the activities of those organizations that are subject to international law will be of most interest. Usually, those organizations will have a number of characteristics in common although, in conformity with the fact that their founding fathers are relatively free to establish whatever they wish, those characteristics are not more than characteristics. The fact that they do not always hold true does not, as such, deny their value in general.

...created between states...

One of those characteristics is that international organizations are usually created between states,[24] or rather, as states themselves are abstractions, by duly

---

[22] In much the same way as notions such as state sovereignty are socially construed. Compare, e.g., Thomas J. Biersteker and Cynthia Weber (eds.), *State Sovereignty as Social Construct* (Cambridge, 1996). For a very lucid philosophical account, see John R. Searle, *The Construction of Social Reality* (London, 1995).

[23] Compare, e.g., the role of the Red Cross under the 1949 Geneva Conventions.

[24] This implies a minimum of two; an example of such a small organization is the Office Franco-Allemand pour la Jeunesse, defendant in *Klarsfeld* v. *Office Franco-Allemand pour la*

authorized representatives of states.[25] This, however, does not tell the whole story. For one thing, there are international organizations which are themselves members of other international organizations – sometimes even founding members. For instance, the EC is a member of the FAO, and a founding member of the WTO. Still, we do not exclude the WTO and the FAO from the scope of international organizations simply because they count another organization among their members. Generally, then, it is not a hard and fast rule that international organizations can only be created by states.[26]

Secondly, not all creatures created by states are generally considered to be international organizations.[27] For example, states may establish a legal person under some domestic legal systems. Perhaps an example is the Basle-Mulhouse airport authority, a joint venture, if you will, between France and Switzerland and governed by French law.[28] On the other hand, an arbitral tribunal found in 2002 that the Basle-based Bank for International Settlements (BIS), established by states but partly governed by Swiss law and having private shareholders, qualified as an international organization.[29]

Moreover, sometimes treaties are to be implemented with the help of one or more organs. For instance, the European Court of Human Rights

---

Jeunesse before the Paris Court of Appeal, 18 June 1968. See 72 *ILR* 191. The Inter-American Tropical Tuna Commission, currently counting sixteen member states, started with two in 1950: the United States and Costa Rica. Still, the EC withdrew from the Convention on Fishing and Conservation of the Living Resources in the Baltic Sea and Belts after most other parties had denounced it following their accession to the EU. This would have left the organization based on the Convention with only Russia and the EC as members, something the EC held to be 'disproportionate and inefficient'. See Council Decision 2004/890/EC.

[25] As the Permanent Court of International Justice already held in 1923, states can only act by and through their agents: *Certain questions relating to settlers of German origin in the territory ceded by Germany to Poland*, advisory opinion, [1923] Publ. PCIJ, Series B, no. 6, at 22. Which agents (of which agencies) are concerned is a different matter altogether. In 1962, Lord Strang could observe, somewhat awestruck, that, within the British government, some twenty departments bore responsibility for maintaining relations with international organizations. See Lord Strang, *The Diplomatic Career* (London, 1962), p. 107.

[26] There is at least one international organization which is created exclusively by other organizations: the Joint Vienna Institute (essentially established in 1994 to help eastern European states in their transition to market-based economies, text in (1994) 33 *ILM* 1505). This was the creation of the BIS, EBRD, IBRD, IMF and OECD. A curious example of a different nature (an organization created not so much by, as in order to aid, a different organization) is the Advisory Centre on WTO Law, which aims to assist developing nations in their dealings with the WTO. For a brief overview, see Claudia Orozco, 'The WTO Solution: The Advisory Centre on WTO Law' (2001) 4 *Journal of World Intellectual Property*, 245–9.

[27] Conversely, sometimes non-governmental organizations may be regarded as intergovernmental for some purposes. See, with respect to IATA, the Swiss Federal Tribunal's decision in *Jenni and others* v. *Conseil d'Etat of the Canton of Geneva*, 4 October 1978, in 75 *ILR* 99.

[28] On such creatures generally see the several volume work by H. T. Adam, *Les organismes internationaux spécialisés* (Paris). See also Ignaz Seidl-Hohenveldern, *Corporations in and under International Law* (Cambridge, 1987).

[29] See *Reineccius and others* v. *Bank for International Settlements*, partial award of 22 November 2002, Permanent Court of Arbitration, paras. 104–18. For discussion, see David J. Bederman, 'The Unique Legal Status of the Bank for International Settlements Comes into Focus' (2003) 16 *Leiden JIL*, 787–94.

is entrusted with supervising the implementation of the European Convention on Human Rights. Yet, the Court is not considered to be an international organization in its own right; it is, instead, often referred to as a treaty organ.

In what exactly the distinction between an organization and a treaty organ resides is unclear, and perhaps it may be argued that its importance is diminishing at any rate: scholars writing in the field of, for example, environmental law, have more or less started to unite the two forms of co-operation, and use the rather more generic term of 'international institutions' – encompassing both treaty organs and international organizations.[30] Others have pointed out that treaty organs endowed with decision-making powers may well be international organizations in disguise.[31] In political science literature, reference is often made to 'international regimes'[32] or, again, 'institutions'.[33]

. . . on the basis of a treaty . . .

A second characteristic that many (but again, not all) organizations have in common is that they are established by means of a treaty. Their creation was not brought about by some legal act under some domestic legal system, but was done in the form of a treaty, which international law in general terms defines as a written agreement, governed by international law.[34] And as the treaty will be governed by international law, so too will the organization.

Not all organizations derive directly from a treaty, though. Some have been created not by treaty, but by the legal act of an already existing organization. The United Nations General Assembly, for instance, has created several organizations by resolution: the United Nations Industrial Development Organization

---

[30] See, e.g., Alan E. Boyle, 'Saving the World? Implementation and Enforcement of International Environmental Law through International Institutions' (1991) 3 *Journal of Environmental Law*, 229–45. See also Robin R. Churchill and Geir Ulfstein, 'Autonomous Institutional Arrangements in Multilateral Environmental Agreements: A Little-Noticed Phenomenon in International Law' (2000), 94 *AJIL*, 623–59.

[31] See, e.g., Deirdre Curtin, 'EU Police Cooperation and Human Rights Protection: Building the Trellis and Training the Vine'. In Ami Barav *et al.*, *Scritti in onore di Giuseppe Federico Mancini, Volume II* (Milan, 1998), pp. 227–56. Curtin refers to such bodies as 'unidentified international organizations'.

[32] See, e.g., Stephen D. Krasner (ed.), *International Regimes* (Ithaca, 1983).

[33] See Daniel Wincott, 'Political Theory, Law and European Union'. In Jo Shaw and Gillian More (eds.), *New Legal Dynamics of European Union* (Oxford, 1995), pp. 293–311. Note also that some recent creations self-consciously style themselves not as organizations, but rather as informal groups or networks, despite having all the characteristics of organizations. Examples include the International Network for Bamboo and Rattan (INBAR) and the International Jute Study Group. For an intelligent exploration of the concept of network, see Annelise Riles, *The Network Inside Out* (Ann Arbor, 2000).

[34] Thus Article 2(1)(a) of the 1969 Vienna Convention on the Law of Treaties. See generally Klabbers, *Concept of Treaty*.

(UNIDO)[35] and the United Nations Children's Fund (UNICEF) come to mind, as do various institutions set up by the Nordic Council, including financial institutions such as the Nordic Investment Bank.[36] Indeed, the Nordic Council itself originated as a form of co-operation between the parliaments of the five states concerned (Denmark, Finland, Iceland, Norway and Sweden), rather than being clearly treaty-based.[37] The importance of this characteristic, then, is above all to indicate that the creation of an international organization is an intentional act. Organizations rest upon conscious decisions of the states involved; they do not come out of the blue, and are not created by accident.

That said, a discernible tendency is to remain nebulous about intentions when creating international institutions. Organizations such as the Organization for Security and Co-operation in Europe (OSCE),[38] Asia-Pacific Economic Co-operation (APEC),[39] the Arctic Council[40] and the Wassenaar Arrangement[41] have been established, but it remains unclear whether they are all to be regarded as full-blown organizations rather than, say, frameworks for occasional diplomacy, and even whether their constituent agreements constitute treaties or not. The legal status and structure of the European Union has, likewise, been subject to debate,[42] and the G–7 (or G–8; the confusion is telling in itself) defies any attempt at definition and classification.[43]

Nonetheless, despite informal ambitions, typically some degree of formalization will take place. A good example is the Council of Baltic Sea States,

[35] UNIDO was first set up as an organ of the General Assembly and was supposed to function as an 'autonomous organization' within the UN. Only later did it become a separate organization. See Schermers and Blokker, *International Institutional Law*, p. 30.

[36] On the NIB, see Siv Hellén, 'The Establishment and Development of the Nordic Investment Bank – An Institution Sui Generis'. In Sabine Schlemmer-Schulte and Ko-Yung Tung (eds.), *Liber Amicorum Ibrahim F.I. Shihata* (The Hague, 2001), pp. 401–27. Another example is the creation, in 1955, of the European Civil Aviation Conference (ECAC) by ICAO at the behest of the Council of Europe. For more details, see www.ecac-ceac.org/uk (visited 18 December 2001).

[37] See generally Frantz Wendt, *The Nordic Council and Co-operation in Scandinavia* (Copenhagen, 1959).

[38] See David Galbreath, *The Organization for Security and Cooperation in Europe* (London, 2007); Christine Bertrand, 'La nature juridique de l'Organisation pour la Sécurité et de la Coopération en Europe (OSCE)' (1998) 98 *RGDIP* 365–406; Ignaz Seidl-Hohenveldern, 'Internationale Organisationen aufgrund von soft law'. In Ulrich Beyerlin *et al.* (eds.), *Recht zwischen Umbruch und Bewahrung: Festschrift für Rudolf Bernhardt* (Berlin, 1995), pp. 229–39. The Paris Club, an informal but highly influential grouping of creditor countries, views itself as a 'non-institution', according to its website. See www.clubdeparis.org (last visited 14 May 2008).

[39] See Melissa Castan, 'APEC: International Institution? A Pacific Solution' (1996) 15 *University of Tasmania Law Review*, 52–76.

[40] See generally Timo Koivurova, 'The Legal Status of Arctic Cooperation'. In Lassi Heininen and Gunnar Lassinantti (eds.), *Security in the European North: From 'Hard' to 'Soft'* (Rovaniemi, 1999), pp. 143–60.

[41] See Christoph Hoelscher and Hans-Michael Wolffgang, 'The Wassenaar-Arrangement Between International Trade, Non-proliferation, and Export Controls' (1998/I) 32 *JWT*, 45–63.

[42] See, e.g., Deirdre Curtin, 'The Constitutional Structure of the Union: A Europe of Bits and Pieces' (1993) 30 *CMLRev*, 17–69.

[43] See generally Jan Klabbers, 'Institutional Ambivalence by Design: Soft Organizations in International Law' (2001) 70 *Nordic JIL*, 403–21.

which started as a loose framework in 1992 but felt the need, having operated for a few years, to establish a permanent secretariat (in 1998) and also now speaks of its participants as 'member states', suggesting a degree of formalization not usually associated with informal co-operation. Likewise, the Black Sea Economic Co-operation, also created as a loose framework in 1992, became a formal organization in 1999. The Shanghai Co-operation Organization grew out of a series of regular conferences between central Asian states, and turned formal in 2001.[44] And after CSCE had become OSCE, the organization started to wonder about privileges and immunities and other things usually associated with formal 'organizationhood'.[45]

... an organ with a distinct will ... *noted*

In order to distinguish the international organization from other forms of international co-operation, another often-mentioned characteristic holds that the organization must possess at least one organ which has a will distinct from the will of its member states. Where the collectivity merely expresses the aggregate opinion of its members, giving it the legal form of an international organization would, in the extreme, be a useless act. One might as well have appointed a spokesperson.[46]

Important though the characteristic of a 'distinct will' is, it is also the most difficult in terms of both practice and theory. As several authorities have noted, in practice not all organizations usually referred to as international organizations possess this characteristic.[47] In theoretical terms, the characteristic of the distinct will goes to the heart of the entire concept of international organization: the problematic relationship between the organization and its member states.

In one way, the international organization is little more than the tool in the hands of the member states, and viewed from this perspective, the distinct will of the organization is little more than a legal fiction.[48] Yet, the international organization, in order to justify its *raison d'être* and its somewhat special status in international law, must insist on having such a distinct will. Otherwise, it becomes indistinguishable from other forms of co-operation, and, if so, it will become extremely difficult to justify why, for example, the constituent treaties of

---

[44] See Mutlaq Al-Qahtani, 'The Shanghai Cooperation Organization and the Law of International Organizations' (2006) 5 *Chinese JIL*, 129–47.

[45] See OSCE Permanent Council Decision 383 of 26 November 2000.

[46] Nonetheless, the position that organizations are little more than standing international conferences comes close. For an example, see G. R. Berridge, *Diplomacy: Theory and Practice* (London, 1995). Similarly state-centric is Gaetano Arangio-Ruiz, 'The "Federal Analogy" and UN Charter Interpretation: A Crucial Issue', (1997) 8 *EJIL*, 1–28.

[47] Compare Schermers and Blokker, *International Institutional Law*, p. 34. For further theoretical elaboration, see Jan Klabbers, 'Two Concepts of International Organization', (2005) 2 *IOLR*, 277–93.

[48] Compare Reinhold Reutersward, 'The Legal Nature of International Organizations' (1980) 49 *Nordisk TIR*, 14–30.

organizations warrant teleological interpretation, as is so often claimed, or why such constituent treaties appear to possess far greater possibilities for deriving implied clauses (in the form of implied powers) from them than regular treaties are said to do.

These are problems that will be dealt with properly later on, and which might ultimately defy any easy solution. For the moment, it is important to realize that the '*volonté distincte*' of international organizations is often mentioned as their quintessential characteristic, but is itself not an unproblematic concept.

The layout of this book

It is slightly problematic to find a decent way of structuring a study which is not limited to a single legal system. When studying a single legal system, one can always ask oneself what that system's sources are, what its subjects are, what its rules say, and how it copes with disputes; with a book such as this, however, which is comparing various legal subsystems and placing them within the larger framework of international law, those questions offer but limited guidance.

Therefore, it is perhaps wiser simply to apply a more or less chronological method. Follow international organizations from their creation through to their possible demise, and deal with a variety of questions that may arise along the way. It is this idea (borrowed from Amerasinghe) that guides the succession of chapters in this book, although the reader should realize that the idea itself is an abstraction, which does not necessarily do full and complete justice to real life.

Thus, I will discuss the creation of international organizations as legal entities, examine the links between the law of international organizations and the general rules of international law (in particular the law of treaties), discuss issues of membership and financing, outline the legal rules relating to privileges and immunities, discuss the adoption of legal acts by the organization as well as what to do when those legal acts may give rise to doubts, debate the external activities of international organizations and issues of responsibility under international law. I will conclude by examining the possible dissolution of international organizations.

I will not, however, engage in comparative research or description: such has been done brilliantly by Schermers and Blokker, and it is not my ambition to try and improve on their seminal work. Instead, my aim is to study the general problems organizations have in common, and the range of possible solutions, and to analyze why so few of the solutions can be offered with any great amount of confidence or certainty.

In doing so, two international organizations will often be singled out for illustrative purposes: the United Nations, and the European Community. The reason for choosing the United Nations will be obvious: it is the single most important existing international organization, aiming to provide peace and security for the whole of mankind. Moreover, and a bit more to the point, in many respects the activities of the UN have served, and continue to serve, as models for other organizations. To name but one example: the privileges and immunities of many international organizations are modelled upon those of the UN.

The choice of the European Communities requires perhaps some explanation, especially in light of the fact that many writers think that the EC is so unique that it warrants separate treatment: what may hold good for international organizations, generally, may not hold good for the EC.[49] Yet, precisely because of its unique features, the EC may serve as a blueprint or a source of inspiration for possible future developments. For, if the phenomenon of international organization is to develop, it is not unlikely that future organizations will to some extent take the EC as a model and, perhaps, learn from its mistakes. Moreover, while acknowledging that the EC is an organization *sui generis* that in many respects cannot be compared to other organizations, it is, nevertheless, still an international organization,[50] at least to the international lawyer.[51]

A book such as the present one cannot just plunge into the thick of things. Before actually starting, some points of a more general nature must be made. These include a short historical survey of the rise of organizations generally, but also some considerations of a more theoretical nature. After all, although we may often forget it, in a world which has often been characterized by the fighting of all against all, and with two world wars still part of recent history, the very existence of international organizations, and their apparent success, demands an explanation.

Moreover, not just the very existence and success of international organizations has been subjected to various explanations, but so too has the operation of international law in respect of international organizations. In other words: why does the law say what it says? Are there explanations for the particular contents of rules of law, and, if so, are such explanations convincing? In a general sense, these questions underlie much of this book, rendering it what one might call (if somewhat tongue in cheek perhaps) a textbook with attitude. The next chapter, however, will look at such questions from a somewhat wider perspective: focusing on general questions and explanations rather than specific ones.

---

[49] Thus, Amerasinghe, *Principles*, is practically silent on the EC, as is a monograph such as Tetsuo Sato, *Evolving Constitutions of International Organizations* (The Hague, 1996).

[50] And arguably losing some of its *sui generis* qualities and therewith becoming more like a 'regular' organization. See briefly Jan Klabbers, 'On Babies, Bathwater, and the Three Musketeers, or the Beginning of the End of European Integration'. In Veijo Heiskanen and Kati Kulovesi (eds.), *Function and Future of European Law* (Helsinki, 1999), pp. 275–81.

[51] It is one of the brilliant curiosities of the EC that we can all project our own professional identities onto it. Many constitutional lawyers are wont to see the EC as a sort of constitution beyond the nation-state; for private lawyers, it has above all to do with the free movement of goods, services, capital and workers, and competition law, and is thus predominantly a form of organizing a market across frontiers. For the international lawyer, it is an international organization: it may be an organization *sui generis*, as is often argued, but an organization it still is.

2

The rise of international organizations

Introduction

Traditionally, public international law has long been thought of as largely a law of co-existence:[1] rules of international law were created, either by custom or by bilateral treaty, for the purpose of delimiting spheres of influence between states, but not much else. For the better part, international law regulated the practical aspects of sovereign states living together on Planet Earth, dealing with such issues as the jurisdiction of states, access to each other's courts, delimitation of maritime zones, and other similar issues.

To the extent that co-operation took place at all, it was of the sort which follows naturally from this co-existential character of the law. Thus, if the spheres of jurisdiction of states have been strictly delimited, it follows that rules and procedures are required, for example, to make possible the extradition of criminals captured abroad, or the enforcement of contracts concluded with foreign partners.[2]

Although embryonic forms of international organization have been present throughout recorded history, for instance in the form of the so-called amphictyonic councils of ancient Greece,[3] the late-medieval Hanseatic League[4] or such precursors as the Swiss Confederation and the United Provinces of the Netherlands,[5] it was not until the nineteenth century that international organizations as we know them today were first established.[6] Moreover, it was not until

---

[1] As a theoretical concern, this conception owes much to the work of Wolfgang Friedmann, especially his *The Changing Structure of International Law* (New York, 1964).

[2] A useful introduction to the history of international law is Arthur Nussbaum, *A Concise History of the Law of Nations* (rev. edn, New York, 1954).

[3] But see, sceptically, A. E. R. Boak, 'Greek Interstate Associations and the League of Nations', (1921) 15 *AJIL*, 375–83.

[4] Compare Gerard J. Mangone, *A Short History of International Organizations* (New York, 1954), p. 19. More on the Hanseatic League and how it compares to the sovereign state can be found in Hendrik Spruyt, *The Sovereign State and its Competitors* (Princeton, 1994).

[5] These are mentioned as forerunners in Sir Frederick Pollock, *League of Nations* (2nd edn, London, 1922), p. 4.

[6] For a brief overview of the development of the law of international organizations, see Jan Klabbers, 'The Life and Times of the Law of International Organizations' (2001) 70 *Nordic JIL*, 287–317.

the nineteenth century that the international system of states (at least within Europe) had become sufficiently stable to allow those states to seek forms of co-operation.[7]

After the watershed Westphalian Peace of 1648, so-called international 'congresses' had become a regular mode of diplomacy:[8] whenever a problem arose, a conference was convened to discuss it and, if at all possible, take steps towards a solution. After the defeat of Napoleon, a new development took place: it was thought convenient to organize those meetings on a more or less regular basis. Moreover, the Congress of Vienna (1815) and its aftermath launched some other novelties as well, the most remarkable of which was perhaps the creation of a supranational military force under the command of Wellington.[9]

In addition, the peace conferences of The Hague, organized in 1899 and 1907, had given the small states a taste for international activism. The 1907 conference approached universal participation, with 44 states being represented. Moreover, due in part to its near-universal participation, organizational experiments took place, one of them being that recommendations (so-called 'voeux') of the conference were passed by a majority vote, instead of unanimity.[10]

Finally, the nineteenth century saw the creation of such institutions as the Rhine Commission, in order to deal with issues of navigation or pollution, on a regular basis. Following the establishment of the Rhine Commission in 1815, in Europe a number of other river commissions were established – managing the Elbe (1821), the Douro (1835), the Po (1849) – and, after the end of the Crimean War, the European Commission for the Danube in 1856.[11]

At roughly the same time, organizations started to be established by private citizens, in order to deal with international issues. Thus, in 1840, the World Anti-Slavery Convention was established, and in 1863 a Swiss philanthropist (and rather unsuccessful businessman) Henry Dunant, created the Red Cross.[12] Around the same time, a certain Karl Marx became involved in the creation of the International Working Men's Association.[13] Even the legal profession became internationalized, when about a decade later a number of lawyers came together to form the Institut de Droit International.[14]

---

[7] Compare Clive Archer, *International Organizations* (2dn edn, London, 1992), pp. 4–5.

[8] Mangone, *Short History*, p. 25.   [9] *Ibid.*, p. 40.

[10] See Inis L. Claude, Jr, *Swords into Plowshares: The Problems and Progress of International Organization* (4th edn, New York, 1984), pp. 28–34.

[11] Later there would also be an International Commission for the Danube, established by the 1919 Peace Treaties.

[12] On the latter, see Angela Bennett, *The Geneva Convention: The Hidden Origins of the Red Cross* (Stroud, 2005).

[13] See Francis Wheen, *Karl Marx* (London, 1999), pp. 272–88.

[14] See generally Martti Koskenniemi, *The Gentle Civilizer of Nations: The Rise and Fall of International Law 1870–1960* (Cambridge, 2001).

Sacrificing sovereignty ?

The rise of modern organizations

It became clear that in many areas, international co-operation was not only required, but also possible. True enough, states were sovereign and powerful, but as the river commissions showed, they could sometimes sacrifice some of their sovereign prerogatives in order to facilitate the management of common problems.

The most obvious area in which international co-operation may be required is perhaps that of transport and communication, as indicated by the creation of those river commissions. Regulation of other modes of transport and communication quickly followed: in 1865 the International Telegraphic Union was established, followed in 1874 by the Universal Postal Union and in 1890 by the International Union of Railway Freight Transportation.[15] The term 'international organization' was first coined, reportedly by the Scottish jurist James Lorimer.[16]

Other areas did not lag behind: in 1903 the International Office of Public Health was created, and in the field of economics the establishment of the Metric Union (1875), the International Copyright Union (1886), the International Sugar Union (1902) and the International Institute for Agriculture (1905) may be mentioned as early forerunners of present day international organizations.[17] Indeed, some of these are still in existence, albeit under a different name and on the basis of a different constituent treaty: there runs a direct connection, for example, from the early International Institute for Agriculture to today's FAO. Slowly but surely, more and more international organizations were established, so much so that public international law gradually transformed (or is said to be gradually transforming) from a law of co-existence to a law of co-operation. Many of the substantive fields of public international law are no longer geared merely to delimiting the spheres of influence of the various states, but are rather geared towards establishing more or less permanent mechanisms for co-operation. Around the turn of the twentieth century it appeared indeed to be common knowledge that the organization of interstate co-operation had become well accepted in international law. As the legendary Swiss international lawyer Max Huber could write in 1910, states concluded treaties for basically two reasons: one was the pursuit of self-interest, the other was the pursuit of common interests.[18]

[15] Marxists might claim that these administrative unions were created out of necessity: the logic of ever-increasing international economic relations at the end of the nineteenth century (the internationalization of capital) brought with it the need to organize these relations. For such an argument in brief, see B. S. Chimni, *International Law and World Order: A Critique of Contemporary Approaches* (New Delhi, 1993), pp. 234–5. More recently he explored the proposition that international organizations function as the institutions of global empire. See B. S. Chimni, 'International Institutions Today: An Imperial Global State in the Making' (2004) 15 *EJIL*, 1–37.

[16] See Pitman B. Potter, 'Origin of the Term International Organization', (1945) 39 *AJIL*, 803–6.

[17] Compare Mangone, Short *History*, Ch. 3.

[18] Max Huber, *Die soziologischen Grundlagen des Völkerrechts* (Berlin, 1928, first published in 1910).

The major breakthrough for international organization, however, would be the year 1919 and the Versailles Peace Settlement which followed the First World War.[19] On 8 January 1918, US president Woodrow Wilson made his famous 'fourteen points' speech, in which he called for the creation of a 'general association of nations . . . under specific covenants for the purpose of affording mutual guarantees of political independence and territorial integrity to great and small states alike'.[20]

Wilson's plea was carried on the waves of public opinion in many states[21] and would lead to the formation of the League of Nations. And not only that: the International Labour Organization was also established at the 1919 Peace Conference. Both proved to be influential in their own right: the League because of its comprehensive character and, perhaps, its dramatic failure as well; the ILO because of its unique representation structures and clever modes of regulation.[22]

The League of Nations was the first international organization which was designed not just to organize co-operation between states in areas which some have referred to as 'low politics', such as transport and communication, or the more mundane aspects of economic co-operation as exemplified by the Metric Union, but to have as its specific aims to guarantee peace and the establishment of a system of collective security, following which an attack against one of the member states of the League would give the rest the right to come to the attacked state's rescue. As Wilson himself noted in 1919, the beauty of the League was that it was to have 'unlimited rights of discussion. I mean of discussion of anything that falls within the field of international relations – and that it is especially agreed that war or international misunderstandings or anything that may lead to friction or trouble is everybody's business, because it may affect the peace of the world.'[23] History, in all its cruelty, has made clear that Wilson's hopes would remain futile. True enough, the League became a place of unlimited discussion, and true enough, it paved the way for future developments: without the League, the United Nations would have looked different indeed. Some

---

[19]   For some, the First World War marks the beginning of the end of the era known as 'modernity': the devastations of the war invited a re-appraisal of the sovereign state, which in turn facilitated the establishment of international institutions. See, e.g., Stephen Toulmin, *Cosmopolis: The Hidden Agenda of Modernity* (Chicago, 1990), esp. p. 152. A highly readable account of the creation of the League is Margaret MacMillan, *Paris 1919: Six Months that Changed the World* (New York, 2001).

[20]   Point XIV of the Fourteen Points. The text of the speech has been reproduced in Richard Hofstadter and Beatrice K. Hofstadter (eds.), *Great Issues in American History, Vol. III: From Reconstruction to the Present Day, 1864–1981* (rev. edn, New York, 1982), pp. 215–19. It has been argued that some elements of the League can be traced back to the 1815 Concert, which already envisaged regular meetings of government representatives on issues of war and peace. See Richard Langhorne, 'Establishing International Organisations: The Concert and the League' (1990) 1 *Diplomacy and Statecraft*, 1–18.

[21]   Pollock, *League of Nations*, pp. 74–5 and 84–6, refers to activism in favour of international organizations in many western states as well as in, e.g., China.

[22]   See below, Chapters 6 and 10, respectively.

[23]   Speech to a plenary session of the Peace Conference, reproduced in Hofstadter and Hofstadter (eds.), *Great Issues*, pp. 219–23.

practices developed in the UN had already been tried and tested within the League, peace-keeping being a prominent example.[24] But the League failed in its own overriding purpose: preventing war.

Arguably, while drafting the Covenant, the politics of international law had temporarily been lost on the wave of good intentions.[25] The Covenant made no meaningful distinction between great powers and small powers (except in the composition of the Council[26]) and made it possible, moreover, for its members to withdraw easily from the League: the option was gratefully used by, among others, Japan and Germany.[27]

Moreover, in one of those great ironies of history, the United States Senate refused to grant approval to the American government to ratify the Covenant thus leaving the newborn organization not only without one of its spiritual and intellectual parents,[28] but also, and more importantly, without one of the two states that had emerged from the First World War as a global powerhouse.[29] To add insult to injury, the other powerhouse-to-be (the USSR) was not admitted until late in the League's existence, joining in 1934, only to be expelled again in 1939 after it invaded Finland.

From the ruins of the Second World War, the urge to organize was given a new impetus. As early as August 1941, American President Roosevelt and British Prime Minister Churchill had concluded the Atlantic Charter,[30] a declaration of principles which would serve as the basis, first, for a Declaration of the wartime allies, and later, after the State Department had overcome President Roosevelt's initial reluctance to commit himself to the creation of a post-war organization, for the Charter of the United Nations.[31]

---

[24] On the League's peace-keeping mission to the Saar and Dutch foreign policy, a fine study in Dutch is Remco van Diepen, *Voor Volkenbond en vrede: Nederland en het streven naar een nieuwe wereldorde 1919–1946* (Amsterdam, 1999).

[25] As novelist George Orwell memorably put it, the 1930s turned out to be a decade starting off 'in the hangover of the "enlightened" post-war age', with 'the League of Nations flapping vague wings in the background', thus illustrating a general sentiment of discomfort. See George Orwell, *Collected Essays, Journalism and Letters, Volume I: An Age Like This 1920–1940* (1968; Harmondsworth, 1970), p. 585.

[26] Under Article 4 of the Covenant, the principal allied and associated powers had a permanent seat, but no extra voting prerogatives: decisions were to be taken by unanimity. For a discussion, see Bengt Broms, *The Doctrine of Equality of States as Applied in International Organizations* (Helsinki, 1959), pp. 138–45.

[27] The very first article (symbolically, surely) of the Covenant dealt in part with withdrawal from the League.

[28] The Covenant was largely based on a mixture of British and American plans. See Mangone, *Short History*, pp. 130–1; see also Robert Lansing, *The Peace Negotiations: A Personal Narrative* (Boston, MA, 1921), Ch. 3.

[29] Historian Michael Howard tantalizingly suggests that democracy and international peace may be difficult to bring together, as democracies are reluctant to provide the armed forces necessary to maintain peace. See Michael Howard, *The Invention of Peace: Reflections on War and International Order* (London, 2000), esp. pp. 65–6.

[30] The Atlantic Charter has been said to pick up the legacy of Wilson. See Ian Clark, *Globalization and Fragmentation: International Relations in the Twentieth Century* (Oxford, 1997), p. 113.

[31] See Lloyd C. Gardner, *Architects of Illusion: Men and Ideas in American Foreign Policy 1941–1949* (Chicago, 1970), p. 35. The establishment of the United Nations is well described in

In drafting the Charter, some of the lessons learned from the League's failure were kept in mind.[32] First, a notorious distinction was to be made between the major powers and ordinary states. The major powers were to become permanent members of a new institution, a Security Council, which would only be able to take decisions if the five major powers[33] were in agreement. Second, perhaps mostly of psychological interest, but interesting nonetheless, the Charter did not and does not contain a withdrawal clause. Admittedly, this may not make withdrawal legally impossible, but it does create something of a political and psychological barrier. Indeed, in the more than fifty years of its existence, no state has formally withdrawn from the United Nations.[34]

Also during the war, in 1944, the future of economic co-operation was mapped in Bretton Woods, where agreement was reached on the need to co-operate on monetary and trade issues, eventually leading to the creation of the International Monetary Fund (IMF) and the General Agreement on Tariffs and Trade (GATT), among others.

The resurrection of the largest battlefield of the Second World War, Europe, also came accompanied by the rise of a number of organizations. The Council of Europe was a first attempt, born out of Churchill's avowed desire to create the United States of Europe, so that Europe could become an important power alongside the US and the UK.[35] To channel the American Marshall aid, the Organization for European Economic Co-operation was created (in 1960 transformed into the Organization for Economic Co-operation and Development), and a relatively small number of European states started a unique experiment when, in 1951, they created the supranational European Coal and Steel Community, followed some years later by the European Economic Community and the European Community for Atomic Energy, all three of which have now been subsumed into the European Union.[36] The northern and western states that remained outside this experiment would later create an alternative in

Stephen C. Schlesinger, *Act of Creation: The Founding of the United Nations* (Boulder, CO, 2003) and Paul Kennedy, *The Parliament of Man: The Past, Present, and Future of the United Nations* (New York, 2006).

[32] Thus, intelligent observers such as Harold Nicolson noted with some regret that, technically, the Charter may well have marked an improvement over the Covenant, the latter being based on a view of human nature which would have rendered any Covenant unnecessary. The Charter, by contrast, could not be viewed as a liberal document: Harold Nicolson, *Comments 1944–1948* (London, 1948), p. 209.

[33] Article 23 of the UN Charter mentions the Republic of China (now the People's Republic of China), France, the USSR (now Russia), the United Kingdom and the United States. For discussion, see Gerry Simpson, *Great Powers and Outlaw States: Unequal Sovereigns in the International Legal Order* (Cambridge, 2004).

[34] There is some uncertainty as regards Indonesia's attempt to withdraw in 1965. See below, Chapter 6.

[35] He famously advocated the creation of the United States of Europe, in a speech delivered in Zürich in 1946. The speech is reproduced in David Cannadine (ed.), *The Speeches of Winston Churchill* (London, 1990), pp. 310–14.

[36] The six founders were Belgium, France, Germany, Italy, Luxembourg and the Netherlands. Denmark, Ireland and the UK joined in 1973, Greece in 1981, Spain and Portugal in 1986, and Austria, Finland and Sweden in 1995. In 2004, no less than ten states joined (Cyprus, the Czech

the form of the European Free Trade Area, while the state-run economies of the east replied with the creation of the Council for Mutual Economic Assistance (usually referred to as Comecon).

The influence of the Cold War also made itself felt through military co-operation in Europe. Western Europe saw the creation of the Pact of Brussels (which later became the Western European Union) and the North Atlantic Treaty Organization;[37] Eastern Europe saw the creation of the Warsaw Pact, while east and west would meet, from the 1970s onwards, within the framework of the Conference on Security and Co-operation in Europe (CSCE), which in 1995 changed its name to reflect its increased organizational structure into the Organization for Security and Co-operation in Europe (OSCE).[38]

Moreover, elsewhere too, organizations mushroomed. On the American continent, the early Pan-American Conference was recreated so as to become the Organization of American States. There are also more localized organizations such as Caricom and Mercosur.

In Africa, the wave of independence of the 1950s and early 1960s made possible the establishment of the Organization of African Unity in 1963,[39] with later such regional organizations as ECOCAS (in central Africa) and ECOWAS (western Africa) being added. In Asia, some states assembled in ASEAN, and, for their security, Australia and New Zealand joined the US in ANZUS. A relaxed form of co-operation in the Pacific Rim area, moreover, is channelled through Asia-Pacific Economic Co-operation (APEC).[40]

In short, there is not a part of the globe which is not covered by the work of some international organization or other; there is hardly a human activity which is not, to some extent, governed by the work of an international organization. Even academic research is at the heart of the work of some organizations, most notably perhaps the International Council for the Exploration of the Sea (ICES), originally set up as a scientist's club, having Fridtjof Nansen as one of its founders, but later 'internationalized'.[41]

Republic, Estonia, Hungary, Latvia, Lithuania, Malta, Poland, Slovakia and Slovenia), followed in 2007 by Bulgaria and Romania.

[37] A proposed defence alliance between the Nordic states never got off the ground. See Gerard Aalders, 'The Failure of the Scandinavian Defence Union, 1948–1949' (1990) 15 *Scandinavian Journal of History*, 125–53.

[38] See, briefly, Miriam Sapiro, 'Changing the CSCE into the OSCE: Legal Aspects of a Political Transformation' (1995) 89 *AJIL*, 631–7.

[39] Since 2000, the OAU has been replaced by the African Union. For a useful overview, see Konstantinos Magliveras and Gino Naldi, *The African Union and the Predecessor Organization of African Unity* (The Hague, 2004).

[40] On the perceived dearth of organizations in the area, see José E. Alvarez, 'Institutionalised Legislation and the Asia-Pacific "Region"' (2007) 5 *New Zealand Journal of Public and International Law*, 9–27.

[41] See generally A. E. J. Went, *Seventy Years Agrowing: A History of the International Council for the Exploration of the Sea 1902–1972* (Copenhagen, 1972). Much the same applies to the European Forest Institute, which transformed from an association of forestry research institutes under Finnish law to an international organization in 2003.

Classifying international organizations

An academic textbook on international organizations is not complete without an attempt to classify the various organizations into different types, sorts, forms or categories. Perhaps the main reason for making such classifications resides in the academic psyche: all academic disciplines engage in classification for the purpose of organizing knowledge, if nothing else, so legal academics should do the same.

As long as it remains clear that classification has the function of organizing knowledge, but no greater ambition, classification may be a useful exercise. As long as the aim is to show that organizations are not monolithic, built according to one and the same eternally valid blueprint, but are wide-ranging in variety, classifying them may even be illuminating. But the suggestion oozing from most classification attempts that there are also legal differences between the various categories is, by and large, unwarranted. In a very important sense, for the lawyer, each international organization is unique, based as it is on its own constituent document and influenced as its development will be by peculiar political configurations. Thus, labels should never be substituted for analysis, as Brownlie has pointed out.[42]

Functions

A first point often made by scholars is that organizations may be classified in accordance with their stated functions. Thus, quite a few are active in the economic field; others are engaged in peace and security, or can be classified as military alliances. Yet others deal with issues of nutrition, public health, telecommunications or fisheries conservation, to name just a few possibilities. Here immediately a caveat should be made: whether or not we think of an organization as active in the economic sphere depends most of all on how we define economics. Some would not hesitate to include telecommunications, whereas other might be at pains to exclude it.

Moreover, there is the distinct possibility that even if we think that telecommunications is not, properly speaking, an economic issue, there is still a chance that an economically oriented organization can deal with the topic if it can be seen to have economic repercussions. Following a similar kind of reasoning, the European Community in particular has developed from a purely economic organization into one that also deals with other aspects of life, provided there is an economic side to those aspects.

A good example of that type of reasoning is to be found in the famous *Bosman* decision of the European Court of Justice.[43] In this case, the

---

[42] Brownlie, *Principles of Public International Law*, p. 131. This would seem to imply also that labelling the EU as being *sui generis* is of little help: at the end of the day, all organizations are *sui generis*.

[43] Case C-415/93, *Union Royale Belge des Sociétés de Football Association ASBL and others* v. *Jean-Marc Bosman and others* [1995] ECR I-4921, paras. 73, 76.

question at issue was whether the transfer system in football (i.e., soccer), according to which professional players could only switch clubs upon payment of a transfer fee from the new club to the old one, was in contravention of some of the basic principles of the EC Treaty, in particular the free movement of workers as guaranteed by Article 48 (nowadays Article 39) of the Treaty establishing the EC. The Court held that, indeed, the transfer system was not in conformity with Article 48, but in order to do so it first had to reach a finding as to whether professional football came within the scope of the Treaty to begin with. This was found to be the case because professional football, whatever else it may be (hobby, entertainment, leisure activity), also constitutes an economic activity. Therefore, and to that extent, the EC rules apply to professional football, and, therefore, the Court could rule that the transfer system violated Article 48 of the TEC. The case indicates, if nothing else, that the boundaries between topics or issues may be very fuzzy indeed.

Membership

Other classifications point to the membership of organizations as being of distinctive value. Thus, some organizations aspire to universal or near-universal membership, in principle inviting all states to join. The United Nations is a typical example, in principle open to all states as long as they meet certain requirements. Hence, the UN is often referred to as an 'open' organization, as are (although their membership does not compare to that of the UN) such organizations as the World Health Organization (WHO) and the World Trade Organization (WTO).

Other organizations, however, may rest satisfied with a limited membership, and usually such limitations may derive from their overall purpose. Thus, many regional organizations, aiming to organize activities in a certain geographical region, are open only to states from that region. The European Union is only open to European states; no Asian state can join the Organization of African Unity, and the Organization of American States can only be joined by states from the Americas.

The limitation is not always based on considerations of geography, though. For instance, the Organization of Petroleum Exporting Countries (OPEC) is a limited organization, but its membership spans the globe, including states from the Middle East, Latin America and Africa.[44] Here, the ties are economic. Similarly, the Organization for Economic Co-operation and Development (OECD) has also, in addition to a large number of western European member states, members from the Americas, Asia and Oceania, and the North Atlantic Treaty Organization (NATO) does justice to the Atlanticism in its name by including

---

[44] To be sure, there is also the geographically more limited OAPEC (which only has Arab member states).

members from western and southern Europe as well as the US and Canada, whereas the French-speaking countries are united in an organization devoted to *francophonie*.[45] Where membership is limited to states from a certain region, such organizations may be referred to as 'regional', but the more generic term used is often 'closed'.

Political v. functional

A distinction sometimes made which refers to notions of integration theory is that between political and functional organizations. Some integration theorists have held that the chances of international integration, or even mere co-operation occurring are larger when the purpose of co-operation is limited to some technical task: a clearly circumscribed function. The underlying idea is that technical functions (such as, say, the regulation of telecommunications) do not involve great political sentiments; co-operation can thus take place unencumbered by unproductive debates and disagreements. As there can hardly be disagreement about the necessity and benefits of regulation, integration can proceed by focusing on substance, and through the work of engineers and other experts rather than politicians. On such views, it is no coincidence that organizations first arose in order to manage practical problems such as transport and communication, and it is no coincidence that the levels of co-operation are more intense in these organizations than in organizations devoted to more 'political' tasks.

Unfortunately, while the distinction is one that makes intuitive sense, it is not a distinction which can easily be captured in comprehensive definitions and descriptions. If under 'politics' we would refer predominantly to issues of peace and security, then there is only one universal political organization at present: the UN (perhaps accompanied by several regional organizations such as the Organization for Security and Co-operation in Europe (OSCE)). And if so, then the distinction might not be overly effective.

Moreover, there is but a fine line between what some would appreciate as political and what others would regard as rather functional, and much may depend on one's position. As the International Court of Justice acknowledged in the early 1970s, a state such as Iceland is disproportionately dependent on fisheries.[46] It would seem to follow that issues that will hardly deprive the Swiss or Austrians of their sleep, such as fisheries, might have serious political overtones for Iceland. Conversely, Iceland will not be overly interested in issues that may bother, say, the Ethiopians, such as co-operation with respect to shared waterways.

---

[45] The organization is the Organisation Internationale de la Francophonie, which used to be headed by former UN Secretary-General Boutros Boutros-Ghali.

[46] See the *Fisheries Jurisdiction Case* (*UK* v. *Iceland*), jurisdiction, [1973] ICJ Reports 3, paras. 41–2.

Finally, there is the fundamental problem that arguments stressing the facility of technical co-operation are based on the untenable misconception that technical issues are, somehow, beyond politics. The better view is that even seemingly technical and 'non-political' issues such as the regulation of telecommunications have profound political aspects and consequences, for example, when it comes to the organization of the information society.[47]

Intergovernmental or supranational?

Finally, a distinction often made is that between intergovernmental and supranational organizations, but here as well we may wonder about the value of the distinction: does it really clarify anything? As things stand, there is only one organization which is usually held to be supranational in character: the EC. Hence, any description of supranational organizations will inevitably be based on the EC.

In comparison with other organizations, the EC possesses a few features which, in combination, render it distinct from the rest. First, under its constituent treaties, decisions which will bind the member states can be taken by majority vote.[48] Thus, it is entirely possible that a member state will have to adopt a certain course of behaviour which it itself vehemently opposes. Second, the product of those decisions is EC law, which attains supremacy over conflicting domestic law, regardless of what the laws of the member state stipulate and regardless of which one was enacted later.[49] Third, much of the law promulgated by the EC may be directly effective in the legal systems of the member states.[50] Thus, much EC law may be invoked not just by one member state against another, but also by a citizen of one of the member states against his or her own government, or in relations with employers or other relations of a private nature. It is in this sense that people often say that the member states have transferred parts of their sovereignty to the EC, and it is in this sense that the EC stands, in an almost literal way, above its member states (hence the term 'supranational').

Some would go further and claim that on occasion, the member states are no longer allowed even to attempt to regulate behaviour:[51] the doctrine of

---

[47] For a brilliant analysis (though not focusing on international telecommunications), see James Boyle, *Shamans, Software, and Spleens: Law and the Construction of the Information Society* (Cambridge, MA, 1996).

[48] Compare, e.g., Arts. 251 (ex Art. 189b) and 252 (ex Art. 189c) TEC.

[49] Case 6/64, *Flaminio Costa* v. *ENEL* [1964] ECR 585.

[50] This follows in some circumstances literally from Art. 249 (ex Art. 189) TEC, and has also been proclaimed by the European Court in landmark cases such as Case 26/62, *Van Gend & Loos* v. *Administratie der Nederlandse Belastingen* [1963] ECR 1.

[51] For a useful discussion in Dutch, see Jan H. Jans, 'Autonomie van de wetgever? Voorafgaande bemoeienis van Europese instellingen met nationale regelgeving'. In Leonard Besselink *et al.*, *Europese Unie en nationale soevereiniteit* (Deventer, 1997), pp. 51–113. An English version hereof is published as Jan H. Jans, 'National Legislative Autonomy? The Procedural Constraints of European Law' (1998/I) 25 *LIEI*, 25–58. See also Eugene D. Cross, 'Pre-emption of Member

In tergovernmental/
tein im/ (handwritten margin note)

pre-emption not only holds that member state action can be overruled, but goes beyond this in saying that member state action is no longer acceptable in some areas.[52]

By contrast, the general rule among international organizations is that binding law-making decisions, at least on issues of substantive policy, can usually only be taken by unanimity, or consensus; that such rules do not usually work directly in the domestic legal orders of the member states; and most assuredly that the member states are not pre-empted from legislating. Here then, the organization does not rise above its members, but remains between its members (intergovernmental).[53]

Why co-operate?

International organizations are, as outlined earlier, perhaps the most obvious and typical vehicles for interstate co-operation. It is difficult to think of any organization which is not intended to foster co-operation in some way, although obviously some organizations provide for larger degrees of co-operation than others. Thus, the EC, being 'supranational', establishes a very intensive form of co-operation; it has even been possible to argue that the EC has risen beyond mere co-operation, and is slowly but surely integrating, something which can loosely be defined as reaching such a level of co-operation that previously independent entities start to form a new one which they cannot undo at will.[54] As some people would have it, due to the state of European integration, the member states alone are no longer in full control of their destinies and that of the EC; they are no longer 'Herren der Verträge': they are no longer masters of the treaty.[55] Indeed, much of the debate nowadays concentrates on the

State Law in the European Economic Community: A Framework for Analysis' (1992) 29 *CMLRev*, 447–72.

[52] For a critique, see Stephen Weatherill, 'Beyond Preemption? Shared Competence and Institutional Change in the European Community'. In David O'Keeffe and Patrick Twomey (eds.), *Legal Issues of the Maastricht Treaty* (London, 1994), pp. 13–33.

[53] Anthropologists intriguingly note a strong parallel between the post-war creation of organizations (entities whose members remain sovereign and therewith respect the local) and the post-war rise of global companies whose products celebrate something that distinctive local but which also has a global, universal appeal. Perhaps the prime example is Coca Cola, the symbol both of everything American and of something universal – but much the same might apply to McDonalds or Pizza Hut. Or Pepsi, for that matter. See Robert J. Foster, *Coca-Globalization: Following Soft Drinks from New York to New Guinea* (New York, 2008), p. 43.

[54] This definition has been gleaned from J. K. de Vree, *Political Integration: The Formation of Theory and its Problems* (The Hague, 1972).

[55] Among the most prominent is Ulrich Everling, 'Sind die Mitgliedstaaten der Europäischen Gemeinschaft noch Herren der Verträge? Zum Verhältnis von Europäischem Gemeinschaftsrecht und Völkerrecht'. In Rudolf Bernhardt *et al.* (eds.), *Völkerrecht als Rechtsordnung, internationale Gerichtsbarkeit, Menschenrechte: Festschrift für Hermann Mosler* (Berlin, 1983), pp. 173–91; see also Ulrich Everling, 'Zur Stellung der Mitgliedstaaten der Europäischen Union als "Herren der Verträge"'. In Ulrich Beyerlin *et al.* (eds.), *Recht zwischen Umbruch und Bewahrung; Festschrift für Rudolf Bernhardt* (Berlin, 1995), pp. 1161–76.

need or desirability of a constitution for the EC, despite the defeat of the Treaty establishing a Constitution for Europe in referenda in France and the Netherlands in 2005, which suggests that the integration process is considered as irreversible and as having found a life of its own.[56]

With other organizations, the degree of co-operation is considerably less intensive. Thus, the central provision of the NATO treaty has been held to be fairly non-committal:[57] under Article 5 NATO, member states are obliged to do what they 'deem necessary' where one of them comes under attack.[58] Clearly, such an obligation leaves the member states a rather wide margin of discretion to determine their actions but, equally clearly, some form of co-operation does take place within NATO, if only in the form of joint military exercises and commands.[59]

Throughout history, observers have had a hard time explaining co-operation. That holds true both in domestic societies and, perhaps *a fortiori*, when international relations are concerned. The question as to why actors will co-operate is one of the central questions of the social sciences, and is particularly prominent in international relations theory.[60]

Arguably the most dominant strand of international relations theory, at least since the Second World War, is what is known as 'realism', or, nowadays, 'neo-realism'.[61] Realists and neo-realists start from the proposition that the world is a jungle, an anarchy, where it is a fight of man against man and state against state. In order to ensure survival, the state must guarantee at the very least that its competitors do not become more powerful, and preferably that it itself gains power.[62]

In such a scheme, co-operation is almost by definition doomed either to remain temporary, or to be the result of submission or coercion. Military alliances, for instance, are not unknown to realists; indeed, they are presumably central tenets of realism.[63] International organizations, however, are harder to

---

[56] On constitutionalization see, e.g., Paul Craig, 'Constitutions, Constitutionalism, and the European Union' (2001) 7 *European Law Journal*, 125–50; Oliver Gerstenberg, 'Denationalization and the Very Idea of Democratic Constitutionalism: The Case of the European Community' (2001) 14 *Ratio Juris*, 298–325; Trevor C. Hartley, 'The Constitutional Foundations of the European Union' (2001) 117 *Law Quarterly Review*, 225–46.

[57] See Michael J. Glennon, *Constitutional Diplomacy* (Princeton, 1990), p. 214.

[58] Moreover, it would take more than half a century before that provision was first seriously invoked: only after 9/11 were the member states agreed that an 'article 5 situation' existed.

[59] For rationalist explanations for such differences in set-up, see Barbara Koremonos, Charles Lipson and Duncan Snidal (eds.), *The Rational Design of International Institutions* (Cambridge, 2004).

[60] A useful overview of international organizations in international relations scholarship is J. Samuel Barkin, *International Organization: Theories and Institutions* (New York, 2006).

[61] The starting point of modern realism (while not blind to its limitations) was, arguably, the publication of E. H. Carr, *The Twenty Years' Crisis 1919–1939* (1939; London, 1981).

[62] The seminal work is Hans J. Morgenthau, *Politics Among Nations: The Struggle for Power and Peace* (2nd edn, New York, 1955).

[63] Similarly Alexander Wendt, *Social Theory of International Politics* (Cambridge, 1999), pp. 299–302.

realism

explain, particularly as these are perceived to be created for longer periods of time. One of the central propositions of realism is, after all, that states will pursue their own interests; as long as organizations can be seen to be helpful in that pursuit, realists will typically be able to explain their existence and functioning. But realists will have a hard time explaining forms of co-operation that apparently go against the national self-interest.[64]

It is here that the efforts of other schools of thought come in. Typically, some authors claim that realists have too bleak an outlook on life. Life, so they argue, is a bit more than a war of all against all and the ensuing struggle for survival: social actors may also strive to co-operate in order to combat problems that would typically require a joint effort (this sort of thinking is sometimes referred to as functionalism or neo-functionalism, particularly if followed by the proposition that co-operation in one sector leads to co-operation in other sectors), and if push comes to shove, co-operation may even take place out of sheer altruism or some similar incentive.[65] Of course, here the main riddle is how to explain failures of co-operation, or the lack of co-operation in situations where it could theoretically have been expected. And moreover, as idealist thinking is based on a sunny view of human nature, it is intuitively perhaps more difficult to accept than the premises of realism.[66]

A more normative school of thought takes these views somewhat further, and defends the thesis that democracies are naturally inclined to co-operate or, at least, not to go to war with one another.[67] Based on the works of Immanuel Kant, especially his short treatise *Zum ewigen Frieden*[68] – with greater or lesser degrees of accuracy – some advocates of the 'democratic peace' thesis might even go so far as to denounce all ties with non-democracies.[69]

More moderate voices, while still allowing for a distinction between different types of states based on their domestic political systems and ideologies, advocate far-reaching co-operation in various forms between like-minded states. Under this liberal theory, liberal states become embedded in a transnational society; a society, in other words, that comprises trans-boundary relationships between private actors. Co-operation in this 'world of liberal states' takes place not just

---

[64] Hence the empty universe of Goldsmith and Posner, positing a view of international society consisting of only two states, and not encompassing international organizations. See Jack L. Goldsmith and Eric A. Posner, *The Limits of International Law* (Oxford, 2005).

[65] Interestingly, Frost's adaptation of the value of recognition in international life, as a means of initiating the new into established practices, comes pretty close. See Mervyn Frost, *Ethics and International Relations: A Constitutive Theory* (Cambridge, 1996), pp. 153–5.

[66] Indeed, it is no coincidence that idealism is not known as realism, but usually goes under such labels as 'institutionalism'. More apposite, many idealists position themselves, and quite understandably so, as realists.

[67] For an empirical critique of the thesis that democracies do not fight each other, see Joanne Gowa, *Ballots and Bullets: The Elusive Democratic Peace* (Princeton, 1999). Also critical is Alexander Wendt, *Social Theory*, Ch. 6, arguing that there is no direct relationship between a shared culture and either co-operation or conflict.

[68] Immanuel Kant, *Zum ewigen Frieden: Ein philosophischer Entwurf* (1795; Stuttgart, 1984).

[69] So, e.g., Fernando Tesón, *A Philosophy of International Law* (Boulder, CO, 1999).

within formal institutions,[70] but also, and perhaps more importantly, through informal mechanisms, ranging from occasional meetings of judges from various jurisdictions to regular meetings of civil servants.[71]

The main problem for theory appears to be how to reconcile observable patterns of co-operation with realist premises. For whatever realists may say, co-operation does take place more often than their theories would warrant; and whatever idealists may say, it is hard to believe that states will do anything for a reason which cannot in one way or another be traced back to self-interest.

A recent answer, which may help explain why dominant states help to set up organizations rather than attempting to dominate them by the exercise of naked power, focuses on bargains between dominant states and other states: the dominant state promises to limit the exercise of its power in return for participation by other states.[72]

A more general answer (not necessarily limited to organizations involving dominant states) rose to prominence, especially in US international relations-thinking during the 1970s and 1980s, and has achieved fame as 'regime theory'. Leaving the differences between various authors aside,[73] one of the central propositions of regime theory was that states can and do co-operate on the basis of the realist premise of enlightened self-interest.[74] And this was made possible, so regime theory claimed, because co-operation can yield greater net results than going it alone. In other words: if co-operation makes the cake grow bigger, then an equal share of the cake as before will nonetheless result in a bigger piece. Thus, in most situations states would actually have an interest in co-operation, since co-operation was generally thought to result in a greater common good.

While it took some time to be formulated, realism's answer, in the form of a seminal article by Joseph Grieco, proved incisive.[75] Where regime theory went wrong, Grieco argued, was in claiming that the realist premise holds that states are interested in increasing their absolute gains. That was based on a misunderstanding. Instead, states are interested in an increase of their relative power positions; they are interested in an increase of their position *vis-à-vis*

---

[70] Indeed, as Falk astutely observed, the liberal approach does not require institutions or organizational structures; it insists, instead, on the inner orientation of states. See Richard A. Falk, *Human Rights Horizons* (New York, 2000), p. 18.

[71] The most explicit proponent of this approach is Anne-Marie Slaughter. See in particular her *A New World Order* (Princeton, 2004).

[72] See G. John Ikenberry, 'Institutions, Strategic Restraint, and the Persistence of American Postwar Order' (1998–9) 23 *International Security*, 43–78. Aspects of the UN's architecture are explained along similar lines in Ian Hurd's excellent *After Anarchy: Legitimacy and Power in the United Nations Security Council* (Princeton, 2007).

[73] For an excellent overview, see Stephan Haggard and Beth A. Simmons, 'Theories of International Regimes' (1987) 41 *International Organization*, 491–517.

[74] One of the leading works is Robert O. Keohane, *After Hegemony: Cooperation and Discord in the World Political Economy* (Princeton, 1984).

[75] Joseph M. Grieco, 'Anarchy and the Limits of Cooperation' (1988) 42 *International Organization*, 485–508.

their main rivals.[76] They will prefer an absolute decrease which grants them a relative increase any time over the converse. They are not interested in a bigger piece as such, but in a bigger piece than their rivals.

Apart from this critique, regime theory suffered on some other points as well. Perhaps its main proposition was that states record their co-operation not just in formal legal rules and procedures, but in informal rules and procedures as well. That was, of course, what was supposed to set regime theory aside from the legalistic study of patterns of co-operation traditionally associated with lawyers, yet it has proved less than successful: by and large regime theorists have come up with precious few examples of informal rules and procedures, which ironically meant that regime theory and international law turned out to have more in common than both might actually care to admit.[77]

Recent theorizing concentrates on the role of domestic forces in fostering international co-operation. According to what its main representative calls 'republican liberalism', co-operation takes place neither for the self-interest of states nor out of altruism, but rather because domestic forces wish to 'lock' their positions. Thus, a weak democracy might join a human rights treaty precisely as a means for ensuring that democracy will not be overturned; by the same token, governments may join organizations to strengthen their own positions.[78] Indeed, it has been argued with great conviction that both the OAU and the Arab League were predominantly set up so as to preserve and strengthen the sovereignty of their member states.[79]

Additionally, it has plausibly been suggested that states may join organizations because the cost of staying out may be too high: this might help to explain why many European states have been (and others still are) keen to join the EU, and why Canada and Mexico joined NAFTA.[80] It may be hypothesized though that this logic is strongest with economic organizations: the same logic may not apply with equal force to other organizations, as the long debate in Finland over whether to join NATO suggests. This debate is cast not in terms of a cost–benefit analysis, but rather in terms of the likely effect on external threats.

[76] The insight was already mentioned (albeit somewhat in passing) in one of the classics of realist theory. See Kenneth N. Waltz, *Man, the State, and War* (New York, 1959), p. 198.

[77] Thus, e.g., Anne-Marie Slaughter Burley, 'International Law and International Relations: A Dual Agenda' (1993) 87 *AJIL*, 205–39. See also Michael Byers, *Custom, Power, and the Power of Rules* (Cambridge, 1999).

[78] See Andrew Moravcsik, 'The Origins of Human Rights Regimes: Democratic Delegation in Postwar Europe' (2000) 54 *International Organization*, 217–52. For a more culturally inclined view (but also stressing domestic factors), see Erik Ringmar, 'Re-imagining Sweden: The Rhetorical Battle over EU Membership' (1998) 23 *Scandinavian Journal of History*, 45–63.

[79] See Jeffrey Herbst, 'Crafting Regional Cooperation in Africa'. In Amitav Acharya and Alastair Iain Johnston (eds.), *Crafting Cooperation: Regional International Institutions in Comparative Perspective* (Cambridge, 2007), pp. 129–44, and Michael Barnett and Etel Solingen, 'Designed to Fail or Failure of Design? The Origins and Legacy of the Arab League'. In *ibid.*, pp. 180–220.

[80] See Lloyd Gruber, 'Power Politics and the Free Trade Bandwagon' (2001) 34 *Comparative Political Studies*, 703–41.

Finally, and difficult to capture in theoretical terms, states may engage in what looks like co-operation primarily to have a scapegoat for policy failure or, alternatively, as a means of suggesting that activities are taking place.[81] Thus, former US diplomat Robert Murphy recalls how Secretary of State John Foster Dulles occasionally saw the UN as something of a storage room for thorny problems which remained unsolved.[82]

In addition to asking why co-operation takes place, we may also ask ourselves which roles organizations, once established, can and do play, and here a more constructivist school of thought has taken the lead. While for many realists and regime theorists alike, international organizations are mere arenas for power struggles between states, the central tenet of constructivism is rather that organizations are more than mere clearing houses for the opinions of their member states: they take on a role and dynamics all their own.[83] Organizations may become actors on their own stage, so to speak.[84] Indeed, this has become one of the core propositions of the constructivist approach to international relations, which argues that existing rules and institutions help shape not just our behaviour, but also the very world we live in.[85]

Perhaps the most obvious example is the case of the European Community which, due to its (partly) supranational character, may well be able to take on dynamics of its own. The belief that similar considerations also hold with respect to more intergovernmental organizations has sometimes been posited, but not unconditionally. Still, it has been noted that organizational leadership and the capacity of organizations to 'learn' offer possibilities for enhanced co-operation.[86]

Either way, what emerges as one of the central problems faced by social scientists in explaining the role and impact of international organizations is the relation between the organization and its member states: is the organization but a forum, convenient for compiling the aggregate wishes of the various member

[81] See in a similar vein Martin Wight, 'Why is There No International Theory?'. In Herbert Butterfield and Martin Wight (eds.), *Diplomatic Investigations: Essays in the Theory of International Politics* (London, 1966), pp. 17–34, esp. p. 23.

[82] Robert Murphy, *Diplomat among Warriors* (London, 1964), p. 443.

[83] For an excellent overview, see Michael N. Barnett and Martha Finnemore, 'The Politics, Power and Pathologies of International Organizations' (1999) 53 *International Organization*, 699–732.

[84] For an intelligent discussion of how the financial institutions have used poverty as an excuse for expanding their own activities, see Balakrishnan Rajagopal, 'From Resistance to Renewal: The Third World, Social Movements, and the Expansion of International Institutions' (2000) 41 *Harvard ILJ*, 529–78.

[85] Its main representatives include John Gerard Ruggie, *Constructing the World Polity* (London, 1998); Alexander Wendt, *Social Theory*; Nicholas G. Onuf, *World of Our Making* (Columbia, SC, 1989), and Friedrich Kratochwil, *Rules, Norms, and Decisions* (Cambridge, 1989). Institutionalists do not necessarily adopt the constructivist thesis in full, but do note that the 'centralization' and 'independence' offered by organizations make them attractive vehicles for international co-operation. See, e.g., Kenneth W. Abbott and Duncan Snidal, 'Why States Act through Formal International Organizations' (1998) 42 *Journal of Conflict Resolution*, 3–32.

[86] Thus, already, Ernst B. Haas in his classic study of the International Labour Organization, *Beyond the Nation-State* (Stanford, 1964).

states, or does it present itself as something that is distinct from its member states? The same problem also haunts the science of law.

Legal theory and international organizations

Legal theorists ordinarily have little business in trying to explain why states co-operate: this belongs to the social sciences. Moreover, the legal theorist is generally ill-equipped to perform such a task: whenever lawyers engage in political analysis, more often than not the results fail to persuade professional political scientists.

More properly, the task of the legal scholar is to explain the incidence of various legal rules relating to international organizations. This, in turn, calls for a background theory concerning the legal nature of international organizations, but no convincing theory has so far been developed, as far as I am aware.

Traditionally, theorists sought refuge in the concept of the state.[87] Thus, organizations were viewed as would-be states, with, in particular, the federal model being an attraction.[88] This line of thinking was dispelled when the ICJ, trying to come to terms with the UN, pronounced that the UN was not the same as a state, let alone a superstate.[89]

One of the leading studies of the law of international organizations, Amerasinghe's textbook,[90] is (its outstanding qualities notwithstanding) illustrative of the theoretical confusion concerning the legal nature of international organizations, and more specifically of what appears to be the heart of the problem: the way the organization relates to its member states.

At some points, Amerasinghe treats the member states of an organization as if they are third parties. In creating the organization, they have created a distinct legal entity, and have therewith limited their individual liability for any actions the organization might take. Precisely because they are considered to be third parties in relation to the organization, they can escape being held liable for its acts.

Clearly, that is a respectable point of view, held by many international lawyers, and usually defended by pointing out that, since states cannot be bound by obligations they have not freely consented to,[91] it follows that obligations incurred by international organizations cannot, as such, bind their member states. After all, that is precisely why they may have created the organization to begin with.

---

[87] For a good overview, indicating that often organizations were thought of as states writ large, see Daniele Archibugi, 'Models of International Organization in Perpetual Peace Projects' (1992) 18 *Review of International Studies*, 295–317.

[88] As noted by Michel Virally, *L'organisation mondiale* (Paris, 1972), pp. 19–24.

[89] *Reparation for Injuries Suffered in the Service of the United Nations*, advisory opinion, [1949] ICJ Reports 174, p. 179.

[90] C. F. Amerasinghe, *Principles of the Institutional Law of International Organizations* (Cambridge, 1996).

[91] This point of departure has found recognition, in, e.g., Arts. 34 and following of the 1969 Vienna Convention on the Law of Treaties.

Elsewhere, though, Amerasinghe is forced to abandon this view, because, taken to the extreme, it would imply that documents which the organization sends to its member states lose their privileged status. As long as those documents circulate on the organization's premises, they can be regarded as internal and privileged documents, but if they are sent to third parties (such as member states) they will inevitably lose that status. Hence, on this point Amerasinghe stops treating member states as third parties, and therewith renders himself vulnerable to the charge of incoherence.

Clearly, such problems call for theoretical explorations; equally clearly, though, so far few such explorations have been undertaken.[92] Instead, lawyers usually invoke a different concept to take the place of theory, and seek refuge in the notion of 'functional necessity'.[93]

Discarding the functional necessity theory

Functional necessity is based, conceptually, on the idea that international law does not automatically grant any substantive rights or obligations to international organizations. When it comes to states, the simple fact of statehood brings with it certain rights. Thus, heads of state can command universal respect, states will generally be immune from suit for their governmental activities (*acta jure imperii*), and will, for example, have the right to accede to numerous treaties.

Similar considerations do not necessarily apply to international organizations. If any legal rights and obligations flow automatically from 'organizationhood' at all (and the classic *Reparation for Injuries* opinion of the International Court offers some support for this proposition[94]), they are limited to those of a more or less procedural character. Thus, organizations may have an inherent right to bring claims under international law, or they may have the inherent right to enter into treaty relations, but they are not automatically immune from suit. Indeed, it can even be wondered if they are capable of exercising governmental activities to begin with.

And if organizationhood itself provides no, or at best limited, answers, then the answers must be sought elsewhere: it is here that the idea of functional necessity comes in. Many scholars maintain that organizations can reasonably claim such rights and privileges as would enable them to function effectively;

---

[92] Steyger, quite typically limits herself to providing an overview of the relationship between the EC and its member states without exploring the theoretical possibilities. See Elies Steyger, *Europe and Its Members: A Constitutional Approach* (Aldershot, 1995).

[93] Arguably first systematically elaborated by Michel Virally, 'La notion de fonction dans la théorie de l'organisation internationale'. In Suzanne Bastid *et al.*, *Mélanges offerts à Charles Rousseau: la communauté internationale* (Paris, 1974), pp. 277–300, although hints are already discernible in his *L'organisation mondiale*.

[94] This opinion will be discussed more appropriately in the next chapter.

their legal position at international law is geared to, literally, their functional requirements, the necessities which flow from their functions. Thus organizations generally are considered to possess the types of legal immunities which are necessary for them to work without interference from their host state, or their member states; at the same time, their prerogatives are limited to their functions.[95]

The functional necessity concept has considerable explanatory power, in that it can help to explain why states create organizations in the first place. Yet, its ingenuity notwithstanding, functional necessity suffers from some serious problems. First, it is biased in favour of international organizations, and is therefore based on the view that international organizations are necessarily a good thing.[96] Thus, it is one thing to say that organizations shall be immune from suit to the extent necessary for their functioning, but why should third parties who have seen a deal gone sour, be victimized by the necessities of the organization? For if the organization is immune from suit, its creditors (for instance) cannot touch it.

The main problem here is the assumption that international organizations are, necessarily, a good thing, an assumption which often takes the place of argument, even before the ICJ: 'The stability and efficiency of the international organizations, of which the United Nations is the supreme example, are . . . of such paramount importance to world order, that the Court should not fail to assist a subsidiary body of the United Nations General Assembly in putting its operation upon a firm and secure foundation.'[97] But are international organizations really humankind's main hope for salvation, or does this depend on their aims and activities?[98] The presumption is perhaps best regarded as the outgrowth of historical developments, for, whatever their flaws, organizations are usually, as Broms reminds us, a step up from the type of co-operation exercised earlier. Respect for the individual consent of member states replaced the situation where powerful states could simply impose their wishes on others.[99]

In part, also, the appeal of organizations to most students of their activities stems from their pivotal role in what has been referred to as the 'international

---

95 See below, Chapter 8.
96 As Singh once put it, in terms characteristic of the sentiment: 'international organisations have a great role to play in the salvation of mankind'. See Nagendra Singh, *Termination of Membership of International Organisations* (London, 1958), p. vii.
97 *Application for Review of Judgement No. 273 of the United Nations Administrative Tribunal*, advisory opinion, [1982] ICJ Reports 325, 347.
98 It may be noted that western observers have on occasion tried to argue that the Warsaw Pact and Comecon did not really constitute international organizations (usually because of their being dominated by a single member state). This would allow the fiction that organizations are by definition beneficial to continue: we simply dismiss those we deem detrimental. For a rendition of such an argument, see Bryan Schwartz and Elliot Leven, 'International Organizations: What Makes Them Work?' (1992) 30 *Can YIL*, 165–94, 178.
99 Broms, *Equality of States*, p. 152.

project' of internationalists.[100] On this line of thinking, to be an international lawyer (or international political scientist, for that matter[101]) is to somehow be in favour of anything international, and it stands to reason that international organizations have benefited greatly from this sentiment in terms of the analysis of their functioning and activities.[102]

In the end, the question of the attraction of organizations answers itself: inasmuch as there can be (and are) undoubtedly many international organizations whose work can command general support, there is at least the hypothetical possibility that international organizations can be used for less than worthy purposes.[103] Where the organization becomes a cover for exploitation or invasion, there appears to be less and less reason to promote anything which would facilitate its functioning.

Moreover, even member states of an organization are generally keen to keep their creation in check, as is witnessed by the popularity in the present-day European Union of notions such as subsidiarity, opting out and 'flexibility'.[104] This very phenomenon runs counter to the idea that organizations should prosper and therefore that their functional needs be honoured.

A second problem with the notion of functional necessity is that it is itself rather empty to begin with. For what is the functional necessity of any given organization? Who is to determine such issues? What yardstick is to be used? Thus, the notion itself warrants theoretical elaboration. Instead of providing a theory, it merely shifts any problems stemming from the lack of theory, and hides the absence thereof.

Indeed, close observation reveals a shift in the notion of what constitutes functional necessity over time. The concept appears to have been considerably narrowed down from the early 1990s onwards, indicating that it is too flexible to be of much use as a theoretical device, indicating that its explanatory force is

---

[100] Anything international, moreover, has often been considered to carry with it an escape from politics, and has been deemed attractive for that reason alone. See David Kennedy, 'Receiving the International' (1994) 10 *Conn JIL*, 1–26.

[101] See, e.g., J. Martin Rochester, 'The Rise and Fall of International Organization as a Field of Study' (1986) 40 *International Organization*, 777–813.

[102] The argument is perhaps most pressingly formulated in David Kennedy, 'A New World Order: Yesterday, Today, and Tomorrow' (1994) 4 *Transnational Law and Contemporary Problems*, 1–47. See also Michael N. Barnett, 'Bringing in the New World Order: Liberalism, Legitimacy, and the United Nations' (1997) 49 *World Politics*, 526–51.

[103] Such a possible exception was Mussolini's plan, launched in the 1930s, to create a formal directorate of the four leading European powers at the time (i.e., France, Britain, Italy and Hitler's Germany). See Van Diepen, *Voor Volkenbond en vrede*, p. 143. During the spring of 2008, there was some discussion in the US (including its Congress) about the possibility of suing OPEC for causing high oil prices. This would entail re-branding OPEC as a cartel, which would also feed the suggestion that not everything international organizations do is inherently good. See, e.g., 'House Votes to Allow US to File Suit vs. OPEC', *Boston Globe*, 21 May 2008, available at www.boston.com/bostonglobe (last visited 17 July 2008).

[104] See generally Filip Tuytschaever, *Differentiation in European Union Law* (Oxford, 1999). For an insightful analysis of subsidiarity (and its limits), see Gareth Davies, 'Subsidiarity: The Wrong Idea, in the Wrong Place, at the Wrong Time', (2006) 43 *CMLRev*, 63–84.

limited – too limited, at any rate, to qualify as a general theory of international institutional law.[105]

Third, as a matter of theory, the idea of 'functional necessity' suffers from the drawback that organizations are rarely, if at all, created according to blueprints involving preconceived theoretical or quasi-theoretical notions. Instead, they are the result, invariably, of negotiations, and therewith of power struggles and struggles between competing ideas. And while surely 'functional necessity' may be among the ideas launched, its acceptance by negotiating partners is by no means guaranteed. Instead, they are likely to entertain different ideas on the functional necessities of any given organization at any given moment in time. And thus, as a unifying theme underlying the law of international organizations, the concept of 'functional necessity' simply will not do.

That is not to say that the notion of functional necessity is completely useless. In good hands, it may facilitate the solution of practical problems. There can be little doubt that courts and tribunals at times resort to the notion in order to solve disputes before them, and the result may well be a fair one. In addition, it may occasionally constitute, as we shall see, a fair description *ex post facto*.

Organizations and their members

Instead of trying to offer the false security of the functional necessity theory, this book is written on the basis of the idea (theory is too big a word) that much of the law of international organizations is the result of the fundamental tension between the organization and its members.[106]

In popular thinking, organizations are probably pretty much perceived as entities which somehow would stand (or at least would have to stand) above their members. This common position is well summarized by the novelist George Orwell in the following quotation, written in 1946, just a few months after the creation of the UN:

In order to have any efficiency whatever, a world organization must be able to override big states as well as small ones. It must have power to inspect and limit armaments, which means that its officials must have access to every square inch of every country. It must also have at its disposal an armed force bigger than any other armed force and responsible to the organization itself. The two or three great states that really matter have never even pretended to agree to any of these conditions, and they have so arranged the constitution of UNO that their own actions cannot even be discussed. In other words, UNO's usefulness as an instrument of world peace is nil. This was just as obvious before it began

---

[105] See, in particular, Chapter 8 below.
[106] For further elaboration, see Jan Klabbers, 'Two Concepts of International Organization', (2005) 2 *IOLR*, 277–93. Differently conceived and organized, but not dissimilar in tenor, is John H. Barton, 'Two Ideas of International Organization', (1983–4) 82 *Michigan Law Review*, 1520–32. See also Niels M. Blokker, 'International Organizations and their Members' (2004) 1 *IOLR*, 139–61.

functioning as it is now. Yet only a few months ago millions of well-informed people believed that it was going to be a success.[107]

The interesting aspect is that Orwell does not stop after having proclaimed that organizations should stand above their members. Instead, he starts by describing an ideal type, then blames the member states for not creating this ideal type, and finally blames the organization for not living up to the ideal type. In other words, Orwell unwittingly captured the fundamental tension between international organizations and their member states: organizations are, at one and the same time, independent of their members (or at least ought to be so), and fundamentally dependent on them.[108] And that idea as such is hardly novel; the French jurist Paul Reuter, without developing it to the fullest extent in his subsequent analysis, could already approach the field in much the same way in 1967.[109]

In short, many of the ambiguities that the law of international organizations appears to be so particularly rich in become understandable when examined against the background of the relationship between the organization and its members. The idea behind this book is to explore that tension in relation to a variety of topics.[110]

Seemingly endless discussions on issues such as the implied powers doctrine, the teleological interpretation of constituent documents, or whether member states retain a hold on an organization are indeed, quite literally, endless. A common characteristic of such debates is that one can either occupy a position favouring the member states or occupy a position favouring the organization without being able to say which is the better view, at least not without lapsing into the type of normative thinking which supposedly ought not to form a part of the law. Thus, as we shall see below, it is easy to advocate the implied powers doctrine with a view to the needs of the organization, but in the end, that is merely subjecting a purported legal rule (i.e., the implied powers doctrine) to a political opinion (i.e., the needs of the organization must be taken into account). Yet without such a political opinion, the argument becomes merely one among various possible candidates. Without having the needs of the organization in view, advocacy of the implied powers doctrine simply falls flat, and has little to offer: its attraction resides precisely in its being hooked up to a normative proposition.

---

[107] See George Orwell, *The Collected Essays, Journalism and Letters of George Orwell. Volume 4: In Front of Your Nose 1945–1950* (1968; Harmondsworth, 1970), pp. 152–3.

[108] The same tension informs influential politicians and statesmen. For an example, see Richard von Weiszäcker, 'All Depends on Member States'. In Georges Abi-Saab *et al.*, *Paix, développement, démocratie. Boutros Boutros-Ghali Amicorum Discipulorumque Liber* (Brussels, 1999), pp. 827–37. Von Weiszäcker is a former President of Germany, and co-chaired one of the more serious working groups on UN reform in the first half of the 1990s.

[109] Paul Reuter, *Institutions internationales* (Paris, 1967), p. 204.

[110] Greater than the number of topics relating to organizations contained in Reuter's *Institutions internationales* and probably less inclined to proclaim a given equilibrium as reflecting the law.

If this is correct, then it follows that large branches of the law of international organizations are fundamentally uncertain: if we change our normative propositions, we find different legal rules to be hooked up with. If, instead of favouring the needs of the organization, we take the side of the members, then the implied powers doctrine loses its attraction and may easily be replaced by the doctrine of attributed powers.[111]

Part of the relation between the organization and its members, moreover, is coloured by the curious circumstance that, in some respects, the organization and its members may well be indistinguishable from each other. That holds true in the rather obvious sense that behind the organization there are always its members, but also in the less obvious sense of observers not being able to tell, at any given moment, whether an act is undertaken by an organization or by its members *en groupe*.[112] It is this curious circumstance which influences to a large extent many of the uncertainties characterizing the law when it comes to the external activities of organizations, from treaty-making to issues of accountability. And as I shall explore in somewhat more depth in the closing chapter, this fading into each other of organizations and their members also has some wider theoretical ramifications, in particular when it concerns the position of international organizations in international society.

---

[111] As Chapter 4 below will demonstrate, things can be taken even further: in the end, there is fairly little which distinguishes the two seemingly opposed doctrines.

[112] Indeed, developments such as creating a European Union of doubtful legal quality or ostensible 'non-organizations' such as the OSCE tap into precisely this fundamental equivalence.

3

The legal position of international organizations

Introduction

International organizations are generally counted among the subjects of international law, together with states, individuals and perhaps some other entities as well.[1] Thus, in accordance with the standard definition of 'subject', they are deemed capable of independently bearing rights and obligations under international law.[2]

This has not always been the case. In the late nineteenth and early twentieth centuries, it was customary for international lawyers to claim that states, and states alone, could independently bear rights and obligations under international law.[3] Other entities were not to be considered as subjects or, at best, were analysed in state-centric terms: as gatherings of states, or as derogations from statehood (e.g., servitudes) or as essentially unclassifiable experiments.[4] And the question as to whether international organizations could be regarded as subjects of international law reverberated well into the second half of the twentieth century.[5]

As the International Court of Justice recognized in the *Reparation for Injuries* opinion, the subjects of international law may come in various shapes and guises. The Court held that: '[t]he subjects of law in any legal system are not

---

[1] International corporations, national liberation movements and belligerents are also sometimes counted among the subjects of international law.

[2] Compare, e.g., Bin Cheng, 'Introduction to Subjects of International Law'. In Mohammed Bedjaoui (ed.), *International Law: Achievements and Prospects* (Dordrecht, 1991), pp. 23–40. A rare study of the EC as a subject of international law is to be found in Jan Vanhamme, *Volkenrechtelijke beginselen in het Europees recht* (Groningen, 2001).

[3] See David J. Bederman, 'The Souls of International Organizations: Legal Personality and the Lighthouse at Cape Spartel' (1996) 36 *VaJIL*, 275–377.

[4] Thus, Verzijl treats the League of Nations and the UN under the heading of 'exceptional and unique persons', alongside belligerents, internationalized territories and the Pope. See J. H. W. Verzijl, *International Law in Historical Perspective. Part II: International Persons* (Leiden, 1969), esp. pp. 303–5.

[5] See, e.g., John Fischer Williams, 'The Status of the League of Nations in International Law', reprinted in his *Chapters on Current International Law and the League of Nations* (London, 1929), pp. 477–500; C. Wilfred Jenks, *Law In the World Community* (London, 1967), esp. p. 7; also C. N. Okeke, *Controversial Subjects of Contemporary International Law* (Rotterdam, 1974), Chapters 10–11.

necessarily identical in their nature or in the extent of their rights, and their nature depends on the needs of the community.[6]

There is no standard set of rights and obligations for each and every subject of international law; instead, 'subject' is a relative notion, the precise contents of which may differ from subject to subject and even between various subjects of the same category. While is it generally recognized that at least international organizations and individuals can be viewed as subjects of international law, not all individuals enjoy the exact same bundle of rights and obligations: it may well make a difference whether one lives in Norway or in Myanmar. Similarly, not all organizations possess identical sets of rights and obligations.

Indicators of 'subjectivity'

The idea of 'subjects' of the international legal system is a confusing idea, and the confusion stems in part from being conflated with the notion of international legal personality. For many authors, understandably, subjectivity and legal personality are one and the same, and there is nothing particularly wrong with treating them as such in pragmatic fashion.[7] Yet, strictly speaking, they are not identical. To be a subject of international law is to be given an academic label: a subject of international law is the legitimate subject of international legal research and reflection. Any attempt by an international lawyer to study, for example, the workings of the city of Amsterdam, or of the Finnish Icehockey Association, or the Roman Catholic church, can be challenged in terms of subjectivity: as these are not generally regarded as subjects of international law, the international legal scholar may have to address claims that he or she could have spent his or her time better.

While subjectivity is, thus, a status conferred by the academic community (and thus by definition inaccurate and sketchy), personality is, in principle at any rate, a status conferred by the legal system.[8] The confusion then stems from the circumstance that the international legal system does not have a single authority endowed with the power to confer personality; indeed, in an important sense, the academic community makes up the legal system.[9]

Given the fluid nature of the very notion of subjects of international law, and the circumstance that different subjects may entertain different sets of rights and obligations under international law, the precise degree of rights and obligations

[6] *Reparation for Injuries Suffered in the Service of the United Nations,* advisory opinion, [1949] ICJ Reports 174, p. 178.

[7] So, e.g., Bengt Broms, 'Subjects: Entitlements in the International Legal System'. In R. St J. MacDonald and D. M. Johnston (eds.), *The Structure and Process of International Law* (The Hague, 1983), pp. 383–423.

[8] See Jan Klabbers, 'The Concept of Legal Personality', (2005) 11 *Ius Gentium,* 35–66. The same type of thinking underlies Schachter's famous conception of the 'invisible college of international lawyers'. See Oscar Schachter, 'The Invisible College of International Lawyers' (1977) 72 *Northwestern University Law Review,* 217–26.

is a matter of analysis, and as a starting point most international lawyers will determine the extent of 'subjectivity'[10] of any possible subject with the help of three indicators.[11] The first is, whether the subject in question possesses the right to enter into international agreements; the second is whether they have the right to send and receive legations; and the third is whether they can bring and receive international claims. These are not, to be sure, strictly legal requirements; we cannot maintain that if an organization does not exercise one of them, it therefore ceases to be an organization.[12] Much less do they constitute a comprehensive definition of subjects of international law. At best, they can be viewed as indicators: to the extent that proposed subjects score on any of these indicators, they can be deemed to be subjects of international law.

Where those indicators themselves come from is a different matter altogether.[13] The International Court, in the *Reparation for Injuries* opinion, alluded to the existence of at least two of them (the right to enter into treaties, and the right to bring claims), but without specifying their source. Presumably, then, those indicators are best viewed as the result of inductive analysis: as all subjects of international law are seen to possess at least one of those character-istics, together they become a decent yardstick by which to measure the degree of subjectivity. Whereas states possess all three simply by reason of being states, other subjects usually do not, or at least not in an unlimited fashion.

Treaty-making capacity?

The treaty-making capacity (*jus tractatuum*) of international organizations has long been subject to some debate. Judges Fitzmaurice and Spender, for example, in their joint dissenting opinion to the first *South West Africa cases*,[14] wondered aloud whether the League of Nations ever possessed such capacity and could thus have been a party to the mandate South Africa held over South West Africa (nowadays known as Namibia).

---

[10] The word is a Germanism, and not a very pretty one at that. Unfortunately, I cannot think of an alternative.

[11] This derives loosely from Ian Brownlie, *Principles of Public International Law* (4th edn, Oxford, 1990), p. 58. A similar list, with the addition of privileges and immunities (which, apparently, are regarded as being granted automatically through operation of law) is used by Amir A. Majid, *Legal Status of International Institutions: SITA, INMARSAT and EUROCONTROL Examined* (Aldershot, 1996), pp. 176–84. The approach is, admittedly, not without flaws, as the yardstick used is the state. See Broms, 'Subjects', p. 383.

[12] With respect to the EU, such an argument is made by Astéris Pliakos, 'La nature juridique de l'Union européenne' (1993) 29 *RTDE*, 187–224.

[13] As a matter of method, perhaps the idea as such was inspired by Hohfeldian analysis. Hohfeld held, in a nutshell, that all legal relationships can be analysed by using four different terms, their negatives and their opposites: Wesley N. Hohfeld, *Fundamental Legal Conceptions as Applied in Judicial Reasoning* (1919; Westport, CN, 1978).

[14] *South West Africa Cases* (*Ethiopia* v. *South Africa*; *Liberia* v. *South Africa*) preliminary objections, [1962] ICJ Reports 319, esp. pp. 495ff.

At present, the treaty-making capacity of international organizations has, in general, been accepted.[15] What is still a matter of debate, though, is where this capacity springs from, the main bone of contention being whether such power derives directly from public international law or rather from the constituent instrument of the organization in question. If it is the former, then the capacity is, in principle, unlimited; if the latter holds good, then the capacity to enter into treaties is, in principle, limited unless the constituent treaty grants the organization a blank cheque.

The 1986 Vienna Convention on the Law of Treaties concluded with or between International Organizations appears, eventually, to choose the first option. According to its preamble, 'international organizations possess the capacity to conclude treaties which is necessary for the exercise of their functions and the fulfillment of their purposes'; the formulation appears to suggest that capacity derives from international law.[16] While it may be limited by the reference to the functions and purposes of the organization, such criteria are rather flexible to begin with and, moreover, can be changed at will by the member states.

Article 6 of the 1986 Convention further specifies in holding that '[t]he capacity of international organizations to conclude treaties is governed by the rules of that organization'.[17] Thus, while capacity stems from public international law, it is governed (and thus potentially limited) by the specific rules of the organization, and those are described as including 'the constituent instruments, decisions and resolutions adopted in accordance with them and established practice of the organization'.[18]

As will be demonstrated below, this must also include implied powers or even inherent powers of organizations (if these exist at all), as with many organizations specific powers to enter into specific kinds of agreements are not granted explicitly. If they exist at all, they are usually deemed to be implied somehow in the rules of the organization, or perhaps considered to be inherent in the fact of 'organizationhood'.

And if the capacity to conclude treaties flows directly from international law, then at least on this point the position of organizations is akin to that of states.

---

[15] See generally, below, Chapter 13.

[16] Karl Zemanek, 'The United Nations Conference on the Law of Treaties Between States and International Organizations or Between International Organizations: The Unrecorded History of its General Agreement'. In Karl-Heinz Böckstiegel *et al.* (eds.), *Völkerrecht, Recht der internationalen Organisationen, Weltwirtschaftsrecht: Festschrift für Ignaz Seidl-Hohenveldern* (Cologne, 1988), pp. 665–79. Seyersted argued in 1983 that it could not be any other way; see Finn Seyersted, 'Treaty-making Capacity of Intergovernmental Organizations: Article 6 of the International Law Commission's Draft Articles on the Law of Treaties between States and International Organizations or between International Organizations' (1983) 34 *ÖZöRV*, 261–7. See more generally Finn Seyersted, *Common Law of International Organizations* (Leiden, 2008), p. 373.

[17] Seyersted's 'Treaty-making Capacity', offers a vigorous critique.

[18] Article 2(1)(j) of the 1986 Convention.

For, with states too, their capacity derives directly from international law, and with states too, it is not unusual that the capacity is, in turn, hemmed in by 'internal' concerns. The clearest example thereof is perhaps that enshrined in the Japanese constitution (the renunciation of war and the threat or use of force), which also makes the participation of Japan in international military operations extremely controversial.[19]

The right to send and receive legations?

Do organizations, generally speaking, have the right to send and receive missions (*jus missionis*)? The answer must be in the affirmative, as practice reveals that, generally speaking, a number of international organizations have permanent missions with states, and that states have permanent missions with international organizations.

By way of illustration, in December 1995, some 125 states had diplomats accredited to the European Community. Most of those combine their EC accreditation with being their state's ambassador to Belgium and perhaps some other states as well.[20] The EC itself also has missions, for instance in Geneva, Tokyo and Washington, DC.

Moreover, it is not only states that may have missions with international organizations, and *vice versa*. It is far from unique for international organizations to have missions with one another, and as the International Court of Justice implicitly confirmed in 1988, other entities may have missions as well. *In casu*, the issue related to the observer mission of the Palestine Liberation Organization with the UN, which had been in existence since 1974.[21]

The existence of the *jus missionis* is also indicated by the conclusion of the 1975 Vienna Convention on the Representation of States in their Relations with International Organizations of a Universal Character. The Convention purports to regulate the diplomatic relations engaged in by a group of international organizations, which already indicates that there is something to be regulated. The fact that, despite having been concluded in 1975, it still awaits its entry into force does not in any way affect that conclusion.[22]

---

[19] For a useful overview, see Hisashi Owada, 'Japan's Constitutional Power to Participate in Peace-keeping' (1997) 27 *New York University Journal of International Law & Politics*, 271–84.

[20] The information is derived from Commission Européenne, *Corps diplomatique accrédité auprès des Communautés européennes et représentations auprès de la Commission: Décembre 1995* (Luxembourg, 1995).

[21] *Applicability of the Obligation to Arbitrate under Section 21 of the United Nations Headquarters Agreement of 26 June 1947*, advisory opinion, [1988] ICJ Reports 12. The European Community's accreditation list (see previous note) mentions nineteen non-state entities, ranging from international organizations such as the UN to territories such as Hong Kong and Macao, and the Maltese Sovereign Order.

[22] The Convention requires, in accordance with Article 89, the consent to be bound of thirty-five states.

Right to bring and receive claims?

Finally, as early as 1949 the International Court of Justice affirmed that international organizations may have the capacity to bring international claims. It did so in its *Reparation for Injuries* opinion, and the Court appeared to imply that the right to bring claims was inherent in being an organization. At any rate, it failed to indicate the specific source of the right, stating simply that '[i]t cannot be doubted'[23] that the UN could lodge a claim against a member state, and that the right to present claims regarding damage done to the UN itself was 'clear'.[24]

The content of the right to bring claims was also clear, in the Court's view:

> Competence to bring an international claim is, for those possessing it, the capacity to resort to the customary methods recognized by international law for the establishment, the presentation and the settlement of claims. Among these methods may be mentioned protest, request for an enquiry, negotiation, and request for submission to an arbitral tribunal or to the Court in so far as this may be authorized by the [ICJ's] Statute.[25]

As a practical matter, the possibilities for international organizations to bring claims may be subject to limitations. Thus, there is no doubt that, at present, they cannot be a party before the ICJ in contentious proceedings.[26] Article 34(1) of the ICJ Statute specifies clearly that '[o]nly states may be parties in cases before the Court'.

No considerations of principle, however, stand in the way of international organizations bringing (or receiving) claims before other tribunals. The courts of various states have had the opportunity to address claims brought by or against international organizations, and organizations have also appeared before various arbitral tribunals. However, while no considerations of principle stand in the way, whether it is actually possible for international organizations to sue or be sued may depend on issues of immunity (to be discussed elsewhere[27]).

---

[23] *Reparation for Injuries*, p. 180.   [24] *Ibid.*

[25] *Reparation for Injuries*, p. 177. Note that, in the Court's view, notions such as the 'competence' and 'capacity' of international organizations are synonymous. Sometimes, in the literature, much stress is placed on a distinction between the two, but such appears unwarranted. At the very least, it may be remarked that the distinction does not, as such, play a very prominent role in other legal systems.

[26] Nevertheless various authors have advocated a *jus standi* for international organizations before the ICJ. See, e.g., Paul Szasz, 'Granting International Organizations *Ius Standi* in the International Court of Justice'. In A. S. Muller *et al.* (eds.), *The International Court of Justice: Its Future Role After Fifty Years* (The Hague, 1997), pp. 169–88. Elihu Lauterpacht has proposed to vest suitable organizations with the power to present claims to the ICJ not so much in relation to their own rights as legal entities, but rather on behalf of the international community at large. See Elihu Lauterpacht, *Aspects of the Administration of International Justice* (Cambridge, 1991), pp. 62–4.

[27] See below, Chapter 8.

as well as on whether or not they have standing,[28] which in turn may or may not depend on whether they are to be considered as having legal personality.

Legal personality under domestic law

Hypothetically, entities can possess legal personality under any legal system, dependent on whether they meet the requirements which that legal system posits for acceptance of the entity's personality. Each legal system is, essentially, free to develop its own requirements; requirements may thus differ from state to state. The requirements under Brazilian law may differ from those of the US, which in turn may be substantially different from those of Kuwait, or from those (if any) posited by the international legal system.

That is not to say that those various differing legal personalities are unrelated. For one thing, as will be indicated below, a legal person under the laws of state X may often be recognized as having personality by state Y, as comity may demand that state Y will not debate the validity of grants of personality by state X. But there is also a connection (or at least there used to be) between domestic and international legal personality. As Bederman reminds us, in the first half of the twentieth century domestic legal systems often looked to international law for guidance: entities could be granted domestic personality on the basis of them having already been granted international legal personality.[29]

In order to overcome this roundabout way of doing things, many constituent treaties of international organizations nowadays make some form of provision as regards their personality under the domestic law of their member states.[30] Thus, Article 104 of the UN Charter states: 'The Organization shall enjoy in the territory of each of its Members such legal capacity as may be necessary for the exercise of its functions and the fulfillment of its purposes.'

The formula used in Article 104 of the Charter comes close to being a blank cheque, and reflects something of a 'functional necessity' test, speaking as it does of 'such legal capacity as may be necessary for the exercise of its functions and the fulfillment of its purposes'. Generally, this is taken to imply that the organization possesses the largest possible degree of personality as recognized in domestic law.

Something similar applies to the EC, under Article 282 (ex-Article 211) TEC. This provision starts by saying that '[i]n each of the member states, the Community shall enjoy the most extensive legal capacity accorded to legal persons under their laws'.

---

[28] See, e.g., *Arab Monetary Fund* v. *Hashim and others*, decision of 21 February 1991, UK House of Lords, 85 *ILR* 1. For an illustrative example regarding a non-governmental organization before the EC Court, see Case C-321/95 P, *Stichting Greenpeace Council and others* v. *Commission* [1998] ECR I-1651.

[29] Bederman, 'The Souls of International Organizations', p. 351.

[30] Not all, though. The constituent documents of, *inter alia*, the Western European Union, the North Atlantic Treaty Organization and the Council of Europe are silent on the issue.

Again, thus, the provision grants a broad scope of personality under domestic law. Article 282 (ex-Article 211) TEC proceeds by giving some illustrations: the Community 'may, in particular, acquire or dispose of movable and immovable property and may be a party to legal proceedings'.

Of course, such provisions can only affect the organization's position within its member states. The EC, for example, cannot itself decide whether it also has legal personality in, say, Ethiopia: such would depend on Ethiopian law. This follows logically from an important principle of the law of treaties: the *pacta tertiis* maxim, as codified in Article 34 of the 1969 Vienna Convention on the Law of Treaties and holding that states cannot create rights or obligations for third parties without the consent of those third parties.[31]

Should the EC wish to sue an Ethiopian company in Ethiopia, then it is up to the Ethiopian courts whether or not to allow the EC to do so. In such a case, the courts may well ask the advice of the government. If, for example, the Ethiopian government has recognized the EC, this may not be much of a problem. The point is, however, that international law is silent on this issue: it all depends on Ethiopian law.

A nice case in point is the case of the *Arab Monetary Fund* v. *Hashim and others*.[32] The Arab Monetary Fund, established in 1976 as an organization comprising twenty Arab states plus the Palestine Liberation Organization (PLO), brought proceedings in the English courts against its former Director-General, Dr Hashim, and some other individuals, claiming a misappropriation of AMF funds. The defendants moved to strike, claiming that the AMF did not possess personality under English law. The House of Lords would eventually hold that the AMF could sue Dr Hashim; their Lordships held, *per* Lord Templeman, that the Fund was given legal personality by the United Arab Emirates (where it had its seat), and that comity required that the 'status of an international organisation incorporated by at least one foreign state should also be recognised by the Courts of the United Kingdom'.[33]

The point to note is, of course, that considerations of international law hardly entered the picture.[34] The House of Lords argued that under English law, recognition of foreign corporate bodies is a matter of comity, provided the foreign states where those bodies are registered are themselves recognized by the Crown.[35] Moreover, the legal personality of the Fund in the United Arab

---

31 For explicit recognition hereof, see e.g., Article 44 EBRD.

32 For an analysis, see Geoffrey Marston, 'The Personality of International Organisations in English Law' (1997) 2 *Hofstra Law & Policy Symposium*, 75–115, esp. pp. 98–103.

33 *Arab Monetary Fund*, p. 13. The earlier decisions of the High Court and the Court of Appeal are reproduced in 83 *ILR* 243.

34 See similarly the decision of the Utrecht Distict Court (The Netherlands) of 23 February 1949 in *UNRRA* v. *Daan,* in 16 *AD* (1949) 337.

35 And note that the reason that caused Lord Lowry to dissent also resided in considerations of English law: the status of international organizations in English law was controlled by the International Organizations Act of 1968, which in essence provides that organizations are

Emirates was itself, so the House of Lords held, a matter which had been decided by the law of the United Arab Emirates. As Lord Templeman put it:

> when sovereign states enter into an agreement by treaty to confer legal personality on an international organisation, the treaty does not create a corporate body. But when the AMF agreement was registered in the UAE by means of Federal Decree No. 35 that registration conferred on the international organisation legal personality and thus created a corporate body which the English courts can and should recognise.[36]

The *Arab Monetary Fund* v. *Hashim* case conveniently illustrates to what extent issues of international and domestic law may get entangled when it comes to personality under domestic law, and it also illustrates a fundamental degree of uncertainty concerning the legal nature of international organizations them-selves. Thus, the respondents felt fit to argue that the AMF had created not just one legal person, but that there had been twenty-one legal personalities (one each for every member state and the PLO) and that 'it is not clear whether Dr Hashim embezzled the money from the UAE fund or the money of a fund established by some other Arab state'.[37] Whereas the argument failed to con-vince both the majority and the dissenting Lord, it is telling in its own right that it was made to begin with.

The domestic legal personality of an organization may also extend to its organs, and even its subsidiary bodies. Thus in 1990, the UN's Office of Legal Affairs unhesitatingly advised a Director at a subsidiary body of the General Assembly, the UN Development Programme (UNDP), that representatives of UNDP have the authority to conclude contractual arrangements. According to the Office of Legal Affairs, this authority flows from the Charter's provision on personality in Article 104.[38] The authority does not go so far, however, as to allow a subsidiary body to participate in the creation of a corporate body under some domestic legal system, largely because such would be difficult to reconcile with the international status of the organ and its staff.[39]

International legal personality

The position of international organizations in various domestic legal systems is usually explicitly provided for in the constituent treaty of the organiza-tion; the main problem to overcome then is the position in non-member states. By contrast, the international legal personality of organizations has traditionally given rise to serious and heated doctrinal debates. In essence,

---

recognized by means of an Order in Council. No such order had been made concerning the AMF.

[36] *Arab Monetary Fund*, p. 5.   [37] As rendered by Lord Templeman, *ibid.*, p. 7.

[38] See *UNJY* (1990), pp. 276–7. The same position was taken with respect to the personality of the UN Council for Namibia in municipal law (see *UNJY* (1982), pp. 164–5), as well as in a reply to a questionnaire from the Institut de Droit International (see *UNJY* (1976), pp. 159–77).

[39] *UNJY* (1990), pp. 259–60, again concerning UNDP.

the debate has been dominated by two contending theories,[40] both of which invoke the International Court's opinion in *Reparation for Injuries* in support: the 'will theory' (or 'subjective theory', perhaps) and the 'objective theory' of personality.

The *Reparation for Injuries* opinion arose out of the establishment of the state of Israel, which created enough unrest in the Middle East for the UN to send a mediator: the Swedish Count Folke Bernadotte. Unfortunately, Count Bernadotte and several of his associates lost their lives, and consequently the UN wondered whether it could bring a legal claim against the entity it held responsible. Consequently, the General Assembly of the United Nations asked the Court whether the UN would possess such a right, and, as already noted, the Court answered in the affirmative.

In the process, the Court devoted some attention to the question of international legal personality, presumably for two related reasons. First, the UN Charter itself did not contain anything on the possibility of the UN bringing a claim. Second, even if the Charter had contained something, Israel was, at the time, not yet a member state, and there remained thus the question as to whether a right to bring a claim would be opposable against Israel to begin with.

The Court would reach the conclusion that indeed the UN was to be regarded as having international legal personality and as having the right to bring a claim, both in its own name and in the name of its employees, but, unfortunately, it remains something of a mystery as to why exactly the Court reached that conclusion. And that, in turn, makes it possible to invoke the decision in support of two diametrically opposed theories.

Under the 'will theory' (by far the more popular of the two), it is the will of the founders of the organization which decides on the organization's legal personality. Thus, if the founders intend to endow their creation with personality under international law, then such will be the case. If they wish to withhold legal personality from their creation, then here too their intention will control the issue.

The main attraction of the will theory resides, no doubt, in being in conformity with positivist notions. Generally, international law is thought to be based on the freely expressed consent of states,[41] and therefore the same should apply to the creation of international organizations. It is difficult to go against states' wishes in international law, so when states have clear intentions concerning the legal personality of international organizations they have established, then those intentions must be respected.[42]

---

[40] Kuyper identifies four contending theories, but acknowledges that not all of these are, as it were, active. See Pieter Jan Kuyper, 'The Netherlands and International Organizations'. In H. F. van Panhuys *et al.* (eds.), *International Law In the Netherlands, Volume II* (Alphen aan den Rijn, 1979), pp. 3–41, esp. pp. 15–19.

[41] In accordance with the classic *Case of the SS Lotus*, [1927] Publ. PCIJ, Series A, no. 10.

[42] The UN's Office of Legal Affairs seems to work on this theory. See, e.g., its opinion on a proposed Asian Clearing Union, in *UNJY* (1971), pp. 215–18.

A serious problem is, however, that relatively few constituent treaties explicitly provide for the international legal personality of organizations.[43] The UN Charter, for one, lacks such a provision: the topic was considered during the drafting of the Charter, but the subcommittee bearing responsibility for what was to become Article 104 (quoted above) eventually rejected a proposal to refer to international legal personality alongside domestic legal personality: they did not think any explicit reference was necessary.[44]

Another problem for the will theory is that it opens up the possibility that the international legal personality of an organization is an empty concept: what if a number of states decided to create an international organization and endow it with international legal personality, yet no one is willing to enter into any engagements with it? Under such a scenario, personality would be an empty concept, devoid of meaning, something which might exist on paper, but with no empirical reverberations.

In order to overcome this problem, many advocates of the will theory resort to recognition by third parties of an organization's international legal capacity, but that renders the will theory incoherent: if the question of an organization's international legal personality depends ultimately (or even partly) on recognition by third parties, then the importance of the will of the founders becomes difficult to sustain.[45]

Indeed, some scholars have seen fit to reverse the situation, to such an extent that the will theory can hardly be deemed to be based on the will of the founders anymore. Thus, Bieber purposefully lists recognition as the decisive factor,[46] and Timmermans, re-writing the pertinent chapter in Kapteyn and VerLoren van Themaat's classic Dutch language textbook on European Community law, even goes so far as to proclaim that since the EC has been recognized by so many states, its international legal personality has become objective.[47] In other words: those (if they exist at all) who do not wish to do business with the EC have no choice but to accept its personality, simply because

---

[43] At best, the provisions are ambiguous, providing quite simply that the organization concerned 'shall have legal personality' or similar terms. Thus, e.g., Art. 281 (formerly Art. 210) TEC. Also not devoid from ambiguity is Art. XVI(1) of the FAO constitution, which holds that the FAO 'shall have the capacity of a legal person to perform any legal act appropriate to its purpose which is not beyond the powers granted to it by this Constitution'. Clearly limited to domestic legal personality are, *inter alia*, Art. 39 ILO, Art. 66 WTO, Art. 47 ICAO and Art. 95(2) Benelux.

[44] As the UNESCO constitution incorporates Art. 104 of the Charter (see Art. XII UNESCO), here too an explicit endowment with international legal personality is absent.

[45] Recognition is, in any event, something of a misnomer, as Köck correctly argues. He goes on to posit the somewhat curious argument that, since recognition is a purely political act anyway, there is no legal answer to the question of whether an organization should be recognized. See H. F. Köck, 'Questions Related to the Recognition of the European Communities' (1997) 2 *ARIEL*, 49–68.

[46] Compare the introduction to his *Draft of a Consolidated Treaty of the European Union*, European Parliament, Directorate-General for Research, Working Paper, Political series W-17/Rev., March 1996, p. 15.

[47] P. J. G. Kapteyn and P. VerLoren van Themaat, *Inleiding tot het recht van de Europese Gemeenschappen na Maastricht* (5th edn, Deventer, 1995), pp. 63–4.

so many before them have done so. Clearly, the point as such makes sense, but equally clearly it cannot be explained by relying solely on the will of the founding states, and it is this circumstance which renders the will theory incoherent.[48]

Some of these objections are met by the main rival of the will theory, the so-called 'objective theory' of personality as devised, in the early 1960s, by Norwegian international lawyer Finn Seyersted.[49] According to Seyersted, the legal personality of international organizations follows the same pattern as that of states: as soon as an entity exists as a matter of law, (i.e., meets the requirements that international law attaches to its establishment) that entity possesses international legal personality. For states, this follows from their acquisition of statehood; for organizations, then, it follows from acquisition of 'organizationhood'. Importantly, then, the will of the founders does not decide on personality as a separate matter.

An obvious question then is: what are the requirements of international law with respect to 'organizationhood'? Seyersted's main criterion was that the organization must possess a distinct will of its own,[50] but that raises the problem of the extent to which such a distinct will is more than a useful legal fiction. As long as an organization is not empowered to take decisions binding its membership by a mere majority of its members, one can hardly speak, in any literal sense, of the organization having a 'distinct will';[51] unanimous decisions, after all, can always be traced back to the member states.

Moreover, and more fundamentally, Seyersted's objective theory raises the prospect of going against the intentions of the founders, and therewith elevates itself to *jus cogens* status. Surely, if states intend their creation to be devoid of international legal personality, then such intention ought to be respected, and cannot be overruled by a rule of general international law saying that organizations shall have international legal personality irrespective of a clear contrary intention on the part of the founders. Or rather, such a rule would be meaningless if one cannot force the organization to act as an international legal person.

It should come as no surprise, then, that practice has shown a more pragmatic approach to questions of international legal personality, perhaps best captured by the phrase 'presumptive personality': as soon as an organization performs acts which can only be explained on the basis of international legal personality,

---

[48] Perhaps it is also useful to note that explicit acts of recognition of organizations are extremely rare.

[49] More recently, Seyersted's approach has found some support in Nigel D. White, *The Law of International Organisations* (Manchester, 1996).

[50] See Finn Seyersted, *Objective International Personality of Intergovernmental Organizations: Do their Capacities Really Depend on the Conventions Establishing them?* (Copenhagen, 1963), esp. p. 47. See also Seyersted, *Common Law*, Chapter 8.

[51] Indeed, as late as 1980, the idea of a 'distinct will' was vehemently denied. See Reinhold Reutersward, 'The Legal Nature of International Organizations' (1980) 49 *Nordisk TIR*, 14–30.

such an organization will be presumed to be in possession of international legal personality.[52]

The notion of presumptive personality is supported by the above-mentioned *Reparation for Injuries* opinion of the International Court of Justice. In an oft-quoted passage, the Court held 'that fifty States, representing the vast majority of the members of the international community, had the power, in conformity with international law, to bring into being an entity possessing objective international personality, and not merely personality recognized by them alone, together with capacity to bring claims'.[53] The surprising element in this passage is that the Court did not specify if those fifty states had actually used their power to create an entity with international legal personality. The Court merely presumed this to be the case, and as no one bothered to rebut the presumption, it survived.[54]

That presumption, moreover, could hardly have been related to the intentions of the founders. These, as noted earlier, actively decided not to provide for the personality at international law of the UN, holding such a provision to be 'superfluous'. Instead, the drafters argued, the issue of personality 'will be determined implicitly from the provisions of the Charter taken as a whole'.[55]

The one drawback (if it is a drawback) of the presumptive approach is that it tends to make a mockery of the few instances where founders have actually made a provision granting their creation international legal personality. If it is true that an organization will be presumed to have international legal personality unless and until the opposite can be shown, does that not imply that a grant of personality is utterly useless?

The answer must be in the negative. At the very least, as Amerasinghe has pointed out, explicitly to endow an organization with personality under international law indicates that the founders wish to create an entity which is somehow separate from their aggregate, and that circumstance may be of evidentiary value when it comes to, for example, deciding on whether or not the member states of an organization incur liability for the activities of the organization.[56]

---

[52] See, for more details, Jan Klabbers, 'Presumptive Personality: The European Union in International Law'. In Martti Koskenniemi (ed.), *International Law Aspects of the European Union* (The Hague, 1998), pp. 231–53.

[53] *Reparation for Injuries*, p. 185. The reference to 'objective' personality is sometimes taken to mean that the UN is somehow qualitatively different because of its creation by what was at the time the vast majority of states. Thus, e.g., Köck, 'Recognition of the European Communities'.

[54] The emphasis political scientists place on the actual activities of the organization suggests a similar approach. See, e.g., Teija Tiilikainen, 'To Be or Not to Be? An Analysis of the Legal and Political Elements of Statehood in the EU's External Identity' (2001) 6 *European Foreign Affairs Review*, 223–41.

[55] *United Nations Conference on International Organization* (Documents), Vol. 13 (London, 1945), p. 817.

[56] C. F. Amerasinghe, *Principles of the Institutional Law of International Organizations* (Cambridge, 1996), pp. 68–70, and Chapter 9. The Italian Court of Cassation, in *Cristiani v. Italian Latin-American Institute* (decision of 25 November 1985, in 87 *ILR* 20), seems to have treated a grant of personality as the basis of jurisdictional immunity, through the working of the *par in parem non habet jurisdictionem* maxim.

Likewise, international legal personality may be thought to facilitate the acquisition of privileges and immunities, as suggested by Article 28 of the revised Benelux Treaty.[57] While the attribution of personality alone is not (and cannot be) decisive, it does provide an indication of what the drafters may have had in mind.

Concluding remarks

Presumably, the main position regarding the personality of international organizations in domestic law is that personality is controlled by the rules of the organization. However, under international law personality is, pragmatically, treated as a presumption, to be rebutted if the evidence points in the other direction. Thus, if the organization's constituent documents are silent on personality, and the organization performs no acts which point to personality, then personality will be absent. However, the absence of an explicit attribution alone will not settle the issue: many organizations can be seen to perform international legal activities despite the absence of an explicit grant of personality, and at times their preparatory works may even indicate, as with the UN, that the absence of any reference was intended.

This, then, points to another, more general consideration: perhaps we should be careful not to make too much of the very notion of personality (at least under international law) to begin with.[58] After all is said and done, personality in international law, like 'subjectivity', is but a descriptive notion: useful to describe a state of affairs, but normatively empty, as neither rights nor obligations flow automatically from it.[59]

Indeed, it is otherwise difficult to explain how an entity such as the EU, which is not explicitly endowed with international legal personality, and, therefore, many feel, does not possess international legal personality, can nonetheless perform international acts. Issues of personality notwithstanding, the EU does conclude agreements, does make the type of unilateral statements which may involve legally binding commitments, and has even taken on the administration of a town (Mostar) in the aftermath of the crisis in the Balkans?[60] Such activities are inexplicable in the absence of international legal personality, unless

---

[57] It provides that the Benelux Union enjoys international legal personality 'with a view to the granting of privileges and immunities' (translation mine – JK). The revised treaty was concluded in 2008; it is not yet in force.

[58] In a similar vein, Ige Dekker and Ramses Wessel, '"Lowering the Corporate Veil": Het recht der internationale organisaties vanuit de institutionele rechtstheorie'. In M. A. Heldeweg *et al.* (eds.), *De regel meester: Opstellen voor Dick W. P. Ruiter* (Enschede, 2001), pp. 5–22, esp. p. 10.

[59] Except, arguably, a very abstract sort of rights, such as the right to conclude treaties; still, those rights may also pertain to non-persons. After all, as practice indicates time and again, entities of doubtful legal personality engage in acts such as treaty-making. See, e.g., by way of illustration, Paola Gaeta, 'The Dayton Agreements and International Law' (1996) 7 *EJIL*, 147–63.

[60] See, e.g., Outi Korhonen, Jutta Gras and Katja Creutz, *International Post-Conflict Situations: New Challenges for Co-operative Governance*, (2nd edn, Helsinki, 2006), pp. 107–26.

international legal personality is itself a normatively empty (and essentially descriptive) concept.[61]

It would seem, then (despite the International Court's suggestion in *Reparation for Injuries*[62]) that personality is by no means a threshold which must be crossed before an entity can participate in international legal relations; instead, once an entity does participate, it may be usefully described as having a degree of international legal personality.

Some even go further, and argue that the very metaphor of personality is at least partly misleading. Bederman has observed that to think of organizations as 'persons' is, in effect, to deny their fundamental nature as 'communities'. Organizations, as Bederman points out, 'see themselves as the legal embodiment of communities, with complex interplays of equal and subordinate relations with states, with other organizations, and within the organs of the entity itself'.[63] To use the metaphor of 'personality' fails to do justice to this complexity, and may even be misleading. In Bederman's view, organizations are more important 'as places for the harmonization of policies, the exchange of ideas and even the making of friends than as centers of power in the international system'.[64]

While Bederman surely has a point in suggesting that the notion of 'personality' is not terribly helpful, one may wonder whether the 'community' notion will be more helpful. Or rather, it seems he does not go far enough. He is, as the title of his wonderful essay indicates, in search of the souls of international organizations; but what if organizations do not have a recognizable soul to begin with?

Indeed, the point was made earlier that the soul of organizations (to adopt Bederman's metaphor) swirls around in the midst of a tension between viewing the organization as a distinct entity (be it a 'person' or a 'community'[65]) and seeing it as merely the vehicle of its member states. Upon such a vision, it is the very fact that organizations are represented in one form or another which warrants scrutiny.

---

[61] The legal personality of the EU has given rise to an impressive body of literature. Some of the more thoughtful essays on both sides of the divide include Ramses A. Wessel, 'The International Legal Status of the European Union' (1997) 2 *European Foreign Affairs Review*, 109–29 (claiming personality partly to be implied), and Esa Paasivirta, 'The European Union: From an Aggregate of States to a Legal Person?' (1997) 2 *Hofstra Law & Policy Symposium*, 37–59 (urging a grant of personality).

[62] After all, the Court started its analysis of the UN's right to bring claims by establishing its personality, thus suggesting that personality is a threshold.

[63] Bederman, 'The Souls of International Organizations', p. 371.

[64] *Ibid.*, p. 372 (emphasis omitted).

[65] The two may be conceptually closer than would appear at first sight; it is telling that organizations are described as the 'embodiment' (as physical a metaphor as 'personality') of communities.

4

The foundations for the powers of organizations

Introduction

International organizations, it is generally agreed, can only work on the basis of their legal powers. Thus, organizations have acquired certain powers to found their actions on, and once they act beyond those powers, their acts may be declared invalid, at least in theory. To give a simple example: it is reasonably clear that a predominantly economic organization such as the OECD will not be able to enter into a military pact; if and when it does, the act by which such a pact was concluded will, if all works according to plan, be invalidated.[1]

That raises the fundamental question of where organizations derive their powers from, and, if anything, it is this precise question which has boggled our minds for decades and is likely to continue to do so.[2] Surprisingly, analysis as well as conceptualization has rarely been forthcoming; most authors content themselves with making a few general remarks on the powers of organizations before moving on to their specific topic of investigation. Monographs are, in other words, scarce, as are scholarly articles on the topic.[3]

Fortunately, though, there is a wealth of court decisions on the powers of organizations, going back to the early 1920s. Questions as to the origin and scope of the powers of international organizations[4] arose in one of the first requests

---

[1] As a jurisprudential matter, the above is in conformity with the notion of a legal power as a power of decision, rather than with the traditionally popular notion of a legal power as the power to exercise a choice. Compare Andrew Halpin, 'The Concept of a Legal Power', (1996) 16 *Oxford Journal of Legal Studies*, 129–52.

[2] The dominant explanation is along the lines of a delegation of powers from the member states. For a thoughtful discussion, see Bruno de Witte, 'Sovereignty and European Integration: The Weight of Tradition'. In Anne-Marie Slaughter *et al.* (eds.), *The European Court and National Courts: Doctrine and Jurisprudence* (Oxford, 1998), pp. 277–304.

[3] A rare exception is the ground-breaking study by Dan Sarooshi, *International Organizations and their Exercise of Sovereign Powers* (Oxford, 2005), which distinguishes three modes: agency, delegation, and transfer.

[4] A different question is that of the powers of specific organs of the organization in question. As Köck reminds us, here too the doctrine of implied powers may have a role to play. See Heribert Franz Köck, 'Die "implied powers" der Europäischen Gemeinschaften als Anwendungsfall der "implied powers" internationaler Organisationen überhaupt'. In Karl-Heinz Böckstiegel *et al.* (eds.), *Völkerrecht, Recht der internationalen Organisationen, Weltwirtschaftsrecht: Festschrift für Ignaz Seidl-Hohenveldern* (Cologne, 1988), pp. 279–99.

Int Labor Organisation

for an advisory opinion submitted to the Permanent Court of International Justice, in 1922. The International Labour Organization, set up with the task of regulating labour relations, wondered whether its powers extended to regulation of the conditions of labour in the agricultural sector.[5] The Court had yet to be convinced of the principled significance of the request, and remarked merrily that no issues of substance were involved: 'The Question before the Court relates simply to the competency of the International Labour Organisation as to agricultural labour. No point arises on this question as to the expediency or the opportuneness of the application to agriculture of any particular proposal.'[6] And, seemingly not quite aware of the principled significance of the request, the Court proceeded:

> It was much urged in argument that the establishment of the International Labour Organisation involved an abandonment of rights derived from national sovereignty, and that the competence of the Organisation therefore should not be extended by interpretation. There may be some force in this argument, but the question in every case must resolve itself into what the terms of the Treaty actually mean, and it is from this point of view that the Court proposes to examine the question.[7]

Thus, the question of the proper scope of the powers of international organizations was regarded, in 1922, merely as a matter of interpretation, and an interpretation of the terms used in their context led the Court to the conclusion that under the constitution of the ILO, the organization was indeed empowered to regulate labour relations in the agricultural sector.[8]

On the same day, the Court gave another advisory opinion, again relating to the powers of the ILO in the field of agriculture, and again upholding the idea that the scope of powers must 'depend entirely upon the construction to be given to the same treaty provisions from which, and from which alone, that Organisation derives its powers'.[9] In this case, the Court eventually held that interpretation pointed to the absence of a power on the part of the ILO to discuss the modes of agricultural production *per se,* when such modes did not relate to the specific points regarding which the ILO had been given powers.

Four years later, in an opinion on the power to regulate incidentally, as a by-product of protecting employees, the activities of employers, the Court once

---

[5] *Competence of the ILO to Regulate the Conditions of Labour of Persons Employed in Agriculture,* advisory opinion, [1922] Publ. PCIJ, Series B, nos. 2 and 3. The opinion was requested in response to French actions to keep the ILO on a tight leash. See David A. Morse, *The Origin and Evolution of the ILO and Its Role in the World Community* (Ithaca, NY, 1969), p. 15.

[6] *Competence of the ILO,* p. 21.   [7] *Ibid.,* p. 23.

[8] The main argument against ILO competence had been the occasional reference to 'industry' or derivations thereof. The Court held that such terms would 'in their primary and general sense' include agriculture, while acknowledging that they have also a more limited meaning. The context, then, made clear that the general and primary meaning was intended. *Ibid.,* p. 35.

[9] *Competence of the ILO to Examine Proposals for the Organisation and Development of Methods of Agricultural Production,* advisory opinion, [1922] Publ. PCIJ, Series B, nos. 2 and 3, pp. 53–5.

more sought to find an answer in simply interpreting the pertinent provisions of the Treaty of Versailles by which the ILO had been called into existence.[10] Interestingly, though, under reference to its advisory opinion no. 2 and the relationship between an organization's powers and national sovereignty (which some states had urged the Court to consider),[11] the Court sternly remarked that it was not to be engaged in such flights of theoretical fancy:

> So, in the present instance, without regard to the question whether the functions entrusted to the International Labour Organization are or are not in the nature of delegated powers, the province of the Court is to ascertain what it was the Contracting Parties agreed to. The Court, in interpreting Part XIII [of the Versailles Treaty], is called upon to perform a judicial function, and, taking the question actually before it in connection with the terms of the Treaty, there appears to be no room for the discussion and application of political principles or social theories, of which, it may be observed, no mention is made in the Treaty.[12]

Thus, the Permanent Court's first attempts to address the relatively new phenomena of international organizations were still a bit hesitant. Those first cases indicate that the Court was not yet fully aware of the special nature (whichever special nature that may be) of organizations, and tried to answer questions relating to their operation simply by looking at the constituent documents as everyday treaties. No doctrine emerged out of those first opinions: legal questions were simply to be answered by reference to the established canons of treaty interpretation, rather than political principles or social theories.[13]

The doctrine of attributed powers

However, a year and a half after opinion no. 13 on the ILO's power to regulate incidentally the activities of employers, the Court would formulate a general rule. Having had some time to reflect and having become aware of the circumstance that organizational documents go beyond the mere contractual,[14] the Court presumably reached the conclusion that to answer every request for an advisory opinion by simply pointing to interpretation would, eventually, create uncertainty, and it must have thought that the time was ripe to offer some guidance. Confronted with the question of the precise scope of the powers of the

---

[10] *Competence of the International Labour Organization to Regulate, Incidentally, the Personal Work of the Employer*, advisory opinion, [1926] Publ. PCIJ, no. 13.

[11] See above, text accompanying notes 4–7.   [12] Advisory opinion no. 13, p. 23.

[13] See more generally Jan Klabbers, 'The Life and Times of the Law of International Organizations' (2001) 70 *Nordic JIL*, 287–317.

[14] The distinction between various sorts of treaties started to gain ground in the contemporary literature. Thus, McNair, in an influential article, specifically distinguished 'treaties akin to charters of incorporation' from contractual and law-making treaties, and from conveyance-like treaties: A. D. McNair, 'The Function and Differing Legal Character of Treaties' (1930), reproduced in Lord McNair, *The Law of Treaties* (Oxford, 1961), pp. 739–54.

European Commission for the Danube, which had been created by a so-called Definitive Statute, the Court answered famously that 'As the European Commission is not a State, but an international institution with a special purpose, it only has the functions bestowed upon it by the Definitive Statute with a view to the fulfillment of that purpose, but it has power to exercise these functions to their full extent, in so far as the Statute does not impose restrictions upon it.'[15] The Court formulated what would later be called the principle of speciality or the principle of attribution, and despite the fact that the Court used the word 'functions' rather than 'powers', it is clear that the Court's opinion relates to 'powers'.

The idea that organizations can only work on the basis of powers specifically attributed to them squares nicely with the prevailing positivist mode of thinking in international law, a mode that, moreover, acquired judicial recognition around the same time as the principle of attribution was first formulated. Especially in the 1927 *Case of the SS Lotus*,[16] the Permanent Court had made it clear that, as a matter of principle, restrictions on sovereign freedoms are not lightly to be presumed. Instead, the rules of international law emanate from the free will of sovereign states, as the Court famously held,[17] and from there it is only a small step to proclaiming that organizations must remain within the powers conferred upon them. After all, if rules cannot be thrust upon states against their will, then organizations too must function in accordance with the will of the member states. It is no coincidence then that the idea was popular in particular (but not exclusively) in the classic Soviet doctrine on international organizations, which held in a nutshell that organizations should not circumvent states and their sovereign rights.[18]

The idea behind attribution is, quite simply, that international organizations, and their organs, can only do those things for which they are empowered.[19] Perhaps the clearest expressions hereof are to be found in Articles 5 and 7 (formerly Articles 3b and 4, respectively) of the TEC. Article 5 (formerly Article 3b) not only contains the famous principle of subsidiarity, but starts by saying that '[t]he Community shall act within the limits of the powers conferred upon it by this Treaty and of the objectives assigned to it therein'.[20]

---

[15] *Jurisdiction of the European Commission of the Danube between Galatz and Braila*, Advisory opinion, [1926] Publ. PCIJ, Series B, no. 14, p. 64.

[16] *Case of the SS Lotus*, [1927] Publ. PCIJ, Series A, no. 10.   [17] *Ibid.*, p. 18.

[18] The classic statement of the Soviet position is Grigory I. Tunkin, 'The Legal Nature of the United Nations' (1966/II) 119 *RdC*, 1–67.

[19] It follows that decisions can no longer be taken on the basis of expired treaty provisions, such as the ECSC provisions. For an illustration before the EC's CFI, see Joined cases T-27/03, T-46/03, T-58/03, T-79/03, T-80/03, T-97/03 and T-98/03, *Sp SpA and others* v. *Commission*, judgment of 25 October 2007 (nyr).

[20] Article 5 was only inserted by means of the Maastricht Treaty (in 1991), but the underlying principle was already recognized by the EC Court in some of its earliest decisions. See, e.g., case 20/59, *Italy* v. *High Authority* [1960] ECR 325, and case 25/59, *The Netherlands* v. *High Authority* [1960] ECR 355.

That sounds unequivocal enough: clearly, the Community can only do those things which the member states have told it that it can do. The same holds true for the separate institutions of the EC. Article 7 (formerly Article 4) of the TEC specifies: 'Each institution shall act within the limits of the powers conferred upon it by this Treaty.'

Again, a clear and unequivocal statement limits the remit of the individual things which the various organizations' organs can do, and similar provisions using different wordings may be found in the constituent treaties of other international organizations.

Thus, the organs of Ecowas 'shall perform the functions and act within the limits of the powers conferred upon them by or under' the constitution and protocols thereto;[21] the legal capacity of the FAO is limited to the powers granted by the constituent document;[22] and the Charter of the OAS provides that the OAS Permanent Council shall act within 'the limits of the Charter', while the General Assembly of the OAS is urged to exercise its powers 'in accordance with the provisions of the Charter'.[23]

The UN Charter too promises member states that the UN shall not intervene in matters which are essentially within their domestic jurisdiction (Article 2, para. 7). Admittedly, this is not as clear as Article 5 (formerly Article 3b) of the TEC,[24] and the Permanent Court of International Justice has already held in 1923 that the question of domestic jurisdiction is 'an essentially relative' question, which develops in accordance with international relations generally.[25] Nonetheless, at any rate in the literature, Article 2, para. 7 UN is often invoked as an expression of the constitutional limit of activities that the organization may legitimately engage itself within.[26]

Moreover, Article 24, para. 2 UN provides that the Security Council shall act in accordance with the purposes and principles of the UN Charter (those are broad, though), and Article 11 *juncto* Article 10 UN make clear that there are some limits to the powers of the General Assembly.

Its obvious attractions notwithstanding, the principle of attribution encounters at least two problems, one more or less theoretical, the other far more practical. Theoretically (or hypothetically, perhaps), if the notion of attribution

---

[21] Article 4, para. 2 ECOWAS.   [22] Article XVI, para. 1 FAO.

[23] Articles 80 and 52 OAS, respectively.

[24] Moreover, an opinion of the Office of Legal Affairs, answering a member state's request to supervise elections, seems to suggest that the scope of the very notion of domestic jurisdiction may be altered upon the will of the UN: 'the Secretary-General does not feel he could properly involve the United Nations Secretariat as an observer in a national election without authorization for such involvement being granted by a competent deliberative organ of the United Nations'. See UNJY (1984), pp. 178–9.

[25] *Nationality Decrees Issued in Tunis and Morocco (French Zone)*, advisory opinion, [1923] Publ. PCIJ, Series B, no. 4, p. 24.

[26] Thus, e.g., Jochen A. Frowein, 'Are There Limits to the Amendment Procedures in Treaties Constituting International Organisations?' In Gerhard Hafner *et al.* (eds.), *Liber Amicorum Professor Ignaz Seidl-Hohenveldern in Honour of His 80th Birthday* (The Hague, 1998), pp. 201–18, esp. p. 209.

is taken to its extreme, then organizations are little more than the mouthpieces of their member states, and, if that is so, then their very *raison d'être* comes into question. If an organization's powers are limited to those powers explicitly granted, then the organization remains, in effect, merely a vehicle for its members rather than an entity with a distinct will of its own, and if it is merely a vehicle for its member states, then it is difficult to see why the particular form of an organization was chosen by those members over, say, a series of occasional conferences, or perhaps even the simple appointment of a joint public relations officer.

An objection with far more fundamental consequences in practice, however, is that while the notion of attribution may be a nice point of departure when it comes to discussing the powers of international organizations, organizations are usually held to be dynamic and living creatures, in constant development, and it is accepted that their founding fathers can never completely envisage the future.[27]

The practical problems this may bring with it are nicely illustrated by the recollection of a former adviser to the UN on peace-keeping (peace-keeping not being explicitly referred to in the Charter):

> Since peace-keeping operations are not known in the Charter, I could not have a place on the official organizational chart – nor even an office, I suppose. But the work had to be done. Because I was 'independent', I could not receive a salary from the permanent UN budget, either. For those many years, my salary was in fact paid as part of the expenses of one or another peace-keeping operation that was in progress.[28]

The constituent documents of organizations necessarily come with gaps, simply because the drafters cannot be expected to think of every possible contingency, and because it may be expected, perhaps even hoped, that internal dynamics will move the organization forward. In those circumstances, the organization should not be limited by those powers granted to it upon its creation; instead, the organization must be allowed some flexibility. It must be allowed certain powers which, while not expressly granted, are granted by implication.[29] And it is this thought, the so-called doctrine of implied powers, which is at the heart of most of the talk about the powers of international organizations. There is (or at least there used to be) virtual agreement amongst statesmen and scholars alike that implied powers exist and are, generally, a good thing. The main disagreement concerning the doctrine of implied powers relates to the

---

[27] See, e.g., Alan Dashwood, 'The Limits of European Community Powers' (1996) 21 *ELR*, 113–28, esp. p. 125.

[28] Lauri Koho, 'Military Advisor in the Office of the Secretary-General'. In Kimmo Kiljunen (ed.), *Finns in the United Nations* (Helsinki, 1996), pp. 105–33, p. 112.

[29] See generally Viljam Engström, 'Implied Powers of International Organizations: On the Character of a Legal Doctrine', (2003) 14 *Finnish Yearbook of International Law*, 129–57.

justification of specific implied powers, something which in turn hinges on the exact basis on which the implication takes place.

The doctrine of implied powers

A pivotal role in the development of the law of international organizations has been played by the doctrine of implied powers, first developed to come to terms with power struggles between central government and local authorities in the context of federal states.[30] Most observers appear to agree that there are at least two ways in which implied powers can be, and have been, found to exist.[31] The first, and relatively innocent version, holds that implied powers flow from a rule of interpretation which itself holds that treaty rules must be interpreted in such a way as to guarantee their 'effet utile':[32] they must be interpreted so as to guarantee their fullest effect.

This particular version of the implied powers doctrine has already been embraced by the Permanent Court of International Justice in its advisory opinion of 1928 on *Interpretation of the Greco-Turkish Agreement of December 1st, 1926*.[33] The Greco-Turkish agreement had created a mixed commission and laid down, in cases where the mixed commission could not reach agreement, that resort to arbitration might be had. It failed to identify the party or parties entitled to resort to arbitration, however, and the Court found that 'from the very silence of the article on this point, it is possible and natural to deduce that the power to refer a matter to the arbitrator rests with the Mixed Commission when that body finds itself confronted with questions of the nature indicated'.[34] Thus, the Court found a power to be implied in the existence of another, explicit power, in much the same way as it is sometimes said that treaties generally may contain implied clauses.[35]

The Court of Justice of the (then) European Community for Coal and Steel approached the matter in similar fashion, in the classic *Fédéchar* case.[36] At issue was whether the Community's executive body, the High Authority, had the

---

[30] See generally Joachim Becker, *Die Anwendbarkeit der Theorie von den implied powers im Recht der Europäischen Gemeinschaften* (Münster, 1976), esp. pp. 1–43.

[31] See Bernard Rouyer-Hameray, *Les compétences implicites des organisations internationales* (Paris, 1962). See also Christine Denys, *Impliciete bevoegdheden in de Europese Economische Gemeenschap: Een onderzoek naar de betekenis van 'implied powers'* (Antwerp, 1990), distinguishing between instrumental and substantive implied powers.

[32] Note, though, that the doctrine is not itself, as is sometimes suggested, a rule of interpretation. Instead, it serves to justify using a particular interpretative device. Compare also Becker, *Die Anwendbarkeit*, p. 53.

[33] [1928] Publ. PCIJ, Series B, no. 16   [34] *Ibid.*, p. 20.

[35] But with a twist: usually, implied treaty clauses serve to protect state sovereignty. Thus, it has been argued for a long time that treaties contain an implied *clausula rebus sic stantibus*: treaties are binding, but only as long as the circumstances of their conclusion remain present. Various other examples are listed in Sir Gerald Fitzmaurice, 'Fourth Report on the Law of Treaties' (1959/II) *YbILC*, pp. 46–7, and 70–4.

[36] Case 8/55, *Fédération Charbonnière de Belgique* v. *High Authority* [1954–6] ECR 292.

power to fix prices as part of a recognized power to regulate the market. The applicant had argued that no such power existed, simply because it remained unmentioned in the Treaty establishing the European Coal and Steel Community. The Court, however, held differently, and argued that indeed the power to regulate implied the power to fix prices, for without such power, the regulatory power would be deprived of its 'effet utile': 'the rules laid down by an international treaty or a law presuppose the rules without which that treaty or law would have no meaning or could not be reasonably and usefully applied'.[37]

The Court of Justice of (later) the European Community essentially upheld the same principle in a decision on the power of the Commission to take binding decisions as a consequence of its power to promote close co-operation between the Community's member states in the field of social policy. The Court found the specific power to be implied in the more general power, again on the basis of effective interpretation. The Court was, however, quick to point out that the substantial scope of the power was not too grand: since Article 118 (now Article 137) of the TEC does not give the Commission wide 'stimulation' powers, it cannot give the Commission wide 'decision-making' powers either.[38]

Perhaps this rather careful approach to the implied powers doctrine was best formulated by Judge Green Hackworth, in his dissenting opinion to the International Court's advisory opinion in *Reparation for Injuries*. In a famous passage, Judge Hackworth wrote that '[p]owers not expressed cannot freely be implied. Implied powers flow from a grant of express powers, and are limited to those that are "necessary" to the exercise of powers expressly granted.'[39]

Judge Hackworth thus disagreed with the majority in *Reparation for Injuries*, and held that the majority used an unduly wide version of the implied powers doctrine by relating the power to be implied not to an express provision, but rather to the functions and objectives of the organization concerned. As the majority had put it:

> Under international law, the Organisation must be deemed to have those powers which, though not expressly provided in the Charter, are conferred upon it by necessary implication as being essential to the performance of its duties. This principle of law was applied by the Permanent Court of International Justice to the International Labour Organisation in its Advisory Opinion No. 13 of July 23rd, 1926, and must be applied to the United Nations.[40]

Several aspects of the passage just quoted require comments. First of all, it is debatable whether the precedent invoked by the Court was actually on point. In the Opinion mentioned, the Permanent Court, as illustrated above, made a point of not making a point. It affirmed that it was engaged in answering a

---

37 *Ibid.*, p. 299.
38 Joined cases 281, 283–5 and 287/85, *Germany & others* v. *Commission* [1987] ECR 3203.
39 *Reparation for Injuries Suffered in the Service of the United Nations*, advisory opinion, [1949] ICJ Reports 174, Hackworth J dissenting, p. 198.
40 *Reparation for Injuries*, majority opinion, p. 182 (reference omitted).

question of law, and its question of law turned out to be, in effect, a question of interpretation.[41] The Permanent Court did not find any powers to exist by necessary implication only; and it most certainly did not derive such powers as it did find to exist solely from the functions or objectives of the ILO's constituent document.

Second, the yardstick created by the Court ('essential to the performance of its duties') is by its very nature a highly flexible one, and very much dependent for concretization on the eye of the beholder. Yet, who actually is the beholder in any given case? And who determines who shall be the beholder?[42] Reasonable people can and do differ concerning what they hold to be essential for the performance of an organization's duties, and while such disagreement is in all probability inevitable (or rather, perhaps: precisely because it is inevitable), the criterion of 'essential to the performance of duties' is not conducive to the creation of legal certainty.

Nonetheless, it is this wider version that is often thought to prevail, and there are indeed other judicial decisions which seem to point in the same direction. One of them is the 1954 advisory opinion of the International Court of Justice in the *Effect of Awards* case.[43] The Court was asked, *inter alia*, whether the General Assembly of the United Nations had the power to establish an administrative tribunal which itself would be capable of taking binding decisions, and the Court answered in the affirmative.

Under explicit reference to its earlier opinion in *Reparation for Injuries*, the Court held that the power of the General Assembly to create an administrative tribunal arose 'by necessary intendment' out of the United Nations Charter.[44] The Court reasoned that since the United Nations has the expressed aim of promoting freedom and justice for individuals, and since disgruntled staff members may be precluded from bringing suit against the UN in domestic courts due to possible jurisdictional immunities, it followed that, as the Court put it, 'the power to establish a tribunal, to do justice as between the Organization and the staff members, was essential to ensure the efficient working of the Secretariat, and to give effect to the paramount consideration of securing the highest standards of efficiency, competence and integrity'.[45] Here then, somewhat curiously perhaps, the well-being of the organization at large (the ostensible justification for implying a power) is reformulated in terms of the efficient working of one of its organs, the Secretariat. If anything, that even extends the scope of the implied powers doctrine: if it is not just the well-being of the organization but also that

---

[41] See on this point also Krzysztof Skubiszewski, 'Implied Powers of International Organizations'. In Yoram Dinstein (ed.), *International Law at a Time of Perplexity: Essays in Honour of Shabtai Rosenne* (Dordrecht, 1989), pp. 855–68, esp. pp. 863–4.

[42] See also H. W. A. Thirlway, 'The Law and Procedure of the International Court of Justice 1960–1989, Part 8' (1996) 67 *BYIL*, 1–73, p. 32.

[43] *Effect of Awards of Compensation Made by the United Nations Administrative Tribunal*, [1954] ICJ Reports 47.

[44] *Ibid.*, p. 57.   [45] *Ibid.*

of its individual organs which must be taken into consideration in determining implied powers, then there is virtually no end to the powers that can be implied. The Court must have felt that, somehow, its reasoning on this point required some bolstering, and added that the power to create an administrative tribunal derived in the end from the necessity 'to do justice as between the Organization and the staff members'.

In other opinions too the Court paid heed to the notion that some of the UN's powers could have been granted to it by implication. Thus, in *Certain Expenses*, it formulated the rule that: 'when the Organization takes action which warrants the assertion that it was appropriate for the fulfillment of one of the stated purposes of the United Nations, the presumption is that such action is not *ultra vires* the Organization'.[46] In other words, powers of the UN (and presumably those of other organizations as well, although the Court limited itself, wisely, to the UN) may be implied if they can be hooked up to the purposes of the organization; the conception is so broad as to have inspired some authors to launch a concept of inherent powers.[47]

Another example sometimes mentioned[48] is the 1971 *Namibia* opinion,[49] in which the Court found that the General Assembly had the power to terminate South Africa's Mandate over South West Africa. Yet, while it is true that the Court did not point to an explicit power grant, it goes perhaps too far to explain this by the notion of implied powers. The Court built its entire reasoning in this opinion on the idea that the Assembly had succeeded to the supervisory role of the League of Nations; its power to terminate the Mandate rested upon this idea of succession, as the League's power to terminate was beyond debate.[50]

The decision of the Court of Justice of the European Community in *ERTA*[51] is also often offered in support of the wider version of the implied powers doctrine. Faced with the question as to whether the European Community was competent to conclude an agreement relating to road transport with third parties, the Court answered affirmatively, on the basis of the fact that since the Community was internally competent to legislate in matters of road transport,

---

[46] *Certain Expenses of the United Nations (Article 17, Paragraph 2, of the Charter)*, advisory opinion, [1962] ICJ Reports 151, p. 168 (italics in original). In the World Bank, activities such as providing technical assistance and grants are typically justified on the basis of implied powers, as is the case with the bank's participation in other entities, such as the Global Environmental Facility or the Consultative group on International Agricultural Research. See Andres Rigo Sureda, 'The Law Applicable to the Activities of International Development Banks' (2004) 308 *RdC*, 9-252, pp. 154, 168.

[47] See below, pp. 66–9.

[48] So, e.g., Nigel D. White, 'The UN Charter and Peacekeeping Forces: Constitutional Issues' (1996) 3 *International Peacekeeping*, 43–63, esp. 45.

[49] *Legal Consequences for States of the Continued Presence of South Africa in Namibia (South West Africa) notwithstanding Security Council Resolution 276 (1970)*, advisory opinion, [1971] ICJ Reports 16.

[50] *Ibid.*, esp. paras. 102–3. Whether the Court's theory of succession was itself plausible is a different matter altogether.

[51] Case 22/70, *Commission v. Council (European Road Transport Agreement)* [1971] ECR 273.

such internal competence must have an external counterpart in order not to be circumvented: 'the Member States no longer have the right, acting individually or even collectively, to undertake obligations with third countries which affect those [internal] rules'.[52]

The reason why the *ERTA* decision is usually mentioned in support of a wide conception of implied powers resides in the fact that the Court ultimately sought a justification not so much in the 'effet utile' of the 'internal' transport provisions, but rather in the objectives of the Treaty and the duty of Community solidarity. As the Court put it:

> Under Article 3(e), the adoption of a common policy in the sphere of transport is especially mentioned amongst the objectives of the Community.
>
> Under Article 5, the Member States are required on the one hand to take all appropriate measures to ensure fulfillment of the obligations arising out of the Treaty or resulting from action taken by the institutions and, on the other hand, to abstain from any measure which might jeopardize the attainment of the objective of the Treaty.
>
> If these two provisions are read in conjunction, it follows that to the extent to which Community rules are promulgated for the attainment of the objectives of the Treaty, the Member States cannot, outside the framework of the Community institutions, assume obligations which might affect those rules or alter their scope.[53]

Teleological though the reasoning clearly is, it is doubtful whether it is inspired by the same type of thinking as was demonstrated by the International Court of Justice in *Reparation for Injuries* or *Effect of Awards*. Instead of simply deriving a power from the functions or objectives of the treaty, the *ERTA* court derives it from what may loosely be termed a requirement of legal unity. The EC does not, strictly speaking, need an external transport power in order to function effectively or to attain its objectives. One could very well imagine that the EC would not be any worse off had the external power rested with the individual member states, on condition that they did nothing to endanger the *acquis communautaire*. The basis of implication is, rather, to safeguard the unity of Community law.

Either way, the implied powers doctrine has proved immensely seductive,[54] appealing as it does to both our instrumentalist sentiments (we tend to think that law is made for a purpose, and thus the reaching of this purpose ought to be facilitated[55]) and our internationalist sentiments. The notion of attribution,

---

[52] *Ibid.*, para. 17.   [53] *Ibid.*, paras. 20–2.

[54] See also Jerzy Makarczyk, 'The International Court of Justice on the Implied Powers of International Organizations'. In Jerzy Makarczyk (ed.), *Essays in International Law in Honour of Judge Manfred Lachs* (The Hague, 1984), pp. 501–19, esp. p. 505, arguing that there are few provisions of constituent documents which are not or cannot be used to enhance the organization's room to operate.

[55] The insight derives from John Griffiths, 'Is Law Important?' (1979) 54 *New York University Law Review*, 339–74. For an illustration, explicitly defending implied powers on grounds of

by contrast, has generally been seen as the handmaiden of sovereignty, and sovereignty is, in the eyes of many international lawyers, a 'bad word'.[56]

Nonetheless, there is another side to this, and it largely reflects the attractions and repulsions of both doctrines in reverse. Thus, while sovereignty is a bad word to some, to others it is an empowering word: the notion of sovereign statehood enables, indeed delimits, political communities, within which people can map out a common existence together. In this framework, international organizations, and indeed international law generally, are seen as potential intruders, capable of disturbing political balances within the state, and undermining democratic procedure.[57] Hence, their powers must be kept in check, as any extension of powers (by implication or otherwise) will be at the expense of the position of some group in society. Thus, if an organization claims a power to occupy itself with topic X, then the parliament of member state A loses some of its powers to deal with the topic, and in the worst-case scenario (which comes true all too often), judicial review by the courts of state A is relinquished as well without being replaced by review or control within the organization. This may lead to more effective international governance, but not necessarily to greater democracy or legitimacy, and may undermine the legal position of individual citizens.[58] The attractions of the implied powers doctrine are, in the end, the mirror image of what we dislike about the attribution doctrine, whereas the advantages of the attribution doctrine are the attractions of implied powers in reverse.

Reconciling the two doctrines

It will be clear that there is a certain tension between the doctrine of attribution on the one hand, and the doctrine of implied powers on the other. The doctrine of attribution finds its rationale, ultimately, in the manifest will of the founders: they have found it necessary to grant their organization certain powers, and that will must be respected. It stresses considerations of state sovereignty rather than the interests of the international community at large. From the same consideration it follows that powers not expressly granted are the result of intentional omissions, and here too then the intention (in this case, to withhold a power) must be respected. On this view, then, taken to the extreme, what you see is what you get; there is no room in the reasoning to imply any powers.

---

instrumentalist logic (acceptance of a goal implies acceptance of the means to reach that goal), see Köck, 'Implied Powers'.

[56] This quip was famously made by Louis Henkin, *International Law: Politics and Values* (Dordrecht, 1995), p. 8.

[57] One of the more sophisticated versions of the argument is Jed Rubenfeld, 'Unilateralism and Constitutionalism', (2004) 79 *New York University Law Review*, 1971–2028.

[58] See Jan Klabbers, 'Over het leerstuk der impliciete bevoegdheden in het recht der internationale organisaties'. In Hanneke Steenbergen (ed.), *Ongebogen recht. Opstellen aangeboden aan prof. dr. H. Meijers* (The Hague, 1998), 1–11.

answer

The standard reply is, however, that drafters cannot be omniscient, and that there may be circumstances where the organization would need a power not expressly granted, simply to be able to function effectively, and because such a power is simply necessary, it may well be implied. After all, so the argument runs, had the founders only thought of it, they would no doubt have granted the particular power without further ado. This argument, then, starts from the different premise of the needs of the organization (or perhaps international society at large), rather than the exigencies of state sovereignty.

Still, with this standard reply the reasoning is also based on, ultimately, the intentions of the drafters: had they only realized the need for a certain power, they would no doubt have intended their creation to be so endowed. And indeed this is the standard way in which the International Court of Justice at least has habitually justified any finding of implied powers, however broad: implied powers are usually said to have arisen 'by necessary intendment'[59] and to have, their implicit nature notwithstanding, been 'conferred' upon the organization.[60]

Perhaps a better way out is to limit the applicability of the doctrine of implied powers, and it is this that Judge Hackworth had in mind when dissenting from the majority in *Reparation for Injuries*. In his view, what mattered for an implied power was that there had to be an explicit power from which the implied power could, quite literally, be implied. The mere 'necessity' of some power was insufficient, if only because necessity as such is a blank cheque.

A similar idea is laid down in Article 300 (formerly Article 235) of the EC treaty: 'If action by the Community should prove necessary to attain . . . one of the objectives of the Community and this Treaty has not provided the necessary powers, the Council shall . . . take the appropriate measures'.

The wording of Article 300 of the TEC oozes the same spirit as Judge Hackworth's dissent: if a power is necessary for the objectives of the EC, then Article 300 can be used. Thus, there is no need to go around creating new powers with the help of the implied powers doctrine: Article 300 can simply be used, which automatically means that the implied powers doctrine should be of limited application only. And indeed, due to the existence of a dynamic clause such as Article 300, the implied powers doctrine in Community law has been used mainly in the field of the Community's external relations,[61] probably for the reason (in itself telling enough) that the connection between external action

---

[59] This is the formula used in *Effect of Awards*.   [60] This is the verb used in *Reparation for Injuries*.

[61] Useful illustrations are I. MacLeod, I. D. Hendry and Stephen Hyett, *The External Relations of the European Communities* (Oxford, 1996), and Dominic McGoldrick, *International Relations Law of the European Union* (London, 1997). Note also that recent proposals to amend the EU treaties (the Treaty establishing a Constitution for Europe as well as the 2007 Lisbon Treaty) have invariably contained a clause limiting the scope of the implied powers doctrine. Thus, according to the Lisbon Treaty, 'competences not conferred upon the Union in the Treaties remain with the Member States'.

and the objectives of the Community (as required by Article 300 of the TEC) is sometimes not so clear as to allow the member states by unanimity to expand the Community's powers.

Inherent powers? — 3rd source

In order to overcome the drawbacks of both the attribution doctrine (often thought to be too rigid) and the implied powers doctrine (sometimes thought to be not rigid enough), some writers have proposed a third source of powers. Already in the 1960s, some such conception was launched by Finn Seyersted, as an adjunct to his 'objective theory' of personality of international organizations.[62] Organizations, on this view, once established, would possess inherent powers to perform all those acts which they need to perform to attain their aims, not due to any specific source of organizational power (note, incidentally, how this underlines the fundamental identity between attribution and implication), but simply because they inhere in organizationhood. As long as acts are not prohibited in the organization's constituent documents, they must be deemed legally valid.[63]

While Seyersted's views, on both legal personality and inherent powers, were for a long time deemed somewhat exotic (while immensely respected, he never gained much of a following), the idea of inherent powers has recently been revived in the context of both the UN and the EC.

As far as the UN goes, the inherent powers doctrine has been revived out of dissatisfaction with the implied powers doctrine. Calling the latter a 'sham', Nigel White points out that the search for a basis of implication is often cumbersome, rarely completely convincing and, in fact, not even necessary: where organizations have inherent powers, there is no need to resort to contrived findings of powers being implied by founders of organizations.[64]

The advantages of the inherent powers doctrine are twofold, as White explains. First, it is thoroughly functional: it helps organizations reach their aims without being 'hidebound by the legal niceties of its individual, and often obscurely drafted, provisions'.[65] Second, it makes legal control easier in that it reduces the number of legal controls on the organization's functioning to two: first, the act must aim to achieve the organization's purpose, and second, it may not be expressly prohibited.[66]

---

[62] See Chapter 3.

[63] See Finn Seyersted, *Objective International Personality of Intergovernmental Organizations: Do Their Capacities Really Depend upon the Conventions Establishing Them?* (Copenhagen, 1963), p. 28. Still, Seyersted would leave some room for delegated powers, under the heading 'extended jurisdiction'. See in particular Finn Seyersted, *Common Law of International Organizations* (Leiden, 2008), pp. 65–70.

[64] Nigel White, 'Constitutional Issues'. The word 'sham' appears in the article's abstract, p. 43; I have assumed White's authorship thereof.

[65] *Ibid.*, p. 48.   [66] *Ibid.*

In the context of Community law, the inherent powers notion is relaunched by Alan Dashwood, largely out of a growing sense of unease from viewing the external relations powers of the EC as being almost exclusively based on implied powers. After all, if the implied powers doctrine is taken seriously, this would mean that the drafters of the EC Treaty were keen on granting the EC external powers, had every intention of endowing the EC with external powers, but had never bothered to write those into the treaty, with the exception of specific powers in the field of commercial policy and, perhaps, the power to conclude association agreements (which says little about the substantive fields those may or may not cover).[67] Such a conception is indeed not entirely plausible perhaps: it takes a leap of faith to find such a wide array of powers implied despite the absence of any specific grant.

Analytically unsatisfactory as the implied powers doctrine may be, it is not immediately obvious that an inherent powers doctrine would be more plausible.[68] One serious drawback (which also attaches to its spiritual cousin, the objective theory of personality) is that it possibly goes against the wishes of the drafters. Indeed, ironically, a finding that a specific act is not expressly prohibited in a constituent document (and thus must be deemed permitted, under the inherent powers doctrine) may always be countered by the argument that if not expressly prohibited, it may have been prohibited by implication.

Thus, instead of arguing that an action was lawful because it was based on an implied power, the tables might turn so as to argue that the action was unlawful because it was not in conformity with an implied prohibition. The only way to overcome this possibility is by completely ignoring the intentions (whether spelled out or implied) of the drafters and that, in turn, is difficult to reconcile with our usual insistence on the importance of intent.

Indeed, at the risk of engaging in semantic squabbles, the doctrine is incoherent by its insistence that a power is inherent as long as it is not expressly prohibited by the drafters: if the very notion of an inherent power is taken seriously, then whether the drafters prohibit the activity is, quite literally, irrelevant. A power that is inherent in organizationhood cannot be cast aside by founders, for if it can be set aside, then it is not, in any meaningful sense of the word, 'inherent'.[69]

---

[67] Compare Dashwood, 'The Limits'; see also Alan Dashwood, 'Implied External Competence of the EC'. In Martti Koskenniemi (ed.), *International Law Aspects of the European Union* (The Hague, 1998), pp. 113–23, and, for a reformulated version, Alan Dashwood and Joni Heliskoski, 'The Classic Authorities Revisited'. In Alan Dashwood and Christophe Hillion (eds.), *The General Law of EC External Relations* (London, 2000), pp. 3–19.

[68] Except perhaps in the moderate version in which the WTO can be said to have an inherent power to address competition problems to the extent that they form market barriers. For such an argument, see René Uruena, 'The Underlying Question: The World Trade Organization and its Powers to Adopt a Competition Policy', (2006) 3 *IOLR*, 55–91.

[69] By way of analogy, Art. 51 of the UN Charter recognizes that states have an 'inherent' right to defend themselves; this is sometimes taken to mean they cannot do away with this right. While

Another problem with the inherent powers doctrine is that it seems to rely on a solid vision of the nature of international organizations. It is, after all, not nothing to call something 'inherent': taken seriously, this must mean that there is something in the nature of organizations which warrants the conclusion that certain things 'inhere' in them. Judging the historical record, at least it must be recognized that whatever is inherent in organizations has nonetheless kept itself from view for roughly a century-and-a-half, until the 1990s (and even that is on the generous proposition that the doctrine has many more adherents than the ones mentioned above).

But also on a more practical level things may not be quite as clear as they seem. Thus, the test that an action must be aimed at contributing to one of the purposes of the organization is, in practice, not terribly strict: there will be few activities which do not meet this requirement, particularly when the majority of the member states support the activity as being in conformity with the organization's constituent documents. By way of example, the ECJ was rather quick to see a connection between illicit trade in small arms and light weapons on the one hand, and development on the other. The reasoning went more or less as follows: trade in small arms contributes to violence and instability; violence and instability are not conducive to a well-functioning economy; a well-functioning economy will be a growing one; hence, there is a connection between illicit trade in small arms and light weapons, and development.[70]

Things can even be taken further: should the EC Council decide on the desirability of engaging in warfare, then there is fairly little that can be done about it as long as the Council decides this in accordance with the prescribed procedure. *In casu*, absent any specific power to engage in warfare, the procedure to follow would probably be that of Article 300 (ex Article 235) of the TEC, which provides for unanimity. But if the Council is indeed unanimous on the desirability of engaging in warfare in light of its contribution to the completion of the internal market (the prerequisite mentioned in Article 300 itself), then any form of legal control is immediately exhausted. Thus, the inherent powers doctrine presumes a degree of objectivity which is no doubt unattainable (objectively, it may be difficult to see the link between warfare and the EC's purposes, but if everyone who matters sees such a link, however subjectively, then such a link exists, for all legal purposes) and, what is more, presumes an objective third party to effectuate this objectivity. It presumes, in short, an Archimedean point from which to evaluate behaviour (as well as a wise Archimedes), but such a point is, sadly perhaps, lacking.[71] The EC Court is probably the closest thing to

---

they may temporarily choose not to use their right of self-defence, they may always change their minds.

[70] As a result, the Court annulled a Council decision which had failed to recognize this connection and had therewith not been taken on the proper legal basis. See Case C-91/05, *Commission* v. *Council*, decision of 20 May 2008, nyr.

[71] Useful on this point (and many others) is Terry Nardin, *Law, Morality, and the Relations of States* (Princeton, 1983).

an Archimedean institution in the law of international organizations; in other settings judicial review hardly even exists.[72]

All this is not to deny, as White correctly observes, that some of the advisory opinions of the ICJ come close to supporting what looks like an inherent powers doctrine, despite making use of the terminology of implied powers. In particular in the *Certain Expenses* opinion the reasoning pushes the bounds of the implied powers to their breaking point, or perhaps even beyond.[73] But that in itself does not underline for the correctness of the inherent powers doctrine; instead, if anything, it testifies to the uncertainties at its core.[74]

Implied powers under fire

The limits of, in particular, the implied powers doctrine have come to be increasingly realized during the 1990s, not just by scholarly calls to recognize the inherent powers doctrine, but also as evidenced by a few judicial decisions. While it is clear that the doctrine played a useful role while organizations were still in development, and in particular when the very phenomenon of the international organization was still developing, it would seem that, at least in some of the more settled organizations, the doctrine has passed its heyday.

Thus, within the European Community, the Court of Justice has, on several occasions, refused to find the Community endowed with a certain power only by implication, and such refusals are difficult to reconcile with earlier wide-ranging applications of the doctrine. When asked whether the Community would possess exclusive competence to enter into international agreements concerning trade in services, the Court found no such power to exist, not even by implication, except where trade in services resembles trade in goods.[75] Similarly, when asked whether the Community would have the power to accede to the European Convention on Human Rights, the Court once again answered in the negative.[76] Of course, in both cases, the Court's answers are as such

---

[72] On an optimistic note, the EC Court would probably do its best to find a way to prevent the EC from engaging in illegal (but unanimously endorsed) activities, but it would have a hard time doing so on the basis of the test prescribed by White.

[73] Compare also Nigel D. White, *The Law of International Organisations* (Manchester, 1996), p. 131. Seyersted strongly suggests that in *Certain Expenses*, the Court adopted his ideas (set out in a forthcoming article) but still only labelled them as 'implied powers'. See Seyersted, *Common Law*, e.g., p. 31.

[74] White himself has a hard time telling them apart. He seems to conflate them when speaking of peace-keeping as possibly being founded on 'implied, or perhaps more accurately, inherent, powers' ('Constitutional Issues', p. 43) and also when noting that the Security Council has a plausible 'implied or inherent power' to create peace-keeping forces (*ibid.*, p. 51). Surely, if words mean anything at all, then inherent powers must be different from implied powers; the two doctrines cannot be used interchangeably at will, particularly if implied powers depend, somehow, on a grant by the members (albeit implied) while inherent powers do not depend on a grant by the members.

[75] *Opinion 1/94 (re WTO Agreement)* [1994] ECR I-5267.

[76] *Opinion 2/94 (Re European Convention on Human Rights)* [1996] ECR I-1759.

defensible;[77] what is striking though is the marked reluctance to find any implied powers, whereas in earlier years a finding of implied powers would have been almost a foregone conclusion.

Even more fundamentally, the Court flatly acknowledged the doctrine of attributed powers in a decision taken in October 2000 in the so-called *Tobacco Directive* case.[78] Here, the Court found, probably for the first time in its history, that the Community lacked altogether the power to engage in a certain activity (banning the advertising of tobacco products). The Community's powers, so the Court affirmed, were limited to those specifically conferred on the Community. While the Community does have the power to legislate on specific issues related to Europe's internal market, this does not mean that it has been given a general, possibly unlimited, power to regulate the internal market; the principle of attributed powers would not tolerate such a broad construction.[79]

A similar trend to interpret organizational powers rather more narrowly than in the past is visible in the recent decisions and opinions of the International Court of Justice. Asked for an advisory opinion by the World Health Assembly concerning the legality of nuclear weapons, the ICJ found that the World Health Organization's constitution did not grant it the power to address issues concerning the legality of weapons systems.[80] The Court reasoned that, while the WHO would be abundantly empowered to deal with the effects of the use of nuclear weapons on health, its activities had no bearing on the question of legality: 'none of the functions of the WHO is dependent upon the legality of the situations upon which it must act',[81] and to the extent that the WHO is competent to address the health effects of activities, 'the competence of the WHO to deal with them is not dependent on the legality of the acts that caused them'.[82] Indeed, for the first time since the Permanent Court's opinion on the *Jurisdiction of the European Commission of the Danube*, the doctrine of attributed powers was invoked.[83]

---

[77] At least on the point of the absence of implied powers. Whether the Court's somewhat contrived rendition (in *Opinion 1/94*) of trade in services as really concerning the movement of persons is defensible is a different question altogether.

[78] Case C-376/98, *Germany* v. *European Parliament and Council* [2000] ECR I-8419.

[79] *Ibid.*, para. 83.

[80] For a brief commentary, illustrating how easy it would have been to find the WHO implicitly empowered to deal with the legality of nuclear weapons, see Pierre Klein, 'Quelques réflexions sur le principe de spécialité et la "politisation" des institutions spécialisées'. In Laurence Boisson de Chazournes and Philippe Sands (eds.), *International Law, The International Court of Justice and Nuclear Weapons* (Cambridge, 1999), pp. 78–91.

[81] *Legality of the use by a state of nuclear weapons in armed conflict*, advisory opinion, [1996] *ICJ Reports* 66, para. 20.

[82] *Ibid.*, para. 21.

[83] And in part defended, somewhat controversially, on the basis of the proper role of the WHO in the UN system: the UN deals with peace and security, whereas the specialized agencies deal with their own functional activities. For a critique, see Klein, 'Quelques réflexions'. See generally also C. F. Amerasinghe, 'The Advisory Opinion of the International Court of Justice in the WHO Nuclear Weapons Case: A Critique', (1997) 10 *Leiden JIL*, 525–39.

The message, then, seems clear: the more well-established international organizations have reached the limits, at least for the time being, of what they can actually engage in. Their initial developmental stages are behind us, and now is not the time to add new powers, but instead to fulfil their main tasks as envisaged. It is surely no coincidence that, during the 1990s, the European Community was enriched with the notion of subsidiarity (which specifies that Community action must be justified, rather than automatic), and that, indeed, the very principle of attribution was explicitly inserted.[84] Both indicate strongly that, at least in the eyes of the member states of the Community, the Community's expansion had gone far enough.

Re-thinking powers?

It is not just the implied powers doctrine that has come under fire. On a deeper level, thinking in terms of powers more generally is slowly subjected to critiques, albeit often implicitly so. Two manifestations of this have become visible. First, and predominantly within the EU, practice suggests that the classic 'powers' perspective is no longer sufficient in order to explain what is going on. It is no longer considered accurate to suggest that a power either belongs to the member states, or to the EU, for in the EU's practice it turns out that even when a member state is exercising a power, it is still possible to interfere with the exercise of powers of the EU. As a result, powers can no longer be conceptualized as communicating barrels (or a zero-sum game).

A good illustration is *SPUC* v. *Grogan*, a judgment from 1992 in a case which revolved, surprisingly, around abortion.[85] While the EC had (and has) no powers whatsoever to address abortion, it turned out that it would be possible that by exercising its own proper powers on abortion, Ireland would come to interfere with the Community's freedom of movement of services. For under Community law, a strong argument can be made that to the extent that advertising abortion possibilities in Europe can be considered a service, local authorities are at liberty to prohibit such advertising. And if this is correct, then there is little point in insisting on powers anymore, because the proper powers of the member states and the Union constantly interfere.

The same is visible in the Union's external practice,[86] where recently there have been intense debates as to whether the power to conclude air traffic agreements, or investment treaties, would still remain with the member states. The

---

[84] Both can be found in Art. 5 (ex Art. 3b) TEC.

[85] See Case C-159/90, *Society for the Protection of Unborn Children Ireland Ltd* v. *Stephen Grogan and others* [1991] ECR I-4685. For a groundbreaking discussion, see Gráinne de Búrca, 'Fundamental Human Rights and the Reach of EC Law', (1993) 13 *Oxford Journal of Legal Studies*, 283–319.

[86] See generally Marise Cremona, 'External Relations and External Competence: The Emergence of an Integrated Policy'. In Paul Craig and Gráinne de Búrca (eds.), *The Evolution of EU Law* (Oxford, 1999), pp. 137–75; Jan Klabbers, 'Restraints on the Treaty-Making Powers of Member States Deriving from EU Law: Towards a Framework for Analysis'. In Enzo Cannizzaro (ed.), *The European Union as an Actor in International Relations* (The Hague, 2002), pp. 151–75.

Court has decided with respect to air traffic that the member states can no longer conclude such agreements, not so much because they would have delegated or transferred a power to do so to the Union, but rather because the principle of Community fidelity (*Gemeinschaftstreue*) pre-empts them from interfering (if only potentially) with Community law.[87] While at the time of writing the cases concerning investment treaties are still pending,[88] the expectation is that here too the Court will find that the Community rules on free movement of capital, protected through the notion of *Gemeinschaftstreue*, pre-empt the member states from concluding their own treaties on investment protection.

More generally, it is no coincidence that precisely in external relations, the TEC often speaks of 'shared' or 'complementary' powers. By the same token, the so-called 'open method of co-ordination' (the latest thing in EU decision-making), by stressing such things as benchmarking, self-reporting by member states, and best practices, seems to tap into uncertainties about power divisions between the organization and its member states.[89]

A second manifestation of the growing sense of dissatisfaction with a 'powers prism' resides in the ICJ's opinion on the WHO's request relating to nuclear weapons. Here the Court construed the scope of powers of the WHO as not only being dependent on what the WHO's own constituent document says (therewith tapping into the intentions of the member states), but it also seemed to put some value on the place of the WHO within the larger family of UN-related organizations. On this reasoning, the WHO had no business engaging with the legality of weaponry; this properly belonged to the sphere of competences of the UN General Assembly.[90] The point to note, though, is that in this construction a power derives not solely from the member states, but also from other circumstances, such as the WHO's place within the larger scheme of things.

Concluding remarks

Given the central importance of the implied powers doctrine in the law of international organizations (it helped to justify pretty much any activity that organizations have been involved in), it may be hypothesized that a change in

---

[87] There have been a number of such decisions. Representative is Case C-467/98, *Commission* v. *Denmark* [2002] ECR I-9519. For further discussion, see e.g., Panos Koutrakos, *EU International Relations Law* (Oxford, 2006), pp. 117–28; Jan Klabbers, *Treaty Conflict and the European Union* (Cambridge, 2009).

[88] Those cases are Case C-205/06, *Commission* v. *Austria*; C-249/06, *Commission* v. *Sweden*; and C-118/07, *Commission* v. *Finland*.

[89] For a good discussion, see Dermot Hodson and Imelda Maher, 'The Open Method as a New Mode of Governance: The Case of Soft Economic Policy Coordination' (2001) 39 *JCMS*, 719–46. Less sanguine is Vassilis Hatzopoulos, 'Why the Open Method of Coordination is Bad for You: A Letter to the EU' (2007) 13 *European Law Journal*, 309–42.

[90] See WHO opinion, esp. para. 26, where the Court held that the WHO constitution can only be interpreted by taking into account 'the logic of the overall system contemplated by the Charter'. The WHO's powers 'cannot encroach on the responsibilities of other parts of the United Nations system'.

our ideas on the implied powers doctrine reflects a change in the way we think of organizations generally. Or, in other words, the fact that the implied powers doctrine is losing some of its appeal, as evidenced by judicial decisions, recent treaty provisions, and by scholarly writings which are keen to replace it with a new concept, may well indicate that organizations themselves are losing some of their appeal. In addition, it is probably also fair to say that there is some dissatisfaction with the state of thinking on powers generally.

5

International organizations and the law of treaties

Introduction

The constituent documents of international organizations are strange creatures, often said to occupy a special place in international law. On the one hand, they are treaties,[1] concluded between duly authorized representatives of states, and as such no different from other treaties.[2] Thus, one would expect, they are simply subject to the general law of treaties.

Yet, such constituent documents are not ordinary treaties: they establish an international organization, and, for that reason, most authors appear inclined to grant those treaties a separate status, from which follows the applicability of some special rules, or, in the reverse, the argument that in some circumstances different rules apply to treaties establishing international organizations may lead to the conclusion that therefore, these instruments occupy a special place.[3] As Zacklin once put it, constituent treaties have an 'organic-constitutive element' which distinguishes them from other multilateral treaties and influences their working.[4]

As a theoretical matter, the claim that constituent documents are somehow different from other treaties has yet to find serious elaboration and substantiation; authors usually limit themselves to detailing in what respects organizational charters differ in practice from other treaties.[5] Thus, for some, an important difference is that constituent documents are often concluded for an indefinite period; may only be amended or terminated with the help of the organization's pertinent organs; and are often interpreted in light of the

---

[1] Barring the exceptional cases where an organization is not directly based on a treaty. See, generally, above, Chapter 1.

[2] Compare generally Jan Klabbers, *The Concept of Treaty in International Law* (The Hague, 1996).

[3] For a brilliant study along these lines, see Shabtai Rosenne, 'Is the Constituent Instrument of an International Organization an International Treaty?' in his *Developments in the Law of Treaties 1945–1986* (Cambridge, 1989), pp. 181–258. Most far-reaching perhaps is Bardo Fassbender, 'The United Nations Charter as Constitution of the International Community' (1998) 36 *Columbia Journal of Transnational Law*, 529–619.

[4] Ralph Zacklin, *The Amendment of the Constitutive Instruments of the United Nations and Specialized Agencies* (Leyden, 1968), p. 8.

[5] But see the fine conceptual study by Catherine Brölmann, *The Institutional Veil in Public International Law: International Organisations and the Law of Treaties* (Oxford, 2007).

organization's goals.[6] Others find the special position of constituent documents predominantly in the common purpose served by organizations: constitutions are then characterized by the circumstance that power is used in the pursuit of a common goal, rather than, as with other treaties, in the pursuit of concurring goals.[7]

The 1969 Vienna Convention on the Law of Treaties, without actually deciding the issue, seems to support the view that the constituent documents of international organizations form a class of their own. It stipulates, for example, in Article 5, that the relevant rules of international organizations themselves may depart from the law of treaties, and it also honours a somewhat special position for international organizations when it comes to various other issues. Thus, for example, organs of organizations may have a role to play in testing the compatibility of reservations made by states, following Article 20, para. 3. Such exceptions notwithstanding, though, the Vienna Convention generally applies to treaties constituting international organizations and treaties adopted under the auspices of international organizations. Nonetheless, according to many authorities, treaties constituting international organizations are separate phenomena, and should be treated differently.

Indeed, in some cases there are clear differences. An obvious example relates to membership of organizations. Normally, when a state accedes to a treaty concluded between others, the accession is a unilateral act. If a treaty is open for accession, then normally speaking, third states can either use their right of accession or not; it is up to them to do so.

However, with international organizations it is often different, in that the accession of new members is not merely a unilateral act by the aspiring new member, but most often entails a positive decision to allow that state to become a member by some organ of the organization concerned. In the United Nations, for example, admission of new members requires a positive recommendation by the Security Council and a decision by the General Assembly.[8]

In the European Union, the admission of a new member state depends upon the unanimous approval of the Council, having consulted the Commission and obtained the assent of the European Parliament.[9] Moreover, accession is preceded (as is also the case with the WTO) by intense negotiations. Clearly, then, admission procedures of international organizations may depart from the general law of treaties, although in those cases where admission will materialize on the basis of an accession treaty between the organization and the new member

---

[6] So, e.g., Riccardo Monaco, 'Le caractère constitutionnel des actes institutifs d'organisations internationales'. In Suzanne Bastid et al. (eds.), *Mélanges offerts à Charles Rousseau* (Paris, 1974), pp. 153–72.

[7] So, e.g., Eric Suy, 'The Constitutional Character of Constituent Treaties of International Organizations and the Hierarchy of Norms'. In Ulrich Beyerlin et al. (eds.), *Recht zwischen Umbruch und Bewahrung: Festschrift für Rudolf Bernhardt* (Berlin, 1995), pp. 267–77.

[8] Article 4, para. 2 UN Charter.   [9] Article 49 TEU.

(as is the case with the EU), the accession treaty will itself be governed by the general law of treaties.

Four separate issues warrant discussion here:[10] the facility of making reservations to constituent documents, revision of constituent documents, termination of such documents and interpretation of constituent documents. It is regarding these issues in particular that the law of international organizations may depart from the general law of treaties.

Reservations

The Vienna Convention on the Law of Treaties has created a complicated, somewhat awkward system of rules relating to making reservations to treaties. When a treaty provides that no reservations are permissible, or that only specified reservations are permissible, then the matter will be governed by those provisions.[11]

Problems occur, though, when a treaty is silent on the issue of reservations. In such a case, it has become standard to adopt the position first outlined by the International Court of Justice in its advisory opinion on *Reservations to the Genocide Convention* in 1951. Here the Court, in an attempt to reconcile the aim of universality of a treaty regime with the idea of its integrity, formulated the 'object and purpose' test: where a treaty is silent on the making of reservations, states may make reservations unless these are incompatible with the object and purpose of the treaty concerned.

That is, in itself, already a vague enough criterion: determining what the object and purpose of any given treaty is, is a difficult enterprise, and opinions may (and will) differ widely.[12] Things get even more difficult with respect to finding out who shall determine whether a reservation is incompatible with a treaty's object and purpose. At the end of the day, that is a decision usually made by each of the treaty partners individually, which may lead to the obviously awkward situation that what state A deems to be incompatible has never for a single moment worried state B or, if it does worry B, it may not do so enough for B to lodge an objection. Thus, the compatibility of reservations with treaties, generally, remains in the eye of the beholder, and the beholder means each and every individual treaty partner.

---

[10] These may be separate, but they are theoretically related in that they embody the classic struggle between exit and voice: leaving things behind, or trying to change things from within. The *locus classicus* is Albert O. Hirschman, *Exit, Voice, and Loyalty: Responses to Decline in Firms, Organizations, and States* (Cambridge, MA, 1970).

[11] Which is not to say that no problems will arise; in particular, the precise scope of reservations often becomes a subject of discussion. See the classic *Anglo-French Continental Shelf* arbitration (1979) 18 *ILM* 397.

[12] Compare generally Jan Klabbers, 'Some Problems regarding the Object and Purpose of Treaties' (1997) 8 *FYIL*, 138–60; also Isabelle Buffard and Karl Zemanek, 'The "Object and Purpose" of a Treaty: An Enigma?' (1998) 3 *ARIEL*, 311–43.

Surely, that is not, from certain perspectives, a very desirable state of affairs, and it is no surprise therefore that in some cases organs established by treaty have appropriated the authority to make final determinations concerning the compatibility of reservations. Thus, in the 1983 *Temeltasch* case,[13] the European Commission of Human Rights claimed to be competent to consider reservations, and derived its competence to consider the compatibility of reservations from the very system of the European Convention on Human Rights and the fact that the Convention established a supervisory mechanism to begin with.[14] Without being overly generous with arguments, the European Court of Human Rights, for its part, claimed its own authority to consider the compatibility of reservations in the 1988 *Belilos* case.[15]

In an analogous situation, the UN has assumed some authority to instruct its member states on the desirability of proposed reservations to the Convention on Privileges and Immunities of the United Nations and the Convention on Privileges and Immunities of the Specialized Agencies. Although the UN is not a party to either of these conventions, it has nonetheless assumed a supervisory role, albeit usually in modest, mainly advisory terms.[16] Thus, on several occasions it has urged states to withdraw proposed reservations.[17]

It would appear that the authority of these treaty organs to address issues relating to reservations has been well established. However, attempts by the Human Rights Committee of the UN to appropriate a similar power in respect of the International Covenant on Civil and Political Rights,[18] were met with serious and vigorous criticism, and do not appear to have met with general acceptance.[19] The main criticism was that the Human Rights Committee does not have the power to make binding decisions in any case, so therefore, it does not have the power to make binding decisions in respect of reservations either.

When it comes to international organizations,[20] the Vienna Convention on the Law of Treaties provides in Article 20, para. 3: 'When a treaty is a constituent

---

13 *Temeltasch* v. *Switzerland*, reproduced in part in 88 *ILR* 619.

14 *Ibid.*, in particular paras. 62–5. Based on a similar type of reasoning, the Inter-American Court of Human Rights established its own prerogatives in these matters and those of the Inter-American Commission on Human Rights in its 1982 advisory opinion on *Effect of Reservations*, in 67 *ILR* 558, esp. paras. 12–16.

15 *Belilos* v. *Switzerland*, reproduced in 88 *ILR* 648. See especially para. 50. For a useful discussion of these cases, see Liesbeth Lijnzaad, *Reservations to UN Human Rights Treaties: Ratify and Ruin?* (Dordrecht, 1995), esp. pp. 116–27.

16 But see UNJY (1964), pp. 266–8, where the UN's Office of Legal Affairs informs a member state that the consent of a Specialized Agency is necessary before a reservation altering its own privileges and immunities under the Convention on Privileges and Immunities of the Specialized Agencies can become effective.

17 See, e.g., UNJY (1963), pp. 188–91, and UNJY (1965), pp. 234–7. The reason for the UN's involvement is, it seems, the notion that the two conventions aspire to give effect to Article 105 UN; the proposed reservations would be incompatible with the UN Charter.

18 See the Committee's General Comment No. 24, reproduced in 107 *ILR* 64.

19 For the response of the United Kingdom government see, e.g., (1995) 66 *BYIL*, 655–6.

20 The seminal study is M. H. Mendelson, 'Reservations to the Constitutions of International Organizations' (1971) 45 *BYIL*, 137–71.

hoca: hangi organ scrutiny'e [*?*] *careful* [*?*]

instrument of an international organization and unless it otherwise provides, a reservation requires the acceptance of the competent organ of that organization.'

That is, so practice seems to suggest, a difficult hurdle to take: few constituent instruments spell out which organ is deemed to be competent to deal with reservations.[21] Still, it could be argued that, since the Vienna Convention's provisions on reservations are included in the part of the Convention dealing with the conclusion of treaties (rather than with, say, their application), it follows that the organ competent to decide on admission must be the one competent to address issues relating to reservations as well.[22]

It would seem that most constituent documents are silent on the issue of reservations at any rate, but then again, it was for such situations that the rule was devised.[23] The International Law Commission, commenting on what was Article 17 of its draft articles on the law of treaties, explained that 'in the case of instruments which form the constitutions of international organizations, the integrity of the instrument is a consideration which outweighs other considerations and that it must be for the members of the organization, acting through its competent organ, to determine how far any relaxation of the integrity of the instrument is acceptable'.[24] At any rate, the standard test of compatibility with a treaty's 'object and purpose' will hardly be able to do justice to the specific characteristics of treaties constituting international organizations. It may very well be argued, for example, that decision-making procedures, or voting procedures, form part of the object and purpose of a treaty establishing an organization, despite the fact that a more material aim may be, say, the safeguarding of the supply of precious metals on the world market. In those cases, there are few if any reservations which would not go against the treaty's object and purpose, rendering the test unworkable. And it is indeed a tell-tale sign that few organizational charters have met with reservations.[25]

Nonetheless, there may still be circumstances where states may wish to join an organization, but on their own terms and not on those of the organization. As the

---

[21] For an early comparison of UPU practice with the Vienna Convention's regime, see UNJY (1971), pp. 230–6.

[22] For such an argument, see Rosenne, 'The Constituent Instrument'. In *Developments*, p. 219. See also, with some nuances, Mendelson, 'Reservations to the Constitutions', esp. pp. 153–4.

[23] The UN's Office of Legal Affairs opined, in connection with a declaration made by a state upon joining IMCO, that a reservation to a treaty establishing an international organization, 'unless it provides otherwise, requires the acceptance of the competent organ of that organization'. See UNJY (1969), pp. 223–5, esp. p. 223.

[24] (1966/II) *YbILC*, 207, para. 20. Prior to the Vienna Convention, a rule of unanimous acceptance seems to have been applied in some organizations. See, e.g., Thomas Buergenthal, *Law-making in the International Civil Aviation Organization* (New York, 1969), pp. 24–9.

[25] Some constitutions explicitly prohibit reservations. So, for instance, Art. XXII of the Convention on the prohibition of the development, production, stockpiling and use of chemical weapons and on their destruction, establishing the Organization for the Prohibition of Chemical Weapons. The text is reproduced in (1993) 32 *ILM* 800. Reservations are also prohibited under Art. 32 of the Black Sea Economic Cooperation. A rare example of a reservation (and one successfully invoked in judicial proceedings) was Italy's reservation related to an organization's immunity from suit. See *Bari Institute of the International Centre for Advanced Mediterranean Agronomic Studies* v. *Jasbez*, reproduced in 77 *ILR* 602.

Declaration

making of reservations is impracticable, practice has witnessed the rise of several other devices. One of those is a phenomenon also known from treaty regimes which do not purport to establish an organization: the so-called declarative interpretation. Where the making of reservations is prohibited, states can claim that a declarative interpretation they make falls just short of a reservation, and therefore remains outside the scope of the prohibition.[26]

The same phenomenon has also reached the constituent documents of international organizations.[27] Thus, although the Chemical Weapons Convention (which creates the Organization for the Prohibition of Chemical Weapons) does not allow the making of reservations, some states have seen fit to make declarations.[28]

Opting-out Clauses

Another way, most popular perhaps in the context of the European Union, is to insist on the use of opting-out clauses and the like.[29] This may lead to highly complicated legal situations. For example, the UK opt out from the social charter,[30] accepted by the other members, presumably meant that the UK was not going to be bound by anything adopted under the charter. Did this imply that the UK member of the Council of Ministers had no say in the matter? Or the UK members of the European Parliament or the Economic and Social Committee? At any rate, the point to note is that as a functional matter, opt-out procedures or interpretative declarations perform many of the same functions as reservations.[31]

2. Revision

When it comes to the revision of treaties, the problem[32] is the existence of a certain tension between, on the one hand, the possible need to adapt

---

[26] For a general study, see Frank Horn, *Reservations and Interpretative Declarations to Multilateral Treaties* (Amsterdam, 1988).

[27] See, e.g., discussing a declaration made by India upon joining the IMCO, UNJY (1969), pp. 223–5. India's declaration was declared admissible by the IMCO Council after India had specified that no legal effects were intended.

[28] And some of those come close to being reservations, even on points where the Convention itself would seem to offer states enough leeway. Thus, despite the fact that the Convention makes unilateral withdrawal relatively easy (Art. XVI), Iran declared to reserve a right to withdraw in some circumstances, e.g., in case of 'non-compliance with the principle of equal treatment of all States parties in implementation of all relevant provisions of the Convention'. Iran's declaration is registered with the UN's Secretary-General.

[29] The leading study is Filip Tuytschaever, *Differentiation in European Union Law* (Oxford, 1999).

[30] The social charter was appended to the Maastricht Treaty under the lengthy title 'Agreement on social policy between the member states of the European Community with the exception of the United Kingdom of Great Britain and Northern Ireland'.

[31] In this light, the conclusion that the Vienna Convention's regime rules on reservations to constitutions work well with respect to constituent documents is perhaps drawn a bit too hastily. See Daniel N. Hylton, 'Default Breakdown: The Vienna Convention on the Law of Treaties' Inadequate Framework on Reservations' (1994) 27 *Vanderbilt JTL*, 419–51, p. 448.

[32] This is generally a rather neglected field of the law of treaties, and even more so when the constituent documents of international organizations are concerned. See M. J. Bowman, 'The Multilateral Treaty Amendment Process – A Case Study' (1995) 44 *ICLQ*, 540–59.

issue

constituent documents so as to reflect the possibility that circumstances may have changed and, on the other hand, the possible need to pay attention to considerations of state sovereignty. This translates itself into the question of whether amendments need to be accepted by all members of the organization, or whether, once accepted by a majority, the outvoted minority will also be bound.[33]

Many constituent documents contain some specific provisions on their revision. Thus, the Treaty on European Union provides in Article 48 that amendments are to be discussed at intergovernmental conferences especially convened, and that they shall enter into force after being ratified by all members. Thus, the TEU lays down a requirement of unanimity, an example followed by some other organizations of limited membership.[34] The constituent documents of other such organizations are less specific, with the Charter of the OAU providing, for example, that amendments shall become effective when approved by a two-thirds majority of all members, but without specifying what happens to the outvoted members.[35]

It may be hypothesized that the situation could be different with organizations of (potentially) universal membership. After all, to insist on unanimity implies that every member can veto a proposed amendment, so the bigger the numbers, the more useful some form of majoritarian revision. Where no specific provision is made, or where the amendment concerns a topic on which the constitution is not clear whether amendments require unanimity or majoritarian decision making (or which majority), constitutional debate may evolve. In addressing such a situation, the Director of the WHO's Legal Division opined that in particular the weight of the Organization's practice and the drafting history of the pertinent provision were to be taken into consideration.[36]

The UN Charter

The prime example of an express majority provision is the UN Charter.[37] Article 109 of the UN Charter provides that a General Conference may be held to review the Charter, with Article 108 stating that amendments to the Charter must be adopted by a vote of two-thirds of the members of the General Assembly. They must, moreover, be ratified by two-thirds of the member states, including the permanent members of the Security Council. Such amendments, then, shall bind all members of the UN, even those who have not accepted the

---

[33] For a study of a few issues relating to the time factor, see Sienho Yee, 'The Time Limit for the Ratification of Proposed Amendments to the Constitutions of International Organizations' (2000) 4 *Max Planck Yearbook of United Nations Law*, 185–213.

[34] Compare Art. 147 in conjunction with 145 of the OAS Charter.

[35] Article XXXIII. Other founding documents do not refer to the precise modalities of amendment or revision at all: compare the NATO treaty which does, however, allow for a review conference (Art. 12).

[36] See UNJY (1979), pp. 199–200.

[37] For a first-hand account of the mechanics of Charter revision, see Bengt Broms, 'The Slow Renewal Process of the United Nations'. In Kimmo Kiljunen (ed.), *Finns in the United Nations* (Helsinki, 1996), pp. 270–89.

amendments.[38] Amendments shall be registered with the UN Secretariat,[39] and instruments of acceptance of amendments shall be deposited with the Secretary-General (the Charter itself has the US government as its depository).[40]

Still, hypotheses aside, the circumstance that amendments bind all members makes the Charter relatively special.[41] Constituent documents more usually provide either that those states who do not accept an amendment cease to be members of the organization,[42] or that amendments may become effective upon acceptance by a certain qualified majority (usually two-thirds), but without specifying what will happen to the states who do not accept a particular amendment,[43] or specifying that amendments will only come to bind those states that have accepted them.[44]

In those cases, then, the outcome may be that different members are bound by different versions of the constituent document: member A may be bound by the original version, while members B and C, having accepted the amendment, are bound by the constituent document as amended.

Where amendments are of marginal importance, they will not pose unmanageable problems. Where amendments relate to substantive law, to have different regimes may be awkward, perhaps even unfair, but is still not necessarily very problematic. It becomes very difficult, though, when those amendments relate to such issues as voting or decision-making procedures.

Several modalities have been invented to overcome such difficulties, although none is overly elegant. One possible solution is simply to create a new treaty which then replaces the old treaty, thus creating a chain of conventions. The most prominent example of this is perhaps the situation within the International Telecommunication Union (ITU), where the constituent document is replaced at regular intervals by a new constituent document.[45] Something similar applied to the subsumption of GATT by the WTO; thus, as Hoekman and Kostecki observe, the creation of the WTO allowed GATT's member states to overcome the need to amend the old GATT.[46] Still, here the question remains what to

---

[38] Nonetheless, the *travaux préparatoires* suggest something of a tacit right of withdrawal for states unable or unwilling to accept amendments to the Charter. Compare Edwin C. Hoyt, *The Unanimity Rule in the Revision of Treaties: A Re-examination* (The Hague, 1959), esp. p. 65.

[39] See UNJY (1966), p. 261, reproducing an internal secretariat memorandum.

[40] See UNJY (1964), p. 249.   [41] But see Art. 73 WHO, containing a similar provision.

[42] This was, e.g., the case with the League of Nations. See Art. 26, para. 2 Covenant.

[43] Thus, e.g., Art. 36 ILO; Art. XIII UNESCO.

[44] Thus, e.g., Art. 94 ICAO; Art. XX FAO; Art. 28 WMO.

[45] Compare G. W. Maas Geesteranus, 'Recht en praktijk in het verdragenrecht'. In E. W. Vierdag and G. W. Maas Geesteranus, *Spanningen tussen recht en praktijk in het verdragenrecht* (Deventer, 1989), 91–122, esp. pp. 108–13. For an interesting proposal along these lines with respect to the United Nations, see Ernst-Ulrich Petersmann, 'How to Reform the UN System? Constitutionalism, International Law, and International Organizations' (1997) 10 *Leiden JIL*, 421–74.

[46] Bernard Hoekman and Michel Kostecki, *The Political Economy of the World Trading System: From GATT to WTO* (Oxford, 1995), p. 19. For largely the same reason, the earlier GATT became accompanied by a number of so-called side agreements (such as the Subsidies Code):

do with states that do not accept the new constituent document. Presumably, given the wording used in the ITU treaties, these are no longer bound, as the new treaties normally 'abrogate' the old ones.

Another way to adapt treaties to changed circumstances is to bypass formal amendment procedures, and instead legislate (or use quasi-legislation, or have a practice develop) to reach the same result.[47] After all, there is but a fine line between a formal amendment and a collective decision to engage in a certain practice that was unforeseen in the constituent document. The most obvious example perhaps is where the United Nations is heavily engaged in peace-keeping activities without the Charter even whispering the term. Another example is how NATO has dramatically changed its activities since the end of the Cold War by means of summit declarations and new strategic concepts.[48] The drawback then is, of course, that any new practice is always vulnerable to the criticism that the organization lacks the competence to engage in it. And while it may be plausible, as the International Court of Justice has suggested,[49] that the presumption must be that organizations and their organs act *intra vires*,[50] nonetheless the point remains that the grafting of such activities onto the basic documents of the organization remains somewhat suspect, and may contribute to a loss of legitimacy of the organization, which in turn may result in an unwillingness to transfer the appropriate funds.[51]

In order to facilitate flexibility, it is not uncommon to distinguish between amendments which create new obligations, and amendments which do not create new obligations but are, instead, merely technical or perhaps executive (i.e., intended merely to execute a previous agreement). Sometimes such a distinction

---

this was considered easier than amending GATT itself. See John H. Jackson, 'Dispute Settlement and the WTO: Emerging Problems' (1998) 1 *JIEL*, 329–51, pp. 345–6.

[47] For an impressive (and somewhat disturbing) overview of how the rules relating to the UN Security Council have changed over the years with little by way of formal amendment, see Frederic L. Kirgis, Jr, 'The Security Council's First Fifty Years' (1995) 89 *AJIL*, 506–39. See also Nico Schrijver, 'The Future of the Charter of the United Nations' (2006) 10 *Max Planck Yearbook of United Nations Law*, 1–34. Much the same happens elsewhere: see, e.g., Gian Luca Burci, 'Institutional Adaptation without Reform: WHO and the Challenges of Globalization' (2005) 2 *IOLR*, 437–43.

[48] This was given the stamp of approval by the German Federal Constitutional Court in *Case 2 B v. E 6/99*, judgment of 22 November 2001, available at www.bundesverfassungsgericht.de (last visited 28 August 2008). The same court later explained NATO's actions in Afghanistan as falling within the scope of self-defence. See the *Tornado* case, judgment of 3 July 2007, *ILDC* 819 (DE 2007). A useful study is Stefan Bölingen, *Die Transformation der NATO im Spiegel der Vertragsentwicklung: Zwischen sicherheitspolitischen Herausforderungen und völkerrechtlicher Legitimität* (Saarbrücken, 2007).

[49] See in particular the ICJ's opinion in *Certain Expenses of the United Nations (Article 17, Paragraph 2, of the Charter)*, advisory opinion, [1962] ICJ Reports 151, and the discussion below on interpretation.

[50] For an interesting illustration see also the decision of the German Federal Constitutional Court in the *International Military Operations (German Participation)* case, decision of 12 July 1994, reproduced in 106 *ILR* 319.

[51] It is for this reason perhaps that the EC Court strongly urged against the bypassing of amendment procedures in case 43/75, *Defrenne v. Sabena* [1976] ECR 455.

can be found in domestic law relating to the approval of treaties,[52] sometimes also in international treaty regimes,[53] and sometimes in constituent documents (and secondary instruments[54]) of international organizations.[55] The idea, then, is to increase flexibility in three ways. First, the procedure for approving unimportant amendments may be less strenuous than the procedure involving new obligations, for example requiring the support of a simple majority instead of a two-thirds majority. Second, provisions relating to the entry into force of amendments may be more relaxed: often amendments involving no new obligations may enter into force upon adoption, whereas those involving new obligations will need to be ratified by the member states in accordance with their domestic procedures. Third, amendments not involving new obligations will usually be deemed binding on all members, even those who voted against them; amendments involving new obligations are usually only binding upon those member states that have accepted them.

At any rate, such provisions provoke a host of legal questions, not the least of which is the question of who shall be empowered to make the determination that a proposed amendment involves a new obligation.[56] It is here that the difficult relation between an organization and its members may arise again.

Thus, in the context of discussing amendments to the WMO constitution, some states claimed that the power to determine whether or not an amendment involves a new obligation would, in the absence of any provision in the constituent documents itself, rest with the individual member states. As the United States representative saw it, a sovereign state has the exclusive right to decide for itself whether an amendment involves a new obligation.[57] Others, however, countered by claiming that, at the very least, such a position would be highly impractical, and for that reason alone the power to determine whether

---

[52] Thus, the 1994 Dutch law on approval of treaties in several places makes special reference to executive agreements as opposed to those which involve new obligations. For a brief comment, see Jan Klabbers, 'The New Dutch Law on the Approval of Treaties' (1995) 44 *ICLQ*, 629–43.

[53] The regime protecting the ozone layer makes a distinction between amendments of such documents as the 1985 Vienna Convention for the Protection of the Ozone Layer or the 1987 Montreal Protocol on Substances that Deplete the Ozone Layer, and the so-called adjustments of the annexes thereto. For the text of the two treaties, see (1987) 26 *ILM*, 1516 and 1541 respectively.

[54] See generally A. O. Adede, 'Amendment Procedures for Conventions with Technical Annexes: The IMCO Experience' (1977) 17 *VaJIL*, 201–15.

[55] See, e.g., Art. XX FAO, distinguishing between amendments that involve new obligations, and those that do not; also Art. XIII UNESCO, which lays down a special rule for amendments 'which involve fundamental alterations in the aims of the Organization or new obligations for the Member States'.

[56] Knowing who may make the determination will exercise huge influence on the procedure to be used in making that determination.

[57] See the lengthy report on procedures for amending the Convention of the WMO, addressed to its Secretary-General and reproduced in UNJY (1967), pp. 338–71, esp. p. 351.

Vienna convention

amendments / revisions

inter se

amendments involve new obligations should rest with one of the organs of the organization concerned; preferably its plenary organ.[58]

Where organizational documents are silent on issues of amendment or revision, the general law of treaties may be looked at for guidance. Articles 40 and 41 of the 1969 Vienna Convention state two possible positions. Article 40, para. 4 provides, in essence, that amendments to multilateral treaties do not (in the absence of any contrary provision contained in the treaty itself) bind states which do not become parties to the amendment. It refers, moreover, to Article 30, para. 4(b) which in turn provides that, in such a case, relations between parties are governed by the version to which both have subscribed.[59] This, then, implies a certain protection of sovereign prerogatives: a state cannot be bound by obligations which it has not accepted.

Another way to prevent institutional paralysis is to modify between certain of the parties *inter se*.[60] Article 41 offers this possibility, subject to two conditions: a modification between some parties *inter se* may not affect the rights and obligations of the other parties, and must not relate to a provision, derogation of which is incompatible with the effective execution of the object and purpose of the treaty as a whole.

Withdrawal and termination

As already alluded to above, especially in relation to amendments not accepted by all members, it may be useful to have some sort of provision concerning the possibility of withdrawal from the organization. After all, members who are forced to remain members against their wishes may find several ways of sabotaging the functioning of the organization, for instance by refusing to implement decisions or by implementing them incorrectly.[61]

The issue assumed some prominence during the drafting of the United Nations Charter, when the drafters had to decide whether or not to insert a specific provision allowing for the withdrawal of a member state. Earlier, with the League of Nations, a withdrawal provision had been given pride of place in the very opening article of the Covenant, in order to appease the expected opposition in the US Senate.[62] With the UN, in the end, a withdrawal provision

---

[58] *Ibid.*, p. 343. The report also invokes the drafting history and standing practice in support of the organization's power to make this determination.

[59] This displays, incidentally, a view of multilateral treaties as bundles of bilateral relations, and such a view is hard put to do justice to the special characteristics of international organizations. See also Rosenne, 'The Constituent Instrument', in *Developments*.

[60] In practice, this may be indistinguishable from an amendment not unanimously accepted. The difference then resides in the point of departure: planning an amendment across the board or a more modest modification.

[61] For an overview of the various possibilities, see Joseph H. H. Weiler, 'Alternatives to Withdrawal from an International Organization: The Case of the European Economic Community' (1985) 20 *Israel Law Review*, 282–98.

[62] Which refused to approve at any rate. See Jan Willem Schulte Nordholt, *Woodrow Wilson: Een leven voor de wereldvrede. Een biografie* (Amsterdam, 1990), p. 325.

was not included, but on the idea, or so it seems, that such would be redundant rather than contrary to prevailing international law. Some argued that a right of withdrawal was customary in nature, others that it was merely an application of the *rebus sic stantibus* doctrine, and yet others that it was rather best perceived as inherent, following from the sovereignty of states.[63]

Again, to the extent that constituent documents remain silent on the issue (which seems to be the standard case), some guidance can be found in the Vienna Convention on the Law of Treaties. Article 56 thereof deals with withdrawal from a treaty containing no withdrawal provisions, and lays down, as a general rule, that in such a case the treaty is not subject to withdrawal. Yet, Article 56 specifies two possible exceptions. First, where a right of withdrawal can nonetheless be established to have been the intention of the drafters, such intention must be honoured.[64] Second, Article 56 provides that, in some cases, a right of withdrawal may be implied in the nature of an agreement. The thinking here, apparently, went first and foremost in the direction of treaties of alliance.[65]

The guidance offered by Article 56, then, is of limited help when it comes to treaties establishing international organizations, and legal problems may well be aggravated by the circumstance that in case of a possible withdrawal not just the other member states of the organization are concerned, but possibly also some of the organization's organs. Thus, it may well be argued that withdrawal from the European Union may involve the consent of the European Parliament, or at the very least a proposal from the Commission. And that, in turn, has given rise to the thought that the member states are no longer the sole masters of the treaty.[66]

In the view of the World Court, the guidance offered by Article 56 is also limited when it comes to treaties concluded with or between international organizations. In its 1980 advisory opinion concerning the headquarters of the WHO's regional office in Alexandria,[67] the ICJ was somewhat hesitant on Article 56. Due to tensions in the Middle East following the Egyptian–Israeli peace, a number of middle eastern states had started a lobby within the World Health Organization (WHO) to move the regional office from Alexandria (Egypt) to somewhere else (Amman in Jordan was named as a possible candidate).

The main problem before the Court was that it was unclear on what legal basis the regional office had come to be established in Alexandria: was this by virtue of the 1951 Host Agreement, or by means of a more informal agreement dating back to 1949?

---

[63] See generally the discussion in Hoyt, *Unanimity Rule*, pp. 62–6.

[64] See generally also the ILC's commentary to the final draft of Art. 53, (1966/II) *YbILC*, 250–1.

[65] *Ibid.*, although the draft Art. 53 did not yet contain this provision.

[66] The argument is made most famously by Ulrich Everling, 'Sind die Mitgliedstaaten der Europäischen Gemeinschaft noch Herren der Verträge? Zum Verhältnis von Europäischem Gemeinschaftsrecht und Völkerrecht'. In Rudolf Bernhardt *et al.* (eds.), *Völkerrecht als Rechtsordnung, internationale Gerichtsbarkeit, Menschenrechte: Festschrift für Hermann Mosler* (Berlin, 1983), pp. 173–91.

[67] *Interpretation of the Agreement of 25 March 1951 between the WHO and Egypt, Advisory Opinion*, [1980] ICJ Reports 73.

The 1951 agreement provided for termination; the 1949 agreement, being more informal, did not. In the end the Court refused to take sides, merely holding that negotiations in good faith between the WHO and Egypt were called for.[68] In doing so, it informed the parties, somewhat curiously perhaps, that the question of the period of notice of termination to be given was something which necessarily varies 'according to the requirements of the particular case'.[69] The Court did not wish to go further than providing 'some indications', such as the twelve months mentioned in Article 56 of the Vienna Convention and its corresponding article in what was at the time still the draft of the Vienna Convention on the Law of Treaties with or between International Organizations.

In this *WHO–Egypt* case, the Court did its best to defuse a potentially explosive political situation, and clearly thought that negotiations would be by far the most advisable solution. Within that framework, it follows that Article 56 of the Vienna Convention is not a hard and fast rule, which must be applied if the parties are at odds and have failed to provide themselves for termination, but rather more in the nature of a guideline: if they so wish, Article 56 may provide a useful indication.

Interpretation

'In the case of language, of any form of discourse or text, of any speech-act', so George Steiner reminds us, 'words seek out words. There is no *à priori* limit to the ways in which this search, this quest for meaning, can be conducted.'[70]

Much of the business of lawyers has to do with the interpretation of documents, and while interpretation is as much art as it is science (or perhaps even, as someone once put it, art masquerading as science[71]), it is no cause for great surprise that general international law has developed something of a general rule of interpretation.

This general rule is laid down in Article 31 of the Vienna Convention on the Law of Treaties, which tells us first and foremost that a 'treaty shall be interpreted in good faith in accordance with the ordinary meaning to be given to the terms of the treaty in their context and in the light of its object and purpose'.

Thus, the general rule embodies something of a compromise (or oscillation perhaps) between what writers usually refer to as the textual approach and the teleological approach, stressing both the text and the treaty's object and purpose; it also allows resort to later agreements or subsequent practice between the parties. Moreover, the Vienna Convention allows parties to resort to a more historical approach in case the general rule leads to absurd or

---

[68] See also Klabbers, *Concept of Treaty*, pp. 202–3.   [69] *WHO–Egypt* case, p. 96.

[70] George Steiner, *Errata: An Examined Life* (London, 1997), p. 18.

[71] See Sir Robert Y. Jennings, 'General Course on Principles of International Law' (1967/II) 121 *RdC*, 323–606, p. 544.

unreasonable results, or leaves the meaning of a term or provision ambiguous or obscure.[72]

The general rule of interpretation appears to function reasonably well with respect to 'ordinary' treaties. This circumstance may well be due to the International Law Commission's point of departure that interpretation 'is the elucidation of the meaning of the text', on the assumption that the text most accurately reflects the intentions of its drafters.[73]

Nonetheless, an important branch of international legal scholarship feels that there are good grounds to exclude some treaties from the straitjackets of the general rule, and instead adopt a more goal-oriented mode of interpretation. And the groups of treaties most often mentioned are treaties for the protection of human rights,[74] and treaties establishing international organizations.[75]

As a matter of observation, there is some truth in saying that international courts and tribunals, by and large, are in the habit of interpreting constituent documents with a view to the goals for which the institutions concerned were created, or, rather, with a view to those goals as perceived by those courts and tribunals themselves.[76] Indeed, a crucial doctrine such as the implied powers doctrine is premised on teleological interpretation.[77]

The most clearcut example of teleological interpretation is undoubtedly contained in much of the case-law of the Court of Justice of the EC, especially in its earlier decisions. In classic decisions such as *Van Gend & Loos*[78] and *Costa v. ENEL*,[79] the Court of Justice established that the Union (at the time still the European Community) was to be regarded as a new and unique legal order, directly effective in the law of the member states, and even superior to the law of the member states.

At the time those cases came before the Court (in particular *Van Gend & Loos*), several member states made the argument that the issue of whether or

---

[72] For a wonderful illustration of how various different techniques can support a single conclusion, see the arbitral award of 19 September 1949 in the *UNESCO (Constitution)* case, 16 *AD* 331.

[73] (1966/II) *YbILC*, p. 220, para. 11. Subtly different quests would involve interpretation as a search for the intentions of the drafters, or as a search for the goal of a text. See generally Jan Klabbers, 'On Rationalism in Politics: Interpretation of Treaties and the World Trade Organization', (2005) 74 *Nordic Journal of International Law*, 405–28.

[74] Compare generally (and cautiously), e.g., J. G. Merrills, *The Development of International Law by the European Court of Human Rights* (2nd edn, Manchester, 1993).

[75] For a useful and balanced study, see Tetsuo Sato, *Evolving Constitutions of International Organizations* (The Hague, 1996). See also Elihu Lauterpacht, 'The Development of the Law of International Organization by the Decisions of International Tribunals' (1976/IV) 152 *RdC*, 381–478.

[76] Compare, e.g., Rosenne, 'The Constituent Instrument', in *Developments*.

[77] So also Benedetto Conforti, *The Law and Practice of the United Nations* (The Hague, 1997), pp. 12–13.

[78] Case 26/62, *Van Gend & Loos* v. *Nederlandse Administratie der Belastingen* [1963] ECR 1.

[79] Case 6/64, *Flaminio Costa* v. *ENEL* [1964] ECR 585.

not Community law could have direct effect was to be decided in accordance with national constitutional law (as is usually the case with treaties).[80]

The Court disagreed, and found that the direct effect of EC law stems from EC law itself, founding this opinion on a rather extensive interpretation of the EC Treaty. The Court noted, first of all, that the objective of the EC is the creation of a common market, which was considered to be of direct concern to the citizens of Europe. Thus, the EC treaty was more than an agreement creating mere mutual obligations between states.[81]

The Court further referred to the preamble of the EC Treaty, which refers not only to governments, but also to the peoples of Europe. Additionally, the Court pointed to the existence of the European Parliament and the Economic and Social Committee as evidence of a desire to involve the people of Europe in the functioning of the EC, and much the same was derived from the existence of the preliminary ruling procedure of Article 177 (nowadays Article 234) of the TEC, which allows national courts to ask the EC Court's advice. Thus, as the Court held:

> The conclusion to be drawn from this is that the Community constitutes a new legal order of international law for the benefit of which the states have limited their sovereign rights, albeit within limited fields, and the subjects of which comprise not only Member States but also their nationals. Independently of the legislation of Member States, Community law therefore not only imposes obligations on individuals but is also intended to confer upon them rights which become part of their legal heritage.[82]

That was a bold conclusion to reach, and a more conservative court would perhaps have reached a different conclusion. It goes to show that within international organizations (most of all perhaps, but not exclusively, the EC) interpretation may be a little more teleological than with regular treaties.

In turn, that gives rise to two questions. First, how can teleological interpretation legally be justified? And second, does not the very possibility of a teleological interpretation presuppose agreement on the precise goal or *telos* of the organization concerned?

While the political or philosophical justification for teleological interpretation may well be that international organizations are generally a good thing,[83] the legal justification is decidedly harder to find. Of course, if and when an international organization has its own rules of interpretation, then those will take precedence over the Vienna Convention, by virtue of Article 5 of the latter.

Yet, few international organizations have any specific rules on interpretation. There is, for example, nothing in the EC Treaty ordering the EC Court to use a

---

80 *Van Gend & Loos*, esp. pp. 7–9.   81 *Ibid.*, p. 12.
82 *Ibid.* Note that the Court without hesitation claims that its construction on the question of direct effect was the one 'intended' by the drafters.
83 See in particular above, Chapter 2.

teleological interpretation. There is nothing in the UN Charter on interpretation either. So why then insist so much on teleology, to the detriment of the more balanced rule of the general law of treaties?[84]

Indeed, if it is realized that, traditionally, the interpretation of treaties has often been regarded as the quest for the intentions of parties, the problem becomes even more serious: it may well be argued that the drafters of the EC treaty envisaged nothing so bold as *Van Gend & Loos*: they may have intended to create a common market, but it is doubtful whether they ever actively thought of giving EC law direct effect, or contemplated granting EC law supremacy over national law. Had they contemplated issues such as direct effect or supremacy, it is by no means self-evident (in light of the member states' opinions issued at the time *Van Gend & Loos* was decided) that they would have written them into the treaties.

Of course, in a very real sense, all approaches to treaty interpretation find their rationale in the quest for the intentions of the drafters. It is just that they differ on the best ways of grasping those intentions: is teleology better than 'ordinary meaning'? Here, opinions differ widely, and often reflect disagreements of a political nature, in the sense that the method to be employed is often dictated by the desired result.[85]

In this light, it is telling that, in its most explicit constitutional interpretation, the International Court of Justice (ICJ) in no way referred to teleological interpretation. In the case of the *IMCO Maritime Safety Committee*,[86] decided in 1960, the Court instead appears to have embraced more of an 'ordinary meaning' approach to interpretation.[87]

The constituent document of the Intergovernmental Maritime Consultative Organization (IMCO, nowadays IMO) provided, in Article 28, that its Maritime Safety Committee be composed of representatives of fourteen states, which should include the eight largest ship-owning nations. Looking purely at registered tonnage, this would have to include two 'flag of convenience' states, to wit Liberia (the third largest) and Panama (ranked number eight by Lloyds). Some western nations, in particular the UK and the Netherlands, objected, and succeeded in bypassing Liberia and Panama. Thereupon, Liberia asked the Secretary-General of IMCO to ask the ICJ for advice.

---

[84] By contrast, the Dispute Settlement Understanding of the WTO refers back (in Article 3) to the customary rules of interpretation, which is, for all practical purposes, a reference to the general rules of the Vienna Convention. These general rules come close to excluding a historical approach to interpretation – this was possibly inspired by a desire to counter possible US 'originalism'.

[85] See generally on the open-ended nature of interpretation, Martti Koskenniemi, *From Apology to Utopia: The Structure of International Legal Argument* (Helsinki, 1989), pp. 291–302.

[86] *Constitution of the Maritime Safety Committee of the Inter-Governmental Maritime Consultative Organization*, Advisory Opinion, [1960] ICJ Reports 150.

[87] And arguably bolstered its approach by paying, as Elihu Lauterpacht somewhat bemusedly observed ('The Development', pp. 443–4), an unusual amount of attention to the preparatory works, thus deflecting attention from anything more teleologically inspired.

Thus, amongst other things, the Court was called upon to interpret the notion of 'largest ship-owning nations'. Did that mean purely looking at registered tonnage, or rather at nationality of ownership? The Court found, based on a purely textual approach, that one should only look at registered tonnage, and it bolstered its conclusion by pointing to the drafting history of Article 28 and maritime usage in general. Interestingly, at no point did it invoke the purpose of IMCO, or the purpose of the Maritime Safety Committee, or anything similar.

Had the Court referred to IMCO's purpose, and the supposed role of the Maritime Safety Committee, it could possibly have reached a different conclusion: after all, it is no secret that 'flags of convenience' do not necessarily devote much effort to improving safety in shipping – perhaps even the contrary. Indeed, this was, albeit in disguise, the argument made by the Netherlands and the UK, but the Court was not too impressed by it.

The point arising from the *IMCO* case, then, is that it is by no means self-evident that constituent treaties always require teleological interpretation: a justification in legal terms is mostly lacking, and in what is arguably its leading case on constitutional interpretation, the ICJ simply used the plain old textual approach. In a similar vein, after having conducted a careful and thorough review of the case law, Professor Sato concludes that where the text of a treaty is sufficiently clear, interpreting bodies do not usually look further.[88]

It is doubtful, then, whether there is a special rule regarding the interpretation of constitutional treaties, which is not to deny that often, a more teleologically inspired interpretation takes place when it concerns constituent instruments. Perhaps the better view is not to insist on the existence of any rigid rule, but to allow for changes in emphasis as the case may demand.[89]

The power to interpret

Another important question relating to interpretation is the question of who is entitled to interpret constituent treaties. With normal treaties, the point of departure is inevitably that each party is, at first instance, responsible for its own interpretation of the treaty. Indeed, it could hardly be otherwise.

With international organizations, however, things may well be different, for we are not only dealing with states, but also with the organs of organizations. The general principle appears to be that each organ is, at first, responsible for interpreting the constituent documents. Thus, the balance of power shifts away from member states to organs; and it seems clear that member states will have to conform to interpretations offered by organs, at least at first instance. If the Security Council decides, for example, on the meaning of a certain term in the

---

[88] Sato, *Evolving Constitutions*, p. 153 (emphasis omitted). Indeed, his own preference for teleological interpretation is emphatically proposed *de lege ferenda* (at xiii).

[89] In a similar vein, C. F. Amerasinghe, *Principles of the Institutional Law of International Organizations* (Cambridge, 1996), p. 59.

United Nations Charter, then it is doubtful whether any individual member state may attach a radically opposed meaning to that term.

Indeed, in the 1962 *Certain Expenses* case, the ICJ confirmed as much with respect to the UN: 'each organ must, in the first place at least, determine its own jurisdiction'.[90] That is not to say that the interpretation by such organ is necessarily authoritative: it might depend on the institutional balance created by the constitution. The Charter does not create any balance, or, depending on where you stand, creates the ultimate balance: there is no legal hierarchy between the various organs when it comes to interpreting the Charter.[91]

The UN itself, in the meantime, is sometimes said to be in a privileged position due to the fact that many treaties are concluded under its auspices. This, so the argument goes, means that even if the UN itself is not a party to such treaties, it may nevertheless assume a role in the process of interpretation, or request an authoritative interpretation from the ICJ.[92]

Whereas the UN system creates a balance between the various principal organs, within the EC the balance tilts clearly in favour of the Court of Justice, following Article 220 (formerly Article 164) of the TEC. The other institutions, so the Court affirmed in the 1995 *Bosman* case, do not have the power to render an authoritative interpretation of the EC Treaty. Or rather, their interpretations remain subject to review by the Court. As the Court put it with respect to the Commission's role: 'except where such powers are expressly conferred upon it, the Commission may not give guarantees concerning the compatibility of specific practices with the Treaty. In no circumstances does it have the power to authorize practices which are contrary to the Treaty.'[93]

Concluding remarks

The treaties establishing international organizations are often regarded as being somehow different from ordinary, more or less contractual arrangements, and therefore, so the argument goes, warrant special treatment in international law. The argument is attractive, and makes sense at least on the level of intuition. Indeed, it can hardly be denied that organizations are often created for an indefinite period of time; that often such issues as revision are formally dependent on the co-operation of the organization's organs; and that interpretation should preferably have the organization's goals or purposes in mind.

Yet, attractive as this may seem, it is only part of the story. Despite being created for an indefinite period of time, most organizations will probably not

---

[90] *Certain Expenses*, p. 168.
[91] See generally Jan Klabbers, 'Checks and Balances in the Law of International Organizations'. In Mortimer Sellers (ed.), *Autonomy in the Law* (Dordrecht, 2007), pp. 141–63.
[92] See, e.g., Rosalyn Higgins, *The Development of International Law through the Political Organs of the United Nations* (Oxford, 1963), p. 326.
[93] Case C-415/93, *Union Royale Belge des Sociétés de Football Association ASBL and others* v. *Jean-Marc Bosman and others* [1995] ECR I-4921, para. 136 (references omitted).

last indefinitely,[94] and indeed some (the ECSC is a prominent example) are initially created for a limited period of time. In addition, the imperative that interpretation be teleological does not find unanimous support, and meets with the practical objection that states may simply not wish their creations to become too independent from them. Where revision formally often entails the co-operation (or even consent) of the pertinent organs, the member states may and do circumvent such procedures by informal revisions.

There is also another consideration which militates against the easy conclusion that constitutions are somehow special – the consideration that the same case can be made (indeed even using the same arguments) for so-called law-making treaties. Thus, human rights treaties, or treaties protecting the environment, are often said to warrant teleological interpretation, are rarely concluded for a short period of time only, and may even give birth to institutions or organs which may desire a say in, for example, revision or, as noted earlier with respect to the European human rights bodies and the UN's Human Rights Committee, concerning the admissibility of reservations.[95] Where two different phenomena can be explained by the same logic and the same arguments, one may wonder how different they really are from each other. At any rate, the imprecise (and ill-worked-out) underlying notion that organizational charters are different because they create something with an institutional life of its own loses some of its plausibility.

In short, then, to put it in circular terms, the attractiveness of viewing constitutions as a special class of treaties may well find its main inspiration in, precisely, its attractiveness: viewing constitutions as a special class of treaty satisfies our intuition as well as our sentiment that to create, say, the United Nations is somehow of more weight than to conclude an agreement on trade in lightbulbs, or some other mundane matter. It is doubtful, however, whether these sentiments alone justify the application of different rules (except insofar as allowed by Article 5 of the Vienna Convention on the Law of Treaties) when organizational charters themselves are silent.

---

[94] See also Chapter 15 below, on the dissolution and succession of organizations.

[95] For an argument to this effect in the context of state succession, see Menno T. Kamminga, 'State Succession in Respect of Human Rights Treaties' (1996) 7 *EJIL*, 469–84.

6

Issues of membership

Introduction

Usually, the constituent treaties of international organizations control who can join the organization, under what conditions, and following which procedure. Often a distinction is made between original members and those who join later, with the original members (or the founder members) being those states that have expressed their consent to be bound by the Organization's terms before the Organization's constituent instrument entered into force, or before a certain specified date, or perhaps a combination thereof. Thus, Article 3 of the UN Charter provides that original members are those who either took part in the negotiations of the Charter and signed and ratified it, or had previously signed the 1942 Declaration by United Nations and subsequently signed and ratified the Charter. The latter construction was chosen to accommodate Poland, which had not been in a position to take part in the negotiations in San Francisco.[1]

The distinction between original members and 'normal' members is, however, only rarely of great legal significance. Unless special provisions are made,[2] normally speaking the difference entails certain practical benefits in favour of the original members; perhaps, as has been argued in a slightly different context, in order to compensate for the fact that original members may for quite some time be subjected to obligations such as not to defeat the organization's object and purpose prior to its establishment.[3] Thus, an original member does not have to apply for membership, and may be able to participate in all sorts

---

[1] Compare Benedetto Conforti, *The Law and Practice of the United Nations* (The Hague, 1997), p. 4.

[2] Vignes mentions that with OPEC and the Antarctic system, the unanimous consent of original members is required in decisions on admission of new members. See Daniel Vignes, 'La participation aux organisations internationales'. In René-Jean Dupuy (ed.), *Manuel sur les organisations internationales* (2nd edn, The Hague, 1998), pp. 61–87, esp. p. 75.

[3] Under Art. 18 of the Vienna Convention on the Law of Treaties, states are to refrain from any behaviour which may jeopardize the attainment of the object and purpose of a treaty prior to its entry into force. For the argument that this obligation is the corollary to certain rights that signatories possess from the time of signing, see E. W. Vierdag, 'The ICJ and the Law of Treaties'. In A. V. Lowe and Malgosia Fitzmaurice (eds.), *Fifty Years of the International Court of Justice* (Cambridge, 1996), pp. 145–66.

of Preparatory Committees. Those not present, however, may be subjected to admission procedures.

Membership

When it comes to deciding on membership, the point of departure is that each and every organization will have its own rules on the matter. Thus, by way of example, Article 4, para. 1 of the UN Charter provides: 'Membership in the United Nations is open to all other peace-loving states which accept the obligations contained in the present Charter and, in the judgment of the Organization, are able and willing to carry out these obligations.' Article 4, then, lays down four conditions for membership. First, only states are allowed to join; other entities cannot join, although the founding members of the UN included several states which were not yet independent at the time: the two USSR republics Belarus and Ukraine as well as the British colony of India (which had already been a member of the League of Nations). Moreover, the status of Lebanon, Syria and the Philippines as independent states was not yet completely settled.[4]

With the UN, membership is not open to other international organizations. Other organizations may have different rules, though, and on this basis the European Community has become a member of such organizations as the Food and Agriculture Organization (FAO).[5]

What exactly constitutes a state is a different matter altogether, and as the UN Charter does not provide a definition, usually resort is had to general international law. Unfortunately, though, general international law is also not very precise on the requirements of statehood. While it is clear that most entities which have an effective government, territory and population, and the capacity to enter into international relations,[6] will qualify as states, the matter is obfuscated in no small measure by issues of recognition. Thus, it may happen that an entity that some consider to be a state will not qualify in the eyes of others; indeed, nowadays, admission to the very United Nations establishes a strong presumption that an entity is a state.[7] After all, how could it possibly have been admitted otherwise? This does not mean that all individual member states will be considered to have recognized the successful applicant, but at least those that voted in favour would be estopped from claiming never to have recognized the applicant.[8] Clearly, there is a certain amount of circularity in the

---

[4] For more details, see Bengt Broms, *The Doctrine of Equality of States as Applied to International Organizations* (Helsinki, 1959), pp. 126–9, 172–9.

[5] Note also that the WMO accepts as members dependent territories, provided they have their own meteorological service. The WTO, moreover, accepts separate customs territories.

[6] These criteria derive from the unratified 1933 Montevideo Convention, and are generally considered to be the point of departure for any discussion on statehood.

[7] See John Dugard, *Recognition and the United Nations* (Cambridge, 1987), esp. p. 164.

[8] The Commercial Tribunal of Luxembourg went further in *USSR* v. *Luxembourg & Saar Company* (decision of 2 March 1935, (1935–7) 8 AD, 114–15), holding that admission also constituted recognition by outvoted or abstaining states.

discussion on admission and recognition, but, equally clearly, such circularity is by no means exceptional in law,[9] and is, as some would have it, perhaps even inevitable.[10]

Secondly, states applying for admission must be peace-loving, according to Article 4. Surely, that is an understandable requirement, seen in its historical context, and may have served for some time to come to terms with the aggressors of the Second World War and Franco's Spain.[11] Presently, however, as a requirement for admission, the criterion of being peace-loving does not appear to carry too much weight, and understandably so.[12] Not only is this criterion to a large extent in the eye of the beholder, but it is also often thought that the best way to ensure a peace-loving attitude is actually to incorporate a potentially aggressive state in the UN. For, as long as it remains outside, it is also, as a matter of law, well-nigh untouchable; the cure of non-admission, then, may well be worse than the disease.

Third, aspirant UN members must accept the obligations of the Charter. This requirement amounts to little more than stating the obvious:[13] an aspirant member that does not accept the Charter obligations clearly acts in bad faith, and reservations to the Charter, while not explicitly prohibited, are difficult to envisage. After all, reservations are not supposed to affect the object and purpose of the organization, following the International Court of Justice in its 1951 *Reservations to the Genocide Convention*[14] opinion as well as the Vienna Convention on the Law of Treaties. Since the object and purpose of the Charter are quite broad by any standard, it follows that no reservation will stand a chance of success.

Fourth, aspiring members must be able and willing to carry out the obligations of the Charter. As a criterion, this too has not given rise to many problems recently; few states have ever been refused due to an alleged lack of ability to carry out the obligations flowing from membership. A similar criterion was used, however, in 1920 to deny the admission of Liechtenstein into the League of Nations. Liechtenstein, being a micro-state in Europe, has traditionally placed

---

[9] See, e.g., Gunther Teubner, *Law as an Autopoietic System* (Oxford, 1993, trans. Adler and Bankowska).

[10] Sir Gerald Fitzmaurice, 'Some Problems Regarding the Formal Sources of International Law'. In F. M. van Asbeck *et al.* (eds.), *Symbolae Verzijl* (The Hague, 1958), pp. 153–76.

[11] Compare Inis L. Claude, Jr, *Swords into Plowshares: The Problems and Progress of International Organization* (4th edn, New York, 1984), p. 88. See also Broms, *Equality of States*, pp. 180–1. Compare also a provision such as Article 107 UN, which creates something of a separate position for the aggressors of the Second World War.

[12] Presently, however, at least in the academic literature, the related distinction between liberal and illiberal states is gaining ground. For a useful overview, see Gerry Simpson, 'Two Liberalisms' (2001) 12 *EJIL*, 537–71.

[13] But see the award of the Arbitration Tribunal of the International Chamber of Commerce in *Dalmia Cement Ltd* v. *National Bank of Pakistan* (award of 18 December 1976), where sole arbitrator Lalive held that a war between members of the UN is not lightly to be presumed, precisely because it must be taken that 'each Member State, if and when it is using force, intends to use it in a manner consistent with its obligations under the Charter'. See 67 *ILR* 611, at 619.

[14] *Reservations to the Convention on the Prevention and Punishment of the Crime of Genocide* (advisory opinion), [1951] ICJ Reports 15.

many of its external affairs in the hands of Switzerland. Therefore, the Assembly of the League thought Liechtenstein would not be able to fulfil all obligations under the Covenant by which the League of Nations was established.[15]

Strictly speaking, a similar type of reasoning could have delayed the admission of Germany and Japan for years. As they were not allowed constitutionally to engage in military activities, arguably they were unable to meet the obligations associated with the system of collective security. Indeed, in Germany, such a situation was finally only settled by a decision of the Federal Supreme Court in 1994,[16] with the Court holding that participation in collective security measures would not infringe the German constitution.

In UN practice, of course, the matter has always been treated in pragmatic fashion: the practice not to order, but at most to authorize enforcement action, has made it easy for states with some form of neutrality, such as Austria,[17] to reconcile their neutrality with membership of the UN.[18]

As the example of Liechtenstein has already indicated, admission is to some extent based on considerations that are not expressly mentioned in Article 4 of the Charter. Liechtenstein is still a small state, and still lets Switzerland handle most of its external affairs, but it was nonetheless admitted into the UN in 1990. Apparently, nowadays the opinion prevails that Liechtenstein might be able to comply with its obligations under the Charter.

The political nature of admission also follows from the little caveat in Article 4: what matters is the judgment of the Organization. Thus, in theory it is possible that a state could apply for membership and would objectively meet all requirements, but still be refused, because a majority within the UN did not want it to be a member.

Such a situation occurred in the late 1940s when a number of states applied for membership but did not get in, for reasons only loosely related to Article 4 (it concerned, amongst others, a number of states that had collaborated with Germany during the Second World War). The General Assembly, ultimately responsible for issues of admission, could not agree on whether to admit them, and it was decided to ask the ICJ for advice.

The ICJ held that the conditions mentioned in Article 4 are exhaustive:[19] thus, states may not be refused for reasons other than those mentioned in Article 4,

---

[15] Article 1, para. 2 of the Covenant required of an aspiring member state that it 'shall give effective guarantees of its sincere intention to observe its international obligations, and shall accept such regulations as may be prescribed by the League in regard to its military, naval and air forces and armaments'.

[16] See the decision of the Federal Constitutional Court in the *International Military Operations (German Participation)* case (decision of 12 July 1994), in 106 *ILR* 319.

[17] The debate on Austria's admission to the UN is discussed in Broms, *Equality of States*, pp. 208–13.

[18] See, on some other possible problems for neutral states, Conforti, *The United Nations*, pp. 28–33.

[19] *Conditions of Admission of a State to Membership in the United Nations (Article 4 of the Charter)*, advisory opinion, [1948] ICJ Reports 57.

although it conceded that Article 4 itself is cast in broad terms and 'does not forbid the taking into account of any factor which it is possible reasonably and in good faith to connect with the conditions laid down' in it.[20] Still, since admission depends on the judgment of the Organization,[21] in the end all that can be said is that applications should be judged in good faith. Needless to say, this did little to resolve the problem which gave rise to the *First Admissions* case discussed above, which was only solved in 1955 when sixteen new members were admitted by way of a package deal between East and West.[22]

As Conforti correctly indicates, on the issue of membership the tension between the organization and its members may manifest itself. In his view, there are no limits on the freedom of the organs to decide on admission. Yet, the member states voting as members of the organs are under the obligation to do so in good faith, as follows from Article 2, para. 2 of the Charter.[23]

Conforti is correct, of course, in suggesting that no good faith obligation is specifically provided for in the Charter as far as the organs are concerned.[24] Yet, to distinguish between the organs and its members in this fashion goes a long way towards denying any form of independence for the organs, relegating them to little more than meeting places for their members. The consequence of this is ultimately to deny them a distinct will, and therewith a *raison d'être*.

Article 4, para. 2, indicates the proper procedure for the admission of new member states to the United Nations: the Security Council recommends, the General Assembly decides. As simple as this provision looks, it too came before the International Court of Justice (ICJ). In this case, the *Second Admissions* opinion of 1950,[25] the main problem was the meaning of the word 'recommendation'. The General Assembly argued that, as the Security Council is only given the power to recommend (as opposed to making a binding determination), the General Assembly can also admit a member if the Council casts a negative vote.

The Court, however, disagreed: if the Security Council does not recommend a state for membership, then there is really no recommendation, and thus no

[20] *Ibid.*, p. 63.
[21] In a powerful joint dissenting opinion, Judges Basdevant, Winiarski, McNair and Read underlined that resolutions on admission 'are decisions of a political character; they emanate from political organs; by general consent they involve the examination of political factors, with a view to deciding whether the applicant State possesses the qualifications prescribed by paragraph 1 of Article 4; they produce a political effect by changing the condition of the applicant State in making it a Member of the United Nations . . . The admission of a new Member is pre-eminently a political act, and a political act of the greatest importance': [1948] ICJ Reports 57, p. 85.
[22] For a detailed description see Broms, *Equality of States*, pp. 189–207.
[23] Conforti, *The United Nations*, pp. 33–7. Article 2, para. 2 specifies that members 'shall fulfil in good faith the obligations assumed by them'.
[24] And strict positivism would probably have to argue that no such obligations could be included in any meaningful way without the consent of the organs themselves.
[25] *Competence of the General Assembly for the Admission of a State to the United Nations*, advisory opinion, [1950] ICJ Reports 4.

basis for the General Assembly to act upon. Clearly, so the Court argued, the Charter had wanted to create some kind of balance between the two institutions, and thus made action by the Assembly conditional upon action by the Council. Neither could decide on membership in isolation. As the Court put it: 'The word "recommendation", and the word "upon" preceding it, imply the idea that the recommendation is the foundation of the decision to admit, and that the latter rests upon the recommendation. Both these acts are indispensable to form the judgment of the organization.'[26] Indeed, the Council's recommendation, as the Court put it in unequivocal terms, is the 'condition precedent' to the Assembly's decision.[27] An important implication is that, within the Security Council, the permanent members can use their veto. Thus, in 1975, the US vetoed the application of the two Vietnams.[28]

In organizations other than the UN, admission of new members may be based on different considerations. Thus the ILO Constitution is open to UN members as well as other states aspiring to membership; no formal conditions are attached.[29] The FAO Constitution provides that, next to original members, states may be allowed to join by a two-thirds majority provided they formally declare acceptance of the obligations of the Constitution.[30] And the WHO Constitution simply says to 'be open to all States'.[31]

Matters are a lot more complicated with the European Union, though. Article 49 (formerly Article O) of the TEU holds that membership shall be decided unanimously by the Council, having consulted the Commission and having received the assent of the European Parliament. Apart from the consideration that, since the entry into force of the Amsterdam amendments in 1999, there are general requirements relating to respect for liberty, human rights, democracy and the rule of law, the difficulty resides especially in the circumstance that the precise conditions of membership are subject to agreement between the members of the Union and the applicant states.[32] Such accession agreement

---

[26] *Ibid.*, p. 7. See also Jan Klabbers, 'Checks and Balances in the Law of International Organizations'. In Mortimer Sellers (ed.), *Autonomy in the Law* (Dordrecht, 2007), pp. 141–63.

[27] *Admissions II*, p. 8.　　[28] Compare Conforti, *The United Nations*, p. 34.

[29] See paras. 3 and 4 of Art. 1 ILO. The main requirement for non-UN members is that they muster the support of a two-thirds majority of the government delegates voting. UN members merely have to communicate their formal acceptance of the ILO Constitution. See generally Ebere Osieke, *Constitutional Law and Practice in the International Labour Organisation* (Dordrecht, 1985), p. 17.

[30] Article II, para. 2 FAO.

[31] Article 3. A simple majority decision suffices for admission, according to Art. 6.

[32] Until the entry into force of the Amsterdam amendments, accession could not, formally, take the shape of an agreement between the Union itself and the applicant, as the Union supposedly had no legal personality and no treaty-making powers. This has not stopped the Union from occasionally entering into treaty relations though. Compare, e.g., the agreement with Finland, Austria, Sweden and Norway, in *Official Journal* (1994), C 241/399. Since the Amsterdam amendments, there is a limited treaty-making power laid down in Art. 24 of the TEU; as this refers expressly to the Union's Foreign and Security Policy as well as Police and Judicial Co-operation, it remains unlikely that this clause would cover accession agreements. For a brief

shall also be subjected to approval procedures in each of the member states, making it possible that in the end the parliament of a single member state is in a position to reject the application of an aspirant state.

In some cases, the connection between various organizations is so close that membership of one is impossible without membership of the other. Thus, membership of the World Bank is only open to members of the International Monetary Fund;[33] with the ILO, membership follows by right for UN member states, whereas for non-UN members a special procedure is envisaged; and it has always been clear that a state could only join all three European Communities at the same time, not just one.[34]

Other forms of membership?

In the normal course of events, organizations tend to have only one class of member. Nonetheless, sometimes organizations allow for such phenomena as associate membership, partial membership and affiliate membership, and usually such anomalous forms of membership constitute pragmatic answers to problems which would be difficult to solve following prescribed procedures.[35]

Associate membership appears usually to be membership with limited rights, possibly leading up to full membership at a later date. It normally entails that nationals of the associate member cannot hold office within the organization concerned, and the associate member has no voting rights, although things may differ from one international organization to the next.

Interestingly, spurred by the newly found independence of many small states who subsequently applied for UN membership, in the late 1960s and early 1970s, both the US and the UK forwarded proposals to reflect the special position of mini-states or micro-states within the UN. The US proposed an associate membership for those states who might not be fully able to carry out all obligations arising out of membership; the UK proposed full membership, but in conjunction with a renunciation of some of the rights of membership. Neither proposal was adopted.[36]

Within some organizations, associate membership is envisaged for entities (territories) which are not themselves responsible for the conduct of their

---

analysis, see Alan Dashwood, 'External Relations Provisions of the Amsterdam Treaty' (1998) 35 *CMLRev*, 1019–45, esp. 1038–41.

[33] Compare Art. II, para. 1 of the IBRD's Articles of Agreement.

[34] Except of course during the few years between 1952 and 1958 when only the European Coal and Steel Community was in existence.

[35] The Stockholm-based Institute for Democracy and Electoral Assistance (IDEA) uses associate membership as a way to accommodate non-governmental organizations. See IDEA's homepage at www.idea.int/institute/1–00.html (last visited 28 November 2001). Likewise, in EFI, European research institutes have the status of associate members, while non-European research institutes may qualify as affiliate members.

[36] See Stephen M. Schwebel, 'Mini-states and a More Effective United Nations', in his *Justice in International Law* (Cambridge, 1994), pp. 326–36.

international relations.[37] Thus, the FAO Constitution provides that such territories may become associate members, provided that the state that is responsible for the territory's international relations accepts the obligations of associate membership.[38] Something similar applies to other organizations, such as the WHO,[39] UNESCO[40] and the ITU.[41]

Another class, sometimes mentioned in the pertinent literature,[42] is that of partial membership, whereby a state is a full member of some organs without being a member of the parent organization itself. Thus, for a long time Switzerland was not a member of the UN (it only joined in 2002), but nonetheless was a member of the UN's Economic Commission for Europe as well as a party to the Statute of the ICJ. As far as the latter is concerned, Switzerland made use of a provision explicitly envisaged in the UN Charter.[43] An important caveat though is that, in this case, the term 'partial membership' is hardly a term of art: it is a useful academic description, but one from which no legal consequences follow.

Yet another possibility is that occasionally entities which are not themselves responsible for the conduct of their international relations (i.e., dependent territories) have been granted associate membership of certain specified UN organs, in particular of the regional economic commissions of ECOSOC. The typical construction is that such entities are entitled to participate fully in the work of the organ, but do not have a right to vote.[44]

It may also happen that organizations give some states, or other entities, the status of observer, usually through the adoption of a resolution to that effect by the competent organ.[45] The precise meaning thereof may differ between organizations, and even from observer to observer. Sometimes it is, again, meant as something of a substitute, or starting point, for full membership: sometimes it is also to accommodate entities which cannot become members because they are not states. Thus, the Palestine Liberation Organization (PLO) has had observer status with the UN since the 1970s (the PLO, incidentally, has been a full member of some regional organizations in the Middle East since the late 1960s and 1970s, despite lacking statehood).[46] At any rate, it is a flexible way of reflecting the political significance of such entities, for, surely, the

---

[37] At one point in time, the Council of Europe counted the Saar among its associate members, until in 1956 it was included in the Federal Republic of Germany. Compare Broms, *Equality of States*, p. 311.

[38] Article II, para. 3 FAO. This is, of course, a remnant of colonial days.   [39] Article 8 WHO.

[40] Article II, para. 3 UNESCO.

[41] Article 1, para. 3(b). Note that in ITU, associate membership also serves as a substitute for full membership for states.

[42] So, e.g., H. G. Schermers and Niels M. Blokker, *International Institutional Law* (4th edn, Leiden, 2003), pp. 126–9.

[43] Article 93, para. 2.   [44] See, e.g., UNJY (1983), p. 186.

[45] For a general analysis, see Eric Suy, 'The Status of Observers in International Organizations' (1978/II) 160 *RdC*, 75–179.

[46] Arguably, the decision to grant the PLO observer status may have been inspired (at least partly) by the General Assembly's then-popular pastime of Israel-bashing. For a suggestion to this

Middle East situation requires the participation of the PLO if a solution is ever to be reached. Hence, there is something to be said for having the PLO participate in the work of the UN.[47] By the same token, the revolutionary changes in eastern Europe in the early 1990s have incited the Western European Union (WEU) to try and accommodate eastern European states by granting them a status as 'associated partners'.[48]

Still, an organization's member states do not always warmly embrace observers, despite the possible benefits of involving them in the political process at hand. For one thing, observers generally do not pay contributions, and are thus capable of being thought of as 'free riders'. More importantly perhaps, the rights associated with membership status may be jealously guarded by members, even to the extent of undermining the activities of the organization, for what is good for the organization is not necessarily always good for its individual member states.[49]

Thus, the rights of observers are not full rights.[50] Observers usually cannot vote; they usually cannot circulate documents as official documents unless with special permission; and if the observer has a proposal relating to the organization's field of activities, it may need a full member to table the motion. It is here that the distinction between observers and full members may be most acutely visible although, as Suy cheerfully notes, observers at the UN are normally invited to receptions or cocktail parties and therewith have access to the informal decision-making arenas.[51] In addition, observers normally represent politically important entities, and are thus usually granted privileges and immunities similar to those of full members.[52]

Intriguingly, the World Tourism Organization (abbreviated as UNWTO, in order to avoid confusion with that other WTO) comprises many of the above categories. In addition to normal member states, it has affiliate members (companies, NGOs and the like), associate members (mainly non-independent territories, such as Hong Kong, Aruba, and the Flemish Community of Belgium), while the Holy See and the PLO have observer status.

---

effect, see Thomas M. Franck, *Nation against Nation: What Happened to the UN Dream and What the US Can Do about it* (Oxford, 1985), esp. Chapter 11.

[47] The same rationale applies to participation of non-member states in Preparatory Committees of international conferences: if their involvement is deemed useful, they may be allowed to participate. See UNJY (1974), pp. 175–81.

[48] Compare, e.g., Daniel Dormoy, 'Recent Developments Regarding the Law on Participation in International Organisations'. In Karel Wellens (ed.), *International Law: Theory and Practice. Essays in Honour of Eric Suy* (The Hague, 1998), pp. 323–32.

[49] Suy, 'The Status of Observers', 141–2, provides some telling examples of UN members insisting that some rights are for members only and should not be extended to observers.

[50] Even so, they may be asked to present credentials; see UNJY (1971), pp. 193–5.

[51] Suy, 'The Status of Observers', 119.

[52] The UN's Office of Legal Affairs has stipulated as much with respect to, e.g., SWAPO and the PLO. See UNJY (1983), p. 227, and UNJY (1979), pp. 169–70, respectively. See also, below, Chapter 8.

A final observation is that sometimes international organizations themselves may have observer status with other organizations. This applies in particular to the UN, which has been accepted as an observer by a number of other organizations.

State succession and membership

When states fall apart, come together, merge or gain independence, an important question is what will happen to the obligations incurred by the predecessor states. As far as obligations under customary international law are concerned, there is usually not thought to be much of a problem: a successor state will be as much bound by existing customary rules as its predecessor or predecessors.

With treaty obligations, things are already a lot less clear cut. One thing to note is that succession does not guarantee continuity; in other words, a successor state may have (or be allowed) to start from scratch. In some cases it is said that succession is, or ought to be perhaps, automatic; in other cases, so-called 'newly independent' states are held to have the right to start with a clean slate, meaning that they do not succeed to any treaty obligations incurred by their predecessors.[53] As it is, the International Court of Justice has so far steered clear of the controversy, despite having had a few opportunities to contribute to clarification of the matter.[54]

Obviously, where a succession of states occurs, it may have important consequences when it comes to membership of international organizations.[55] Again, the point of departure is that the rules of each international organization will prevail. The problem, however, is that few organizations have their own rules on the topic, perhaps for two reasons. One is that issues of succession are relatively rare (or, more accurately, were thought to be rare when most constituent documents were drafted) and tend to come in waves. Thus, decolonization took place largely in the early 1960s; the map of Europe was seriously shaken in the early 1990s. Second, it is notoriously difficult to make rules on succession because the modalities of succession may differ greatly from case to case. While the merger of two states and the dissolution of another may both be classified as cases of succession, the differences between them are probably greater than what they have in common.

---

[53] Compare in general terms the 1978 Vienna Convention on Succession between States in respect of Treaties, in (1978) 17 *ILM* 1488.

[54] See, e.g., the *Application of the Convention on the Prevention and Punishment of the Crime of Genocide* case (*Bosnia and Herzegovina* v. *Yugoslavia*), preliminary objections, [1996] ICJ Reports 595, and the *Legality of Use of Force* case (*Yugoslavia* v. *Belgium*), [1999] ICJ Reports 124, as well as the *Case Concerning the Gabcikovo-Nagymaros Project* (*Hungary/Slovakia*), [1997] ICJ Reports 7.

[55] See generally Konrad G. Bühler, *State Succession and Membership in International Organizations: Legal Theories versus Political Pragmatism* (The Hague, 2001).

merger

Germany

If two members merge and become one, then there is not much of a membership problem: the new state simply takes over, including possible obligations that one of the two previously existing states still needed to fulfil. That said, there may be some debate as to the exact scope or amount of those obligations. Moreover, when, as with German unification, the leading theory holds that the situation was not one of succession *per se* but rather of accession of a number of *Länder* to an entity which itself continued to exist in law,[56] then it seems to follow that no obligations were strictly speaking succeeded to.[57]

What may pose a problem though is the question of the fate of treaties concluded under auspices of an international organization. Thus, the ILO usually casts its law-making activities in the form of a treaty; some members ratify, some members do not. In the context of German unification, the question arose whether the new Germany would be bound by ILO-sponsored conventions to which the former GDR had been a party; the new Germany denied this to be the case, and is probably correct in doing so, for one of at least two reasons. For one thing, on the theory that German unification concerned an accession rather than a merger, there is no rule of international law which stipulates that the obligations of the acceding entities become obligations of the new whole. At best, the old entities themselves remain bound (but not other parts of the new entity), although responsibility for the correct implementation and execution would come to rest with the new entity. But the territorial scope of the obligations would not necessarily and automatically alter.

Second, some authors feel that, in such a case, the *rebus sic stantibus* doctrine can play a useful role.[58] Under this doctrine, states are allowed to escape from their treaty obligations upon the occurrence of a fundamental change of circumstances, and for some the very fact of state succession constitutes such a fundamental change. While this position is difficult to reconcile both with the historical origins of the *rebus sic stantibus* doctrine and with the systematization of the law of treaties in recent decades (with a special convention being devoted to issues of state succession in respect of treaties[59]), it is also obvious that, in the absence of a possible reliance on *rebus sic stantibus*, states could end up being forced to adhere to onerous obligations that they themselves never

---

[56] When, in 1963, Malaysia added three new components to its federation, the UN's Office of Legal Affairs commented that Malaysia's membership was not in the least affected. See UNJY (1963), pp. 161–4.

[57] Germany made such an argument to the UN with respect to outstanding financial obligations of the former GDR. For more details, see Jan Klabbers and Martti Koskenniemi, 'Succession in Respect of State Property, Archives and Debts, and Nationality'. In Jan Klabbers *et al.* (eds.), *State Practice regarding State Succession and Issues of Recognition* (The Hague, 1999), pp. 118–45, esp. pp. 120–4. Similar discussions took place within UNIDO and the International Cocoa Organization. See UNJY (1990), pp. 313–14, and UNJY (1991), pp. 315–17, respectively.

[58] So, e.g., Stefan Oeter, 'German Unification and State Succession' (1991) 51 *ZaöRV*, 349–83.

[59] Note also that Art. 73 of the Vienna Convention on the Law of Treaties claims that issues of state succession are explicitly beyond its scope, which seems to suggest that applying the *rebus sic stantibus* doctrine to cases of succession is, at the very least, not what the Convention's drafters had in mind.

even incurred; and clearly, in such circumstances, states may well be tempted to ignore those obligations.

Things become even more complicated when at issue is not merger or accession, but where a state dissolves. Prime recent examples of dissolution involve the Union of Soviet Socialist Republics (USSR) and the Socialist Federal Republic of Yugoslavia (SFRY).

Generally speaking, cases of succession to membership were traditionally considered from certain viewpoints: membership was deemed to be personal, attached to the (artificial) person of the state, and hence when a state disappeared its place could at best be taken by one successor state only. This remained, in a nutshell, the basic idea underlying discussions concerning succession of membership in recent cases.[60]

The case of the former USSR was relatively simple: all old USSR members agreed that Russia would be the continuation of the USSR, and therefore the Russian Federation continued to be a member of international organizations, while the other republics simply applied for admission as new states (except, with respect to the UN, Ukraine and Belarus, which had, curiously, been original members). As an important consequence, Russia could also take up the USSR's vacant seat in the Security Council, but it took a unique meeting of the Security Council at the level of Heads of State or Government, to seal Russia's continuity claim within the UN.[61] The alternative would have been to open up membership of the Council, but clearly that alternative was not to the liking of, in particular, the UK and France, who accordingly were in something of a hurry to settle the question of Russia filling the USSR's seat.[62]

Other types of problems arose in other settings. For instance, some organizations provide that the more important member states in a certain issue-area will have a governing function. Thus, in the ILO, the ten most industrialized member states are allowed to appoint members of the Governing Body. The USSR had qualified as such, but did the Russian Federation? In the end, it was decided in the affirmative.[63] Here, Russia's continuity thesis could not, as a matter of law, control the matter.

With Czechoslovakia, no continuation was identified, and both the Czech Republic and Slovakia applied again for membership of most international

---

[60] See generally, with respect to UN membership, Michael P. Scharf, 'Musical Chairs: The Dissolution of States and Membership in the United Nations' (1995) 28 *Cornell ILJ*, 29–69. Incidentally, the word 'traditionally' is a bit of an exaggeration, as the tradition consisted solely of the partitioning in 1947 of British India into India and Pakistan. Scharf argues, moreover, that the position taken by the UN at the time was not very coherent.

[61] Thus the interpretation of N. D. White, *The Law of International Organisations* (Manchester, 1996), p. 68. Others have noted that Russia already occupied the USSR's seat before the special Security Council meeting, and do not refer to that meeting at all. So, e.g., Scharf, 'Musical Chairs'.

[62] As recalled by the former President of Finland, Mauno Koivisto, *Witness to History* (London, 1997), p. 212.

[63] See Schermers and Blokker, *International Institutional Law*, p. 84.

organizations, and were accepted without problems. Here, too, the main situation was easy, as both states had agreed to start from scratch. Neither claimed to be the continuation of the former Czechoslovakia.

Nonetheless, within some organizations the two new republics had themselves agreed that one of them would be the successor to the old Czechoslovakia, so that one of them would be entitled to continue to hold a position on governing bodies. This, however, did not work. The two countries were generally treated as new members, thus no succession was deemed to have occurred. After all, if membership is indeed supposed to be personal, then it would seem to follow that succession is limited to one country at a time, and ceases when that country no longer exists.

Serious legal problems arose in connection with the dissolution of the Socialist Federal Republic of Yugoslavia. Here, the issue of the continuation state was controversial. Since Slovenia, Macedonia, Croatia and Bosnia-Herzegovina had all left the SFRY, Serbia argued that it (together with Montenegro) was the only one left in the end, and thus it was the logical continuation of the SFRY. In strict law, the argument appears rather sound, especially in light of the recent success of a similar claim by the Russian Federation; nevertheless, the world community disagreed, and by and large refused to treat Serbia as the continuation of the SFRY. Instead, it was treated merely as one of the five successor states to the former SFRY, and thus had to file for admission as a member of most international organizations that the SFRY had been a member of.

A curious and rather painful situation materialized in the UN, when the General Assembly adopted a resolution (Resolution 47/1) according to which the SFRY could no longer participate in the Assembly's work. However, according to the UN Office of Legal Affairs, this did not imply that membership had come to an end:

> Yugoslav missions at United Nations Headquarters and offices may continue to function and may receive and circulate documents. At Headquarters, the Secretariat will continue to fly the flag of the old Yugoslavia as it is the last flag of Yugoslavia used by the Secretariat. The resolution does not take away the right of Yugoslavia to participate in the work of organs other than Assembly bodies.[64]

After a messy interval, Serbia applied and was admitted as a new member state in 2002. This caused problems, however, in light of litigation involving Serbia before the ICJ. In the early 1990s, Bosnia had started proceedings against Serbia, which presupposes that the respondent state is a party to the ICJ Statute, something that follows from UN membership. In other words, if Serbia was not a UN member at the relevant time, the conclusion could well be that the ICJ would have no authority over Serbia. Indeed, in 2004, after Serbia itself had brought a string of cases to NATO member states over their involvement with NATO's intervention in Kosovo in the late 1990s, the Court used precisely

---

[64] See UNJY (1992), pp. 428–9.

this argument to dismiss the applications: as Serbia was not a member state of the UN in 1999, when those cases were brought, the Court could not entertain Serbia's complaints.[65]

In light of this, it should come as no surprise that Serbia also tried to apply this finding to the case brought by Bosnia. Here though, another difficulty set in: earlier, in 1996, the Court had already found that it had jurisdiction to address Bosnia's complaint.[66] Here it had based itself on an assumption of continued UN membership. In the end, when judging on the merits in 2007, the Court could only insist that its 1996 finding was *res judicata*: 'the judicial truth within the context of a case is as the Court has determined it . . . '. This followed, so the Court explained, from the nature of the judicial function, as well as from considerations of legal certainty.[67]

It is not too hard to sympathize with the Court, which found itself in a difficult situation because of the activities of the political organs of the UN. Both the Security Council and the General Assembly wanted to take a stand against Serbia, but without literally expelling the Serbs. As a result, vague language was chosen over clear solutions, and the statement of the UN's Office of Legal Affairs, quoted above, suggests that this Office had already realized that the non-membership of Serbia could have consequences for the pending litigation. Wittich's conclusion, in the end, is plausible: the outcome of the meanderings was a 'legally absurd result that did not lend itself to an easy solution by the ICJ'.[68]

The alternative to treating none of the new states in the former Yugoslavia as successor members would have been to treat all successor states as successor members but, as noted, such an approach would be difficult to reconcile with the idea that membership of organizations is personal and limited to one state at a time. Nonetheless, collective succession to membership is exactly what took place with respect to both the former Yugoslavia and Czechoslovakia within the context of the IMF and the World Bank. To preserve the assets of successor states, they were allowed to succeed collectively, if a number of conditions (including an acceptance of a proposed distribution of assets) were met. Another condition applied to the Yugoslavia case, derived somewhat loosely from the constituent documents, was that successors must be able to carry out the obligations of membership, and as the new Yugoslavia (i.e., Serbia and Montenegro) was subject to international sanctions, the Fund could easily, if transparently, reach the conclusion that the new Yugoslavia did not meet the conditions for succession.[69]

---

[65] See *Case Concerning Legality of Use of Force (Serbia and Montenegro v. Belgium)*, preliminary objections, [2004] ICJ Reports 279, e.g., para. 79.

[66] See *Application of the Convention on the Prevention and Punishment of the Crime of Genocide (Bosnia and Herzegovina v. Yugoslavia)*, preliminary objections, [1996] ICJ Reports 595.

[67] See *Application of the Convention on the Prevention and Punishment of the Crime of Genocide (Bosnia and Herzegovina v. Serbia and Montenegro)*, judgment of 26 February 2007, para. 139.

[68] See Stephan Wittich, 'Permissible Derogation from Mandatory Rules? The Problem of Party Status in the Genocide Case', (2007) 18 *EJIL*, 519–618.

[69] The World Bank managed to avoid this problem since states can only join if they are members of the IMF. For a useful overview, see Paul R. Williams, 'State Succession and the International

Organizations may entertain different rules on how to handle, in cases of state succession, obligations incurred under the organization's auspices (think, for example, of a treaty concluded under sponsorship of the General Assembly). While membership itself is often regarded as personal, commitments entered into under the organization's auspices need not be. Indeed, from the organization's point of view, continuity of commitment will be an important consideration; for the new state, however, its own newly found sovereign right to consent to commitments may weigh more heavily than the organization's desire for continuity.[70]

Article 4 of the 1978 Vienna Convention on Succession of States in respect of Treaties provides that, generally, the rules embodied in that Convention apply also to treaties adopted within international organizations, but 'without prejudice to any relevant rules of the organization'.[71]

Generally, the 1978 Vienna Convention favours continuity of treaty commitments, but with one important exception: so-called 'Newly Independent States' (i.e., former colonies) are allowed to start independence with a clean slate, and there is no reason to assume that this would not apply to treaties adopted within international organizations.[72]

Representation

An issue related to membership, but nevertheless distinct, is representation: which government is supposed to represent a state within an international organization? The classic problem concerned the representation of China: is this to be done by the government of mainland China, or rather by those governing Taiwan?[73]

Here, too, political sympathies (or their opposite) may be influential. Generally speaking, the constituent treaties do not address the issue of representation, although it may be dealt with in the rules of procedure of the organization, and perhaps even in the various organs of the same organization.

Thus, within the Security Council a majority decision is needed to dismiss an individual's credentials. In 1971, the representative of Taiwan was dismissed in this way from the Security Council: nine members opposed his credentials

Financial Institutions: Political Criteria v. Protection of Outstanding Financial Obligations' (1994) 43 *ICLQ*, 776–808.

[70] The arguments are usefully summarized in UNJY (1972), pp. 195–9.

[71] Note that it has been plausibly argued that, due to this Art. 4 of the 1978 Vienna Convention, the topic of succession to membership fits more appropriately in the law of international organizations than in the law on state succession; see Bühler, *State Succession and Membership*, pp. 290–1.

[72] Compare, e.g., Art. 16 of the 1978 Vienna Convention.

[73] In the context of the UN, Singh launches the curious opinion that, prior to 1971, the effective government of China (i.e., mainland China) had lost its right of representation and therewith, for all practical purposes, had ceased to be a member of the UN. See Nagendra Singh, *Termination of Membership of International Organisations* (London, 1958), p. 146.

for representing China. In the General Assembly as well there was agreement in 1971 to dismiss the representatives from Taiwan and let in those from the mainland: here the required two-thirds majority was mobilized.

While arguably the use of credentials in the China incident was defensible, if a mite unprincipled, at times the credentials of individuals can also be used for other reasons.[74] Thus, during most of the 1970s and the 1980s, the credentials of the representatives of South Africa were not accepted by the General Assembly, with the result that South Africa could not participate in the Assembly's work.[75] The same tactics have sometimes been tried with respect to Israel, but with less success.

This use of credentials is of doubtful legality. It is, after all, not what credentials of representatives are supposed to be used for: credentials are supposed to certify that Mr X rightfully represents the government of the state he claims to represent;[76] verification of credentials is not supposed to amount to an analysis of the policies of the government concerned.[77]

Nevertheless, this use of credentials may turn out to be a reasonable political solution if the choice is the stark one of either letting a state fully co-operate, or expelling that state from the organization altogether or suspending its rights.[78] Clearly, the political climate of much of the 1970s and 1980s was not conducive to letting South Africa participate in activities without some form of condemnation of its policies; yet, to expel South Africa from the UN was not considered a viable option by some of the Security Council's permanent members. And where the Charter provides no middle way, it is only to be expected that some such middle way arises in practice.[79]

And in addition, although this does not apply to the UN, with some organizations expulsion is legally difficult to attain: some constituent documents do not expressly provide for expulsion. While in such cases expulsion is perhaps not necessarily completely excluded, clearly a less strenuous management technique may be given preference.

[74] It may also happen that not everyone whose credentials are accepted actually participates: it has been observed that some delegates merely wish to add to their curricula vitae rather than actually participate. See Sergio Marchisio and Antonietta di Blase, *The Food and Agriculture Organization* (Dordrecht, 1991), p. 180.

[75] Note that decisions of the Assembly on credentials are not considered automatically binding on the UN's other principal organs, although they are thought to provide authoritative guidance. See UNJY (1985), pp. 128–30.

[76] It follows that they do not by definition contain full powers of signature for treaties concluded under the organization's auspices or similar matters. See UNJY (1977), p. 191.

[77] The UN Office of Legal Affairs has traditionally been somewhat hesitant to accept dual or multiple representation (i.e., an individual representing more than one state at the same time), largely on the ground that it might complicate voting, in particular when done by show of hands. See UNJY (1967), pp. 317–20. On the other hand, surely member states have a right to decide for themselves by whom they wish to be represented.

[78] Higgins additionally suggests that if states wish to express disapproval of governments, they might consider breaking off diplomatic relations. See Rosalyn Higgins, *The Development of International Law through the Political Organs of the United Nations* (Oxford, 1963), p. 159.

[79] For an illuminating analysis, see Dan Ciobanu, 'Credentials of Delegations and Representation of Member States at the United Nations' (1976) 25 *ICLQ*, 351–81.

Termination of membership

Like the Covenant of the League of Nations,[80] the UN Charter provides for expulsion. Article 6 holds that the General Assembly, upon recommendation of the Security Council, may expel a member if it 'has persistently violated the Principles' contained in the Charter.

That is, to put it mildly, a rather tall order. One of the Security Council's permanent members might veto expulsion; the General Assembly may not reach the required two-thirds majority (the decision to expel is considered an important decision under Article 18 of the Charter, and thus requires a two-thirds majority); and even so, it is not a decision lightly taken, and for a good reason: if you expel a state, you also lose control over it. Thus, it may be better to keep the state in, and try and make them feel in other ways that their behaviour cannot be tolerated.[81]

Nonetheless, expulsion from organizations does occasionally take place. Thus, the IMF envisages expulsion if a member fails to meet its obligations although, with a nice euphemism, the Fund's Articles of Agreement refer to compulsory withdrawal rather than expulsion.[82] On this basis, Czechoslovakia's membership came to an end in 1954.[83]

A classic episode in the history of the Council of Europe concerned the situation of the Greek, 'colonel's regime' in the late 1960s. Greece, threatened by expulsion for its neglect of human rights,[84] withdrew just before expulsion materialized. Similarly, in 1966, just before a constitutional amendment allowing for expulsion of member states entered into force, South Africa decided to withdraw from the ILO.[85]

Another method which tries to persuade reluctant member states of the errors of their ways, and is somewhat softer than expulsion, is, with respect to the UN, laid down in Article 5 of the Charter: suspension of rights and privileges of membership – and this usually relates to voting. The Article 5 situation can only be applied to members against whom preventative or enforcement action is being taken. To date, it appears never to have been used.[86]

---

[80] The League expelled the USSR in December 1939, after the invasion of Finland. The incident is somehow treated as a case of voluntary withdrawal by Konstantinos D. Magliveras, *Exclusion from Participation in International Organisations: The Law and Practice behind Member States' Expulsion and Suspension of Membership* (The Hague, 1999), p. 25.

[81] For a general analysis, see Magliveras, *Exclusion from Participation*. See also Jerzy Makarczyk, 'Legal Basis for Suspension and Expulsion of a State from an International Organization' (1982) 25 *GYIL*, 476–89.

[82] Article XV, para. 2 IMF.   [83] Czechoslovakia was admitted again in 1990.

[84] Compare Art. 3 *juncto* 8 of the Statute of the Council of Europe.

[85] See David A. Morse, *The Origin and Evolution of the ILO and its Role in the World Community* (Ithaca, NY, 1969).

[86] In 1968, a permanent subsidiary organ (UNCTAD) suspended South Africa, much to the chagrin of the UN's Office of Legal Affairs which held that the decision to suspend ought to be taken by the Assembly rather than by subsidiary organs, following the terms of Art. 5 of the UN Charter. See UNJY (1968), pp. 195–200. South Africa's delegation has sometimes been expelled from plenary meetings of the UPU (seemingly without this affecting membership as such); see, e.g., UNJY (1969), pp. 118–19. See also Magliveras, *Exclusion from Participation*,

In particular in recent years, though, it has become a rather popular practice to legislate on what will happen once a member state breaches the organization's rules. Instead of using the notion of material breach (as laid down in Article 60 of the Vienna Convention on the Law of Treaties), the constituent documents of organizations increasingly prescribe their own systems of sanctions, and they usually refer to suspension of rights and privileges. An example is the Organization for the Prohibition of Chemical Weapons, where expulsion is even prohibited.[87] The gravest sanction is reference to the Security Council, possibly in the hope of enforcement action. Another example is the inclusion, in Articles 6 and 7 of the TEU (as amended at Amsterdam), of essential bases of membership, in combination with sanctions when those essential bases (respect for liberty, democracy, human rights and the rule of law) are violated: certain rights attaching to membership, including voting rights, may be suspended.[88]

A sanction similar to that of Article 5 of the Charter is provided for in Article 19 of the UN Charter: if a member is in arrears (i.e., does not pay its contributions) it may be stripped of its voting rights within the General Assembly.[89] It has been used against Haiti, in 1963, and against the Dominican Republic in 1968. Those temporarily lost their voting rights in the General Assembly.

On paper the sanction looks automatic ('shall have no vote', and 'the General Assembly may, nevertheless, permit').[90] In practice, there does not seem to be such automatic application; indeed, the Assembly has on occasion resorted to decision making by consensus when member states ran the risk of losing their voting rights after being in arrears due to a disagreement of principle on the propriety of certain expenses of the UN. At any rate, it is important to realize that a suspension under Article 19 only amounts to a suspension of rights of the member state, not to a suspension of obligations or a suspension of membership status.[91]

---

pp. 74–5, who seems to treat the episode as one in which formal membership came to an end.

[87] Article VIII, para. 2 CWC: 'All States parties to this Convention shall be members of the Organization. A State Party shall not be deprived of its membership in the Organization.' Hence, as long as one remains a party to the CWC, one cannot be expelled from the OPCW; whether the treaty relationship itself can be terminated against a member's will is unclear.

[88] See Art. 7 of the TEU. The situation concerning Austria in 1999–2000, after the election of a rather right-wing government, illustrates the difficulties, political and otherwise, in actually applying Art. 7. Not surprisingly, the report of the 'wise men' appointed to defuse the crisis ended up recommending prevention and monitoring mechanisms. See the 'Wise Men Report on the Austrian Government's Commitment to the Common European Values, in particular concerning the Rights of Minorities, Refugees and the Evolution of the Political Nature of the FPÖ' (2001) 40 *ILM* 102. The Treaty of Nice, if it enters into force, will add a procedural complement to Art. 7, essentially to safeguard the position of the accused member state and to smoothen the process somewhat.

[89] This is not normally considered to affect such things as an organ's quorum, or the majorities required for valid decision making. See, with respect to WMO, UNJY (1983), pp. 182–3.

[90] For a forceful argument to this effect, first published in 1964, see Stephen M. Schwebel, 'Article 19 of the Charter of the United Nations: Memorandum of Law', included in his *Justice in International Law*, pp. 337–63.

[91] See also below, Chapter 7.

Whether expulsion or suspension may take place in the absence of an explicit provision to that effect is debated. Some argue that, as constituent documents contain the terms upon which states join the organization, no additional sanctions may be created without their consent;[92] others might claim, however, that constituent documents are living instruments which are there to serve the organization and the majority of its membership. If this occasionally results in large-scale agreement to do something not initially envisaged (such as suspending a member's rights), then so be it. If other powers may be implied, then why not a power to suspend or even expel?

While expulsion may be the most dramatic way of terminating a state's membership of an international organization, it is by no means the only way. Obviously, termination of membership will also take place when the organization is dissolved. This does not happen every day, and the most prominent example to date is presumably the dissolution of the League of Nations. While already practically defunct, and superseded (rather than succeeded) by the United Nations, the League Assembly formally dissolved the League at a meeting in April 1946, having first settled some outstanding matters.[93]

Membership may also come to an end by means of withdrawal, or in connection with an amendment of the constituent treaty. Some organizations specifically grant a right of withdrawal, usually upon a certain period of notice,[94] and on condition that all obligations have been fulfilled.[95] In some cases, moreover, a constituent treaty provides that withdrawal is precluded for the first number of years.[96] But as already discussed in Chapter 5, where no specific provision is included, the general law of treaties is most likely to be applicable. After all, as Singh tersely observes with respect to the UN, if a member wishes to withdraw, it is not the purpose of the organization to persuade it to continue to co-operate.[97]

---

[92] So, very firmly, Singh, *Termination of Membership*, pp. 79–80. See also the opinion of the legal advisor of the ITU, in UNJY (1982), pp. 214–17.

[93] Aufricht suggests that dissolution of the organization does not automatically entail the termination of the underlying treaties. See Hans Aufricht, 'Supersession of Treaties in International Law', (1951–2) 37 *Cornell Law Quarterly*, 655–700, esp. 697.

[94] This may give withdrawing members the time to change their mind, as happened when Spain decided not to withdraw from the League of Nations in 1928, shortly before its notice would have taken effect. For more details, see Broms, *Equality of States*, p. 133. At least within the context of the ILO, it has been held that an extension of the notice of withdrawal seems legally permissible. See UNJY (1977), pp. 248–50.

[95] Singh notes that even Germany settled its financial obligations before withdrawing from the League of Nations. See Singh, *Termination of Membership*, p. 34. At least with respect to UNIDO, it has been considered that those obligations (including financial obligations) continue until the date on which the withdrawal becomes effective. See UNJY (1987), pp. 234–5.

[96] See e.g., Art. 13 NATO, providing that withdrawal is not possible until twenty years after the entry into force of the treaty.

[97] Singh, *Termination of Membership*, p. 93. Indeed, Singh claims that there is an 'inherent right of withdrawal' which states enjoy on account of their sovereignty (*ibid.*, p. 27). As Weiler points out, moreover, to insist on the impossibility of withdrawal might be counterproductive. See Joseph H. H. Weiler, 'Alternatives to Withdrawal from an International Organization: The Case of the European Economic Community' (1985) 20 *Israel Law Review*, 282–98.

A curious situation arose in the UN in 1965 and 1966. In January 1965 Indonesia announced that it was to withdraw from the UN, something which not all the other members appeared to accept. Nothing much happened, although Indonesia did indeed no longer participate in the organization's work, until in September 1966 it announced it was 'to resume full co-operation'. This was accepted without much further discussion, so it appears that Indonesia merely did not participate for a while. It was not regarded as having actually withdrawn, and did not have to apply for membership again.[98] A compromise was also reached over its contributions during the period of absence: Indonesia paid 10 per cent of what it would have paid had it continued to participate. Still, the legal situation is not entirely clear. For the year 1965, the UN Yearbook does not list Indonesia as a member; it was not listed in the 1965 resolution on the assessment of contributions, and was replaced on various commissions and subcommissions.[99]

Similar situations have happened in other organizations.[100] When the Soviet bloc withdrew from the World Health Organization in the 1950s, it was subtly treated not as withdrawal but as cessation of participation; and the same applied when Poland, Hungary and Czechoslovakia 'withdrew' from UNESCO between 1954 and 1963.[101] Of course if a state genuinely withdraws, but changes its mind a couple of years later, it will generally have to apply for membership all over again.

A remarkable situation arose when France withdrew from NATO, but withdrew only partially. It remained a member, but withdrew from what, arguably, constitutes NATO's showpiece: its integrated military structure.[102] France managed to justify its behaviour in legal terms by distinguishing between the original treaty and the organization founded on the treaty: it remained a party to the former but not the latter.[103]

 A less spectacular, more technical way by which membership may come to an end is by amending the constituent treaty. Some international organizations provide that if the treaty is amended and a party does not accept the amendment, that state stops being a member state.[104]

---

[98] The UN followed the suggestion of the Secretary-General that Indonesia's absence be regarded as a 'cessation of co-operation' rather than a withdrawal. See UNJY (1966), pp. 222–3.

[99] Conforti, *The United Nations*, p. 38, treats the Indonesia episode as one of withdrawal followed by readmission in simplified form.

[100] No member state has withdrawn from the EU, although EU law (EC law, at the time) stopped applying to Greenland in 1985. On the legal possibilities with respect to withdrawal from the EU, see generally Arved Waltemathe, *Austritt aus der EU: Sind die Mitgliedstaaten noch souverän?* (Frankfurt am Main, 2000).

[101] See UNJY (1966), pp. 267–9. There are, however, also 'real' examples of withdrawal, one of them being the withdrawal of the Union of South Africa from UNESCO in 1956 and its withdrawal from ILO in 1964. In 1977, the US left ILO, only to be admitted again in 1980.

[102] To complicate matters further, in 1966 France did so before it would under the NATO Treaty itself be entitled to withdraw, for this was only deemed allowable after the first twenty years, a period that ended in 1969.

[103] For more details, see Vignes, 'La participation', p. 82.

[104] So, e.g., Art. 26, para. 2, of the League of Nations Covenant.

Withdrawal (and the same applies, *mutatis mutandis*, to other ways of terminating membership) may lead to all sorts of practical questions and problems. What, for example, should happen to the permanent delegation of the withdrawing state? What will be the fate of employees of the organization who are nationals of the withdrawing state? What will happen to the organization's offices on the territory of the withdrawing state? Can nationals of the withdrawing state still be eligible for scholarships sponsored by the organization? And should the withdrawing member pay its outstanding contributions, or are the remaining members free to accept another solution?[105] As membership of the state in the organization determines the bond between the organization and both the state and its nationals, it would seem that upon breaking the bonds of membership, any benefits for both the state and its nationals will also be terminated, but having said that, much will depend on a case-by-case analysis. Some constitutions may, for example, provide that only nationals of member states may be employees unless no qualified nationals can be found; this, in turn, might help save the employment of a national of a withdrawing state.[106]

Finally, membership may also come to an end if the state ceases to exist. This happened when, in 1958, Egypt and Syria merged for a short period of time.[107] Obviously, too, the former USSR and Yugoslavia are no longer members of any international organization. Still, having said that, statehood does not cease to exist very quickly. There appears to be a strong presumption in public international law in favour of the continuity of statehood, even if some of the requirements for statehood are no longer met. Thus, we may well argue that Somalia lacked effective government during most of the 1990s, but it has not seriously been argued that Somalia stopped being a state.[108] Instead, UN activities in Somalia were all geared towards re-establishing effective government. Consequently, this is not the most obvious reason for membership to wither away.

Concluding remarks

Even with a seemingly mundane topic such as that of membership, it is noteworthy that much of the law (or rather, much of the uncertainty of the law) can be traced back to different conceptions of the relation between the organization and its member states. Those who favour state consent are reluctant to read a right to expel a member state into the organization's constitution when no specific expulsion clause is drafted; the potential usefulness of observers to

---

[105] This latter option was chosen when South Africa, having given the ILO notice of withdrawal in 1964, left without paying its arrears. See Osieke, *The International Labour Organisation*, p. 35.

[106] For an extensive overview of the questions that may arise, see UNJY (1985), pp. 156–83.

[107] Syria was later re-admitted following a simplified procedure, according to Conforti, *The United Nations*, p. 38. See also Broms, *Equality of States*, p. 150.

[108] On this sort of issue generally, see Riikka Koskenmäki, 'Legal Implications Resulting from State Failure in Light of the Case of Somalia', (2004) 73 *Nordic JIL*, 1–36.

the organization's functioning is sometimes impeded, or at least limited, by the jealousy of members, and two camps can be discerned even on so eso-teric a topic as whether or not to accept multiple representation: those who claim that the functioning of the organization should not be made more diffi-cult by uncertainties as to who represents whom, and those who would claim that surely member states have a right to decide themselves whom they will appoint as their representatives, and if their chosen representative happens also to represent another member, so what?

Hence, even on issues of membership, the law is far from clear, and even on issues of membership, much depends on policy preferences. There is, of course, nothing particularly wrong with this, as long as it is remembered that the law is to a large extent coloured by policy preferences. While this is most visible in decisions to admit or to expel a member, the same considerations apply on a great number of somewhat less spectacular issues.

As Vignes[109] has suggested, membership issues are ultimately founded on two grand ideas. One is that sovereign states submit themselves voluntarily to inter-national organizations by becoming members; the other is that sovereign states, despite submitting themselves to organizations, nevertheless retain control over both themselves and their organizations. It is this tension which colours much of the law relating to membership.

---

[109]   Vignes, 'La participation', esp. 61–2.

7

Financing

Introduction

An oft-heard complaint about the UN is that it does not deliver what it promises. The organization carries the promise of universal peace and security, but often fails to show up in crisis situations, or shows up too late, or does too little. One of the standard replies on the part of the organization is that it lacks the funds, and could do a lot more if only its member states would pay their contributions, and would pay them on time and in good order. And that, in turn, signifies that, however esoteric the topic may seem, the financing of international organizations is of the utmost practical relevance. As Singer put it in the early 1960s: 'Until the policy decisions of the various organs are translated into budget items, there is no visiting mission to encourage Togoland's movement toward eventual self-government, no ceasefire observer in the Middle East, no rehabilitation commission in South Korea, and no public administration advisor in Santiago.'[1]

Member states usually have an obligation to pay some form of fee or contribution; if they do not pay, they are in violation of the obligations assumed upon membership, and certain consequences can follow. In addition, there may be voluntary contributions. The financing of the EC, however, provides a special case, as it is the one organization which can boast its own resources. And in a different way, the financial institutions also form a special case.

In most cases, the contributions are supposed to cover at the very least the costs of running the organization *qua* organization: the administrative costs, as opposed to possible operational costs. Occasionally, constituent documents provide that the expenses of member states' delegations will be borne by the member states themselves,[2] and occasionally this even includes appointees on organs and committees.[3]

---

[1] J. David Singer, *Financing International Organization: The United Nations Budget Process* (The Hague, 1961), p. vii.
[2] So, e.g., Art. 49 IMO.   [3] Compare Art. 63 ICAO.

The politics of procedure

Both estimated income and estimated expenditures will be laid down in the organization's budget, usually prepared by the organization's administrative organ and, after several advisory bodies have had their say, submitted for decision to its plenary body. Indeed, probably the only legally significant principle is that the budget must be approved in accordance with the appropriate procedure by the appropriate organ.[4]

Thus, in the UN, the various departments of the Secretariat come up with proposals concerning their own activities, the Secretary-General makes a comprehensive draft, which then goes for scrutiny to an advisory organ of the Secretariat (the Programme Planning and Budgeting Board) before it is submitted to one of the standing committees of the General Assembly (the Advisory Committee on Administrative and Budgetary Questions) and, later, to the Fifth Committee of the General Assembly. The General Assembly will then adopt (or revise and adopt) by a two-thirds majority.[5]

It is here also that political considerations enter the picture, for the budget is precisely the way to get one's political visions across. There are various ways in which politics enter the budget process (or, put less charitably, various moments at which the budget process may be politicized). A first consideration is to decide on which organ shall have 'the power of the purse' and at least within the UN heated debates have taken place, even before the actual drafting of the Charter, on whether the budgetary power should be the sole prerogative of the General Assembly or whether the Security Council should also have a say; as it turns out, the Council has been left out of the budget process.[6]

A second potential politicizing moment arrives when it is time to decide on how the budget itself shall be adopted. Preparing for the UN Charter, in 1944 the US proposed a system of weighted voting on the budget and on its apportionment (i.e., voting rights in relation to a member state's financial input); however, the proposal disappeared rapidly, and would only find acceptance within the IMF and the World Bank.[7] Nonetheless, the so-called 'Kassebaum amendment', adopted by the US Congress in 1985, once again introduced the idea of weighted voting in the General Assembly on budgetary issues; as this requires an amendment of the Charter, however, the proposal has not proved to be a resounding success.[8]

[margin handwriting: budget = politics]

---

[4] See also C. F. Amerasinghe, 'Financing'. In René-Jean Dupuy (ed.), *Manuel sur les organisations internationales* (2nd edn, The Hague, 1998), pp. 313–37, esp. p. 315.

[5] The procedure is derived from Bengt Broms, *United Nations* (Helsinki, 1990), pp. 171–2.

[6] In the League of Nations, it was left open which organ should exercise the budgetary power. This gave rise to serious power struggles, which only ended when the League's Assembly came out on top in 1930. Compare Singer, *Financing International Organization*, pp. 2–3.

[7] *Ibid.*, p. 3.

[8] See generally Richard W. Nelson, 'International Law and US Withholding of Payments to International Organizations' (1986) 80 *AJIL*, 973–83, esp. 974–6.

Another moment for politics is the decision whether the preparation and execution of the budget (not so much its formal adoption) should be entrusted to a political organ, or whether it is best left to ostensibly disinterested civil servants.[9] After some in-fighting at the first session of the General Assembly, the UN Secretariat came out victorious, despite a French proposal that the UN's Advisory Committee on Administrative and Budgetary Questions (a representative, 'political' organ) be given broad powers.[10]

Budgeting techniques themselves are also not nearly as neutral as they would seem. Controversial pet projects may be sponsored by methods of 'budgetary concealment': instead of reserving money for the project under a single heading, money may be reserved in bits and pieces under various different, innocuous-sounding headings. A favoured technique for influencing the basis of financial assessments is to vary the base period (the period of time on the basis of which calculations are made), as a newly rich state may benefit from a long base period which takes its previous poverty into account.[11] Moreover, a tightly compartmentalized budget may also become a straitjacket: if a budget contains specific items for each of the agencies and departments and offices at, for example, the Secretariat of the organization, then the Secretary-General has less freedom to transfer staff or posts from one agency to the other than he has when the budget treats the Secretariat as a single entity.[12]

Expenditure

The regular expenditure of international organizations is mostly related to their organizational existence: the lease or rent of offices, the salaries of staff, the travels of staff members and invited guests, the organization of conferences, the purchase and maintenance of office equipment and libraries, et cetera.[13] Sometimes the organization pays for the representation of members, either in whole or in part, and sometimes the organization pays for some of its members to be present at meetings: usually the poorest ones.

Most organizations will, however, also incur some operational expenses. Thus, the United Nations sends peace-keepers all over the world, among them special rapporteurs, fact-finding missions, and election monitors; the WMO helps its members to improve their meteorological facilities, while the ICAO

---

[9] The same type of debate took place when creating the European Central Bank: should it have autonomous powers, or should it be subservient to the wishes of the finance ministers of its members?

[10] See Singer, *Financing International Organization*, p. 81.

[11] See Thomas M. Franck, *Nation against Nation: What Happened to the UN Dream and What the US can do about it* (Oxford, 1985), p. 257.

[12] The example derives from Singer, *Financing International Organization*, p. 65.

[13] See generally Bernd-Roland Killmann, 'Procurement Activities of International Organizations – An Attempt at a First Insight in Evolving Legal Principles' (2003) 8 *ARIEL*, 277–300.

helps its member states to improve airport safety;[14] the financial institutions lend large sums of money to members in need. In short, organizations generally provide some form of service which, of course, brings expenditure with it.

The main legal question arising in connection with the expenses of an international organization is whether they are the type of expense that the organization is empowered to incur to begin with, or whether it is beyond the scope of proper activities of the organization. Related (so much so as often to be indistinguishable) is the question of who should bear the expenses incurred. These questions came before the International Court of Justice in 1962, when the Court was asked to render an advisory opinion following the reluctance of some member states of the UN to contribute to peace-keeping activities undertaken under auspices of the General Assembly. This opinion will be discussed in some detail in the next section.

Problems and crises

With the UN, the budget is initially governed by Article 17 of the Charter, which provides that the budget of the organization shall be considered and approved by the General Assembly, and that the Assembly also approves of the apportioning of the budget. Thus, the Assembly decides which states shall pay how much, and does so with binding force and by a two-thirds majority.[15]

In doing so, the Assembly makes use of the so-called 'scale of assessment principle': a member state's assessment is based on its perceived capacity to pay which, in turn, depends largely on such things as national income, national *per capita* income and the general level of development.[16] While based on such factors, it is useful to bear in mind that any decision on assessment is, in essence, a political decision by the Assembly. The scale of assessment principle is used in most organizations. Exceptionally, some organizations (such as OPEC) use a system of equal contributions, while some others (UPU, ITU) allow their member states to choose from a number of contribution possibilities.[17]

In case a member state is in arrears, Article 19 of the UN Charter provides for a sanction: if the amount of arrears equals or exceeds the amount of contributions due from it for the preceding two full years, then that member state 'shall have no vote' in the General Assembly.[18] The language employed by Article 19 suggests

---

[14] The examples are taken from Henry G. Schermers and Niels M. Blokker, *International Institutional Law* (4th edn, Leiden, 2003), p. 610.

[15] Compare Art. 18, para. 2 UN Charter. In the EC, the budgetary power is exercised by the Council and the European Parliament together; the procedure is set out in Art. 272 of the TEC.

[16] In 1987, when Cuba offered to pay its contribution to UNIDO by means of services in the field of translation and interpretation rather than by means of cash, the offer was rejected for want of a legal basis: there was no basis to accept contributions in currencies other than money. See UNJY (1987), p. 233.

[17] See Amerasinghe, 'Financing', p. 318.

[18] An interesting early Dutch proposal was not adopted: the proposal held that the seat of any member state on the Security Council would be forfeited if the member was in arrears. See J. D. Singer, *Financing International Organization*, p. 7.

that the suspension of voting rights occurs automatically, as the automatic consequence to be attached to non-payment.[19] And this is confirmed by the closing sentence of Article 19: should a member state be able to show that failure to pay is due to circumstances beyond its control, then that member may be permitted to vote;[20] this would make no sense if the Assembly would first have to vote in favour of sanctions.[21] The decision to allow a state in arrears nonetheless to exercise voting rights is to be taken by the General Assembly itself, by a two-thirds majority.[22]

The relative textual clarity of Article 19, para. 1, notwithstanding, practice appears to be in two minds. Thus, Conforti can confidently claim that the suspension of voting rights envisaged in Article 19 occurs automatically, and does not depend on a decision by the General Assembly. Yet, in the same breath he suggests that the Article ought to have been applied in the early 1960s, when several member states refused to contribute to peace-keeping operations in the Middle East and the Congo. Instead, as Conforti notes with a sense of drama, the Assembly proceedings were suspended: no session was held in 1964.[23]

Indeed, others are less confident about the automatic application of the sanction of Article 19, with one author mentioning that it has never been applied,[24] while another notes that the crisis of the 1960s was in practice circumvented simply by agreeing not to vote.[25] And where no vote takes place, no voting rights need to be suspended. This, in turn, has been interpreted as a choice by the Assembly not to enforce decisions on contributions, with the result that 'it is now open to any state to refuse payment on the ground that a UN activity is beyond the powers of the organ that authorized it, and against that state's interest'.[26]

The main crisis referred to arose when the General Assembly, stepping into the vacuum created by the indecisiveness of the Security Council, decided to organize peace-keeping operations in the Middle East (UNEF, 1956) and Congo

---

[19] This is also the position consistently held by the UN's Legal Counsel and Office of Legal Affairs: suspension of rights occurs automatically, but may be lifted by the General Assembly. See UNJY (1968), pp. 186–8, and UNJY (1974), pp. 156–7.

[20] For examples, see Res. 50/207 B, exempting Liberia and Rwanda from Art. 19, and Res. 51/212 A, doing the same for the Comoros.

[21] See also Christian Tomuschat, 'Article 19'. In Bruno Simma (ed.), *The United Nations: A Commentary* (Oxford, 1994), pp. 327–39, esp. p. 332.

[22] The decision cannot be taken by the Secretary-General only to be approved *ex post facto* by the Assembly. See, a request by the UN's Deputy Special Representative in Cambodia to that effect, UNJY (1992), pp. 438–9.

[23] Benedetto Conforti, *The Law and Practice of the United Nations* (The Hague, 1997), p. 39. According to Nelson, 'US Withholding of Payments', p. 979, the General Assembly reached an informal agreement to operate without a formal vote.

[24] C. F. Amerasinghe, *Principles of the Institutional Law of International Organizations* (Cambridge, 1996), pp. 317–18. This seems difficult to reconcile with the large amount of examples provided by Tomuschat, 'Article 19'.

[25] Wilfried Koschorreck, 'Financial Crisis'. In Rüdiger Wolfrum (ed.), *United Nations: Law, Policies and Practice, Volume I* (Munich, 1995), pp. 523–31, esp. p. 526.

[26] See Franck, *Nation against Nation*, p. 259.

(ONUC, 1960).[27] Two of the permanent members of the Security Council, not particularly appreciative of being outflanked by the Assembly's cunning manoeuvre, refused to pay their contributions, on the theory that, as the peace-keeping was not ordained by the Security Council, it was illegal under the Charter, and member states could hardly be expected to help finance illegal activities.

The matter was submitted to the International Court of Justice for an advisory opinion, the question submitted being whether expenditures authorized by the Assembly for peace-keeping purposes constituted 'expenses of the Organization' within the meaning of Article 17 of the Charter.[28] The Court started its analysis by observing that it was not being asked to say anything about the apportionment of the budget; the question before it was limited to finding out whether or not peace-keeping expenses authorized by the Assembly were to be considered as expenses of the organization (therewith falling under the regular budget) or rather as extraordinary expenses (which would require separate modes of financing). The Court, moreover, warned against too abstract an approach, and underlined that it was asked a concrete question rather than to define 'expenses' in the abstract.

Having made these preliminary remarks, the Court proceeded by noting that drawing a distinction between administrative expenses and operational expenses was rejected by the drafters of the Charter. While such a distinction is envisaged in the Assembly's power to make recommendations to the Specialized Agencies concerning their budget,[29] it is not made in paras. 1 and 2 of Article 17, and had never been accepted in the practice of the UN.[30] Consequently, such a distinction ought not to be read into the text of Article 17.

Still, that alone would have done little to dispel doubts concerning allegedly illegal activities: do even activities not warranted by the Charter nonetheless constitute expenses of the Organization, and are they thus to be borne by the member states?

The Court, accordingly, addressed several arguments relating to the legality of Assembly ordained peace-keeping, and struck down arguments which held that the financing of peace-keeping was to be negotiated with member states under Article 43 of the Charter, or that the Assembly would not be empowered to occupy itself with the maintenance of peace and security at all. Instead, although peace and security are clearly the primary responsibility of the Security Council,[31] they are not the exclusive province of the Council; nothing hinders the Assembly from engaging itself with such issues, except that it lacks

[27] Luck suggests that nowadays, when the General Assembly convenes an emergency meeting, it owes more to the wish to highlight the absence of Council action than as a heartfelt desire on the part of the Assembly to intervene. See Edward C. Luck, *The Security Council: Practice and Promise* (London, 2006), p. 70.

[28] *Certain Expenses of the United Nations (Article 17, paragraph 2, of the Charter)*, advisory opinion, [1962] ICJ Reports 151.

[29] Compare Art. 17, para. 3 UN Charter.   [30] *Certain Expenses*, pp. 159, 160.   [31] *Ibid.*, p. 163.

the power actually to bind the member states to participate in peace-keeping activities.

Thus, the Court arrived at the intermediary conclusion that the General Assembly could well occupy itself, within limits, with the maintenance of international peace and security, and that legitimate expenses incurred in the process would no doubt qualify as expenses of the Organization.

At this point, however, things got decidedly more obfuscated, for how can it be determined whether a particular expenditure is indeed in conformity with the Charter? As long as the Charter explicitly spells out certain expenditures, the matter may be easily solved, but the problem was rather that the Charter remained silent on peace-keeping activities organized under the Assembly's auspices. Thus, the Court had to find some form of yardstick to test the legality of the expenses at issue, and it found this by testing them in light of their compatibility with the purposes of the UN, for 'if an expenditure were made for a purpose which is not one of the purposes of the United Nations, it could not be considered an "expense of the Organization".[32] And given the broad nature of the purposes of the Organization (as the Court itself also, with some seeming embarrassment, pointed out), it was almost inevitable that the Court would reach the conclusion that the expenses at issue constituted expenses of the United Nations.[33] Even if the wrong organ has taken the decision (thus acting *ultra vires*), the decision is not by definition falling outside the regular budget.[34]

Arguably, the Court could have stopped here, simply outlining the argument of principle and telling the objecting states that, as the expenses at issue fell within the scope of the 'expenses of the Organization', their objections would have to be dismissed and they would be expected to contribute in full. Yet, the Court must have realized that such a stand would not necessarily persuade the objecting states completely. After all, it would not be inconceivable for them to take issue with the Court's chosen yardstick of relating expenditure to the UN's purposes, the inevitable counter-argument being that, as sending troops by the Assembly is not explicitly provided for in the Charter, there is no reason why member states should carry financial burdens for activities that they did not agree to. Hence, the Court bolstered its conclusion by pointing out that when the issue of sending troops to the Middle East and Congo had been discussed in the General Assembly, no objections were raised. Since the argument concerned the illegality of expenditure, the states concerned should have made known their objections at the moment the Assembly was apprised of the issue. Objections to the legality of an organ's acts, so the Court implied, ought to be raised when the organ is acting. When they are not raised at that moment, acquiescence may be presumed.[35]

---

[32] *Ibid.*, p. 167.   [33] *Ibid.*, p. 168.

[34] Some commentators have seen in this the launch (or re-launch) of the notion of inherent powers. See, e.g., Nigel D. White, *The Law of International Organisations* (Manchester, 1996), esp. p. 131. But see above, Chapter 4.

[35] This is in line with general international law.

Over four decades later, the financing of peace-keeping operations is still a controversial topic. What is clear, since the *Certain Expenses* case, is that peace-keeping expenses are to be considered as expenses of the organization within the meaning of Article 17 of the Charter, and are thus subject to binding determinations by the General Assembly. This does not mean that peace-keeping is automatically part of the regular budget and indeed, it hardly could be, given its usually unforeseeable nature. Hence, although some operations have been part of the regular budget, most have had their own budget, so to speak.[36]

Attempts to establish a single comprehensive budget for all peace-keeping operations have so far failed, but at least something approaching a single system has been set up to apportion the costs.[37] By Resolution 3101 (XXVIII) the General Assembly divided the membership of the UN into four groups: the Security Council's permanent members, developed nations, less developed members, and finally a group of specifically named less developed members. The last group is assessed for only a very modest share of peace-keeping expenses (together a mere 0.05%), whereas the first group bears most (roughly 60%) of the costs. This has given rise to some dissent. As Dormoy, for example, puts it: why should the permanent members bear the main financial burden of what are, at the end of the day, activities of the Organization? It does not follow from the Council's primary responsibility in matters of peace and security (in accordance with Article 24 UN) that therefore its permanent members should pick up most of the tab.[38] At any rate, due to the reluctance of member states to pay their share, special measures were required, resulting in the creation of a Peace-keeping Reserve Fund as of 1 January 1993,[39] comprising a reserve of US$150 million.[40]

The most notorious instance in recent years relating to incomplete payment in general is the position of the United States, which at one point was estimated to have arrears of roughly $1.3 billion.[41] The United States is by far the biggest contributor to the UN budget (in 2000, the maximum the US will have to pay

---

[36] For a lucid overview, see Susan R. Mills, 'The Financing of UN Peacekeeping Operations: The Need for a Sound Financial Basis'. In Indar Jit Rikhye and Kjell Skjelsbaek (eds.), *The United Nations and Peacekeeping: Results, Limitations and Prospects* (Houndmills, 1990), pp. 91–110. Useful also is William J. Durch, 'Paying the Tab: Financial Crises'. In William J. Durch (ed.), *The Evolution of UN Peacekeeping: Case Studies and Comparative Analysis* (New York, 1993), pp. 39–58.

[37] Note though, that some operations have been paid largely out of voluntary contributions, and at least twice the parties involved have themselves borne the costs. See generally Mills, 'The Financing of UN Peacekeeping Operations'.

[38] See Daniel Dormoy, 'Aspects récents de la question du financement des opérations de maintien de la paix de l'Organisation des Nations Unies' (1993) 39 *AFDI*, 131–56, esp. p. 148.

[39] Set up by GA Res. 47/217. In connection with the regular budget, there has always been a Working Capital Fund on which to draw in times of emergency.

[40] See generally also Dormoy, 'La question du financement'.

[41] See Michael P. Scharf and Tamara A. Shaw, 'International Institutions' (1999) 33 *International Lawyer*, 567–86, esp. p. 567. Also useful is Klaus Hüfner, 'Financing the United Nations: The Role of the United States'. In Dennis Dijkzeul and Yves Beigbeder (eds.), *Rethinking International Organizations: Pathology and Promise* (New York, 2003), pp. 29–53.

was set at 22% of the regular budget), and therewith exercises considerable power over the UN's fate. Some American politicians have seized this particular circumstance to pursue their own agendas, illustrating that international affairs are not necessarily susceptible to explanations based on logic or instrumental considerations.[42]

Sometimes states promise to pay provided the Organization meets certain unilaterally determined requirements. Such linkage raises a handful of legal questions. First, the question arises as to whether the Organization should indeed make the promises demanded of it, and the short answer is most likely to be in the negative. After all, the member states, when founding or joining the Organization, undertook an obligation to meet its financial burdens; they cannot, later, demand something else in return and thus renege on their initial commitment. Second, if the Organization were to make such promises, what would be their status in law? Surely, any commitment made under financial duress must be deemed legally invalid. Upon joining, the member states can possibly extract valid promises, but to do so later on, under threat of withholding contributions it is duty bound to pay, is legally dubious.[43]

Another issue is the precise scope of the sanction provided for in Article 19: the loss of the right to vote in the Assembly. Does that also cover sub-organs and committees set up by the Assembly? The answer is, most likely, in the negative, as often membership of (and therewith voting rights in) sub-organs and committees is based on the representation of a group of member states. To disallow voting to the representative of a group of member states would disadvantage the entire group.[44] In addition, the loss of voting rights of a member state is not normally thought to affect quorum requirements or the required majorities for decision making.[45]

Finally, the legal situation concerning contributions when a succession of member states occurs is far from clear. To the extent that a member state breaks up, few problems arise, as usually all new states will have to apply for membership anew. And where, as with the Russian Federation, membership is deemed to be continuous, outstanding payments will most likely simply be transferred.[46]

However, a curious situation arose in the UN with respect to Belarus and Ukraine: after the break-up of the USSR, the General Assembly's Committee

---

[42] For an analysis of the effectiveness of withholding as a political tool, see Paul Taylor, 'The United Nations System under Stress: Financial Pressures and their Consequences' (1991) 17 *Review of International Studies*, 365–82. On legal considerations, see above all José E. Alvarez, 'Legal Remedies and the United Nations' à la Carte Problem' (1991) 12 *Michigan JIL*, 229–311. A belated reply of sorts is Francesco Francioni, 'Multilateralism à la Carte: The Limits to Unilateral Withholdings of Assessed Contributions to the UN Budget' (2000) 11 *EJIL*, 43–59.

[43] See similarly Michael P. Scharf, 'Dead Beat Dead End: A Critique of the New US Plan for Payment of UN Arrears' (2000) 6 *New England International & Comparative Law Annual*, 1–4 (I have used the electronic version, available at www.nesl.edu/annual/vol6index.htm (visited 13 June 2001)).

[44] Similarly Tomuschat, 'Article 19'.   [45] See, with respect to the WMO, UNJY (1983), pp. 182–3.

[46] See generally above, Chapter 6.

on Contributions (an advisory body) proposed a change in the assessment of Belarus and Ukraine, on the theory that the break-up of the USSR had made them similar to new member states. However, as they had never left the UN, the UN's legal counsel opined that they had already, in conformity with the rules, been assessed for the next few years, and that any new assessment would be legally objectionable, unless the member states decided not to apply the pertinent rules. But this, the Legal Counsel continued, 'is a course of action that I, as Legal Counsel of this Organization, cannot recommend'.[47]

If dissolution normally does not give rise to great difficulties, things are more difficult with unification, as the unification of the two Germanys illustrates. The UN presumed that with the GDR joining the FRG, the latter would take over all financial obligations of the GDR, therewith following an 'inheritance' theory of state succession.

The German government thought differently, pointing out that the situation could also be regarded as the UN losing a member state (the former GDR). On that scenario, it would be far from self-evident that the new Germany would have to pay the outstanding financial contributions of the former GDR. In the end, after some heated discussions going back and forth, a compromise was reached, with FRG paying something extra, while denying any legal obligation to do so.[48]

In other organizations as well, financing takes place through membership fees. Thus, in the OAS, the General Assembly determines the contribution of each member state, taking into account their ability to pay, as well as, somewhat curiously perhaps, 'their determination to contribute in an equitable manner'.[49] The OAS Charter does not contain any explicit provision on what to do in case contributions are not forthcoming, which presumably means that general principles of the law of treaties and the law of state responsibility will apply.

Much the same applies to other organizations.[50] Thus, the OECD demands a fee, to be decided upon by its Council, but without mentioning any sanctions on non-payment.[51] So too with the Council of Europe, where the apportionment is decided upon by the Committee of Ministers,[52] while in the OAU contributions are decided by the Council of Ministers, in accordance with UN scales.[53] Again, sanctions are not specifically foreseen.

An exception is the ILO, which follows roughly the UN model (as amended): under conditions which are reminiscent of Article 19 of the UN Charter, the

---

[47] See UNJY (1992), pp. 435–8, esp. p. 438.

[48] For more details, see Jan Klabbers and Martti Koskenniemi, 'Succession in Respect of State Property, Archives and Debts, and Nationality'. In Jan Klabbers *et al.* (eds.), *State Practice regarding State Succession and Issues of Recognition* (The Hague, 1999), pp. 118–45. See also documents D/62 and D/83 reproduced in the same volume. A similar discussion took place over East Germany's obligations towards the International Cocoa Organization. See UNJY (1991), pp. 315–17.

[49] Article 53 OAS.

[50] Apart from the ones mentioned here, see also Art. XVIII FAO and Art. IX UNESCO.

[51] Article 20 OECD.   [52] Article 38 of the Council of Europe Statute.   [53] Article XXIII OAU.

member state in arrears 'shall have no vote in the Conference, in the Governing Body, in any committee, or in elections of members of the Governing Body'.[54] Thus, the sanction is more comprehensive than in the UN, as voting rights are suspended not just in the plenary body (as with the UN).[55]

In the WHO, sanctions for non-payment are also foreseen, but do not follow automatically. Instead, the World Health Assembly (the plenary body) may suspend voting rights and services to which members are entitled 'on such conditions as it thinks proper'.[56] Suspension of voting rights is also foreseen in the ICAO Constitution, but here too the suspension does not automatically follow when states fail to discharge their financial obligations towards the organization.[57]

Sources of income

Leaving compulsory contributions aside, in practice large parts of the income of organizations may stem from voluntary contributions. In some constitutions, this is explicitly foreseen. Thus, Article XIV, para. F IAEA refers to the possibility of the Agency receiving voluntary contributions, whereas Article 57 WHO envisages the possibility of receiving gifts and bequests. Wisely, perhaps, the same article stipulates that any conditions attached to gifts or bequests must be acceptable and must be 'consistent with the objective and policies of the Organization'.

As the WHO provision indicates, gifts may come from natural persons as well as states. Possibly the most famous example of the former is the well-publicized gift by billionaire Ted Turner to the UN, in 1997.[58] Other gifts are handled with somewhat less publicity; thus, in 1987 the UN accepted the gift of a new limousine for exclusive use by the Secretary-General, but refrained from making a public demonstration of the event.[59]

It is perhaps inevitable in an increasingly privatizing world[60] that international organizations too, have come to rely on the private sector.[61] In addition to the individual gifts mentioned above, many organizations accept contributions or donations from corporations. Thus, the website of UNHCR reports that in 2008, donations were received from such companies as All Nippon Airways and

---

[54] Article 13, para. 4 ILO.   [55] Compare similarly Art. 52 IMO.
[56] Article 7 WHO.   [57] Article 62 ICAO.
[58] See 'Ted Turner Saves World ... and Taxes', *The Economist*, 27 September 1997, p. 53.
[59] As reported in UNJY (1987), pp. 170–1.
[60] See e.g., Naomi Klein, *The Shock Doctrine* (London, 2007).
[61] Or start to behave like private actors. While this has probably always applied to the financial institutions, an interesting novel example is that the WHO has co-founded what its legal counsel calls 'a virtual R&D company (albeit not-for-profit)': the Medicines for Malaria Venture. See Gian Luca Burci, 'Institutional Adaptation without Reform: WHO and the Challenges of Globalization' (2005) 2 *IOLR*, 437–43.

Statoil Iran, while the largest donation was received from the Bill and Melinda Gates Foundation.[62]

Of greater structural relevance, perhaps, is where organizations engage with the private sector in all sorts of public–private partnerships. To this end, the UN has even set up an Office for Partnership, which manages the UN's relations with various private partners, including companies such as BP, Coca Cola, De Beers, and Microsoft, in addition to non-governmental entities. Not all partnerships revolve directly around money; sometimes it takes on the form of assistance in kind, such as when Coca Cola lent the UN refrigerated trucks to transport polio vaccines through Africa.[63]

Finally, private sector involvement may also take the form of sponsoring conferences or meetings. Thus, reportedly, the ill-fated Seattle Ministerial Conference of the WTO in 1999 was sponsored by a number of private companies, including Boeing, Ford and Microsoft.[64] The obvious risk here is that of 'selling out': government representatives wined and dined on corporate expense accounts may find it difficult to take decisions that would negatively affect those corporations.

There are situations where an organization's constitution prohibits the acceptance of some private gifts. Thus, the General Assembly resolution establishing UNIDO, while allowing acceptance of certain specific gifts, does not tolerate gifts which aim to form a permanent source of financing, at least according to the UN's Office of Legal Affairs.[65]

More usually, voluntary contributions are granted by an organization's member states, and the main advantage for states of doing this is that they can usually wield considerable political influence by using voluntary contributions: they can generally control what these are being used for, and thus sponsor pet projects, programmes or agencies while ignoring others.[66] This immediately raises the main objection to voluntary contributions: an inordinate amount of influence is exercised by a handful (usually of course the most wealthy) of member states, thus potentially eroding the Organization from the inside.

While a voluntary contribution is, of course, voluntary, it nonetheless may give rise to a legal obligation on the part of the state pledging the voluntary contribution. Once a commitment has been made, and in particular after the funds have been budgeted and spent, a member state must make good on its commitment. Here the legal obligation is not based on a specific provision of

---

[62]   See www.unhcr.org/partners/PARTNERS/483c14692.pdf, last visited 25 July 2008.

[63]   See Amir A. Dossal, 'United Nations Partnerships: Working Together for a Better World'. In Roy S. Lee (ed.), *Swords into Plowshares: Building Peace Through the United Nations* (Leiden, 2006), pp. 139–57, esp. pp. 154–5. Likewise, Kofi Annan has been travelling across Africa in a jet borrowed from the emir of Qatar. See James Traub, *The Best Intentions: Kofi Annan and the UN in the Era of American World Power* (New York, 2006), p. 221.

[64]   See Schermers and Blokker, *International Institutional Law*, p. 616.

[65]   See UNJY (1974), pp. 174–5.

[66]   See José E. Alvarez, 'Financial Responsibility'. In Christopher C. Joyner (ed.), *The United Nations and International Law* (Cambridge, 1997), pp. 409–31, esp. p. 410.

the constituent document, but rather on more general notions of good faith and estoppel.[67]

Within the FAO, the practice has arisen of establishing Trust Funds, through which FAO members channel their bilateral assistance to other members (this is sometimes awkwardly referred to as 'multibilateral' assistance). While generally considered useful, one danger is nonetheless that it turns the FAO into some sort of 'service management agency', whose purpose is merely to serve donor states.[68]

In addition to voluntary contributions, some organizations derive some income from providing services or selling goods on commercial terms. For instance, organizations in the field of nuclear technology (IAEA, Euratom) also charge for services or facilities rendered.[69] UNICEF, as is well known, raises considerable sums of money from the sale of greeting cards, while sometimes organizations issue special stamps to raise funds. The UN itself weathered a financial crisis in the early 1960s in part by issuing bonds worth US$200 million.[70] Some organizations derive income from the sale of publications and from catering services, whereas the budget of WIPO consists in part of fees paid by private parties for the registration of patents, marks, industrial designs and the like.[71] Some impose a form of internal taxation on their staff (who are usually exempt from state taxes[72]) which in itself provides a source of income.

The financial institutions (IMF and World Bank in particular, but much the same applies to regional financial institutions such as the Nordic Investment Bank) diverge from the general pattern. Typically, their income stems not from member state contributions, but from their lending activities. As a result (and perhaps partly explaining why the work of the institutions is sometimes criticized as being insufficiently guided by purely economic considerations[73]), the institutions are under intense pressure to increase their lending. Astonishingly, (and rather disturbing, really), the income generated covers not just the organizations' expenses, but is also channelled back to the wealthier donor countries. They are being paid, so to speak, for backing the loans – a far cry from the image of the IMF and the World Bank as public welfare agencies.[74]

---

[67] In the same vein, Nelson, 'US Withholding of Payments', p. 977.

[68] See Sergio Marchisio and Antonietta di Blase, *The Food and Agriculture Organization* (Dordrecht, 1991), esp. pp. 151–3.

[69] Compare Schermers and Blokker, *International Institutional Law*, pp. 672–3.

[70] Although eventually only $169 million dollars' worth were actually sold. See Mills, 'The Financing of UN Peacekeeping Operations', p. 97.

[71] See Christopher May, *The World Intellectual Property Organization: Resurgence and the Development Agenda* (New York, 2007), p. 25 (noting also that this has prevented richer member states from capturing WIPO).

[72] See generally below, Chapter 8.

[73] For such a critique from within, by a former leading World Bank economist (and Nobel laureate), see Joseph E. Stiglitz, *Globalization and its Discontents* (London, 2002).

[74] See the excellent study by Ngaire Woods, *The Globalizers: The IMF, the World Bank, and their Borrowers* (Ithaca NY, 2006), pp. 194–200. Incidentally, this does give the poor states some leverage, however meagre perhaps, for without their borrowing, there would be no institutions.

While a reputable organization such as the UN could considerably increase its income by using its name and emblem for commercial purposes, the Office of Legal Affairs of the Secretariat has vehemently opposed such use, as explicitly prohibited by the General Assembly. If the UN were to let its name and emblems be used, 'such use could create the erroneous impression of United Nations endorsement or sponsorship of those products, or of an official connection between the firm and the United Nations'.[75]

As a matter of principle, the Office of Legal Affairs surely has a point: the image of the UN as being above and beyond the world of finance and commerce would be unlikely to survive unscathed from such corporate connections. Yet, curiously perhaps, in the same memorandum the Office of Legal Affairs sees no legal objection to specific UN-associated emblems (in this case the emblem of the UN Decade of Disabled Persons) being used for commercial purposes.[76]

A special case is that of the European Community which boasts a system of so-called 'own resources'.[77] Early on in the existence of the Community it became clear that the scope of its operational expenditures could never be matched by a system of membership fees alone.[78] After all, one of its main expenditures (and for many years a rapidly growing one) was the Common Agricultural Policy.

As envisaged in the constituent document, a system of 'own resources' was devised, and adopted in the form of a series of decisions. The first of these, adopted by the Council in 1970, provided for three resources. First, there were the customs duties; with the Community forming a customs area, anything coming from outside the Community is subject, at least potentially, to a Community customs duty (which takes the place, of course, of duties formerly levied by the individual member states). Second, agricultural levies formed part of the Community resources. Third, it was agreed that the member states would pay part of their Value Added Tax (VAT) collections to the Community – this in turn was justified by pointing to the harmonization of VAT systems and rates within the Community. Initially the maximum ceiling was set at 1% of VAT income; this has met with various amendments upwards since then.

The idea that organizations have their own resources has proved attractive to others as well. Thus, it was proposed already in the 1950s and 1960s that the UN ought to find sources of income over which the member states would not exercise control. The UN system at large could benefit from taxes on international travel or such activities as air traffic or mail services, and might also gain revenues from the exploration of the Antarctic, ocean resources and outer space.[79] More

---

[75] See UNJY (1987), pp. 170–1, esp. p. 171.

[76] *Ibid.* Note also that FC Barcelona, one of the world's leading football (i.e., soccer) teams, has a reverse sponsorship deal with UNICEF, paying UNICEF for carrying its name on their shirts.

[77] For an analysis, see C. D. Ehlermann, 'The Financing of the Community: The Distinction between Financial Contributions and Own Resources' (1982) 19 *CMLRev*, 571–89.

[78] The budget of the Community also covers the Union's administrative expenditure on foreign and security policy as well as co-operation on justice and home affairs, and may cover operational expenditure incurred under those headings. Compare Art. 268 of the TEC.

[79] See John G. Stoessinger and associates, *Financing the United Nations System* (Washington, 1964), pp. 265–92.

recently, old ideas about a UN lottery have surfaced again, while newer ideas include a tax on environmental pollutants.[80]

Still, a system of own resources is not as unproblematic as it looks. The problem arising almost inevitably in the Community system of more or less automatic transfers of money to the Community (thus preventing haggling over the income side of the budget), and de-nationalized transfers back to the member states (e.g., in the form of agricultural subsidies) is the problem of equitable distribution. The possibility arises that member states contribute far more to the Community budget than they will receive from the system, and the UK in particular has forcefully indicated its discontent. Consequently, something of a compromise was laid down in the 1985 own-resources decision, boiling down to a decrease of the British VAT ceiling, to be compensated for by the other members.[81] Not surprisingly, some other countries have also started to demand a 'juste retour', most remarkably perhaps the Dutch.

This should not come as a surprise, for the very term 'own resources' is something of a misnomer. While always presented in opposition to dependence on member state contributions,[82] the EC experience demonstrates that, at the end of the day, the member states cannot so easily be outmanoeuvred as the term 'own resources' may suggest.[83] After all, the Community's resources will still have to be collected by the member states (e.g., the EC does not have its own customs officers but uses those of the member states), but, more fundamentally, any revenue flowing to the organization is revenue which does not flow to the members. States may well view the income of organizations as a zero-sum game: whatever the organization gains, the members lose, even if it concerns income which did not exist before (think of taxes on environmental pollutants; the members may be reluctant to let the organization benefit, rather than they themselves).

The counter-argument that the members are still under the legal obligation to hand over the Community's own resources which would therefore guarantee the Community's independence is, while correct as such, not much to the point. After all, generally the obligation to pay compulsory contributions is also a legal obligation. If all members fulfilled this obligation, there would be little need even to think of establishing a system of own resources.

Concluding remarks

The power of the purse is as important in international organizations as it is in domestic societies: payment (or threatening to withhold it) is an important tool in the exercise of political influence. This political importance ensures that

---

[80] As mentioned in Dormoy, 'La question du financement', p. 151.
[81] In far more detail, P. J. G. Kapteyn and P. VerLoren van Themaat, *Inleiding tot het recht van de Europese Gemeenschappen na Maastricht* (5th rev. edn, Deventer, 1995), pp. 213–17.
[82] See, e.g., Ehlermann, 'The Financing of the Community', p. 571.
[83] Ehlermann acknowledges as much, holding that the distinction between contributions and own resources does not appear to have much basis in reality. *Ibid.*, p. 575.

the law relating to the financing of international organizations is more volatile than is sometimes imagined.

As noted earlier, there are various moments in which the budgetary process lends itself to political use (and occasionally abuse). But, more fundamentally, here too the complicated relationship between the organization and its members causes uncertainties in the law. Thus, while the General Assembly unmistakably may decide on the apportionment of the budget, it is also understandable that the outcome in which the permanent members of the Security Council bear the lion's share of peace-keeping expenses (and a sizeable proportion of the regular budget as well – together the permanent members are responsible for nearly half of the total budget) is questioned. If peace-keeping is indeed an activity of the Organization, then why single out some members? To do this is to suggest that the organization is predominantly a vehicle for their individual activities rather than an entity with a separate existence and its own preferences.[84]

Conversely, the discussion on own resources is an uncomfortable reminder that the interests of organizations and their members need not always coincide: what is good for the organization may not be welcomed by the members, as, indeed, is demonstrated by the occasional financial crisis of an organization such as the UN to begin with. Here too, then, there are no easy answers and few easily applicable rules: even as clear a rule as Article 19 of the Charter has, in practice, given rise to all sorts of complications.

Indeed, as Alvarez[85] has pointed out, part of the problem is that arguments can usually be reversed: some member states may sincerely believe that withholding payments from an organization, even if it violates the constituent document, may nevertheless be in the interest of the organization, and may even be (morally) obligatory if the organization is 'running wild' – where it is doing things it should not be doing, withholding may serve to save the organization from itself.

[84] This is further strengthened by the political claims of large contributors. Thus, in particular Japan has made no secret of its feeling that its large contribution to the UN (Japan is the second-largest contributor, paying some 20% of the regular budget) should be rewarded e.g., by a permanent seat on the Security Council.

[85] See José E. Alvarez, 'Multilateralism and its Discontents' (2000) 11 *EJIL*, 393–411, esp. pp. 406–7.

8

Privileges and immunities

Introduction

One of the classic branches of international law is the law of immunity. States, their (political) leaders and their diplomatic representatives claim, and are usually granted, privileges and immunities in their mutual relations. Diplomats cannot, generally, be sued unless their immunity is waived, and diplomatic agents are exempt from certain forms of taxation and civil duties in the state where they are accredited. Moreover, diplomatic missions and belongings are generally inviolable. As far as the privileges and immunities of diplomatic agents go, these are usually explained with the help of the theory that, without immunities and privileges, diplomats cannot freely do their work. If a diplomat risks being arrested on frivolous charges at the whim of the host state, international relations can hardly be maintained. Some observers speak therefore of a theory of 'functional necessity' as underlying the granting of privileges and immunities to diplomatic agents and others in the service.[1]

States and their leaders can also boast some privileges and immunities, most important among these being the immunity from suit in the courts of a foreign state, at least for acts which may be qualified as governmental (*acta jure imperii*) rather than commercial (*acta jure gestionis*).[2] Here, however, a 'functional necessity' theory is already less convincing, and it would seem that sovereign immunity is largely based on the idea that states require a space for the conduct of unencumbered politics without fear of legal ramifications,[3] rather than on functional necessity. Indeed, since the functions of states are rather broad, any attempt to link immunities to their functional necessity would amount to creating rather broad immunities.

---

[1] See generally, e.g., Grant V. McClanahan, *Diplomatic Immunity: Principles, Practices, Problems* (London, 1989), esp. pp. 27–34. The theory that embassies are part of the territory of the sending state has long passed its sell-by date, and is nowadays only upheld by ill-informed novelists. Perhaps the best example is Dan Brown, *The Da Vinci Code* (New York, 2003), p. 116.

[2] The distinction between the two is not always easy to draw, and it is usually domestic legislation which prescribes what test to use: whether what matters is the purpose of the activity or rather its nature. The latter appears to be the dominant test.

[3] See further Jan Klabbers, 'The General, the Lords, and the Possible End of State Immunity' (1999) 68 *Nordic JIL*, 85–95.

In much the same way as states enjoy privileges and immunities, so too do international organizations. In much the same ways as diplomats have immunities and privileges, so too do people working for international organizations, and people accredited to such organizations or representing such organizations on specific missions.

The theoretical basis of privileges and immunities

International organizations have no territory of their own, and are not properly to be considered sovereigns either. While on occasion courts have referred to the 'sovereignty' of an organization, or its exercise of 'sovereign powers', such instances are best regarded as examples of courts struggling to come to terms with the nature of international organizations rather than as clear-cut affirmations of sovereignty.[4]

This entails that resort is usually had to a theory of 'functional necessity' in order to explain and delimit the privileges and immunities of organizations. The idea, then, is that organizations enjoy such immunities as are necessary for their effective functioning: international organizations enjoy what is necessary for the exercise of their functions in the fulfilment of their purposes. Moreover, this is often deemed to be a normative proposition: not only do organizations in fact enjoy privileges and immunities on the basis of functional necessity, they are actually entitled to such privileges and immunities, so the argument goes.[5]

There is some linguistic support for the 'functional necessity' thesis when it comes to international organizations. For instance, Article 105, para. 1 of the United Nations Charter provides that the UN shall enjoy in its member states 'such privileges and immunities as are necessary for the fulfillment of its purposes', with para. 2 adding a similar provision with respect to representatives of member states and UN officials. Article 105 is referred to in the preamble

---

[4] See, e.g., *Branno* v. *Ministry of War*, decision of 14 June 1954 by the Italian Court of Cassation, in 22 *ILR*, 756–7, holding that NATO's 'member States cannot exercise judicial functions with regard to any public law activity of the North Atlantic Treaty Organization connected with its organization or with regard to acts performed on the basis of its sovereignty'. In *Maida* v. *Administration for International Assistance*, the Italian Court of Cassation referred to the 'sovereign functions' of an organization: decision of 27 May 1955, in 23 *ILR*, 510–15. See also, as late as 1982, *Food and Agriculture Organization* v. *INPDAI*, decision of the Italian Court of Cassation referring to the FAO's 'sovereign powers' (87 *ILR*, 1–10, esp. 8). The EC Court, in its classic decision in Case 26/62, *Van Gend & Loos* v. *Nederlandse Administratie der Belastingen*, [1963] ECR 1, held that the EC institutions are 'endowed with sovereign rights' (at p. 12). For an example from the literature, see Philpott, who argues that the EU constitutes a political entity with 'formal sovereign prerogatives': Daniel Philpott, 'Sovereignty: An Introduction and Brief History' (1995) 48 *Journal of International Affairs*, 353–68, esp. p. 367.

[5] See, e.g., Peter H. F. Bekker, *The Legal Position of Intergovernmental Organizations* (Dordrecht, 1994), p. 5. But see the discussion below.

to the 1946 Convention on the UN's Privileges and Immunities, and the same thought recurs in s. 27 of the UN–US Headquarters Agreement.[6]

Indeed, several decisions of courts and tribunals, both national and international, can be cited in support of the functional necessity thesis, although their number is surprisingly limited.[7] Moreover, the functional necessity thesis has an intuitive appeal, in that it would seem to be self-evident that the organization must be protected against outside interference; and it is of course in particular the host state that could interfere if the organization were devoid of privileges and immunities.

Still, the functional necessity thesis has some considerable weaknesses as well.[8] For one thing, it may well adopt too instrumentalist a view of international life and ignore that the granting of privileges and immunities is usually, quite simply, the result of negotiations between the organization and its host state rather than the application of any blueprint. To be sure, while the needs of the organization will usually be considered during such negotiations, so too will be other factors: past practice of the host state concerned or of the organization concerned if the establishment of a regional or branch office is at issue; the interests of possible third parties, et cetera.

Participating in such negotiations are also often representatives of the various relevant ministries in the host states, which may hold widely different views on the desirability of certain provisions. Tax authorities might be reluctant to grant broad tax exemptions; social security authorities might not wish to see exceptions for international civil servants from domestic security schemes in the host states; the labour ministry might have its own views on the need for work permits for spouses of international civil servants, et cetera.

Moreover, there is always the role of negotiating power and the quality of the negotiators, as well as the chemistry (or absence thereof) between negotiators. In addition, negotiators may hold widely divergent views as to what the functional needs of their proposed creation amount to.[9]

---

[6] In a similar vein, the circumstance that the immunity of financial institutions is typically limited by excluding their borrowing activities may be explained by functionalist arguments: immunity for borrowing would make it well-nigh impossible to attract creditors. See Andres Rigo Sureda, 'The Law Applicable to the Activities of International Development Banks' (2004) 308 *RdC*, 9–252, pp. 45–8.

[7] Possible examples may include the decision of Italy's Tribunal of First Instance in *Porru* v. *FAO* (decision of 25 June 1969, in 71 *ILR* 240, p. 241), holding that FAO was deemed immune 'with regard to the activities by which it pursues its specific activities', and the decision of Italy's Court of Cassation in *Minnini* v. *Bari Institute of the International Centre for Advanced Mediterranean Agronomic Studies* (decision of 4 April 1986, in 87 *ILR* 28). Bekker, *The Legal Position*, pays much attention to the 1990 *European Molecular Biology Laboratory* arbitration: *EMBL* v. *Federal Republic of Germany*, 105 *ILR* 1.

[8] See also, Chapter 2.

[9] And, as Kunz reminds us, the idea of granting privileges and immunities to organizations to begin with remained rather exceptional until the 1940s. See Josef L. Kunz, 'Privileges and Immunities of International Organizations' (1947) 41 *AJIL*, 828–62, esp. 829–30.

weakness

Indeed, another drawback of the functional necessity thesis (but probably also the main source of its attraction) is precisely its open texture. As Reinisch succinctly puts it: 'The fundamental problem is clearly that functional immunity means different, and indeed contradictory, things to different people or rather different judges and states.'[10] The determination of the functional needs of an organization is essentially in the eye of the beholder, and as good an illustration as any is the case which arose before the US Federal Communications Commission (FCC) in 1953, *Re International Bank for Reconstruction and Development and International Monetary Fund v. All America Cables & Radio, Inc. and other Cable Companies.*[12] At issue was a claim on behalf of the World Bank and the IMF in order to lower the rates they had to pay for their official telecommunications messages. Both the organizations in question and their opponents, the cable operators, based themselves on functional necessities considerations. The World Bank and the IMF argued, as the FCC put it, that the purpose of granting privileges and immunities to organizations is 'to protect the operation of these organizations from unreasonable interference (including protection against unreasonably high rates)'. The defendant cable companies argued, on the other hand, that 'there has been no showing that the Bank and Fund need lower-than-commercial rates to carry out their functions',[13] thus arguing on the basis of a radically different conception of the needs of the organizations.

The very idea of functional necessity has occasionally also caused confusion on the conceptual level. Thus, in *United States v. Melekh et al.*, in which the defendant (a UN official) was charged with espionage, it was argued that since espionage is not part of the functions of the United Nations, it is not an activity to which immunity could possibly apply.[14] Yet, the activity itself may well be engaged in to further the purposes of the organization, or in the course of doing something else which would in itself clearly be defensible as an official activity. While this may, admittedly, be difficult to visualize when it comes to espionage, it is easier to imagine when it comes to words spoken or written down in an official capacity which might amount to libel or slander; surely, much of that determination is in the eye of the beholder.

The purpose of immunity then is at least partly to prevent the very classification of behaviour as libellous (or, for that matter, as espionage) from being

---

[10] August Reinisch, *International Organizations before National Courts* (Cambridge, 2000), p. 206. Elsewhere in the same work, he refers to functional immunity as 'very elusive' (p. 331).

[11] Compare also Jenks's astute observation that whether any particular privilege or immunity is called for is a matter of judgment rather than of principle: C. Wilfred Jenks, *International Immunities* (London, 1961), p. 26.

[12] Decision of 23 March 1953, in 22 *ILR*, 705–12.

[13] *Ibid.*, both quotations at 709. In the end, the FCC would find in favour of the Bank and Fund, but for reasons unconnected to functional necessity, which in itself should tell us something.

[14] Decision by the US District Court for the Southern District of New York, 28 November 1960, and confirmed (after proceedings had been moved) by the District Court, Northern District, Illinois, on 20 March 1961. In 32 *ILR*, 308–34.

made by people who are in a position to interfere with the organization's work. The point is not that espionage should not be an official activity; the point is that the determination of the legality of behaviour should not come before the courts of the host state because that might obstruct the organization's work.[15] It is too simple then merely to look at the activity concerned and condemn it as being inexcusable and thus outside the scope of immunity from suit. This would lead, eventually, to the untenable position that immunity from suit is no longer required because only lawful behaviour qualifies.[16]

It turns out that concrete decisions relating to the scope of an organization's privileges and immunities are almost unpredictable.[17] At the one extreme, one can find a case such as *Broadbent* v. *Organization of American States*,[18] coming close to granting absolute immunity to the organization, whereas at the other end of the continuum there are decisions in which the scope of immunities is considered to be much more narrow. Indeed, even a single dispute gives rise to various conceptions, and a perfectly useful illustration thereof is the case of *Iran–United States Claims Tribunal* v. *A.S.* In this dispute involving the labour relationship between Mr S. and the Tribunal, the Local Court of The Hague initially found that translation activities performed for the Tribunal could not be captured by the notion of *acta jure imperii*. The District Court of The Hague, though, affirmed by the Dutch Supreme Court, found that Mr S.'s activities were 'so clearly connected with *acta jure imperii*' that the decision of the lower court was well-nigh incomprehensible.[19]

Yet another problem with anything like the functional necessity thesis has recently been observed to reside in the possibility that the organization can commit violations of public order, or even of human rights, under the shield of its functional necessity.[20] Thus, while it may happen that functional necessity

---

[15] For this reason the Dutch Supreme Court (Hoge Raad) in 2007 quashed an order of the Amsterdam District Court according to which Euratom could not claim immunity for alleged crimes. See Case S 01984/07 CW, *Greenpeace* v. *Euratom*, judgment of 13 November 2007.

[16] In addition, while it might be difficult to regard espionage as an official activity, it is also difficult to think of espionage in such circumstances as being done purely for personal gain, and as a purely private activity.

[17] As also the supporters of the functional necessity thesis acknowledge. See, e.g., Niels M. Blokker and Henry G. Schermers, 'Mission Impossible? On the Immunities of Staff Members of International Organizations on Mission'. In Gerhard Hafner *et al.* (eds.), *Liber Amicorum Professor Ignaz Seidl-Hohenveldern in Honour of his 80th Birthday* (The Hague, 1998), pp. 37–54, esp. p. 41.

[18] Decision of 28 March 1978 by the US District Court for the District of Columbia, 63 *ILR*, 162–3. Compare also *Weidner* v. *International Telecommunications Satellite Organization*, decision of 21 September 1978 by the US Court of Appeals for the District of Columbia, in 63 *ILR*, 191–4.

[19] The three decisions can be found in 94 *ILR*, 321–30. The European Commission of Human Rights would later hold in respect of the same case, in its 1988 decision in *Spaans* v. *Netherlands*, that it did not consider that a grant of immunity 'gives rise to an issue' under the European Convention on Human Rights. See 107 *ILR*, 1, at 5.

[20] The debate was partly sparked by the decision of the US Court of Appeals for the DC Circuit in *Mendaro* v. *World Bank*, decision of 27 September 1983, in 99 *ILR*, 92.

requires that an organization's labour policies are not subject to local jurisdiction, where those labour policies condone discrimination or sexual harassment, the balance between the organization and the individual may tilt too strongly in favour of the organization.[21]

It is surely no coincidence that in recent years, the insight has gained ground that far-reaching immunities may come to affect access to justice. The leading case is *Waite and Kennedy* v. *Germany*, a 1999 decision of the European Court of Human Rights in which it accepted that the immunity from suit of organizations may have 'implications as to the protection of human rights'.[22] While *in casu* the Court found that no violation had occurred, the decision is usually taken to entail that international organizations may have to compensate for their immunities from suit before domestic courts (at least in employment cases) by invoking or creating alternative mechanisms to guarantee access to justice: internal administrative tribunals would be prominent examples.[23]

There seems to be, in the end, a more basic flaw in the very idea of functional necessity: it is almost by definition biased in favour of international organizations, to the possible detriment of others. At the very least, the idea that the functional needs of organizations are worthy of protection, and perhaps more so than the needs of others, requires some form of justification, yet none has so far been forthcoming. Of course, the argument may be made (and has been made[24]) that people engaging in some sort of relationship with an organization are, and should be, well aware of the organization's immunities, but that answer, if valid at all (it may be seen to ignore economic considerations), surely cannot extend to those who end up on the wrong side of, say, a traffic accident.

Finally, on a more academic note, it would seem that the idea of functional necessity would require the legal position of international organizations to remain relatively stable. After all, it is unlikely that the needs of an organization change overnight, as long as other circumstances remain constant. And while it is probably true that different observers can come up with different views of an organization's functional needs, the variety of judicial pronunciations on the

---

[21] Compare Michael Singer, 'Jurisdictional Immunity of International Organizations: Human Rights and Functional Necessity Concerns' (1995) 36 *VaJIL*, 53–165. Reinisch expresses similar concerns, and adds the argument that the host state may be under conflicting obligations: an obligation towards the organization to grant immunity, and a human rights obligation to grant access to courts. See Reinisch, *International Organizations before National Courts*, e.g., pp. 278ff.

[22] Reported in 118 *ILR* 121, esp. para. 67.

[23] For a fine discussion, see August Reinisch and Ulf Andreas Weber, 'In the Shadow of Waite and Kennedy' (2004) 1 *IOLR*, 59–110.

[24] It is a variation on the more common argument that where states engage in contractual activities, their partners are well aware of what they get themselves into. See generally Hazel Fox, 'State Responsibility and Tort Proceedings against a Foreign State in Municipal Courts' (1989) 20 *Neth YIL*, 3–34.

scope of organizational privileges and immunities suggests that predictability remains difficult to attain.[25]

That does not mean that the idea of functional necessity is totally without value. It may serve as a useful shorthand way of describing what people may have in mind when granting privileges and immunities, and when assessing them. The problem then resides not so much in the description, but in the fact that this description has taken on normative dimensions. It is one thing to say that privileges and immunities are usually granted on the basis of what negotiators have considered to be the functional needs of an organization. Such may be descriptively accurate, albeit probably too abstract to offer much insight. But it does not follow, as is sometimes suggested,[26] that therefore the description turns, or ought to turn, into the norm.

Applicable law

A separate but highly relevant issue is the question of the law applicable to international organizations in light of their immunities: does immunity mean that the law of the host state does not apply at all? Or is the better view that host state law is in principle applicable, but cannot in reality be applied due to the existence of immunities? There are strong arguments to uphold the view that host state law continues to apply, at least as something of a default position.[27] Some of those reasons are purely pragmatic: surely, an organization would be ill-advised to ignore a host state's traffic rules, for instance, or municipal ordinances relating to garbage collection or similar activities. Likewise, where the acts of organizations require licences (think, for instance, of acts that may affect the natural environment, or even simply expanding the premises), the only feasible possibility is that those licences will be granted by local authorities and, thus, will be in accordance with local legislation.[28]

Moreover, the very concept of immunity would seem to imply that there is something to be immune from, and that something can hardly be anything other than the local legal system. Sometimes this is spelled out more or less explicitly (e.g., sections 7 and 8, of the UN–US Headquarters Agreement make clear that US law continues to apply except where set aside by UN regulations).

---

[25] Indeed, recent case law suggests a more narrow interpretation of functional necessity than current in earlier times. For instance, in *Food and Agriculture Organization* v. *INPDAI* (above, note 4), the Italian Court of Cassation refused to regard a contract of tenancy as functionally necessary for the FAO.

[26] For a rather blunt statement that necessity entails legal entitlements, see A. S. Muller, *International Organizations and their Host States* (The Hague, 1995), p. 151.

[27] See, along similar lines, August Reinisch, 'Accountability of International Organizations According to National Courts' (2005) 36 *NYIL*, 119–67.

[28] Note that in *Euratom*, the organization was accused of having violated licences that had been granted by the Dutch authorities.

But even where it is not spelled out, it would seem to be consistent with the idea of immunity that local law remains applicable.

Indeed, it could hardly be otherwise, if only because there will not be many organizations drafting their own rules on what to do in case one official assaults another[29] or, more mundane perhaps, on whether superiors will be entitled to read the work-related correspondence, including e-mails, of their subordinates. On such topics few organizations will bother to create their own rules, something which also reduces the chances that an applicable general principle of institutional law will ever emerge.[30]

Distinguishing rationales

Apart from the circumstances that international organizations do not, as a rule, have their own territory or population, but are always located in the midst of the territory and population of a state[31] (usually, but not invariably, a member state of the organization concerned[32]), there are several other reasons why organizations would warrant a treatment different from that accorded to states when it comes to privileges and immunities. First, as Ahluwalia sums up:

> Unlike diplomatic agents, international officials are neither accredited to the government of a particular country nor are representatives of one. They are servants of the international organization in the true sense of the term and act in its name. Unlike diplomatic agents, they exercise their functions not in the territory of a single but several States including sometimes their own.[33]

In other words, while it is unthinkable (as a matter of law) that a state diplomat would require protection against his own state, it is by no means implausible to suggest that officials of organizations may need protection against the states of which they are nationals.[34] Indeed, the two pertinent advisory opinions of the

---

[29] This was alleged to have happened in *In re Romach-Le Guludec*, involving staff at EPO. See ILOAT, judgment no. 1581, 30 January 1997.

[30] As envisaged by Finn Seyersted, *Common Law of International Organizations* (Leiden, 2008).

[31] And are thought to require freedom from interference by the host state. See the Italian Court of Cassation in *International Institute of Agriculture* v. *Profili*, decision of 26 February 1931 (1929–30) 5 *AD*, 414–15.

[32] An exception is OPEC, having its headquarters in Austria. The UN has its European headquarters in what used to be a non-member state, Switzerland.

[33] Kuljit Ahluwalia, *The Legal Status, Privileges and Immunities of the Specialized Agencies of the United Nations and Certain Other International Organizations* (The Hague, 1964), p. 105.

[34] As underlined by the UN's Legal Office in an *aide-mémoire* to a member state; see UNJY (1963), pp. 188–91. There is a converse to this point: whereas diplomats of states may be immune abroad, their acts may well be scrutinized and penalized in their own states; with officials of organizations, however, there is no home authority to resort to. While a state diplomat may be prosecuted for murder back home, this is far less plausible when it comes to officials of organizations (unless immunity is waived), in particular where immunity is deemed absolute. For an implicit confirmation on the part of the UN Secretary-General (promising 'quick and effective action' by the UN), see UNJY (1985), pp. 150–2.

International Court of Justice (ICJ) both involved situations where the national state of the official in question was putting obstacles in his way.[35]

Another factor distinguishing the diplomatic relations of states and their representatives from those of organizations and their agents may well have to do with the far greater variety among organizations. States may be rich or poor, strong or weak, liberal or illiberal, but will not be either universal or regional, open or closed as far as membership is concerned, functional or rather comprehensive in terms of proposed activities.

Finally, all states are both host and sending states when it comes to diplomatic relations with other states; indeed, diplomatic law is one of the branches of the law often explained by pointing to reciprocity.[36] Yet, with organizations, this is not the case. While most states will be members of several organizations (and thus be sending states), the amount of host states is relatively limited: organizations are to a considerable extent concentrated in locations such as Austria, Switzerland and the United States, creating a clear imbalance when it comes to interests between sending states and host states.

This imbalance, and its translation into treaty form, may well have been among the reasons for the failure of the Vienna Convention on the Representation of States in Their Relations with International Organizations of a Universal Character, concluded in 1975 but not in force. This Convention, heavily tilted towards the interests of the sending states while mostly neglecting those of host states,[37] has failed to attract the required number of instruments of ratification; it is not likely ever to enter into force.[38]

In stark contrast to the diplomatic relations between states, which are by and large governed by a single, almost universally accepted treaty,[39] no one document governs the diplomatic relations involving international organizations and their staff, and those representing states to those organizations.[40]

Instead, the law relating to privileges and immunities of organizations is a labyrinth of treaties and other legal instruments, including domestic legislation. Some of those instruments are of universal ambition. Thus, the 1946 Convention on the Privileges and Immunities of the United Nations has attracted an impressive number of states; its scope, however, is limited to the United

---

[35] See, below, the discussion of the Court's opinions in *Mazilu* and *Cumaraswamy*, pp. 143–5.

[36] So, classically, Stanley Hoffmann, 'International Systems and International Law'. In Klaus Knorr and Sydney Verba (eds.), *The International System: Theoretical Essays* (Princeton, 1961), pp. 205–37, esp. p. 213.

[37] See J. G. Fennessy, 'The 1975 Vienna Convention on the Representation of States in their Relations with International Organizations of a Universal Character' (1976) 70 *AJIL*, 62–72.

[38] For the argument that much of the 1975 Convention nonetheless corresponded to existing state practice, see G. E. do Nascimento e Silva, 'Privileges and Immunities of Permanent Missions to International Organizations' (1978) 21 *GYIL*, 9–26.

[39] The 1961 Vienna Convention on Diplomatic Relations, which in many respects codified well-settled custom.

[40] Note, incidentally, that sovereign immunities are also not subject to universal agreement. In Europe, the 1972 Convention on State Immunity, sponsored by the Council of Europe, is of importance.

Nations.[41] The 1947 Specialized Agencies Convention is, as its title indicates, limited to the Specialized agencies of the UN, and is at any rate strongly modelled on the 1946 UN Convention. Indeed, it is usually the case that each organization, or group of related organizations (such as the organizations and institutions comprising the European Union), will have its own treaty on privileges and immunities.

There exists a special bond between the organization and its host state,[42] and this bond cannot be well regulated in a convention of general scope. Consequently, in many cases there is a separate Headquarters Agreement, concluded between the organization and its host state or, alternatively (and sometimes simultaneously), relations between the host state and an organization on its territory may be regulated by domestic legislation. Thus, the sources of the law on privileges and immunities of international organizations, their staff, and members of delegations are varied, and often comprise, in addition to general conventions and headquarters agreements, national legislation as well.

The UN Convention

Perhaps the most important document is the Convention on the Privileges and Immunities of the United Nations, as it provides a model for many other similar documents and in particular for the Specialized Agencies Convention, concluded in 1947. The UN Convention starts, surprisingly, by pointing to the juridical personality of the UN, but then proceeds more or less along the lines to be expected.[43] Analytically, the Convention creates four different subjects of attention. There is, first of all, the organization itself:[44] Article II holds that the UN, its property[45] and its assets shall be immune from legal process,[46] unless immunity is waived.[47]

---

[41] Note that the UN itself is not a party, although it is often treated as one, e.g., by the UN's Legal Counsel, as indicated by a speech to the Sixth Committee (i.e., the legal committee) of the General Assembly. See UNJY (1967), pp. 311–14. For an intelligent discussion, concluding that the UN is not so much a party as rather a beneficiary, see Reinisch, *International Organizations before National Courts*, pp. 141–4.

[42] For a recent exploration, see Muller, *International Organizations and their Host States*.

[43] Somewhat unexpectedly, a decision by Argentina's labour tribunal (decision of 19 March 1958 of the Cámara Nacional de Apelaciones del Trabajo de la Capital Federal), in *Bergaveche v. United Nations Information Centre*, seems to suggest the possible retroactive force of the Convention. See 26 *ILR*, 620.

[44] And, by extension, its organs, according to the decision of New York's Eastern District Court in *Boimah v. United Nations General Assembly*, decision of 24 July 1987, in 113 *ILR*, 499.

[45] The concept of property will usually include immovables. See, e.g., with respect to the OEEC, the decision of the French Court of Cassation in *Procureur Général v. Syndicate of Co-owners of the Alfred Dehodencq Property Company* (decision of 6 July 1954), in 21 *ILR*, 279.

[46] Incidentally, the immunity of an organization is no bar to the institution of proceedings by the organization itself. See, e.g., *International Refugee Organization v. Republic S. S. Corp. et al.*, decided by the US Court of Appeals, 4th Circuit, on 11 May 1951 (in 18 *ILR*, 447). More hesitant was the US District Court for the Northern District of California in *Balfour, Guthrie & Co., Limited et al. v. United States et al.*, decision of 5 May 1950, in 17 *ILR*, 323.

[47] There is broad agreement that in general waiver must be express, for waiver 'is not to be presumed against a sovereign or an organisation that enjoys immunity. If anything, the

The premises of the UN,[48] as well as its archives and documents, are inviolable, and the UN shall be exempt from direct taxes[49] and customs duties and restrictions. Article III, moreover, accords the UN most-favoured-nation status with respect to communication facilities; it also confirms that 'no censorship shall be applied'.

The second subject of attention consists of the representatives of the UN's member states.[50] Those occupy, as Kunz already observed, a somewhat ambivalent position: they are both national organs and part of an international organ.[51]

Article IV creates a number of immunities (e.g., from personal arrest) and exemptions (e.g., exemption from immigration restrictions), and contains the fall-back clause that representatives of member states shall generally enjoy the same privileges, immunities and facilities as diplomatic envoys usually enjoy, with the exception of exemptions from customs duties, excise duties or sales taxes. Importantly, freedom of speech is guaranteed, as well as immunity from suit for acts, words and writings.[52]

The UN Convention does not specifically refer to entities with observer status, yet it is generally accepted that these too can often rely on a similar degree of protection.[53] However, practice seems to make an exception for observers from liberation movements and non-governmental organizations; these are often granted less extensive privileges and immunities than other observers, presumably since the authority such entities exercise over their members is generally considered to fall short of the degree of control exercised by states over their nationals.[54]

---

presumption must be that there is no waiver until the evidence shows to the contrary.' Thus Nigeria's Supreme Court in *African Reinsurance Corporation* v. *Abate Fantaye*, decision of 20 June 1986, in 86 *ILR*, 655, p. 674 (emphasis omitted). See also *Dutto* v. *UN High Commissioner for Refugees*, decision of Argentina's National Labour Court of Appeal of 31 May 1989 in 89 *ILR*, 90. Often though, alternative means of dispute resolution (such as arbitration) are agreed upon in contracts between the organization and private parties. See, e.g., UNJY (1987), pp. 203–5.

[48] Whether these are the UN's property or merely rented or leased is not relevant for purposes of inviolability; see UNJY (1965), pp. 219–20.

[49] On the difference between direct and indirect taxes, see the useful article by A. S. Muller, 'International Organizations and their Officials: To Tax or Not to Tax?' (1993) 6 *Leiden JIL*, 47–72.

[50] According to the UN's Office of Legal Affairs, a position as permanent representative of a member state cannot be reconciled with a position as that same member state's foreign minister. See UNJY (1992), pp. 490–1.

[51] See Kunz, 'Privileges and Immunities', p. 843; see also Edvard Hambro, 'Permanent Representatives to International Organizations' (1976) 30 *Yearbook of World Affairs*, 30–41. Perhaps this ambivalence is most visible in those cases where permanent representatives play an institutionalized role in decision making, an example being the role of COREPER within the EC.

[52] This may also cover the relatives of representatives. See *People* v. *Von Otter*, decision of the City Court of La Rochelle (New York) of 30 July 1952, in 19 *ILR*, 385.

[53] See, e.g., with respect to the PLO, UNJY (1979), pp. 169–70. The circumstance that observers are not expressly mentioned in the UN–US Headquarters Agreement, however, made the US Court of Appeals for the Second Circuit decide not to grant immunity to the PLO in *Klinghoffer and others* v. *SNC Achille Lauro and others* (decision of 21 June 1991, in 91 *ILR*, 68).

[54] R. G. Sybesma-Knol, *The Status of Observers in the United Nations* (Brussels, 1981), p. 41.

Article IV does posit two important limitations to the privileges and immunities of representatives of member states. First, it specifically states that the privileges and immunities are granted in order to safeguard the exercise of functions in connection with the UN.[55] It follows, Article IV continues, that member states are under a duty to waive immunity if they feel that continued immunity would impede the course of justice, and can be waived without prejudice to the function for which the immunity was granted.

A second limitation is the explicit provision in Article IV, section 15, detailing what has sometimes been referred to as the principle of nationality discrimination:[56] if the representative of a member state happens to be a national of the host state, then no privileges and immunities apply.[57]

The third subject demanding specific attention is the category of officials of the UN.[58] Article V grants a number of privileges and immunities, including exemption from national service obligations, immunity from suit for acts performed in an official capacity,[59] and exemptions from direct taxes[60] on their salaries and emoluments.[61] The highest-ranking officials (the Secretary-General and the Assistant Secretaries-General) are elevated to the same level as diplomatic envoys.

Article V does not contain a clause relating to nationality discrimination[62] but, similar to Article IV in respect of member states' representatives, it spells

---

[55] A similar provision in the IAEA constitution proved decisive in the *IAEA Representative Immunity* case, decided by Bavaria's Supreme Court on 30 September 1971 (in 70 *ILR*, 413). With the FAO, however, this limitation apparently does not apply to representatives of ambassadorial rank. See the decision of Italy's Court of Cassation of 10 July 1969 in *Re Pisani Balestra di Mottola*, 71 *ILR*, 565.

[56] For instance by Ahluwalia, *The Legal Status*, e.g., p. 132.

[57] 'The provisions of sections 11, 12 and 13 are not applicable as between a representative and the authorities of the State of which he is a national or of which he is or has been the representative.' Bear in mind here that at issue is the Convention covering the UN, including all its possible regional branches.

[58] For in-depth discussion, see Anthony J. Miller, 'Privileges and Immunities of UN Officials' (2007) 4 *IOLR*, 169–257.

[59] The UN's Office of Legal Affairs has confirmed that officials do not enjoy immunity for acts unrelated to their official duties. See UNJY (1963), p. 188.

[60] The concept of direct taxes does not necessarily include such things as compulsory church dues. For an example relating to an IAEA employee, see *Evangelical Church (Ausburg and Helvitic Confessions [sic]) in Austria* v. *Grezda*, decision of Austria's Supreme Court of 27 February 1962, in 38 *ILR*, 453. Nor does it automatically entail that exempt income may not be counted as part of a family's total income; see the decision of Austria's Administrative Court in *Karl M.* v. *Provincial Revenue Office for Vienna*, decision of 20 November 1970, in 71 *ILR*, 573.

[61] Moreover, garnishment or attachment of salary (e.g., to recover an official's debts) is null and void as far as the UN is concerned. See UNJY (1983), pp. 213–14. See also, on sequestration, the decision of New York's Family Court in *Means* v. *Means* of 6 August 1969, in 53 *ILR*, 588. The seemingly contrasting decision of the Swiss Federal Tribunal in *In Re Poncet* (decision of 12 January 1948, (1948) 15 *AD*, 346–8) owed much to a *modus vivendi* between Geneva and the UN on garnishment.

[62] See, e.g., UNJY (1975), pp. 183–4 and (with respect to the Specialized Agencies Convention), pp. 184–6. Should a member state feel reluctant to grant privileges and immunities to officials who are its nationals, a possible circumvention (particularly useful with short-term projects) may be that the nationals in question are hired by the member state and assigned or seconded to the organization. See UNJY (1973), pp. 167–8.

out that privileges and immunities are granted in the interest of the UN: where the course of justice would be impeded, the Secretary-General has the duty to waive immunity, and if it concerns the Secretary-General himself, this duty falls upon the Security Council. Moreover, as if to underline the limits of the perks of officials, Article V concludes by pointing out that the UN shall at all times co-operate with the authorities of its member states 'to facilitate the proper administration of justice, secure the observance of police regulations, and prevent the occurrence of any abuse'.

What exactly constitutes abuse is open for debate. The Philippine Supreme Court suggested in *WHO and Verstuyft* v. *Aquino and others* that the determination of abuse is the province of executive discretion, and added a delightful note that, according to the Philippine State Department, the importation of 120 bottles of wine by a diplomat is 'ordinary in diplomatic practice'.[63]

The fourth and final subject of attention is the somewhat random category of experts on mission for the UN,[64] and the Convention concludes with a number of general issues, including the United Nations *laissez-passer* which may be granted to officials,[65] an elaborate and interesting provision on dispute settlement,[66] and some provisions on the Convention's entry into force and related issues.

In several cases, the ICJ has had occasion to clarify the meaning of the provision relating to experts on mission.[67] In 1989, it rendered an advisory opinion on the scope of the very notion of experts on mission,[68] whereas ten years later it gave an opinion on how to determine whether section 22 applies.

In 1984, Mr Dumitru Mazilu had been recommended by his country, Romania, to be a member of the United Nations Sub-Commission on the Prevention of Discrimination and Protection of Minorities, which was, at the time, a sub-commission of the Commission on Human Rights which itself used to be a subsidiary organ of the UN's ECOSOC.[69]

---

[63] Decision of 29 November 1972, in 52 *ILR* 389, p. 392, note 2.

[64] See, extensively, Anthony J. Miller, 'United Nations Experts on Mission and their Privileges and Immunities' (2007) 4 *IOLR*, 11–56.

[65] The proposal to create a UN passport was obstructed by some states who felt that issuing passports was a prerogative of sovereigns only. See, e.g., Kunz, 'Privileges and Immunities', p. 856. Other organizations too have adopted the idea of a *laissez-passer*; compare Art. 7 of the Protocol on the Privileges and Immunities of the European Communities.

[66] For more details, see below, Chapter 12.

[67] In some organizations, consultants or experts are given staff appointments, and thus benefit from the privileges and immunities of regular staff (see, e.g., with respect to the World Bank, Ibrahim Shihata, *The European Bank for Reconstruction and Development* (London, 1990), p. 93). In others, they are treated as a separate category (see, e.g., with respect to the FAO, the decision of Madagascar's Court of Appeal in *La Hausse de la Louvière* v. *Brouard*, decision of 25 May 1972, in 71 *ILR* 562).

[68] *Applicability of Article VI, Section 22, of the Convention on the Privileges and Immunities of the United Nations (Mazilu)*, advisory opinion, [1989] ICJ Reports 177.

[69] It was replaced, in 2006, by the Human Rights Council, in an effort (most likely in vain) to counter what was perceived as the politicization of human rights. For more details, see Jan Klabbers, 'Reflections on the Politics of Institutional Reform'. In Peter Danchin and Horst

Mr Mazilu was appointed as a member of the Sub-Commission for three years (until the end of 1987), and was given the task, in 1985, to report on human rights and youth. Here things started to go wrong. Apparently, Mr Mazilu started to advance some thoughts which turned out to be difficult to reconcile with Romania's official policy. Romania seemed to hinder him in his work, declaring that Mr Mazilu was seriously ill and not mentally capable of finishing the report. Mr Mazilu was also stripped of his travel rights.

This provoked the question, which ECOSOC asked of the Court, whether the General Convention is applicable also to people such as Mr Mazilu (not staff of the UN, not delegates of a member state), and also in relations with their own states. The Court answered unanimously that indeed, section 22 of the General Convention, relating to experts on mission, was applicable in such cases. It presented a rather wide definition of experts on mission: 'The Court takes the view that Section 22 of the General Convention is applicable to persons (other than UN officials) to whom a mission has been entrusted by the organization'.[70] The Court, having noted that the Convention did not itself define 'experts on mission', and that the *travaux préparatoires* were of little help, based itself predominantly on the practice of the UN: members of peace-keeping forces, technical assistants, members of committees and commissions, all had consistently been treated as experts on mission within the meaning of section 22.

In other words: as long as Mr Mazilu was writing his report (even after his membership of the Sub-Commission had expired) he was entitled to the privileges and immunities guaranteed by section 22 of the General Convention, which include the immunity from personal arrest or detention and immunity from suit. Still, as experts on mission are not on the UN payroll, there are no provisions on such things as taxation.[71]

Section 22 provides for immunity for official acts only, but fails to specify when an act is to be considered as official, and does not indicate who shall make such determinations either. This may, on occasion, lead to controversy, as when Mr Cumaraswamy, the UN's special rapporteur on the independence of the judiciary, found himself confronted with libel suits in his native Malaysia. The question arose whether utterances he made during an interview were to be regarded as words spoken in the course of the performance of his mission and, most importantly, whether the Secretary-General of the UN would have the final say on such matters.[72] The UN position has traditionally been that

---

Fischer (eds.), *United Nations Reform and the New Collective Security* (Cambridge 2009, forthcoming).

[70] *Mazilu*, para. 52.

[71] What is clear though is that experts on mission are not generally exempt from domestic taxation on their UN honorariums. See UNJY (1983), p. 217.

[72] *Difference relating to immunity from legal process of a special rapporteur of the Commission of Human Rights (Cumaraswamy)*, [1999] ICJ Reports 62 (hereinafter referred to as *Cumaraswamy* case).

this determination is the exclusive province of the Secretary-General, arguing that if national courts could make such determinations, then 'a mass of conflicting decisions would be inevitable, given the many countries in which the Organization operates. In many cases it would be tantamount to a total denial of immunity.'[73]

The International Court of Justice agreed that the Secretary-General, 'as the chief administrative officer of the Organization, has the authority and the responsibility to exercise the necessary protection where required'.[74] Consequently, where a domestic court is confronted with a legal issue in which the immunity of a UN agent is involved, it should immediately be notified of the Secretary-General's opinion, for this opinion 'creates a presumption which can only be set aside for the most compelling reasons'.[75]

Still, that stops short of saying that the Secretary-General has the final say; it leaves open the possibility of rebuttal of the strong presumption created by the Secretary-General.[76] And rightly so, of course, if only because the Secretary-General will have the natural and understandable inclination to construe immunity as widely as possible.

Headquarters Agreement

A number of things were left out of the UN Convention, and consequently had to be addressed in the Headquarters Agreement, concluded in 1947 between the UN and the USA. The Headquarters Agreement, moreover, specifies that it is to be read against the background of the 1946 Convention on Privileges and Immunities.

The seat of the UN is in New York City, in an area called the Headquarters District.[77] Generally, US law (federal, state and local) continues to apply in this area,[78] and the general rule of section 7 also provides that the US courts will have jurisdiction, except 'as otherwise provided in this agreement'. This means, generally speaking, that the privileges and immunities of the UN are to be viewed as exceptions to US jurisdiction, and therefore warrant a restrictive interpretation.[79] The same follows, one could argue, from section 27: 'This

---

[73] Thus the UN's Office of Legal Affairs, in UNJY (1976), pp. 236–9, esp. p. 238.

[74] *Cumaraswamy* case, para. 50.   [75] *Ibid.*, para. 61.

[76] In a similar vein, Hazel Fox, 'The Advisory Opinion on the Difference Relating to Immunity from Legal Process of a Special Rapporteur of the Commission of Human Rights: Who has the Last Word on Judicial Independence?' (1999) 12 *Leiden JIL*, 889–918.

[77] Premises located outside the original Headquarters District may be (and have been) included by means of supplemental agreements. See UNJY (1985), pp. 144–6.

[78] Although service of legal process within the District requires the consent of the Secretary-General, as affirmed by the US Court of Appeals for the 2nd Circuit in the Joined cases *Kadic* v. *Karadzic* and *Doe I and Doe II* v. *Karadzic*, decision of 13 October 1995, in 104 *ILR* 135.

[79] As much is evidenced by judicial decisions, in which the protection offered by the Agreement has been restrictively interpreted. Thus, immunity from legal process has been held by the US Court of Appeals for the 2nd Circuit to apply neither to observers nor to invitees. See,

agreement shall be construed in the light of its primary purpose to enable the United Nations at its headquarters in the United States, fully and efficiently to discharge its responsibilities and fulfill its purposes.' This 'primary purpose' also entails that the host state is under an obligation to protect the organization, its staff members and their families.[80] Where the host state is unable (or unwilling) to do so, the organization itself may well be under an obligation to protect its employees and their families (at least those who are not nationals of the host state), for example by providing for evacuation in situations of emergency.[81]

The Headquarters District is inviolable, according to section 9: the US authorities may not enter except with the consent of the Secretary-General, and then only in accordance with conditions agreed by the Secretary-General. Still, the UN has the duty not to let the Headquarters District become a refuge for persons avoiding arrest.

Under section 11, the USA shall not restrict the travel[82] to and from the Headquarters District of various categories of persons:

- representatives of members of the UN, its officials, representatives to or officials of specialized agencies, and their families;
- experts performing missions for the UN;
- media representatives, provided they have been accredited by the UN (in consultation with the US);
- representatives of non-governmental organizations (NGOs) recognized by the UN;
- other persons invited, on official business with the UN. The USA shall also offer appropriate protection.[83]

Of some historical importance is that section 11 applies irrespective of political relations between the USA and the state to whom a person may belong (section 12). Thus, the USA will also have to respect representatives from states which it has not recognized.[84]

Generally speaking, the representatives of member states to the UN enjoy the same diplomatic privileges and immunities as normal diplomats, and they

---

respectively, *Klinghoffer and others* v. *SNC Achille Lauro and others* (above, note 53), and the various *Karadzic* cases (above, note 78).

[80] For a suggestion that such an obligation is not dependent on a particular treaty relation between the organization and its host state, see Muller, *International Organizations and their Host States*, pp. 194–6.

[81] See, e.g., UNJY (1983), pp. 197–8. The obligation of the organization is construed as a moral obligation.

[82] This does not amount to an exemption of visa requirements, but obliges the US to grant them without charge and as speedily as possible. See UNJY (1985), pp. 147–9.

[83] The applicability of the Agreement in general was confirmed by the International Court of Justice in 1988, despite the existence of later US legislation which would on some points have negated the agreement. See *Applicability of the Obligation to Arbitrate under Section 21 of the United Nations Headquarters Agreement of 26 June 1947*, advisory opinion, [1988] ICJ Reports 12. For a scathing comment (in particular on the US attitudes involved), see W. Michael Reisman, 'An International Farce: The Sad Case of the PLO Mission' (1989) 14 *Yale JIL*, 412–32.

[84] This provision has lost much of its utility with the end of the Cold War.

enjoy them throughout the whole territory of the USA (section 15). However, representatives of member states not recognized by the US only enjoy privileges and immunities in the Headquarters District, at their residences and offices outside the District, and in transit, either from those residences to the District or on official business to and from overseas locations.

While a decent argument can be made that headquarters agreements may be terminated in accordance with the law of treaties,[85] it is less certain that such agreements can be unilaterally modified by the host states. Early this century a minor diplomatic storm broke out when it became clear that the Dutch authorities were planning to undo, or had already undone, earlier concessions to international organizations located in The Hague: Brower spoke of 'the progressive reduction of previously granted, and in some cases previously agreed, financial incentives . . .', and hinted that this would hurt The Hague's image as the self-proclaimed Legal Capital of the World.[86] Likewise, a new Swiss law on privileges and immunities envisages the unilateral withdrawal, by the Swiss authorities, of specific privileges and immunities in specific cases.[87]

Other sources of law

Similar provisions to those included in the 1946 Convention on the Privileges and Immunities of the UN, or the 1947 UN–US Headquarters Agreement, surface regularly in other conventions. Differences in the level of privileges and immunities between the various organizations, then, are usually a matter of detail rather than of principle, and it would seem that the granting of privileges and immunities to any particular organization is dependent to a large extent on the prevailing political climate.

Thus, some organizations shall not be restricted by financial controls, regulations or moratoria;[88] with others, one looks in vain for such a clause. With some organizations, the staff's exemptions from taxation are so strong as to guarantee that the member states do not take exempt income into account when assessing the amount of tax for income from other sources;[89] with others, however, this

---

[85] As much would seem to follow from *Interpretation of the Agreement of 25 March 1951 between the WHO and Egypt*, advisory opinion, [1980] ICJ Reports 73. See also the discussion on termination in Chapter 5 above.

[86] See Charles H. Brower, 'The Hague as Leading Host of International Organizations'. In Agata Fijalkowski (ed.), *International Institutional Reform: 2005 Hague Joint Conference on Contemporary Issues of International Law* (The Hague, 2007), pp. 344–6, esp. p. 345.

[87] See the Gaststaatgesetz, in force since 1 January 2008, Art. 31. Such a position had already been accepted by the Swiss Federal Supreme Court in *A v. B* (judgment of 8 April 2004, ILDC 343 (CH 2004)). The court acknowledged a rather soft obligation to consult with the organization at issue, at least when it concerns the status of a representative of a member state to that organization.

[88] Compare Art. 6 of the 1949 General Agreement on Privileges and Immunities of the Council of Europe, in *European Treaty Series*, No. 2.

[89] This is the position upheld within the UN family (see, e.g., referring to the Specialized Agencies Convention, UNJY (1972), pp. 193–4). See also UNJY (1983), p. 216.

is ruled out, and exempt income may be taken into account when calculating the taxation over income from other sources.[90]

With academic institutions, it is not uncommon to guarantee specifically the organization's academic freedom.[91] Some Headquarters Agreements also lay down a duty on the host state to ensure that the premises of the organization shall be supplied with the necessary public utilities, which could sound a little facetious if it were not for the consideration that there are many subtle and not so subtle ways in which privileges and immunities may be circumvented.[92]

There is one organization where many of the pertinent cases end up before that organization's own court, and that is the EC. In a number of cases, the Court of Justice of the EC has applied and interpreted the Protocol on the Privileges and Immunities of the European Communities. Those cases have involved lots of different issues, ranging from employees with problems about the level of taxation imposed upon them,[93] to questions concerning the distinction between taxation (for which immunity would apply) and public utility charges where no immunity applies,[94] to cases involving the disclosure of documents by Community institutions and authorization to give evidence in criminal proceedings.[95]

The Protocol applies to the EC itself and its officials and the representatives of member states, but also to members of the European Parliament and officials of the Court[96] and to an affiliated institution such as the European Investment Bank.[97] The Protocol provides, moreover, in Article 17 that missions of third countries accredited to the EC shall be accorded privileges and immunities by the EC's host state.

Apart from being provided for in numerous treaties, it is sometimes argued that there is also an obligation under customary international law to grant privileges and immunities.[98] There are so many treaties on the topic, so the

---

[90] Compare Art. 53, para. 6 EBRD.

[91] So, e.g., Art. IV of the Agreement between Finland and the United Nations University regarding the World Institute for Development Economics Research.

[92] Former Finnish President Koivisto recalls that former USSR Foreign Minister Gromyko was unable to attend the 1984 meeting of the General Assembly because the US authorities would not authorize Gromyko's plane to land: Mauno Koivisto, *Witness to History* (London, 1997), p. 4.

[93] So, e.g., case 6/60, *Jean-E. Humblet* v. *Belgium* [1960] ECR 559.

[94] So, e.g., case C-191/94, *AGF Belgium* v. *EEC and others* [1996] ECR I-1873.

[95] See the Court's order in case 2/88, *J. J. Zwartveld and others* [1990] ECR I-4405.

[96] The Court underlined as much in its order in case C-17/98, *Emesa Sugar* v. *Aruba* [2000] ECR I-665.

[97] As confirmed in, e.g., case 85/86, *Commission* v. *Board of Governors EIB* [1988] ECR 1281.

[98] See, e.g., the Maastricht District Court in *Eckhardt* v. *Eurocontrol (No 2.)*, holding that Eurocontrol 'is entitled to immunity from jurisdiction on the grounds of customary international law to the extent that it is necessary for the operation of its public service': decision of 12 January 1984, in 94 *ILR* 331, at 338. See also Ignaz Seidl-Hohenveldern, 'Functional Immunity of International Organizations and Human Rights'. In Wolfgang Benedek *et al.* (eds.), *Development and Developing International and European Law: Essays in Honour of Konrad Ginther on the Occasion of his 65th Birthday* (Frankfurt am Main, 1999), pp. 137–49, esp. p. 138.

argument goes, that their sheer abundance provides evidence of both state practice and the required *opinio juris*. While it may indeed be the case that there is a customary rule to grant privileges and immunities, such a rule is bound to remain fairly abstract, for what is usually at issue is not so much privileges and immunities *per se*, but rather their precise scope. It will do little good to plead privileges and immunities without being able to delimit them with some degree of precision.

The only way out is to continue the argument by stating that the precise scope need not be defined because privileges and immunities are absolute. The reasoning behind this position would go as follows. Organizations can only act within their powers – anything else is *ultra vires*. Since immunity will be granted for official acts, it follows that the scope of *intra vires* activities is identical to the scope of the organization's official acts. Hence, immunity by definition will cover all acts of the organization. Elegant as the reasoning is, it puts quite a premium on the assumption that organizations never engage in activities that could be regarded as *ultra vires*.[99] For that reason alone it ought to be dismissed.[100]

Domestic law

There are various ways in which domestic law may play a part in the framework of an organization's privileges and immunities. One way is, obviously, by means of an act incorporating the organization and its status in domestic law. Another, and more intricate way, is to provide for a general act on international organizations in conjunction with decrees establishing which organizations shall qualify for privileges and immunities under the act. This is the system which prevails in both the UK and the US.[101] In the UK, the government decides which organizations qualify by Order in Council; in the US, this is done by presidential decree. It is a matter of some controversy whether such instruments are constitutive of the organization's legal existence in the legal system concerned, or whether they merely serve to declare and, perhaps, specify the organization's existence in law. The view that they would be constitutive is difficult to reconcile with the oft-found provision in treaties establishing organizations that they shall have such capacity as may be necessary for their functioning within domestic

---

[99] See also below, Chapter 11.

[100] Still, the UN's Office of Legal Affairs (which has something at stake, of course) has stipulated that the nature of immunities of organizations is such as to render these immunities absolute. See UNJY (1984), pp. 188–9. For a defence of absolute immunity, see also Richard J. Oparil, 'Immunity of International Organizations in United States Courts: Absolute or Restrictive?' (1991) 24 *Vanderbilt JTL*, 689–710.

[101] For a useful discussion of the position of organizations in US domestic law, enriched with excerpts from pertinent documents and cases, see Frederick L. Kirgis, Jr, *International Organizations in their Legal Setting* (2nd edn, St Paul, MN, 1993), 19–53. A recent example of the application of the Foreign Sovereign Immunities Act in respect of a mission to the UN, see *Permanent Mission of India to the UN* v. *City of New York*, US Supreme Court, 14 June 2007 (holding that immunities under the FSIA would not cover a tax lien on immovable property held by the Indian government but used for housing low-ranking officials).

systems. The better view, then, is that Orders in Council and presidential decrees mostly serve to specify the precise scope of the legal position of the organization within a state, including the scope of privileges and immunities.[102]

In some cases, where there is no Headquarters Agreement, it may well be that its place is taken by the terms of an Order in Council or a presidential decree. The most famous example perhaps was the situation of the Intergovernmental Maritime Consultative Organization (IMCO) in London.

In some cases, privileges and immunities are directly granted by domestic law, and, in some cases, domestic law may even grant privileges and immunities to NGOs. Thus, Austria has a general law dealing with privileges and immunities of NGOs with more or less public functions,[103] as well as a few special laws dealing with specific NGOs. The classic example probably concerns the International Institute for Applied Systems Analysis (IIASA).[104] In other cases, it was precisely the desire for privileges and immunities which spurred an NGO to transform itself into an international organization.[105]

Some domestic laws may also provide for the regular granting of privileges and immunities in case of meetings by organs of organizations. Thus, in Finland two Laws on Privileges and Immunities for International Conferences and Special Representatives routinely grant privileges and immunities with respect to meetings taking place in Finland. The first of these laws[106] spells out the privileges and immunities concerned, covering wide categories of persons, whereas the second mainly specifies the organizations and organs to which the laws apply.[107] Coverage includes most European organizations, but also an entity such as the Customs Co-operation Council.

Concluding remarks

As in other branches of the law of international organizations, the field of privileges and immunities is rich in illustrations of the tensions between the organization and its members.[108] For example, the view that an organization,

---

[102] In a similar vein, Geoffrey Marston, 'The Origin of the Personality of International Organisations in United Kingdom Law' (1991) 40 *ICLQ*, 403–24.

[103] BGBl no. 174/1992.

[104] BGBl no. 441/1979; no. 219/1981. Similar laws are made with respect to the Unabhängige Kommission für Fragen der Abrüstung unter die Sicherheit (BGBl no. 293/1981) and the Aktionsrat Ehemaliger Regierungschefs für Internationale Zusammenarbeit (BGBl no. 531/1983).

[105] This applies, e.g., to ICES and to EFI. Note also how the Benelux States will be granted international legal personality precisely with a view to obtaining privileges and immunities, as discussed in Chapter 3 above.

[106] No. 572 of 15 June 1973, as amended in 1991. Reproduced in II *Suomen Laki* (1996), 404.

[107] No. 728 of 14 September 1973, as amended in 1991. Reproduced in II *Suomen Laki* (1996), 406.

[108] And it would seem that the balance is shifting towards a restrictive concept of immunity: see Emmanuel Gaillard and Isabelle Pingel-Lenuzza, 'International Organisations and Immunity from Jurisdiction: To Restrict or to Bypass?' (2002) 51 *ICLQ*, 1–15.

while not a signatory to a convention on its privileges and immunities, can nevertheless be regarded as a party to that convention, is doubly illustrative of this complex relationship. On the one hand, it may signify that the organization is nothing but a vehicle for its members: if the members are bound, then so is the organization. Yet, and curiously at first sight, it can also be seen as an illustration of the separate identity of the organization: precisely because it bestows rights and privileges on the organization, it makes sense to consider it a party,[109] even in the absence of signature and ratification.

The same tension comes to the fore in connection with the functional necessity doctrine, which is arguably mostly referred to in the context of the privileges and immunities of organizations. What is functionally necessary is, however, in the beholder's eye, and the members may have rather different conceptions from the organization itself; differences of opinion will also exist among members, and perhaps even among organs of one and the same organization.

Indeed, even organizations themselves may well realize that what to their mind is functionally necessary may not always be the most practical policy to follow. While very much aware of being immune from suit, the UN nonetheless complies with requirements that it arguably should not be burdened with, such as a domestic law requirement to obtain export licences: 'The reason for this is pragmatic rather than legal. The United Nations wants to avoid difficulties which might hinder future projects.'[110]

Finally, there is the paradoxical consideration that, as the level of integration increases, the logic of the reason for being granted privileges and immunities may become less convincing. Illustrative hereof is the outbreak of much debate (at least in German legal circles[111]) upon granting privileges and immunities to Europol and its staff. For this could mean that police officers would be able to act without even the possibility of judicial control.[112]

Likewise, when it comes to the policing tasks involved in the administration of territory by organizations (e.g., think of the administration of Kosovo by the UN, or earlier its presence in East Timor), there is tension between privileges and immunities and the very idea of the rule of law. As the Ombudsperson for Kosovo unequivocally put it: granting privileges and immunities in such circumstances 'is incompatible with recognised international human rights standards'.[113]

---

[109] This seems to have been the opinion of the ICJ in *Reparation for Injuries Suffered in the Service of the United Nations* (advisory opinion), [1949] ICJ Reports 174, at p. 179, referring to the 1946 General Convention as an example of an agreement which would indicate the legal personality of the UN.

[110] See UNJY (1983), pp. 180–1.

[111] For a critical analysis, see Burkhard Hirsch, 'Immunität für Europol – eine Polizei über dem Gesetz?' (1998) 31 *Zeitschrift für Rechtspolitik*, 10–13. Fewer dangers are anticipated by Kay Hailbronner, 'Die Immunität von Europol-Bediensteten' (1998) 53 *Juristenzeitung*, 283–9.

[112] Compare also Ulrich Daum, 'INTERPOL – öffentliche Gewalt ohne Kontrolle' (1980) 35 *Juristenzeitung*, 798–801.

[113] See Ombudsperson in Kosovo, *Special Report No. 1*, 26 April 2001, para. 28.

By the same token, the finding that practitioners working for international organizations (medical doctors, engineers, architects, lawyers) are not subject to administrative or disciplinary proceedings from professional organizations[114] might mean that their activities end up without any supervision or control whatsoever. In short, as soon as the organization aims to act as more than a co-ordination and focus point for its members and actually develops activities of its own, its activities become indistinguishable from those of others: whether veterinary services are performed by a veterinarian on the payroll of the FAO or in private practice appears quite irrelevant for the service to be performed. In this light, there does not seem to be any particular reason why a surgeon working for the FAO should not be subject to peer group control if his colleagues working for private hospitals or even national governments would be subjected to control from within their disciplines.

---

[114] See the opinion of the FAO's Legal Counsel, in UNJY (1986), pp. 330–1.

9

Institutional structures

Introduction

Most international organizations possess a variety of organs, set up to perform various distinct functions and, perhaps, also to keep each other in check. Within the EC, the idea of the institutional balance as a principle behind the distribution of powers has gained some prominence, and has traditionally been honoured by the EC Court.[1] And with respect to the UN, as Martti Koskenniemi has noted, something similar may be seen:

> The Security Council should establish/maintain order: for this purpose, its composition and procedures are justifiable. The Assembly should deal with the acceptability of that order: its composition and powers are understandable from this perspective. Both bodies provide a check on each other. The Council's functional effectiveness is a guarantee against the Assembly's inability to agree creating chaos; the Assembly's competence to discuss the benefits of any policy – including the policy of the Council – provides, in principle, a public check on the Great Powers' capacity to turn the organization into an instrument of imperialism.[2]

In much the same way as state organs constitute the machinery of states, performing tasks in the name of the state,[3] so too do the organs of international organizations perform tasks in the name of the organization. Usually they lack a separate legal personality,[4] which indicates that they are not to be considered as actors in their own right.

While it seems to be reasonably clear that states acting together can create organizations and endow those with organs, two questions may occasionally give rise to problems. First, can organs themselves create other organs, and,

---

[1] See, e.g., Case 9/56, *Meroni and others v. High Authority* [1957/8] ECR 133.

[2] See Martti Koskenniemi, 'The Police in the Temple. Order, Justice and the UN: A Dialectical View' (1995) 6 *EJIL*, 325–48, p. 339. See generally also Jan Klabbers, 'Checks and Balances in the Law of International Organizations'. In Mortimer Sellers (ed.), *Autonomy in the Law* (Dordrecht, 2007), pp. 141–63.

[3] See, e.g., Jan-Erik Lane, *Constitutions and Political Theory* (Manchester, 1996), p. 90.

[4] Within the EC, this was confirmed by the ECJ in case C-327/91, *France v. Commission* [1994] ECR I-3641, where it found that an international agreement concluded by the Commission would bind the EC as a whole, despite the Commission's argument to the contrary.

if so, under what conditions? Second, what exactly is the position of member states of the organization: are they to be considered not just as creators of the organization, but also as its organs? The latter may sound like a quaint question, but that is not what it is: it goes to the heart of the law of international organizations, in that it problematizes the relationship between the organization and its members – where the member states help fulfil the tasks of the organization, why do we still insist on thinking in terms of organizations?

Regular organs

The European Union, created in Maastricht in late 1991, has only one formal institution: the European Council, consisting of the heads of state and government of the member states,[5] although it is often said to be able to 'borrow' the EC's institutions.[6] The EC itself, in existence since 1952,[7] has five institutions: the Council of Ministers, the Commission, the European Parliament, the Court of Justice and, since the amendments incorporated in the Maastricht Treaty, the Court of Auditors. The EC can also boast a number of subsidiary and auxiliary organs, such as the Committee of the Regions or the Cohesion Fund. There are a number of more or less independent bodies which are nonetheless in some way tied to the EC. Thus, monetary policy is made by the European Central Bank (a separate entity with its own personality[8]), and the European Investment Bank, similarly not an institution or organ of the EC, is envisaged in the EC Treaty,[9] and within the scope of the Community's protocol on privileges and immunities. The EIB's independence is well illustrated by the circumstance that it is itself among the founding members of the EBRD, together with the EC.

Where the EC Treaty speaks of institutions, the United Nations Charter speaks of principal organs: Article 7, para. 1 lists six of those principal organs,[10] while Article 7, para. 2 allows for the establishment of such subsidiary organs 'as may be found necessary'. These have been of great variety, including such bodies as the International Law Commission and the Yugoslavia and Rwanda Tribunals,

---

[5] This may give rise to domestic squabbles: in Finland, this is a function appropriated by the president against expectations. According to a former president, the idea was that Finland should be represented by its prime minister. See Mauno Koivisto, *Witness to History* (London, 1997), p. 237.

[6] Thus, e.g., Ulrich Everling, 'Reflections on the Structure of the European Union' (1992) 29 *CMLRev*, 1053–77, esp. 1061.

[7] The ECSC Treaty entered into force in 1952; the EEC and Euratom were created in 1958. The present-day EU comprises these three Communities as well as two so-called 'pillars' dealing with other more or less common policies: a common foreign and security policy, and co-operation in police and judicial matters.

[8] See Art. 107 EC (formerly Art. 106). Some aspects are discussed in Chiara Zilioli and Martin Selmayr, 'The External Relations of the Euro Area: Legal Aspects' (1999) 36 *CMLRev*, 273–349.

[9] See Art. 266 EC (formerly Art. 198d).

[10] The Security Council, the General Assembly, the Economic and Social Council, the Trusteeship Council, the Secretariat and the International Court of Justice.

the various Sanctions Committees, and the Claims Compensation Commission to deal with the aftermath of the Gulf War.[11]

Organizations will generally have at least three main organs. First, they will usually have a plenary body: a body where all members meet at more or less regular intervals (once a year, or once every two or three years, occasionally once every five years). Usually, the persons composing the plenary will represent their government, but this is not necessarily the case. A well-known exception is the ILO, whose plenary body consists half of government representatives, and half of representatives of employers and employees.[12] The latter should act independently from their governments. Unique as this modality of representation is, it does reflect political considerations: tripartism is merely among various possible ways of arranging industrial economies.[13]

The tasks of the plenary body are, typically, to set standards common to all, at least as far as the internal functioning of the organizations is concerned, and, where external effects are envisaged, these also usually (if not invariably) emanate from the plenary. Thus, within the EC, it is the plenary Council of Ministers that is generally endowed with legislative powers, increasingly in conjunction with the European Parliament. Within the UN, however, the powers of the plenary General Assembly are largely limited to making decisions on the internal functioning of the organization, such as determining and apportioning the budget. Indeed, in an important sense, the UN lacks a legislative body.

Second, organizations typically have an executive body, which meets and may take decisions on shorter notice. Some of those have been granted the power to make binding decisions (the Security Council is an example[14]), whereas others are largely engaged in regulatory and executive activities. The EC Commission may largely, but not completely,[15] be cited as an example of the latter.

With executive bodies, the question is usually how to compose them. The old GATT found an easy solution: its Council used to consist of those members willing to accept membership of the Council. Other organizations follow slightly more intricate procedures, which are usually based on the idea of representation,

---

[11] For a fine study on the circumstances under which delegation of powers by the Security Council may lawfully take place, see Danesh Sarooshi, *The United Nations and the Development of Collective Security: The Delegation by the UN Security Council of its Chapter VII Powers* (Oxford, 1999).

[12] Article 3, para. 1 ILO. In nominating representatives of employers and employees, so the PCIJ has held, 'the persons nominated should have been chosen in agreement with the organisations most representative of employers or workpeople, as the case may be'. See *Nomination of the Worker's Delegate for the Netherlands*, advisory opinion, [1922] Publ. PCIJ, Series B, no. 1, at 19.

[13] See generally Robert W. Cox, *Production, Power, and World Order: Social Forces in the Making of History* (New York, 1987).

[14] But, as Alvarez notes, it is difficult to distinguish legislative acts from decisions applying the law. See José E. Alvarez, *International Organizations as Law-makers* (Oxford, 2005).

[15] It has the power to make binding determinations, sometimes derived directly from the Treaty, sometimes also delegated by the Council.

in one form or another.[16] The Security Council, its five permanent members apart (who, incidentally, also represent at least an idea that was once current: the major allied powers of the Second World War), consists of group representatives according to a more or less fixed key: five African and Asian states, one from eastern Europe, two from Latin America and the Caribbean, and two from western Europe 'and others', which include Canada and Australia.[17]

The idea of representation is stronger, though, in some other international organizations. For instance, the executive board of the International Monetary Fund (IMF) consists of twenty-four members. Five of those are appointed by the member states that have the largest amount of quotas (i.e., money) invested in the IMF. If not among those five, other big lenders may also appoint an executive director. Thus, in 2008, eight states had an appointee on the board: the US, the UK, France, Germany, Japan, Saudi Arabia, Russia and China.

The remaining sixteen members of the executive board are elected by the plenary body (the Board of Governors), and all represent groupings of a number of states. Thus, the Italian member represents not just the interests of Italy, but also those of Greece, Portugal, Malta, San Marino and East Timor. The EC Commission, by contrast, consists of one representative per member state, appointed by the common accord of the member states with the approval of the European Parliament.[18]

Third, organizations typically possess an administrative body, a secretariat or suchlike.[19] Here, of course, there is generally little notion of actual representation, although it is scarcely a coincidence that the IMF's director traditionally hails from Europe, while an American national traditionally heads the World Bank. The international civil service is usually thought to be neutral or impartial, working only for the interests of the organization as a whole. As Article 100, para. 1 of the UN Charter puts it, the staff are 'responsible only to the Organization'. The old practice of largely employing staff on loan from the host state, popular before the First World War, has lost its attraction (although staff may be seconded from the member states[20]). And there never was much attraction in Italy's 1927 law which provided that international civil servants were

---

[16] Note that, as far as individuals go, there is support for the proposition that where they cease to be members of their national delegations they are also no longer eligible to function in executive bodies. See the *UNESCO (Constitution) Case*, decided on 19 September 1949 by a special arbitral tribunal (1949) 16 *AD*, 331.

[17] The non-permanent members are elected by the General Assembly. Inability on the part of the Assembly to make up its mind does not immediately prevent the Council from functioning. See UNJY (1979), pp. 164–6.

[18] See Art. 214 EC (formerly Art. 158).

[19] Indeed, as Claude puts it, the identity of every organization is lodged in its staff: 'The staff, in a fundamental sense, *is* the organization': Inis L. Claude, Jr, *Swords into Plowshares: The Problems and Progress of International Organization* (4th edn, New York, 1984), p. 191 (emphasis in original).

[20] On the modalities of secondment, see UNJY (1983), pp. 204–5.

first screened by the government, and were required to give up their position if the government so demanded.[21] Still, while negotiating the UN Charter the Soviet Union echoed this position that only candidates approved by their national governments would qualify for UN posts; its proposal was ultimately defeated.[22]

That is not to say that secretariats, or, more particularly Secretaries-General, are necessarily passive observers performing strictly delimited administrative tasks.[23] Under Article 99 UN Charter, for example, the UN Secretary-General has a clear political role to fulfil, as Article 99 allows the Secretary-General to bring problems to the attention of the Security Council.[24] However, a problem is often how to play out that role, and where to find the limits. After all, it is here that the supposed neutrality of the Secretary-General may be put to the test: to bring a matter to the attention of the Council will most often be seen as already taking a stand on the political issue involved.[25]

This is well-illustrated by the situation of Mr Bustani, appointed as Director-General of the OPCW in 1997. His contract was renewed in 2000. Problems started in 2001, when the US aspired to oust him for being overly active. The interesting thing is that the US had a hard time deciding what exactly it expected from a Director-General: on the one hand, he was expected to follow orders from the policy-making organs, yet on the other hand he was 'not a mere functionary who is restricted to following explicit orders'. He should show initiative, be energetic, and be something of a visionary but, on the other hand, not 'free-lance on controversial issues' or 'push the boundaries'.[26] In other words, Bustani was expected to be both political and non-political at the same time, and much the same holds true with organizational leaders generally.[27]

---

[21] As reported in Stephen M. Schwebel, 'The International Character of the Secretariat of the United Nations'. In his *Justice in International Law* (Cambridge, 1994), pp. 248–96, esp. p. 251. Schwebel seems to suggest that the practice of screening was perhaps more widespread than one may have expected.

[22] See Kurt Jansson, 'The United Nations Before and Now'. In Kimmo Kiljunen (ed.), *Finns in the United Nations* (Helsinki, 1996), pp. 33–60, esp. p. 35.

[23] For a general, if brief, overview, see Javier Pérez de Cuellar, 'The Role of the UN Secretary-General'. In Adam Roberts and Benedict Kingsbury (eds.), *United Nations, Divided World* (2nd edn, Oxford, 1993), pp. 125–42. A useful survey of the administrative tasks of the UN Secretary-General can be found in UNJY (1982), pp. 189–200. Also highly informative is Paul C. Szasz, 'The Role of the UN Secretary-General: Some Legal Aspects' (1991) 24 *New York University Journal of International Law & Politics*, 161–98.

[24] And a subtle way to influence things, as Franck notes, is to have the Office of Legal Affairs prepare legal opinions. See Thomas M. Franck, *Nation against Nation: What Happened to the UN Dream and What the US can do about it* (Oxford, 1985), p. 126.

[25] Compare also Stephen M. Schwebel, 'The Origins and Development of Article 99 of the Charter'. In Schwebel, *Justice in International Law*, pp. 233–47.

[26] The quotes are taken from a statement by Donald A. Mahley, 'The Role of the Director-General', available at www.state.gov (last visited 6 October 2003). At the time, Mahley was the US permanent representative to the OPCW.

[27] Bustani complained to the ILOAT (which has jurisdiction over OPCW staff cases), and won. See ILOAT, *In re Bustani*, Judgment No. 2232, 16 July 2003. For a brief comment, see Jan

The Secretary-General of the UN, because of the special importance of the organization, occupies something of a special place among Secretaries-General. Apart from the political powers under Article 99, it is widely accepted that the UN Secretary-General may engage in other more or less political activities as well (e.g., in mediating disputes between member states).[28] The UN Charter does not provide a specific legal basis for such activities; so it has been argued that such activities are allowed on the basis of customary international law, circumscribed by the specific powers of other organs.[29] In addition, it may also be the case that authorization flows from a decision of the General Assembly or the Security Council, or even from an agreement between disputing states.[30]

Still, sometimes Secretaries-General are seen as too keen, and powerful member states start to resist them. Thus, when the United States found Boutros Boutros Ghali too arrogant (and possibly too unfriendly in his policies), they made sure he would not be re-elected.[31] Earlier, following the 1950 Korea crisis, the USSR vetoed the re-nomination of the Secretary-General at the time, Trygve Lie. When the US threatened, in response, to veto any other candidate, a constitutional smokescreen was created: without formally re-appointing Lie, he was 'continued in office' for another three years, based on a vote in the General Assembly without the required Security Council recommendation.[32]

In other organizations too, administering functions are not always limited to administration pure and simple. In the EC, it is not uncommon for prominent Commission members to entertain conflict-ridden relationships with leading politicians in the member states, which in itself suggests that the Commission does not limit itself to mere administration. Former EC Commissioners such as Hirsch and Hallstein reportedly did not really see eye-to-eye with one-time French President Charles de Gaulle, a pattern repeated in the 1980s by the relationship between UK Prime Minister Margaret Thatcher and another dynamic Commission president, Jacques Delors. Indeed, the stimulating role of the Commission preparing to achieve both a single market and Economic and Monetary Union is generally acknowledged as an example of pro-active

---

Klabbers, The *Bustani* Case before the ILOAT: Constitutionalism in Disguise?' (2004) 53 *ICLQ*, 455–64.

[28] An example is Secretary-General Pérez de Cuellar's role in the *Rainbow Warrior* dispute between New Zealand and France; his ruling of 6 July 1986 is reproduced in XIX UNRIAA, 199–215.

[29] Thus, where the Security Council bears, under the Charter, primary responsibility for peace and security, any independent acts on the part of the Secretary-General might encroach on the Council's powers. For a brief analysis, see Roberto Lavalle, 'The "Inherent" Powers of the UN Secretary-General in the Political Sphere: A Legal Analysis' (1990) 37 *Neth ILR*, 22–36.

[30] See, for a broad overview of the Secretary-General's activities, Thomas M. Franck and Georg Nolte, 'The Good Offices Function of the UN Secretary-General'. In Roberts and Kingsbury (eds.), *United Nations, Divided World*, pp. 143–82.

[31] See James Traub, *The Best Intentions: Kofi Annan and the UN in the Era of American Power* (New York, 2006), pp. 63–8.

[32] See H. G. Nicholas, *The United Nations as a Political Institution*, (3rd edn, Oxford, 1967), p. 56.

administration.[33] In a similar vein, it has been argued that the GATT Uruguay Round was only successfully concluded, in the early 1990s, because Peter Sutherland was a skilful enough Director-General to iron out any remaining rifts between the negotiating parties.[34]

The staff employed in the secretariats are usually selected on the basis of something approximating neutrality,[35] while taking adequate geographical representation into account. Thus, Article 101, para. 3 UN Charter puts it as follows: 'The paramount consideration in the employment of the staff and in the determination of the conditions of service shall be the necessity of securing the highest standards of efficiency, competence, and integrity. Due regard shall be paid to the importance of recruiting the staff on as wide a geographical basis as possible.'[36] It is clear that there may on occasion be something of a tension between the requirements of capability on the one hand, and geographical representation on the other,[37] and to some extent the peculiar outlook of the organization's senior management may be as much responsible for this tension as anything else. Julian Huxley, for example, the first Director-General of UNESCO, recalls with some disdain the difficulties, immediately after the Second World War, of finding 'a coloured person' of sufficient suitability. In the end, UNESCO employed a Haitian schoolteacher on its staff, but seemingly with mixed results.[38]

Nonetheless, while often derided, there is at least one advantage in trying to secure a broad basis of representation. As Claude astutely observed, a principle of geographical distribution 'is a concession to political necessity. It licenses a kind of international spoils system in which states seek to nourish their national self-esteem by securing an adequate quota of international jobs for their citizens. Ironically, perhaps, because it is politically necessary, it is also politically

---

[33] It has been argued that the Commission's influence not only stems from its agenda-setting role, but is exercised in other ways as well. One of those ways is that, by threatening legal action before the EC Court, the Commission can persuade member states to give in. See Susanne K. Schmidt, 'Only an Agenda Setter? The European Commission: Power over the Council of Ministers' (2000) 1 *European Union Politics*, 37–61.

[34] For an argument that personal characteristics alone are not determinative of a leadership role, see Michael G. Schechter, 'Leadership in International Organizations: Systemic, Organizational and Personality Factors' (1987) 13 *Review of International Studies*, 197–220.

[35] Within the UN, appointments are the exclusive competence of the Secretary-General. Objections of member states cannot be accepted, least of all when the candidates are not nationals of the objecting state. See UNJY (1983), p. 203.

[36] Note that gender is never referred to. On the under-representation of women in the UN (and more generally), see Hilary Charlesworth and Christine Chinkin, *The Boundaries of International Law: A Feminist Analysis* (Manchester, 2000), esp. Chapter 6.

[37] Also in the unexpected way that sometimes member states, in particular, fear a brain drain if a great number of their qualified nationals leave the country in order to become international officials. In such cases, the Secretary-General may be willing to consult with the state in question. See UNJY (1969), pp. 228–9.

[38] Julian Huxley, *Memories II* (Harmondsworth, 1973), p. 19. As if to apologize, he adds a footnote according to which 'with the newly won independence of so many colonies, coloured staff are now a numerous and valuable element in UNESCO'.

and administratively desirable.'[39] Apart from geographical concerns, political considerations too may occasionally creep in, and the witch-hunt of people with leftist inclinations in the US of the early 1950s, known as McCarthyism, even resulted, albeit in an incidental manner, in an opinion of the ICJ after the contracts of several of UNESCO's employees were not renewed despite initial promises to that effect.[40] On the other hand, reportedly the ILO did hire Jewish refugees from Germany in the 1930s, a prominent example being the political theorist Hannah Arendt.[41]

Some other bodies

Some organizations are in the luxurious position of being endowed with judicial bodies.[42] These can be created to solve disputes between member states (which can be said to be the case, albeit roughly so, with the ICJ) or to solve disputes between the organization and its staff (the various administrative tribunals). Sometimes, as with the EC Court, the functions are combined,[43] although, since 2005, all staff cases in the Community end up before the Civil Service Tribunal. The EC Court (which also comprises a Court of First Instance (CFI)) also settles disputes between its institutions and member states, and even between the Community's various institutions. In addition, it famously serves as a point of reference for domestic courts, due to the preliminary ruling procedure of Article 234 (ex-Article 177). Under this procedure, the courts of the member states may (and sometimes must) ask the EC Court's opinion on questions concerning the interpretation and validity of Community law; more or less colloquially, therefore, domestic courts are often regarded as Community organs.[44]

Of course, when it comes to judicial organs the idea of representation is anathema (or rather, ought to be anathema perhaps[45]): Article 2 ICJ Statute holds, for example, that the Court shall be composed of independent judges,

---

[39] Claude, *Swords into Plowshares*, p. 197.

[40] See the Court's advisory opinion in *Judgments of the Administrative Tribunal of the International Labour Organization upon Complaints made against the United Nations Educational, Scientific and Cultural Organization*, [1956] ICJ Reports 77. The opinion deals mainly with issues of competence.

[41] See Elisabeth Young-Bruehl, *Hannah Arendt: For Love of the World* (New Haven, 1982), p. 107. Arendt enjoyed a brief secretarial spell at the ILO.

[42] While the ILO itself has several procedures to address issues of non-compliance with ILO-sponsored conventions, nonetheless judicial settlement is left to the ICJ, by virtue of Art. 37, para. 1 ILO. For a useful study of the ILO, see Ebere Osieke, *Constitutional Law and Practice in the International Labour Organisation* (Dordrecht, 1985).

[43] Inter-state disputes before the ECJ are, however, extremely rare. One of the few that comes to mind is Case 141/78, *France v. United Kingdom* [1979] ECR 2923.

[44] Thus, it has been observed that the EC Court has been able to use national courts in constructing the EC legal system. See Joseph H. H. Weiler, Anne-Marie Slaughter and Alec Stone Sweet, 'Prologue – The European Courts of Justice'. In Anne-Marie Slaughter, Alec Stone Sweet and Joseph H. H. Weiler (eds.), *The European Courts and National Courts: Doctrine and Jurisprudence* (Oxford, 1998), v–xiv, p. xiii.

[45] For a passionate plea to this effect, see Hersch Lauterpacht, *The Function of Law in the International Community* (Oxford, 1933), Chapter 10.

'elected regardless of their nationality'. In actual practice, though, the five permanent members of the Security Council always have their own judge on the ICJ, and, there is the possibility of appointing an *ad hoc* judge to make sure that the parties to the dispute are both represented on the bench.[46] In addition, the Statute provides that, while no requirements of nationality may be posed, nonetheless the Court is supposed to represent the main forms of civilization and the principal legal systems of the world.[47]

In the EC Court, and the CFI as well, all member states are naturally represented; with the European Court of Human Rights, however, the number of judges shall equal the number of parties to the Convention, which gives rise to the possibility that judges need not necessarily be nationals of the state proposing them. Indeed, both San Marino and Liechtenstein have appointed nationals of other states as their judges.[48]

Some organizations also possess a parliamentary body. The most famous among these is doubtless the European Parliament (one of the institutions of the European Community), but other organizations also have assemblies, an example being the Council of Europe.[49] In the case of NATO, the parliamentary body is based on agreement between the participating parliaments; therefore, it is not an official organ of NATO.

While the European Parliament has some real powers, other assemblies are usually purely advisory bodies. Here, of course, the idea of representation is in the foreground, but at least the European Parliament represents not so much the member states' governments, as the peoples of Europe: since 1979, it is directly chosen by the European electorate every five years. As far as representation goes, something similar holds true with respect to other assemblies, albeit less obviously perhaps: the construction that is used most often is that assemblies are composed of members elected by and from the national parliaments of the member states, who accordingly are said to hold a 'dual mandate'.

An institution in its own right, although not universally regarded as an international organization but mostly as an NGO, is the Interparliamentary Union, created by national parliaments and strictly limited to co-operation between parliaments.[50]

Comitology

In particular within the EU, there are numerous committees which help the institutions in their tasks of policy making and decision making or represent various interest groups at some stage in the decision-making process; so much

---

[46] Article 31, paras. 2 and 3 ICJ Statute.   [47] Article 9 ICJ Statute.

[48] Writing in 2008, Liechtenstein's appointee is the Swiss international lawyer Mark Villiger.

[49] For a proposal to transform the UN General Assembly into something resembling a parliament, partly based on direct elections, see Thomas M. Franck, *Fairness in International Law and Institutions* (Oxford, 1995), pp. 483–4.

[50] See, e.g., H. G. Schermers and Niels Blokker, *International Institutional Law* (4th edn, Leiden, 2003), p. 28.

so, indeed, that the word 'comitology' has become a catch-phrase (albeit not a very accurate one) to describe the plethora of committees which help make up the structure of the EU.[51]

The creation of such committees creates a few serious legal problems.[52] One relates to the question whether the creation of committees left, right and centre does not disturb the vision of the founding fathers too much, in particular their system of institutional checks and balances. Another question relates to democracy and transparency: where decision making takes place in committees, far from the public eye, it follows that any form of control is difficult to realize. A third problem has to do with the composition of, in particular, advisory committees: which interest groups are represented and can they exercise some influence on decision making?

The growth of such committees in relative disregard of constituent documents is presumably inevitable, for it represents two intuitions of timeless quality. On the one hand, there is our need to take politics out of politics, as it were: the idea that decisions are best left to committees of experts, or at least ought to be taken upon the advice of expert committees, has a strong hold on our collective imagination. As a result, many organizations boast committees consisting of experts (scientists, often) which give advice or even take decisions on a seemingly disinterested basis. The spirit, if not the actual phenomenon of comitology itself, is probably best captured by the circumstance that the US delegation to the Versailles Conference which would create the League of Nations included historians, geographers and ethnologists. This was done, as US President Wilson explained, so that conclusions could be reached on the basis of facts;[53] scientific objectivity, in other words, should take the place of passionate politics.

On the other hand, there is also a strong desire to politicize things, in the sense of making sure that those who take decisions can in some way be held accountable, or at least do not drift away too much from the scrutiny of the public view.[54] Hence, committees tend to be created as watchdogs over those who are to prepare or implement policy, and committees are created to have various diverse interests represented in the decision-making process. Much as we would like to leave the running of our lives to those who know best, we

---

[51] For a useful overview, see Ellen Vos, 'EU Committees: The Evolution of Unforeseen Institutional Actors in European Product Regulation'. In Christian Joerges and Ellen Vos (eds.), *EU Committees: Social Regulation, Law and Politics* (Oxford, 1999), pp. 19–47.

[52] On the more limited (as not all committees exercise delegated powers) topic of delegation of powers, see generally Sarooshi, *The Development of Collective Security*, Chapter 1.

[53] As referred to in Thomas M. Franck, *The Power of Legitimacy among Nations* (Oxford, 1990), p. 154.

[54] In other terms, we seem to be oscillating between form and substance, between the formalism of procedures and the desirability of giving effect to substance. Our substantive designs may well render formalism expendable, yet without formalism we have no guarantee that we will not become victimized by someone else's substantive designs. See generally Roberto M. Unger, *Law and Modern Society: Toward a Criticism of Social Theory* (New York, 1976).

also dimly realize that we cannot escape taking some responsibility ourselves, and that amounts to putting the politics back into politics, albeit without great enthusiasm. Kennedy has brilliantly portrayed this ambivalence with respect to the EU, which to his mind has become 'a broad political culture with a technocrat and legal face, in which politics is treated as having somehow already happened elsewhere – in the treaty, the European Summit, in the Member States or in the Council and so forth'.[55] Kennedy also noted that there is nothing really unique about the EU: the same type of thing can be seen within states, as well as, it may be added, international organizations generally.[56]

Creating organs

The standard method of creating organs is by means of the constituent treaty, and when a new organ is added, it is often done by amending the constituent treaty. Thus, while the UN continues to consist of six principal organs, the structure of the EC received its fifth institution in 1993, when the Maastricht Treaty entered into force: the Court of Auditors.

The reason why the most obvious method of creating organs is by means of an amendment of the constitution is that it may cause problems with member states if existing organs are to create organs on the same hierarchical level. The member states would probably not appreciate such a venture, as it may be considered to erode their sovereignty. Indeed, in such a case they tend to prefer the creation of separate, independent organizations instead of organs. Thus, the World Bank group has seen the creation, over the years, of IDA, IFC and MIGA; within the FAO, the Indian Ocean Tuna Commission has been created as a separate organization.

Nonetheless, it is generally accepted that organs may create subsidiary organs. Thus, for example, the General Assembly has created such subsidiary organs as UNCTAD; under the Charter, the authority for doing so derives from Article 7, para. 2, which provides that '[s]uch subsidiary organs as may be found necessary may be established in accordance with the present Charter'.

In addition to the general power to create subsidiary organs granted by Article 7, para. 2, the Charter also grants a specific power to do so to the General Assembly (Article 22), the Security Council (Article 29) and, arguably, to the Economic and Social Council (Article 68). The precise relationship between these powers has been the subject of some academic debate, the main question being whether in establishing subsidiary organs the principal organs ought to rely on the specific powers to do so, or rather on the more general power of Article 7, para. 2.

---

[55] David Kennedy, 'Receiving the International' (1994) 10 *Conn JIL*, 1–26, p. 22.
[56] See generally also Martti Koskenniemi, 'The Fate of Public International Law: Between Technique and Politics' (2007) 70 *Modern Law Review*, 1–30.

The answer, some suggest,[57] depends on the nature of the subsidiary organ to be established. Judging by their wording, Articles 22 and 29 limit the power to establish subsidiary organs for the Assembly and the Council, respectively, to such subsidiary organs as are deemed necessary for the exercise of their respective functions. Article 7, para. 2 is framed in broader terms though: the reference to the principal organ's functions is absent, and thus, under Article 7, para. 2, a principal organ can establish subsidiary organs which may perform functions that the principal organ itself cannot perform. Under a strict reading of Articles 22 and 29, the creation of such an organ would be more difficult to defend.[58]

Effect of awards

In the late 1940s, the General Assembly had created an administrative tribunal: a court to hear disputes between UN staff and the UN (UNAT).[59] That caused no particular problems, until UNAT began to issue awards of compensation: the UN was to compensate staff members whose complaints had been found to be justified.

Accordingly, the Secretary-General asked the General Assembly to reserve some financial resources to that effect in the budget, and it was here that some member states started to object, denying that the Assembly could be bound by judgments of UNAT. The Assembly could not solve the puzzle, and asked the ICJ for advice: does the General Assembly have the right to refuse to give effect to an award of compensation made by the Tribunal?[60]

The Court started its analysis by delimiting, and perhaps somewhat redefining, the question. The Court noted that it was only concerned with situations where the legality of the award was not in doubt: ultra vires considerations could easily be left aside. The first thing the Court did was look at the statute of the Tribunal: what did the General Assembly intend to do when it created the UNAT? Since the Statute spoke freely of 'Tribunal', 'Judgment', et cetera, and since Article 10 of the Statute held that UNAT's (judgments) were 'final and without appeal', the Court found that the Assembly had intended to create a judicial body, not just an advisory committee. It followed that decisions of a judicial body were *res judicata*, having binding force between the parties to the dispute. The next question, then, was to identify the parties to an administrative dispute.

---

[57] See generally Danesh Sarooshi, 'The Legal Framework Governing United Nations Subsidiary Organs' (1996) 67 *BYIL*, 413–78.

[58] See also Sarooshi, *The Development of Collective Security*, pp. 92–8.

[59] In the summer of 2008, far-developed plans exist to terminate UNAT and replace it with a new UN Dispute Tribunal. See UN Doc. A/62/748 of 14 March 2008.

[60] *Effect of Awards of Compensation made by the United Nations Administrative Tribunal*, advisory opinion, [1954] ICJ Reports 47.

One side was easy to identify: disgruntled staff members. The other side of the equation was perhaps a bit more difficult, but the Court did not let itself get worried by that: the other party was the United Nations Organization, represented by its highest administrative officer, the Secretary-General. And since the UN was bound by judgments of UNAT, so too were the organs of the UN, such as the General Assembly.

The Court could perhaps have left it at this, but did not: it felt the need to refute some arguments that had been made before it. One of these arguments was that the Assembly did not have the power to create UNAT: nothing in the Charter would give it this power.

This is a potentially powerful argument, but it could easily be overcome with the help of the implied powers doctrine. The Court simply noted that while the power to create UNAT was indeed not specified in the Charter, it could nonetheless be implied from the Charter 'by necessary intendment'.[61] After all, as the Court astutely remarked, the express aim of the Charter is to promote freedom and justice for individuals; it would hardly be consistent with this expressed aim if the UN should not afford its own staff judicial remedies to settle employment disputes.

The other arguments were a bit less fundamental perhaps and served to bolster the legitimacy of the Court's finding of an implied power. Some states had argued that having to compensate in order to do justice to UNAT judgments would erode the budgetary power of the General Assembly. This argument was cogently dismissed by the Court, holding that organizations do have all kinds of expenses which the budgetary power has no choice but to honour. One cannot seriously regard these as eroding budgetary powers.

Others had argued that, by creating UNAT, the Assembly interfered with the powers of the Secretary-General, being the highest administrative officer. This too was given short shrift by the Court: it observed that the General Assembly had the power to make staff regulations (Article 101) and thus to interfere with the Secretary-General's work. There was a solid legal basis for such interference.

The most important counter-argument, however, was that UNAT was but a secondary or subsidiary organ: consequently, it could not bind its own creator, the General Assembly. Here the Court noted that this argument was based on the assumption that the Assembly had created an organ necessary for the performance of the Assembly's own functions. In other words: the argument presupposed a mere delegation of powers to have taken place. The Court, however, held otherwise: the General Assembly was not delegating the performance of its own functions, but rather exercising a power it had under the Charter.[62]

---

[61] *Ibid.*, at 57.
[62] Incidentally, the Court never seriously addressed the proper legal basis of UNAT's creation (Art. 7 or Art. 22 of the Charter).

The Court confirmed the broad scope of the power to create subsidiary organs in its opinion in *Application for Review of Judgement No. 158*,[63] after a staff member had raised objections to a decision of UNAT and had asked the Committee on Applications for Review of Administrative Tribunal Judgements to ask the ICJ for an advisory opinion. The question arose as to whether this Committee could properly be regarded as an organ of the General Assembly (otherwise, it might lack the power to ask for advisory opinions), and the Court held in the affirmative.

The Court argued that Article 22 of the Charter was clear enough, and 'specifically leaves it to the General Assembly to appreciate the need for any particular organ, and the sole restriction placed by that Article on the General Assembly's power to establish such organs is that they should be "necessary for the performance of its functions"'.[64]

Limits? The *Tadic* case

What the *Effect of Awards* case leaves by and large unanswered is whether there may be limits to the powers of an organ to establish subsidiary organs. Such a question arose in October 1995 in connection with the International Criminal Tribunal for the Former Yugoslavia. The Appeals Chamber of the Tribunal was asked to investigate whether the Security Council had the power to establish the Tribunal,[65] or whether it had acted *ultra vires*.[66]

Not too surprisingly perhaps,[67] the Appeals Chamber of the Yugoslavia Tribunal found that the Yugoslavia Tribunal had been established in accordance with the powers of the Security Council.[68] Mr Tadic, accused of war crimes, had claimed before the Trial Chamber that the Tribunal was unconstitutional. The Trial Chamber had dismissed his argument (citing a lack of jurisdiction to decide on the legality of the Tribunal's creation), and he appealed to the Appeals Chamber.

---

[63] *Application for Review of Judgement No. 158 of the United Nations Administrative Tribunal*, advisory opinion, [1973] ICJ Reports 166. The opinion is occasionally referred to as the *Fasla* opinion, after the staff member whose situation gave rise to it.

[64] *Ibid.*, para. 16.

[65] This was far from self-evident for, as Zacklin notes, the Council's competence does not normally involve the creation of legal bodies. See Ralph Zacklin, 'The Role of the International Lawyer in an International Organisation'. In Chanaka Wickremasinghe (ed.), *The International Lawyer as Practitioner* (London, 2000), pp. 57–68, esp. p. 67.

[66] *Prosecutor* v. *Dusko Tadic*, reproduced in 35 *ILM* (1996) 32. For a general comment, see José E. Alvarez, 'Nuremberg Revisited: The *Tadic* Case' (1996) 7 *EJIL*, 245–64.

[67] In a similar vein, G. P. Politakis, 'Enforcing International Humanitarian Law: The Decision of the Appeals Chamber of the War Crimes Tribunal in the Dusko Tadic Case (Jurisdiction)' (1997) 52 *ZöR*, 283–329, esp. p. 291.

[68] The General Assembly was initially not happy with the creation of the Tribunal, and demonstrated as much by leaving the Tribunal without a budget for its first year. See Mohammed Bedjaoui, *The New World Order and the Security Council: Testing the Legality of its Acts* (Dordrecht, 1994), p. 123.

The Appeals Chamber reasoned as follows: under Article 39 of the UN Charter, the Security Council has the power to determine whether there is a breach of the peace, threat to the peace, or an act of aggression. This power is a very wide one, although perhaps not unlimited: after all, under Article 24, para. 2, the Council must act within the principles and purposes of the Charter. Nonetheless, the power under Article 39 is a wide discretionary power.

The Appeals Chamber continued that if the Council determines that an Article 39 situation exists, it can take such measures as it deems necessary. Under Article 40, it can take provisional measures; under Article 42, it can take measures involving armed force. Clearly, both do not apply to the establishment of a tribunal.

Instead, the Appeals Chamber argued that the Security Council had acted under Article 41, which provides in part that '[t]he Security Council may decide what measures not involving the use of armed force are to be employed to give effect to its decisions, and it may call upon the members of the United Nations to apply such measures'.

Article 41 continues by providing some examples (not including the establishment of a tribunal), but the Appeals Chamber argued that these were, indeed, merely examples; the list of Article 41 does not constitute an exhaustive enumeration.

In other words: under Article 41 the Security Council has a wide discretionary power to take whatever measures it wants to take, as long as those (in the terms of Article 39) 'maintain or restore international peace and security'. In setting up the Tribunal, the Security Council had considered that the Tribunal 'would contribute to the restoration and maintenance of peace' and thus, the Tribunal argued, there was nothing *ultra vires* about its establishment.

As a matter of law, the Appeals Chamber's decision is clearly defensible: the discretionary powers of the Security Council are wide indeed, and may well include the power to establish a tribunal with a view to the maintenance or restoration of international peace. Nonetheless, a jump of some magnitude must be made, and that is the jump that the establishment of a tribunal will indeed (or at least may be expected to) contribute to the maintenance or restoration of peace. As a matter of law, that jump can be made; as a practical matter, however, it need not necessarily be very credible. On the other hand, as the Appeals Chamber quite rightly remarked, the expected success or failure of policy cannot be a criterion of the legality or validity of that policy.[69] In short, the conclusion presents itself that, at the very least, there is an extremely strong presumption that Security Council acts will be *intra vires*. After all, the same wide discretion also applies to other acts.

As a basic principle, much the same will apply to and within other organizations. In the absence of express prohibitions to create subsidiary organs, existing organs must be deemed to be allowed to create sub-organs within the

---

[69] *Tadic* case, para. 39.

limits set by their constituent documents. Those limits are, invariably, flexible and, moreover, in the normal course of events each organ will itself be the first to determine whether it has acted *intra vires*. In good faith, then, the creation of subsidiary organs will normally go unchallenged. Indeed, where it is challenged by a majority of the organization's members, the subsidiary organ will simply not be created.

Inter-relationship: hierarchy or not?

Even if the Security Council were to act *ultra vires*, it remains to be seen what could possibly be done about it. Can *ultra vires* acts be nullified? If so, on what grounds? And by whom? The substantial questions will be discussed elsewhere,[70] but at this juncture some attention for the more general question is warranted: can organs of international organizations control each other, and, if so, under what conditions?

The topic has gained some special importance in recent years, due to the activities of the Security Council with respect to Iraq, Yugoslavia, Rwanda and Libya. In the above-mentioned *Tadic* case, the question arose whether the Appeals Chamber was competent to hear such a question, relating to its own establishment. In terminology derived from continental administrative law: did the Chamber have the *Kompetenz-Kompetenz*?[71]

The answer is by no means self-evident. At the very least it must be noted that the Statute of the Yugoslavia Tribunal does not provide anything in this regard: the Tribunal's competence is limited, under Article 1, to 'the power to prosecute persons responsible for serious violations of international humanitarian law committed in the territory of the former Yugoslavia since 1991'.

Thus, the Tribunal's competence is clearly subject to various limitations. There is, first, a temporal limitation ('since 1991'). Second, competence is territorially limited to 'the territory of the former Yugoslavia', and third, there is a substantive limitation: 'serious violations of international humanitarian law'.

The Appeals Chamber itself, however, saw little problem, and used a two-step technique to give itself the competence to pronounce on its own establishment. First of all, although the Statute remained silent, the Tribunal had created its own Rules of Procedure, and in one of those rules had given itself an unlimited power to decide preliminary issues. The Trial Chamber was given the power to decide all preliminary motions, and, moreover, if jurisdiction was in doubt, then the Appeals Chamber could be activated.

The second step, then, was to regard the Tribunal's creation as somehow a matter of jurisdiction. The prosecutor, no doubt keen to come up with a verdict, had argued that the validity of the creation of the Tribunal could not be regarded as a matter of jurisdiction. The Appeals Chamber disagreed, however,

---

[70] See below, Chapter 11.   [71] *Tadic* case, para. 18.

and argued that the prosecutor's conception of jurisdiction was 'narrow', and 'falls foul of a modern vision of the administration of justice'.[72]

Interestingly, the pertinent paragraph of the judgment is almost completely made up of rhetorical questions. The Tribunal gives no legal arguments; such arguments as it does give are based on 'the higher interest of justice', and on 'common sense'.[73] Presumably, the Appeals Chamber was keen on coming up with a decision favouring the legality of its own creation, for, if not answered at that moment, the question would come back to haunt it: if not answered there and then, any conviction of Mr Tadic would always remain tainted and the question of its legality would inevitably surface in subsequent cases.[74] Presumably, this was a justified fear on the part of the Appeals Chamber.

Still, its chosen solution remains debatable, for various reasons. One reason is that the Statute itself remains silent, and, as noted, it clearly describes and limits the competence of the Tribunal. Second, to paraphrase the Appeals Chamber, the modern administration of justice does not just have to listen to demands of common sense and the higher interests of justice, but also places a premium on reasoning at the basis of an opinion. Legal reasoning is, as Judge Higgins put it in the *Nuclear Weapons* opinion of the ICJ, an 'essential step in the judicial process'.[75] And legal reasoning is more than just invoking common sense and justice.[76] Third, while it is one thing to have the competence to decide on your own competence, as a matter of principle it is somewhat mystifying to judge on the validity of your own creation.[77]

In this light, perhaps the Appeals Chamber would have done better to ask the ICJ for an advisory opinion. Perhaps the outcome would have been the same; perhaps the ICJ would have reached the conclusion that the creation of the Tribunal would have been a perfectly valid act in contemporary international law. But at least such a conclusion from the ICJ would have possessed a higher degree of legitimacy than the same conclusion reached by the Appeals Chamber.

Leaving issues of *Kompetenz-Kompetenz* aside, the ICJ has always been very careful not to come to a conclusion that favours any hierarchy between the principal organs of the UN, in particular between the General Assembly, the Security Council and the ICJ itself, and, as will be discussed below, probably for good reasons.[78]

---

[72] *Ibid.*, para. 6.
[73] And, some paragraphs later, the Appeals Chamber invokes the decentralized nature of international law as a reason for rejecting too narrow a concept of jurisdiction. *Ibid.*, para. 11.
[74] See also Politakis, 'Enforcing International Humanitarian Law', p. 325.
[75] *Legality of the threat or use of nuclear weapons*, advisory opinion, reproduced in [1996] ICJ Reports 226, Judge Higgins dissenting, para. 9.
[76] See Neil MacCormick's classic *Legal Reasoning and Legal Theory* (Oxford, 1978).
[77] See also Alvarez, 'Nuremberg Revisited'.
[78] When it comes to the possibility of judicial review of Security Council acts, Alvarez makes the useful argument that we should not expect too much from judicial review by the ICJ, and that the ICJ is not the only actor which may have important things to say about the legality of Security Council acts. See Alvarez, 'Judging the Security Council'.

The situation with respect to the remaining principal organs of the United Nations is relatively clear. Under Article 87 of the Charter, the Trusteeship Council is clearly subordinate to the General Assembly; somewhat less explicitly, something similar follows from Article 66 with respect to ECOSOC. The Secretary-General,[79] in turn, has very few powers of his own, and such powers as he does have are fairly general. They are not described as 'exclusive' or something similar, thus the question of hierarchy hardly presents itself; rather, his powers in many areas are complementary. While the Secretary-General has the power to bring matters to the attention of the Security Council (Article 99), this is clearly discretionary, and moreover does not get in the way of the powers of other organs.[80]

Things are different, though, with the remaining three principal organs. The 1962 *Certain Expenses* case[81] was the result of the inactivity of the Security Council in the 1950s when it came to peace-keeping. In 1950, the Council had allowed the UN to do something about the conflict in Korea, due to the absence of the USSR at the crucial moment.

The General Assembly, understanding that such a fortunate situation was not likely to happen again, adopted its famous Uniting for Peace resolution,[82] granting itself the power to send missions to the world's hot-spots. And indeed, in the 1950s, peace-keeping missions went to the Middle East (UNEF), and, in the early 1960s to the Congo (ONUC), more or less under authority of the General Assembly.[83]

As such, that presented few problems. Obviously, the General Assembly cannot take binding decisions, and thus cannot force member states to send troops. Moreover, it cannot act under Chapter VII of the Charter, so both UNEF and ONUC were established with the consent of the parties involved.

The question that did arise, though, related to the topic of the financing of peace-keeping operations. France and the USSR argued that, sending troops was the sole prerogative of the Security Council, and, accordingly, the General Assembly had no binding powers concerning peace and security, and, therefore, the costs should not form part of the regular budget.

---

[79] Incidentally, the Secretary-General is not an organ of the UN; the Secretariat is.

[80] Which is not to deny that any conflicts ever take place between the Secretary-General and other organs. For an insightful discussion of the power struggles between Secretary-General Hammarskjöld and the Security Council, often revolving around the interpretation of the latter's resolutions, see generally Georges Abi-Saab, *The United Nations Operation in the Congo 1960–1964* (Oxford, 1978). On the relationship between the Secretary-General and the ICJ, see Carl-August Fleischhauer, 'The Constitutional Relationship between the Secretary-General of the United Nations and the International Court of Justice'. In Georges Abi-Saab *et al.*, *Paix, développement, démocratie: Boutros Boutros-Ghali Amicorum Discipulorumque* (Brussels, 1999), pp. 451–74.

[81] *Certain Expenses of the United Nations (Article 17, paragraph 2, of the Charter)*, advisory opinion, [1962] ICJ Reports 151.

[82] Resolution 377 A(V), of 3 November 1950.

[83] With respect to ONUC, the General Assembly only intervened for a short period of time. See generally Abi-Saab, *The United Nations Operation*.

Asked to give an advisory opinion, the Court disagreed on this point, and found that since the Assembly had some responsibilities when it came to peace and security, costs made in that connection qualified as 'expenses of the Organization' within the meaning of Article 17, and could therefore simply be put in the normal budget.[84]

That, however, is not so important for present purposes. What is important, however, is the way the Court reached its conclusions. The Court refused to create a hierarchy between the Security Council and the General Assembly, and could use the text of the Charter for that purpose. Under Article 24, para. 1, the Security Council bears 'primary' responsibility for the maintenance of international peace and security, and, thus, it followed that the Council's powers were precisely that: primary. They were not, however, exclusive, as also appeared from the Assembly's power to recommend measures, for example, under Article 14. This implied, according to the Court, that the Assembly is empowered to take 'some kind of action'.[85] In other words: the Assembly's power to deal with peace and security was complementary.

There was but one important limitation: under the Charter, only the Security Council could take enforcement action (i.e., action going against the wishes of the state concerned – action under Chapter VII). Most importantly for present purposes is the following quotation:

> In the legal systems of States, there is often some procedure for determining the validity of even a legislative or governmental act, but no analogous procedure is to be found in the structure of the United Nations. Proposals made during the drafting of the Charter to place the ultimate authority to interpret the Charter in the International Court of Justice were not accepted; the opinion which the Court is in course of rendering is an *advisory* opinion. As anticipated in 1945, therefore, each organ must, in the first place at least, determine its own jurisdiction.[86]

The message appears to be clear but, upon closer scrutiny, is not. Obviously, the Court did not wish to establish a hierarchy there and then, but, equally obviously, it did not reach a final verdict: the qualification that each organ determines its own jurisdiction 'in the first place at least' keeps the door open for a more final determination. None has yet been issued.

This hands-off approach, letting organs do as they please as long as they remain within their competence and hoping that no irreconcilable conflicts will result, also seems to be the approach guiding practice between the Security Council and the General Assembly,[87] and even between committees of a single organ.[88]

---

[84] *Certain Expenses*, 151. See also the discussion above, in Chapter 8.
[85] *Ibid.*, at 163.   [86] *Ibid.*, p. 168 (emphasis in original).
[87] See UNJY (1964), pp. 228–37. See also UNJY (1968), p. 185, for a skilful circumvention of possible jurisdictional conflict.
[88] See UNJY (1969), p. 211.

The International Court of Justice had another opportunity to look at the hierarchy issue in the *Lockerbie* case, in 1992.[89] As is well known, after a bomb exploded aboard a plane over Lockerbie, Scotland, the suspicion grew that two Libyan citizens were responsible. Libya was asked to hand them over to either the US or the UK, and, upon Libya's refusal to do so, the Security Council imposed sanctions. Libya went to the ICJ to ask the Court for interim measures of protection against the USA and the UK, arguing that these states were in breach of the 1971 Montreal Convention on safety of civil aviation, which provides that states will either extradite or carry out prosecution themselves.[90]

Libya thus started proceedings against the USA and the UK (separately) for hindering Libya from fulfilling its obligations under the Montreal Convention. Moreover, Libya claimed that its territorial integrity was threatened, although it never actually referred to the Security Council. By contrast, the UK and the USA pointed out that the Security Council was also apprised of the matter; therefore, the Court should not indicate provisional measures. Indeed, the Court refrained from indicating provisional measures, but not simply because the Security Council was seized of the matter. Instead, the Court found a way out of a difficult situation by combining the fact that it was a request for provisional measures with the provision of Article 103 of the Charter, according to which, in cases of conflict between treaties, the provisions of the Charter prevail.

The Court emphasized that, because of Article 103, which was *prima facie* applicable and which *prima facie* gave rise to the supreme binding force of Council resolutions under Article 25, the Court could not regard the rights claimed by Libya under the Montreal Convention as 'appropriate for protection',[91] given the very existence of Security Council involvement. It even mentioned, slightly maliciously perhaps, that indicating measures to protect Libya might impair the rights of the USA and the UK under the Council resolutions. Still, most importantly, the Court underlined four times in the last five paragraphs of the 1992 order that it was not making any definitive findings regarding the legal effect of Security Council Resolution 748.[92]

In February 1998, the Court finally gave a judgment on some of the preliminary objections raised by the USA and the UK. The respondents made the argument that the matter was to be governed by Council Resolutions 748

---

[89] *Case concerning questions of interpretation and application of the 1971 Montreal Convention arising from the aerial incident at Lockerbie (Libya v. United Kingdom)*, Order [1992] ICJ Reports 3. Parallel proceedings between Libya and the United States are to be found in *ibid.*, 114. The case would eventually be discontinued in 2003.

[90] According to some, it was this request for extradition (without using that term) which intersected the judicial work of the Court with the political work of the Council, and therewith provoked the question of judicial control. See, e.g., Bedjaoui, *The New World Order*, p. 46.

[91] *Lockerbie* case, paras. 40 (UK) and 43 (US).

[92] In a similar vein, Thomas M. Franck, 'The "Powers of Appreciation": Who is the Ultimate Guardian of UN Legality?' (1992) 86 *AJIL*, 519–23.

(1992) and 883 (1993). Both were 'determinative of any dispute over which the Court might have jurisdiction'.[93] The Court disagreed, pointing out that Libya's claim had already been brought before the Council had adopted Resolution 748 (1992). The only resolution adopted at the moment Libya filed its application was Resolution 731 (1992), but this could not be an impediment to admissibility 'because it was a mere recommendation without binding effect'.[94]

The respondents also argued that Libya's claim was rendered without object due to the effect of the later Council resolutions. Under the Rules of Court, so they claimed, this implied that the Court should make the application inadmissible before it proceeded with the merits; otherwise, the Court would run the risk of having to dismiss later on an exclusively preliminary point.[95] While the Court agreed in principle, it denied that the overriding effect of the Council resolution constituted an argument of an exclusively preliminary character. Instead, the Court observed, any decision thereon entails at least two decisions on the merits: first, it would entail a decision that Libya's rights under the Montreal Convention are incompatible with the Council resolutions, and second, it would imply that those Council resolutions prevail. Therefore, the argument of respondents was not of an exclusively preliminary character, and, therefore, the Court could not decide the claim inadmissible.

In doing so, the Court still left open the issue of hierarchy between itself and the Security Council: it could afford not to address it on the theory that Libya filed its application before the two main resolutions were adopted,[96] and what matters for admissibility is the situation at the moment of filing the application. The only obstacle was that Resolution 731 had already been adopted; yet the Court could find this resolution to be a mere recommendation.[97]

In other organizations, the hierarchy between the various organs may be more clearly posited. Thus, within the European Community, the Court of Justice is the ultimate guardian of legality: 'The Court of Justice shall ensure that in the interpretation and application of this Treaty the law is observed', as Article 220 EC (formerly Article 164) puts it. Still, while this may hold true for the European Community, it does not cover all activities of the European Union, as the Court is largely left out of the loop when it comes to both the

---

[93] *Case concerning questions of interpretation and application of the 1971 Montreal Convention arising from the aerial incident at Lockerbie (Libya v. UK)*, preliminary objections, [1998] ICJ Reports 9, para. 41.

[94] *Ibid.*, para. 44.

[95] This happened, indeed, in the *Case concerning the Barcelona Traction, Light and Power Company, Limited* (Belgium v. Spain), second phase, [1970] ICJ Reports 3, where the Court in the merits phase decided that the claim was inadmissible for being of the wrong nationality. As a result, the Rules of Court were amended in 1972 so as to prevent such a situation.

[96] For a scathing critique of the Council's actions by a former judge at the ICJ, see Bedjaoui, *The New World Order*, p. 73.

[97] The Court did not devote any argument to why Resolution 731 would merely be a recommendation. Its wording is, indeed, hortatory, but it is not self-evident that the wording alone determines the issue. See also below, Chapter 10.

Union's Common Foreign and Security Policy and its co-operation in matters of justice and crime.

Moreover, while the Court is the ultimate guardian of legality, that is not to imply that it occupies a higher position in other walks of life. Surely, the Council, the Commission and even the European Parliament may have political prerogatives which are not for the Court to touch, and if push really comes to shove, the member states remain free simply to change the law (perhaps against the grain of the Court's suggestions), and arguably remain free to limit the effects of the Court's decisions.[98] After all, if need be, the member states can amend the treaties, insert new provisions or delete old ones, and there is little that the Court can do about it.[99] Indeed, there is little to protect individuals or businesses from such activities; at best, the principle of legitimate expectations may offer an initial shield against all-too-abrupt changes.

Similar considerations apply across the board. The general picture is that in most cases, regardless of any formal power distributions, the member states remain masters of the treaty, and it is here of course that the distinction between the member states acting together and the plenary organ becomes very fine. For even where a plenary organ would be subordinated to another organ, acting outside the confines of the plenary, the very same states can circumvent that other organ.

The position of member states

Most organizations have but limited resources and, consequently, limited staff. Such staff as there is is typically engaged in arranging meetings and preparing decisions, facilitating contacts between member states and their representatives, and similar activities. In other words, few officials are engaged in actually implementing the decisions taken by the organization. To put it succinctly: the Security Council may authorize armed action, but it does not have its own troops;[100] while the EU sets tariffs at its external boundaries, it does not have its own customs officers. In short: much of the implementation of decisions of international organizations rests with the member states, and that raises the question of the exact position of those member states within these organizations.

---

[98] Moreover, at least in the early years of the EC, the Commission would refrain from starting proceedings if it suspected that the member state concerned would ignore the decision. See Miguel Poiares Maduro, *We, the Court: The European Court of Justice and the European Economic Constitution* (Oxford, 1998), p. 10 (citing a former head of the Commission's legal service).

[99] Indeed, there appears to be no principled bar against the member states taking powers 'back' from the Community. See Daniela Obradovic, 'Repatriation of Powers in the European Community' (1997) 34 *CMLRev*, 59–88.

[100] Those are foreseen in Art. 43 of the Charter though, and, curiously enough, the implementation of Art. 43 was long (and perhaps still is) regarded as only a matter of time. Thus, a memorandum from the UN's Office of Legal Affairs, written as late as 1982, treated the topic as one whose time would still come. See UNJY (1982), pp. 183–5.

This question, as might have been expected, defies an easy answer. Clearly, it appears counterintuitive to speak of member states as organs of the organization. After all, member states exist before the organization does – indeed, they are the creators of the organization – so how could they be among its organs at the same time? Member states are, moreover, lacking some of the elements that usually characterize organs: well-described tasks and powers, instructions as to composition, et cetera.

On the other hand, in many organizations the member states are in part subordinate to the organization.[101] This is partly expressed in the circumstance that in some organizations, binding decisions can be made even against the wishes of one or more members (this is, however, relatively rare), but partly also in more general clauses laying down duties of co-operation, often referred to as a duty of community solidarity (*Gemeinschaftstreue*, in German). The most famous among the pertinent provisions[102] is no doubt Article 10 (formerly Article 5) of the TEC, which provides 'Member States shall take all appropriate measures, whether general or particular, to ensure fulfilment of the obligations arising out of this Treaty or resulting from action taken by the institutions of the Community. They shall facilitate the achievement of the Community's tasks. They shall abstain from any measure which could jeopardise the attainment of the objectives of this Treaty.' Other organizations have similar provisions, albeit less explicit. Article 2, para. 2 of the UN Charter orders UN members to 'fulfil in good faith the obligations assumed by them', with para. 5 of the same article adding that the members 'shall give the United Nations every assistance in any action it takes' in accordance with the Charter. The OECD Convention provides for duties of consultation and co-operation,[103] whereas the Statute of the Council of Europe calls for sincere and effective collaboration among the members.[104] The International Bauxite Association has a clause instructing its members 'to take all appropriate measures to ensure that obligations ... are carried out',[105] with the Statute of the IAEA endorsing that members shall fulfil obligations assumed by them.[106]

On one level, such provisions read as little more than confirmations of the time-honoured *pacta sunt servanda* principle, yet as such they would be redundant, for it goes without saying that commitments are to be honoured. Hence, rather than merely confirming that *pacta sunt servanda*, such solidarity clauses remind the member states of organizations that they may be called

---

[101] Note also that Sarooshi can confidently write about the delegation of Security Council powers to the UN member states, which would seem to presuppose a conception of the member states as organs of the organization. See Sarooshi, *The Development of Collective Security*, chs. 4 and 5.

[102] But see also, e.g., Art. 300, para. 7 (formerly Art. 228, para. 7) of the TEC, which explicitly treats the member states and the institutions on an equal footing when it comes to the binding nature of treaties concluded by the Community.

[103] Article 3 OECD.   [104] Article 3 Council of Europe Statute.

[105] Article V of the Agreement establishing the International Bauxite Association.

[106] Article IV, para. (c) IAEA.

upon to do things which are not to their liking and which they may never even have expected;[107] rather than merely replicating the *pacta sunt servanda* norm (without which treaty-making would be unthinkable to begin with), they remind the member states that they enter into a relationship which aspires to create 'an ever closer union', as the EC Treaty poetically puts it. Much in the same way as marriage is somehow more than a mere contractual arrangement, so too the creation of an organization is an act which involves not just the normal good-faith duty to give effect to one's commitments, but also a spirit of loyalty, camaraderie and mutual support.

With this in mind, given the reliance of organizations on the implementing acts of their member states, it becomes all of a sudden less eccentric to think of member states as organs of the organization. After all, carrying out the organization's programme is pretty much what one would associate with organs rather than creators.[108]

Perhaps the easiest (but not a final) way to come to terms with this duality is to adopt the classic notion of 'dédoublement fonctionnel', a term once coined by French jurist Georges Scelle to describe the similarly problematic relationship of states (and their organs and representatives) with international law:[109] state organs act as state organs when they operate in the national legal system, but once they operate in the international system, they act as international agents.[110]

Concluding remarks

Again we have seen that there are several ways in which the relationship between organizations and their members colours the law of international organizations. The very question of whether the member states must be considered as organs of the organization pays testimony to this problematic relationship, as do attempts to politicize and depoliticize decision making simultaneously through the creation of committees, making sure that either the interests of the member states are guaranteed, or that those interests are circumvented in the name of expertise

---

[107] For an impressive overview of the possible obligations which may in whole or in part be derived from the notion of Community solidarity, see John Temple Lang, 'Community Constitutional Law: Article 5 EEC Treaty' (1990) 27 *CMLRev*, 645–81.

[108] Austria's Supreme Court followed a similar line when holding that the United States was immune from suit for not having paid airport fees when using an Austrian airport in the framework of a NATO operation: see *Airport L. v. United States of America*, 28 August 2003, *ILDC* 3 (AT 2003). Interestingly, the Court looked only at state immunity, suggesting that acts to implement an organization's decision qualify by definition as *acta jure imperii*; at no point did the Court look at organizational immunities.

[109] Note also Kelsen's insistence that individual states can be characterized as organs of the international legal community. See Hans Kelsen, *Introduction to the Problems of Legal Theory* (1934: Oxford, 1992, trans. Litschewski Paulson and Paulson), esp. pp. 122–4.

[110] Cassese has suggested that Scelle's work (including the notion of 'dédoublement fonctionnel') may have great explanatory potential with respect to, especially, the EC legal system. See Antonio Cassese, 'Remarks on Scelle's Theory of "Role Splitting" (*dédoublement fonctionnel*) in International Law' (1990) 1 *EJIL*, 210–31, esp. p. 231.

and objectivity (in which case no doubt another committee will see to it that the members' interests are represented after all).

Also the more formal creation of subsidiary organs may profitably be analysed in terms of the position of the member states, for the members will eventually have to succumb, in one way or another, to the activities of such organs: the activities of a subsidiary organ may curtail the members' room to manoeuvre; the members may lose certain prerogatives with the creation of new organs; and, ultimately, they will have to pay for the organ's expenses as well. In those circumstances, it becomes imperative that the creation of new organs be done with care and caution, lest the organ is devoid of legitimacy before it even starts to operate.[111]

---

[111] Witness the resistance in the General Assembly to the creation, by the Security Council, of the Yugoslavia Tribunal. See, e.g., Julian J. E. Schutte, 'Legal and Practical Implications, from the Perspective of the Host Country, Relating to the Establishment of the International Tribunal for the Former Yugoslavia' (1994) 5 *Criminal Law Forum*, 423–50.

10

Legal instruments

Introduction

The very idea of international organizations suggests that those entities are capable of performing acts; creating an entity with a separate identity only makes sense (instrumental sense, at any rate), if that entity can subsequently do certain things. In order to do those things, the organization must be able to adopt or create legal instruments.[1]

The scope of acts that organizations may adopt will differ from organization to organization, and is essentially a question of the organization's powers;[2] what is at issue in the present chapter is not so much the scope, but rather the type of acts: what are the legal instruments that organizations may create, and where does their binding character – if any – stem from?

The legal nature of instruments of international organizations, and the ways those instruments are created, are in principle determined by what the constituent treaty says. That is, however, not all that can be said, for at least two reasons. One is that the constituent documents of organizations are not always clear on the types of acts (and their nature) to be adopted. Second, even where the constituent document is relatively clear (as in the European Community), practice tends to come up with examples that do not fit the mould of the constituent document.

The topic of legal instruments is perhaps most usefully approached with the help of a variety of questions. First, what types of instruments can be distinguished? Second, how are the various legal instruments adopted (or, in other words, what are typical decision-making procedures)? Third, are there rules relating to the validity of an organization's legal instruments? And fourth, if so, does this presuppose a hierarchy between various legal instruments? The

---

[1] Note that the very term 'instruments' suggests (not quite fortunately perhaps) a problem-oriented approach: any problem may be solved provided the right tools are available. However, alternative generic terms come with their own drawbacks: 'decisions' are also specific instruments within the EC, whereas the term 'legal acts' opens up entire jurisprudential avenues that, for present purposes, best remain closed. See, e.g., Alan R. White, *Grounds of Liability* (Oxford, 1985), pp. 23–34.

[2] See in particular Chapter 4 above.

latter three questions will be addressed in Chapter 11; the first one is the subject of this chapter.

Before going there, though, it is useful to remember that any thoughts on law-making by international organizations depend on two preliminary issues. First, opinions on law-making depend greatly on the underlying concept of law. Thus, for some (Alvarez is an important recent example), law consists of those things that states – or others – actually live up to.[3] Such an approach, inspired by the social sciences, tends to downplay the role of formalities: if actors give effect to a resolution, then it must be law. If they don't, then it was not law after all. Such an approach makes it fairly easy to reach the conclusion that international organizations are engaged in much law-making activity for, empirically, much of the output of organizations tends to be complied with, regardless of the formal status of that output. On the other hand, the approach comes with two drawbacks. One is that it makes it difficult to say in advance what the law says: one always has to await the 'normative ripples' emanating from an instrument. Second, it becomes problematic to separate law from non-law: differences between law and morality, law and etiquette, law and power even, tend to evaporate.

For those reasons, legal theorists tend to agree, by and large, that what matters is not only the behaviour of actors, but also their sense of being under a legal obligation (not dissimilar to the *opinio juris* requirement of customary international law), the 'internal point of view', as Hart calls it.[4] And for actors to understand themselves as being under a legal obligation, such formal things as whether or not the institution in question is endowed with legislative powers becomes an important question.

Second, much may also depend on the underlying concept of international organizations.[5] Those who view organizations as mere aggregates of states will be reluctant to concede that they can make law, for on such a conception, acts of organizations are, really, just the acts of a bunch of states acting together. Arguably, the treaty analogy (to be discussed below) stems from such a concept. If, on the other hand, one thinks of organizations as separate actors, then all of a sudden it makes a lot more sense to think of them as being engaged, in a meaningful way, in law-making activities.[6]

---

[3] Obviously this short description does an injustice to Alvarez's rich and varied discussion; see José E. Alvarez, *International Organizations as Law-makers* (Oxford, 2005). For a more in-depth engagement, see Jan Klabbers, book review of José E. Alvarez, *International Organizations as Law-makers* (2006) 3 *IOLR*, 153–7.

[4] See H. L. A. Hart, *The Concept of Law* (Oxford, 1961), p. 86. This insistence on the relevance of an internal perspective unites positivists and natural lawyers. See, e.g., Frederick Schauer, *Playing by the Rules: A Philosophical Examination of Rule-based Decision-making in Law and in Life* (Oxford, 1991) and Lon L. Fuller, *The Morality of Law* (rev. edn, New Haven CT, 1969).

[5] For a general discussion, see Jan Klabbers, 'Two Concepts of International Organization' (2005) 2 *IOLR*, 277–93.

[6] Arguably the most systematic analysis to date is Edward Yemin, *Legislative Powers in the United Nations and Specialized Agencies* (Leiden, 1969). Yemin enthusiastically embraces this second

Sketching the problem: the Mandate

It is imperative first to make some distinctions as to the types of instruments which international organizations can adopt. That may sound like a relatively simple exercise, but it is not. Obviously, the bottom line is always to refer to the constituent treaty, but even then some issues are likely to remain problematic. Thus, the ICJ has wrestled on several occasions with the qualification of the legal nature of South Africa's Mandate over Namibia.

One of the more interesting phenomena accompanying the establishment of the League of Nations was the creation of a mandate system, by which some of the former territories of Germany and the Ottoman Empire were to be helped on the road to independence, in the name of the 'sacred trust of civilization'. Under the auspices of another state and under final supervision of the League, these territories were to be developed prior to becoming independent, based on the theory that they were 'inhabited by peoples not yet able to stand by themselves under the strenuous conditions of the modern world'.[7]

The precise operation turned out to be problematic,[8] and the biggest problem of all involved South West Africa (nowadays known as Namibia). South West Africa was to be placed under the tutelage of its large neighbour, South Africa, and, after the Second World War, with the demise of the League of Nations, South Africa started to raise claims according to which South West Africa was no longer a Mandate territory, but had become part of South Africa. That claim raised many issues, one of which was the legal nature of the Mandate. As the Mandate over South West Africa was not cast in treaty form, the episode gave rise to heated and protracted debate on the precise legal nature of the Mandate, which serves as a useful reminder of some of the intricacies of the law of international organizations.

The League Covenant was silent on the question of the legal nature of the Mandate, thus providing ample space for contending theories. Some thought the Mandate was an executive act of the League Council. Others thought, rather, that it was an agreement between South Africa and the people of Namibia. Still others argued that the Mandate was simply a treaty between the League and South Africa, along the lines of the British Mandate over Iraq.[9] Another group held that the South West Africa Mandate may have been a treaty concluded between the League of Nations and South Africa, but that it expired due to the dissolution of the League, which was not, as such, succeeded to. Still others agreed that it was such a treaty, but claimed that the League had been succeeded to, at least in respect of supervision over the Mandate, with the result

---

perspective, and therewith can conclude that at least in some organizations law-making does take place.

[7] See Art. 22, para. 1, of the Covenant.

[8] Suffice it to recall that mandate territories included territories which would later see violence, such as Iraq, Palestine and Lebanon.

[9] The Iraq Mandate was the only mandate which was explicitly cast in the form of a treaty.

that the Mandate had also been succeeded to. And then finally (but by no means exhaustively), there were those who pointed out that, while colloquially it could be deemed to be a treaty between the League and South Africa, it remained less than clear who was actually bound. The League as such? Only the League Council? The member states of the League? Or a combination of these options?[10]

All this may give the impression of being something of an esoteric discussion, but there are at least two points of relevance. First, if the Mandate was not, in the 1960s, a treaty or convention in force, it could not serve as the basis for the ICJ to exercise jurisdiction over any issues arising under the Mandate (in contentious proceedings; there would of course still be the possibility to ask for advisory opinions). The Mandate itself provided that recourse to the PCIJ was possible in disputes between South Africa and 'another member of the League'. If the Mandate could be considered a treaty in force, then it was possible to argue that jurisdiction was thus transferred to the ICJ, in accordance with Art. 37 of the ICJ Statute. If, however, the Mandate was nothing but an expired treaty, then obviously this compromissory clause would also have expired.

Secondly, if not a treaty but an executive decision of the League, then who could actually start proceedings against whom before the Court? The ICJ is only open to states, not international organizations. So even if the compromissory clause would have survived, it would remain unclear as to who could go to Court over the Mandate. In the end even the ICJ itself could not solve the riddles. It dealt with the Namibia Mandate on no less than six occasions, and addressed the Mandate's legal nature a few times, but only swerved in its opinions.[11]

The life and times of the Mandate go to show that there may be good reasons to devote some time to the analysis of the legal nature of instruments created by international organizations. While, as a matter of substantive law, what usually matters is simply the existence of legal rights and obligations, from a more procedural point of view it may well be important what form those rights and obligations have been given: ultimately the legitimacy of substantive norms may well depend (at least in part) on the form in which those norms are cast.[12]

Categories of instruments

A distinction is often made among various types of legal instruments according to what those instruments are supposed to do. Some aspire to be of a law-making nature, laying down more or less general abstract rules of general application, binding upon all subjects of a given legal system. EC regulations are perhaps the prime example: they aspire, so Article 249 (formerly Article 189) of the

---

[10] See generally the discussion in Jan Klabbers, *The Concept of Treaty in International Law* (The Hague, 1996), pp. 182–7.

[11] *Ibid.*, esp. pp. 186–7.

[12] For a general discussion, see Oscar Schachter, 'Alf Ross Memorial Lecture: The Crisis of Legitimation in the United Nations' (1981) 50 *Nordisk TIR*, 3–19.

TEC states, to bind all member states and they aspire to be directly applicable within those member states. And for some, much the same would apply to at least some of the decisions of the General Assembly. These too are thought by some observers to bind at least all member states of the UN, although pleas as to direct effect, or direct applicability, are heard less often.

Apart from acts aspiring to law-making, we may also distinguish acts that are more in the nature of applying the law to certain configurations of facts: more or less the equivalent of administrative acts. Examples are so-called 'decisions' in EC law, and perhaps also decisions taken by the Security Council.[13] The idea behind the latter was to create not so much a law-making organ, but rather an organ with the task of applying the law.

Third, then, there is the category of acts of a 'household nature'. While the term does not sound very sophisticated, it conveys with a reasonable degree of accuracy the idea that it involves acts relating to the (largely internal) functioning of the organization. Decisions relating to such things as the making of the budget or the election or selection of officials do not try to regulate behaviour in a general and abstract way.

And fourth, there is a large category of acts which aims to influence behaviour, but without creating law: many organs of many organizations habitually adopt recommendations, declarations, codes of conduct or generally non-binding resolutions.[14] This category also includes model laws on a given topic, which member states would be well advised (but not obligated) to implement.

As Tammes explains, the curious phenomenon of the non-binding instrument is the pragmatic answer to the dilemma that will inevitably face international organizations. If they provide that all decisions have to be taken unanimously, then the organization will be unworkable; majoritarian decision making will, however, scare off the states that have something to lose; hence, the non-binding resolution forms a halfway house, a useful device for taking action by majority decision, the only cost being that action thus taken creates no legal obligations.[15] That cost, however, may not be overly great, as many have observed that non-legally binding instruments may be quite as effective (or ineffective) as legally binding ones.[16]

---

[13] Increasingly, or so it seems, the Security Council makes use of a category invented in practice: presidential statements are used as the slightly less formal alternative to resolutions. See briefly Michael C. Wood, 'Security Council Working Methods and Procedure: Recent Developments' (1996) 45 *ICLQ*, 150–61, esp. p. 154. Incidentally, the effect of Security Council resolutions in domestic law is a matter of domestic law. See, e.g., the decision of the US Court of Appeals (D.C. Circuit) in *Diggs* v. *Schultz*, decision of 31 October 1971, in 60 *ILR* 393.

[14] The EC Treaty, in Art. 249 (formerly Art. 189), seems to recognize some of these (recommendations and opinions) as valuable policy instruments, but quickly adds that they 'shall have no binding force'.

[15] See A. J. P. Tammes, 'Decisions of International Organs as a Source of International Law' (1958/II) 94 *RdC*, 265–363, p. 304.

[16] A useful overview, suggesting that the distinction between legally binding and legally non-binding norms is not generally thought to be of great relevance, is Benedict Kingsbury, 'The Concept of Compliance as a Function of Competing Conceptions of International Law'.

In addition to the categories of clearly binding rules and clearly non-binding recommendations, many observers have seen fit to posit the grey in-between category of 'soft' law; although defined in various distinct ways, usually the concept of 'soft' law entails the notion that rules may exert influence without being clearly 'hard' law. Resolutions of organizations would typically come within this category: strictly speaking, they may not be law but they cannot be deemed to be devoid of legal effects.[17]

Popular as the idea of 'soft' law has become among scholars, it must be discarded. It is premised on the jurisprudentially dubious notion that legal rules may be more or less binding, and meets with little or no support in the decisions of judicial tribunals. Moreover, as 'soft' law typically is conceived as informal standard-setting without any control, it becomes a convenient tool for the exercise of naked political power by the powers that be.[18]

The division between law-making, the application of law and household acts is, of course, arbitrary (as is the distinction between legally binding and legally non-binding), and at times the dividing lines may be seriously blurred.[19] Moreover, there may also be instruments which, while clearly legal in one way or another, nevertheless do not fit in: a prime example is the directive in EC law, which leaves the member states free to decide on how to achieve a binding result.

Finally, there is the amorphous category of instruments adopted by the member states (rather than organs) of an organization, or by its organs but seemingly outside the regular decision-making procedures. An example is the declaration adopted by the Security Council meeting at the level of heads of states and governments (rather than the regular ambassadorial level) in January 1992; yet, it is especially around the EU that such instruments are concluded. The Charter on Fundamental Rights of the EU is but one of the more recent examples.[20]

The attraction of this type of instrument for negotiators resides, we may assume, precisely in their legally nebulous status. It often remains unclear whether such instruments are to be regarded as acts of the organization or

In Edith Brown Weiss (ed.), *International Compliance with Non-binding Accords* (Washington, 1997), 49–80.

[17] For a fairly representative example, see Paul C. Szasz, 'General Law-making Processes'. In Christopher C. Joyner (ed.), *The United Nations and International Law* (Cambridge 1997), pp. 27–64. With respect to the EC, see Francis Snyder, 'The Effectiveness of European Community Law: Institutions, Processes, Tools and Techniques' (1993) 56 *Modern Law Review*, 19–54, and K. C. Wellens and G. M. Borchardt, 'Soft Law in European Community Law' (1989) 14 *ELR*, 267–321. A rare monograph on the topic is Wolfgang Heusel, *'Weiches' Völkerrecht* (Baden Baden, 1991).

[18] See further Jan Klabbers, 'The Redundancy of Soft Law' (1996) 65 *Nordic JIL*, 167–82, and, by the same author, 'The Undesirability of Soft Law' (1998) 67 *Nordic JIL*, 381–91.

[19] Also due to the presence of hardly enforceable provisions in binding treaties. A classic example is Part IV of GATT.

[20] On the drafting thereof (itself unconventional), see Gráinne de Búrca, 'The Drafting of the European Union Charter of Fundamental Rights' (2001) 26 *ELR*, 126–38.

as acts of the member states *en groupe* (or *en petit comité*, as the case may be); consequently, it also remains unclear which legal effects such instruments engender. This, in turn, liberates the decision makers: where the law is unclear, executive power can act unchecked.

Three theories of law-making

Generally speaking, the constituent documents of international organizations will control the issue of law-making by international organizations, in various ways. Not only will they usually provide which legal acts may be taken by which organ, and according to which decision-making procedures, but they may also state the grounds for invalidity of those legal acts.

Those constituent instruments will shortly be discussed, but for the moment it is important to realize that while the constitution will, initially, control the issue, it will not be able to control it exhaustively. In other words: in practice all types of instruments may emerge which have not been envisaged in the constitutions, and law-making may also take place outside constitutionally controlled conditions.

This, in turn, makes it profitable to subject law-making within international organizations to a somewhat more theoretical analysis. Three main theories ('theories' is, actually, too grandiose a term) abound: the treaty-analogy, the theory of delegation and the theory of legislation. The first is largely discarded; the third is often considered as somewhat esoteric. Accordingly, the theory of delegation is most often adhered to.

The treaty-analogy underpinned the judgment of the Permanent Court of International Justice in the 1931 *Railway Traffic* case between Lithuania and Poland.[21] Poland and Lithuania had had some problems concerning the resumption of railway traffic between them after the First World War, and had submitted the matter to the Council of the League of Nations. The Council had issued a resolution to the effect that both parties were supposed to enter into negotiations. In 1931, the Court held this to be a binding obligation, albeit of rather limited scope.[22]

The interesting question is why the Court ascribed binding force to the terms of this resolution. The Covenant itself was silent on the legal force of resolutions: the Covenant of the League of Nations merely specified that decisions and resolutions were to be adopted by unanimity, save in purely procedural matters where a simple majority would suffice.

Still, the Court found that Lithuania and Poland were bound by the terms of the resolution, and explained this, with a fine disregard for theory, simply

---

[21] *Railway Traffic between Lithuania and Poland (Railway Sector Landwarów–Kaisiadorys)*, [1931] Publ. PCIJ, Series A/B, no. 42.

[22] The case is therefore often cited as authority on *pacta de negotiando*; for an overview, see Ulrich Beyerlin, 'Pactum de contrahendo und pactum de negotiando im Völkerrecht?' (1976) 36 *ZaöRV*, 407–43.

by pointing out that representatives of both states had 'participated in the adoption' of the resolution; they were 'bound by their acceptance'.[23]

Without putting too fine a point on it, the Court based its conclusion on what might be called the 'treaty analogy. Following this analogy, decisions of international bodies, if and where they require unanimity, can be considered as analogous to treaties, formulating the combined will of the participating states.[24] Therefore, when a member state has participated in the discussions and has not used its veto, its consent to be bound has been established, in much the same way as such consent is normally established by signature or ratification. And thus, it could be argued (and the Court apparently did so in 1931, without being very explicit), that decisions or resolutions of international organizations are really to be considered along the lines of treaties.

Nowadays, the theory that decisions of international organizations are to be regarded as somehow similar to treaties is largely discarded,[25] mainly because the theory is unable to explain the binding nature of majority decisions. After all, with majority decisions, one simply cannot say that all members have expressed their consent to be bound. Moreover, the treaty analogy, by reducing acts of organizations to treaties, in effect comes close to denying that the organization has an existence of its own: if there is no difference between a treaty and an organizational act, then what is the point of having an organization to begin with? Consequently, there must be something specific about legal acts of organizations: their binding nature, or otherwise as the case may be, must be explained on another basis.[26]

The most popular theoretical basis espoused (albeit rarely explicitly referred to) nowadays appears to be that the binding nature of acts of organizations can be explained on the basis of a delegation of powers.[27] In this view, the member states, when consenting to be bound to the constitution of an organization, may or may not give that organization the power to create binding rules of law. If and when they do, they can be seen to have delegated some law-making powers to that particular organization.[28]

---

[23] *Railway Traffic* case, p. 116.

[24] Or, perhaps more accurately, amounting to their 'disagreement reduced to writing', as Allott once defined treaties. See Philip Allott, 'The Concept of International Law' (1999) 10 *EJIL*, 31–50, p. 43.

[25] But see the decision of the EC Court in Case C-311/94, *Ijssel-Vliet Combinatie BV* v. *Ministry of Economic Affairs* [1996] ECR I-5023, arguing that the Netherlands had become bound by so-called 'guidelines' by virtue of having participated in their adoption.

[26] Detter, in a pioneering (if somewhat erratic) study, initially captures this by saying that legal instruments of organizations contain both consensual and statutory elements. See Ingrid Detter, *Law Making by International Organizations* (Stockholm, 1965), p. 54. Later she appears to discard the statutory element somewhat.

[27] So, e.g., *ibid.*, p. 322.

[28] Whether this is to be regarded as delegation in the classic sense is debatable: if it is true that delegates may not delegate further, as some contend (*delegatus non potest delegare*), then it would seem that treating any transfer of powers to an organization as an act of delegation makes delegation within the organization impossible. Thus, there must be two kinds of

The theory is strengthened by the consideration that, in some cases, domestic constitutions actually speak of delegating powers to international organizations. Thus, Article 92 of the Dutch Constitution provides that legislative, administrative and judicial powers may be delegated or assigned to international organizations.[29] On this view, then, the organization carries out the tasks assigned to it by its members; those members have given the organization the authority to do so, and have promised to accept valid decisions as binding. Here too, then, the binding effect derives ultimately from the consent of member states.

Both the treaty analogy and the delegation theory are founded upon positivist premises, and thus derive much of their attraction from fitting nicely into the main mode of international legal thinking. Both, after all, stress the importance of consent. While the delegation theory claims that expressing consent upon joining the organization suffices, the treaty analogy insists on consent with respect to every single instrument adopted. But the relevant point to note is that, in both cases, the consent of the member states is deemed decisive.

Still, inasmuch as the positivism underlying both theories has its traditional counterpart in natural law thinking, so too do these theories have their counterpart in the theory that some acts of international organizations can be explained, rather controversially, as instances of international legislation. The basic idea behind this notion is that the consent of states need not always be decisive, and may at times be overruled for the sake of the interests of mankind.

While this 'legislation' theory could possibly be employed to explain why formally binding decisions are binding, it is more often invoked to add legal force to the type of instruments which, according to the constituent documents from which they derive their authority, are non-binding. Thus, it is mostly encountered with respect to recommendations, declarations and the like, in particular those emanating from the single most comprehensive and universal organ the world knows: the General Assembly of the United Nations. In radical versions of the legislation theory, the General Assembly is sometimes even explicitly compared to an international parliament, which as such can simply create binding rules of law by majority.[30]

At their extremes, both the delegation theory (and the treaty-analogy) and the legislation theory are not completely satisfactory. If consent is all-decisive, then we might have problems not only in justifying the finding of implied law-making powers, but also in explaining the acknowledged effect that acts of

delegation: one from states to organizations, and one from organs to other organs. The leading study (which does not address this problem, though) is Danesh Sarooshi, *The United Nations and the Development of Collective Security: The Delegation by the UN Security Council of its Chapter VII Powers* (Oxford, 1999).

[29] The actual verb used is 'opdragen', the literal translation of which (i.e., 'to order') does not quite do it justice.

[30] See, e.g., T. O. Elias, 'Modern Sources of International Law'. In Wolfgang Friedmann *et al.* (eds.), *Transnational Law in a Changing Society: Essays in Honor of Philip C. Jessup* (New York, 1972), pp. 34–69, p. 51.

organizations may have on the development of custom. Thus, in the *Nicaragua* case,[31] the ICJ has held that at the very least some resolutions adopted by the General Assembly can be evidence of *opinio juris*, and, indeed, so much so that if there is plenty of evidence of *opinio juris*, then there is no overwhelming need to find evidence of state practice. And if we take that to the extreme, then we come closer to the legislation theory than to the delegation theory.

The legislation theory, on the other hand, cannot fully overcome the absence of an explicit power to legislate in the constituent documents of international organizations and, moreover, has problems in living up to its name. As we will see, it is still relatively rare that binding instruments are adopted; it is rarer still that binding instruments are adopted against the wishes of member states.[32]

Still, some organizations can meaningfully be said to have law-making powers, however limited. An example is the International Civil Aviation Authority (ICAO) which, on the basis of Article 12 of the Chicago Convention, has the power to establish rules regulating aircraft flying over the high seas.[33] Other instruments emanating from ICAO come close: states are expected to implement Standards and Recommended Practices to the extent practicable. These, Yemin suggests, therewith carry a qualified legal force.[34]

Similarly, the WHO can, on the basis of Article 21 WHO, enact regulations on such issues as the names to be used to describe diseases, or sanitary and quarantine regulations. These become binding on member states, unless a state opts out within a fixed period of time.[35] Likewise, within the North East Atlantic Fisheries Commission, so-called 'recommendations' nonetheless acquire binding force for those who do not object to them.[36] While the sceptic could argue that opting out embodies a contractual element, others might say that such regulations nonetheless become binding without specific consent by states: states need not consent; instead, they need to express dissent if they wish to prevent being bound by the regulation.[37]

While not directly binding on its member states, safety standards adopted by the International Atomic Energy Agency (IAEA) are binding on IAEA's own operations and, more importantly, on all operation by states in which IAEA somehow participates.[38] Alvarez suggests, moreover, that IAEA standards may become binding on states by virtue of having been incorporated in another

---

[31] *Military and paramilitary activities in and against Nicaragua* (*Nicaragua* v. *USA*), merits, [1986] ICJ Reports 14.

[32] Note also that this entails that the legislation theory, ostensibly the opposite of the treaty-analogy, actually becomes indistinguishable from it as long as unanimity is required.

[33] See Art. 12 ICAO; an early discussion is Yemin, Legislative Powers, pp. 146–7.

[34] *Ibid.*, p. 149.

[35] See, e.g., David Fidler, 'The Future of the World Health Organization: What Role for International Law?', (1998) 31 *Vanderbilt JTL*, 1079–1126, esp. 1086–9.

[36] See Philippe Sands and Pierre Klein, *Bowett's Law of International Institutions*, 5th edn (London, 2001), p. 283. The new constituent document of NEAFC, dated 2007, leaves this intact (see Art. 12).

[37] For such an approach, see Yemin, *Legislative Powers*, pp. 201–2.

[38] For brief discussion, see Hans Blix, 'The Role of the IAEA in the Development of International Law' (1989) 58 *Nordic JIL*, 231–42.

instrument, in this case a Security Council resolution.[39] A similar technique ascribes legal force to the Codex Alimentarius: this initially non-binding set of guidelines on food safety, a joint venture of the Food and Agriculture Organization (FAO) and WHO, may be relied on by WTO member states to justify domestic food safety standards under the WTO's Agreement on the Application of Sanitary and Phytosanitary Measures.[40]

More broadly, the WTO is said to have legislative powers in the field of food safety (on the basis of Article 4 of the same Agreement) and on standard setting in the field of services (with respect to such things as recognition of professional qualifications), although it has been reluctant to make full use of the latter, seemingly preferring the treaty form for the time being.[41]

Most prominently, perhaps, it has been suggested that in recent years the Security Council has started to legislate.[42] Some of the Council's resolutions on terrorism and disarmament are seen to go beyond merely applying existing law and, instead, seem to lay down new rules.

That is not to say law-making by the Council is by definition normatively desirable: while some claim that the Council, being a small and relatively nimble organ, can enact in accordance with the needs of international community,[43] others may point out that the Council's composition is not very representative of that international community, and thus is hardly in a position to define its needs. As a result, Council legislation may always be tainted by a lack of legitimacy, unless it becomes, somehow, more representative.[44]

Non-binding instruments

Under the United Nations Charter, the powers of the General Assembly are rather limited. In certain household matters, the power of the Assembly to take binding decisions is undisputed. Thus, as discussed earlier, under Article 4 the Assembly has the final say about admission of members, and under Article 17 it has the power of the purse: not only can it approve the budget, it can also decide on the apportionment. To this may be added the power to suspend rights and privileges under Article 5 as well as under Article 19. To some extent those are

---

[39] See Alvarez, *Law-makers*, p. 231. It concerns Security Council Resolution 1540.

[40] *Ibid.*, p. 222 (referring to the WTO's Technical Barriers to Trade agreement, though).

[41] See the discussion in Mary E. Footer, *An Institutional and Normative Analysis of the World Trade Organization* (Leiden, 2006), pp. 282–91.

[42] See, briefly, Paul Szasz, 'The Security Council Starts Legislating' (2002) 96 *AJIL*, 901–5; Matthew Happold, 'Security Council Resolution 1373 and the Constitution of the United Nations' (2003) 16 *Leiden JIL*, 593–610.

[43] See Eric Rosand, 'The Security Council as "Global Legislator": *Ultra Vires* or Ultra Innovative?' (2004–5) 28 *Fordham International Law Journal*, 542–90.

[44] For an overview of the debate, see Jan Klabbers, 'Reflections on the Politics of Institutional Reform'. In Peter Danchin and Horst Fischer (eds.), *United Nations Reform and the New Collective Security* (Cambridge 2009, forthcoming). An excellent discussion on how the Council is used, in turn, to legitimize national policies is Ian Hurd, *After Anarchy: Legitimacy and Power in the United Nations Security Council* (Princeton, 2007).

household matters; to another extent they are administrative in nature, thus already indicating the difficulties involved in drawing the line.

However, there is no explicit law-making power to be found in the Charter, and no tribunal has ever reached the conclusion that the General Assembly has a general implied power to make law. Perhaps the closest has been a decision of the Guatemalan Supreme Court in 1952, in the *Klahr Ehlert* case, where it held the Universal Declaration on Human Rights (adopted by the Assembly in 1948) to be superior to conflicting domestic law.[45]

Short of this case, however, there have been few such exercises. That is not to say that occasionally General Assembly resolutions have not been treated as being legally relevant by courts, because they have. Indeed, sometimes domestic courts have a hard time distinguishing between various sorts of legal instruments, and may easily confuse Assembly resolutions with treaties.[46] Still, in its 1966 decision on South West Africa, the ICJ remarked flatly and clearly that whatever persuasive force Assembly resolutions might possess (and this could be very considerable), this force operated on the political and not the legal level.[47]

In the absence of a general law-making power vested in the General Assembly, the legal effects of General Assembly resolutions have been explained along a couple of lines.[48] Thus, following a first line of argument, they may reflect 'authoritative interpretations' of the UN Charter.[49] For instance, if the Assembly decides on the meaning of 'aggression',[50] for example, this could be taken as an interpretation of the word 'aggression' as used in the Charter, and coming from the Assembly such an interpretation would be more authoritative than if it were suggested by, for example, some textbook writer.

There are, however, two problems with this approach. One is that the Charter does not explicitly authorize the General Assembly to make authoritative interpretations,[51] although it does not forbid it either. At any rate, the power of

---

[45] As referred to in Krzysztof Skubiszewski, 'Recommendations of the United Nations and Municipal Courts' (1972–3) 46 *BYIL*, 353–64.

[46] Thus, in *Huynh Thi Anh and another* v. *Levi and others*, the US Court of Appeals for the 6th Circuit argued that the Universal Declaration of Human Rights (i.e., a General Assembly resolution) was not self-executing, a term arguably more properly used in connection with treaties: decision of 20 October 1978, in 95 *ILR* 494.

[47] *South West Africa Cases* (*Ethiopia* v. *South Africa*; *Liberia* v. *South Africa*), second phase, [1966] ICJ Reports 6, para. 98.

[48] For a comprehensive overview, see Blaine Sloan, 'General Assembly Resolutions Revisited (Forty Years Later)' (1987) 58 *BYIL*, 39–150. Arguably the most sophisticated discussion has been conducted in the pages of *AJIL* between Richard Falk and Nicholas Onuf in the late 1960s. The discussion is reproduced in Jan Klabbers (ed.), *International Organizations* (Aldershot, 2005), pp. 297–313.

[49] See, e.g., with some approval, G. J. H. van Hoof, *Rethinking the Sources of International Law* (Deventer, 1983), p. 181.

[50] See resolution 3314 (XXIX) of 14 December 1974.

[51] In a similar vein, Gennady M. Danilenko, *Law-making in the International Community* (Dordrecht, 1994), p. 205. See also the decision of the US Court of Appeals (9th Circuit) in *Karadzole et al.* v. *Artukovic* (decision of 24 June 1957, in 24 *ILR* 510), emphasizing that

the Assembly to make such authoritative interpretation is thus itself in need of justification, and absent an explicit power, most writers adhere to some form of implied or perhaps inherent power.[52]

Second, it still leaves the position of states who voted against any particular resolution unclear: should they abide by the majority position, or not? Of course, if the Charter itself would provide an explicit power, a version of the delegation theory could be invoked, but with implied powers this will be more difficult: unless the 'implication' is overly obvious, member states may always argue that they never intended the Assembly to have powers to make authoritative interpretations, and that these therefore may not too easily be implied.

 A second approach has been to regard at least some resolutions as being declarative of international law.[53] Thus, if the Assembly prohibits the resort to aggression, it does not create law, but merely declares law. But as such, apart again from the lack of an explicit power to declare the state of the law, the one problem is of course that as a matter of principle a declaration made by the Assembly as to the state of international law is not inherently different from that made by any other body. The difference is one of degree, not necessarily one of kind.

Having said that, though, at the very least General Assembly resolutions can be seen as evidence of *opinio juris*, as indeed the ICJ clarified in 1986 in the *Nicaragua* case,[54] and confirmed in its opinion on the legality of nuclear weapons.[55] And that leads to a third explanation, which comes in various shades: General Assembly resolutions as customary international law. Well settled, already before the *Nicaragua* decision, is the version which says that indeed they may reflect *opinio juris*.[56] But then again, as such that does not mean too much: *opinio juris* alone is not law-creative, according to traditional sources doctrine, but needs to be accompanied by state practice, and, moreover,

Assembly resolutions 'have not sufficient force of law to modify long standing interpretations of similar treaty provisions'.

[52] See, e.g., Obed Y. Asamoah, *The Legal Significance of the Declarations of the General Assembly of the United Nations* (The Hague, 1966), esp. pp. 34–5.

[53] Indeed, some resolutions are given the title 'Declaration', which suggests a degree of importance that ordinary resolutions lack. However, as the UN's Office of Legal Affairs explains: 'In the practice of the United Nations a Declaration is a formal and solemn instrument suitable for those occasions when principles considered to be of special importance are being enunciated. Apart from the solemnity and formality associated with a declaration there is legally no distinction between a declaration and a recommendation which is less formal.' See UNJY (1981), p. 149.

[54] *Nicaragua* case, para. 188. Strikingly though, the ICJ often conceptualizes General Assembly resolutions as representing the *opinio juris* of the UN's member states (rather than that of the Assembly). See Jan Klabbers, 'International Organizations in the Formation of Customary International Law'. In Enzo Cannizzaro and Paolo Palchetti (eds.), *Customary International Law on the Use of Force* (Leiden, 2005), pp. 179–95.

[55] *Legality of the threat or use of nuclear weapons*, advisory opinion, [1996] ICJ Reports 226, para. 70.

[56] Compare, e.g., Van Hoof, *Rethinking the Sources*, p. 182.

states who vote against, and perhaps even those who abstain, thereby indicate that they do not share the *opinio juris* of the majority.[57]

So the question arose of what to do with state practice. In the 1960s, inspired by the rapid acceptance of a few Assembly resolutions on outer space, Professor Bin Cheng suggested the concept of 'instant custom', which is, of course, a contradiction in terms.[58] In his view, if the nature of a certain topic was such as to render any state practice scarce by definition (after all, how many astronauts and space ships are there?), then the element of practice would not truly be necessary.

Others have argued that the practice of states within the Assembly itself should qualify as state practice for purposes of the formation of customary law.[59] Thus, voting and debating should be worth the same as, or perhaps even more than, actual behaviour. Still others have pointed out that this may border on the absurd, because the only practice in the Assembly is indeed that of debating and voting. So at best customary rules could arise relating to debating behaviour and voting procedures, but not much else.[60]

Yet another explanation, of limited scope, comes close to the treaty-analogy mentioned above. On this view, resolutions may embody the agreement of the states that voted for them and can therefore be considered as agreements in simplified form. The limitation is clear, however: due to the rule that treaties can create neither rights nor obligations for states without their consent, resolutions as treaties in simplified form cannot bind those who abstained from voting or voted against them.[61]

A final explanation for the legal effects of General Assembly resolutions has centred around the notion of estoppel. Under this version, at the very least a state which has voted for something would be precluded from practising the opposite, not because General Assembly resolutions are legally binding, but because you cannot give false impressions; you cannot blow hot and cold.[62]

---

[57] It has, however, been argued that the traditional doctrine of customary law is going through an identity crisis. For a critical assessment, see Bruno Simma and Philip Alston, 'The Sources of Human Rights Law: Custom, Jus Cogens, and General Principles' (1992) 12 *Australian YIL*, 82–108.

[58] Bin Cheng, 'United Nations Resolutions on Outer Space: "Instant" International Customary Law?'. Reproduced in Bin Cheng (ed.), *International Law: Teaching and Practice* (London, 1982), pp. 237–62.

[59] So, e.g., Asamoah, *Declarations of the General Assembly*, p. 54, holding that votes amount to state practice because voting is a formal act, and all formal acts would qualify as state practice.

[60] A witty example is Iain MacGibbon, 'General Assembly Resolutions: Custom, Practice and Mistaken Identity'. In Bin Cheng (ed.), *Teaching and Practice*, pp. 10–26.

[61] See, e.g., Asamoah, *Declarations of the General Assembly*, pp. 63–7. Note that in such a view the specific nature of an organizational act gets lost; instead, the resolution becomes the collective act of individual states, which effectively denies the organization its separate identity.

[62] So, e.g., seemingly, Tammes (his words are not unambiguous), 'Decisions of International Organs', p. 338, claiming that a government that voted in favour of a resolution may be 'legally estopped from refusing to accept the instrument'.

Here too, however, criticism has been easily forthcoming, and rather predictable: the estoppel argument is vulnerable to the criticism that voting is not the same as making promises or acting so as to give rise to expectations. Of course, if you make a promise, you have to make good on it; if you consistently act in a certain way, you cannot later deny doing so, but if you vote in favour of a resolution urging South Africa to abolish apartheid, can you be considered as bound by that resolution? You would be estopped from denying that you ever said apartheid was a bad thing, but not necessarily from much more, which indicates that, at most, the estoppel explanation has but a limited range.

At best, then, there is the point Sir Hersch Lauterpacht made long ago: resolutions of the General Assembly are binding in the sense that United Nations members must consider them in good faith,[63] and Lauterpacht, with characteristic seriousness and optimism,[64] underlined that this was not an empty obligation.

On the other hand, as the ICJ stated in 1988 in the *Transborder Armed Action* case between Honduras and Nicaragua, good faith itself does not create legal obligations.[65] While legal obligations must be fulfilled in good faith (without good faith, it is difficult to think of law at all), good faith cannot turn an obligation which is not legal into one that is. In short: even if states would be (as Lauterpacht probably meant) under the moral obligation to consider resolutions in good faith, that alone cannot turn them into law.[66]

The main reason why so much attention has been paid to Assembly resolutions is the simple fact that the UN is the only universal organization of broad competence. The UN is a forum where all states (with only a handful of exceptions) meet regularly to discuss a whole range of topics.[67] It is somewhat curious and unsatisfactory to consider the possibility that all this work may be legally inconsequential, or at best have indirect consequences: for instance through the back door of custom. This may perhaps also explain why the debates concerning the legal effect of formally non-binding acts have been less prominent in other settings.

---

[63] *Voting procedure on questions relating to reports and petitions concerning the territory of South-West Africa*, advisory opinion, [1955] ICJ Reports 67, separate opinion Judge Lauterpacht, at 118–19: A resolution recommending a specific course of action 'creates *some* legal obligation which, however rudimentary, elastic and imperfect, is nevertheless a legal obligation . . . The State in question, while not bound to accept the recommendation, is bound to give it due consideration in good faith' (emphasis in original).

[64] For a wonderful analysis of Lauterpacht's thinking, see Martti Koskenniemi, 'Lauterpacht: The Victorian Tradition in International Law' (1997) 8 *EJIL*, 215–63.

[65] *Border and transborder armed actions* (*Nicaragua* v. *Honduras*), jurisdiction of the Court and admissibility of the application, [1988] ICJ Reports 69, para. 94.

[66] As Tammes, 'Decisions of International Organs', p. 341, put it succinctly, the very idea behind non-binding instruments is that they leave the addressee freedom to act.

[67] It has also been observed that as a global body with broad jurisdiction, the General Assembly is less likely to be captured by special interests than organizations with more limited mandates. See Alan Boyle and Christine Chinkin, *The Making of International Law* (Oxford, 2007), pp. 117–8.

Perhaps most curious is the case of the OECD. Within the OECD, there has arisen the habit of adopting only documents which are formally non-binding: guidelines, model agreements, et cetera. And those non-binding instruments purport to regulate quite important things: credit insurance, restrictive business practices – in short, important economic and financial issues. Yet, adherence to them is not legally required, but, in practice, those instruments are among the most successful (in terms of compliance) international legal instruments. It turns out that many members of the OECD give effect to those instruments in their national legislations, and that domestic courts do not shy away from applying them, even if no transformation has taken place.

A leading illustration is the 1977 *Badger* case. Desiring to shut down its Belgian subsidiary, Badger US planned to let the Belgian company (organized as an independent entity) go bankrupt rather than use its US funds to help pay the separation payment prescribed by Belgian law. Still, after an OECD Committee had found that, under the 1976 Guidelines for Multinational Enterprises, parent companies sometimes are 'morally responsible' for the liabilities of their subsidiaries, the company reconsidered and a compromise was reached.[68]

And, as if to illustrate the fluidity of categories, OECD acts come interestingly close to such phenomena as self-regulation by industries. A good example thereof is constituted by the standard-setting activities, in terms both of quality control of products and of environmental certification, of the International Organization for Standardization (ISO), an organization comprised of national standardization organizations and as such non-governmental rather than governmental.[69]

It has also been suggested that even the non-deontic acts of international organizations (i.e., acts that do not purport to recommend or command) may nonetheless engender legal effects. Thus, the OECD exercises quite a bit of influence on national education policies through its Program on International Student Assessment (PISA), despite the fact that PISA does not purport to set any standards. It merely tests students and ranks the results, but that alone has been seen to exercise a considerable hold over national policy-makers in the field of education.[70]

EC instruments

In some organizations, there can be no misunderstandings about the legal nature of particular acts. Thus, Article 249 (ex-Article 189) of the TEC clearly

[68] For more details, see Ignaz Seidl-Hohenveldern, 'International Economic "Soft Law"' (1979/II) 163 *RdC*, 165–246, pp. 209–10.
[69] For a brief overview, see Naomi Roht-Arriaza, 'Compliance with Private Voluntary Standards: The Example of the International Organization for Standardization's ISO 14000 Environmental Management and Related Standards'. In Brown Weiss (ed.), *International Compliance with Nonbinding Accords*, pp. 205–18.
[70] See the ground-breaking article by Armin von Bogdandy and Matthias Goldmann, 'The Exercise of Public Authority through National Policy Assessment' (2008) 5 *IOLR* (forthcoming).

indicates that regulations, directives and decisions are binding.[71] In contrast, recommendations and opinions 'shall have no binding force'.

That sounds simple and convenient, but in practice is a bit more resilient, largely for two reasons. First of all, the boundaries between the various types of instruments mentioned in Article 249 may at times be blurred; and secondly, in practice the Community institutions have created a whole range of instruments not mentioned in the treaty, whose legal nature is therefore sometimes in doubt.[72]

Regulations are *par excellence* the instruments for EC law-making, binding as they are in their entirety and being directly applicable.[73] That has two important consequences. First, a regulation, being directly applicable, enters the domestic legal orders of the member states without further ado, and is superior to domestic law, even if the latter is later in time.[74] Second, the member states are not supposed to tamper with regulations, are not even supposed to perform any transformation operation, for doing so might make inroads into their direct applicability and result in local differences.[75]

Directives, on the other hand, are only binding as far as their result is concerned, and leave the member states the choice as to how to achieve that result. This, in turn, implies a transformation of some sort, and therefore directives come with deadlines: they must be transposed within a certain period of time. If not, then the member state can be held liable,[76] and it has become clear that individuals can derive some benefits from directives which have passed their deadlines without being (properly) implemented.[77]

Decisions, finally, are best regarded as administrative acts. The Commission, for example, may decide whether or not a proposed merger between two companies meets with the requirements of the merger regulation. It may also decide whether the behaviour of a company amounts to abuse of a dominant position, or whether public health concerns may make it necessary to ban the export of British beef.

These decisions are, of course, binding (Article 249 says so explicitly), but generally speaking they do not create abstract and generally applicable rules of

---

[71] Still useful is Richard H. Lauwaars, *Lawfulness and Legal Force of Community Decisions* (Leiden, 1973), esp. pp. 5–54.

[72] Compare generally Jan Klabbers, 'Informal Instruments before the European Court of Justice' (1994) 31 *CMLRev*, 997–1023.

[73] On the notion of direct applicability, see J. A. Winter, 'Direct Applicability and Direct Effect: Two Distinct and Different Concepts in Community Law' (1972) 9 *CMLRev*, 425–38; see also Pavlos Eleftheriadis, 'The Direct Effect of Community Law: Conceptual Issues' (1996) 16 *YEL*, 205–21.

[74] The seminal case is case 6/64, *Flaminio Costa* v. *ENEL* [1964] ECR 585.

[75] See, e.g., case 50/76, *Amsterdam Bulb* v. *Produktschap voor Siergewassen* [1977] ECR 137, para. 7: the members may not adopt 'any measure which would conceal the Community nature and effects' of a regulation.

[76] See, e.g., joined cases C-6/90 and C-9/90, *Andrea Francovich and others* v. *Italy* [1991] ECR I-5357.

[77] See, e.g., case 14/83, *Von Colson and Kamann* v. *Land Nordrhein-Westphalen* [1984] ECR 1891.

behaviour. Still, while they are formally binding upon their addressee only, they may be addressed to all member states. It may at times be difficult to distinguish a decision from a regulation, or to distinguish a regulation from a directive. As a general rule, the ECJ has indicated that one should judge them by their contents, not by their designation. Thus, a so-called regulation may well turn out to be a decision in disguise; a so-called directive may well turn out to be a regulation. Speaking generally, the Court has developed several rules of thumb to distinguish them: if general and abstract, then it is probably not a decision, but either a directive or a regulation. If it leaves member states a lot of discretion, then it will be a directive; if it leaves member states hardly any discretion at all, then we might be in the presence of a regulation.[78]

The implications are especially important from the point of view of legal protection: individuals and companies may go to the Court to have the legality of decisions reviewed (but not of regulations or decisions addressed to others, unless these are of direct and individual concern to them[79]), and may perhaps attack a regulation through the back door of the so-called 'plea of illegality' provided for in Article 241 (ex-Article 184) TEC, but have no means to combat directives.

Either way, it is clear that regulations, directives and decisions derive their binding nature from the Treaty. However, this is not the case with other instruments.[80] The Community has adopted, for instance, action programmes, not mentioned in the treaty. In some cases, the institutions issue guidelines, or codes of conduct, or resolutions. Again, these are not mentioned in Article 249 of the TEC. Still, by focusing on their contents, the Court has most often found some legal obligation to be contained in them, presumably on the theory that such instruments would not be made if there was not the intention to have them adhered to.[81] The only exceptions, broadly speaking, have related to cases where other pertinent rules of law interfered. Thus, for example, the Court has not been very friendly towards instruments adopted by the Council which went against the basic treaty. This the Court considered to be tantamount to an amendment, and, since the treaty has prescribed an amendment procedure, the Court left the Council instrument without legal effect.[82]

A new development, and perhaps somewhat typical of the EC, is the so-called 'inter-institutional agreement'.[83] Sometimes Council, Commission and

---

[78] See, e.g., case 6/68, *Zuckerfabrik Watenstedt* v. *Council* [1968] ECR 409.

[79] And the Court has approached this rather strictly. See, e.g., case 25/62, *Plaumann & Co.* v. *Commission* [1963] ECR 95.

[80] Although the amorphous category of so-called '*sui generis* decisions' (a catch-all phrase which, paradoxically, does not catch all things left unmentioned in Art. 249 EC) seems to have attained a quasi-formal character, at least with textbook writers. For an early analysis, see Lauwaars, *Lawfulness and Legal Force*, pp. 50–4.

[81] See generally Klabbers, 'Informal Instruments'.

[82] Case 43/75, *Defrenne* v. *Sabena* [1976] ECR 455.

[83] See Jörg Monar, 'Interinstitutional Agreements: The Phenomenon and its New Dynamics after Maastricht' (1994) 31 *CMLRev*, 693–719.

Parliament (in various combinations) issue a joint declaration or conclude a joint agreement, for example on the budget procedure. How should these be treated? Nothing in the EC Treaty refers to such instruments, but again the Court appears to have treated them as binding upon the institutions.

Here, again, a jurisprudential problem may arise: are they also binding upon the member states? Obviously, an inter-institutional agreement between the Commission and the EP cannot bind member states, since neither the Commission nor the EP is to be viewed as representing member states. But what if the Council is involved? Here things are less clear. If we regard the Council as representing members individually and jointly, then Council participation may well bind the member states. The one remaining problem would be one of voting behaviour: if a state voted against the agreement, it may escape its binding force. Presumably, though, such agreements are not the result of majority voting, but either of unanimity or of consensus, so this particular risk is not all that great. If, however, we view the Council as a separate institution with a separate identity, then things are less clear. On such a theory, we could argue that Council acts can only bind the Council, not its individual members.

Presumably, though, the Court will be somewhat hesitant to let member states hide behind the Council, purely for practical reasons: separating the Council from the members would render it possible for any individual member state to undermine EC law. If the separation were allowed, the Council could make deals, but all individual member states could later claim not to be bound, and therefore do as they please. Clearly, this would spell disaster for the integration process.

Some scholars have explained the binding force of inter-institutional agreements on the basis of a so-called 'Organtreue': a duty of the Community institutions to co-operate.[84] As the member states themselves are under a duty to co-operate which is found in Article 10 of the TEC (ex-Article 5, laying down the notion of 'Gemeinschaftstreue'), so too the institutions would be subject to 'Organtreue'.[85] The Final Act of the Nice Conference, adopted in February 2001, confirmed as much: it contains a declaration according to which the Conference 'recalls' that the duty of solidarity also comprises the institutions. Accordingly, the Conference is firmly of the view that inter-institutional agreements bind the institutions by virtue of 'Organtreue', and linked this 'Organtreue' explicitly to the 'Gemeinschaftstreue' of Article 10 of the TEC. It adds, understandably, that

---

[84] See Marijke Gauweiler, *Die rechtliche Qualifikation interorganschaftlicher Absprachen im Europarecht* (Mainz, 1988).

[85] Sometimes reference is made to Case 204/86, *Greece* v. *Council* [1988] ECR 5323. The Court here spoke of 'mutual duties of sincere cooperation' between the institutions (in para. 16), but did so in the context of the budgetary procedure envisaged in the Treaty itself rather than by pointing to an inter-institutional agreement. It also pointed to an earlier decision in which it had derived a duty of obligation between institutions and member states from Art. 10 (formerly Art. 5) of the TEC, notwithstanding the circumstance that Art. 10 does not address the institutions at all.

inter-institutional agreements may not amend or supplement the EC Treaty itself.[86]

While this sends a clear enough signal from the member states, it is perhaps useful to note that the legal status of declarations of this sort is itself subject to debate.[87] In this light, we might still ground the legal force of inter-institutional agreements in considerations of utility: why conclude such inter-institutional agreements, if not to undertake certain duties and have your counterpart reciprocate?[88]

Occasionally, the EC Court goes (or so it seems) beyond Article 249 (ex-Article 189) of the TEC. For instance, in 1989, it held that a recommendation had certain legal effects, despite the explicit wording of Article 249. The case concerned a Mr Salvatore Grimaldi, an Italian-born miner who had been living and working in Belgium for thirty years.[89] He contracted an occupational disease, and was no longer fit to do his job. Under Belgian law, he would be entitled to some compensation had he been a Belgian national. Alas, he did not have Belgian nationality, but had always remained an Italian national. EC law was silent on the point: there were no regulations or directives. There was only a recommendation, to the effect that member states should extend benefits for occupational diseases to those Community nationals living in their territory.

The Court found that, although the recommendation had no binding effect, in the absence of binding EC law it had to be taken into account when interpreting domestic law. Thus, the Belgian courts could apply Belgian law, but had to take the recommendation into account – that could only mean one thing: the recommendation produced legal effects after all.

The precise legal basis for the Court's decision remains somewhat unclear. Perhaps the Court simply felt sorry for Mr Grimaldi; perhaps it was displeased with Belgium for ignoring the recommendation (which itself would require an explanation); perhaps again it argued that, where there is an instrument, adopting the instrument cannot, despite the terms of Article 249, be a completely gratuitous act.

Decisions taken under the so-called 'second and third pillars' of the EU (foreign policy decisions and criminal policy decisions, respectively) also come under various headings, most notably as 'common positions' and as 'joint actions'. Both types are generally adopted by unanimous agreement of the member states, and are generally considered to bind those member states, at least towards each other. Whether they can also bind the EU itself *vis-à-vis* third

---

[86] Final Act of the Conference of the Representatives of the Governments of the Member States, Nice, February 2001, Declaration No. 3.

[87] See, e.g., A. G. Toth, 'The Legal Status of the Declarations Annexed to the Single European Act' (1986) 23 *CMLRev*, 803–12.

[88] This appears to be the reasoning underlying Monar's finding that inter-institutional agreements generally are not devoid of legal effects. See Monar, 'Interinstitutional Agreements'.

[89] Case C-322/88, *Salvatore Grimaldi* v. *Fonds des maladies professionelles* [1989] ECR I-4407.

parties depends on such factors as the intent underlying them, as well as good faith and estoppel.[90]

In other organizations things are, generally speaking, a lot less complicated than in the EU, and are to some extent still comparable to the classic treaty analogy: a decision of an organization reflects the unanimous agreement of its member states in much the same way as a treaty does. The main differences relate to formalities: thus, adoption by a vote or by consensus will be viewed as the expression of consent to be bound; ratification or signature are not specifically required. And there may also be other differences of a more or less formal nature. Thus, the decisions may perhaps be revised by adopting a new decision, whereas a regular treaty would require either an amendment or a completely new agreement, both of which may be harder to attain. Still, the number of organizations that can take binding decisions by some form of majority procedure (thus outvoting some member states) remains low,[91] and where binding decisions can be made they relate predominantly to procedural matters.

Adopting conventions

It is much more usual for organizations to contribute to the development of international law by sponsoring the conclusion of treaties.[92] Here, of course, consent is of fundamental importance; in that respect there is no difference from treaties concluded outside the frameworks of international organizations.

What is different though is that the drafting will be done differently.[93] Thus, at least within the UN system, an important role is played by the International Law Commission, which, responsible as it is for the codification and progressive development of international law, has been the breeding ground for a number of important conventions, such as the 1969 Vienna Convention on the Law of Treaties.

Another difference with the drafting of treaties within international organizations as compared to regular treaties is that those drafted within organizations

---

[90] See, e.g., Leonard Besselink, 'Tussen supranationaliteit en soevereiniteit: over het nietcommunautaire recht van de Europese Unie'. In Leonard Besselink *et al.*, *Europese Unie en nationale soevereiniteit* (Deventer, 1997), pp. 125–58; see also Martti Koskenniemi, 'International Law Aspects of the Common Foreign and Security Policy'. In Martti Koskenniemi (ed.), *International Law Aspects of the European Union* (The Hague, 1998), pp. 27–44.

[91] Similarly, Felice Morgenstern, *Legal Problems of International Organizations* (Cambridge, 1986), p. 91; see generally also Frederic L. Kirgis, Jr, 'Specialized Law-making Processes'. In Joyner (ed.), *The United Nations and International Law*, pp. 65–94.

[92] See Morgenstern, *Legal Problems*, p. 104, referring to the multilateral treaty as the 'favourite tool' in the standard-setting activities of international organizations.

[93] For a discussion relating to the erstwhile OAU and addressing the drafting of the Protocol on the Establishment of an African Court on Human and Peoples' Rights, see Tiyanjana Maluwa, 'International Law-making in the Organisation of African Unity: An Overview' (2000) 12 *African Journal of International & Comparative Law*, 201–25.

will usually involve all members of the organization, including those that have no intention whatsoever of becoming contracting parties to the treaty under negotiation.[94] And even the life of the treaty once it has entered into force may involve what are still non-parties, for instance when the organization is given a role in the supervision of the agreement or the amendment of its provisions.[95]

International organizations may use different techniques when it comes to sponsoring treaties. The standard technique is simply to draft a treaty which will then become binding upon those who ratify it. This is frequently resorted to by the General Assembly, prime examples being the 1948 Genocide Convention and the two Human Rights Covenants of 1966. Thus, the Assembly drafts and adopts a convention (often on the basis of an earlier resolution or a set of resolutions), after which it will typically be opened for signature and ratification.

Similarly, a number of treaties have been concluded within the framework of the Council of Europe, including the European Human Rights Convention and the European Social Charter. In essence, their main practical difference from regular treaties is that they have been drafted under the auspices of an organization, and that may imply that the drafting conference does not establish its own procedures, but uses those of the organization in question.[96]

A second technique is to adopt conventions but, instead of insisting on ratification, to allow rather for so-called 'opting-out' procedures. Thus, member states will have a certain period of time in which they can make it known that they do not accept a certain convention. Several organizations use variations on this theme. Thus, as noted above, the WHO can adopt 'regulations' which require opting-out,[97] whereas ICAO adopts so-called 'international standards' which come close enough (the way to escape is to specify that your national standards are different).[98]

Such opting-out procedures may appear to be a decent compromise between traditional reliance on opting-in (ratification) and majority decision making. Yet, they are not unproblematic. It has been noted that with ICAO, for example,

---

[94] See also Shabtai Rosenne, 'United Nations Treaty Practice' (1954/II) 86 *RdC*, 281–443, pp. 308–9 and esp. pp. 330–46.

[95] Thus, Art. 90, para. 2, of the 1990 International Convention on the Protection of the Rights of all Migrant Workers and Members of their Families provides that amendments require the approval of the General Assembly plus acceptance by a majority of the parties to the Convention. The text is reproduced in (1991) 30 *ILM* 1517.

[96] Likewise, the World Bank played an important facilitating role in the creation of the Multilateral Investment Guarantee Agency. See Ibrahim Shihata, 'The Multilateral Investment Guarantee Agency (MIGA) and the Legal Treatment of Foreign Investment' (1987/III) 203 *RdC*, 95–320, esp. 142–7.

[97] Article 22 WHO. It has been noted though that the WHO has made scant use of this facility: using it only twice in its first fifty years. See Fidler, 'The Future of the World Health Organization', esp. pp. 1087–9.

[98] Article 38 ICAO. Art. 8 UNESCO obligates member states to report on their practice concerning Conventions and Recommendations, but does not go further. See Nico Schrijver, 'UNESCO's Role in the Development and Application of International Law: An Assessment'. In Abdulqawi A. Yusuf (ed.), *Standard-setting in UNESCO: Normative Action in Education, Science and Culture. Volume I* (Leiden, 2007), pp. 365–84.

some member states refrained from giving any indication at all for years.[99] Technically they may be bound, but it is highly doubtful whether they actually apply the rules in question.

Third – and a variation on the same theme, designed to speed up the process a bit – is to have a lengthy opting-out period, but to start applying the terms of the convention provisionally, awaiting the decision of the member states either to opt-in or to opt-out. International law can well live with this procedure;[100] whether domestic law can also live with it depends on domestic law. The Dutch pertinent rule, for example, allows provisional application, unless it runs counter to the Dutch constitution.[101]

Of course, it is a matter of perspective to claim that such instruments are really to be considered legislative instruments, or whether they should still somehow be seen as consent-based treaties.[102] While their conclusion is not completely identical to the ordinary conclusion of treaties, mostly they might still stop short of being binding decisions. At best, the organization's decision to adopt a convention may oblige the member states to submit the convention to their competent national authorities;[103] and it is perhaps no coincidence that some mostly speak of 'quasi-legislation'.[104]

Internal and household matters

At the end of the day, there are few international organizations which actually come close to having organized some form of 'legislation', however defined. Most organizations still insist on the requirement of consent when it comes to making binding rules of law, either by insisting that normative rules will only be adopted by unanimity, or at least consensus, or by having those rules only become binding upon those who actually accept them.

The main exception thereto is when the organization aims at creating rules relating to its own functioning: not so much normatively, but rather practically. Here, decisions can usually be taken by some form of majority, yet are to be binding upon all member states.

Once more, the example of the General Assembly may prove instructive. One of its powers in this category is the power to 'consider and approve the budget'

---

[99] See, highly critical, Thomas Buergenthal, *Law-making in the International Civil Aviation Organization* (New York, 1969), esp. pp. 96–101.

[100] See Art. 25 of the Vienna Convention on the Law of Treaties.

[101] See Art. 15 of the 1994 State Law on Approval and Promulgation of Treaties. For a brief comment, see Jan Klabbers, 'The New Dutch Law on the Approval of Treaties' (1995) 44 *ICLQ*, 629–43.

[102] But see Blokker, who feels that their link to the organization is strong enough to warrant qualification as decisions: Niels M. Blokker, 'Decisions of International Organizations: The Case of the European Union' (1999) 30 *Neth YIL*, 3–44, esp. p. 14.

[103] So already the Canadian Supreme Court in an advisory judgment in the early 1920s. See *In the Matter of Legislative Jurisdiction over Hours of Labour*, in (1925–6) 3 *AD*, 393.

[104] So, e.g., Yemin, *Legislative Powers*.

(Article 17, para. 1), another is the power to apportion the budget (Article 17, para. 2). Others include those relating to the admission of new member states (Article 4), suspension of rights of member states (Articles 5 and 19), the appointment of the Secretary-General (Article 97) and the election of the judges of the ICJ (Arts. 8 and 10 Statute ICJ). In addition, the General Assembly (as well as many other organs) may determine staff regulations, financial regulations and its own rules of procedure.[105]

With other organizations the situation is similar. For instance, the only binding decision that can be taken by a majority within the OAS is a decision on whether to convene a Meeting of Consultation,[106] and that is a household matter if there ever was one. Within the EC, many treaty provisions are devoted to the internal functioning of the organization and the precise relationship among the various institutions.

Applying the law

There are organizations which have given some organ the task of applying the law, and thus of acting pretty much as the executive, in Montesquieuan terms. Perhaps the clearest example is the Commission of the EC. While its tasks are varied, and include an initiating role in the law-making process, among its main prerogatives is the facility to enact a so-called 'decision' which, under Article 249 (ex-Article 189) of the TEC, shall be binding in its entirety upon its addressee. Article 249 of the TEC is quite vague as to the potential scope of decisions, and it turns out that they are taken in a number of circumstances. Among the more famous ones, at least since March 1996 when trade in British beef became an issue, are the Commission's powers in the field of agriculture.

Similarly, the Commission has far-reaching powers in the field of competition law. It is the Commission that decides whether or not companies are violating the EC rules on antitrust, and while those decisions can be reviewed, they do highlight the Commission's administrative role. By the same token, it is the Commission that has the power to issue permits in the field of (again) competition law, and in the field of state aids, and it is usually the Commission that decides on anti-dumping duties against foreign exporters, or whether or not foreign companies engage in illicit commercial practices. In short, the administration of the EC is to a large extent in the hands of the Commission, and by definition, administration implies the application of rules of law.

In other organizations things are less clear-cut. Generally, most executive bodies seem to have some administrative powers, but subject usually, to approval or disapproval by the plenary body. Generally, executive bodies are given the task of implementing the decisions taken by the plenary. But, usually, they are

---

[105] For a useful overview, see Jorge Castaneda, *Legal Effects of United Nations Resolutions* (New York, 1969), pp. 22–69.
[106] Article 60 OAS.

not given any autonomous decision-making powers; where decision-making powers exist, there is generally always a method for political review (more so than legal review: the plenary may overrule administrative decisions).

Apart from the EC Commission, the main exception is the Security Council of the UN which has the power to take binding decisions under Chapter VII of the Charter and, according to some, even beyond that. The power to take binding decisions is laid down in Article 25, holding that the members of the UN 'agree to accept and carry out the decisions' of the SC in accordance with the present Charter'.

The interesting consideration is that Article 25 is not part of Chapter VII, but rather part of the general chapter on the Security Council (Chapter V), and does not even specifically refer to Chapter VII. Indeed, that very argument was used by the ICJ when it held a resolution on Namibia (Resolution 276 of 1970) to be binding, mainly because it was cast in mandatory terms.[107] Unfortunately, the resolution did not specify its basis in the Charter; in its preamble, it merely referred to earlier resolutions, which in turn only referred to earlier resolutions, which in turn only referred to earlier resolutions of either the Security Council or the General Assembly! In short, it is even unclear whether this particular resolution had any direct basis in the Charter, but this did not stop the ICJ from having a close look and pronouncing it to be binding upon the member states and even, to some extent, upon non-member states.

The Court's method for finding so was not the formal test of whether the Charter authorized the Security Council to take binding decisions on Namibia. Instead, the Court held in general terms that the legal effect of Security Council resolutions is to be determined 'having regard to the term of the resolution to be interpreted, the discussions leading to it, the Charter provisions invoked and, in general, all circumstances that might assist in determining the legal consequences of the resolution of the Security Council'.[108]

At any rate, it would seem that the powers of the Security Council are limited to making decisions, and do not include law-making. Therefore, the Council's activities may perhaps be compared to administrative acts, rather than legislation. Having said that, though, there is but a fine line between making law and applying law, and, especially with the Security Council, the problem may take on rather large proportions, as its decision-making powers are rather wide to begin with.[109] At least when it comes to discharging its duties

---

[107] *Legal consequences for states of the continued presence of South Africa in Namibia (South West Africa) notwithstanding Security Council Resolution 276 (1970)*, advisory opinion, [1971] ICJ Reports 16.

[108] *Ibid.*, para. 114.

[109] See also José E. Alvarez, 'Judging the Security Council' (1996) 90 *AJIL*, 1–39. Incidentally, the technical quality of Security Council resolutions is not always beyond debate. Thus, Resolution 1373 (2001) formulates a number of obligations of states in the fight against terrorism (this alone is questionable, as it assumes law-making powers), but fails to make clear what is meant by terrorism.

in matters of peace and security, the Security Council is admonished to act in accordance with the purposes and principles of the UN.[110] These are not overly specific, and are enumerated in Articles 1 and 2 of the Charter. Presumably, they do not place many substantive obstacles in the way of the Security Council: it will be relatively easy to justify a decision in terms of justice, international law, peace and security, et cetera. Thus, not many activities of the Council (not even, arguably, law-making activities) are likely to be *ultra vires*.[111]

Concluding remarks

The great puzzle when it comes to legal instruments is to explain their binding force upon the organization's members. The delegation theory, although popular, has serious problems in explaining majority decisions which are based on the implied powers doctrine: an outvoted member state can always claim that it never consented to the activity in question simply because the decision's legal basis is not spelled out in the constituent document.

Conversely, while the legislation theory does away with the need for consent, it stumbles over the rather principled objection that the founding fathers of international organizations have never given the legislation theory pride of place. Put differently, there are simply no organizations with regard to which it can convincingly be argued that they may engage in law-making as that term is usually understood: the creation of abstract rules of general application by some form of majority decision.

With that in mind, it is perhaps no coincidence that the treaty analogy occasionally surfaces, despite the fact that convincing arguments against it can be made: it cannot deal with unanimity decisions, and ignores, in a sense, the separate identity of the organization. Still, the treaty analogy has the distinct advantage of being able to point to the consent of the state or states concerned, which effectively kills off any further discussion. Thus, in particular where the legal status of an instrument is doubtful, the treaty analogy may be of help.

All this entails that the law of international organizations is still looking for a convincing way to explain the binding force of decisions of international organizations,[112] and it seems more than likely that such a convincing explanation is impossible to find: the law must do justice to the dual demands of

---

[110] Article 24, para. 2. A useful overview of how the Council has galvanized the idea of international public order is Vera Gowlland-Debbas, 'The Function of the United Nations Security Council in the International Legal System'. In Michael Byers (ed.), *The Role of Law in International Politics: Essays in International Relations and International Law* (Oxford, 2000), 277–313.

[111] But note that the Council's decision to put a binding gloss on the boundary between Kuwait and Iraq, after the work of the Iraq–Kuwait Boundary Demarcation Commission, has been qualified as unprecedented. See Maurice Mendelson and Susan Hulton, 'The Iraq–Kuwait Boundary: Legal Aspects' (1990) 23 *RBDI*, 293–332, p. 294.

[112] See, in a similar vein, Alvarez, *Law-makers*.

catering to the needs of the organization (which would seem to favour the legislation theory) and those of its members (which would favour a consent-based theory).[113] Those demands are, however, mutually exclusive: the law cannot do both at the same time. Or rather, to the extent that those two demands can be met, the price to pay is that the organization and its members fade into one and become indistinguishable from one another.[114] But this, needless to say, cannot easily be reconciled with the separation of identities between the organization and its members.

That does not imply that practical difficulties abound, for in practice the clear-cut situations seem reasonably well accepted. Few would deny the binding force of decisions of the Security Council (at least those taken under Chapter VII), or of regulations adopted by the EC Council. Where the situation is less clear-cut (EC guidelines, General Assembly resolutions, even Security Council decisions not taken under Chapter VII of the Charter), the debate will inevitably turn into a debate on the legal nature of the instrument involved. It is here, at the fringes as it were, that the search for a convincing explanation assumes importance.

---

[113] This ambiguity is wonderfully (if inadvertently perhaps) captured by Schermers: 'we may conclude that international organizations have taken over international law making. They draft most of the treaties and through their discussions general principles of law – and in the long run customary law is developed. Since international organizations are composed of States, the change is not fundamental.' See Henry G. Schermers, 'International Organizations and the Law of Treaties' (1999) 42 *GYIL*, 56–65, esp. p. 62.

[114] A good example is Asamoah, *Declarations of the General Assembly*, pp. 15 and 29, for whom acts of international organizations are, in fact, collective acts of the member states.

11

Decision making and judicial review

Introduction

Whereas the previous chapter dealt with the various sorts of legal instruments that may be created by and within international organizations, this chapter deals with two related aspects. The first is the question of how those legal instruments are adopted. Second, one may wonder to what extent the adoption of instruments is governed and controlled by legal factors. In other words: are there possibilities for judicial review, and, if so, on what grounds? This entails in particular the topic of the validity of legal instruments. Studying the validity of legal instruments, in turn, leads almost inevitably to discussion of a third topic: the possibility of a hierarchy between various categories of legal instruments.[1]

With all these issues, the complicated relationship between the organization and its member states once more comes to the fore,[2] and the complication can perhaps best be described as one of how to protect the interests of a minority of members against the wishes of the majority. One obvious way to protect the minority is through the decision-making procedure itself; another method is by facilitating judicial review, which will in turn be greatly facilitated if there is a clear hierarchy between legal instruments.

But there is more to it than that. Most decisions will somehow also engender effects outside the limited confines of the organization itself and its member states. Obviously, this is the case when the organization decides to conclude an agreement with a third party. Here, the interests of the third party concerned may be pitted against those of an outvoted minority: should the agreement be kept even if it was invalidly concluded (so as to protect the third party), or should it be annulled (so as to protect an outvoted minority)? It is also, albeit less obviously, the case where an organization takes action against one of its member

---

[1] This is to be distinguished from the question of a hierarchy between organs; see above, Chapter 9.

[2] Indeed, as Dekker and Wessel remind us, it is the very existence of established decision-making procedures which help to distinguish organizations from mere gatherings of states. See Ige Dekker and Ramses Wessel, '"Lowering the Corporate Veil": Het recht der internationale organisaties vanuit de institutionele rechtstheorie'. In M. A. Heldeweg *et al.* (eds.), *De regel meester: Opstellen voor Dick W. P. Ruiter* (Enschede, 2001), pp. 5–22, esp. p. 14.

states, as most likely this action will also affect individuals or companies within the member states. Here then, it is the rights of those individuals or companies which may be pitted against those of the majority to steer the organization (the rights of the minority and the affected individual or company will most likely coincide, in that both would seek annulment).

And that leaves still unmentioned a more abstract form of interest: not only has the outvoted minority a right to be protected against the majority, and not only may third parties warrant some form of protection, but it is also often thought that the interests of the world community at large ought to be taken into account; and the interests of the world community then entail the proposition that, generally speaking, international organizations perform worthwhile functions and should, in principle, be free to pursue their activities with as little interference as possible,[3] as well as (sometimes opposing, sometimes coinciding with the previous point) a general interest in seeing that the rule of law is upheld, which then translates into an interest in organizations acting strictly in conformity with their constituent documents.[4] After all, the very legitimacy of the organization and its organs is often judged at least partly by the extent to which the organization can be seen to be working in accordance with established procedures and within the parameters of its constitutional document.[5]

Adopting legal instruments

Perhaps still the classic method of adopting legal acts, at least when it comes to adopting binding acts, is to do so by unanimity.[6] Obviously, this is based on classic notions of state sovereignty: states cannot be bound against their will. Moreover, as Tammes already observed, the idea of unanimity radiates a strong 'metaphysical symbolism', denoting unity and harmony rather than discord and in-fighting.[7] It follows that the point of departure will usually be that binding decisions must be adopted unanimously.

---

[3] Such a stand is often taken in literature on the liability of organizations towards third parties. See, e.g., Moshe Hirsch, *The Responsibility of International Organizations toward Third Parties: Some Basic Principles* (Dordrecht, 1995).

[4] Such strands are visible in the work of Ernst-Ulrich Petersmann. See, e.g., his 'How to Constitutionalize International Law and Foreign Policy for the Benefit of Civil Society?' (1998) 20 *Michigan JIL*, 1–30.

[5] Additionally, procedures and rules themselves are often criticized from the (elusive) vantage point of legitimacy. See generally David D. Caron, 'The Legitimacy of the Collective Authority of the Security Council' (1993) 87 *AJIL*, 552–88.

[6] For an illuminating study on how decision making tends to gravitate towards unanimity, see Fritz W. Scharpf, 'The Joint-decision Trap: Lessons from German Federalism and European Integration' (1988) 66 *Public Administration*, 239–78. For an update and elaboration, see Fritz W. Scharpf, 'The Joint-decision Trap Revisited' (2006) 44 *JCMS*, 845–64.

[7] See A. J. P. Tammes, *Hoofdstukken van international organisatie* (The Hague 1951), p. 16. Tammes spoke of 'bovenzinnelijke symboliek' and pointed out that as a result, the ideal of unanimity might well legitimize coercion.

Indeed, the Permanent Court of International Justice (PCIJ) could confidently state in 1925 that, with respect to bodies composed of representatives of governments 'from whom they receive instructions and whose responsibility they engage . . . observance of the rule of unanimity is naturally and even necessarily indicated. Only if the decisions of the Council have the support of the unanimous consent of the Powers composing it, will they possess the degree of authority which they must have'.[8] It is this same connection with ideas of sovereignty and equality which is the main advantage of the unanimity rule (if advantage it is): it does justice to the notion that states cannot be forced to accept obligations without their consent.[9]

The drawback, as often perceived, is that unanimity gives all member states the possibility to block unwelcome proposals, therewith leading to paralysis of the organization and more generally arresting the development of international law.[10] A side-effect, moreover, is that insistence on unanimity often invites recourse to other, legally nebulous, means of pushing developments: by informal instruments, informal amendments, authoritative interpretations and the like. Indeed, some have explained the very existence of the phenomenon of non-binding recommendations within international organizations along these lines.[11]

As demonstrated earlier, the unanimity rule applies, in one way or another, to most binding decisions of most international organizations,[12] and for that reason most of them can be considered, still, as intergovernmental. Or, more accurately, the setting of abstract standards of behaviour occurs usually on the basis of unanimity.[13]

Another method of decision making is to adopt decisions by consensus, once somewhat tersely described by Pierre Pescatore as 'a state of non-objection, a resigned let-it-go'.[14] Usually, consensus is taken to mean that no participant seriously objects: while some may still have their doubts, they have decided not to stand in the way of the adoption of the instrument at hand. The UN's Office

---

[8] *Interpretation of Article 3, paragraph 2, of the Treaty of Lausanne*, advisory opinion, [1925] Publ. PCIJ, Series B, No. 12, p. 29.

[9] The virtues of this type of thinking are eloquently set out by Prosper Weil, 'Towards Relative Normativity in International Law?' (1983) 77 *AJIL*, 413–42.

[10] Hence, the literature contains quite a number of excursions into the question of whether states can be bound by international law in the absence of their consent. Influential examples include Christian Tomuschat, 'Obligations Arising for States without or against Their Will' (1993/IV) 241 *RdC*, 195–374, and Jonathan Charney, 'Universal International Law' (1993) 87 *AJIL*, 529–51.

[11] So, e.g., A. J. P. Tammes, 'Decisions of International Organs as a Source of International Law' (1958/II) 94 *RdC*, 265–363, at p. 304.

[12] See also Abram Chayes and Antonia Handler Chayes, *The New Sovereignty: Compliance with International Regulatory Agreements* (Cambridge, MA, 1995), esp. p. 129.

[13] In contrast, concrete issues (say, an organization's budget) may often be decided upon by majority.

[14] Pierre Pescatore, 'The GATT Dispute Settlement Mechanism: Its Present Situation and its Prospects' (1993/2) 27 *JWT*, 5–20, esp. 13.

of Legal Affairs defines it as follows: 'consensus is generally understood to mean adoption of a decision without formal objections and vote; this being possible only when no delegation formally objects to a consensus being recorded, though some delegations may have reservations to the substantive matter at issue or a part of it'.[15] Usually, deciding by consensus implies that possible opponents of a decision have been bought off, as it were: there is a natural relationship, one might say, between voting by consensus and the conclusion of package deals. In practice, as a Swedish political scientist found in 1988, there is precious little difference between deciding by unanimity and deciding by consensus. In both cases, each and every participant in the decision-making process retains a right of veto.[16] While initially, in the 1960s and early 1970s, consensus was heralded as a new form of decision making, finding a balance between unanimity and qualified majority voting[17] and uniquely geared to foster negotiation and compromise,[18] it has turned out to be less beneficial than some expected.[19]

Indeed, the connection with package deals even carries a serious legal danger: if an instrument is supposed to codify existing customary law, but is decided upon by means of consensus and package deals, it may well happen that the resulting instrument reflects the package deals rather than the initial customary rules. In other words: there is the danger of customary international law actually being weakened rather than codified. The classic illustration of the problem is the Third UN Conference on the Law of the Sea, not an organization itself, but a highly structured and organized round of negotiations where decision making was to take place on the basis of consensus. As a result, it has been argued that some traditionally well-settled customary rules may have been weakened.[20]

Not surprisingly, where formal provision for consensus is made, it is often accompanied by a reference to qualified majority voting (QMV, in jargon), so as to prevent consensus from lapsing completely into unanimity. Thus, the WTO agreement provides that in both its plenary and its executive organs (the Ministerial Conference and the General Council) decisions will be taken by

---

[15] See UNJY (1987), pp. 174–5, at p. 174.

[16] Ulf Lindell, *Modern Multilateral Negotiation: The Consensus Rule and its Implications in International Conferences* (Lund, 1988). That said, consensus decisions may be accompanied by reservations or declarations on the matter at issue.

[17] See generally Anthony d'Amato, 'On Consensus' (1970) 8 *Can YIL*, 104–22.

[18] For a brief but balanced assessment, Antonio Cassese, 'Consensus and Some of its Pitfalls' (1975) 58 *Rivista di Diritto Internazionale*, 754–61.

[19] Despite also Jenks's high hopes. See C. Wilfred Jenks, 'Unanimity, the Veto, Weighted Voting, Special and Simple Majorities and Consensus as Modes of Decision in International Organisations'. In D. W. Bowett *et al.*, *Cambridge Essays in International Law: Essays in Honour of Lord McNair* (London, 1965), pp. 48–63, esp. p. 63.

[20] See Sir Robert Y. Jennings, 'Law-making and Package Deals'. In Roberto Ago *et al.* (eds.), *Mélanges offerts à Paul Reuter. Le droit international: unité et diversité* (Paris, 1981), pp. 347–55. Eldar is less worried, arguing that things such as vote trading (and package trading, it may be presumed) may enhance general welfare. See Ofer Eldar, 'Vote-trading in International Institutions' (2008) 19 *EJIL*, 3–41.

consensus, or, failing consensus, by majority.[21] Similar provisions can also be found elsewhere. Thus, under the regime for the protection of the ozone layer, amendments are to be accepted by consensus or, if that is out of reach, by a three-quarters majority.[22]

There are many possible ways of voting by a qualified majority, and in a sense the term itself (or at least the adjective) is meaningless, as any majority requirement will be 'qualified' in one way or another. Even if a simple majority suffices to adopt a legal act, it still means that the necessary majority has been qualified: it must be a simple one, which usually signifies the majority of those members that are present and voting. An absolute majority is, usually, considered to connote something slightly different: it refers to a majority of the members of an organization, or an organ of the organization, rather than of those present and voting.[23]

Nonetheless, usually the term 'qualified majority' is supposed to mean something more than just a simple or absolute majority. An example is voting in the Security Council, at least on substantive issues: it requires the affirmative vote of nine members (out of fifteen), including the five permanent members.[24] Thus, the majority is qualified: it must be three-fifths of the members and it must include the five permanent members. In practice, though, the rule has become a bit more lenient: as long as the five permanent members do not object, a proposal can be carried.

This practice, which famously became visible during the Korea crisis of the early 1950s, has been given the stamp of legal approval by the ICJ, in its 1971 *Namibia* opinion. The Security Council had, ever since the USSR's boycott of meetings during the Korea crisis, developed the practice that an abstention could be regarded as a 'concurrent vote' in terms of Article 27, para. 3. As the Court said, the records reflect that the members of the Council 'have consistently and uniformly interpreted the practice of voluntary abstention by a permanent member as not constituting a bar to the adoption of resolutions'.[25] This, the Court continued, had been generally accepted by the UN's membership, and 'evidences a general practice of that Organization'.[26]

Interestingly, the Court left the exact legal status somewhat in doubt. On the one hand, it comes close to accepting the practice as customary law: yet, it stops

---

[21] Article IX, para. 1 WTO.

[22] Article 9, para. 3 of the 1985 Vienna Convention for the Protection of the Ozone Layer. The text is reproduced in (1987) 26 *ILM* 1529.

[23] Reasons for non-presence may be plentiful, including the sometimes tedious preparatory work required. Thus, a prominent US delegate in the early days of the UN confesses that, having received her first sets of documents, she struggled to stay awake and make sense of it all. See Eleanor Roosevelt, *The Autobiography of Eleanor Roosevelt* (Boston, 1984), p. 300.

[24] Compare Art. 27, para. 3 UN Charter.

[25] *Legal consequences for states of the continued presence of South Africa in Namibia (South West Africa) notwithstanding Security Council Resolution 276 (1970)*, Advisory Opinion, [1971] ICJ Reports 16, para. 22.

[26] *Ibid.*

just short of doing that, calling the decision-making practice 'a general practice of that Organization' instead. And, presumably, it could not have gone further, for three reasons. First, the practice of the permanent members is, in the end, the practice of five states only. Of course, it is their practice that matters (they are the states whose interests are specially affected, in terms borrowed from the *North Sea Continental Shelf* cases[27]) – but still, as a matter of principle, it is difficult to construe the practice of five states within an organization of near-universal membership as giving rise to customary law effective for the entire membership. Second, the Court at no point investigates whether the practice is accompanied by *opinio juris*, and arguably evidence of *opinio juris* would be hard to find. Third, and perhaps most importantly, had the Court opted for claiming the decision-making procedure as being of customary law nature, then it would have had to pronounce itself on the possibility of customary law developing within the UN to begin with: Article 108 (the amendment article) may militate against such a conclusion.

Clearly, the Court had in mind that this general practice was somehow legally consequential, and presumably what the Court had in mind was that at the very least the 'general practice' could be regarded as 'subsequent practice' for the purpose of interpretation of the Charter. Under Article 31, para. 3(b) of the Vienna Convention, when interpreting a treaty 'there shall be taken into account, amongst other things, any subsequent practice in the application of the treaty which establishes the agreement of the parties regarding its interpretation'. That still leaves the exact legal status of the Security Council's decision-making practice somewhat in doubt, but is probably the most forceful explanation.[28]

The voting provisions relating to the Security Council may well be characterized as an example of weighted voting: voting is not done according to the idea that all members have identical numbers of votes, but rather follows the idea that, on some issues, the votes of some states should carry more weight than the votes of others. Another decision-making method along similar lines is the way the IMF has institutionalized weighted voting. In the IMF, the number of votes of each member state is dependent on the contribution of that member state to the IMF, and the stability of its currency: if a member has to borrow heavily, it may lose some of its votes. In the end, most decisions are taken by a majority of the votes cast (i.e., a simple majority).[29]

---

[27] *North Sea Continental Shelf* cases (*Federal Republic of Germany/Denmark*; *Federal Republic of Germany/Netherlands*), [1969] ICJ Reports 3, para. 73.

[28] The UN's Office of Legal Affairs suggests that the practice constitutes 'an authentic example of a *de facto* modification of a constitutive instrument . . . through the manner of its implementation by Member States'. See UNJY (1991), pp. 290–1, esp. p. 291. It is not specified how this can be reconciled with the presence of a formal amendment procedure. For a useful analysis of some aspects of decision making in the Security Council, see Loie Feuerle, 'Informal Consultation: A Mechanism in Security Council Decision-making' (1985) 18 *New York University Journal of International Law and Politics*, 267–308.

[29] See Art. XII, s. 5(c) IMF. Woods suggests that the system has outlived its utility, in that most of the income of IMF and World Bank is nowadays generated through loans to borrowing

Systems of weighted voting may be looked at in different ways.[30] Some would say that weighted voting is difficult to reconcile with the idea that states are supposed to be equal, as is laid down, e.g., in Article 2, para. 1 of the UN Charter: the UN is based on the sovereign equality of its members.[31] The five permanent members of the Security Council, though, are, to paraphrase Orwell, somewhat more equal than others.

On the other hand, in real life states are of course unequal. For better or for worse, the United States is a little more important than Liechtenstein; Germany is a little more important than Luxembourg. While doctrinally attractive, Vattel's famous words according to which the dwarf and the giant are alike holds little footing in sociological realities.[32] To insist on their equality is to neglect politics, and neglecting politics is usually something that one does only at one's peril.

Another question then is, of course, whether it is wise to carve existing power configurations in stone, as is done in the Charter. Nowadays, after all, it would seem that the USA is the only superpower left, and China is perhaps only now on its way to becoming one. Instead, other candidates have come to the fore, and thus it is no coincidence that every now and then arguments are made with respect to changing the composition of the Security Council.

It is perhaps inevitable that states try to circumvent existing frameworks when these are deemed to be too cumbersome: in politics, the end all too often justifies the means. In the Security Council, this has resulted in the 'pre-cooking' of decisions in smaller groups: while the Council nominally has fifteen members, many decisions are, in effect, prepared by the five permanent members (P-5), and within the P-5 it is often the United States that dominates.[33] Likewise, within the WTO, the path to decision making is often prepared in so-called mini-ministerials and 'green room' meetings, in which powerful member states aim to persuade certain other states, in the hope that once these are on board, the rest will follow.[34] While this upgrades the prestige and power of states such as Brazil or India, it stands in tension with fundamental notions of transparency and proper decision making.[35]

---

countries. In other words, the poor countries contribute most, but under the existing voting rules have the least power. See Ngaire Woods, *The Globalizers: The IMF, the World Bank, and Their Borrowers* (Ithaca, NY, 2006), p. 199.

[30] Incidentally, voting by proxy (one person voting for two or more states) has always been deemed undesirable in settings where 'one state, one vote' holds true, precisely because it would come close to weighted voting. See UNJY (1965), pp. 223–4.

[31] Moreover, weighted voting can be seen to highlight the idea that the organization is just a vehicle for some of its more powerful members: it undermines the international and separate character of organizations.

[32] Emmerich de Vattel, *The Law of Nations* (1758; New York, n.d., Chitty trans.), p. lxii.

[33] See, e.g., Linda Fasulo, *An Insider's Guide to the UN* (New Haven, CT, 2004), p. 41.

[34] See generally Fatoumata Jawara and Aileen Kwa, *Behind the Scenes at the WTO: The Real World of International Trade Negotiations*, updated edn (London, 2004). See also Mary Footer, *An Institutional and Normative Analysis of the World Trade Organization* (Leiden, 2006), pp. 163–73.

[35] For the argument that in advocating procedural reform, many NGOs help to keep unjust organizational regimes in place, see Ruth Buchanan, 'Perpetual Peace or Perpetual Process:

European Community

When it comes to qualified majority voting, the European Community does things in accordance with a pre-negotiated distribution of votes. Within the Council of Ministers, each member state has been given a certain number of votes: the four biggest members (Germany, France, the United Kingdom and Italy) have 29 votes each, small Malta has only 3, and the rest have something in between. Since Bulgaria's and Romania's accession, this totals 345 votes; and the treaty prescribes that a minimum of 255 is required to make a decision following this procedure.[36]

The EC system is, therefore, an elaborate form of weighted voting. Those who drafted it have spent some serious time and attention negotiating the precise weight to be accorded to each member state, and setting the threshold for decision making. Indeed, every enlargement or treaty review of the Union gives rise to serious (and understandable) political haggling between the members, usually resulting in a temporary compromise, to be renegotiated at the next round of accessions. And sometimes difficult compromises on voting arrangements are concluded in other circumstances, such as the infamous Luxembourg Compromise which, following French remonstrations in the mid-1960s, allowed for a departure from majority decision making whenever a member state invoked a national interest of vital importance, or even merely threatened to do so.[37] Although often qualified as 'constitutionally invalid',[38] the Luxembourg Compromise nonetheless managed to influence the Community's decision-making procedure for many years.[39]

Moreover, decision making involves other actors as well. Thus, EC regulations and directives usually originate in a Commission proposal, and require either the advice or consent of the European Parliament.[40] In a number of cases, moreover, advisory bodies such as the Economic and Social Committee or the Committee of the Regions (or both) must be heard.[41]

A peculiar feature of decision making within the Community is that many of the Council's legal acts are, in fact, adopted by high-ranking civil servants, assembled in the Committee of Permanent Representatives (COREPER). One

---

Global Civil Society and Cosmopolitan Legality at the World Trade Organization' (2003) 16 *Leiden JIL*, 673–99.

[36] Article 205 (ex-Art. 148) TEC, in conjunction with Article 22 of the Accession Protocol. The text of the latter can be found in OJ, 21–6-2005, L 157/29.

[37] For a brief overview, see Anthony L. Teasdale, 'The Life and Death of the Luxembourg Compromise' (1993) 31 *JCMS*, 567–79.

[38] Compare, e.g., Dominic Lasok and J. W. Bridge, *Law and Institutions of the European Community* (5th edn, London, 1991), p. 239.

[39] The best analysis of the role of the Luxembourg Compromise is, without a doubt, contained in the work of Joseph H. H. Weiler. See in particular his 'The Community System: The Dual Character of Supranationalism', (1981) 1 *YEL*, 267–306.

[40] See in particular Arts. 251 (ex-Art. 189b) and 252 (ex-Art. 189c) TEC.

[41] Compare Art. 148 (ex-Art. 125) TEC.

well-placed observer (a former British government minister) put it like this in his diaries:

> Everything is decided, horse traded off, by officials at COREPER, the Council [*sic*] of Permanent Representatives. The Ministers arrive on the scene at the last minute hot, tired, ill, or drunk (sometimes all of these together), read out their piece, and depart. Strange, really. Because the EC constitution is quite well drawn. The Council of Ministers is sovereign [*sic*], and can/could boss COREPER around. But, as always in politics everywhere, democratic or autocratic, it's the chaps on the spot who call the shot [*sic*]. The civil servants beaver away, massage and congratulate each other, while the politicians treat attendance as a chore.[42]

While Clark's experience may be somewhat colourful, it does contain a kernel of truth.[43] European summit meetings, on the other hand, are often occasions for political leaders to show their gamesmanship qualities, with lots of opportunities to engage in devious leaking or to offer misleading guidance.[44] Still, leaving summitry aside, many complain that everyday decision making has become a labyrinthine affair, where it is difficult to trace lines of responsibility and authority due to, COREPER aside, an abundance of advisory or preparatory committees.[45]

Validity

The various types of legal acts that may be taken by various organs of various international organizations were discussed above, and it has been noted that there is the possibility that some decisions at least may be subjected to certain conditions of validity.[46]

If and where international organizations perform administrative acts or adopt legislative acts, it makes sense if the various subjects of the law of that particular organization can protest[47] or appeal against those administrative or legislative acts. Whether they can do so in the courts of the various member states, or whether review is only possible before organs of the organization itself, is under debate. The French Conseil d'Etat, for instance, has held in 1994 that French administrative courts have no competence to examine the legal justification of decisions taken by an international body.[48] On the other hand, in 1998, the

---

[42] Alan Clark, *Diaries* (1993; London, 1999), p. 139 (tabs omitted).

[43] In addition, the Court of Justice has observed (in itself telling) that whatever the practice may be, formal responsibilities still rest with the Council. See case C-25/94, *Commission* v. *Council* [1996] ECR I-1469, para. 27: 'Coreper's function of carrying out the tasks assigned to it by the Council does not give it the power to take decisions which belong, under the Treaty, to the Council.'

[44] See, e.g., John Dickie, *Inside the Foreign Office* (London, 1992), esp. pp. 155–7.

[45] See also above, Chapter 9.   [46] See above, Chapter 10.

[47] On the utility of protest, see Nicolas Angelet, 'Protest against Security Council Decisions'. In Karel Wellens (ed.), *International Law: Theory and Practice. Essays in Honour of Eric Suy* (The Hague, 1998), pp. 277–85.

[48] Decision of 22 July 1994 in *Chambre Syndicale des Transports Aériens*, in 111 *ILR* 500.

Danish Supreme Court seemed to endorse a review of EC law by Danish courts, holding that 'the courts of law cannot be deprived of their right to try questions as to whether an EC act of law exceeds the limits for the transfer of sovereignty' involved in joining the EC.[49] In its turn, in a few controversial cases the Court of First Instance (CFI) has assumed the power to review Security Council acts at least to the extent that these can be said to be in conflict with *jus cogens* norms, while declining more general powers of review.[50]

Elihu Lauterpacht has given a convenient overview of the types of unlawful acts usually at issue in the context of international organizations. To his mind, an element of the illegality of the act 'involves a reference to the special nature of international organisations as artificial legal persons deriving all their powers from a conventional or statutory source and bound to act only within the limits and in accordance with the terms of the grant made to them'.[51] The types of acts it concerns then may include instruments adopted not in accordance with the prescribed procedure, or by an organ lacking the requisite power to adopt the measure in question, suspension or expulsion without justification, wrongful apportionment of expenses, the improper exercise of a discretionary power, et cetera.[52] In addition, defects that result from a violation of a substantive rule of law may occasionally prove a ground for invalidity,[53] although here the organizational element as such is of little special relevance. Put differently, whether a treaty to commit genocide is concluded between two states or between two organizations has little bearing on its validity, whereas such things as wrongful apportionment of expenses presuppose the existence of an organization somewhere in the background.

The case-law of the World Court has so far not provided much guidance beyond setting a very rough guideline. This was already implicit in the classic PCIJ opinions on the competences of the International Labour Organization (ILO).[54] As Osieke summarizes the gist of these opinions, the constitutionality of the ILO's acts was to be tested against the objects and purposes of the ILO.[55]

This rather broad principle has also been upheld in other opinions, most notably the 1962 *Certain Expenses* opinion. In this case, confronted with the question of whether expenses incurred for peace-keeping (not foreseen in the

---

[49] *Carlsen et al.* v. *Rasmussen*, decision of 6 April 1998, para. 9.6. Incidentally, the Court continues by stating that Danish courts cannot declare EC law invalid; but they can declare it inapplicable in Denmark. I have used the unauthorized translation available at the website of Denmark's foreign ministry, at www.um.dk.udenrigspolitik/.

[50] See case T-306/01, *Yusuf and Al Barakaat* v. *Council* [2005] ECR II-3533, and Case T-315/01, *Kadi* v. *Council* [2005] ECR II-3649.

[51] Elihu Lauterpacht, 'The Legal Effect of Illegal Acts of International Organisations'. In Bowett *et al.*, *Cambridge Essays*, pp. 88–121, esp. p. 89.

[52] See also, for a general and very useful overview, Felice Morgenstern, 'Legality in International Organizations' (1976–7) 48 *BYIL*, 241–57.

[53] See generally Karl Doehring, 'Unlawful Resolutions of the Security Council and their Legal Consequences' (1997) 1 *Max Planck Yearbook of United Nations Law*, pp. 91–109.

[54] See, for a full discussion, Chapter 4 above.

[55] Ebere Osieke, 'Ultra Vires Acts in International Organizations – The Experience of the International Labour Organization' (1976–7) 48 *BYIL*, 259–80, esp. 266–7.

UN Charter) could qualify as regular expenses and could thus be part of the regular budget, the Court stated that 'such expenditures must be tested by their relationship to the purposes of the United Nations in the sense that if an expenditure were made for a purpose which is not one of the purposes of the United Nations, it could not be considered an "expense of the Organization"'.[56] And the Court then made the point more general, when it held that 'when the Organization takes action which warrants the assertion that it was appropriate for the fulfilment of one of the stated purposes of the United Nations, the presumption is that such action is not *ultra vires* the Organization'.[57] In other words: as long as an act of an organization can somehow be fitted into the scheme of that organization's purposes, there is at least a presumption that the organization was entitled to undertake that activity.[58] Given the generally broad nature of the purposes of most organizations (the Court acknowledged as much with respect to the UN), chances are that in practice the presumption of legality cannot be rebutted, except perhaps in the most blatant of cases.[59] But even then, as we shall shortly see, the legality of the decision may still stand due to such factors as acceptance or approval.[60]

Only rarely has the ICJ declared that an international decision had been adopted unconstitutionally. A first example is the 1960 opinion on the IMCO's Maritime Safety Committee, where the Court found that the decision composing the Maritime Safety Committee failed to comply with the relevant article of IMCO's constituent document. Curiously though, the Court here seemed to have reversed its test: it is not testing a decision against the organization's purposes (in which case it would probably have given its approval), but is interpreting the document concerned and then testing whether its alternative interpretation is consistent with the organization's purposes.

The Court's approach here was one, eventually, of treaty interpretation: it stipulated that '[t]he words of Article 28(a) must be read in their natural and ordinary meaning, in the sense which they would normally have in their context'.[61] It bolsters its conclusion by referring to the drafting history of the

---

[56] *Certain Expenses of the United Nations (Article 17, Paragraph 2, of the Charter)*, advisory opinion, [1962] ICJ Reports 151, p. 167.

[57] *Ibid.*, p. 168.

[58] And, as Osieke explains, the fact that review bodies rarely have the jurisdiction to interfere on their own motions, but need a reference from a member state or an organ of the organization, contributes to this strong presumption of validity: there will be a presumption of validity unless a formal complaint is lodged. See Ebere Osieke, 'The Legal Validity of *Ultra Vires* Decisions of International Organizations', (1983) 77 *AJIL*, 239–56.

[59] Compare also Osieke's observation that, in the more than fifty years since the establishment of the ILO, not a single act has been declared illegal or unconstitutional: Osieke, '*Ultra Vires* Acts', p. 275.

[60] Note also that the EC Court already in its early days created a similar construction, without bothering to refer back to the Community's (in this case the ECSC's) purposes: 'The adoption of an administrative measure creates a presumption as to its validity.' See joined cases 7/56 and 3–7/57, *Algera and others v. Common Assembly* [1957–8] ECR 39, p. 61.

[61] *Constitution of the Maritime Safety Committee of the Inter-governmental Maritime Consultative Organization*, advisory opinion, [1960] ICJ Reports 150, p. 159.

provision concerned,[62] and then goes on to interpret the provision in more detail. At no point does it refer to the purposes of IMCO, except towards the end of its opinion, when it holds that the 'interpretation the Court gives to Article 28(a) is consistent with the general purpose of the Convention and the special functions of the Maritime Safety Committee'.[63]

By virtue of its unique reversal of the traditional test (not linking an organization's decision to the purposes of that organization, but rather bringing an alternative interpretation within the scope of the organization's purposes), it is doubtful whether the opinion on IMCO's Maritime Safety Committee adds a lot to the law of international organizations beyond the proposition that it provides authority for procedural challenges. Clearly, it illustrates that there may be limits to how organizations can use their powers; they ought not to be able to use them in procedurally incorrect ways.[64] But no points of more general application are developed, nor does the Court explain why it departs from the test it had used and would use again in other cases.

The second occasion on which the Court found an organizational decision unconstitutional arose in 1996, when the World Health Assembly (WHO) had approached the Court with the question whether the use of nuclear weapons would be contrary to international law including the WHO constitution.[65] As the Court would hold, it was 'essentially immaterial' for the functioning of the WHO whether behaviour was legal or illegal: 'their effects on health would be the same'.[66]

Here, the Court did explicitly tie the contested decision (i.e., the request to the Court) to the organization's purposes, and found that the purposes of the WHO did not warrant its involvement with the question of the legality of nuclear weapons; not their legality under international law generally, and not even their legality in light of the WHO constitution in particular, since 'the WHO is not empowered to seek an opinion on the interpretation of its Constitution in relation to matters outside the scope of its functions'.[67]

The possible consequences of invalidity of a decision of an international organization are varied. A first possible consequence is that the act is invalid *ab initio* and thus never considered as legally effective. This is, in general international law, the situation when a treaty is concluded under duress or in violation

---

[62] *Ibid.*, pp. 161–5.   [63] *Ibid.*, at 170.

[64] See also Elihu Lauterpacht, 'Judicial Review of the Acts of International Organizations'. In Laurence Boisson de Chazournes and Philippe Sands (eds.), *International Law, the International Court of Justice and Nuclear Weapons* (Cambridge, 1999), pp. 92–102, esp. p. 93.

[65] *Legality of the use by a state of nuclear weapons in armed conflict*, advisory opinion, [1996] ICJ Reports 66.

[66] *Ibid.*, para. 22.

[67] *Ibid.*, para. 28. Here the reasoning is curious, to say the least: surely a request for interpretation may signify that the organization itself is not quite clear as to whether a matter falls within its powers; to prohibit requests in such cases is to foreclose all judicial clarification except in those cases where everything is clear and clarification is thus not needed.

of a norm of *jus cogens*[68] (provided such peremptory norms exist), and, by analogy, it has been argued that the same could possibly apply to decisions of international organizations.

Thus, when confronted with the effects of a Security Council arms embargo encompassing all parties in the Yugoslav crisis, Bosnia argued before the ICJ that, since its starting position in terms of arms possession was so bad when compared to that of its enemies, the resolution unwittingly contributed to the genocide of the Bosnian population. Therewith, the resolution violated the prohibition of genocide in international law (a norm of *jus cogens*, according to many) and should thus be considered void *ab initio*.[69]

The second and, within the context of international organizations, probably more current consequence is that invalidity does not occur *ab initio*, but will be declared without retroactive effects. After all, the invalid act may have engendered legal effects in the period between entry into force and the finding of invalidity and the position of parties that have acted in good faith on the basis of the invalid decision may well need to be preserved.

A third possible consequence is partial invalidity. Where only part of an organizational act is tainted by a defect, it might be sensible, if and when possible, to invalidate merely the tainted part, while leaving the remainder of the act valid. Obviously, this is not likely to occur in cases where the defect stems from a procedural violation: but one can imagine cases where a substantive defect affects only a small portion of the act concerned, for example, where only a minor provision of a resolution is in conflict with a norm of general international law.

Much depends, of course, on whether severability of provisions is itself acceptable, and the dominant position would appear to be that severability is indeed acceptable unless the tainted provision forms an essential part of the organizational decision. While there is little directly relevant case law (with the exception perhaps of judgments of the EC Court), in the different context of severability of provisions in a declaration of acceptance of the compulsory jurisdiction of the ICJ, Judge Hersch Lauterpacht opined in *Norwegian Loans* that severability would not be permissible where the contested part is an essential element of the decision concerned.[70] By implication, where it does not constitute an essential element, severability could be permissible.[71]

---

[68] See Arts. 51–3 of the Vienna Convention on the Law of Treaties.

[69] The ICJ itself did not pick up on the argument; however, *ad hoc* Judge Lauterpacht did, and, while sympathetic to the argument, he concluded that there were some debatable links in the chain of reasoning. Incidentally, to his mind a possible (but not overly realistic) legal consequence could be (see para. 103 of his separate opinion) that the resolution at issue ceased to be valid as soon as its operation began to make the member states of the UN accessories to genocide. Thus, invalidity would set in as soon as a certain effect was created, rather than *ab initio* strictly speaking. For more details, see also below, pp. 248–9.

[70] *Case of certain Norwegian loans (France* v. *Norway)*, [1957] ICJ Reports 9, separate opinion Judge Lauterpacht, esp. pp. 50–4.

[71] In a similar vein, E. Lauterpacht, 'The Legal Effect of Illegal Acts', p. 120.

There is a final possible consequence, and that is of the utmost (if somewhat unexpected) importance in the law of international organizations: except where acts are void *ab initio* (and arguably even in such a situation), many a defect may be cured, as it were, through the operation of acceptance, acquiescence or estoppel.[72] Thus, even if it is clear that an organ acts *ultra vires*, but none of the organization's members (or anyone else affected, for that matter) objects, then in all likelihood the decision will stand. In fact, one might even go further and argue that there is fairly little legal protection against acts adopted *ultra vires*, precisely because many acts which might be, on the face of it, *ultra vires*, are nonetheless accepted by the organization's membership.[73] As the Danish government once put it: 'it would be meaningless to maintain that action taken with the active support of an overwhelming majority of the Member States in a situation of extreme gravity should be considered illegal'.[74]

Indeed, many possibly illegal acts have been warmly welcomed by the membership of the organization concerned, ranging from usurpation of powers to debatable use of credentials procedures. In turn, this creates the following situation: if a healthy majority agrees with the activity, then it can hardly be deemed illegal, for, if it were illegal, how could a healthy majority possibly accept it?[75]

Then again (or moreover, perhaps), the *ultra vires* doctrine may be convenient when an organization (or one of its organs) is reluctant to engage in action: one can always claim that the proposed course of action would possibly be *ultra vires*. An example from the UN's early days suggests as much: asked by the General Assembly to furnish a commission overseeing the partition of Palestine with enforcement powers, the Security Council refused, citing the *ultra vires* argument.[76] The one problem then, from the organization's point of view, is that of precedent: if something is *ultra vires* today, it will be difficult to sell as *intra vires* tomorrow, even if the organization has changed its mind.

It is no surprise perhaps that, in one of the few cases on point, the ICJ could lay down a strong presumption that organizational acts be considered as legal; while it may be possible to interpret the Court's opinion in *Certain Expenses* as containing a possibility of finding an illegal act, as Elihu Lauterpacht

---

[72] Indeed, as Morgenstern reminds us, the functioning of international organizations is based on acquiescence. See Morgenstern, 'Legality', p. 256.

[73] Note that in US corporate law, the *ultra vires* doctrine was already largely discarded by the 1930s. A wonderful discussion is Morton J. Horwitz, *The Transformation of American Law 1870–1960: The Crisis of Legal Orthodoxy* (Oxford, 1992), pp. 77–8.

[74] Quoted in R. Y. Jennings, 'Nullity and Effectiveness in International Law'. In Bowett *et al.*, *Cambridge Essays*, pp. 64–87, esp. p. 86. Jennings quoted from the Danish memorandum presented to the ICJ in connection with the *Certain Expenses* opinion.

[75] An in-depth study of the transformation of the FAO into an organization actively engaged in technical assistance and even discussing human rights and environmental issues suggests, indeed, that the transformation took place on the basis of sheer acceptance by the member states. It was not even deemed necessary to invoke the implied powers doctrine in support. See Sergio Marchisio and Antonietta di Blase, *The Food and Agriculture Organization* (Dordrecht, 1991).

[76] See H. G. Nicholas, *The United Nations as a Political Institution* (3rd edn, Oxford, 1967), p. 88.

contends,[77] in practice it would seem that this possibility will not occur too often. As Franck puts it succinctly, 'constitutional authority is sometimes nothing more than what you can get away with'.[78] Indeed, it is perhaps telling that the ICJ has so far only found the presumption of legality rebutted in circumstances where an organizational decision (that of the World Health Assembly to request an advisory opinion on the legality of the use of nuclear weapons) would have asked it to do the impossible[79] and, in addition, was sufficiently similar to another request to create a serious risk of duplication.[80]

Additionally, for many commentators the doctrine of *ultra vires* is so bound up with the possibility of judicial review, that, in the absence of a well-developed system of judicial review, the *ultra vires* doctrine has little chance of successful application. It is this consideration which often informs discussion of the *ultra vires* doctrine in domestic legal settings,[81] and which also informed the separate opinion of Judge Morelli in *Certain expenses*. For Judge Morelli, the absence of judicial possibilities meant that decisions were either absolute nullities, or fully valid; the middle category of voidable acts was not a possibility within the law of international organizations, as there was no one capable of actually voiding an instrument. As a result, this made it necessary:

> to put a very strict construction on the rules by which the conditions for the validity of acts of the Organization are determined, and hence to regard to a large extent the non-conformity of the act with a legal rule as a mere irregularity having no effect on the validity of the act. It is only in especially serious cases that an act of the Organization could be regarded as invalid, and hence an absolute nullity.[82]

Either way then, whether a limited possibility of judicial review is accepted or denied altogether, at the end of the day the standard situation in many organizations is that only in the most blatant cases may instruments possibly be regarded as invalid. The one safeguard that the law has created against the abuse of executive power turns out to be a reluctant safeguard: the doctrine of *ultra vires*, and the related doctrine of procedural irregularity, are incapable of putting a stop to illegal but accepted exercises of power. The only possible remaining defence then is to try and stop an illegal decision from being taken

---

[77] E. Lauterpacht, 'The Legal Effect of Illegal Acts', p. 111.

[78] See Thomas M. Franck, *Nation against Nation: What Happened to the UN Dream and What the US Can Do about it* (Oxford, 1985), p. 146.

[79] On the lack of wisdom involved in asking the World Court to decide on the legality of nuclear weapons, see Martti Koskenniemi, 'Faith, Identity, and the Killing of the Innocent: International Lawyers and Nuclear Weapons' (1997) 10 *Leiden JIL*, 137–62.

[80] At roughly the same time, the UN General Assembly had requested a similar opinion from the Court. See *Legality of the Threat or Use of Nuclear Weapons*, advisory opinion, [1996] ICJ Reports 226.

[81] See Mark Elliott, 'The Ultra Vires Doctrine in a Constitutional Setting: Still the Central Principle of Administrative Law' (1999) 58 *Cambridge Law Journal*, 129–58.

[82] *Certain Expenses* opinion, separate opinion Judge Morelli, p. 223.

by trying to persuade the organization's other members of its undesirability, but that, typically, is an exercise in politics.

Judicial review in the EC

Not surprisingly in light of the often posited correlation between the existence of tribunals and the very possibility of meaningfully talking about *ultra vires* and related issues, the most elaborate system of judicial review exists in the EC, and it is largely laid down in Article 230 (ex-Article 173) of the TEC. As one observer noted, it is difficult to think of an unlawful act of the Community's institutions which would remain outside the catalogue of Article 230.[83]

Article 230 is rather complicated, especially with respect to *locus standi*. The bottom line is that the EC's members, its institutions in most cases,[84] and sometimes also individuals and companies, can ask the ECJ to review the legality of legal acts adopted by the EC. The latter, however, can only do so against decisions addressed to them or decisions which are of direct and individual concern to them, and this notion has traditionally been rather restrictively interpreted by the EC Court.[85] Moreover, the Court has confirmed that an action on behalf of others or on behalf of the community at large is not covered by Article 230.[86]

Article 230 mentions four grounds for annulment, which are largely inspired by French administrative law. The first of these is perhaps the most obvious: lack of competence. Thus, if the Commission adopts an act which according to the Treaty should have been adopted by the Council, then the act can be annulled.[87] This of course is again putting a premium on the principle of attribution of powers, and thus is occasionally difficult to reconcile with the implied powers doctrine. It may mean that sometimes it is the Court which finds a competence somewhere in the Treaty.

---

[83] E. Lauterpacht, 'The Legal Effect of Illegal Acts', p. 95.

[84] As far as the European Parliament, the European Central Bank, and the Court of Auditors are concerned, their standing is limited to the protection of their own prerogatives. The driving force to include this at all has been the European Parliament, which urged the Court in the *Chernobyl* case that such standing would only be logical. Case C-70/88, *European Parliament* v. *Council (Chernobyl)* [1990] ECR I-2041.

[85] See already case 25/62, *Plaumann and Co* v. *Commission* [1963] ECR 95. Lauwaars explains this out of the need for effective administration. See Richard H. Lauwaars, *Lawfulness and Legal Force of Community Decisions* (Leiden, 1973), p. 307. The CFI attempted a broader interpretation some years ago, but was quickly called to order by the ECJ. See Case T-177/01, *Jégo-Quéré* v. *Commission* [2002] ECR II-2365, and Case C-263/02 P, *Commission* v. *Jégo-Quéré* [2004] ECR I-3425.

[86] See case C-321/95 P, *Stichting Greenpeace Council and others* v. *Commission* [1998] ECR I-1651, esp. paras. 28–9.

[87] So, e.g., case C-327/91, *France* v. *Commission* [1994] ECR I-3641. In case C-376/98, *Germany* v. *European Parliament and Council (Tobacco Directive)* [2000] ECR I-8419, the Court annulled a directive on grounds of lack of competence of the Community as such.

The second ground for annulment is the infringement of an essential procedural requirement. Thus, if the Council adopts something without consulting the European Parliament or the Economic and Social Committee, while such consultation is prescribed, the measure will be annulled.[88]

Third, more substantively, if a legal act infringes the EC Treaty or any rule relating to its application, it may be annulled. And this, the Court has held, is fairly inclusive: it includes not just the Treaty itself, but also secondary legislation, and even international treaties to which the EC is a party.[89]

Finally, a measure can be annulled on the grounds of misuse of powers, and that is perhaps the most arbitrary (or elusive) of grounds. The basic idea is, obviously, that if any of the institutions uses a power it has for purposes other than those for which the power has been granted, such use could render the measure annulled (e.g., the organization cannot write job descriptions so as to fit specific individuals at the exclusion of others).[90] The possibility of misusing powers presupposes that it is possible to figure out for what purpose a certain power was granted; in the absence of published *travaux préparatoires*, however, this is not very easily established, and is almost by definition a matter of inference and conjecture.

Finally, it is worth mentioning that the EC Court's jurisdiction remains limited in connection with activities undertaken under the so-called 'second and third pillars' of the EU. The Court has fairly little power when it comes to the legality of decisions in the field of foreign and security policy or co-operation in criminal matters.[91]

Judicial review of Security Council Acts

While the Community system of judicial review of administrative acts is clearly the most developed, we may wonder whether other organizations do not also have some rules relating to the validity of their decisions. Arguably, some of them do; but equally arguably, their rules are so broadly circumscribed as to be incapable of any practical application.

As noted earlier, the UN Security Council should stay, generally speaking, within the purposes and principles of the Charter, at least for those who entertain

---

[88] The advisory nature of consultation is no reason to disrespect the prescribed procedure. See Case 138/79, *Roquette Frères* v. *Council* [1980] ECR 3333, esp. para. 33: 'Due consultation of the Parliament in the cases provided for in the Treaty . . . constitutes an essential formality disregard of which means that the measure concerned is void.'

[89] The principle was already laid down in joined cases 21–24/72, *International Fruit Company* v. *Produktschap voor Groenten en Fruit*, [1972] ECR 1219. Its precise application by the Court has, however, been puzzling on occasion. Thus, it remains unclear why judicial review would only be possible when the treaty provisions at stake are self-executing, as the Court found in the first *Banana* case, Case C-280/93, *Germany* v. *Council* [1994] ECR I-4973 and confirmed in case C-149/96, *Portugal* v. *Council*, [1999] ECR I-8395. See generally Jan Klabbers, 'International Law in Community Law: The Law and Politics of Direct Effect' (2002) 21 *YEL*, 263–98.

[90] Case 105/75, *Giuffrida* v. *Council* [1976] ECR 1395.   [91] See generally Art. 46 TEU.

a more or less constitutional vision of the UN (rather than a strictly realist conception).[92] As much follows from Article 24, para. 2,[93] and Article 25 of the Charter.[94] Those purposes and principles are, however, broad.[95] Most famous among them,[96] from a validity point of view, is perhaps Article 2, para. 7, the domestic jurisdiction clause:[97] 'Nothing contained in the present Charter shall authorize the United Nations to intervene in matters which are essentially within the domestic jurisdiction of any state or shall require the Members to submit such matters to settlement under the present Charter; but this principle shall not prejudice the application of enforcement measures under Chapter VII.' Its very inclusion in Article 2 already indicates that the drafters were not too concerned with establishing conditions of validity as such: otherwise, they would have isolated it from a provision which in other paragraphs declares the loftiness of sovereign equality or outlaws the use or threat of force. Article 2, para. 7, is part of the broad principles of the UN and, as Koskenniemi reminds us, those principles and purposes are ambiguous and often pointing in different directions;[98] Article 2, para. 7 was not written as a validity clause, and we should thus not place too much weight upon it.[99]

Nonetheless, it is the closest the Charter comes to a more or less general validity clause, and it has indeed been invoked every now and then to try and prevent the UN, or its organs, from discussing a politically sensitive issue such as human rights. Sometimes states claim that even discussion alone would constitute an intervention in their domestic affairs but that, clearly, goes too

---

[92] On how one's premises may influence one's standpoints, see generally José E. Alvarez, 'Judging the Security Council' (1996) 90 *AJIL*, 1–39.

[93] When it comes to the maintenance of peace and security, the Council 'shall act in accordance with the Purposes and Principles of the United Nations', according to Art. 24, para. 2.

[94] 'The Members of the United Nations agree to accept and carry out the decisions of the Security Council in accordance with the present Charter.' See also Derek Bowett, 'The Impact of Security Council Decisions on Dispute Settlement Procedures' (1994) 5 *EJIL*, 89–101, esp. p. 92.

[95] Indicative is that the Canadian courts (including, finally, the Supreme Court) were divided on whether drugs trafficking fell within the purposes and principles of the UN. In the end, the Supreme Court held that, however serious, drugs trafficking was not contrary to the purposes and principles of the UN. See *Pushpanathan* v. *Canada*, 4 June 1998, ILDC 182 (CA 1998).

[96] Bowett, 'The Impact of Security Council Decisions', p. 96, lists a few other examples relating to the activities of the Security Council. Thus, the Security Council could not impose sanctions without first determining whether a threat or breach of the peace or act of aggression has occurred. Neither could the Council order (only recommend) that states submit to the jurisdiction of the International Court of Justice, nor order a state to transfer part of its territory to another state.

[97] So, e.g., Jochen A. Frowein, 'Are There Limits to the Amendment Procedures in Treaties Constituting International Organisations?'. In Gerhard Hafner *et al.* (eds.), *Liber Amicorum Professor Ignaz Seidl-Hohenveldern in Honour of his 80th Birthday* (The Hague, 1998), pp. 201–18.

[98] Martti Koskenniemi, 'The Police in the Temple. Order, Justice and the UN: A Dialectical View' (1995) 6 *EJIL*, 325–48, esp. p. 327.

[99] Indeed, in its *Namibia* opinion, para. 89, the Court curtly stated that it did not have powers of judicial review over the acts of UN organs to begin with.

far. Under the motto that 'sticks and stones may break your bones, but words can never hurt you', there appears to be a large measure of agreement that mere discussion of a state's policies and practices does not run counter to Article 2, para. 7. Moreover, this already contains an exception: it does not apply to measures taken under Chapter VII; yet, if anything, those are the measures most likely to intervene in a state's domestic affairs.

Another consideration related to Article 2, para. 7, which makes it difficult to apply, is that the PCIJ already held in 1923 that whether something is within a state's domestic jurisdiction is 'an essentially relative question; it depends on the development of international relations'.[100] And if it is accepted that international relations have developed more and more towards interdependence, then it follows that there are not many matters anymore which would undoubtedly fall within a state's domestic jurisdiction. Moreover, the key word is 'essentially': it must concern matters which are 'essentially' within the domestic jurisdiction, and there will not be too many of those around. Indeed, as a basic rule of thumb many commentators use the yardstick of whether a topic has found regulation by international law.

Presumably then, Article 2, para. 7, prohibits the UN from sending fact-finding missions without the consent of the state concerned, as well as sending peace-keepers or human rights rapporteurs without such consent. Whether it goes much further than this appears dubious,[101] and, at any rate, Article 2, para. 7 can safely be circumvented by the Security Council if it acts under Chapter VII of the Charter, as is often the case when setting up schemes which have great domestic impact.[102]

While during the Cold War the Security Council was largely comatose (so much so that a leading textbook on international law in the 1980s could essentially ignore it altogether[103]), its renaissance from the early 1990s onwards has caused quite a bit of concern. The Council has become highly active in imposing sanctions on states and other actors; it has assumed responsibility for the administration of territory in places such as Kosovo and East Timor; and it seems to have usurped some legislative powers as well. All these activities raise issues of legality and validity; consequently, amongst academics, the topic of review of Security Council acts has become a growth industry.[104]

---

[100] *Nationality Decrees Issued in Tunis and Morocco (French Zone)*, advisory opinion, [1923] Publ. PCIJ, Series B, No. 4, p. 24.

[101] Manusama, e.g., using a generous interpretation of Charter law, finds that the Council generally stays within the limits of the law. See Kenneth Manusama, *The United Nations Security Council in the Post-Cold War Era: Applying the Principle of Legality* (Leiden, 2006).

[102] See generally also Steven R. Ratner, *The New UN Peacekeeping: Building Peace in Lands of Conflict after the Cold War* (New York, 1995), pp. 31–3.

[103] See Antonio Cassese, *International Law in a Divided World* (Oxford, 1986).

[104] For an overview of the debate, see Jan Klabbers, 'Straddling Law and Politics: Judicial Review in International Law'. In R. St. J. MacDonald and D. M. Johnston (eds.), *Towards World Constitutionalism* (Leiden, 2005), pp. 809–35.

The leading cases to date illustrate some of the complexities. Whenever it imposes sanctions, the Security Council creates a Sanctions Committee, charged with the task of administering the regime concerned. Messrs Kadi and Yusuf[105] were blacklisted by the Sanctions Committee overseeing the sanctions regime against Afghanistan for having possibly supported terrorist activities. As a result, based on implementing legislation adopted by the EU, their bank accounts were frozen. They claimed this violated some of their human rights, in particular their right to have access to justice and a fair trial, as well as their right to property.[106] Since the UN does not offer the possibility of judicial review, they ended up asking the EU's CFI to review the legality of Security Council acts.[107] The CFI by and large declined, holding that it essentially lacked the jurisdiction to review Security Council acts, even when it concerned human rights. It made one curious exception though. It claimed that it did have the jurisdiction to review the compatibility of Security Council acts with *jus cogens* norms, something it derived most likely from the gravity of such norms.[108]

The cases sparked a lot of discussion on a variety of topics, including such things as the proper relationship between international law and EU law. Most interesting for present purposes though, there have been studies discussing possible substantive limits to Security Council action, aligning Council action with the rule of law.[109] Others have tended to focus somewhat more on procedural issues, accepting that fully-fledged judicial review within the UN is bound to remain a pipe-dream.[110]

Hierarchy between acts

To posit that there are rules relating to the validity of legal acts almost inevitably leads to a discussion of the question whether those rules concerning validity must themselves be of higher status than the legal acts concerned. In other words, there are circumstances where it may be fruitful to think in terms of a hierarchy of norms.

The very idea of a hierarchy of norms within international organizations invites serious political debate, and indeed it seems fair to state that the debate is often hijacked by uncontrollable political arguments. Typically, arguments

---

[105] See the *Kadi* and *Yusuf* cases mentioned above.

[106] The possible human rights implications of sanctions has prompted both the Council of Europe and the UN's Office of Legal Affairs to commission reports. See, respectively, Iain Cameron, 'UN Targeted Sanctions, Legal Safeguards and the European Convention on Human Rights' (2003) 72 *Nordic JIL*, 159–214, and Bardo Fassbender, *Targeted Sanctions and Due Process* (New York, 2006).

[107] See generally also Erika de Wet and André Nollkaemper (eds.), *Review of the Security Council by Member States* (Antwerp, 2003).

[108] This is a rather curious claim in that jurisdiction would seem to be an issue separate from the contents of norms; at no point did the CFI explain its position.

[109] Possibly the most useful of these is Jeremy Matam Farrall, *United Nations Sanctions and the Rule of Law* (Cambridge, 2007).

[110] An example is Jan Klabbers, 'Kadi Justice at the Security Council?' (2007) 4 *IOLR*, 293–304.

against hierarchy proclaim that to organize a hierarchy is to undermine state sovereignty so as to favour the organization, while arguments in favour of hierarchy often proclaim that rules on hierarchy are but technical devices which may facilitate the work of the organization and are most certainly not aimed at undermining the sovereignty of its members.

International law in general has a hard time thinking in terms of a hierarchy of norms. While few would disagree with the statement that the prohibition of genocide is superior to, say, a prohibition on the raising of tariffs, it does not automatically follow that such distinctions can be reflected by the formal status of norms.[111] While in particular the concept of peremptory norms of international law (*jus cogens*) has been forcefully advocated, others have pointed out that such peremptory norms ought to be binding even without a consensual basis, which in turn is difficult to reconcile with the very notion of state sovereignty.[112]

International tribunals have so far not dealt with the effects of *jus cogens* on the activities of international organizations, although the issue was raised before the ICJ in the dispute between Bosnia and Serbia.[113] After the Security Council had imposed an arms embargo by means of Resolution 713 (1991), Bosnia raised the argument that, as the Serbs had been heavily armed whereas the Bosnians had not, the resolution prevented the Bosnians from being able to defend themselves and therewith contributed to the genocide of the Bosnians. And since genocide, so the argument ran, was prohibited as a matter of *jus cogens*, it followed that Security Council Resolution 713 (1991) should be declared invalid.

The majority opinion left the argument unaddressed, but *ad hoc* Judge Elihu Lauterpacht carefully hinted that although the 'chain of hypotheses . . . involves some debatable links', there may nevertheless be some merit in Bosnia's argument. In particular, he felt that the relevance of *jus cogens* should be drawn to the attention of the Security Council. Without (wisely) taking a definitive stand on the effect of *jus cogens* on Security Council resolutions, Judge Lauterpacht did seem to suggest that the Council may be bound to respect *jus cogens*.[114]

Jus cogens aside, there are few provisions of general international law which indicate a possible hierarchy of norms.[115] Perhaps the main example is

---

[111] And perhaps, as has been argued, this is for the better, as an obsession with hierarchy may well result in 'a bureaucratic culture of blind obedience'. See Martti Koskenniemi, 'Hierarchy in International Law: A Sketch' (1997) 8 *EJIL*, 566–82, esp. p. 582.

[112] A famous critique is Weil, 'Towards Relative Normativity'; arguably the most insightful defence is John Tasioulas, 'In Defence of Relative Normativity: Communitarian Values and the *Nicaragua* Case' (1996) 16 *Oxford Journal of Legal Studies*, 85–128.

[113] *Case Concerning Application of the Convention on the Prevention and Punishment of the Crime of Genocide (Bosnia and Herzegovina v. Yugoslavia (Serbia and Montenegro))*, Provisional measures, order of 13 September 1993, [1993] ICJ Reports 325.

[114] See in particular para. 104 of his separate opinion. In the literature, the position that the Council is bound by *jus cogens* is often treated as self-evident. See, e.g., Doehring, 'Unlawful Resolutions'.

[115] Indeed, the Vienna Convention on the Law of Treaties has a hard time dealing with the topic of conflicting treaties, precisely because some possible situations defy solution. The classic study is Guyora Binder, *Treaty Conflict and Political Contradiction: The Dialectic of Duplicity* (New

Article 103 of the UN Charter, which provides that, where conflict arises between obligations under the UN Charter and obligations under other treaties, the UN Charter prevails.

Here too a final judicial determination has yet to be made. In the 1992 *Lockerbie* cases[116] the ICJ limited itself to stating that *prima facie*, the obligations of states arising under the UN Charter (in particular through Security Council resolutions) would indeed seem to prevail over obligations or rights arising under another convention, but the Court was careful to point out that at that precise moment in the proceedings, no definitive findings had been made.[117]

With many international organizations, the question of hierarchy does not give rise to many problems, for it is clear that, normally speaking, the basic rule is that, if there are superior norms at all, these will be contained in the constituent treaty. It is no coincidence that in EC law circles, regulations and other instruments are invariably referred to as 'secondary legislation', while the constituent treaties are dubbed 'primary legislation'. Moreover, there is the assumption that the provisions of the constitution itself will not be contradictory, so that no issues of hierarchy can possibly arise.

However, as the legal system grows and grows, and more and more law is generated, at some point in time some stand on the hierarchy of norms would seem to be desirable. It should come as no surprise that, within the EC, there is some debate as to whether or not a formal hierarchy should be introduced.[118]

Within the WTO, a rough form of hierarchy is established, at least when it concerns the relations between the various documents comprising the world trade regime. Thus, the Marrakesh Agreement establishing the World Trade Organization prevails over any of the substantive Multilateral Trade Agreements,[119] while the Multilateral Trade Agreements themselves, by virtue of a so-called 'General interpretative note', prevail over the provisions of the remnants of the old GATT as amended into GATT 1994.[120]

York, 1988). Also useful is Jan Mus, *Verdragsconflicten voor de Nederlandse rechter* (Zwolle, 1996). Recently, the topic has been studied with special reference to the WTO and the EU. See, respectively, Joost Pauwelyn, *Conflict of Norms in Public International Law* (Cambridge, 2003) and Jan Klabbers, *Treaty Conflict and the European Union* (Cambridge, 2009).

[116] *Case concerning questions of interpretation and application of the 1971 Montreal Convention arising from the aerial incident at Lockerbie (Libya v. UK)*, provisional measures, [1992] ICJ Reports 3; almost parallel proceedings took place between Libya and the USA, [1992] ICJ Reports 114.

[117] Compare in particular paras. 39 (*Libya v. UK*) and 42 (*Libya v. USA*).

[118] See Roland Bieber and Isabelle Salomé, 'Hierarchy of Norms in European Law' (1996) 33 *CMLRev*, 907–30. The defeated Treaty Establishing a Constitution for Europe went a long way towards establishing a formal hierarchy. For a discussion, see Koen Lenaerts and Marlies DeSomer, 'Towards a Hierarchy of Legal Acts in the European Union? Simplification of Legal Instruments and Procedures' (2005) 11 *European Law Journal*, 744–65.

[119] Article XVI, para. 3, Marrakesh Agreement.

[120] This concerns the general interpretative note to Annex 1a, this Annex being the one containing a number of agreements on trade in goods.

Concluding remarks

Issues relating to the validity of legal norms emanating from international organizations are bound to stir up controversy, for the simple reason that so many interests and rights are at issue. Such issues involve the legal positions of the majorities and minorities among the member states of the international organization concerned, but often go beyond this dichotomy in that many decisions may affect individuals or companies as well as member states and organs and may, from the helicopter view, also affect the legitimacy of the organization itself.

Perhaps the establishment of the Yugoslavia Tribunal provides a convenient example. While the decision of the Security Council to establish the Tribunal may well have been justifiable, it nonetheless elicited some serious controversy. The General Assembly, for one, withheld funding for a while; from the defendants' side, the validity of the creation has been contested with the argument that the decision to create the Tribunal was *ultra vires* the Council; in practical terms, not all member states have been equally eager to co-operate; and from other corners, the creation of the Tribunal has been regarded as possibly undermining the Council's legitimacy.[121]

Still, there is no mistaking that it remains difficult to protect oneself against the actions of a majority running wild. The *ultra vires* doctrine, as noted earlier, would be a most suitable defence mechanism, as it is in domestic legal systems, but in practice, it is largely unable to do its job effectively. And even where it could hypothetically be used, it may easily be overruled by acceptance, acquiescence or estoppel.

Small wonder then that many have felt the need to try somehow to put the brakes on illegal decisions of international organizations. Some have proposed a procedural device, such as full judicial review[122] or granting international organizations *locus standi* before the ICJ.[123] Others have tried to envisage more substantive brakes on organizational activities. Thus, for some, membership of an organization entails an inherent right to withhold contributions in cases where the organization engages in activities which may be deemed unlawful.[124]

And for others, organizations are said to be bound by *jus cogens* norms. Members would even have an obligation towards the organization not to give effect to any decisions that may violate such *jus cogens* norms: the loyalty that

---

[121] See, e.g., Koskenniemi, 'The Police in the Temple'.

[122] So, e.g., Geoffrey R. Watson, 'Constitutionalism, Judicial Review, and the World Court' (1993) 34 *Harvard ILJ*, 1–45.

[123] So, e.g., Paul C. Szasz, 'Granting International Organizations *Ius Standi* in the International Court of Justice'. In A. S. Muller *et al.* (eds.), *The International Court of Justice: Its Future Role after Fifty Years* (The Hague, 1997), pp. 169–88.

[124] See Elisabeth Zoller, 'The "Corporate Will" of the United Nations and the Rights of the Minority' (1987) 81 *AJIL*, 610–34, esp. pp. 631–2. She invokes, ironically perhaps, a sort of implied powers doctrine in support, but this time implied powers of member states rather than of the organization.

members owe to the organizations they have created or joined does not extend to violations by those organizations of fundamental rules; in the end, states cannot be compelled to violate peremptory norms of international law.[125]

In particular the two latter positions indicate the structural flexibility of international law in general, and the law of international organizations in particular. Favouring a withholding of payments and a refusal to carry out decisions amounts, in one sense, to calling for disobedience; it amounts to advocating a violation of the constituent document. Yet, in both cases the violation is justified (and with some plausibility) as actually being in the interest of the organization itself: the violation is advocated so as to save the organization from itself, and to protect a minority from the dictates of the majority.[126] And that, in turn, might require a reversal of arguments so as to make sure that the majority does not suffer under the tyranny of the minority.

[125] Doehring, 'Unlawful Resolutions'.   [126] Zoller, 'The Rights of the Minority', p. 614.

12

Dispute settlement

Introduction

All legal systems will have found a way to settle disputes between their subjects in a legally prescribed manner. These may range from having disputes settled by the elders of a tribe or village following their wisdom to highly formal and formalized procedures involving barristers, judges, juries and journalists, following strictly defined rules of law.

A similar variety can be seen within international organizations: most organizations will have some mechanism to settle disputes, and these may range from highly complex and organized ways where a premium is put on application of strict rules (the EC is the paradigm example) to rather more flexible ways where the ironing out of the conflict is deemed more important than the rigid application of strict rules (e.g., the old GATT[1]).

Those different mechanisms may well stem from the consideration that, within an organization made up of a relatively small number of states, strict judicial settlement is somehow incongruous: if those states embark on a common project, it may not be a particularly good idea to have them meet in court on a regular basis; litigation, with its connotations of winners and losers, guilty parties and victims, crime and punishment, is not conducive to fostering the spirit of community. This may explain why advisory opinions are relatively popular within international organizations,[2] whereas binding judicial settlement is reasonably rare and usually deals with the legal protection of individuals or companies rather than with inter-state disputes.

Additionally, the variety of dispute settlement mechanisms reflects a variety of ideas as to the roles of law and of dispute settlement within the organization. In an organization such as the EC, it has always been assumed that the Court of Justice could and should play an important role in 'cementing' the organization. The Court is not just, according to Article 220 (ex-Article 164) of the TEC, the ultimate guardian of legality, but is also assigned the task of

---

[1] The seminal study is Robert E. Hudec, *The GATT Legal System and World Trade Diplomacy* (New York, 1975).

[2] For an overview of the popularity of advisory opinions, see Kenneth J. Keith, *The Extent of the Advisory Jurisdiction of the International Court of Justice* (Leiden, 1971), pp. 16–18.

guaranteeing the unity of Community law (in particular via the preliminary reference procedure of what used to be Article 177 of the TEC[3]) and has traditionally been viewed as the motor of the integration process.[4] Something similar is sometimes expected (or feared) with respect to the WTO's dispute settlement mechanism.[5]

In contrast, dispute settlement procedures in other organizations are usually more limited in ambition: they purport to settle disputes, by legal means if possible, but taking liberties where necessary. Here, then, the dispute settlement mechanism is not envisaged to play an additional role in organizational politics; indeed, the somewhat ironic hypothesis may be formulated according to which the greater the element of politics in dispute settlement is thought to be, the smaller will be the political role of the dispute settlement organ.

The types of disputes to be settled may also vary, and will vary from organization to organization.[6] First and foremost, dispute settlement mechanisms may facilitate the settlement of disputes between member states of the organization.[7] In addition, there may also be disputes between a member state and the organization or a member and one or more organs of the organization. Within the EC, it happens not infrequently that the dispute to be settled is one between various organs of the organization among themselves. A recurring feature, typical of international organizations, is the settlement of staff disputes. And finally, even more typical of international organizations is that some of them provide for the advisory jurisdiction of tribunals.

Where international organizations themselves are involved, formal methods of dispute settlement may not always be utilized: organizations have no standing before the ICJ,[8] and claims before domestic courts may often encounter immunity defences.[9] Hence, recourse is often had to arbitration or to claims commissions.[10] In both cases, the organization remains in control, as its consent is required for the establishment of an arbitral tribunal or claims commission.

---

[3] Nowadays Art. 234 TEC.

[4] So, e.g., Richard H. Lauwaars and C. W. A. Timmermans, *Europees Gemeenschapsrecht in kort bestek* (3rd edn, Groningen, 1994), pp. 21–2; for a balanced (if brief) assessment of the role of law in European integration generally, see T. Koopmans, 'The Role of Law in the Next Stage of European Integration' (1986) 35 *ICLQ*, 925–31.

[5] For a balanced and sophisticated discussion, see Deborah Z. Cass, *The Constitutionalization of the World Trade Organization: Legitimacy, Democracy, and Community in the International Trading System* (Oxford, 2005).

[6] Judicial review of organizational acts is addressed in the previous chapter.

[7] Thus, within the ILO, a procedure of inquiry may be initiated under Art. 26 ILO by a member concerning the degree of observance by another member of any convention concluded under ILO auspices. The first of these was a complaint by Ghana against Portugal in 1962 concerning the Abolition of Forced Labour Convention; see 35 *ILR* 285.

[8] Article 34 Statute ICJ.   [9] See Chapter 8 above.

[10] See, e.g., Mahnoush H. Arsanjani, 'Claims against International Organizations: *Quis Custodiet Ipsos Custodes*' (1981) 7 *Yale Journal of World Public Order*, 131–76, esp. 161–3. See generally also Karel Wellens, *Remedies against International Organisations* (Cambridge, 2002).

The ICJ's advisory jurisdiction

The UN Charter enumerates, in Article 33, a number of methods for the peaceful settlement of disputes. States may resort to negotiations, conciliation, good offices, mediation, arbitration, judicial settlement, et cetera. There is no point in generally describing those, except to say perhaps that, according to some, the duty to settle disputes peacefully is itself a hard and fast rule of international law.[11]

The jurisdiction of the ICJ in cases involving states need not be described here in great detail. In general terms, the ICJ can have jurisdiction in contentious proceedings between states only if those states have somehow consented thereto, and the most prominent means for consenting to the Court's jurisdiction include the conclusion of a *compromis*; providing for the Court's jurisdiction in a more general treaty; and the unilateral acceptance of the Court's jurisdiction as compulsory.[12]

Of course, the ICJ is one of the principal organs of the UN, and there is a clear organizational link between the UN and the ICJ, but the ICJ is more than just the judicial organ of a particular international organization: its ambitions go beyond a merely organizational role, although in particular its advisory role pays homage to the organizational backdrop.

The ICJ does not, in contentious proceedings, grant access to entities other than states, and this renders the possibility of requesting an advisory opinion the sole means by which international organizations (some of them, at any rate) may come before the Court. The facility of rendering advisory opinions is provided for in Article 96 of the UN Charter:

1 The General Assembly or the Security Council may request the International Court of Justice to give an advisory opinion on any legal question.
2 Other organs of the United Nations and specialized agencies, which may at any time be so authorized by the General Assembly, may also request advisory opinions of the Court on legal questions arising within the scope of their activities.

The procedure is further outlined in the Court's Statute, which provides in Article 65 that the question shall be put in writing and shall be as precise as possible. Article 66 proceeds by stating that the registrar of the ICJ will give notice of the request to all states entitled to appear before the Court. It will ask those states, as well as international organizations, for further information. Apart from providing information, states and organizations are also entitled to make substantive comments.

---

[11] A useful overview is J. G. Merrills, *International Dispute Settlement* (2nd edn, Cambridge, 1991).
[12] Article 36 Statute ICJ.

The ICJ has rather consistently held that its advisory power establishes the connection with the UN family: through its advisory powers it is in the position to provide legal counsel to the UN. It follows that the Court has usually been very broad-minded concerning its advisory role.[13] While the power to accept a request is discretionary, there are few, if any, arguments which it will invoke to deny a request for advice, provided of course the request itself is admissible.

Still, the system did not get off to a flying start. One of the first cases ever before the PCIJ, the *Eastern Carelia* case, was a request for advice coming from the League of Nations concerning a dispute between Russia and Finland.[14] They had concluded the Treaty of Dorpat (Tartu) in 1920, but a dispute ensued over the precise legal status of two communities in Eastern Carelia (which had been Finnish territory). The dispute was submitted to the League of Nations. The League, in turn, submitted the dispute to the PCIJ for advice, but the Court refused to become involved, holding that the dispute was in reality a quite contentious one between two states, one of whom had not accepted the Court's jurisdiction in contentious proceedings and was not even a member of the League at the time. Were the Court to give advice in such a case and under such circumstances, it would pronounce on an inter-state dispute through the back door of the advisory power. As the Court put it: 'Answering the question would be substantially equivalent to deciding the dispute between the parties.'[15]

In later cases, however, the Court has been quite willing to lend an ear to requests for advisory opinions, even if the background would involve a clear dispute between states.[16] States have made the most curious arguments in trying to stop the Court from rendering an advisory opinion (the eternal yet desperate favourite being that the question put to the Court is political rather than legal), but as soon as the Court can identify any link between the request and the work of the organization concerned, it will assume that it has the required jurisdiction. As the Court put it in 1950: 'The Court's opinion is given not to the States, but to the Organization which is entitled to request it; the reply of the Court, itself an organ of the United Nations, represents its participation in the activities of the Organization, and, in principle, should not be refused.'[17] The only request which the Court has rejected was that of the World Health Assembly to pronounce on the legality of the use of nuclear weapons. Here the

---

[13] See also Keith, *The Advisory Jurisdiction*, p. 146.

[14] *Request for advisory opinion concerning the Status of Eastern Carelia*, Court's reply, 23 July 1923, [1923] Publ. PCIJ, Series B, no. 5.

[15] *Ibid.*, p. 29.

[16] An example is *Western Sahara*, advisory opinion, [1975] ICJ Reports 12. Here the background involved 'a legal question actually pending' between, at least, Spain and Morocco; as the Court included a Spanish judge, Morocco was entitled to appoint a judge *ad hoc*. See *Western Sahara*, order of 22 May 1975, [1975] ICJ Reports 6. A strongly political background is also visible in *Legal Consequences of the Construction of a Wall in the Occupied Palestinian Territory*, [2004] ICJ Reports 136.

[17] *Interpretation of peace treaties with Bulgaria, Hungary and Romania*, advisory opinion, [1950] ICJ Reports 65, p. 71.

Court found that as the WHO (and thus also the WHA) has no powers to deal with issues of nuclear weapons, it could not possibly have the power to ask the ICJ for an advisory opinion on the topic. After all, 'none of the functions of the WHO is dependent upon the legality of the situations upon which it must act'.[18]

In rendering advisory opinions, the Court has granted itself the liberty to reformulate the questions asked of it, on the theory that sometimes the requesting organ formulates its questions in an unfortunate manner. In attempting to identify what is 'really in issue', the Court is guided by the idea that it should uncover the intentions of the requesting body.[19] The risk, of course, is that by reformulating the question, the Court might end up not answering the initial question at all.

It could be (and has been) argued[20] that there are two kinds of advisory opinions. The first sort is the sort contemplated by the UN Charter and the Court's Statute, where the Court literally gives advice. As the Court itself has put it: 'The Court's reply is only of an advisory character: as such, it has no binding force.'[21]

Thus, if the General Assembly or the Security Council, or any other organ so authorized, files a request on the basis of the Charter and the Statute, it is clear that the Opinion is only advisory. It may be of great weight, and it may be accepted as authoritative and, for all practical purposes, as binding as a judgment,[22] but still, as a formal matter, it is not to be considered binding.

In some cases, however, the power to request an advisory opinion is not based on the Charter and the Statute as such, but on a different convention. An example is offered by Article 30 of the 1946 General Convention on Privileges and Immunities of the UN: 'If a difference arises between the United Nations on the one hand and a Member on the other hand, a request shall be made for an advisory opinion on any legal question involved in accordance with Article 96 of the Charter and Article 65 of the Statute of the Court. The opinion given by the Court shall be accepted as decisive by the parties.' Thus, although in name an advisory opinion, it will be accepted as 'decisive', or final. Several other conventions contain similar clauses, opening up the possibility of adding weight to advisory opinions. It is important to note though, as the Court underlined in its 1999 *Cumaraswamy* opinion, that the binding effect of such opinions

---

[18] *Legality of the use by a state of nuclear weapons in armed conflict*, advisory opinion, [1996] ICJ Reports 66, para. 20.

[19] See, e.g., *Application for review of Judgement No. 333 of the United Nations Administrative Tribunal*, advisory opinion, [1987] ICJ Reports 18, paras. 43–5.

[20] See Roberto Ago, '"Binding" Advisory Opinions of the International Court of Justice' (1991) 85 *AJIL*, 439–51.

[21] *Interpretation of peace treaties*, p. 71. The same argument was happily embraced by South Africa's Supreme Court with respect to the ICJ's 1971 *Namibia* opinion in *Binga* v. *The Administrator-General for South West Africa and others*, decision of 22 June 1984, in 82 *ILR* 465.

[22] See also Keith, *The Advisory Jurisdiction*, pp. 221–2.

stems from a collateral agreement (such as, for example, the 1946 General Convention); the opinion itself remains, as it were, advisory.[23]

In the *Mazilu* case,[24] the possibility of a 'binding' advisory opinion created something of a problem. Romania, Mr Mazilu's state of origin, had made a reservation relating to Article 30 of the General Convention, thus precluding the possibility of asking the Court for a binding advisory opinion. For that reason, it also advanced the argument that no advisory opinions at all could be sought. The Court however disagreed, holding in effect that even if the procedure of Article 30 cannot be used, that still leaves the General Assembly (or, in this case, ECOSOC), free to ask for an advice by way of the procedure envisaged in Charter and Statute. Obviously, Romania's reservation implied that the Court could give no binding advisory opinion; but there was no problem in rendering a non-binding advisory opinion.[25]

Other tribunals within the UN system

While the ICJ is the principal judicial organ of the UN, it is by no means the only one. As observed earlier, an important innovation was the creation of an administrative tribunal by the General Assembly, and quite a number of treaties concluded under the auspices of the UN have included the creation of some organ or other with a judicial or quasi-judicial function.

Thus, a number of specialized human rights treaties concluded under the aegis of the UN all have their own supervisory organs: there is a Committee against Torture, a Committee on the Elimination of Discrimination against Women as well as one on the Elimination of Racial Discrimination, and a Committee on the Rights of the Child.[26] In addition, the two general human rights covenants (those on Civil and Political Rights, and on Economic, Social and Cultural Rights, respectively) also have their own supervisory organs.

Generally speaking, those bodies will receive reports from the parties to the conventions establishing them on the human rights situation, and will proceed, on the basis of those reports, to make suggestions and recommendations. Some may, however, also entertain complaints or communications made by states or even by individuals, provided the state against whom the communication is addressed has recognized the jurisdiction of the body in question and usually insisting that local remedies are exhausted.[27]

---

[23] *Difference relating to immunity of legal process of a special rapporteur of the Commission of Human Rights (Cumaraswamy)*, advisory opinion of 29 April 1999 (nyr), para. 25.

[24] *Applicability of Article VI, Section 22, of the Convention on Privileges and Immunities of the United Nations*, advisory opinion, [1989] ICJ Reports 177.

[25] *Ibid.*, in particular paras. 29–36.

[26] On the work of the latter, see Jutta Gras, *Monitoring the Convention on the Rights of the Child* (Helsinki, 2001).

[27] This applies to the Committee against Torture and to the Human Rights Committee set up to supervise the implementation of the International Covenant on Civil and Political Rights, and may one day also apply to the Committee on the Protection of the Rights of All Migrant

Strictly speaking, all those bodies will hardly qualify as judicial bodies; none of them can make binding decisions in cases before them, and, indeed, actual cases can only come before a few of them to begin with. Nonetheless, their impact is generally felt to be considerable: the statements emanating from those bodies are usually regarded as authoritative interpretations of the underlying conventions, and the absence of the power to make binding determinations has not impeded (in particular) the Human Rights Committee in coming up with an impressive body of 'case law', and much of the contents of the International Covenant on Civil and Political Rights has been further developed by means of General Comments and through questioning states on the basis of their national reports.[28]

More in the nature of judicial bodies are the two *ad hoc* bodies established by the Security Council in the early 1990s. Those do not purport to oversee the implementation of a single convention, but are rather responses to grave atrocities committed. Both the Yugoslavia Tribunal,[29] created in 1993, and the Rwanda Tribunal,[30] created in 1994, allow for binding determinations to be made after cases have been brought by a prosecutor (itself quite an innovation in international law). Defendants may eventually end up in prison once it is established by a Trial Chamber or Appeals Chamber that they have been guilty of violations of humanitarian law, crimes against humanity, or genocide; the death penalty is, however, excluded.

The very creation of the tribunals by the Security Council implies that the consent of states is deemed of lesser importance.[31] Hence, there is no need for optional protocols through which states can recognize the jurisdiction of either of the tribunals, nor are there any parties to the Statutes of either tribunal. Instead, the binding nature of the tribunals' decisions derives from Article 25, in conjunction with Chapter VII, of the Charter. Where a jurisdictional claim of one of the tribunals may overlap with that of a state, the basic notion to be applied is that of primacy: the tribunal has the final say, at least as a formal matter, but may have to respect the position of a recalcitrant member state as it lacks the means to actually take a suspect into custody unless

---

Workers and Members of their Families, which is envisaged in a convention that has yet to enter into force.

[28] The seminal study is Dominic McGoldrick, *The Human Rights Committee: Its Role in the Development of the International Covenant on Civil and Political Rights* (Oxford, 1991).

[29] See generally Daphna Shraga and Ralph Zacklin, 'The International Criminal Tribunal for the Former Yugoslavia' (1994) 5 *EJIL*, 360–80. On the practicalities involved in setting up the Tribunal, see Julian J. E. Schutte, 'Legal and Practical Implications, from the Perspective of the Host Country, Relating to the Establishment of the International Tribunal for the Former Yugoslavia' (1994) 5 *Criminal Law Forum*, 423–50.

[30] See generally Roy S. Lee, 'The Rwanda Tribunal' (1996) 9 *Leiden JIL*, 37–61.

[31] In August 2000, the Security Council gave the green light for the creation of a tribunal dealing with atrocities in Sierra Leone (Resolution 1315). Here, however, the consent of the government of Sierra Leone was envisaged. The UN has also been (or still is) involved in setting up courts in Bosnia, Kosovo, East Timor, and Cambodia. For a useful discussion, see Taru Kuosmanen, *Bringing Justice Closer: Hybrid Courts in Post-conflict Societies* (Helsinki, 2007).

he or she is handed over, short of using shady techniques such as luring or abduction.[32]

Of a different order altogether is the United Nations Compensation Commission, although this too was created by the Security Council. The Compensation Commission grew out of the aftermath of Iraq's invasion of Kuwait, and is designed to provide compensation for war damages on the basis of claims. Such claims could[33] be brought by individuals, corporations, governments and international organizations, although only governments had direct access to the Commission. The Commission, it has been observed, is a political body, despite the fact that its main function consists of the consideration and verification of claims and the determination of any losses. Obviously then, political as it may be, its tasks (and composition) ensure that judicial elements are not entirely absent.[34]

The Yugoslavia and Rwanda Tribunals and the UN Compensation Commission have in common not only that they were all created by the Security Council on the basis of the collective security functions of the Charter, but also that their existence is, in principle, temporary. Their jurisdiction is limited in time, so sooner or later they will have decided all cases or settled all claims before them, after which they can be dissolved. The same applies to the various Sanctions Committees, quasi-judicial bodies set up by the Security Council to monitor and regulate compliance with UN-ordained sanctions.[35]

By contrast, the International Tribunal for the Law of the Sea, created by means of the 1982 Law of the Sea Convention which was concluded under the aegis of the UN, is established for an unlimited period of time. It has jurisdiction in cases arising under (but not limited to) the Law of the Sea Convention, provided that the parties to the dispute have accepted its jurisdiction. Those that have not were nonetheless required to accept another mode of peaceful dispute settlement. A particular competence of the Tribunal is dealing with urgent cases: prescription of interim measures (even if main proceedings are brought elsewhere), and requests concerning the prompt release of vessels and crew. The Tribunal comprises a special Sea-Bed Disputes Chamber, which not only is competent to decide contentious cases but also may render advisory

---

[32] For an argument that abductions may be permissible under certain conditions, see Michael P. Scharf, '*The Prosecutor* v. *Slavko Dokmanovic*: Irregular Rendition and the ICTY' (1998) 11 *Leiden JIL*, 369–82.

[33] The deadline for submitting claims was 1 August 1994.

[34] See Carlos Alzamora, 'The UN Compensation Commission: An Overview'. In Richard B. Lillich (ed.), *The United Nations Compensation Commission* (Irvington, NY, 1995), pp. 3–14. The panellists are invariably drawn from the legal profession.

[35] See, e.g., Martti Koskenniemi, 'Le Comité de Sanctions (créé par la résolution 661 (1990) du Conseil de Sécurité)' (1991) 37 *AFDI*, 119–37; see also Michael P. Scharf and Joshua L. Dorosin, 'Interpreting UN Sanctions: The Rulings and Role of the Yugoslavia Sanctions Committee' (1993) 19 *Brooklyn JIL*, 771–827. For a very useful overview of the operations of sanctions committees, see Jeremy Matam Farrall, *United Nations Sanctions and the Rule of Law* (Cambridge, 2007).

opinions. Also noteworthy is the fact that a right of access is granted to non-state entities.[36]

Dispute settlement in the EC

Within the European Community system, the role of the Court of Justice is of the utmost importance. It shall ensure, as Article 220 (ex-Article 164) TEC puts it, that in the interpretation and application of the EC Treaty the law is observed. To that end, twenty-seven judges (one for each member state) and eight advocates-general[37] deliver well over 100 judgments per year. In addition, the twenty-seven judges of the Court of First Instance (created by virtue of the 1986 Single European Act so as to relieve the Court's workload) decide a similar amount of cases annually. Since 2005, staff cases end up before the newly created Civil Service Tribunal.

Curiously perhaps, traditional inter-state dispute settlement is almost non-existent before the Court. One of the very few cases brought by a member state against another member state involved a dispute between France and Britain over fisheries.[38]

To some extent, this finds its cause no doubt in the circumstance that cases against member states may be, and often are, brought by the Commission, under Article 226 (formerly Article 169) TEC: where the Commission brings a case, individual member states no longer have to feel compelled to do so. Indeed, it may happen that the Commission acts upon the instigation of a member state which would be reluctant to start proceedings itself.

A peculiar feature is the facility (largely under the rubric of judicial review, dealt with in the previous chapter) for the Community's institutions to bring proceedings against each other. Usually, such cases reflect constitutional struggles about which institutions shall exercise what powers, or struggles relating to the proper decision-making procedures to be followed.[39] Here too, in the background, power issues loom large. For a dispute concerning decision-making procedures is often one involving the prerogatives of the institutions involved.

The most innovative feature of the judicial mechanism of the EC is without a doubt the possibility for national courts to refer matters to the EC Court: the preliminary reference procedure of Article 234 (formerly Article 177) TEC. Under this procedure, usually understood as an attempt to institutionalize dialogue between the EC Court and the courts of the member states, the latter can (and if they are the highest national courts, must) ask the EC Court for a

---

[36] For a general overview, see Thomas A. Mensah, 'The International Tribunal for the Law of the Sea' (1998) 11 *Leiden JIL*, 527–46.

[37] Compare Art. 222 (ex-Art. 166) TEC.

[38] Case 141/78, *France* v. *United Kingdom* [1979] ECR 2923.

[39] Or, related, the proper legal basis for Community measures. On this, see Ronald H. van Ooik, *De keuze der rechtsgrondslag voor besluiten van de Europese Unie* (Deventer, 1999).

preliminary ruling on questions relating to (in a nutshell) the interpretation of the Treaty and the interpretation and validity of the acts of the institutions.[40]

The precise circumstances in which the highest national courts must ask for a ruling remain somewhat nebulous though: while the Court has clarified that the obligation to ask for a ruling evaporates when the legal situation has already been clarified (the *acte éclairé* doctrine) or when the answer is abundantly clear (the *acte clair* doctrine), in particular the latter scenario has been given so many caveats by the Court that it could, if it wants, always question the appropriateness of a member state court's invocation of the *acte clair* doctrine.[41]

Finally, apart from the possibility of appearing as a sort of cassation court in cases first brought to the Court of First Instance, the EC Court may also act in something of an advisory capacity when it concerns the conclusion of international agreements by the Community. Under Article 300 (ex-Article 228) of the TEC the Council, the Commission, or any member state may ask the Court for an 'opinion' as to whether 'an agreement envisaged' is compatible with the EC Treaty.[42]

This facility is not always used for the right reasons. Thus, in *Opinion 1/94*[43] (asked for by the Commission and dealing with the EC as a founding member of the WTO), the Court ended up outlining the external powers of the various institutions. But that is hardly what Article 300 (ex-Article 228) sets out to accomplish in concentrating on the compatibility of the agreement with EC law. It takes a rather big leap to subsume internal power struggles also under that heading.[44]

The Commission is not the only one trying to use the Court for more political reasons. Another example is *Opinion 2/94*,[45] this time asked for by the Council, on whether it is at all possible that the EC would accede to the European Convention on Human Rights (ECHR). The Court held, not surprisingly perhaps, such accession to be impossible, since accession to a human rights instrument would remain outside the competences of the EC. The point to note is that the Council asked for advice even prior to contemplating acceding to the European

---

[40] A similar procedure was later created within Benelux; for an application, see the decision of the Benelux Court of Justice in *MBAK and another* v. *Minister for Foreign Affairs*, decision of 20 December 1988, in 99 *ILR* 38.

[41] See case 283/81, *Srl CILFIT* v. *Italian Ministry of Health* [1982] ECR 3415, para. 21, holding that the highest domestic courts need not bother the EC Court when 'the correct application of Community law is so obvious as to leave no scope for any reasonable doubt. The existence of such a possibility must be assessed in the light of the specific characteristics of Community law, the particular difficulties to which its interpretations give rise and the risk of divergences in judicial decisions within the Community.'

[42] In *Opinion 3/94 (Framework Agreement on Bananas)* [1995] ECR I–4577, the Court declined to say anything about an agreement that had already been concluded.

[43] *Opinion 1/94 (WTO)* [1994] ECR I-5267.

[44] Although the leap can be made (if somewhat contrived perhaps) in that, ultimately, the test of compatibility with EC law presupposes that the envisaged treaty topic falls within Community competence to begin with.

[45] *Opinion 2/94 (ECHR)* [1996] ECR I-1759.

Convention. Paragraph 6 of Article 300 (ex-Article 228) of the TEC mentions that the Court can be asked for an opinion on 'an agreement envisaged'. To consider something as abstract as the hypothetical possibility that one day the EC might be willing to accede to the ECHR is stretching that provision just a little bit.[46]

The terms of Article 300 (ex-Article 228) of the TEC are somewhat ambiguous on the legal effect of the Court's opinions, but by and large appear to suggest that they are best regarded as binding. The provision specifies that if the Court finds that an envisaged agreement is adverse to EC law, then the agreement may only enter into force in accordance with Article 48 (ex-Article N) of the TEU. In other words: if a proposed treaty conflicts with the EC Treaty, the EC Treaty should be amended. That itself seems to point in the direction that the Court's opinions are to be regarded as binding.

Still, the more usual practice is not that the EC Treaty will be amended, but rather that the 'envisaged agreement' will be renegotiated: a prime example is the EEA agreement, first rejected by the Court, later renegotiated and given the stamp of approval.[47] That is, of course, a lot easier than amending the EC Treaty itself: the latter would open up Pandora's Box and, ironically perhaps, undermine the very supremacy of EC law.

Dispute settlement in other organizations

Other organizations have, as a rule, less elaborate dispute settlement mechanisms, although the machinery set up to supervise the implementation of the European Convention on Human Rights, concluded under the auspices of the Council of Europe, is impressive in its own right. Other organizations having their own judicial organ include the OSCE,[48] ECOWAS,[49] EFTA, the Andean Common Market, Benelux, the Organization of Central American States, the Organization of Arab Petroleum Exporting Countries, and the Common Market for Eastern and Southern Africa.[50]

Other organizations have difficulties envisaging legal methods of dispute settlement at all. There is, for example, no such thing as a NATO court. What will usually happen if NATO's member states have a serious dispute is that politicians will exercise some deep massage: the remedy will be to look for a compromise between those in dispute – such compromise, needless to say, may not have much to do with applicable rules of law.

---

[46] See also Meinhard Hilf, 'The ECJ's Opinion 1/94 on the WTO – No Surprise, But Wise?' (1995) 6 *EJIL*, 245–59, p. 250, note 15.

[47] *Opinion 1/91 (EEA)* [1991] ECR I-6079, and *Opinion 1/92 (EEA)* [1992] ECR I-2825.

[48] See generally Susanne Jacobi, 'The OSCE Court: An Overview' (1997) 10 *Leiden JIL*, 281–94.

[49] See Koti Ofeng Kufuor, 'Securing Compliance with the Judgments of the ECOWAS Court of Justice' (1996) 8 *African Journal of International & Comparative Law*, 1–11.

[50] See generally Henry G. Schermers and Niels M. Blokker, *International Institutional Law* (4th edn, Leiden, 2003), who also list a number of inactive or not-yet-active tribunals at pp. 442–52.

Indeed, the solutions sought need not necessarily have too much to do with law. In the 1960s when France was getting disheartened by the dominant role of the USA in NATO its strategy was to withdraw from NATO's military structures. Clearly, there is nothing in NATO specifically authorizing such a move: there is no article saying that states may withdraw from the military structure while remaining members of NATO and while still participating in NATO's policy-making.[51] Yet, there is also nothing in the treaty prohibiting such a move, and in the end it must have seemed like a wise compromise to everyone involved: NATO without France does not make too much sense, but France should also not be made more important than it is.

In quite a few organizations, dispute settlement is to a large extent an overtly political mode of dealing with conflicts, applying diplomacy rather than strict legal rules. Thus, organizations such as the Organization of African Unity (OAU) (now replaced by the AU) or the Organization of American States (OAS) provide their good offices or engage in mediation. The OAU, for example, managed to settle a long-standing boundary dispute between Algeria and Morocco in 1963, while in 1972 the President of Somalia mediated in a dispute between Tanzania and Uganda.[52]

Similarly, the OAS successfully intervened in a dispute between Honduras and Nicaragua in 1957 as well as in several disputes involving Nicaragua and Costa Rica in the 1940s and 1950s. The Arab League proved highly instrumental in guaranteeing Kuwait's newly won independence in 1961 against Iraqi claims, while the *ad hoc* Contadora group settled long-standing difficulties in volatile Central America.[53]

In some cases, the creation of special *ad hoc* (quasi-)tribunals can serve useful purposes, and not only legal purposes at that. Perhaps the prime example is the creation by the EC, during the dissolution of Yugoslavia, of the Badinter Commission, which functioned as a high-level policy adviser rather than a settler of disputes. Through a number of opinions on legal questions, it helped the EU to formulate its policy towards Yugoslavia and its offspring. As Craven observed, the Badinter Commission's opinions helped to rationalize an otherwise not always coherent state practice, and guided subsequent practice.[54]

In addition, the very existence of organizations where states may meet both formally and more informally may already provide valuable services relating to dispute settlement. As Merrills notes with respect to NATO and the disputes

---

[51] Indeed, the integrated military structure was initially not even envisaged. For a close-up account of the creation and the early years of NATO, see the brilliant memoirs of Dean Acheson, *Present at the Creation: My Years in the State Department* (New York, 1969).

[52] The OAU's role in determining the boundary between Mali and Burkina Faso proved less successful, finally leading to litigation before the International Court of Justice: *Case Concerning the Frontier Dispute (Burkina Faso v. Mali)*, [1986] ICJ Reports 554.

[53] See generally Merrills, *International Dispute Settlement*, pp. 214–18.

[54] See Matthew C. R. Craven, 'The European Community Arbitration Commission on Yugoslavia' (1995) 66 *BYIL*, 333–413, esp. 335.

over Cyprus (involving Turkey, Greece and Britain) and the British–Icelandic 'cod wars' of the 1970s, 'the fact that all states concerned were members of NATO ensured that the lines of communication remained open, despite a degree of bitterness and hostility which on several occasions led to the use of force'.[55]

To some extent, international courts and tribunals are themselves to be regarded as international organizations. The Iran–US Claims Tribunal, set up on the basis of the 1981 Algiers declarations in the aftermath of the Tehran hostage crisis, has been treated as an international organization by Dutch courts, at least for the purposes of claiming privileges and immunities.[56] Likewise, the International Criminal Court is set up much like an international organization,[57] complete with plenary organ (the Assembly of State Parties) and a Permanent Secretariat, as well as a Headquarters Agreement with its host state.[58]

The GATT/WTO system

Most international dispute settlement is rather political in nature, and is destined to retain that character in most cases. One of the few exceptions thereto is to be found in the world trading regime. Within GATT, dispute settlement procedures developed largely in practice, and while they started out as exercises in trade diplomacy, they have gone through a distinct process of juridification.

GATT was created in 1947 as the General Agreement on Tariffs and Trade. It had been part of the Havana Charter establishing an International Trade Organization (ITO), but since this ITO proved still-born, the provisions on tariffs and other trade restrictions were lifted out of the Havana Charter and turned into a separate agreement, to be provisionally applied by most of its contracting parties. As GATT was but an agreement, it did not mention any institutions, with the exception of a plenary body called the 'Contracting Parties' (rather unimaginatively so).[59] It followed that there was also no dispute settlement mechanism to speak of: if states had a dispute, they called upon the Contracting Parties, and hoped for the best.

When the first disputes arose, already in the 1940s, the Contracting Parties resolved to settle those disputes in a flexible way, and for that purpose started to establish working parties and, later, panels consisting of three or five persons to look into the matter, and to render advice. That was, for a time, the long and the short of GATT dispute settlement. If there was a dispute, parties were supposed

[55] Merrills, *International Dispute Settlement*, p. 213.
[56] See *Iran–US Claims Tribunal* v. *A. S.*, in 94 *ILR* 321.
[57] Some of the issues involved are addressed in A. S. Muller, 'Setting Up the International Criminal Court' (2004) 1 *IOLR*, 189–96.
[58] The Agreement was concluded in 2007; at the time of writing, it was awaiting the approval of the Dutch parliament.
[59] For a general overview, see Kenneth W. Dam, *GATT: Law and International Economic Organization* (Chicago, 1970). The seminal work on substantive GATT law is John H. Jackson, *World Trade and the Law of GATT* (Indianapolis, 1969).

first to enter into consultations,[60] and, if that did not work out, to resort to the Contracting Parties.[61] The Contracting Parties would establish a panel, and the panel would produce a report. If the report met with the approval of the Council, it would qualify as 'accepted', and the advice or the recommendation of the panel would be given the stamp of approval of the Council.

What this meant in legal terms has always remained unclear. First, it has always been uncertain whether panel decisions, once adopted, would be binding upon the parties to the dispute. There are some grounds to suppose this to be the case. For one thing, many adopted decisions have been adhered to, albeit sometimes after a considerable period of time has lapsed. It took the USA, for example, some four years to change a part of its tax laws to bring it into conformity with GATT, after it had blocked adoption of the panel report for another four or five years. Thus, some nine years after the panel itself came to its findings, US law was finally adapted.[62]

Moreover, if states really would have a hard time agreeing to a panel report, they could simply block its adoption: the Council was supposed to adopt the panel's decisions by consensus, effectively giving every Council member a veto.[63] Thus, one could argue that mere adoption meant that the guilty party had already consented to be bound by the findings of the panel.

A second question, however, is whether the panel decisions would also be binding upon others besides the parties directly concerned. Would they contribute to the development of a standing body of GATT law, or would their binding force be limited to the parties involved (if it existed at all)? Opinions diverge. Perhaps the better view is that no binding precedents are created. There is, after all, nothing in GATT to allow for the creation of binding precedent, and it could be argued that such a provision would be important enough to warrant explicit mentioning in the agreement. That said, panels have rather regularly referred to earlier decisions, and at times, where they reached a different conclusion, have been anxious to distinguish the dispute before them from previous decisions.[64]

The dispute settlement has been streamlined and, many think, improved with the creation of the WTO. The most eye-catching innovations are that blocking panel reports is now only possible by consensus,[65] and that an Appellate Body

---

[60] Article XXII GATT.   [61] Article XXIII GATT.

[62] See Jan Klabbers and Annerie Vreugdenhil, 'Dispute Settlement in GATT: DISC and its Successor' (1986/1) *LIEI*, 115–38.

[63] This caught public attention after the US had blocked acceptance of (unfavourable) panel reports concerning US legislation to combat driftnet fishing (*Tuna I* and *Tuna II*). The reports are reproduced in (1991) 30 *ILM* 1594, and (1994) 33 *ILM* 839.

[64] It is perhaps useful to note that general international law does not seem to recognize a doctrine of binding precedent, for reasons intimately connected to state sovereignty.

[65] Insiders speak of a negative consensus, to indicate that what is at issue is the negation of a report. For an excellent analysis of the role of the WTO in a world of sovereign states, see Robert Howse, 'The Legitimacy of the World Trade Organization'. In Jean-Marc Coicaud and Veijo Heiskanen (eds.), *The Legitimacy of International Organizations* (Tokyo, 2001), pp. 355–407.

has been created, which may and does scrutinize panel reports on points of law and has already been considered instrumental in cementing an otherwise rather incoherent body of case law.[66]

On the topic of precedent, the WTO agreement remains less than unequivocal. It states that the WTO 'shall be guided by the decisions, procedures and customary practices followed by the Contracting Parties to GATT 1947 and the bodies established in the framework of GATT 1947'.[67] There is, moreover, an Understanding on Rules and Procedures Governing the Dispute Settlement Procedures, but that too is not very specific, holding that 'members affirm their adherence to the principles for the management of disputes heretofore applied under Articles XXII and XXIII of GATT 1947'.[68]

An intriguing feature of the GATT/WTO dispute settlement mechanism is that it may be activated even without a violation of the organization's rules: under Article XXIII it suffices if a state feels that benefits to which it is entitled are nullified or impaired by another contracting party. Such nullification or impairment may result from a violation of GATT/WTO rules, but such need not necessarily be the case.[69]

In theory, then, this opens the door for having GATT/WTO deal with a number of issues which are not expressly prohibited, but which are nonetheless contrary to the spirit of GATT/WTO. In practice, however, there have not been all that many findings of a nullification or impairment of benefits without a violation, for the obvious reason that if there is no violation, then it is difficult to hold someone responsible. It is one thing to say that behaviour of state X hurts the interests of state Y, but if X can claim that it is really not doing anything illegal, that effectively ends most debate.[70]

Administrative tribunals

When we think of dispute settlement within organizations, we usually think of disputes between member states *inter se*, or disputes between a member and an organ of the organization. But there is also a whole class of disputes that concern the organization and its employees: the staff cases. While these may on occasion challenge the legality of the organization's acts in a more general sense

---

[66] For a balanced assessment, see Rambod Behboodi, 'Legal Reasoning and the International Law of Trade: The First Steps of the Appellate Body of the WTO' (1998/4) 32 *JWT*, 55–99. See also Deborah Z. Cass, 'The "Constitutionalization" of International Trade Law: Judicial Normgeneration as the Engine of Constitutional Development in International Trade' (2001) 12 *EJIL*, 39–75.

[67] Article XVI, para. 1 WTO.   [68] Article 3, para. 1 of the Understanding.

[69] And it has been suggested that a breach which does not nullify or impair benefits may actually be insufficient. See John H. Jackson, 'The Jurisprudence of International Trade: The DISC Case in GATT' (1978) 72 *AJIL*, 747–81, 754.

[70] Indeed, in later disputes it would seem that the order has been reversed, in that a violation would automatically be regarded as nullification or impairment of benefits. See John H. Jackson, 'Dispute Settlement and the WTO: Emerging Problems' (1998) 1 *JIEL*, 329–51, 337.

(if an employee's legal position is influenced by a general instrument[71]), they usually deal with relatively straightforward individual complaints.

Some international organizations have created specialized tribunals to deal with such cases in a more or less legal procedure: as noted earlier, the General Assembly has created such a tribunal under the name United Nations Administrative Tribunal. Other organizations having their own administrative tribunal include the EC (since 2005), World Bank, and the ILO. The ILO Administrative Tribunal is, moreover, authorized to hear cases stemming from other organizations, and a host of them have used this opportunity, ranging from GATT to the FAO, and from the WHO to UNESCO. Administrative tribunals can also be found in a number of regional international organizations, from the League of Arab States to the Asian Development Bank.[72]

Some points concerning the administrative law of international organizations are worth mentioning. First of all, there is a certain logic involved in having a unified system of labour rules for employees and having internal systems to deal with disputes.[73] An obvious reason for this is the fact that employees will usually come from different countries with different labour laws; equally obvious, they should be independent from their home states in all possible respects, including those of employment. Moreover, there should be some remedy against machinations of the organization, and as organizations are usually immune from local jurisdiction, it stands to reason that their servants should have other possibilities for legal recourse.[74]

In essence, international civil servants are hired on two bases. One possibility is employment on the basis of a contract; the other is statutory employment, where the decision to employ Mr or Ms X will be a legal act of the organization concerned. Most organizations use the contract; the EU, however, is an important example of an organization using statutory employment.

While the differences between the two need not necessarily be exaggerated, there are some differences nevertheless: in particular the applicable law will to some extent be inspired either by contractual notions, or by more administrative notions. Thus, there may be differences relating to, for example, the way

---

[71] See Paul C. Szasz, 'Adjudicating Staff Challenges to Legislative Decisions of International Organizations'. In Gerhard Hafner *et al.* (eds.), *Liber Amicorum Professor Ignaz Seidl-Hohenveldern in Honour of his 80th Birthday* (The Hague, 1998), pp. 699–720.

[72] For an overview of the latter, see Kari T. Takamaa, 'Aspects of Procedure and Jurisprudence of the Asian Development Bank Administrative Tribunal 1991–1996' (1997) 8 *FYIL*, 70–137.

[73] See, e.g., the decision of the Tribunal Civil of Versailles of 27 July 1945 in *Chemidlin* v. *International Bureau of Weights and Measures*, in (1943–5) 12 *AD*, 281, holding that the international character of the Bureau meant that French law was not applicable to labour relations between it and its staff. In a similar vein the Conseil d'Etat held on 20 February 1953 (*In re Weiss*) that it had no jurisdiction over labour disputes, not even with respect to French candidates for international positions, in 20 *ILR* 531.

[74] See generally Michael Singer, 'Jurisdictional Immunity of International Organizations: Human Rights and Functional Necessity Concerns' (1995) 36 *VaJIL*, 53–165.

in which the employment relationship may come to an end. Still, according to one authority, the two systems are growing more and more towards each other.[75]

Apart from contract or decision, the employment law of international organizations may have some other sources as well. The most obvious of these is the constituent treaty: if an employment decision or contract would go against the constitution of the organization, it may well be annulled. To name one apposite example: Article 288 (ex-Article 215) of the TEC specifies that the personal liability of EC employers towards the EC will be regulated in Staff Rules and Conditions of Employment. It follows that employment decisions may not ignore such prescriptions.

Of more practical importance, however, than constituent charters are instruments such as staff rules and regulations, and even manuals, circulars and similar documents may be deemed to be 'law-creative'. As a matter of hierarchy, usually staff regulations will be of higher status than staff rules.

Like all legal systems, the administrative law of international organizations also has a place for general principles of law (good faith, for example, or *force majeure*), and some argue that the body of rules making up international civil service employment law often incorporates more specific principles under the banner of general principles of law within the meaning of the Statute of the ICJ.[76]

Issues of administrative law occasionally used to reach the ICJ in the form of a request for an advisory opinion, granting the ICJ a curious form of appellate jurisdiction.[77] Thus, under the Statute of the ILO Administrative Tribunal, the opinion of the ICJ was to be considered as binding.[78] Following the *Effect of Awards* opinion of 1954, the General Assembly even created a special Committee on Applications for Review of Administrative Tribunal Judgments,[79] with the task (inserted into Article 11 of the UNAT's Statute) of screening applications and selecting those which would be suitable as the basis of a request for an advisory opinion.

In this regard, the Court has described its task as follows:

> the task of the Court is not to retry the case but to give its opinion on the questions submitted to it concerning the objections lodged against the Judgment [of the Administrative Tribunal]. The Court is not therefore entitled to substitute its own opinion for that of the Tribunal on the merits of the case adjudicated by the Tribunal. Its role is to determine if the circumstances of the case, whether they

---

[75] C. F. Amerasinghe, *Principles of the Institutional Law of International Organizations* (Cambridge, 1996), p. 334.

[76] So, e.g., Michael Akehurst, *A Modern Introduction to International Law* (6th edn, London, 1987), pp. 34–5.

[77] The General Assembly terminated this possibility in 1996. See Szasz, 'Adjudicating Staff Challenges', p. 715. This termination does not, of course, deprive past decisions of their validity.

[78] Article XII, ILOAT Statute.   [79] By means of General Assembly Resolution 957(X).

relate to merits or procedure, show that any objection made to the Judgment . . . is well founded.[80]

In the early 1950s, several UNESCO employees had seen their contracts expire without renewal, despite the fact that UNESCO's Director-General had earlier issued an administrative memorandum in which he stated that all employees who fulfilled certain conditions and whose services were needed would be offered a new contract. The disgruntled employees figured that they met the conditions and that their services were needed. They thought the only reason their contracts were not renewed was the upsurge of McCarthyism: their leftist sympathies were apparently the cause for their dismissal. They went to the ILO Administrative Tribunal (which also handles UNESCO cases), which found in their favour. In turn, UNESCO appealed to the ICJ.[81]

The Court indicated how its own role could be of use, and how, its own limitations on standing notwithstanding, it could nevertheless guarantee good administration of justice. In particular on the point that the Court is not available to individuals so proceedings would therefore be lacking in equality, the Court found an elegant way out, noting that the difficulty 'was met, on the one hand, by the procedure under which the observations of the officials were made available to the Court through the intermediary of Unesco and, on the other hand, by dispensing with oral proceedings'.[82]

In the 1973 *Fasla* opinion, arising out of the discontent of an employee whose contract was not extended and for whom no other assignment was found, partly due to incorrect information circulating within the UN concerning his qualifications and experience, the Court was asked whether, in not specifically (*eo nomine*) addressing some of Mr Fasla's claims and in awarding Mr Fasla a relatively small amount of compensation, the Tribunal had failed to exercise proper jurisdiction. The Court upheld the idea that tribunals possess a wide margin of discretion when it comes to delimiting their proper jurisdiction and awarding damages.

In respect of the Tribunal's exercise of jurisdiction, the Court's chosen criterion is a formal one: to find out whether the Tribunal 'addresses its mind to a claim or question'.[83] If so, it cannot be accused of failing to exercise its proper jurisdiction. In respect of reparation, the Court affirmed the principle that 'reparation must, as far as possible wipe out all the consequences of the

---

[80] *Application for Review of Judgment No. 158 of the United Nations Administrative Tribunal (Fasla)*, advisory opinion, [1973] ICJ Reports 166, para. 47 (hereinafter referred to as the *Fasla* opinion).

[81] *Judgments of the Administrative Tribunal of the ILO upon Complaints Made Against the UNESCO*, advisory opinion, [1956] ICJ Reports 77.

[82] *Ibid.*, p. 86.

[83] *Fasla* opinion, paras. 59, 70 and 74. In a similar vein, on the claim that an error in procedure had been committed, the Court affirmed the importance of some form of apparent reasoning in a judgment (para. 95).

illegal act and re-establish the situation which would, in all probability, have existed if that act had not been committed'.[84]

At the time of writing (summer 2008) there are well-developed plans within the UN to streamline its system of internal justice. It is envisaged that there will be a two-tier structure with a Dispute Tribunal and an Appeals Tribunal. A temporary Internal Justice Council has been set up to pave the way and to assist in such things as the selection of judges to sit on the new tribunals.

Alternatives

To some extent, the experiences of the latter part of the twentieth century appear to indicate a move away from traditional dispute settlement mechanisms, and towards a replacement by two distinct, but presumably related, phenomena. The first is an increasing emphasis on the management of international regulatory regimes, guiding states towards compliance with norms formulated both within and without international organizations rather than assigning blameworthiness and responsibility. The second is an increasing tendency to settle disputes 'indoors', using the organization's own substantive rules and leaving the general doctrines of international law, most notably the law of treaties and the law of responsibility, aside.

The first trend, a sign of post-modern times perhaps,[85] is to focus increasingly on the management of a regime. In this view, most sophisticatedly set out by Chayes and Handler Chayes,[86] the traditional binary way of legal thought (behaviour is either in conformity with the law or it is not) is gradually replaced by more diverse opinions, where small violations may not be counted or taken seriously, as long as the regime itself is not threatened. That this phenomenon takes place is undeniable; whether it is also a good thing, as Chayes and Handler Chayes seem to suggest, is a different matter. Taking the management approach one step further, it has already been suggested that it is 'incorrect to assume that more compliance is always good',[87] and from there it is only a small step to claiming that whether or not to comply with international law is, really, a matter for the law's subjects to decide for themselves. In some regimes set up under international environmental agreements this is manifested in the establishment of so-called 'compliance procedures' aiming not so much to mete out punishment to states that violate environmental norms (or rather,

---

[84] *Fasla* opinion, para. 65.

[85] It has been argued that the attempt to cast aside politics by technical management is a typical feature of present-day post-modern thinking, which has not left international organizations unaffected. For an argument to this effect, see Veijo Heiskanen, 'The Rationality of the Use of Force and the Evolution of International Organization'. In Coicaud and Heiskanen (eds.), *The Legitimacy of International Organizations*, pp. 155–85.

[86] Abram Chayes and Antonia Handler Chayes, *The New Sovereignty: Compliance with International Regulatory Agreements* (Cambridge, MA, 1995).

[87] See Joel P. Trachtman, 'Bananas, Direct Effect and Compliance' (1999) 10 *EJIL*, 655–78, 657.

states that have 'compliance issues') but, instead, assist states, either technically or financially or both, to reach the standards set in the treaty concerned.[88]

A second trend (arguably) in the law of international organizations relating to dispute settlement is that, increasingly, the law of any given organization tends to become self-contained.[89] While usually general international law will remain present in the background, resort to it will be avoided as much as possible: general international law is increasingly becoming the law of last resort.[90]

Thus, the 1993 Chemical Weapons Convention (CWC),[91] creating the Organization for the Prohibition of Chemical Weapons (OPCW), envisages three types of breach of Article XII. The first is somewhat euphemistically referred to as 'compliance' problems; if these exist, then diplomacy will solve the problems. If that does not work, the rights and privileges of the defaulting state may be restricted or suspended by the OPCW's plenary body (the Conference), upon recommendation of its Executive Council.

Secondly, there may be cases resulting in 'serious damage to the object and purpose' of the Chemical Weapons Convention. If these occur, the Conference may recommend collective measures to state parties, 'in conformity with international law'. Third, in cases of 'particular gravity', the issue may be brought to the attention of the General Assembly and the Security Council.

What is interesting to note is the fact that it was deemed necessary to specify various categories of violations at all, rather than rely on international law's general doctrines. The most plausible practical explanation is a serious dissatisfaction with general international law on this point, which indeed may be said to be lacking in clarity. A more interesting theoretical explanation may well be, however, that international law is increasingly 'fragmenting'. International regimes are increasingly said to be functioning as more or less closed entities: a trading regime, a human rights regime, an environmental regime, et cetera. These would all develop their own internal logics, including what to do in case of a dispute. The upshot then is, that precisely because of these internal logics, disputes between regimes are difficult to solve.[92]

---

[88] See generally Jan Klabbers, 'Compliance Procedures'. In Daniel Bodansky, Jutta Brunnée and Ellen Hey (eds.), *The Oxford Handbook of International Environmental Law* (Oxford, 2007), pp. 995–1009.

[89] The wording is borrowed from the ICJ, which held diplomatic law to be a self-contained regime and thereby presumably meant that no remedies were to be sought outside that regime: *United States Diplomatic and Consular Staff in Tehran*, [1980] ICJ Reports 3, para. 86.

[90] See generally Martti Koskenniemi, 'Breach of Treaty or Non-compliance? Reflections on the Enforcement of the Montreal Protocol' (1992) 3 *Yearbook of International Environmental Law*, 123–62.

[91] Convention on the Prohibition of the Development, Production, Stockpiling and Use of Chemical Weapons and on their Destruction, reproduced in (1993) 32 *ILM* 800. Some aspects of the OPCW's position in international law are discussed in Eric Myjer (ed.), *Issues of Arms Control Law and the Chemical Weapons Convention* (The Hague, 2001).

[92] Quite possibly the most sophisticated theoretical exploration is Andreas Fischer-Lescano and Gunther Teubner, *Regime-Kollisionen: Zur Fragmentierung des globalen Rechts* (Frankfurt am Main, 2006). An authoritative framework for handling this sort of issue is sketched in Martti

Problems of fragmentation are less likely to appear where dispute settlement is mainly left to the political organs, as is the case in the above-mentioned OPCW. This can also be found in other organizations: if they provide for some organ having the power to take binding decisions, it is usually one of the political organs. Within ICAO, for instance, the power rests with the executive body, the Council; and this was unambiguously confirmed by the ICJ in 1972, in a dispute between Pakistan and India. Admittedly though, the ICJ reserved for itself the possibility of functioning as an appeals court, but could of course only do so on the basis of the ICAO Treaty itself: in this case, its jurisdiction to handle appeals against ICAO decisions finds its origin in the ICAO convention.[93]

Concluding remarks

The complex relationship between the organization and its members is also visible in the realm of dispute settlement. On the one hand, where organizations assume judicial settlement functions beyond inter-state disputes, as with the EC Court, or the Yugoslavia Tribunal, the organization is partly relieving its members from some tasks, under the banner of the greater good for all. This is generally considered as a highly welcome development; after all, for the committed internationalist, any international settlement is instinctively preferable to a domestic solution.

Yet, at the same time, the member states jealously guard their sovereign prerogatives. With many human rights treaties, it is no coincidence that the exhaustion of local remedies is a strict condition for the admissibility of complaints, assuring the member states that the organization can only become active if they (the members) let it. While the exhaustion rule allows international tribunals to act as courts of appeal (thus catering to organizational demands), it also narrows down considerably the situations in which appeals may arise, therewith protecting the position of member states.

In other organizations, awkward or ingenious procedures of cooperation are envisaged. Thus, the Yugoslavia and Rwanda Tribunals know full well that, when push comes to shove, they may have the formal final say but lack the means actually to force states to hand over those who are on its territory.[94] The EC has the preliminary reference procedure, but the EC Court has also been forced to

Koskenniemi, *Fragmentation of International Law: Difficulties Arising from the Diversification and Expansion of International Law. Report of the Study Group of the International Law Commission* (Helsinki, 2007).

[93] *Appeal Relating to the Jurisdiction of the ICAO Council (India v. Pakistan)*, [1972] ICJ Reports 46.

[94] The ICC Statute, by contrast, envisages a more 'co-operative' notion of complementarity, but this too leaves jurisdictional conflicts ultimately unresolved. See Immi Tallgren, 'Completing the "International Criminal Order": The Rhetoric of International Repression and the Notion of Complementarity in the Draft Statute for an International Criminal Court', (1998) 67 *Nordic JIL*, 107–37, 123.

devise complex rules on which court has what to say in which circumstances; witness the open-ended nature of the *acte clair* doctrine.

By the same token, it is no coincidence that many of the tribunals that somehow deal with the rights of private citizens either are unable to render binding decisions (think of all the human rights tribunals operating under the flag of the UN) or do not even allow private citizens or companies standing, despite relating, in as far as the substance of their work goes, to the activities of private actors (the WTO dispute settlement mechanism is a good example). And it is no coincidence that advisory, non-binding opinions are at their most popular within international organizations.

Such doctrines, rules and procedures may grow haphazardly, as pragmatic answers to practical questions, but taken together they confirm the by-now familiar pattern: they fit the pattern of the law of international organizations resembling an intricate tug of war between the organization and its members.

13

Treaty-making by international organizations

Introduction

For many years, it has been seriously debated whether international organizations could actually enter into international commitments.[1] In other words: did they have the capacity to conclude treaties? Or was treaty-making rather something they were incapable of doing unless specifically and explicitly empowered to do so? If it was the latter, then how should commitments entered into by organizations be explained in the absence of explicit powers?

The constitutions of the earlier organizations did not contain specific provisions with respect to treaty-making, with the League of Nations Covenant constituting a prime example. Indeed, the absence of any specific provision in the Covenant was one of the reasons why some of the judges of the ICJ, in the various *Mandate* cases, found that the Mandate could not be regarded as a treaty between South Africa and the League of Nations. Such would, they reasoned, presuppose treaty-making competence on the part of the League, and in the absence of a clause conferring such power, treaty-making competence was not lightly to be presumed.[2]

Nowadays, it is reasonably well established that international organizations may conclude treaties, although there is still some debate as to where the capacity to conclude these treaties comes from if no explicit competence is contained in the constituent documents.

At this point, much is often made of a distinction between the capacity to do something and the competence to engage in that activity. The former is abstract, denoting a general capability, whereas the latter is more concrete and specific.[3]

---

[1] As Higgins puts it without further ado, before the creation of the UN, treaties concluded by international organizations were considered to be unusual. See Rosalyn Higgins, *The Development of International Law through the Political Organs of the United Nations* (Oxford, 1963), p. 241.

[2] See in particular the joint dissenting opinion of Judges Spender and Fitzmaurice to the *South West Africa Cases* (*Ethiopia* v. *South Africa*; *Liberia* v. *South Africa*), preliminary objections, [1962] ICJ Reports 319, pp. 483 and 502 (recording the debated capacity of the League of Nations to conclude treaties).

[3] See, e.g., Gunther Hartmann, 'The Capacity of International Organizations to Conclude Treaties'. In Karl Zemanek (ed.), *Agreements of International Organizations and the Vienna Convention on the Law of Treaties* (Vienna, 1971), pp. 127–63, esp. pp. 149–51.

The leading theory holds that capacity, as an abstract notion, derives from general international law; indeed, Professor Hungdah Chiu, in a rich and detailed study in 1966, had already reached the conclusion that organizations had been granted treaty-making capacity by virtue of a rule of customary international law.[4] After all, lots of organizations do indeed conclude agreements both with each other and with states and other entities, and since 1986, there has even been an unratified convention: the 1986 Vienna Convention on the Law of Treaties with or between International Organizations which, moreover, seems to argue that capacity derives directly from international law.[5] Its preamble notes 'that international organizations possess the capacity to conclude treaties which is necessary for the exercise of their functions and the fulfillment of their purposes'.[6]

Where capacity is said to derive from general international law, competence (or power) would derive mainly from the rules of the organization, leading to the situation that an organization would have the capacity under international law to conclude a treaty on a given topic, but might lack the competence to do so under its own rules.

In the end, the discussion on the treaty-making capacity of international organizations is predominantly an historic discussion, evidenced by the circumstance that the main academic studies were written in the 1950s and 1960s.[7] The majority of observers nowadays accept that organizations can and do conclude treaties, and that the specific sorts of treaties they can conclude depend on their constitution. Thus, practice walks the middle ground, more or less ignoring the doctrinal debate on capacity and competence; moreover, with the help of the implied powers doctrine many treaties which the founders had never envisaged have been concluded by international organizations.[8]

Indeed, it is precisely this circumstance which renders the distinction between capacity and competence somewhat artificial; excess reliance on implied powers suggests that competences are not always clear-cut and self-evident, and may well lapse into the more abstract notion of capacity.[9]

---

[4] Hungdah Chiu, *The Capacity of International Organizations to Conclude Treaties, and the Special Legal Aspects of the Treaties so Concluded* (The Hague, 1966), p. 34.

[5] See also Karl Zemanek, 'The United Nations Conference on the Law of Treaties between States and International Organizations or Between International Organizations: The Unrecorded History of its "General Agreement"'. In Karl-Heinz Böckstiegel *et al.* (eds.), *Völkerrecht, Recht der internationalen Organisationen, Weltwirtschaftsrecht: Festschrift für Ignaz Seidl-Hohenveldern* (Cologne, 1988), pp. 665–79.

[6] The Convention was concluded in 1986, but has yet to enter into force. The text is reproduced in (1986) 25 *ILM* 543.

[7] These include, apart from Hungdah Chiu, *The Capacity of International Organizations to Conclude Treaties*, and the collection edited by Zemanek (*Agreements of International Organizations*); see also Karl Zemanek, *Das Vertragsrecht der internationalen Organisationen* (Vienna, 1957).

[8] For an impressive early overview of UN practice, see Higgins, *The Development of International Law*, pp. 241–9.

[9] It is hardly a coincidence that Hartmann, 'The Capacity of International Organizations', p. 143, ends up suggesting the existence of something like inherent (rather than implied) treaty-making powers, which ultimately negates the distinction between competence and capacity.

The 1986 Vienna Convention

Despite the fact that it has yet to enter into force (it had forty parties in 2008[10]), the starting point for our analysis is the 1986 Vienna Convention.[11] The Convention was prepared by the ILC, on the basis of the work of Special Rapporteur Paul Reuter, and finally adopted at a conference which took place in February and March of 1986.[12] Ironically, but tellingly perhaps, international organizations themselves were rather reluctant to participate, and indeed even to see a separate convention drawn up, for a codified law of treaties might impede the liberty which they had enjoyed in treaty-making.[13] Its preamble, as noted, implies that capacity derives from international law generally, and perhaps it is good to realize that the terms of the preamble are also subject to heavy negotiations between the states who conclude a treaty.[14]

Nonetheless, the capacity of organizations to enter into treaties is, so it seems, not unlimited. Article 6 specifies that the capacity of an international organization to conclude treaties is governed by the rules of the organization, and is thereby a wonderful example of a compromise between the demands of the international system and those of individual actors therein (organizations) who, in turn, have to live up to the wishes and desires of their members and for that reason alone cannot claim unfettered capacity.[15]

Those rules of the organization include, according to the definition of Article 2, para. 1(j) of the 1986 Convention, 'in particular, the constituent treaty, decisions and resolutions adopted in accordance with them, and established practice of the organization'.

The organization's rules may also, in rare cases, have a bearing on the validity of an agreement concluded by an organization. Article 46 spells out that a manifest violation of a rule of fundamental importance may possibly be

---

[10] The Convention needs the approval of thirty-five states to enter into force; at present, quite a few of its forty parties are international organizations, whose approval is irrelevant for purposes of the entry into force of the Convention.

[11] For a general overview, see R. G. Sybesma-Knol, 'The New Law of Treaties: The Codification of the Law of Treaties Concluded between States and International Organizations or between Two or More International Organizations' (1985) 15 *Georgia Journal of International and Comparative Law*, 425–52.

[12] For a brief account by a participant, see Gerard Limburg, 'The United Nations Conference on the Law of Treaties between States and International Organizations or between International Organizations' (1986) 33 *Neth ILR*, 195–203.

[13] See G. E. do Nascimento e Silva, 'The 1986 Vienna Convention and the Treaty-making Power of International Organizations' (1986) 29 *GYIL*, 68–85, esp. p. 71.

[14] See, e.g., Martti Koskenniemi, 'The Preamble of the Universal Declaration of Human Rights'. In Gudmundur Alfredsson and Asbjorn Eide (eds.), *The Universal Declaration of Human Rights* (The Hague, 1999), pp. 27–39.

[15] Reportedly, some representatives of Soviet doctrine went so far as to consider the treaty-making powers of organizations to be merely the delegated treaty-making powers of their member states: as mentioned in Liviu Bota, 'The Capacity of International Organizations to Conclude Headquarters Agreements, and Some Features of Those Agreements'. In K. Zemanek (ed.), *Agreements of International Organizations*, pp. 57–104, esp. p. 73.

successfully invoked in order to get the treaty invalidated. The conditions are so strict, however, that no examples are on public record.[16]

Apart from those rules referred to in Article 2 of the 1986 Convention, here too the implied powers doctrine plays a tremendously important role. Many treaties concluded by organizations are difficult to trace back to the constituent treaty, decisions or resolutions, or established practice. Instead, they themselves constitute established practice, and find their justification not in an explicit power, but rather by implication. The external relations law of the EU, to name a well-known example, is based to a large extent on the notion of implied powers.[17]

This gives rise to some curiosity. Thus, while arguably treaties concluded by an organization *ultra vires* would be void, the organization can (almost) always boast that its members supported the conclusion of the agreement, and, if that is the case, how can it possibly be void?

If supported by all members (or even by only a majority), three possible arguments may be used in support of the conclusion of the agreement in question. First, the members were of the apparent conviction that the agreement was *intra vires*; their very support for its conclusion suggests as much. Second, if the power to conclude an agreement is not expressly provided for in the organization's constituent document, it may nonetheless be implied in it. Third, at the very least, the conclusion itself qualifies as subsequent practice of the organization and, if meeting with support, can be deemed to be acquiesced in.[18] In other words, the main mechanism that exists so as to protect an organization's members from excess authority in the organization, i.e., the doctrine of *ultra vires*, may always be manipulated out of existence by those very same member states.[19]

Hence, even where the outside observer may have doubts about the legality (and therewith validity) of an agreement in terms of the powers of the organization concerned, as long as the members do not agree with the outside observer, any finding of invalidity is bound to fall upon deaf ears, and this in turn renders the doctrine of *ultra vires* a paper tiger.

[16] The ICJ dismissed an Art. 46 argument (based on the near-identical 1969 Vienna Convention on the Law of Treaties) in *Land and Maritime Boundary between Cameroon and Nigeria* (*Nigeria* v. *Cameroon*), merits, [2002] ICJ Reports 303, paras. 265–8: Cameroon could not be expected to be intimately familiar with the niceties of Nigeria's constitutional law. For a discussion based on the 1969 Vienna Convention, see Theodor Meron, 'Article 46 of the Vienna Convention on the Law of Treaties (*Ultra Vires* Treaties): Some Recent Cases' (1978) 49 *BYIL*, 175–99. Similarly, under Art. 27, the organization cannot invoke its internal rules to escape from its treaty obligations, as confirmed by an IMF memorandum reproduced in UNJY (1982), pp. 212–13.

[17] See generally I. MacLeod, I. D. Hendry and Stephen Hyett, *The External Relations of the European Communities* (Oxford, 1996), and Panos Koutrakos, *EU International Relations Law* (Oxford, 2006).

[18] It is no surprise then that Hungdah Chiu, *The Capacity of International Organizations to Conclude Treaties*, can write, without blinking an eye, that treaties concluded *ultra vires* are void (p. 83), but also, in the same study, that an absence of specific powers may well be cured by subsequent practice (p. 46, concerning the League of Nations).

[19] See also, on the limits of the *ultra vires* doctrine more generally, Chapter 11 above.

It is perhaps largely symbolic that the 1986 Vienna Convention, although dealing explicitly with the activities of international organizations, still puts organizations on a lesser footing than states. Thus, while international organizations may sign the Convention[20] and may, through acts of 'formal confirmation' (the euphemistic equivalent of ratification[21]), express their consent to be bound, whether the Convention enters into force depends on the number of ratifications received from states.[22] No matter how many organizations confirm their consent to be bound, what matters legally is the acts of states, not those of organizations.[23]

Another element symbolizing the curious position of international organizations is that an agreement between various states and an international organization will be governed by two separate documents: the relations between those states and the organization will be governed by the 1986 Convention, whereas the relations between those states *inter se* will remain within the ambit of the 1969 Convention.[24] In practical terms, this may not be terribly important, but once again the symbolic value need not be underestimated.[25]

The reason why, practically, the precise coverage of the 1986 Convention is not overly relevant resides foremost in the consideration that many of its rules are based on the same principles which underpin the law of treaties generally and which have also found elaboration in the 1969 Vienna Convention on the Law of Treaties between states. While the precise rules duly take into account that organizations are differently structured, the underlying principles are the same, whether it concerns the conclusion of treaties, their application and effect, their validity or their termination.[26]

Treaty-making powers

What then, are the rules of various organizations? There are, actually, not that many explicit treaty-making powers to be found in the constitutions of

---

[20] Although even this was controversial; see Limburg, 'The United Nations Conference', p. 202.

[21] A number of states felt that ratification was a prerogative of sovereigns only, therefore an organization's expression of consent to be bound should be termed differently.

[22] Article 85, para. 1. The only exception, if such it is, was that, at the time, the United Nations Council for Namibia was also to be counted among states, as the Council represented Namibia prior to the latter's independence.

[23] It has been convincingly argued that the international legal system has a hard time accommodating non-state entities such as organizations, and that this difficulty would be visible in particular with respect to the law of treaties. See Catherine M. Brölmann, *The Institutional Veil in Public International Law: International Organisations and the Law of Treaties* (Oxford, 2007).

[24] Article 73. See also E. W. Vierdag, 'Some Remarks on the Relationship between the 1969 and the 1986 Vienna Conventions on the Law of Treaties' (1987) 25 *Archiv des Völkerrechts*, 82–91.

[25] Moreover, as Nascimento e Silva, 'The 1986 Vienna Convention', p. 85, observes, some delegations still felt the treatment accorded to international organizations to be excessive.

[26] On termination of trusteeship agreements, see *UNJY* (1974), pp. 181–2.

international organizations (although many will contain some). In the UN, for example, there are only scant references. Article 43 authorizes the Security Council to enter into agreements with the UN's member states in order to allow military troops to be made available. Articles 57 and 63 empower the Economic and Social Council to conclude agreements with various other international organizations in order to bring them into a relationship with the UN, and Article 105 can be read as suggesting a power to conclude an agreement on the UN's privileges and immunities (without specifying whether the UN will be a party).

Yet, the UN has concluded numerous other agreements.[27] Obvious examples include the Headquarters Agreements with, amongst others, the USA and Switzerland,[28] although here too authority can be read into Article 105, but there are other examples in abundance. For instance, peace-keeping or peace-enforcement operations are, ideally if not invariably,[29] based on agreements with those states that make troops available as well as with host states. Such agreements serve, for example, to outline the legal position of those troops: issues of immunity and so on. Moreover, whenever the UN wishes to offer humanitarian assistance, some form of agreement with the host state will be at the heart of the effort.

In short: the UN concludes treaties on a far grander scale than was ever envisaged by the founders, and while the implied powers doctrine can be of some help in explaining and justifying this situation, one may wonder whether the legal situation has not become strained when most activities can only be explained with the help of implied powers.[30]

Most other organizations will have concluded at least a headquarters agreement, and increasingly organizations participate in activities relating to their field of expertise, and such participation includes the conclusion of treaties. In addition, increasingly organizations are concluding agreements with one another.[31]

---

[27] Usually they are concluded by the Secretary-General upon authorization by the competent organ. See *UNJY* (1981), p. 149.

[28] Hungdah Chiu (*The Capacity of International Organizations*, p. 71) usefully reminds us that the UN is not a party to the 1946 General Convention on Privileges and Immunities, which nonetheless was a factor upon which the ICJ seemed to rely in coming to terms with the legal personality of the UN in *Reparation for Injuries*. See also Chapter 8 above.

[29] See, generally, Robert C. R. Siekmann, *National Contingents in United Nations Peace-keeping Forces* (Dordrecht, 1991).

[30] As Rosenne observed, as early as 1954, the UN uses implied powers far more intensively than express powers. See Shabtai Rosenne, 'United Nations Treaty Practice' (1954/II) 86 *RdC*, 281–443, p. 296. Rosenne also provides the amazing statistic (p. 303) that, between 1945 and the end of 1953, the UN, its subsidiary organs and the Specialized Agencies together had entered into 809 agreements with individual states and fifty-four agreements with other organizations.

[31] See below, pp. 267–9.

The EC in particular concludes agreements on an impressive scale.[32] With respect to the EC, the power to conclude certain types of agreements is explicitly laid down in the constituent treaties.[33] Thus, under Article 133 (ex-Article 113), the Community is entitled to conclude trade agreements; under Article 310 (ex-Article 238), it may conclude association agreements. And, in addition, there are a number of provisions empowering the Community to conclude agreements on other topics: development co-operation,[34] environmental protection,[35] et cetera.

The power to conclude other sorts of agreements has been found to be implied in the treaty.[36] Thus, in the classic *ERTA*[37] case, the power to deal with the external aspects of transport was implied on the basis of the existence of a power to regulate transport within the Community and the need to protect the unity of EC law: if the EC lacked the external power, then member states could circumvent EC law simply by entering into external agreements. Thus, an existing internal regulatory power had to be complemented by an external power.[38]

In *Opinion 1/76*,[39] the Court proceeded on the basis of the same logic, and even extended it a little. In *ERTA*, the power of the EC to act externally was based, in the end, on the thought that, since the EC had already legislated internally, external powers were required to safeguard the integrity of the internal legislation.[40] In *Opinion 1/76*, however, the Court extended this reasoning to apply to situations where the EC had not yet legislated internally. Thus, even the integrity of possible future internal legislation had to be protected.

In *Opinion 1/76*, at issue was whether the EC would be competent to take part, together with Switzerland, in the creation of a fund for vessels engaged in Rhine and Moselle navigation. Clearly, the Court thought that, under EC law, the Community would be competent to do such a thing internally. The problem was, however, that such would be a rather empty gesture without the participation of Switzerland. Since the Rhine springs in Switzerland, it does not

---

[32] For an overview, see Delano Verwey, *The European Community, the European Union and the International Law of Treaties* (The Hague, 2004).

[33] Where the EC's power is exclusive, its member states may have to denounce their own participation. Thus, when the EC joined the Inter-American Tropical Tuna Commission, Spain had to withdraw. See Council Decision 2006/539/EC.

[34] Which may include a human rights component: see case C-268/94, *Portugal* v. *Council* [1996] ECR I-6177. See more generally Jutta Gras, *The European Union and Human Rights Monitoring* (Helsinki, 2000).

[35] See, e.g., Lena Granvik, *The Treaty-making Competence of the European Community in the Field of International Environmental Conventions* (Helsinki, 1999).

[36] A fine overview is offered in Koutrakos, *EU International Relations Law*, Chapter 3.

[37] Case 22/70, *Commission* v. *Council (ERTA)* [1971] ECR 273.

[38] For further discussion, see Chapter 4 above.

[39] *Opinion 1/76 (Laying-up Fund)* [1977] ECR 754.

[40] For an overview of the techniques developed since then, see Jan Klabbers, 'Safeguarding the Organizational *Acquis*: The EU's External Practice' (2007) 4 *IOLR*, 57–89.

make much sense to try and adopt legal rules without Swiss participation. Thus, in order not to render the internal power meaningless, an external power was deemed implied, even though the internal power had not yet been used.

While both *ERTA* and *Opinion 1/76* unabashedly solved a power struggle between the EC and its members by taking the side of the Community, the Court backtracked in its famous (or infamous) *Opinion 1/94*.[41] The Commission had asked the Court for an Opinion on the WTO agreement, and more specifically on who was competent to conclude it. The Commission had argued that, since the World Trade Organization deals with world trade, it falls under the heading of the EC's commercial policy which belongs to the EC's exclusive competence.

The Court, however, disagreed to some extent, and did so in two ways. First, it narrowed down the scope of the phrase 'commercial policy' in what used to be Article 113 TEC,[42] and rather curiously found that commercial policy is basically limited to trade in goods, and only a few aspects of trade in services (those aspects which can be analogized to trade in goods): since other forms of trade involve the movement of persons (e.g., a patient visiting a doctor abroad, a plumber repairing a sink abroad), the Court chose to analyse these types of trade in terms of the EC's internal rules on the free movement of persons, and as it is undisputed that here the Community has to share competences with its members, so too external competences would have to be shared.[43]

But second, it also narrowed down the scope of the implied powers doctrine. Whereas in *ERTA* and *Opinion 1/76*, the Court had been quite liberal (so much so as to warrant the suggestion that it went even beyond the implied powers doctrine), in *Opinion 1/94* it limited the implied external powers of the EC to those cases where Community action would be 'inextricably linked' to the objectives of the EC.

That differs from the *ERTA* and *Opinion 1/76* doctrine in one fundamental respect: the underlying logic has been abandoned. Instead of finding a power to exist because otherwise another, existing power would make little sense, the Court found another basis, far more in line with the ICJ's finding in the *Reparation for Injuries* case – some power can be implied if necessary for the effective functioning of the international organization, and here the EC Court decided, moreover, to subject this to a rather narrow test: a power can only be implied if it is inextricably linked to these objectives.[44] In recent years the

---

[41] See, e.g., Meinhard Hilf, 'The ECJ's Opinion 1/94 on the WTO – No Surprise, But Wise?' (1995) 6 *EJIL*, 245–59, esp. p. 254.

[42] Nowadays Art. 133 TEC.

[43] What puzzles, then, is why the Court found it necessary to analyse these types of trade in services through the prism of movement of persons.

[44] And that, in turn, suggests that the implied powers doctrine never properly applied to cases such as *ERTA* and *Opinion 1/76*, something which is increasingly recognized in the literature. For example, Dashwood prefers to think of such cases as exploring inherent powers. Compare Alan Dashwood, 'The Limits of European Community Powers' (1996) 21 *ELR*, 113–28. See also Chapter 4 above, in particular the section on 'Re-thinking Powers'.

discussion seems to have settled down a bit, with the ECJ focusing not so much on powers as such, but finds member state action precluded on the basis of the notion of Community fidelity (*Gemeinschaftstreue*) laid down in Article 10 of the TEC. Thus, it was largely on the basis of this notion (combined with some secondary legislation) that the Court held, in a string of decisions, that the member states were not in a position to conclude bilateral air traffic agreements with third states. Doing so would potentially interfere with internal rules on services and establishment, and therewith endanger Community law.[45]

The ties that bind

Apart from the question of competence, the conclusion of treaties by international organizations provokes several other legal problems. One problem is to assess which is the exact entity that becomes bound: the organization itself, or, as the case may be, the particular organ of the organization that entered into the agreement? A second problem, not wholly unrelated, has to do with the position of the member states of the organization: if the organization concludes an agreement, are the member states also bound?

Usually, treaties concluded by organizations are concluded by one of the organs of the organization. Thus, with the UN, most agreements are entered into by the Secretary-General (or his representative), although Article 43 keeps open the possibility of agreements being entered into by the Security Council, and other articles envisage yet other possibilities.

Within the EC, the conclusion of agreements is regulated in Article 300 of the TEC (ex-Article 228 TEC, the same article which also allows the Court to be asked for an opinion), and the basic rule is that treaties are entered into by the Council, having been negotiated by the Commission.[46]

The question then is: who exactly becomes bound under international law? In other words: upon whom, all else remaining equal, do international obligations come to rest, and who becomes the bearer of international legal rights? The matter as such has never been subjected to the ICJ, but it stands to reason to hold that, as far as UN treaty-making is concerned, it will be the UN which is bound, not just the Council or the Secretary-General. One argument for this finding springs from considerations of legal logic: neither the Security Council nor the Secretary-General possess treaty-making powers in their own right. Whatever powers they may have to enter into agreements, they have by virtue of being principal organs of the UN.

---

[45] See, e.g., Case C-467/98, *Commission* v. *Denmark* [2002] ECR I-9519. In total there have been nine decisions on these sort of agreements.

[46] Euratom too concludes treaties. An example is a 2005 treaty with Kazakhstan on controlled nuclear fusion (OJ, 7 June 2005). Euratom and the EC together sometimes also conclude treaties with third parties, such as the interim agreement on trade with Tajikistan (OJ, 16 November 2004).

Second, in the *Effect of Awards* case,[47] the ICJ did pronounce itself on the establishment of the Administrative Tribunal, and reached the conclusion that the Tribunal, although having been set up by the Assembly, served the whole of the UN, and that any employment disputes were to be regarded as disputes between the employee and the UN as such, not between the employee and the General Assembly, or between the employee and the Secretariat. By analogy, one may reach the conclusion that agreements entered into by the principal organs (or other organs, for that matter) will come to bind the organization as a whole.

The EC Court has had the opportunity to pronounce itself on the matter, and has found that an agreement entered into by the Commission would be binding upon the whole Community. In September 1991, the Commission had concluded an agreement with the US Department of Justice to co-operate in antitrust affairs. France argued that the Commission, in doing so, had acted *ultra vires*, and went to court, claiming that only the Council can conclude agreements on behalf of the Community.[48]

One of the Commission's arguments was that the agreement would merely be of an administrative nature,[49] binding the Commission but not the Community as a whole.[50] Therefore, there should be no problem. The Court, however, rejected the argument, claiming in essence that there is in international law no such thing as an administrative agreement which can bind only administrative units. Instead, an agreement entered into by the Commission would bind the Community as a whole, and there can be little doubt that the Court was correct in its assessment. International law[51] does not

---

[47] *Effect of awards of compensation made by the United Nations Administrative Tribunal*, advisory opinion, [1954] ICJ Reports 47.

[48] Case C-327/91, *France* v. *Commission* [1994] ECR I-3641. The case highlights difficult problems in the relationship between EC law and international law. For a useful discussion of those aspects, see Christine Kaddous, 'L'Arrêt France c. Commission de 1994 (accord concurrence) et le contrôle de la légalité des accords externes en vertu de l'art. 173 CE: la difficile réconciliation de l'orthodoxie communautaire avec l'orthodoxie internationale' (1996) 32 *CDE*, 613–33.

[49] The same type of argument sometimes surfaces in other organizations. With respect to the treaty-making powers of the UN Secretary-General, see UNJY (1981), p. 149.

[50] The Commission was arguably forced to do so as its own treaty-making powers are rather limited; the most important is the power, under Art. 302 (ex-Art. 229) TEC, to ensure and maintain relations with other international organizations. Article 300, para. 2 (ex-Art. 228, para. 2) TEC moreover suggests that there may be treaty-making powers 'vested in the Commission', but the meaning of that phrase is debated. For a Commission-friendly interpretation, see Alain-Pierre Allo, 'Les accords administratifs entre l'Union Européenne et les organisations internationales'. In Daniel Dormoy (ed.), *L'Union Européenne et les organisations internationales* (Brussels, 1997), pp. 56–67.

[51] All this presupposes that the Community is bound by customary international law, something which, although not immediately self-evident, has increasingly become recognized. See, e.g., case C-286/90, *Anklagemyndigheden* v. *Poulsen and Diva Navigation* [1992] ECR I-6019; case C-405/92, *Mondiet SA* v. *Armement Islais SARL* [1993] ECR I-6133; and, more explicitly, case T-115/94, *Opel Austria GmbH* v. *Council* [1997] ECR II-39. Some problems involved in the Community's relationship with customary international law are discussed in Vaughan Lowe,

readily recognize administrative entities as being capable of bearing independent rights and duties under international law as long as they remain part of another entity.[52]

A more difficult situation arises when it comes to the legal position of member states: if an international organization concludes an agreement, are the member states to be considered as, somehow, parties to that agreement, or are they considered to be third parties?

That is a complicated question, which would require a clear theoretical perspective on the overall position of member states towards their organizations in order to be answered.[53] The International Law Commission, while drafting the 1986 Vienna Convention, tried in vain to develop a general rule. In a famous draft Article 36bis, it opted for the solution that members should be considered as third parties, primarily. They could, generally, only be regarded as being parties to the treaty concluded by their organization if three distinct conditions were met.

First, the treaty concerned must intend to create rights or obligations for the member states of the organization in question. Second, the members must have unanimously agreed to become bound by such a treaty, either by specific act or by virtue of the constituent treaty. And third, the fact that the members will be bound must have been notified to the organization's treaty partner.

The proposal was, ultimately, defeated. What it indicated, though, was that, at least within the International Law Commission, there were some strong opinions generally favouring the view of member states as legally distinct from their organizations, even to be able to hide behind their creations.[54]

The Special Rapporteur drafting this particular article, Professor Paul Reuter, defended his choice in terms of state consent. Since states cannot be held to be bound unless they express their consent to rights and obligations, the same would apply to situations in which the entities they created (i.e., international organizations) entered into commitments.[55]

'Can the European Community Bind the Member States on Questions of Customary International Law?' In Martti Koskenniemi (ed.), *International Law Aspects of the European Union* (The Hague, 1998), pp. 149–68.

[52] Compare Jan Klabbers, *The Concept of Treaty in International Law* (The Hague, 1996), esp. pp. 97–105. The position that administrative agreements would be non-legally binding seems to have been discarded; compare Allo, 'Les accords administratifs'.

[53] For a general analysis, see Catherine M. Brölmann, 'The 1986 Vienna Convention on the Law of Treaties: The History of Draft Article 36bis'. In Jan Klabbers and René Lefeber (eds.), *Essays on the Law of Treaties: A Collection of Essays in Honour of Bert Vierdag* (The Hague, 1998), pp. 121–40.

[54] See also Philippe Manin, 'The European Communities and the Vienna Convention on the Law of Treaties between States and International Organizations or between International Organizations' (1987) 24 *CMLRev*, 457–81.

[55] See in particular Reuter's Tenth Report on the Question of Treaties Concluded between States and International Organizations or Between Two or More International Organizations, in (1981/II) *YbILC*, part one, pp. 43–69, esp. p. 67.

Clearly, the underlying argument is that organizations may and do have a will distinct from the will of their member states; therefore, they can take actions which may not be to the liking of their member states, and therefore it follows that those members cannot be bound to treaties concluded by the organization unless they express consent to be bound.

The question then is, of course, whether such a view is in accord with realities, and here some caution may be in order for, if it is true that decision making (including decisions to conclude treaties) usually takes place by the unanimous consent of the member states, then it follows that the will of the organization is identical to the will of all its members. Therefore, whatever the will of the organization may be, it can usually be considered to be the aggregate will of the member states, rather than the distinct will of the international organization. With that in mind, organizations could simply be regarded as exercising a delegated power: there would be no need for specific acts of consent, because it would be clear that all the organization's acts would be based on consent anyway.

Such a conception, however, would mean getting rid of the element of the distinct will, and therefore getting rid of an important justification for the existence of organizations. For if an organization does not have a distinct will, then why establish one to begin with?

Ironically, the main organization to which the problem may apply, the EC, has dealt with this itself in its constituent treaty. Article 300 (formerly Article 228) of the TEC proclaims, in para. 7, that treaties entered into by the EC shall be binding upon the member states.[56] Indeed, the EC Court has even held that treaties concluded between the Community and a third state may well have direct effect in the laws of the member states. The leading case is *Kupferberg*,[57] in which a German wine importer claimed that German levies on Portuguese wine were in violation of the then-existing association agreement with Portugal. The German Court wondered whether Mr Kupferberg could invoke the provisions of an association agreement before the German courts, and the EC Court held that indeed Mr Kupferberg could do so, provided that the provisions of the association agreement would lend themselves to being directly effective. As it was, *in casu* those provisions were sufficiently precise and unconditional as to be directly effective.[58]

At any rate, it is clear that, under EC law, treaties concluded by the EC and third states bind the member states and the institutions. It is important to

---

[56] Indeed, they 'form an integral part of Community law', although it remains as yet unclear why and how they do so. See case 181/73, *Haegeman* v. *Belgium* [1974] ECR 449, para. 5.

[57] Case 104/81, *Hauptzollamt Mainz* v. *C. A. Kupferberg & Cie* [1982] ECR 3659.

[58] Generally, the Court relies on criteria first established in case 26/62, *Van Gend & Loos* v. *Nederlandse Administratie der Belastingen* [1963] ECR 1. WTO law is usually denied direct effect though, which suggests that the Court functions like a gate-keeper. For a discussion along these lines, see Jan Klabbers, 'International Law in Community Law: The Law and Politics of Direct Effect', (2002) 21 *YEL*, 263–98.

realize, though, that the binding force stems from EC law: it is EC law which proclaims, in Article 300 (ex-Article 228), para. 7 of the TEC, that treaties shall be binding upon the member states and the institutions.[59]

International law itself is less clear about the topic, and perhaps the rule formulated by the International Law Commission, in the defeated draft Article 36*bis*, still stands: member states will only be bound if they have expressed their consent.

While, as noted, the underlying argument may not be entirely persuasive, there is widespread doctrinal support and, more importantly, any other reasoning would presumably be equally unpersuasive: a hypothetical rule that member states are bound by definition is ultimately based on the thought that there is no distinction between the organization and its members, and that, in turn, is difficult to maintain.

As it is, the 1986 Vienna Convention contains nothing on the topic; writers, however, fall back on the 1969 Convention, and since the 1969 Convention prescribes that treaties shall create neither rights nor obligations for third states, neither do treaties concluded by international organizations. Nonetheless, while this seems to be the doctrinal majority position, it is perhaps important to realize that it seems to presuppose its own position: the argument presupposes that member states are indeed to be regarded as third parties, but that is precisely the question.

Mixed agreements

A phenomenon peculiar to international organizations is that of the so-called 'mixed agreement', whereby both an international organization and some or all of its member states become parties to a treaty. The main legal reason for doing this resides in the circumstance that an international convention may deal with topics which are partly within the powers of the organization, and partly within the powers of the organization's member states.

Again, the practical occurrence of this phenomenon is largely limited to the EC,[60] which is a party to a number of treaties, alongside some or all of its member states. The question addressed earlier cannot, strictly speaking, arise: if both the organization and all member states are parties, then both the organization and the member states will be bound. However, the question then becomes

---

[59] Treaties emanating from the 'second and third pillars' (foreign affairs and justice) are already deemed to bind those member states that have accepted them, according to Art. 24 TEU. The Nice Treaty will add, upon entry into force, that they also bind the institutions (Art. 24, para. 6 TEU).

[60] At one point, the UN considered accession to two conventions on nuclear accidents. See UNJY (1987), pp. 173–4. On other occasions, the UN may strive to include international provisions into its internal rules or possibly into bilateral agreements (e.g., on peace-keeping) without actually joining multilateral regimes. This applies, e.g., to the law of armed conflict; see UNJY (1992), pp. 430–1.

slightly different: who is bound to what?[61] For the underlying idea with mixed agreements is that each party, be it the organization or its member, will take care of the things arising within the scope of its own powers.[62]

To determine the distribution of powers, the other contracting parties usually insist that the EC hand over some declaration on this distribution of powers.[63] Thus, upon signing the 1982 United Nations Convention on the Law of the Sea, the EC declared that the member states have transferred competence to it with regard to the conservation and management of sea fishing resources, as well as some powers relating to the protection of the marine environment and commercial policy.[64]

While such a declaration is already rather vague in its own right, the Community obfuscated matters even more by adding: 'The exercise of the competence that the Member States have transferred to the Community under the Treaties is, by its very nature, subject to continuous development. As a result the Community reserves the right to make new declarations at a later date.'[65] It is not uncommon for the EC to issue such declarations on distribution of competencies. The 1992 Climate Change Convention, for example, has been signed by the EC with a similar declaration.[66] It should be noted, though, that usually the obligation to make such a declaration derives from the treaty concerned. Thus, the United Nations Convention on the Law of the Sea specifies that international organizations may become parties under conditions set out in one of the annexes to the Convention: Annex IX.[67]

---

[61] In addition, there may be cases where EC law gives the EC competence, but the EC is not accepted as a treaty partner. In such a case (it applies e.g., to some ILO conventions), the EC's 'external competence may, if necessary, be exercised through the medium of the Member States acting jointly in the Community interest', according to the EC Court. See *Opinion 2/91* (ILO) [1993] ECR I-1061, para. 5. The ILO's position on the matter is set out in UNJY (1991), pp. 340–6. Similar problems may arise with respect to representation within organs; see UNJY (1980), p. 192.

[62] An excellent general analysis is Joseph H. H. Weiler, 'The External Legal Relations of Nonunitary Actors: Mixity and the Federal Principle'. Reproduced in his *The Constitution of Europe* (Cambridge, 1999), pp. 130–87. The leading monograph is Joni Heliskoski, *Mixed Agreements as a Technique for Organizing the International Relations of the European Community and its Member States* (The Hague, 2001).

[63] For a critical view, holding that what is the EC's distribution of competences is not of concern to the EC's treaty partners, see John Temple Lang, 'The Ozone Layer Convention: A New Solution to the Question of Community Participation in "Mixed" International Agreements' (1986) 23 *CMLRev*, 157–76, esp. p. 172.

[64] The text is reproduced in, e.g., the UN publication *Multilateral Treaties Deposited with the Secretary-General: Status as at 31 December 1993* (New York, 1994), pp. 805–6.

[65] Upon depositing its instrument of formal confirmation, on 1 April 1998, the Community confirmed that the scope and exercise of Community competence are, by their very nature, subject to continuous development, and added that 'the Community will complete or amend this declaration, if necessary'. The Declaration can be found at http://untreaty.un.org/ENGLISH/bible/englishinternetbible/partI/chapterXXI/treaty6.asp (visited 14 November 2001).

[66] See *Multilateral Treaties*, p. 889.   [67] Article 305 UNCLOS.

Annex IX, in turn, specifies that the Convention is open to participation by organizations enjoying both competence over substantive law of-the-sea issues and treaty-making powers in respect of those issues,[68] and provided a majority of their member states have ratified.[69] Article 5 of Annex IX demands a declaration be included in the instrument of formal confirmation[70] or accession 'specifying the matters governed by this Convention in respect of which competence has been transferred to the organization by its member States which are parties to this Convention',[71] with Article 6 adding that responsibility for failure to comply shall follow the declaration of competences.

If the treaty concerned remains silent, then there is most likely no obligation to indicate clearly the distribution of competences. A case in point is the Marrakesh Agreement establishing the World Trade Organization, although much clarity (substantively largely unexpected) has been provided by the EC Court of Justice in its *Opinion 1/94*.

Another issue that may sometimes arise is that occasionally the EC has to reserve its internal position. Thus, upon signing the Environmental Impact Assessment Convention of 1991, the EC declared that it signed 'on the understanding that, in their mutual relations, the Community Member States will apply the Convention in accordance with the Community's internal rules ... and without prejudice to appropriate amendments being made to those rules'.[72] More generally, at least with treaties concluded under the auspices of the Council of Europe (in which the EC, with its twenty-seven member states, holds a strong position), the EC typically insists on the inclusion of a so-called 'disconnection clause': a clause allowing the EC members to apply EC law in their mutual relations while applying the Council of Europe convention in relations with non-EC members. As long as other states agree to this (and this is usually the case) there is legally not much of a problem; politically, though, insisting on the inclusion of a disconnection clause smacks a bit of raw power, and for that reason has often been subjected to criticism.[73]

More difficult problems arise when the agreement is a so-called 'incomplete mixed agreement', meaning that the organization and some of its members have become parties, but that some other members have not. Usually, this is defended by pointing out that the subject matter of the treaty at hand does not involve the other member states individually; thus, say, Austria may have little interest in a convention on North Sea cabotage, while Finland will hardly be interested in Rhine shipping. In such circumstances,

---

[68] Annex IX, Art. 1.   [69] *Ibid.*, Art. 3.   [70] The act analogous to ratification.

[71] Article 5, para. 1. Article 2 demands a similar declaration upon signature.

[72] See *Multilateral Treaties*, p. 882.

[73] A useful overview is Constantin P. Economidès and Alexandros G. Kolliopoulos, 'La clause de déconnexion en faveur du droit communautaire: une pratique critiquable' (2006) 110 *RGDIP*, 273–302.

there is no practical reason to insist on the participation of Austria and Finland, respectively.[74]

As a theoretical matter, mixed agreements (whether covering all or only some of the organization's members) are far from elegant solutions to practical problems.[75] They rupture the unity, or would-be unity, of an organization's external actions, and even place question marks around the very idea of unity to begin with. In particular where 'mixity' is inspired not so much by legal necessity but rather by demands arising from concerns relating to the legitimacy of agreements amongst those who have to implement them (i.e., the member states), one may well regard them as a sign of defeatism on the part of the organization concerned: it sends the message that its ambitions cannot be realized without the separate involvement of its member states.

On the other hand, mixity also signifies that there might be situations where an analysis in terms of a distribution of powers between the organization (meaning mostly the EC) and its members is no longer very useful, in the sense that a power analysis might not say a lot about actual restraints on the behaviour of member states arising out of Community law. This might find its cause in the circumstance that, even exercising its proper powers, a member state may nonetheless interfere with EC law,[76] or because Community law increasingly prescribes that Community powers or policies be complementary to member state powers or policies.[77] Where it is no longer possible or useful to separate the powers of the Community from those of its members, mixity becomes an obvious answer when it comes to the conclusion of treaties.[78]

---

[74] It has been pointed out though that in such a case member states that do not become parties to the treaty at hand themselves are subject to the suspicion of attempting 'to secure a form of limited accession . . . with major reservations' by having the Community become a party. Compare Kenneth R. Simmonds, 'The Community's Declaration upon Signature of the UN Convention on the Law of the Sea' (1986) 23 *CMLRev*, 521–44, p. 530. Such a view seems premised upon a conception of organizations being mere vehicles for their member states.

[75] And, additionally, bring their own practical problems with them. A recently discovered problem relates to whether the EC Court has the jurisdiction to apply or interpret an entire mixed agreement, or only those parts which fall within the Community's powers. Case law tends to lean towards jurisdiction over the entire mixed agreement; see, e.g., case C-53/96, *Hermès* v. *FHT* [1998] ECR I-3603. For a brief discussion, see Joni Heliskoski, 'The Jurisdiction of the European Court of Justice to Give Preliminary Rulings on the Interpretation of Mixed Agreements' (2000) 69 *Nordic JIL*, 395–412.

[76] See also Chapter 4 above.

[77] See Marise Cremona, 'External Relations and External Competence: The Emergence of an Integrated Policy'. In Paul Craig and Gráinne de Búrca (eds.), *The Evolution of EU Law* (Oxford, 1999), pp. 137–75. The Treaty of Nice goes even further, and stipulates that certain trade agreements may only be concluded on the basis of mixity. See Art. 133, para. 6 TEC (as amended at Nice).

[78] Note, however, that mixity may engender problems of responsibility. See Martin Björklund, 'Responsibility in the EC for Mixed Agreements – Should Non-member Parties Care?' (2001) 70 *Nordic JIL*, 373–402.

Organizational liaisons

Treaty-making by international organizations is so well established that few eyebrows are raised when organizations enter into relations with one another.[79] There is little doubt that, under general international law, organizations can and do conclude treaties with other organizations, on all possible topics and in all possible forms. Thus, to provide a random example, NATO and WEU, in 1995, signed a Memorandum of Understanding on communications co-operation.[80]

The capacity of international organizations to help create, or join, other international organizations is not yet generally accepted. The UN's Office of Legal Affairs, for one, has expressed some hesitation in a memorandum relating to UNDP: 'International intergovernmental organizations which are the creation of States cannot in and of themselves create new international organizations, endowed with the same legal personality, unless they are specifically mandated by States.'[81] Still, on occasion, organizations have joined other organizations, or have been among the founding members of another organization, and at least one organization is established solely by other organizations without any direct state involvement: the so-called Joint Vienna Institute.[82]

Many of the problems discussed earlier return in this context, albeit in more complicated form. Thus, to take the example of an agreement between NATO and WEU, again the question may arise who is bound: the organizations, or their members? Matters are more complex here, for two reasons. First, and most obvious, there is not one organization involved, but two. Second, and more problematic, those two organizations have overlapping membership: all WEU members are also members of the larger NATO. This seems immediately to make clear that the agreement must be considered to bind only the organizations (and their organs); otherwise, the construction would arise in which at least the states that are members of both would find the agreement reduced to one that they concluded with, among others, themselves: Belgium, NATO-member, cannot meaningfully be considered as having concluded an agreement with Belgium, WEU-member.[83]

---

[79] A useful volume on the connections between the EU and various organizations within the UN family is Jan Wouters, Frank Hoffmeister and Tom Ruys (eds.), *The United Nations and the European Union: An Ever Stronger Partnership* (The Hague, 2006).

[80] See NATO Press Release (95)102 of 27 October 1995.

[81] See UNJY (1991), pp. 296–301, esp. p. 297. This confirmed an earlier opinion, in which the Office held that international organizations 'do not have the legal capacity to establish new organizations', as represented at p. 298. Incidentally, the UN Office of Legal Affairs has also held that UNDP's mandate does not include 'the capacity to establish or participate in the establishment of a legal entity under the national laws' of its members either. See UNJY (1990), pp. 259–60, at p. 259.

[82] The Agreement for the establishment of the Joint Vienna Institute to provide training support, during the transition of central and eastern European countries to market-based economies, entered into force in 1994 and was concluded between the Bank for International Settlements, EBRD, IBRD, IMF and OECD. The text is reproduced in (1994) 33 *ILM* 1505.

[83] Of course, this can only arise where there is overlapping membership.

This, however, may re-introduce questions that are asked when things go wrong: if WEU fails to perform, whom should NATO address? Surely, if WEU remains unwilling to perform and refuses to provide remedies, some recourse to the underlying member states must be possible, even if that means that those member states may have to address themselves.[84]

Other problems are more specific to inter-organizational relations and in particular to the situation where one organization is a member of another organization, such as the question of voting rights and procedure.[85] While practice is hitherto relatively scarce, it would seem that voting rights and voting procedure are to be determined by the target organization (i.e., the organization that comprises another organization). The target organization will also make sure, if only to protect the interests of its other members, that the member organization shall not have more votes than its individual members would have together, and will insist, prior to voting and perhaps even prior to discussing matters, that the member organization provide a detailed overview of the precise distribution of competences between it and its member states, similar to the type of declarations issued upon signing or confirming a treaty (as discussed above). Thus, with FAO meetings, the Community declares, prior to technical sessions, ministerial sessions and meetings of the Committee on Fisheries, what the actual state of distribution of powers is on every specific agenda item, and whether the Community or its member states shall exercise voting rights.[86] Nonetheless, the way those voting rights are exercised is a matter to be decided by the member organization, which shall follow either its usual decision-making procedures or a specific set of rules.[87]

A few other issues are also of relevance. Thus, the constituent document of the target organization must allow accession or membership of international organizations. The few that do[88] have limited the type of organizations able to become members of regional economic integration organizations, and usually state that at least a majority of the members of the prospective member organizations must also (independently) be members of the target organization. Moreover, target organizations usually attach the condition that such an organization must be able to take decisions which bind its members. Hence, in practice the only prominent candidate to date to make use of this facility is the EC, which is a member of a number of international organizations.[89]

In addition, at least ideally, the prospective member organization should have an internal rule granting it the power to join other organizations; it has

---

[84] Matters of responsibility will be further dealt with below (see Chapter 14).

[85] For a useful general overview, see Jörn Sack, 'The European Community's Membership of International Organizations' (1995) 32 *CMLRev*, 1227–56.

[86] For an example of such a declaration, see (1995) 11 *International Organizations and the Law of the Sea Documentary Yearbook*, pp. 782–3.

[87] Compare Case C-25/94, *Commission v. Council (FAO)* [1996] ECR I-1469.

[88] These include a number of commodities agreements. See UNJY (1976), pp. 216–18. The FAO, in 1991, changed its constitution in order to allow the EC to join.

[89] These include the WTO, the EBRD, the FAO, and several fisheries organizations.

been cogently argued that, with respect to the EC, the existence of such a rule is doubtful.[90] While there is little doubt that the EC can substantively act on the fields covered by the organizations of which it is a member, there is no specific accession provision outlining the proper procedure to be followed analogous to the treaty-making procedure of Article 300 (ex-Article 228) of the TEC. As so often though, the absence of a specific rule has not prevented the EC from acting, and as so often, it has been the implied powers doctrine which has come to the rescue: where a substantive power exists, this must be deemed to imply the power to join or even help establish international organizations.[91]

Also of interest is whether an organization, as a member of another organization, can participate in subsidiary bodies set up jointly with other organizations, such as the joint FAO/WHO body Codex Alimentarius. At least the FAO's Legal Counsel answered the question in the affirmative, although it remains unclear whether such bodies allow participation of member organizations in their own right, or rather as exercising the rights of their member states.[92]

Finally, another issue of relevance is the member organization's contribution to the budget. If the member states of the member organization themselves contribute in full, there appears to be little reason to expect an additional contribution from the organization, save perhaps to cover any additional costs arising out of its separate membership. Against this, the argument has sometimes been invoked that to insist on state contributions would prevent the member organization from following its planned road to further integration (separate membership would prevent the proper exercise of possible future exclusive competences)[93] but surely it is not the task of the target organization to stimulate the development of its member organization *vis-à-vis* the member states of the member organization.

Concluding remarks

The intriguing nature of the relationship between an organization and its members becomes perhaps most visible where the organization aspires to take the place of its members (e.g., as a treaty partner or even as a member of yet another organization). There is a constant oscillation between the position of the organization as a party in its own right, and the position of the organization as a vehicle for its own member states.

---

[90] See Rachel Frid, 'The European Economic Community – A Member of a Specialized Agency of the United Nations' (1993) 4 *EJIL*, 239–55, esp. 242–5. More in-depth, see Rachel Frid, *The Relations between the EC and International Organizations: Legal Theory and Practice* (The Hague, 1995).

[91] As much follows from *Opinion 1/76*, where the Court held the EC to have the power to help found a fund. More generally, the EC has always been empowered to conclude association agreements (Art. 310, ex-Art. 238 TEC). Such associations may establish joint organs whose decisions may be directly effective in the legal order of the EC. See, e.g., case C-192/89, *Sevince v. Staatssecretaris van Justitie* [1990] ECR I-3461.

[92] See UNJY (1991), pp. 346–7.   [93] So, e.g., Frid, 'The European Economic Community', p. 255.

Given this complex state of affairs, it should come as no surprise that there are few, if any, hard and fast rules; much depends on the rules of the target organization, as well as on those of the acceding or joining organization, and even then much needs to be decided on a case-by-case basis.

While general doctrines, such as the law of treaties, may remain of help in simple cases (indeed, there is no good reason why an organization should be able to terminate its treaties under conditions which differ from those to which states are subjected), those same general doctrines cannot provide ready-made solutions to questions such as whether a treaty binding an organization also binds its members. Here, the indeterminacy of international law in general shows itself with full force, and with a twist: not only is the regular regime relating to third parties not free from uncertainties, but here it is not even clear whether member states (or organs) are to be regarded as third parties to begin with. The same problem plays an important role when it comes to the responsibility of international organizations.

14

Issues of responsibility

Introduction

It is one of the more settled principles of international law, as authoritatively formulated by the Permanent Court of International Justice in the classic *Chorzow Factory* case,[1] that a violation of international law entails responsibility and the obligation to make reparation in one form or another.[2] When it concerns the activities of states, the basic rule is, all sorts of difficulties notwithstanding, relatively straightforward: states are responsible for internationally wrongful acts that can be attributed to them.[3]

With international organizations, however, the question is whether the organization can be held responsible for internationally wrongful acts and, if so, whose acts qualify and upon whom does responsibility eventually come to rest.[4] While states can by and large be treated, for purposes of international law, as unitary actors,[5] the same is not self-evident when it comes to international organizations, which are, after all, the creations of states. Here, once again,

---

[1] *Case Concerning the Factory at Chorzów (Claim for Indemnity)*, jurisdiction, [1927] Publ. PCIJ, Series A, judgment no. 8, p. 21: 'It is a principle of international law that the breach of an engagement involves an obligation to make reparation in an adequate form.'

[2] For a general study, see Christine Gray, *Judicial Remedies in International Law* (Oxford, 1987).

[3] ILC Draft Article 2: 'There is an internationally wrongful act of a State when conduct consisting of an action or omission: (a) is attributable to the State under international law; and (b) constitutes a breach of an international obligation of the State.' See UN Doc. A/CN.4/L.602/Rev. 1 of 26 July 2001, containing the draft articles adopted by the Drafting Committee on second reading. One of the surprisingly few (relatively) recent monographs on state responsibility is Ian Brownlie, *System of the Law of Nations Part I: State Responsibility* (Oxford, 1983).

[4] The earlier ILC draft articles on state responsibility, while not specifically addressing the responsibility of international organizations or their member states, seemed nonetheless predisposed to accept a separate responsibility for the organization. The present draft articles on state responsibility (see previous note) do not address the issue at all. Host states may arguably incur responsibility if they allow organizations to engage in illicit activities, but then the basis of responsibility is this failure to prevent rather than the illicit activity itself. See also Matthias Hartwig, *Die Haftung der Mitgliedstaaten für Internationale Organisationen* (Berlin, 1993), pp. 49–50.

[5] Although with federal states at least this presumption may no longer be tenable, in light of the ICJ's recent pronouncement that certain obligations are incumbent on the Governor of Arizona. See the *Case Concerning the Vienna Convention on Consular Relations (Germany v. USA)*, [1999] ICJ Reports 9, in particular para. 28.

the layered nature of international organizations becomes visible: behind the 'organizational veil' the contours of the organization's member states can be discerned.[6]

The topic of the responsibility of international organizations had been given scant attention until the mid-1980s, and the few studies that had appeared before then initially found it difficult to come to terms with international organizations to begin with. Thus, Clyde Eagleton, writing in the 1950s, hardly considered the possibility that international organizations might themselves incur responsibility under international law. His lengthy study was based on the premise that the only conceivable form of responsibility in international law would be responsibility of states; organizations, after all, as a general rule, exercise no control over territory.[7] And even as late as 1969, Konrad Ginther's thoughtful study was largely devoted to the question of whether organizations could bear responsibility to begin with.[8]

In the mid-1980s, however, the collapse of the International Tin Council (ITC), and the voluminous litigation that ensued predominantly in the English courts, made it clear that here was a topic which would require further study and analysis. In the 1990s alone several monographs have appeared.[9]

One factor complicating the Tin Council litigation was the absence of any clause on responsibility in the constituent document, and this is indeed a general pattern. Few charters of international organizations contain responsibility clauses; the main exceptions are the financial institutions and some commodity agreements as well as some dealing with satellite activities – in short, organizations whose activities entail financial risks.[10] Here, the standard type of clause envisages a limited liability for the member states.

The ITC litigation makes clear that a first possible distinction to draw is that between responsibility under domestic law and responsibility under international law. The former depends, of course, first and foremost on domestic law (albeit guided perhaps by international law); I will therefore refrain from addressing the issue specifically.[11] Responsibility under international law, however, depends of course on international law.

---

[6] Incidentally, this applies to all complex organizations: behind the organization, there are always its members (or employees, or participants), and *vice versa*. For a useful study from the field of organization theory, see Mark Bovens, *The Quest for Responsibility: Accountability and Citizenship in Complex Organisations* (Cambridge, 1998).

[7] Clyde Eagleton, 'International Organization and the Law of Responsibility' (1959/I) 76 *RdC*, 319–425.

[8] Konrad Ginther, *Die völkerrechtliche Verantwortlichkeit internationaler Organisationen gegenüber Drittstaaten* (Vienna, 1969), esp. pp. 1, 87–8.

[9] These include Hartwig, *Die Haftung der Mitgliedstaaten*; Moshe Hirsch, *The Responsibility of International Organizations toward Third Parties: Some Basic Principles* (Dordrecht, 1995); Pierre Klein, *La responsabilité des organisations internationales dans les ordres juridiques internes et en droit des gens* (Brussels, 1998); Rick Lawson, *Het EVRM en de Europese Gemeenschappen* (Deventer, 1999). A more recent contribution is Kirsten Schmalenbach, *Die Haftung internationaler Organisationen* (Frankfurt am Main, 2004).

[10] See also Hartwig, *Die Haftung der Mitgliedstaaten*, pp. 146–68.

[11] Not everyone appears convinced of the validity or utility of this distinction. Thus, at least in the context of the Tin Council litigation, some doubts are expressed by Ignaz Seidl-Hohenveldern,

A second distinction to draw, this time on the international legal level is whether responsibility is invoked by a member state of the organization concerned, or by a third party, for instance another state, a creditor or perhaps an individual. The former applies predominantly to the UN, to which, after all, there are precious few third parties (or rather, few third states). What follows will deal mostly with responsibility *vis-à-vis* third parties.

Third, it is useful to distinguish between the responsibility of the organization, and any possible subsidiary responsibility of the member states for the organization's behaviour. The responsibility of member states may be subsidiary (German scholars use the wonderful term 'Durchgriffshaftung'[12] or variations thereon, loosely to be translated as 'see-through responsibility'), in that the member states may be responsible if the organization itself is unwilling or unable to bear responsibility. But it may perhaps also be the case, as some scholars have argued, that the member states incur direct responsibility: if the member states fail to exercise proper control over the acts of the organization, then they may be held responsible for negligence.[13]

Finally, there is the situation where an obligation does not, as such, rest upon an organization, but does rest upon all of its members, yet wrongful behaviour must be attributed to the organization as it exercises powers instead of its member states. An example (a somewhat controversial example perhaps) might be the position of the EC with respect to the European Convention on Human Rights: although the EC is not a party to the European Convention on Human Rights, all its members are. In some areas, the EC's members have transferred powers to the EC, and have done so willingly and wittingly: no one forced them to transfer powers, and thus they should not be allowed to invoke this transfer in order to escape responsibility. Consequently, should the EC violate a norm contained in the European Convention, responsibility rests upon the members jointly.[14]

Some preliminary issues

To assign legal responsibility to an entity (or moral responsibility, for that matter) presupposes a few things. First, it presupposes that the entities concerned can be legal or moral agents. This is not quite the same as saying they

'Piercing the Corporate Veil of International Organizations: The International Tin Council Case in the English Court of Appeals' (1989) 32 *GYIL*, 43–54, esp. pp. 49–50.

[12] So, e.g., Ginther, *Die völkerrechtliche Verantwortlichkeit*, p. 172 (more accurately, he speaks of 'Durchgriffsmöglichkeit').

[13] See the brilliant study by Romana Sadurska and Christine M. Chinkin, 'The Collapse of the International Tin Council: A Case of State Responsibility?' (1990) 30 *VaJIL*, 845–90.

[14] For a detailed analysis along these lines, see the excellent study (in Dutch, unfortunately) by Lawson, *Het EVRM*. One might also think of the responsibility of UN members for violations of the laws of armed conflict by UN troops, as the UN is not a party to any convention on humanitarian law. On this topic though, the Secretary-General has unilaterally stated that humanitarian law also applies to UN troops. For the text of the Secretary-General's 'Bulletin', see (1999) 38 *ILM* 1654. See also UNJY (1992), pp. 430–1.

have legal (or moral) personality: after all, many would deem organized crime groups capable of being held responsible for their behaviour, regardless of whether such entities possess legal personality. Likewise, while most people would agree that Al Qaida is not a legal person for purposes of international law, few would add that therefore, it operates outside the law.

Much relevant work in this area has been done by moral theorists rather than lawyers, and those theorists seem to be in agreement that collectivities may be considered moral agents (from which legal agency might be derived).[15] Some put a premium on the presence of a separate identity and the capacity to deliberate: if such a capacity is present within an independent actor (be it individual or collective), then such actor may be deemed a moral agent.[16] Others may be more interested in sketching the consequences for members of a group once the group can be held responsible.[17] But either way, there seems to be common accord that collective entities, including international organizations, can be moral agents, despite having 'no soul to be damned and no body to be kicked', as someone once put it.

Next, to assign responsibility to agents presupposes that it is clear that those agents actually had something to do with the matter (even in the extreme case of command responsibility), and that it is reasonably clear what part of the action was theirs. This now is problematic with international organizations, precisely because it is not always clear where the organization begins and its member states end.[18] With NATO dropping bombs over Belgrade in the late 1990s, should one blame NATO? Should one blame its most influential member state for quite possibly pushing the action through? Should one blame all NATO member states? Or only those who actively participated?[19] These are difficult issues to which there are no easy answers, and the absence of easy answers helps explain why the law on the responsibility of international organizations is far from settled.[20]

---

[15] And note that international law has for centuries accepted, and is founded on, the moral agency of states.

[16] See generally the extremely useful volume by Toni Erskine (ed.), *Can Institutions Have Responsibilities? Collective Moral Agency and International Relations* (Basingstoke, 2003).

[17] See, e.g., Larry May, *Sharing Responsibility* (Chicago, 1992).

[18] It is by no means accidental that recently, a case concerning the fall of Srebrenica was brought to the Dutch courts against both the UN and the Netherlands. A first incidental judgment (upholding the UN's immunity from suit) was rendered on 10 July 2008 by the District Court of The Hague, Case no. 295247 (available in English at www.rechtspraak.nl (visited 12 August 2008)).

[19] Organization theorists sometimes refer to this as the paradox of the 'many hands'. In the words of Boven: 'As the responsibility for any given instance of conduct is scattered across more people, the discrete responsibility of every individual diminishes proportionately.' See Bovens, *The Quest for Responsibility*, p. 46.

[20] The ICJ declined the opportunity to clarify things when dismissing a string of cases brought by Serbia against individual member states of NATO, on the argument that since Serbia was not, at the relevant time, a member of the UN and thus also not a party to the ICJ Statute, it had no access to the ICJ. See *Case concerning the legality of the use of force (Serbia and Montenegro v. Belgium)*, preliminary objections, [2004] ICJ Reports 279.

Third, and most fundamental perhaps, there is what might be called the 'paradox of obligation'.[21] In bureaucracies, of whatever kind, chains of command exist: superiors give orders to subordinates.[22] The more precise the order, the clearer will be the situation with respect to responsibility. An order to 'do X, no matter what', clearly places responsibility with the superior, but does so at the cost of a lack of flexibility: it might be that the activity concerned would be hopelessly inappropriate in the circumstances of the moment. By way of example, an order to sprinkle the lawn makes little sense if, at the relevant time, it is raining hard. Thus, it is generally desirable to leave the subordinate some discretion.[23] But this can only be done by diluting the order: 'sprinkle the lawn, unless it is raining'. The problem then is that there might be other situations as well where sprinkling the lawn would be inappropriate: what if it has started freezing? Or what if a royal parade passes by? Or there is a general shortage of water? Hence, the only order able to cover all these contingencies is the order to sprinkle the lawn unless, in the subordinate's view, there is a good reason not to do so. This then, however, places all responsibility on the shoulders of the subordinate, who shall exercise his discretion whenever he decides to sprinkle the lawn.[24]

This gives rise to two related problems. One is, that somehow the superior can no longer be said to be involved in quite the same way, so the basis for her responsibility must be sought elsewhere: perhaps for a lack of proper oversight, or perhaps for hiring the wrong person (presuming she was involved in hiring the subordinate to begin with). Second, and perhaps more crucial, on this line of reasoning it becomes almost impossible to regulate behaviour in a legally meaningful way: the subordinate can be found guilty, afterwards, for poor judgment and a woeful sense of discretion, but since it is up to him to decide whether or not to act under the prevailing circumstances, his behaviour can no longer be judged with the help of any objective standard, for the more precise the standard, the less discretion the subordinate can exercise, and the less sensitive to context the action on the ground will be.[25]

---

[21] Much of this is based on Michael Harmon, *Responsibility as Paradox: A Critique of Rational Discourse on Government* (Thousand Oaks, CA, 1995).

[22] Note that with international organizations it may not even be clear who is superior, and who is subordinate. While within headquarters such matters may be obvious, with operations in the field it is often highly contested whether the organization authorizes member states, or whether the member states authorize the organization, or even both simultaneously. See generally Niels M. Blokker, 'Is the Authorization Authorized? Powers and Practice of the UN Security Council to Authorize the Use of Force by "Coalitions of the Able and Willing"' (2000) 11 *EJIL* 541–68.

[23] Think, e.g., of the Eichmann trial, to which this sort of concern was central. For an influential analysis, see Hannah Arendt, *Eichmann in Jerusalem: A Report on the Banality of Evil* (New York, 1963).

[24] Michael Walzer makes the same point in the context of armies and warfare, suggesting that the laws of war 'leave the cruelest decisions to be made by the men on the spot with reference only to their ordinary moral notions or the military traditions of the army in which they serve'. See Michael Walzer, *Just and Unjust Wars*, (3rd edn, New York, 2000), p. 152.

[25] Note also that often enough, the rules binding the organization (internal or external) may not be in harmony with the rules of the profession, as pointed out in David Beetham, *Bureaucracy*

Hence, creating a law of responsibility for international organizations is not an easy matter, all the more so since the EU, the one organization most active externally (and thus having most opportunities to encounter issues of responsibility), seems inclined to insist on differentiated treatment: what may be good law with respect to organizations generally, so the EU suggests, may be inappropriate with respect to the EU.[26]

Perhaps, in light of all these difficulties, there is some merit in the consideration that a regime of legal responsibility is but one method for exercising control over actors. While lawyers are professionally inclined to think in terms of responsibility, it is useful to remember that control can come in various forms (e.g., in the form of participation in decision-making, or a market-type of control (are there any clients for the organization's products?), or even self-control).[27]

An illustration: the Tin Council litigation

As noted, the issue of the responsibility of international organizations, and the closely related issue of responsibility of member states for acts of the organization, assumed prominence in the mid-1980s, with the collapse of the International Tin Council (ITC).[28] The ITC was an organization with thirty-two members (including the EC), based on an International Tin Agreement, the sixth version of which was in force in the mid-1980s. The idea behind the Tin Council was that it should buy and sell tin on the world market in order to promote an orderly market and keep prices stable. In 1985, it ran out of money, and in the UK its debt was held to be several hundred million pounds.

Quite a few court cases followed, especially in the UK where the ITC had its headquarters. Some of those cases involved issues of immunity,[29] but others dealt more specifically with issues of responsibility. Tellingly, the various courts reached essentially different conclusions, and some debated the preliminary problem of trying to decide which law to apply.[30]

(2nd edn, Buckingham, 1996), p. 15. Similarly, David Kennedy, 'Challenging Expert Rule: The Politics of Global Governance' (2005) 27 *Sydney Law Review*, 5–28, 17.

[26] See Pieter Jan Kuyper and Esa Paasivirta, 'Further Exploring International Responsibility: The European Community and the ILC's Project on Responsibility of International Organizations' (2004) 1 *IOLR*, 111–38.

[27] A classic discussion is Judith E. Gruber, *Controlling Bureaucracies: Dilemmas in Bureaucratic Governance* (Berkeley, 1987). The point is picked up in more recent discussions of accountability. See, e.g., Deirdre Curtin and André Nollkaemper, 'Conceptualizing Accountability in International and European Law' (2005) 36 *Neth YIL*, 3–20.

[28] For an early but useful overview, see Philippe Sands, 'The Tin Council Litigation in the English Courts' (1987) 34 *Neth ILR*, 367–91.

[29] So, e.g., *Arab Banking Corporation v. International Tin Council*, decision of 15 January 1986, High Court, Queen's Bench Division, in 77 *ILR* 1.

[30] Thus, one of the main (and eventually rejected) arguments in one of the cases was the argument that the Council could, like a company, be wound up by the courts so as to allow creditors to go after the 'shareholders': *In Re International Tin Council*, decision of 22 January 1987, High Court, Chancery Division, in 77 *ILR* 18.

The judgments which are more interesting for present purposes determined that applying international law was more appropriate, but were in disagreement as to what international law says, and more particularly on the question of whether or not the organization must be seen as legally distinct (at international law) from its member states, or rather as little more than an agent of the member states. And to complicate matters, the courts were also confronted with such questions (and did their best to avoid giving an answer[31]) as to whether the ITC was legally distinct from its members for purposes of English law, and whether the personality (if any) of the ITC could not only be invoked against third parties, but against its member states as well.

In *MacLaine Watson* v. *International Tin Council*, the High Court's Chancery Division, *per* Millett J, was unwilling to uphold an application that a receiver be appointed to aid the applicants in retrieving some of the money, awarded them by arbitration, through proceedings against the ITC's member states. The Court argued that while liability of a principal to a third party is governed by the agency contract between principal (i.e., the member states) and agent (i.e., the ITC), in the case at hand the agency contract was an international treaty concluded between sovereign states, and such agreements are not, without more, enforceable by English courts. The counter-argument that the ITC is not a party to its own constituent treaty (and therefore some other source of agency must exist) was swept aside, perhaps too hastily, by Millett J, stating that this was one of those questions 'upon which, as a judge of the national courts of one of the member states only, I have no authority to pronounce'.[32]

After having obtained at least a possibility of assessing the properties and assets of the ITC itself,[33] MacLaine Watson appealed against the earlier decision; the ITC, in the meantime, appealed against the order to disclose information about its properties and assets. Both appeals were dismissed by the Court of Appeal on 27 April 1988, with the Court of Appeal once more underlining that it was not the business of English courts to occupy themselves with applications (such as the receivership claim) which involve claims by the ITC against its members. Those are 'clearly not justiciable in an English court', as Nourse LJ summed up.[34]

In the meantime, MacLaine Watson had started separate proceedings against the British Department of Trade and Industry, representing the British government and therewith one of the member states of the ITC. MacLaine Watson asked for direct payment of the amount awarded in earlier arbitration

---

[31] So, e.g., the Chancery Division of the High Court in *MacLaine Watson & Co. Ltd* v. *International Tin Council*, decision of 13 May 1987, in 77 *ILR* 41, 45.

[32] *Ibid.*, p. 53.

[33] *MacLaine Watson and Co. Ltd* v. *International Tin Council (No. 2)*, decision of 9 July 1987, High Court, Chancery Division, in 77 *ILR* 160. Millett J based himself on the inherent jurisdiction of the Court to order such an assessment.

[34] *MacLaine Watson & Co. Ltd* v. *International Tin Council*, decision of 27 April 1988, Court of Appeal, in 80 *ILR* 191; *MacLaine Watson and Co. Ltd* v. *International Tin Council (No. 2)*, decision of 27 April 1988, Court of Appeal, in 80 *ILR* 211.

proceedings, but the High Court's Chancery Division, once again *per* Millett J, dismissed the action.[35] In doing so, Millett J closely followed the reasoning of Staughton J in a similar case brought against the Department of Trade and Industry,[36] and argued that, since the ITC had been granted the special status of a body corporate in English law,[37] it had 'been granted specifically the legal capacities of a body which is separate and distinct from its members'.[38] As a result:

> the ITC has full juridical personality in the sense that it exists as a separate legal entity distinct from its members; though it is sufficient to dispose of this case to say that it has the characteristic attribute of a body corporate which excludes the liability of the members, that is to say the ability to incur liabilities on its own account which are not the liabilities of the members.[39]

And from this it followed that any official or agent pledging the ITC would have authority only to pledge the ITC and not the separate credit of its member states. Consequently, a direct application against a member state was bound to fail.

The House of Lords dismissed the appeal lodged by MacLaine Watson and others.[40] It confirmed that the ITC 'is a separate legal personality distinct from its members';[41] that the contracts entered into by the ITC did not involve any liability on non-parties (such as the member states); and that an alleged liability of member states under international law could not be enforced by English courts. Nonetheless, some of the Lords expressed some dissatisfaction with this state of affairs. As Lord Griffith summed up, 'the appellants have suffered a grave injustice'.[42]

In the end, the Tin Council litigation allows for few conclusions to be drawn. Many of the decisions depended on English law, hinging in particular on the status of the ITC in English law and relying on all kinds of comparisons with other legal personalities. And to the extent that the issue was not covered by English law, it was generally deemed non-justiciable. Nonetheless, the litigation provides a good picture of some of the issues and complexities involved when it

---

[35] *MacLaine Watson and Co. Ltd* v. *Department of Trade and Industry*, decision of 29 July 1987, High Court, Chancery Division, in 80 *ILR* 39.

[36] *J. H. Rayner (Mincing Lane) Ltd* v. *Department of Trade and Industry and others*, decision of 24 June 1987, High Court, Queen's Bench Division, in 77 *ILR* 55.

[37] This was done by Parliament by Order in Council, in 1972.

[38] *MacLaine Watson* v. *Department of Trade and Industry*, p. 44.   [39] *Ibid.*

[40] *J. H. Rayner (Mincing Lane) Ltd* v. *Department of Trade and Industry and others and related appeals; MacLaine Watson & Co Ltd* v. *Department of Trade and Industry, and MacLaine Watson & Co. Ltd* v. *International Tin Council*, decision of 26 October 1989, House of Lords, in 81 *ILR* 670.

[41] *Ibid.*, p. 678, *per* Lord Templeman.

[42] *Ibid.*, p. 683, *per* Lord Griffiths. Compare also Lord Templeman's opinion, where it is noted that proceedings could not be decided by criticism of the conduct of member states or attaching blame to member states (p. 682).

comes to responsibility of international organizations and their member states *vis-à-vis* third parties.

Whose behaviour?

Any general analysis of the responsibility of organizations and their member states must start from the premise that, in normal circumstances, international organizations will incur responsibility in cases where they violate international law, as well as in those (still rare) situations where international law creates a regime of strict liability and organizations act within those regimes.[43] Thus, the point of departure must be that there is nothing exotic about holding organizations responsible; indeed, as much follows from a recognition of their claim to be independent actors, having a will distinct from that of their member states.

Moreover, in some treaty regimes, in particular with respect to outer space,[44] the possible responsibility of international organizations is clearly taken for granted, and the circumstance that the 1986 Vienna Convention on the Law of Treaties provides for remedies in case of a material breach of a treaty to which an international organization is a party[45] also illustrates (although technically the law of treaties at issue here can be distinguished from the law of responsibility) that organizations, at the very least, are deemed capable of wrongdoing, and therefore almost by definition, of bearing responsibility.

A first question to ask, then, is this: for what sort of behaviour will an organization incur responsibility under international law?[46] Given the paucity of strict liability regimes, organizations will be responsible largely for their internationally wrongful acts, i.e., violations of international law which can be attributed to the organization.[47]

But here problems already start to surface, for when can acts be attributed to an organization? If, for example, a Dutch customs officer in the port of Rotterdam illicitly seizes a shipment of goods coming from Japan while implementing a Community regulation, is his illicit behaviour attributable to the Community?

On one line of reasoning, it is. After all, the customs officer is implementing Community law; the Community, moreover, has exclusive competence regarding trade in goods, meaning that the member states have nothing left to say.

---

[43] Strict liability regimes are to be found mainly in the field of space law and, increasingly, environmental law.

[44] See, e.g., Art. 16 of the Treaty on principles governing the activities of states in the exploration and use of outer space, including the moon and other celestial bodies. Text in (1967) 6 *ILM* 386.

[45] Article 60. The 1986 Vienna Convention is reproduced in (1986) 25 *ILM* 543.

[46] Domestic liability is occasionally addressed in the constituent documents; compare Art. 288 (ex-Art. 215) TEC on the European Community's non-contractual liability. Immunity from jurisdiction, incidentally, may go a long way towards ignoring any issues of liability.

[47] So also Sadurska and Chinkin, 'The Collapse of the International Tin Council', esp. pp. 856–8.

Thus, the customs officer engages in illicit behaviour while acting, for all practical purposes, as an agent of the Community.

There is, however, a counter argument. The customs officer is, most likely, a Dutch civil servant, whose activities are controlled by Dutch supervisors. Indeed, it may even be the case that he works in accordance with Dutch internal guidelines as to how to handle certain shipments. While those guidelines cannot legally detract from the Community regulation (after all, regulations shall not be touched by domestic authorities[48]), it may be the case that in practice they deviate from the regulation, and that such deviation is the result of careless transposition, by the Dutch customs authorities, of the regulation. Thus, blame may be assigned, ultimately, to the Dutch customs authorities, but does liability follow suit?

Here a new counter argument is conceivable, for, whatever the quality of the Dutch guidelines, the fact remains that the Dutch customs authorities, when handling imported goods, merely act as agents of the Community. And so on and so forth: the argumentation can go to and fro without there necessarily being a solution. And this, in turn, goes to show that matters are rarely clear cut when it comes to the responsibility of international organizations: even attribution of the wrongful act to an organization may be a difficult affair.[49]

What adds to the complications is that the organization in question may be perceived as working for the common good and exercising its proper functions. Such a situation forms the backdrop of the 2007 decision of the European Court of Human Rights in *Behrami and Saramati*.[50] Applicants had lodged complaints relating to possible human rights violations in Kosovo while Kosovo was governed by the UN Mission in Kosovo (UNMIK) with NATO troops (KFOR) involved in security. The question then arose whether a claim against member states of the UN and NATO, individually bound by the European Convention, would be admissible before the ECtHR. The Court declined, arguing that the behaviour of KFOR and UNMIK could not be reduced to that of individual member states but, instead, might be attributable to the UN, under whose mandate both entities performed their tasks. However, the Court refused to engage in an analysis of the behaviour of the Security Council: scrutinizing the Council 'would be to interfere with the fulfillment of the UN's key mission' in the field of peace of security.[51]

---

[48] See, e.g., case 50/76, *Amsterdam Bulb BV* v. *Produktschap voor Siergewassen* [1977] ECR 137, esp. paras. 5–7.

[49] Lawson reasonably concludes, invoking some case law from the European Human Rights Commission, that states may be held responsible for violating international norms even when they are only executing international regulations. See Lawson, *Het EVRM*, p. 475. Whether the organization may be held responsible simultaneously for ordering illicit behaviour is a different matter, and much depends on whether the breached norm is actually one that the organization is a party to in its own right.

[50] See *Behrami and Behrami* v. *France* (Application No. 71412/01) and *Saramati* v. *France and Others* (Application No. 78166/01), decision of 2 May 2007, in 133 *ILR* 1.

[51] *Ibid.*, para. 149.

Interesting is the way in which the Court framed the issue: it felt that the case was not so much about the exercise of jurisdiction by ECHR parties outside their own territories (as earlier cases have been construed), but rather whether the Court could scrutinize the contribution of member states to international actors. This then made it lay down an attributability test, something that was not done in those earlier cases. For instance, in *Bankovic*, an earlier case brought against NATO member states concerning NATO's actions in Yugoslavia, the Court saw the problem as one of whether or not actions taken outside the territory of ECHR parties could nonetheless fall within the jurisdiction of the Court, and held that this could exceptionally be the case, namely when the respondent state 'exercises all or some of the public powers normally to be exercised' by governments.[52] The *Bankovic* test then comes close to the *Behrami and Saramati* scenario, the one difference (but possibly a crucial one) being that in *Behrami and Saramati*, public power was not exercised extra-territorially by a single state, but by the UN.

Behrami and Saramati was received rather critically by the human rights community: it seems to suggest that the UN can get away with human rights violations.[53] Still, it is important to spell out the judgment's limits. First, it concerned a decision on admissibility: the Court at no point said that organizations can violate human rights with impunity – it merely specified that such cases may remain outside the Court's reach. Second, the reasoning would seem to limit the ramifications to the UN alone or, even more strictly, to only Security Council action. While that may be cause for concern in its own right, it is doubtful whether the reasoning (relying as it did on the special mission of the Council, and on the supremacy of UN law) can be applied to other organizations.

Where a wrongful act is committed by an organ of the organization,[54] or an official on the organization's payroll, the act will at least primarily be attributable to the organization, but matters are not always clear cut. As far as organs go, it is probably the case that even *ultra vires* acts engage the international responsibility of the organization. At any rate, the case law of the EC Court seems to point in this direction.[55] As far as officials go, though, an intervening factor may be

---

[52] See *Bankovic* v. *Belgium and Sixteen Other States*, Application No. 52207/99, decision of 12 December 2001, para. 71, in 123 *ILR* 94. The case was not brought against the US and Canada: both are members of NATO, but are not parties to the European Convention on Human Rights.

[53] It is precisely to counter this impression that the General Assembly, in 2006, established an Ad Hoc Committee on Criminal Accountability of United Nations Officials and Experts on Mission (Resolution GA 61/29). Member states, moreover, are 'strongly urged' to establish jurisdiction in their domestic criminal law systems. This is without prejudice to possible privileges and immunities though (Resolution GA 62/63).

[54] Where the organ acts on the territory of a state that is not its host (be it for purposes of keeping the peace, providing technical assistance, or other activities), usually those acts are subject to an agreement between the organization and the state concerned; these agreements will usually contain provisions on liability. See UNJY (1975), pp. 153–5.

[55] So, e.g., case C-327/91, *France* v. *Commission* [1994] ECR I-3641, discussed in more detail in Chapter 13 above. In addition, in *Certain expenses*, the ICJ suggested that even where an act is

whether they were acting in an official capacity.[56] Thus, it would be far fetched to hold the UN liable if a UN secretary or interpreter, on his or her Saturday off, attends a demonstration in front of the embassy of Iraq and is seen throwing stones and breaking windows.[57]

Yet another scenario, not uncommon, is that where an organization acts through locally hired agents, or entrusts private companies with the task of carrying out some of the obligations of membership. For instance, peacekeeping troops may hire local civilians as chauffeurs: what to do in case of a traffic accident? The UN, for situations such as these, seems to have adopted a policy of treating the local civilian as a UN official for purposes of insurance, but not for purposes of immunity. Thus, the driver could be sued without being able to claim immunity; if proceedings are successful, the insurance will cover the damages.[58] When it comes to activities outsourced to private companies, there is some (albeit old) support for the thesis that an explicitly limited liability of member states extends to those companies.[59]

The UN will also often use soldiers put at its disposal by the member states, and there is judicial support for the thesis that they remain members of the armed forces of the contributing states and thus remain subject to that state's disciplinary rules and procedures.[60] Should such a soldier violate international humanitarian law, then he (or she) is thought to be subject to prosecution before national courts.[61]

Similarly, the organization might use aircraft and vehicles put at its disposal by member states. Here practice seems to point in the direction of initial

---

    ultra vires an organ, it may still be *intra vires* the organization at large and, as noted, to claim that the organization itself acts *ultra vires* is well-nigh impossible.

[56] Indeed, with respect to peace-keepers, the UN does not accept liability for their off-duty acts; see UNJY (1986), pp. 300–1.

[57] The UN's Legal Counsel has accepted that chauffeurs may be held personally liable for gross negligence (but not mere negligence), even when on official business. See UNJY (1975), pp. 186–8.

[58] See UNJY (1984), pp. 189–90. Where it concerns non-UN personnel being transported by UN vehicles, an individual release is usually required: the passenger shall not hold the UN liable should anything happen. See UNJY (1985), pp. 142–3.

[59] See *Elias and Abdou Noujaim* v. *Eastern Telegraph Co.*, decision of Egypt's Summary Tribunal of Port Said of 21 December 1932, in (1931–2) 6 *AD* 413. See also *Nader* v. *Marconi Radio Telegraph Co. of Egypt*, decision of 12 March 1934 by the Civil Court of Alexandria (1933–4) 7 *AD* 471.

[60] See, e.g., Indiana's Southern District Court in *Jennings* v. *Markley, Warden*, decision of 19 September 1960, in 32 *ILR* 367. With respect to the occupation by British troops of a privately owned hotel on Cyprus, see *Attorney-General* v. *Nissan*, decision of the House of Lords of 11 February 1969, in 44 *ILR* 359. However, Vienna's Superior Provincial Court has held, in *N. K.* v. *Austria* (decision of 26 February 1979, in 77 *ILR* 470), that, substantively, a certain act of an Austrian soldier taking part in a UN peace-keeping mission was attributable to the UN.

[61] See the Secretary-General's 'Bulletin', mentioned in note 14 above. See also Daphna Shraga, 'The United Nations as an Actor Bound by International Humanitarian Law' (1998) 5 *International Peacekeeping*, 64–81. For a fine general discussion, see Chanaka Wickremasinghe and Guglielmo Verdirame, 'Responsibility and Liability for Violations of Human Rights in the Course of UN Field Operations'. In Craig Scott (ed.), *Torture as Tort* (Oxford, 2001), pp. 465–89.

liability of the carrier (i.e., the organization) towards third parties. Yet, where the activities undertaken are paid for by contributions from participating members (which will usually be the case), it may well be that subsidiary responsibility comes to rest with the member which placed the vehicle at the disposal of the organization to begin with.[62] When the vehicle is destroyed while in service, the organization may have to reimburse the state from which it was 'borrowed'.[63] When the vehicle is the property of the organization, of course, such subsidiary responsibility would be less easy to defend.[64]

The wrongful act

Much as with the issue of responsibility of states, it does not seem to matter a great deal what sort of wrongful act is committed. In other words, whether the wrongful act amounts to a breach of a treaty or a breach of a customary rule of international law is, for purposes of assigning responsibility, not terribly relevant: in both cases responsibility will be the result. So too when the organization does not live up to unilateral promises it may have made,[65] or when it violates a general principle of law (although the latter are, by their very nature, difficult to violate).

One of the central tenets of contemporary debates concerning the responsibility of states under international law is the question whether responsibility results from each and every violation, or whether some element of blameworthiness (*culpa, dolus*) must be present.[66] While opinion is divided, there is much force in the argument that one can hardly hold sovereign states liable for wrongful acts which resulted from accidents, or honestly mistaken interpretations. On the other hand, there is also some force in the claim that, regardless of a state's intent, if another party somehow suffers, that party ought to be compensated.

Similar arguments may recur in the setting of international organizations. While not usually considered sovereigns themselves, they are nonetheless usually deemed worthy of at least some form of respect (at least for exercising the almost Arendtian function of being engaged in politics, politics being the laudable way in which mankind discusses and manages its common existence[67]). It would follow that they cannot be held responsible for just about everything that goes wrong; instead, on this line of reasoning, *culpa* or *dolus* would be a *conditio sine qua non*.

---

[62] See UNJY (1980), 184–5.   [63] See UNJY (1976), 177–8.

[64] Here, then, the organization's insurance policy (if any) should ideally cover any contingencies. See UNJY (1981), 158–9.

[65] This assumes some relevance in light of the circumstance that many of the external political acts of the EU are in the form of unilateral statements.

[66] See, e.g., the brief discussion in Brownlie, *State Responsibility*, pp. 35–52. See also René Lefeber, *Transboundary Environmental Interference and the Origin of State Liability* (The Hague, 1996).

[67] Arendt's political philosophy is perhaps most explicitly spelled out in Hannah Arendt, *The Human Condition* (Chicago, 1958). More accessible are the essays brought together in Hannah Arendt, *Between Past and Future* (1961; New York, 1993).

On the other hand, *culpa* and *dolus* presuppose that it is possible to look into the state of mind of an organization. Whereas with states this is already highly unlikely, it is even less likely with complex entities such as organizations, comprising member states, a variety of organs, and individuals who may aspire to a leading role. Whose state of mind does one eventually look for?

While it may take a wrongful act (i.e., a violation of an obligation under international law) to trigger responsibility, it is by no means obvious what sort of obligations international organizations are under to begin with. The ICJ has held, authoritatively, that organizations are subjects of international law and, 'as such, are bound by any obligations incumbent upon them under general rules of international law, under their constitutions, or under international agreements to which they are parties'.[68] This, however, may still be fairly limited: it may mean that organizations are bound by *jus cogens* and by the secondary rules of the system,[69] but that says little about, e.g., human rights or environmental standards. If not *jus cogens*, such norms are typically only binding on the basis of treaty commitments, but typically, organizations are parties neither to human rights treaties nor (with the partial exception of the EU) to environmental treaties. Hence, in the absence of a treaty commitment, it is not always obvious why an organization would be legally bound (as opposed to morally bound) to respect certain rules.[70] That is not to say that organizations can engage in human rights violations with impunity, but it does suggest that the discipline still lacks an adequate theory concerning the basis of obligation for international organizations.[71]

To make matters more complicated still, often enough violations of one norm are the result not of nasty intentions or negligence, but result from the pursuit of otherwise legitimate policy choices. NATO's bombing of Yugoslavia may well have violated international law and resulted in concrete violations of humanitarian law and human rights but was, to many, still justified as a humanitarian intervention.[72] Likewise, World Bank projects may end up displacing people and therewith violating their human rights, but if they are

---

[68] See *Interpretation of the Agreement of 25 March 1951 between the WHO and Egypt*, Advisory opinion, [1980] ICJ Reports 73, para. 37.

[69] The distinction between primary and secondary rules stems from H. L. A. Hart, *The Concept of Law* (Oxford,1961). Secondary rules are those relating to the workings of the legal order (rules on law-making and enforcement), while primary rules are those creating concrete and specific obligations, such as 'thou shalt not kill'.

[70] For an illustration of the difficulties involved in presenting a persuasive legal account, see Sigrun Skogly, *The Human Rights Obligations of the World Bank and the International Monetary Fund* (London, 2003).

[71] This applies to non-state actors more broadly. For a discussion, see Jan Klabbers, '(I Can't Get No) Recognition: Subjects Doctrine and the Emergence of Non-state Actors'. In Jarna Petman and Jan Klabbers (eds.), *Nordic cosmopolitanism: Essays in International Law for Martti Koskenniemi* (Leiden, 2003), pp. 351–69.

[72] See generally Anne Orford, *Reading Humanitarian Intervention* (Cambridge, 2003). It has been noted, however, that NATO's acts were inspired more by Serbia's resistance to being drawn into the western camp of market democracies than by the plight of the people of Kosovo. See

done in the pursuit of economic growth and development with the ultimate aim (at least in the neo-liberal ideology) of contributing to the entire population's welfare, then it somehow becomes too facile to simply adopt the language of legal responsibility.

Further complications follow from the circumstance that sometimes the issue is not so much action but, rather, inaction. What is the situation where we feel someone should have done something, but didn't? Examples abound, from the 'safe-haven' of Srebrenica where Dutch UN troops stood idly while thousands of people were massacred, to the genocide in Rwanda in 1994. Still, legally meaningful accusations of wrongful omissions would seem to presuppose that clear legal obligations exist and, moreover, that those obligations rest on international organizations. Here things can get decidedly tricky.

Thus, concerning Srebrenica, one could even go so far as to claim that Dutchbat did nothing wrong as a matter of law. As peace-keepers, it was within their mandate not to resort to violence except in self-defence; as such, moreover, there was nothing unusual about the mandate either. While it is easy to reach the conclusion, afterwards, that Dutchbat should have acted, this conclusion is easier to reach on moral than on legal grounds, perhaps illustrating the paradox of obligation mentioned above to some extent. In addition, Srebrenica illustrates the problem of the many hands: some commentators suggest that responsibility rests with the UN for not providing air support and for creating the concept of safe haven without actually taking care of adequate protection.[73]

Concerning Rwanda, the argument has been made that in the mid-1990s, after problematic interventions in Yugoslavia and Somalia, the UN reverted to a culture of passivism.[74] While this does not necessarily justify things, it does make it more difficult to think in terms of responsibility: if the organization, its organs, and its most influential member states all seem to feel that it is not the task of the organization to intervene, then assigning responsibility becomes problematic.[75]

Indirect and secondary responsibility

Perhaps the central question in respect of the responsibility of international organizations (as the Tin Council litigation abundantly illustrates) is to figure out what the position of the member states of the organization is, and this,

Naomi Klein, *The Shock Doctrine* (London, 2007), p. 328 (citing John Norris who in turn cites his ex-boss, former US Under-secretary of State Strobe Talbott).

[73] So, e.g., Anthony Lang, Jr, 'The United Nations and the Fall of Srebrenica: Meaningful Responsibility and International Society'. In Erskine (ed.), *Can Institutions Have Responsibilities?*, pp. 183–203.

[74] See Michael Barnett and Martha Finnemore, *Rules for the World: International Organizations in Global Politics* (Princeton, 2004), Chapter 5.

[75] This is, in fact, the poverty of the *ultra vires* argument in action: see above, Chapter 11. Note moreover that to the extent an obligation exists to intervene in cases of genocide (which is arguable on the basis of the Genocide Convention), it would also seem to rest upon states.

[handwritten margin note: Are the meaningful responsible?]

in turn, depends to a great extent on how organizations are viewed to begin with.[76] Thus, for those who view the organization to be a distinct entity from its member states, residuary or subsidiary responsibility of the member states is not a foregone conclusion.[77] After all, if the organization is distinct, any attempt to hold its member states responsible is akin to holding state A responsible for the activities of state B; there simply is no proper justification for doing so. Indeed, it would be difficult to reconcile with the basic notion that an entity can only be responsible for behaviour that can be attributed to it.[78]

Those who view organizations to be mere vehicles for their member states, however, or those who are of the opinion that member states can control the organization's activities to a large extent, may feel that to exclude member state responsibility is too artificial to be of much use. Moreover, they may point out that any rigid exclusion of member state responsibility may give rise to serious unfairness. Surely, a creditor, or a contract partner, or simply the innocent victim of a tort, should have some recourse to justice; to allow member states to hide behind an entity that is, after all is said and done, their own creation, might end up hurting third parties; and it is difficult to think of a justification for doing so.

Consequently, in the literature two distinct forms of residuary responsibility are devised, to make sure that third parties do not suffer unnecessarily. The first of these is referred to as a regime of secondary member state responsibility, and described as follows by Hirsch: 'the injured party is required to present its claim first to the international organization, and then it would be entitled to proceed against the members only if the organization were to default in providing an adequate remedy'.[79] This regime of secondary responsibility finds some support in the (scarce) case-law. Thus, in one of the many Tin Council opinions, Justice Kerr of the Court of Appeals expressed a great deal of sympathy with the idea of secondary responsibility, although expressing doubts in light of the terms of the Tin Agreement and on whether secondary responsibility could be enforced by English courts.[80]

More apposite though is the award of an arbitration court set up by the International Chamber of Commerce in *Westland Helicopters*.[81] Here it concerned

---

[76] Sadurska and Chinkin demonstrate an awareness of this tension, 'The Collapse of the International Tin Council', p. 855.

[77] So, e.g., the Civil Tribunal of Brussels, in *M. v. Organisation des Nations Unies and Etat Belge (Ministre des Affaires Etrangères)*, decision of 11 May 1966 (holding that Belgium was a third party when it came to acts by UN troops in Congo), in 45 *ILR* 446. See generally also Klein, *La responsabilité*, esp. pp. 490–520.

[78] On the philosophical importance hereof in general, see H. L. A. Hart, *Punishment and Responsibility: Essays in the Philosophy of Law* (Oxford, 1968), esp. Chapter 1.

[79] Moshe Hirsch, *The Responsibility*, p. 155.

[80] *MacLaine Watson & Co. Ltd v. Department of Trade and Industry; J. H. Rayner (Mincing Lane) v. Department of Trade and Industry and others, and related appeals*, decision of 27 April 1988, Court of Appeal, in 80 *ILR* 47, pp. 104, 109.

[81] *Westland Helicopters Ltd and Arab Organization for Industrialization, United Arab Emirates, Kingdom of Saudi Arabia, State of Qatar, Arab Republic of Egypt and Arab British Helicopter Company*, award of 5 March 1984, in 80 *ILR* 600, p. 613.

the Arab Organization for Industrialization (AOI), established by four Arab states in order to develop their arms industry. The AOI had created a joint venture with Westland Helicopters in 1978; then, a year later, the AOI announced its liquidation. Arbitration followed, and the arbitrators, basing their thoughts on general principles of law and the notion of good faith, held as follows:

> In the absence of any provision [in the AOI's founding documents] expressly or impliedly excluding the liability of the four States, this liability subsists since, as a general rule, those who engage in transactions of an economic nature are deemed liable for the obligations which flow therefrom. In default by the four States of formal exclusion of their liability, third parties which have contracted with the AOI could legitimately count on their liability.

The award was later annulled by the Court of Justice of Geneva[82] (and the annulment upheld by the Federal Supreme Court[83]), for the different, if somewhat related reason that the arbitrators had assumed jurisdiction over Egypt without Egypt's consent: the fact that a panel has jurisdiction over an international organization does not imply that it also has jurisdiction over the organization's members. In relation to its member states, the Federal Supreme Court noted, the AOI enjoys 'total legal independence', and while the issue of member state liability was not explicitly referred to, the Federal Supreme Court nevertheless expressed serious doubts as to whether it was plausible to state that 'when organs of the AOI deal with third parties they *ipso facto* bind the founding States'.[84]

The second form of subsidiary responsibility is usually referred to as 'indirect' responsibility, and refers to the idea that the member states are responsible to the organization so as to enable the organization to meet its obligations towards third parties.[85] Thus, for example, member states should pay additional contributions if the organization is financially incapable of meeting its obligations.[86] This option too has found some support in parts of the Tin Council litigation,[87] but other support has remained limited to some of the academic literature.

And support has remained limited for the good reason that a regime of indirect responsibility presupposes too much. It presupposes, for example, that the organization is merely unable to meet its obligations; it is of little avail, however, when the core of the problem is the organization's unwillingness (as opposed to inability) to act. Moreover, it presupposes that all problems are financial in nature, or at least can be cast in financial terms. After all, it is difficult to envisage any other way in which member states could come to the aid of their organization. Additionally, a regime of indirect responsibility is also somewhat contrived: if indirect responsibility can be accepted, then why not accept direct

---

[82] *Arab Organization for Industrialization and others* v. *Westland Helicopters Ltd and others*, decision of 23 October 1987, in 80 *ILR* 622.

[83] *Arab Organization for Industrialization and others* v. *Westland Helicopters Ltd*, decision of 19 July 1988, Federal Supreme Court (First Civil Court), in 80 *ILR* 652.

[84] *Ibid.*, p. 658.   [85] This is the conclusion reached by Hartwig, *Die Haftung der Mitgliedstaaten*.

[86] Compare the rendition in Moshe Hirsch, *The Responsibility*, pp. 157–8.

[87] In particular the opinion of Justice Nourse, note 35 above, p. 47.

responsibility? Arguably, a regime of indirect responsibility leaves the separate identity of the organization intact, but if this separate identity is taken seriously, then indirect responsibility is difficult to justify. If the separate identity is not worthy of protection, then indirect responsibility serves no identifiable purpose and may readily be replaced by direct responsibility.

Policy arguments

In the absence of authoritative precedent, writers do not hesitate to invoke policy considerations to buttress their points of view. Needless to say, some of those policy considerations are more persuasive than others. One consideration often heard is that, if public international law were to create some form of residual liability of member states, then international law would interfere with the internal activities of the organization and might even make it unattractive for states to establish or join organizations. In this vision, the main point of restricting the liability of members of organizations is to make it possible for organizations to engage in activities in which the individual member states would hesitate to participate.[88]

Clearly, there is a domestic analogy here: the limited liability corporation may well have been created to facilitate large-scale investments which would contribute to economic life in general. Where investors might shy away if full liability were to exist, they might take huge risks if their liability would remain limited. And society as a whole would benefit from the impetus such investments could bring to the economy.

That may make some sense in domestic contexts, but the question is whether the underlying idea can readily be transposed to international organizations. After all, international organizations are not usually created as profit organizations and, moreover, it is far from clear whether international society unequivocally benefits from the existence of organizations. Admittedly, it will benefit from some, but presumably not from all; and it is by no means impossible that different observers reach radically different conclusions about the desirability of particular organizations, as the strong emotions surrounding the WTO suggest.[89] In short, it is too simple to say that co-operation between states is always and necessarily a good thing and, therefore, aggrieved third states should be willing to make a sacrifice in the greater interest.

By way of counter argument, it is sometimes contended that the aggrieved party knew what it did when it entered into an engagement with an international

---

[88] So, e.g., C. F. Amerasinghe, *Principles of the Institutional Law of International Organizations* (Cambridge, 1996), esp. pp. 283–7.

[89] In a similar vein Sadurska and Chinkin, 'The Collapse of the International Tin Council', pp. 875, 878, doubting the moral standing of an organization aimed at developing an arms industry, such as the Arab Organization for Industrialization at issue in the *Westland Helicopters* litigation.

organization, and therefore should not complain about inequitable situations which may arise out of that self-inflicted situation.[90]

This argument meets with two objections. First of all, the very existence of a debate concerning responsibility of organizations and their members already indicates that it can hardly be expected of an aggrieved party that it knew what it got itself into when it opted to enter into an undertaking with an organization. Indeed, as far as liability goes, constitutions generally do not address the matter. The main exception relates to the financial organizations, such as the World Bank, the IFAD and similar institutions. These provide in their constituent documents, in various formulations, that their member states shall not be liable for the activities of the organization. Here, then, liability is explicitly limited, and here it can meaningfully be argued that aggrieved parties knew what they were getting themselves into. It remains doubtful, however, whether the same applies to other organizations.

A second argument is that it is possible that the organization does not engage in breach of contract, but in tort or perhaps even criminal behaviour,[91] victimizing the aggrieved party without that party being in any way responsible for the legal connection with the organization. A victim of aggression by an organization, or of a human rights violation committed by or on behalf of an organization, or even of a simple traffic accident, cannot in any way be deemed to have wittingly sought for a legal relation with the organization. Hence, the type of thinking that is premised on contractual connections cannot without more be transposed to tort settings.[92]

Limited liability and legal personality

As already alluded to above, in some cases the member states of an organization specifically limit their liability for the activities of organizations of which they are members. Thus, the constituent document of the IBRD provides, *inter alia*, that securities guaranteed or issued by the bank shall explicitly specify that they are not obligations of any government.[93] This, in conjunction with a few other provisions contained in the IBRD's Articles of Agreement, may well be interpreted as evidence that 'it was clearly intended by the parties that

---

[90] It is this which appears to prompt Moshe Hirsch (*The Responsibility*, Chapter 5) to distinguish between voluntary and non-voluntary third parties. Voluntary third parties could invoke the indirect responsibility of member states, whereas non-voluntary third parties could invoke the (stronger) secondary responsibility.

[91] For an argument coming close to regarding NATO's intervention in Kosovo as criminal, see Jules Lobel, 'Benign Hegemony? Kosovo and Art. 2, para. 4 of the UN Charter' (2000) 1 *Chicago JIL*, 19–36.

[92] This also happens in other contexts though, with public law litigation (e.g., concerning human rights) being seen as merely a variation on private law litigation. See, e.g., Harold Hongju Koh, 'Transnational Public Law Litigation' (1991) 100 *Yale Law Journal*, 2347–402.

[93] Article IV, para. 9 IBRD.

members as such should not be liable for the obligations of the organization'.[94]
And, in some cases, the limitation of liability is far more explicit. Thus, Article 3,
para. 4, IFAD provides: 'No member shall be liable, by reason of its membership,
for acts or obligations of the Fund.'

The question though remains as to the effect of such limited liability provisions on third parties.[95] Surely, as noted earlier, such limited liability provisions
(mainly to be found with financial institutions and some commodities arrangements) can serve as warnings to third parties not to rely on the members to
clean up after the organization. Still, that does not exhaust the matter: strictly
speaking, for any third party, whatever the members of an organization agree
remains *res inter alios acta*; it cannot affect those third parties.[96]

On the other hand, and in an intricate irony, the same principle of *pacta
tertiis nec nocent nec prosunt* underlies the idea that member states shall not
be liable at all for organizational acts,[97] at least if the theory is accepted that
organizations have an identity separate from their member states.

Here then, according to some, the attribution of legal personality to an
organization may provide evidence of the intention to create a separate identity.
From this it would follow that the member states will not be held responsible
(at least not at first instance) for activities of the organization: the very fact
of endowing personality may be seen to be an act to limit the liability of the
member states.[98] An obvious ramification must be, however, that where legal
personality is not explicitly granted by the member states, those member states
will be responsible for wrongful activities of the organization. And in light of
the circumstance that personality is not often granted explicitly, this argument
does little to alleviate concerns.

A different way of limiting the liability of member states is simply to provide
for this in agreements with third parties. Thus, the United Nations has been
known to conclude contracts with private parties which would contain a provision according to which neither the member states nor any official of the UN
'shall be charged personally . . . or held liable'.[99]

Useful as such devices may seem, at least two considerations mitigate their
usefulness somewhat. One is that there is a certain power imbalance between a
huge organization such as the UN and a private contractor; the contractor may
not have much choice but to accept such a clause, which renders it dubious as
an expression of mutual intent. Second, the utility of such clauses is limited at

---

[94] So Amerasinghe, *Principles*, p. 268.

[95] Surely, as Lawson suggests, a group of states creating an organization for purposes of nuclear
testing could not dismiss any liability simply through a clause in the constituent document. See
Lawson, *Het EVRM*, p. 281.

[96] Compare also Sadurska and Chinkin, 'The Collapse of the International Tin Council'.

[97] As Amerasinghe points out: *Principles*, pp. 256–7.   [98] *Ibid.*, p. 255.

[99] So, e.g., a contract between the UN and a private contractor for construction of a building in
Thailand, quoted in Mahnoush H. Arsanjani, 'Claims Against International Organizations:
Quis Custodiet Ipsos Custodes' (1981) 7 *Yale Journal of World Public Order*, 131–76, pp. 137–8,
note 20.

any rate to contractual undertakings. By definition, it cannot apply to torts or even crimes committed by the organization.

Piercing the corporate veil

It has sometimes been argued[100] that there may be circumstances where the corporate veil should be pierced. While accepting the starting point that organizations are themselves responsible, rather than their member states, nonetheless there may be situations where to provide no relief at all to injured third parties would be too unfair to be justifiable.

One of those circumstances would be the situation where the organization violates the most basic principles of international law, for instance by committing genocide or aggression. In such a case, international law should ignore the possible responsibility of the organization and go straight to the member states, so the argument goes.[101]

Another circumstance is where it is clear that the organization hides behind the corporate veil: where it abuses its separate personality. Although it is difficult to think of concrete examples, one example sometimes mentioned in the literature is where a state is supposed, following an award, to hand over a piece of territory but cedes it to an organization prior to its execution of the award.

Perhaps another circumstance, nice in theory but difficult in practice, is to ignore an organization's separate personality when it is dominated to such an extent by a single state that it becomes virtually that single state's alter ego. The problem here is one of power politics: how realistic was it to expect the USSR to allow for the piercing of the corporate veil in connection with Comecon or the Warsaw Pact? Or, as some might argue, for the US to allow the corporate veil over NATO to be pierced or lifted?

Case law is, as expected, scarce, but at least it is worthy of note that some of the judges dealing with the Tin Council litigation, and the arbitrators initially deciding *Westland Helicopters*, apparently found that a piercing of the veil could be justified. In a similar vein, the International Court of Justice, in the second phase of its *Lockerbie* proceedings, refused to accept English hints that, as Libya's complaint was actually about the activities of the Security Council, the United Kingdom should not find itself in the position of the accused. The Court, without wasting its words, failed to honour this particular line of reasoning, therewith evidencing some support in favour of the possibility of lifting the organizational veil.

---

[100] See in particular Moshe Hirsch, *The Responsibility*, pp. 169–72.
[101] The problem here is that, at least with respect to aggression, it may be difficult to separate lawful uses from unlawful uses: aggression, after all, can be used for good purposes (think of humanitarian intervention). Genocide is, in this light, easier: while there may be an excuse for aggression, it is hard to think of any justification for genocide.

Concluding remarks

The complicated nature of the relationship between an organization and its members becomes acutely visible where issues of responsibility are at stake. One can imagine an endless shifting of the blame if an organization is accused: the organization can always blame its members (who, after all, are *Herren der Verträge*, or more often *Herren des Vertrags*), while the members can always point to the organization's independence. In the process, the injured third party (be it a third state, or a citizen or company) gets crushed and might look in vain for justice.

With that in mind, and in particular following the Tin Council litigation, it should not come as a surprise that the topic has inspired a great deal of study in recent years, not least within such august bodies as the Institut de Droit International[102] and the International Law Association.[103] Here too the by-now-familiar positions reproduce themselves: whereas the ILA's work, so far, seems to have been inspired above all by a need to protect third parties (leaning towards the conception of organizations being vehicles for their members), the Institut's efforts, more conservatively perhaps, still have state sovereignty as their point of departure (viewing the member states as third parties to the organization).

Either way, though, the practicalities of responsibility may remain problematic, in that organizations rarely have standing (either to sue or be sued) before international tribunals, and may often invoke immunity before domestic courts. A rare (and limited) exception is the possibility, within the EC, of starting proceedings against the various institutions, not only in the form of administrative review but also for torts committed by the Community and for situations arising out of contract.[104]

An interesting novelty, moreover, was the creation in 1993 of the World Bank Inspection Panel, enabling groups of individuals to complain about failure on the part of the World Bank (as well as the IDA) to follow its own policies and procedures in developing projects. While the Inspection Panel has only recommendatory powers, its creation nonetheless signifies that organizations can be held accountable, and what is more, can be held accountable even by private, non-state actors.[105]

---

[102] See the reports by Rosalyn Higgins, in 66 *Annuaire de L'Institut de Droit International* (1995/I) and (1996/II).

[103] The first report of the ILA's Committee on Accountability of International Organisations, prepared by Professors Shaw and Wellens, stressed that the 'exclusive objective of the Committee's work is to consider what measures should be adopted to ensure the accountability' of organizations. See International Law Association, *Report of the Sixty-Eighth Conference (The Taipei Conference)* (London, 1998), 584–608, esp. p. 585.

[104] See Art. 288 (formerly Art. 215) TEC. For a general discussion, see Trevor M. Hartley, *The Foundations of European Community Law* (3rd edn, Oxford, 1994), ch. 17.

[105] Useful overviews include Daniel D. Bradlow and Sabine Schlemmer-Schulte, 'The World Bank's New Inspection Panel: A Constructive Step in the Transformation of the International

If the World Bank's Inspection Panel is an innovative mechanism, within many organizations forms of self-regulation have started to appear. There is a long-standing tradition, obviously, of having financial activities accounted for and audited. More recent is the creation of compliance officers, boards of oversight, inspection units, and the like. The idea here is to provide internal scrutiny, based on staff regulations but also, increasingly perhaps, on the basis of internal codes of conduct or charters of values.[106] In other words: organizations are supposed to control themselves, rather than be held accountable later on by others. As such, this may signify a move away from traditional legal thought about responsibility.

Legal Order' (1994) 54 *ZaöRV*, 392–415, and Ellen Hey, 'The World Bank Inspection Panel: Towards the Recognition of a New Legally Relevant Relationship to International Law' (1997) 2 *Hofstra Law & Policy Symposium*, 61–74.

[106] A useful collection is Chris de Cooker (ed.), *Accountability, Investigation and Due Process in International Organizations* (Leiden, 2005).

15

Dissolution and succession

Introduction

While international organizations are generally created for longer periods of time, indeed usually even without any definite time period in mind,[1] not all of them manage to survive indefinitely. Some simply disappear without being succeeded to in any way; prime examples are the Warsaw Pact and Comecon, both of which were dismantled after the dissolution of the Soviet Union. On 26 June 1991, a ministerial meeting of Comecon members decided to dissolve the organization; the Warsaw Pact was disbanded at a meeting of its Political Consultative Committee in Prague, on 1 July 1991.[2]

In other cases, organizations are remodelled to cope with new or unexpected demands, or are succeeded by new entities providing similar services and exercising similar functions to their predecessors. The most famous example is, in all likelihood, that of the League of Nations which, for all practical if not all legal purposes, has found a successor in the United Nations. Others include the 'reconstitution' of the Organization for European Economic Co-operation (OEEC) into the Organization for Economic Co-operation and Development (OECD), the transformation of the Brussels Pact into the Western European Union (WEU), and the transition from the General Agreement on Tariffs and Trade (GATT) to the World Trade Organization (WTO).

Obviously, there is but a fine line between formal transformation and informal processes of change. In a sense, organizations are constantly evolving. They are changing internal procedures but also, more importantly, their constitutions, either through formal amendment or by informal means, and such processes can be very far-reaching: today's UN may still resemble what the Charter drafters had in mind, but is nonetheless a rather different creature from the UN of 1945. By the same token, NATO has undergone a substantive transformation since the end of the Cold War, but not a formal one, and the United Nations Conference on Trade and Development (UNCTAD) too is said to have

---

[1] An exception was the ECSC, created initially for a period of fifty years, although with the possibility of continuation.

[2] The facts are derived from Clive Archer, *Organizing Europe: The Institutions of Integration* (2nd edn, London, 1994), pp. 252–5.

undergone change.[3] Still, these cases stop short of the things that concern us in this chapter: termination or succession of formally distinct entities, and the legal issues these entail.

The main legal questions arising, whether an organization dissolves or is succeeded to, pertain to the functions, personnel, assets and liabilities of the predecessor organization. Will they disappear? Will they continue to exist? How, if at all, will they be distributed? A preliminary question is whether dissolution (and succession) are possible to begin with, and by what modalities.

Closely related is the question of who has the power to decide on such issues as dissolution. Does such power rest solely with the member states, or does the organization itself have a say in the matter? And if the latter, which organ, and following which procedure? It is here, then, that the tense relationship between the organization and its members manifests itself once again: those who view organizations as mere vehicles for their members will easily be inclined to accept that dissolution is the sole province of the members, whereas proponents of the view that organizations have a separate identity will be more inclined to allow the organization to have some formal powers regarding its own dissolution.

The modalities of dissolution

It would be convenient were the constituent charters of international organizations to contain provisions on when, how and by what means a possible dissolution of the organization could be effected, but, alas, this is not normally the case. And understandably so: an international organization is created with a view to its performance, rather than with a view to its demise, and it might often be difficult to get states to agree on what the organization may do and how it should go about things – so much so that no energy is left to negotiate the topic of dissolution.

There are, however, exceptions.[4] Thus, Article VI, para. 5, of the Articles of Agreement of the World Bank provides for a 'permanent suspension' and subsequent ceasing of all activities of the Bank upon a majority decision of its Board of Governors, and lays down in some detail what will happen with outstanding obligations. Similarly, Article XXVII, s. 2, of the Articles of Agreement of the IMF provides for its liquidation by a decision of the Board of Governors, presumably by majority vote.[5]

---

[3] On the latter, see Matthias Finger and Bérangère Magarinos-Ruchat, 'The Transformation of International Public Organizations: The Case of UNCTAD'. In Dennis Dijkzeul and Yves Beigbeder (eds.), *Rethinking International Organizations: Pathology & Promise* (New York, 2003), pp. 140–65.

[4] See also Art. 28 of the Agreement establishing the Terms of Reference of the International Jute Study Group, which deals with the Group's liquidation. The Agreement was concluded on 13 March 2001 and entered into force in 2002.

[5] Compare Art. XII, s. 5(c) IMF.

Nevertheless, these are exceptions,[6] and since guidance is rarely provided by the constitutions in any explicit terms, it must be sought elsewhere, and it is here (once again) that the precise relationship between the organization and its members may well colour the solution finally chosen.

Thus, on one view, the organization as such has the inherent power to terminate its own existence, regardless of whether or not its constitution makes any reference thereto.[7] On this view, a decision to dissolve should follow the regular decision-making procedure within the organization or, where several such procedures exist, should follow the one reserved for important decisions. Thus, such a decision may come to involve several organs. It could be argued, for example, that termination of the EC would only be possible upon a proposal by the Commission and upon the advice (perhaps even the assent) of the European Parliament; while, with respect to the UN, such an approach would amount to, probably, a decision by the General Assembly upon the recommendation of the Security Council.

While this view is not without attractions, it is not without problems either. One such problem is, as expected, the choice of the proper decision-making procedure to be followed. This alone may cause all sorts of haggling. Another is that a decision to dissolve may, where decisions are to be taken unanimously, be blocked by a single member state. Clearly, this would create an unworkable situation.[8]

On the other hand, the main point (and possible attraction) of scenarios involving the organs of the organization concerned is that they prevent the member states from circumventing the organization, as it were. Thus, as a matter of law, the members of an organization would not be allowed to terminate the organization's existence behind its back, without the consent of the organization itself. Yet, put like this, the theory acquires a distinct air of artificiality. Surely, one might argue (and some *would* argue), at the end of the day the organization is but the aggregate of its members: it was created by them, so it can also be destroyed by them. Others would say, however, that this ignores the separate existence of organizations: while they may be created by states, they become actors in their own right, so surely, if liquidation is at issue, the entity to be liquidated should be consulted as well.

A second approach aims to do at least some justice to the idea that organizations may lead a separate existence, but without going so far as to enable them

---

[6] The fact that provisions on liquidation were included in the first place is attributed to the special financial services provided by the World Bank and the IMF. See H. G. Schermers, *De gespecialiseerde organisaties: Hun bouw en inrichting* (Leiden, 1957), p. 70.

[7] For an example, see *ibid.*, p. 69, finding the right of dissolution to rest with the plenary organ which would have to follow at least the procedure created for amendments.

[8] One of the worries when it came to dissolving the League of Nations was that some members would try 'to hold the Covenant in suspended animation indefinitely'. Another worry was that some would refuse to dissolve at all, and instead simply proclaim the Covenant to be terminated, thus leaving a legal mess. See Denys P. Myers, 'Liquidation of League of Nations Functions' (1948) 42 *AJIL*, 320–54, esp. 330–1.

to decide on their own fate. This approach would allow for termination of an organization by way of concluding a subsequent agreement. Here, unanimity is built-in (in the sense that one would need all parties to the constitution to agree to a new treaty), and it is this unanimity which can be seen as a safeguard for the organization: the organization is protected by the fact that it needs only one member state to block its liquidation.[9]

A third approach, which eventually outsmarts most of the problems of dissolution and succession by refusing to think of itself as dissolution and succession, and which has met with support in both recent practice and recent scholarship,[10] is to graft a new organization onto the remains of the predecessor, or to build a new one around the remains, in whole or in part, of a predecessor.

Thus, the new WTO was built around the framework of the existing GATT, and it could be argued that the EU has also grafted itself onto an already existing structure: that of the European Community. Moreover, the EU incorporates other institutions as well, either by reference (this applies in particular to the WEU[11]) or by adopting the other's *acquis*, as with Schengen.[12] With both the WTO and the EU, the predecessors continue to exist, and the legal problems associated with succession proper simply do not arise, or are solvable in pragmatic fashion.

For instance, there was never any worry that Community officials would lose their jobs upon the creation of the Union; at worst, they needed to get new business cards and office stationery printed. So too, a visible reminder of the continuity between GATT and WTO is that the Secretariat is still located in the same building in Geneva. No transfer of funds, archives or personnel proved necessary.

The drawback is, of course, that in such a case problems of co-ordination may well arise. Where old GATT law continues to exist next to new GATT law, the question of which is deemed supreme will inevitably arise; consequently,

---

[9]   Slightly different is the technique of concluding new constitutional documents while leaving the organization intact. This happens regularly with commodity agreements. Thus, the International Cocoa Organization was created in 1972, but has the Sixth International Cocoa Agreement as its 'constituent' document since its entry into force in 2005.

[10] Compare, e.g., Ernst-Ulrich Petersmann, 'How to Reform the UN System? Constitutionalism, International Law, and International Organizations' (1997) 10 *Leiden JIL*, 421–74.

[11] Article 17 TEU provides that the WEU 'is an integral part of the development' of the EU (para. 1), and that the EU 'will avail itself of the WEU to elaborate and implement decisions and actions' (para. 3). For more details, see Ramses A. Wessel, 'The EU as a Black Widow: Devouring the WEU to Give Birth to a European Security and Defence Policy'. In Vincent Kronenberger (ed.), *The EU and the International Legal Order: Discord or Harmony?* (The Hague, 2001), 405–34. See also Inger Österdahl, 'The EU and its Member States, Other States, and International Organizations – The Common European Security and Defence Policy after Nice' (2001) 70 *Nordic JIL*, 341–72.

[12] See the Protocol integrating the Schengen *acquis* into the framework of the European Union, annexed to the TEU and EC Treaty at Amsterdam and reproduced in *Official Journal* (1997), C-340/93. That the Schengen regime functioned as an international organization is reasonably clear; whether it would qualify as a formal organization is a different matter.

the WTO Agreement had to include a conflict rule,[13] and a separate rule had to be created with respect to existing waivers of GATT obligations.[14]

With respect to the European Community and the European Union, co-ordination questions have arisen regarding, for example, the jurisdiction of the European Court of Justice, whereas the overlap between the 'political' Union activities and 'economic' Community activities has given rise not only to special provisions making it possible to use economic instruments in order to further political goals (i.e., sanctions),[15] but also to case-law where the Court was called upon to figure out which rules were applicable in the case of trade in goods which can serve both a civilian and a military purpose.[16]

In addition to this 'constitutional adaptation' (to adopt Hahn's phrase, which he used to describe the remodelling of the ILO[17] and the WEU, the Organization of American States (OAS) and even already the EC), Hahn reserves the phrase 'automatic succession' to describe the relationship between the League of Nations and the UN.[18] Additionally, he helpfully distinguishes three modes of 'conventional succession': substitution (where one or more successors take the place of a predecessor), merger (where a successor takes over another organization) and transfer (where both continue to exist, but functions are transferred).

Dissolution

Dissolution without any transfer of functions or assets and liabilities to a new or already existing organization is a rare phenomenon, probably for the good reason that the tasks the disbanded organization performed continue to serve a purpose. Thus, the rationale behind an organization will usually continue to exist; it is merely the institutional arrangements which are deemed unsuitable.

Indeed, the few examples of dissolutions proper appear to demonstrate that dissolution without succession is most likely to occur after a dramatic change in political circumstances which renders the very *raison d'être* problematic. Good

---

[13] Article XVI, para. 3 WTO: 'In the event of a conflict between a provision of this Agreement and a provision of any of the Multilateral Trade Agreements, the provision of this Agreement shall prevail to the extent of the conflict.'

[14] Article 2 of the Understanding in respect of waivers of obligations under the General Agreement on Tariffs and Trade 1994 provides: 'Any waiver in effect on the date of the entry into force of the WTO Agreement shall terminate [unless lawfully extended] on the date of its expiry or two years from the date of entry into force of the WTO Agreement, whichever is earlier.'

[15] Article 301 (formerly Art. 228a) TEC.

[16] See, e.g., case C-70/94, *Fritz Werner Industrie-Ausrüstungen GmbH* v. *Germany* [1995] ECR I-3189, and case C-83/94 *Criminal proceedings against Peter Leifer and others* [1995] ECR I-3231.

[17] This had become necessary after the Second World War due to the close institutional ties between the ILO and the disbanded League of Nations. A useful overview is C. Wilfred Jenks, 'The Revision of the Constitution of the International Labour Organization' (1946) 23 *BYIL*, 303–17.

[18] Hugo J. Hahn, 'Continuity in the Law of International Organization' (1964) 13 *ÖZöR*, 167–239.

examples are both the Comecon and the Warsaw Pact, which were rendered obsolete with the end of the Soviet Union and the concomitant end of the Cold War. Still, mere obsolescence is not necessarily enough for, as the experiences of NATO and the WEU demonstrate (the WEU in particular has never had a very active existence), organizations and their members may well search for new tasks to justify their existence. In addition, then, before an organization is dissolved, its continued existence must also have become politically untenable.

Another (if atypical) case of dissolution was the dissolution of Eurochemic, a 'société internationale par actions' with its headquarters in Belgium, but founded on the basis of a treaty between states and governed, largely, by that treaty (and therewith by international law[19]).

Eurochemic, established to provide nuclear energy and educate nuclear scientists, proved to be less than a success as far as its industrial task was concerned, and its General Assembly decided that dissolution and liquidation were in order, a process that was finally completed in 1990.[20] Both the constituent document and Eurochemic's by-laws were silent on its dissolution, except for providing that dissolution was to take place on the basis of an agreement between Eurochemic and Belgium; the agreement concerned was concluded as early as 1978.

The liquidation agreement provided, among other things, that the industrial properties of Eurochemic would be transferred to a new company to be formed or, failing that, to the Belgian state; the new company would take care of the costs of dismantling. As far as nuclear waste was concerned, Eurochemic itself would ensure its evacuation, except for highly charged waste which would be sold to an interested German company. Eurochemic would no longer be responsible for stockpiling nuclear materials, and, to the extent necessary, the newly established company would take over Eurochemic's staff.

A peculiar problem, partly inspired by Eurochemic being engaged in nuclear activities, arose in connection with the payment of the costs of dismantling. Most member states were in agreement that they should bear the costs together, based on the theory that Eurochemic had been, in fact, acting as their agent. However, one member state (Italy) resisted this approach, and rejected any direct or indirect liability: as Eurochemic had been an independent commercial entity, the member states could not be held liable in any way. Eventually a compromise was found, with Italy pledging a voluntary contribution.

Also atypical is the case of the European Coal and Steel Community (ECSC), which has disappeared simply because its founding document has expired. The Nice Treaty kept a number of the ECSC provisions alive (mainly those things the ECSC shared with the other Communities), but the ECSC itself has

---

[19] Belgian law was applicable subsidiarily, and only to the extent that it was in harmony with the constituent document.

[20] Much of this is based on Pierre Strohl, 'Les aspects internationaux de la liquidation de la société Eurochemic' (1990) 36 *AFDI*, 727–38.

disappeared as a separate organization. A special protocol was concluded to deal with the financial ramifications: the Protocol on the financial consequences of the expiry of the ECSC Treaty and the research fund for coal and steel.[21] The Protocol provided that assets and liabilities of the ECSC, as they existed in July 2002, transfer to the EC which, in turn, has used the net worth to set up a Research Fund for Coal and Steel.

A rather curious case is that of the Korean Peninsula Energy Development Organization (KEDO), which was set up in 1995 between the US, Japan and South Korea to help implement an earlier agreement concluded between the US and North Korea to dismantle North Korea's nuclear programme. (Note that while the organization is devoted to providing assistance to North Korea, North Korea itself was never a member.)[22] Part of the plan was that in order to compensate for the loss of nuclear technology, North Korea would be supplied with other sources of energy and KEDO would support the construction of two light-water reactors. After North Korea repeatedly failed to comply with its dismantling obligations, KEDO suspended, and in 2006 finally terminated, both the supply of alternative energy and the construction of those two light-water reactors. As a result, the organization has lost its utility. It is unclear whether it still formally exists, but if it does, it has been emptied of all meaningful activities: an empty shell may be all that is left.[23]

Succession: some basic issues

The most well-known instance of the succession of an organization is, in all likelihood, that of the dissolution of the League of Nations and the creation of the United Nations. Nonetheless, strictly speaking the case was not one of succession, if only for the reason that both organizations existed simultaneously for half a year: the Charter of the UN entered into force on 24 October 1945, whereas the League Assembly decided on the dissolution of the League on 18 April 1946, the dissolution taking effect the next day.[24]

Still, for most practical purposes the UN filled the spot left by the League: its functions are similar, as is, with a few important differences such as the veto, its institutional set-up. The similarities between the two are such that they are usually compared with one another. Indeed, the UN's draftsmen must have realized as much; as Brierly points out, they have attempted to get away

---

[21] This has been appended, by means of the Nice Treaty, to the Treaty establishing the EC.

[22] A number of other states joined later, as did Euratom.

[23] The above information is culled from KEDO's website, www.kedo.org (last visited 14 August 2008), which does not speak of dissolution, nor of termination of the constituent treaty. It merely mentions that KEDO's projects have been terminated.

[24] The League was actually represented at the San Francisco Conference, but only on an 'unofficial' level: the United States wanted to create as much distance as possible between the League and the UN. See H. G. Nicholas, *The United Nations as a Political Institution* (3rd edn, Oxford, 1967), p. 14.

from being associated with the League's not-so-glorious past by using different terms, such as substituting the Security Council for the Council, and the General Assembly for the Assembly.[25]

To the extent that a transfer of functions, assets and liabilities, and staff occurred, it took place on the basis of the mutual agreement of the two organizations concerned (mostly in the form of parallel resolutions), and indeed several legal reasons suggest that it could hardly have been otherwise.[26]

For one thing, there is almost always the problem of different membership. Where the successor organization does not have membership identical to the predecessor organization, anything other than agreement would be difficult to reconcile with the basic idea of consent: why should a member of the successor but not the predecessor be obliged to take on (part of) the predecessor's debts, functions or even staff?[27]

Another problem is that, where a succession of organizations takes place, the usual scenario appears to be that the organizations concerned exist simultaneously for a while: the co-existence of the League and the UN appears to be far from exceptional. Even where there seems to be an explicit case of succession (Art. 33 AU specifies that it 'shall replace the Charter of the Organization of African Unity'), nonetheless something of a transitional period is envisaged where the two co-exist.[28]

Thus, Chiu finds in an authoritative survey that in only one of seven cases was there no simultaneous existence. This concerned the subsumption of the International Technical Committee of Aerial Legal Experts (CITEJA) by the newly created International Civil Aviation Organization (ICAO) in 1947. The case is atypical at any rate as ICAO was created by replacing not one but two predecessors. The other was the International Commission for Air Navigation (CINA), which did co-exist with ICAO for some eight months.[29] Indeed, in a strict sense one can hardly even speak of succession where predecessor and successor exist alongside; it therefore seems to be a case of taking over certain of a predecessor's functions, assets and liabilities, and staff, rather than of succession strictly speaking. Of course it is far from surprising that such 'succession' is practically always based on mutual agreement.[30]

---

[25] Brierly thought this was a little childish. See J. L. Brierly, 'The Covenant and the Charter' (1946) 23 *BYIL*, 83–94, 83.

[26] Article 16(c) of the Agreement establishing the Terms of Reference of the International Jute Study Group provides for agreement in a different way: 'As the legal successor to the International Jute Organization, the Group shall assume responsibility for all the assets and liabilities of the former Organization.'

[27] It may be hypothesized that succeeding to assets will be less problematic, in much the same way as the law of treaties recognizes a difference between the creation of rights and of obligations for third parties.

[28] For more details, see Konstantinos D. Magliveras and Gino Naldi, *The African Union and the Predecessor Organization of African Unity* (The Hague, 2004), pp. 61–4.

[29] Hungdah Chiu, 'Succession in International Organisations' (1965) 14 *ICLQ*, 83–120, 89–91.

[30] Chiu draws the same conclusion (but not on the basis of identical arguments), rejecting any automatic succession theory: *ibid.*, pp. 114–18.

There is, however, one notorious exception when it comes to the functions of an organization, and that is the way the League of Nations' supervisory powers concerning South Africa's Mandate over South West Africa were transferred. As is well known, no explicit transfer thereof had taken place, which did not prevent the General Assembly, in the late 1940s, from claiming supervisory powers. When South Africa resisted, the ICJ was asked for an advisory opinion, and the Court found that indeed a transfer of powers had taken place, but it remains less than clear why exactly the Court thought so. Much in the reasoning suggests wishful thinking on the part of the Court, claiming that, even though the League had disappeared, the necessity of supervision of the Mandate continued to exist. Moreover, as the Court put it, the General Assembly had in practice taken over supervisory functions (never mind South Africa's lack of co-operation), and the 'dissolution resolution' of the League of Nations Assembly, while it remained silent on the topic, was nevertheless interpreted by the Court as 'presupposing' that the supervisory powers would be taken over by the UN.[31]

All in all, there is much conjecture in the Court's reasoning, but then again any other option would also have been vulnerable to criticism, and often to remarkably similar criticism. Thus, a finding that no supervision had been transferred would have an equally dubious basis: can one conclude from the absence of anything explicit on supervision that therefore supervision had come to an end, even in the face of humanitarian concerns? After all, the Mandate was created in the name of the sacred trust of civilization; South Africa's faithful adherence thereto seemed, in the 1940s, at least debatable.

Assets and debts

While successions of organizations are relatively rare (especially when cases of reconstitution or constitutional adaptation are not counted) and follow their own patterns, usually on the basis of mutual agreement between the organizations concerned, nonetheless some generalities tend to recur. Thus, assets of the predecessor organization (as well as archives) tend to fall to the successor organization.[32]

Indeed, there is even some (albeit limited) judicial support for the thesis that such would be the case even without agreement. In *PAU* v. *American Security and Trust Company*,[33] at issue was whether the Pan-American Union (PAU) was entitled to receive the residue of the estate of its deceased Director-General, in accordance with his will. The PAU had become, since 1948, the General Secretariat of the OAS; prior to that, it had been the administrative organ of the Union of American Republics. While the will's executor doubted that the

---

[31] Hahn, 'Continuity', in particular pp. 197–8, suggests that the Court applied the idea of (automatic) succession but refused to call it by that name because of succession's private law overtones.

[32] See O. M. Ribbelink, *Opvolging van internationale organisaties* (The Hague, 1988), p. 212.

[33] Decision of 6 May 1952, US District Court for the District of Columbia, in 18 *ILR* 441.

PAU was still the same entity, the US District Court for the District of Columbia found, in 1952, that the PAU had essentially retained its identity, and reached the conclusion that the PAU, 'as General Secretariat of the Organization of American States, has succeeded to the property and contractual rights it previously held as agent of the Union of American Republics'.[34]

The judgment seems to offer some support for automatic succession of assets and contractual rights, but only in a limited way, as the situation surrounding the various changes of the PAU is too atypical to be able to serve as the basis for general conclusions. Moreover, the PAU as such had not ceased to exist; it had merely taken on another function in a different organization. The more likely scenario is that succession will take place by agreement – this has been the basis of at least one other judicial decision.[35]

When it comes to debts of the predecessor organization, the picture is less clear. Those of the League of Nations were neatly taken care of, but little is known about those of other organizations, such as the debts of the Caribbean and Latin American free trade areas, CARIFTA and LAFTA (succeeded by, respectively, the Caribbean Common Market (Caricom) and the Latin American Integration Association (LAIA)).[36] Where the succession is merely a reconstitution without a change in identity (as with OEEC–OECD), there is no reason why debts or assets would not continue to exist. Indeed, a well-placed observer has argued that the choice for reconstitution rather than the creation of a new legal person was inspired by a desire to prevent precisely these types of problems.[37]

Personnel

With personnel too, matters are uncertain. When the League of Nations disappeared, some of its staff found employment with the UN but, once again, mainly on the basis of agreement.[38] And indeed, the importance of agreement has also been emphasized in other contexts.[39] Thus, the Administrative Tribunal of the ILO held that, in the absence of any agreement to that effect, officials of

---

[34] *Ibid.*, p. 443.
[35] In *United Nations* v. *B*, decision of 27 March 1952, Tribunal Civil of Brussels, in 19 *ILR* 490, the Court found that the defendant was under the obligation to restitute money paid to him by the dissolved United Nations Relief and Rehabilitation Administration (UNRRA) to the UN, which had by agreement taken over UNRRA's rights. The Supreme Court of New York, however, in *Wencak* v. *United States*, found that the UN 'is in no sense the successor of Unrra [sic]', but had merely undertaken to administer UNRRA's liquidation: decision of 18 January 1956, in 22 *ILR* 509.
[36] Compare Ribbelink, Opvolging van internationale organisaties, p. 212.
[37] Hahn, 'Continuity', p. 220. Hahn was a legal adviser with the OEEC at the time of its reconstitution.
[38] See, e.g., Myers, 'Liquidation', p. 336.
[39] With respect to the GATT–WTO succession, the Director of the Legal Affairs Division of the GATT Secretariat proposed an agreement between the WTO and the contracting parties of GATT. See Frieder Roessler, 'The Agreement Establishing the World Trade Organization'. In Jacques H. J. Bourgeois *et al.* (eds.), *The Uruguay Round Results: A European Lawyers' Perspective* (Brussels, 1995), 67–85, 83.

the Pan American Sanitary Bureau could not enjoy the benefits guaranteed to WHO officials, despite the fact that the Pan American Sanitary Bureau acted as the WHO's regional office and was about to become fully integrated into the WHO.[40]

The same applies, by and large, to other cases of succession. Usually, there is no blanket take-over of staff, although some staff members may move along with the predecessor's movable assets. There is, however, often a commitment to help the predecessor's staff to find new employment, and to grant them preferential treatment with the successor organization. And of course, their experiences with the predecessor can prove useful.

Where no proper succession takes place, but is merely constitutional adaptation, often the staff remains in function, at least to the extent that a refashioned organization's new functions need the same type of expertise. Where functions have changed, it may be that a change in staff will also be needed.

Functions

On an abstract level, the transfer of functions brings few problems with it. After all, functions are (in contrast to assets, liabilities and archives) not under anyone's ownership, and at least hypothetically there is no objection to disbanding organization X on Monday and creating a new organization Y on Tuesday with the same functions as the ones earlier given to organization X. Indeed, there is no problem in having both exist simultaneously; and one might hypothetically even reach the conclusion, over time, that organization X has fallen into desuetude.

Nonetheless, on less abstract levels things are not so easy, as (once again) the fate of South Africa's Mandate over Namibia demonstrates. For, with functions usually also come such things as supervision and control, and to leave those to the workings of desuetude, or to simply abandon them by dismantling the organization, will be messy indeed and, more importantly, will not do justice to the functions of either the new or the old organization. In addition, in some circumstances functions may be bestowed upon an organization by others. Thus, the League of Nations exercised functions as a depository of treaties, and had been given functions under conventions dealing with narcotic drugs.

Consequently, some form of transfer of functions may be useful and, once again, such transfer usually takes place on the basis of agreement in one form or another. Thus, the League's functions under drugs conventions were transferred after the acceptance of those functions by the UN had become clear, as were the League's technical functions as treaty depository.[41] As far as other

---

[40] *Brache v. World Health Organization*, decision of 3 November 1969 by the ILO Administrative Tribunal, in 43 *ILR* 459.

[41] See, e.g., H. McKinnon Wood, 'The Dissolution of the League of Nations' (1946) 23 *BYIL*, 317–23, 318.

functions were concerned, after it had become clear that the USSR would oppose any wholesale transfer (having been dismissed from the League in 1939, the USSR was particularly keen to make a fresh start and rejected suggestions of succession), the UN General Assembly asked the UN Economic and Social Council to consider what non-political functions and activities of the League should be taken up by the UN (and some ended up being taken partly by Specialized Agencies such as the WHO or the IMF). These 'non-political' topics were to include such matters as human rights, the status of women, fiscal issues, social issues, and economic issues and employment.[42]

While quite a few instances of transfer of functions and activities were based on precise decisions, Myers has noted that it is well-nigh impossible to figure out exactly what the UN has taken over from the League of Nations,[43] and by way of example he observes that the Economic and Social Council of the UN may be regarded as a development from the League's creation of a Central Committee on Economic and Social Questions.

This alone illustrates the elusive nature of succession of international organizations. To draw general conclusions is bound to remain unconvincing, apart from the (rather obvious) conclusion that a succession based on agreement is generally deemed preferable. This way, the type of problems to which the automatic succession thesis, employed in connection with the Mandate, gave rise can be avoided, and justice can be done to the interests of the organizations concerned as well as their member states and, where appropriate, those of third parties (e.g., creditors).

Concluding remarks

Even the dry and technical area of dissolution and succession, typically lawyer's law if ever such a thing existed, is in the end unable to escape from the workings of politics. The tension between the organization and its members, often considered the political moment *par excellence* in the law of international organizations, also colours the contents of the law in this area, so much so indeed that the law can do little else but advocate solutions based on agreement.

Such a plea for agreement, while useful, hardly exhausts the matter, for it remains to be seen whose agreement is deemed to be necessary or required: agreement between a new organization and its functional predecessor? Or also between the member states of either one (or both of them)? And if the latter is the case, the next question automatically presents itself: is the agreement of all members required, or will a majority suffice? And this, in turn, may depend on which procedure is followed, which is in itself a question to which the answer is often the result of negotiations rather than of the strict application of rules of law.

---

[42] Compare Myers, 'Liquidation', p. 337.   [43] *Ibid.*, p. 352.

But that, of course, is only fitting – international organizations, while endowed with legal characteristics in order to exercise legal powers, are in the end creatures of politics: inasmuch as their creation involves a political act, and inasmuch as their everyday existence involves everyday politics, it should not come as a surprise that their dissolution too is an intensely political affair.

16

Concluding remarks: Towards re-appraisal and control

Introduction

It was stated in the beginning of this book that an important characteristic of the study of international organizations is the absence of a single perspective on them. Instead, as the previous chapters have sought to demonstrate, many of the ideas invoked in the law of international organizations can be traced back to different conceptions of what organizations are, and more specifically to different perspectives on the relationship between international organizations and their member states.

What I hope to have indicated in the preceding chapters is that these contending perspectives are reflected in much of what we usually think of as the law of international organizations. In many respects, this branch of the law is ambiguous, and cannot make up its mind whether to err on the side of the member states, or whether to err on the side of international organizations (although it often ends up doing the latter). Thus, we find implied powers alongside attributed powers; we find residual liability side by side with limited or no liability, while member states and organs are both interested in admitting new members.

That is, we may presume, a structural situation, which finds its origin in the fundamental tension lying at the heart of international law generally, and arguably of all law: the idea that law, in the absence of some form of agreement as to how best to organize our lives, in the absence of some concord on what constitutes the good life, has to cater to two fundamentally irreconcilable demands.

On the one hand, it should aspire to be in touch with the demands, desires and regular behaviour of its subjects, for a law that is out of touch with society will not prove to be a highly successful instrument for the regulation of that society. Yet, on the other hand, law must also distance itself from society in order to be normative, for a law that only states what social actors already do anyway is, again, not very suitable as a regulatory instrument. Instead, it amounts (at best) to little more than descriptive sociology.[1]

---

[1] It is perhaps no coincidence that outsiders tend to look at international law as either descriptive sociology (and thus of little practical effect in terms of constraining states' behaviour) or as a

In international law generally, this fundamental conflict finds itself translated into an everlasting tension between the exigencies of state sovereignty and the imperatives of international order and justice.[2] With international organizations, it translates itself predominantly, but not exclusively, into a tension between the organization and its member states. Additionally, when organizations look outside, third parties immediately enter the picture, and behind them stand, once again, such things as international order and justice, often portrayed as a personified international society (which in turn is sometimes held to be personified, confusingly, in the United Nations[3]).

The idea that much of the law of international organizations derives from the relationship between organizations and their members is far from novel, and goes back to at least the 1950s. Thus, Nagendra Singh, who would later serve as a judge with the ICJ, could in 1958 boldly (and perhaps against his own sentiments) proclaim that 'anything which is not conceded in favour of the international organisation is retained by the member State, which by virtue of its sovereignty must be vested with the residuary jurisdiction'.[4]

And part of the reason why Inis Claude's classic *Swords into Plowshares* still looks fresh, almost half a century after it was first published, is precisely his recognition of 'an ambiguity which is a persistent bane of the existence of international organization. Men and nations want the benefits of international organization, but they also want to retain the privileges of sovereignty, which are inseparable from international disorganization.'[5]

Organizations v. members: a zero-sum game?

Much of the law of international organizations, then, derives from the relationship between the organization and its members, and, more importantly perhaps, is usually seen in terms of a clash between the organization and its members. Much writing in the field is based on the unspoken thought that whatever the law eventually says is the result of a tug of war between the organization and its member states, and then miraculously ends up beyond politics. In short, much writing is based on the thought that this tug of war is a zero-sum game: either

---

branch of ethics (and therewith equally of little practical effect). For an example, see Robert O. Keohane, 'International Relations and International Law: Two Optics' (1997) 38 *Harvard ILJ*, 487–502.

[2] See generally Martti Koskenniemi, *From Apology to Utopia: The Structure of International Legal Argument* (Helsinki, 1989); see also his 'The Politics of International Law' (1990) 1 *EJIL*, 4–32.

[3] For an example, see Jochen A. Frowein, 'Reactions by Not Directly Affected States to Breaches of Public International Law' (1994/IV) 248 *RdC*, 347–437.

[4] See Nagendra Singh, *Termination of Membership of International Organisations* (London, 1958), pp. 80–1. His own sentiments, arguably, went more in the direction of viewing organizations as having 'a great role to play in the salvation of mankind' (*ibid.*, at vii).

[5] Inis L. Claude, Jr, *Swords into Plowshares: The Problems and Progress of International Organization* (4th edn, New York, 1984), p. 39.

the organization wins, or the members win – whatever the organization wins entails a corresponding loss for the members, and *vice versa*.

Indeed, much of this book is based on the same thought, precisely because it is the one thought that dominates the field.[6] But (and this is perhaps where my argument becomes more novel), I do not think that the law of international organizations should only be analysed in terms of a zero-sum game between the organization and its members, where powers exercised by the members on Monday may be transferred to the organization on Tuesday only to flow back again to the members on Wednesday, and so on and so forth. Neither is it a zero-sum game in the more fluid sense of saying that whenever an organization loses power, it can only be to the benefit of states, whereas when states lose power it only benefits organizations. Instead, much as the organization and its members may be in competition when it comes to the exercise of power and powers, they ultimately also represent the same thing: the dream of instrumentality; the dream of regulation; the ideal that we can somehow make and shape society in accordance with our favourite blueprints. States as well as organizations represent organized political life; both ultimately represent the idea that we can make and control our surroundings, and that we can conquer both nature and human nature.

This idea goes back to at least the Enlightenment, and found its culmination in eighteenth- and nineteenth-century pleas to advocate the abolition of such things as poverty by treaty,[7] as well as in the 1950s battle cry of 'World peace through world law'. Law, it was thought (as an adjunct to politics, or perhaps taking the place of politics), could possibly cure all evils, as long as it was informed by science; novelist and would-be futurologist H. G. Wells (most famous for his futuristic *War of the Worlds*), in telling fashion, once sighed in desperation that many of the pitfalls of modern times could have been overcome if only the governance of society had been left to scientists.[8]

It is this Enlightenment ideal that has come increasingly under fire in recent decades; we are no longer convinced that we can shape society according to our wishes.[9] And more fundamentally perhaps, we cannot even agree on what

---

[6] As Schlag has observed, law is 'at once a concrete social form embedded in institutional practices and an abstract conceptual representation of those institutions and practices'. Legal analysis slips inevitably into an analysis of this representation rather than of the concrete social form, for constructing law is a matter of 'collective, projective objectification'. See Pierre Schlag, 'Law as the Continuation of God by Other Means' (1997) 85 *California Law Review*, 427–40, 440 and 439, respectively.

[7] As observed by Oakeshott, the nineteenth-century social reformer Robert Owen once suggested the project of a convention to end ignorance, poverty, sin and a few assorted other things as well. Oakeshott drily adds that even a rationalist might find this a bit eccentric. Compare Michael Oakeshott, 'Rationalism in Politics', in his *Rationalism in Politics and Other Essays* (London, 1962), 1–36, esp. p. 6.

[8] As referred to in Benedetto Croce, *History of Europe in the Nineteenth Century* (New York, 1933, trans. Furst), pp. 256–7.

[9] For an accessible formulation, see Claus Offe, *Modernity and the State* (Cambridge, 1996).

society should look like. While the fall of communism has taught us the lesson that, broadly speaking, such things as liberty, democracy, respect for human rights, and the advantages of the market economy are preferable to their counterparts, the devil is, as they say, in the detail.[10] What exactly does liberty mean, and does it include the liberty to be abusive? What do we mean by democracy, and should not international society be democratic as much as we would like to see domestic societies democratically arranged?[11] What, exactly, are human rights? While most of us – though probably not all of us – may agree on the broad outlines of the good life, there is sufficient ground to debate (and continue to debate) the more specific aspects thereof.[12]

To some extent, this has no doubt been a healthy development: such ideologies as fascism and communism presuppose a commitment to the modernist idea that society is malleable. As Zygmunt Bauman, a leading sociologist, has suggested, there is a direct connection between modernity's idea that society can be transformed at will, and the gas chambers of Auschwitz.[13] Moreover, there is good reason to suppose that world government, once seen as the next phase of international organization, may itself be undesirable: perhaps mankind is better off with a world of smaller political communities instead of a single large polity.

In the midst of all this, international institutions have started to suffer from a bad reputation, especially compared with the optimism of yesteryear's 'international project'. They are deemed to be wasteful bureaucracies, feeding fat cats, without in any way contributing to the solution of global or regional problems. While it is reasonably obvious that some trans-boundary problems require international co-operation, it is no longer equally obvious that the formal international organization is the best-qualified vehicle for such co-operation, Indeed, one could argue that recent attempts to create entities which miss some of the characteristics of formal organizations (think of the OSCE, with its ostensible non-legal hallmarks, or the flexibility provided by G7 or G8) are attempts precisely to overcome the perceived obstacle of a formal style of politics.

A similar tendency is apparent from the names of some recently created organizations. Thus, since 1998, co-operation in the bamboo and rattan sector has taken place through a network – the International Network for Bamboo and Rattan – and the International Jute Organization has been replaced by a toned-down International Jute Study Group, tellingly based

---

[10] For an illustration, see Kerry Rittich, *Recharacterizing Restructuring: Law, Distribution and Gender in Market Reform* (The Hague, 2002).

[11] For an in-depth discussion, see Susan Marks, *The Riddle of All Constitutions: International Law, Democracy, and the Critique of Ideology* (Oxford, 2000).

[12] An imaginative contribution is Andrew Linklater, *The Transformation of Political Community* (Cambridge, 1998).

[13] See, e.g., Zygmunt Bauman, *Modernity and Ambivalence* (Cambridge, 1991), p. 50, arguing that modernity is a necessary (but not sufficient) condition for genocide.

on an agreement establishing terms of reference rather than anything more
formal-sounding.

Transgovernmentalism, civil society and formalism

Taking the place of formal and organized international politics, we have started
to idolize two new (relatively new, at any rate) styles of politics. One is the
reification of transgovernmentalism[14] or, as it has also been called in the slightly
more concentrated context of the EC, infranationalism.[15] We have come to be
content with letting our lives be run by informal networks of decision makers,
and often consider this to be a welcome development: no more bureaucracy,
but effective, goal-oriented management of international issues. Thus, judges
are said to be engaged in international conversations with one another; civil
servants serve their states by informally concluding informal arrangements with
their colleagues elsewhere; bankers set standards at their meetings far from the
spotlights.[16] And to top things off, we often consider that these standards and
arrangements are somehow beyond the realm of the law or, at best, make up
that mushy institution known as soft law.[17]

There is, however, a price to be paid for all this effectiveness and efficiency:
our lives are being run without any control whatsoever.[18] Parliaments cannot
oversee the deals made by civil servants or bankers, and when they claim that
they should at least have a look, they are told not to bother because those
deals are not really law, after all. And the judges are too busy conducting their
transnational conversations to mind much about the details of what others do,
and they too start to believe that what those bankers or civil servants agree upon
is not really law, and, should it be law after all, then perhaps it is not the type of
law that would insist on rigid compliance.[19]

Still, we reify transgovernmentalism because, after all, it is somehow international, and we internationalists have a natural affection for what David Kennedy

---

[14] See in particular Anne-Marie Slaughter, 'The Real New World Order' (1997) 76 *Foreign Affairs*,
183–97. A full account is provided in Anne-Marie Slaughter, *A New World Order* (Princeton,
2004).

[15] Compare Joseph H. H. Weiler, *The Constitution of Europe* (Cambridge, 1999), esp. pp. 96–101.

[16] See, e.g., Lawrence L. C. Lee, 'The Basle Accords as Soft Law: Strengthening International
Banking Supervision' (1998) 39 *VaJIL*, 1–40.

[17] For a critique, see Jan Klabbers, 'Institutional Ambivalence by Design: Soft Organizations in
International Law' (2001) 70 *Nordic JIL*, 403–21.

[18] The same concern underlies, e.g., Deirdre Curtin, *Postnational Democracy: The European
Union in Search of a Political Philosophy* (The Hague, 1997), as well as Larry Siedentop,
Democracy in Europe (London, 2000).

[19] Amazingly, recent scholarship, especially in international trade law, attempts to justify
non-compliance on the rather curious ground that, after all, states do not always comply with
rules, and this should be reflected in the law. A representative example is Joel Trachtman,
'Bananas, Direct Effect and Compliance' (1999) 10 *EJIL*, 655–78. Theoretical underpinnings
are provided by Andrew T. Guzman, *How International Law Works: A Rational Choice Theory*
(Oxford, 2008).

once fortuitously referred to as our 'international project': anything is good, as long as it is international. This, in turn, stems from our distrust of anything parochial: the state stands for nasty things such as sovereignty, human rights violations and warfare. After all, who has (or had, until Kosovo) ever seen an international organ or network go to war? Well then: for us internationalists, the state was, until recently, the root of all evil, so it follows that anything that attempts to reach beyond the state is laudable and praiseworthy, regardless of its precise contents. As Louis Henkin once put it with resonating force, sovereignty is a bad word;[20] state sovereignty needs to be overcome if life is ever to get better.[21]

The second form of politics we have come to appreciate is the politics of what is widely referred to as 'civil society'. We have lost our faith in political parties, and have instead turned to what some call 'new social movements'. We may not turn out at election time, but we are busy raising funds for Greenpeace, writing postcards for Amnesty International, demonstrating in the streets of Seattle, Prague and Genoa, and discussing the pros and cons of prospective international agreements on the Internet.

However laudable such activities may be, once again democracy and account-ability become problematic. Perhaps the *Werdegang* of the planned Multilateral Agreement on Investment, largely ascribed to amorphous and elusive Internet protests, illustrates best what is at stake: power exercised by faceless, nameless and uncontrolled individuals and groups, without any form of supervision and without any form of accountability.[22] While we expect our statesmen to be democrats, and while we try to sell the blessings of it to those that have hith-erto remained deprived of democracy, we simultaneously allow our spirits to be uplifted by the utterly undemocratic politics of civil society, conveniently ignor-ing the circumstance that civil society not only includes our noblest dreams, but may also include our worst nightmares.

And yet, international organizations continue to flourish, both in material terms and in terms of the scope of activities. In material terms, it is worth noting that during the golden years of deregulation, the 1980s of Thatcher and Reagan, the already obese UN organization managed to create a whopping 173 new agencies, while laying to rest a mere 73.[23] Brian Urquhart, a former

---

[20] See Louis Henkin, 'International Law: Politics, Values and Functions' (1989/IV) 216 *RdC*, 9–416, esp. p. 24.

[21] Note, however, that the most serious attempt to present a coherent liberal vision along these lines nevertheless ends up partly defending the state, precisely because of its dual nature: on the one hand, traditionally the violator of human rights and democracy, but on the other capable of protecting (and giving effect to) human rights and democracy. See Thomas M. Franck, *The Empowered Self: Law and Society in the Age of Individualism* (Oxford, 1999).

[22] For a brief discussion, see Alan Boyle and Christine Chinkin, *The Making of International Law* (Oxford, 2007), pp. 76–7.

[23] Cheryl Shanks, Harold K. Jacobson and Jeffrey H. Kaplan, 'Inertia and Change in the Constellation of International Intergovernmental Organizations' (1996) 50 *International Organization*, 593–627, esp. 602–3.

high-ranking UN servant, vividly explains how such things may take place: 'Cock-eyed ideas from member states or other sources begot studies which produced reports which set up staffs which produced more reports which were considered by meetings which asked for further reports and sometimes set up additional bureaucratic appendages which reported to future meetings. The process was self-perpetuating.'[24]

Despite having had a bad press, organizations also flourish in terms of the scope of their activities. The Security Council has never been as active as it is today. Organizations keep usurping tasks not directly related to their constituent treaties, NATO being a prime example. The financial institutions penetrate deeply into national economies – and their political systems. The UN has started to administer territory in places such as Kosovo and East Timor; the EU has done the same in Mostar. Peace-keeping, peace-enforcement, and peace-building missions take place left, right, and centre, with organizations competing for their moment of glory.[25] And whenever a new problem is identified, the creation of some kind of international organization is often considered to be an obvious way of attempting to do something about it.[26]

It thus appears to be recognized that while efficiency and effectiveness are great goods, we run the risk of throwing the baby out with the bathwater if we welcome civil society and transgovernmental networks too warmly: it may well be the case that in order to organize (never mind regulate) our lives, we cannot do without a style of politics where the interests of the minority find some protection, and where it is possible to argue before a court of law that a decision ought never to have been taken, or ought to have been taken by somebody else. It is these ideals that form the basis of modern conceptions of the *Rechtsstaat* or the Rule of Law, and they can only be honoured by means of conducting our politics through agreed-upon procedures and in accordance with agreed-upon standards.

In this light, it is no surprise that the state has met with approval again in recent years, being form without content: precisely because there is nothing natural or authentic about the state (in contrast to the nation), it turns out to be the ideal place in which to conduct politics.[27]

---

[24] Brian Urquhart, *A Life in Peace and War* (New York 1987), p. 108.

[25] As underlined by David Galbreath, *The Organization for Security and Cooperation in Europe* (London, 2007).

[26] Hence, influential sociologists Hutton and Giddens advocate the creation of global institutions to deal with poverty, criminal affairs, security, and the world economy, as well as a World Competition Authority and regulation of currency transactions. See Anthony Giddens and Will Hutton, 'Fighting Back'. In Will Hutton and Anthony Giddens (eds.), *On the Edge: Living with Global Capitalism* (London, 2001), pp. 213–23. Likewise, Beck suggests that international institutions are no luxury, but a bare necessity in globalizing times in order to maintain some form of control over unmitigated corporate action: states are no longer capable of this on their own. See Ulrich Beck, *Was ist Globalisierung?* (Frankfurt am Main, 1997), p. 226.

[27] Compare in particular Martti Koskenniemi, 'The Wonderful Artificiality of States' (1994) 88 *Proceedings of the American Society of International Law*, 22–9; see also his 'The Future of Statehood' (1991) 32 *Harvard ILJ*, 397–410.

Control

It should also not come as a surprise that the issue of control of international organizations has come to occupy a prominent place on the international agenda.[28] While some of this takes the fairly traditional form of discussing the responsibility of international organizations (or, using a broader phrase and broader concept, their accountability), it has also come to take two other forms: debates are conducted on the possibility of constitutionalism in international organizations, and on the possibility of an emerging global administrative law.

Constitutionalism taps into an analogy with the nation state as a political model, and plays out in organizations such as the EU,[29] the WTO,[30] and perhaps most of all the UN.[31] The underlying idea (which, to be sure, comes in many guises and variations) would seem to be that the organizations concerned embody certain values which are deemed especially laudable, so laudable as to deserve being carved in stone.[32] Moreover, those organizations encompass discrete political communities (respectively, the European West, the global trading community, and the global community at large) and do so in ways that cannot be explained on the mere basis of the *pacta sunt servanda* norm; hence, a new conceptual apparatus is required, and often found in the vocabulary of constitutionalism. As so often, this is accompanied by normative propositions: constitutionalism is deemed a good thing, perhaps a necessity: since globalization entails that constitutional guarantees within states are eroding, they need to be compensated for at the international level.[33] Moreover, and with respect to international law generally, situating international regulation within a constitutionalist framework may well enhance the legitimacy of international law.[34]

---

[28] It has also come to dominate domestic agendas, both public and private. For an insightful discussion, see Michael Power, *The Audit Society: Rituals of Verification* (Oxford, 1997).

[29] The seminal article is Eric Stein, 'Lawyers, Judges, and the Making of a Transnational Constitution' (1981) 75 *AJIL*, 1–27. Influential studies include J. H. H. Weiler, *The Constitution of Europe*, and J. H. H. Weiler and Marlene Wind (eds.), *European Constitutionalism Beyond the State* (Cambridge, 2003). An exhaustive overview is Armin von Bogdandy and Jürgen Bast (eds.), *Principles of European Constitutional Law* (Oxford, 2005).

[30] Something of a manifesto by a leading proponent is Ernst-Ulrich Petersmann, 'The WTO Constitution and Human Rights' (2000) 3 *Journal of International Economic Law*, 19–25; a more extensive discussion is John O. McGinnis and Mark L. Movsesian, 'The World Trade Constitution' (2000) 114 *Harvard Law Review*, 511–605. For a balanced discussion, see Deborah Z. Cass, *The Constitutionalization of the World Trade Organization: Legitimacy, Democracy, and Community in the International Trading System* (Oxford, 2005).

[31] See, e.g., Jürgen Habermas, *The Divided West* (Cambridge, 2006, Cronin trans.), pp. 113–93. The seminal article is Bardo Fassbender, 'The United Nations Charter as Constitution of the International Community' (1998) 36 *Columbia JTL*, 529–619.

[32] Highlighting the unifying role of values is Erika de Wet, 'The International Constitutional Order' (2006) 55 *ICLQ*, 51–76.

[33] See Anne Peters, 'Compensatory Constitutionalism: The Function and Potential of Fundamental International Norms and Structures' (2006) 19 *Leiden JIL*, 579–610.

[34] See, e.g., Matthias Kumm, 'The Legitimacy of International Law: A Constitutionalist Framework for Analysis' (2004) 15 *EJIL*, 907–31.

Still, the constitutional position is not without problems. One of these is that to the extent that it claims to be based on universally shared values, it may turn out to be a pipe-dream: the unity of values appearing in the abstract may well dissipate in concrete situations. Put differently, few people would disagree with the proposition that torture is a bad thing; but not all would agree on what exactly constitutes torture, or whether there are or could be situations in which torture would be justifiable.

Second, it remains unclear where those constitutional norms come from. It takes rather a leap of faith to specify not only that organizations may be bound by norms they have never consented to in their own right, but that those norms have even assumed constitutional importance. In some cases this may be overcome by referring to the explicit inclusion of some of these norms in the organization's legal order (as Article 6 of the TEU refers to human rights), but that argument would be difficult to sustain with respect to the WTO, whose constituent document remains silent about human rights.

Indeed, sometimes existing norms seem rather to prevent things. The standard example is the situation of the World Bank which, so many people think, should take human rights into account when making all sorts of decisions. Its constituent document, however, suggests in Article III, section 5, that only economic and efficiency factors may influence decision making, 'without regard to political or other non-economic influences or considerations'. Paradoxically then, control over the World Bank (through human rights norms) can only be achieved by ignoring, or at least re-interpreting, its own constituent document.[35] This suggests, of course, that control as such is not always at issue; often, the organization is the site of a political struggle (in this case between an economic vision and a human rights vision) over the activities of the organization, with 'control' and 'accountability' functioning as part of the vocabulary of that struggle.

Third, and perhaps of most fundamental relevance, even constitutional guarantees are impotent in the face of political agreement. Where all relevant actors agree to circumvent a constitution, the mere fact of there being a constitution will not usually stop them – in politics, usually the end is thought to justify the means, so when the end meets with everyone's approval, the possible unconstitutional nature of the means is not a sufficiently strong argument to stop things. This is visible even within the EU, arguably the most constitutionalized organization (e.g., when in 2003 the provisions of the Stability and Growth Pact were set aside so as not to embarrass France and Germany).[36]

Where constitutionalism seeks to posit immutable legal orders based on universal values, the idea behind global administrative law is more modest. In

---

[35] The standard rendition is Ibrahim Shihata, 'Human Rights, Development and International Financial Institutions' (1992) 8 *American University Journal of International Law and Policy*, 27–37.

[36] For a general critique, see Jan Klabbers, 'Constitutionalism Lite' (2004) 1 *IOLR*, 31–58.

essence, global administrative law is based on the thought that much public authority is exercised by international actors (formal and not so formal), and that it stands to reason that the exercise of public authority can and should be scrutinized.[37] The instruments for doing so are borrowed from domestic administrative law, and focus predominantly on procedure: surely, if standards are set without public participation, or without democratic input, then some form of review ought to be possible. By the same token, if sanctions are imposed on individuals, those individuals should at least have the possibility to defend themselves in court. If UNHCR screens refugee applications in its camps, then surely some procedure must be available should UNHCR do a sloppy job.[38]

This is, at first sight, an attractive idea, partly because it promises to also capture the output of informal decision making, and partly because of its modesty: it does not have to rely on universally shared values in order to appear workable. Moreover, it would seem that as a general matter, people might be happier to agree on the utility of procedural notions (transparency, access to justice, due process, participation) than on matters of substance. Still, some of these attractions may turn out to be deceptive: the distinction between procedural and substantive matters may quickly collapse. Moreover, one of the procedural elements often mentioned is proportionality, but that is, really, difficult to sustain.[39] Partly, this is the case because when applying a proportionality test, it is still relevant to decide against what exactly the behaviour should be proportional, and often enough there are several candidates.[40] Should, a decision to refuse someone refugee status be proportional to the situation in his country of origin? Or proportional to the misery he has already suffered? Or proportional to the possible security risk he represents? Or proportional to the economic situation in the country he wants to go to? Legal standards are often too imprecise, leaving matters to the discretion of decision makers.[41]

Moreover, there remains the vexed issue of where exactly those administrative norms stem from. It has been pointed out that administrative law, even in Europe, embodies radically different traditions: the English tend to think of

---

[37] A very useful guide is provided by Benedict Kingsbury, Nico Krisch and Richard B. Stewart, 'The Emergence of Global Administrative Law' (2005) 68 *Law and Contemporary Problems*, 15–61.

[38] The example is derived from Mark Pallis, 'The Operation of UNHCR's Accountability Mechanisms' (2005) 37 *New York University Journal of International Law and Politics*, 869–918.

[39] Still, the argument has been made that proportionality acts as the 'ultimate rule of law'. See David M. Beatty, *The Ultimate Rule of Law* (Oxford, 2004).

[40] A more philosophical issue is that proportionality inserts an element of utilitarian thinking into what is otherwise a strongly rule-based body of thought, and the two might not be all that easily reconcilable.

[41] By way of analogy, proportionality in armed conflict may mean that an act must be proportional to its immediate goal, or may mean that it must be proportional to the overall goal. See Jan Klabbers, 'Off Limits? International Law and the Excessive Use of Force' (2006) 7 *Theoretical Inquiries in Law*, 59–80.

administrative law as controlling government, whereas the French think less in terms of control and more in terms of action: administrative law is the law relating to government. Moreover, even agreement on procedural principles may dissipate on closer scrutiny: transparency in Scandinavia has dramatically different connotations from the same notion in the UK or Italy.[42] And at any rate, much of the normative framework is Western in origin, marginalizing the global South.[43]

In light of the circumstances that both constitutionalism and global administrative law have problems in particular with specifying the basis of obligation (as does any responsibility regime, as Chapter 14 above has suggested), perhaps a possible complement is to focus not only on applying external standards to the behaviour of international organizations, but also tap into the virtue of those making and applying decisions. In other words, as important as it may be to have constitutional norms is to have a 'constitutional mindset', as Koskenniemi calls it,[44] upholding 'a different style of politics'.[45] Responsible government, after all, requires responsible governors.

There are strands in this direction in the public administration literature,[46] and in ethics too there is some attention for virtue-based approaches,[47] possibly in conjunction with a more traditional rule-based approach.[48] More to the point, in many organizations developments are taking place which appear to be inspired by similar concerns: the creation of offices of internal oversight or compliance officers, monitoring the exercise of proper governance by the organization and those working for it. These will turn out to be a missed opportunity should they focus solely on the application of external norms to the organization's organ and employees, but may also come to embody a more concrete reliance on the individual qualities and characteristics of officials and decision makers.

Nonetheless, miracles should not be expected. For one thing, internal auditors and other watchdogs may not be trusted much by people 'on the ground', who might fear that internal oversight boards may have institutional interests of their own to protect or are merely looking for easy scapegoats. Moreover, such

---

[42] See Carol Harlow, 'Global Administrative Law: The Quest for Principles and Values' (2006) 17 *EJIL*, 187–214. Perhaps this is why Esty speaks of 'administrative tools and practices' rather than 'rules and principles'. See Daniel C. Esty, 'Good Governance at the Supranational Scale: Globalizing Administrative Law' (2006) 115 *Yale Law Journal*, 1490–1562.

[43] See Harlow, The Quest. See also B. S. Chimni, 'Co-option and Resistance: Two Faces of Global Administrative Law' (2005) 37 *New York University Journal of International Law and Politics*, 799–827.

[44] See Martti Koskenniemi, 'Constitutionalism as Mindset: Reflections on Kantian Themes about International Law and Globalization' (2007) 8 *Theoretical Inquiries in Law*, 9–36.

[45] See Klabbers, 'Constitutionalism Lite', p. 57.

[46] Perhaps most prominently Larry D. Terry, *Leadership of Public Bureaucracies: The Administrator as Conservator*, 2nd edn (Armonk, NY: 2003).

[47] A useful overview is Roger Crisp and Michael Slote (eds.), *Virtue Ethics* (Oxford, 1997).

[48] See, e.g., Onora O'Neill, *Towards Justice and Virtue: A Constructive Account of Practical Reasoning* (Cambridge, 1996).

boards may have little understanding of the conditions under which the people 'on the ground' must operate.[49]

More structurally, there is the consideration that decision makers can often only act within the limits set by politics. A fine example is provided by James Traub, recalling how the UN, in the Oil-for-Food enterprise, was not allowed to use American, British or Swiss banks, and thus had little choice but to settle for a French bank – one it had earlier considered not quite suitable.[50] While it will be impossible (and undesirable) to take the politics out of politics, it just might be possible to insist occasionally on a different style of politics, where the ends do not always justify the means but may have to give in to decency, common sense and doing the right thing.

That is not to say that what is needed is a reform of the institutional structures of international organizations. Reform projects tend to be more successful on paper than in practice,[51] and some organizations may be, quite literally, unreformable.[52] Indeed, as Franck observed over two decades ago, it is not so much that we need new forms, but rather that we make more intelligent use of those that already exist while accepting the realities of the general conditions under which we live.[53]

Concluding remarks

The law of international organizations, as this book hopes to have indicated, does not add up to a clear set of plain, unequivocal legal rules: there is much uncertainty in the law of international organizations, and much of that uncertainty finds its cause in the tense and problematic relationship between the organization and its member states – it is difficult to tell the acts of an organization from those of states acting *en groupe*, which in turn allows states and organizations to hide behind one another – even to become indistinguishable. And this is no coincidence, as they stand for the same thing: politics in accordance with the law. That the law itself is unclear in no way diminishes this circumstance.

---

[49] See, for an example, the very readable account by three UN officers sent to places such as Haiti, Cambodia and Bosnia: Kenneth Cain, Heidi Postlewait and Andrew Thomson, *Emergency Sex (and Other Desperate Measures)* (London, 2004), esp. pp. 184–5.

[50] See James Traub, *The Best Intentions: Kofi Annan and the UN in the Era of American World Power* (London, 2006), pp. 300–1.

[51] See, e.g., Maurice Bertrand, 'The Historical Development of Efforts to Reform the UN'. In Adam Roberts and Benedict Kingsbury (eds.), *United Nations, Divided World* (2nd edn, Oxford, 1993), pp. 420–36; see also Rosemary Righter, *Utopia Lost: The United Nations and World Order* (New York, 1995).

[52] For an argument that the UN is unreformable, see Marie-Claude Smouts, 'United Nations Reform: A Strategy of Avoidance'. In Michael G. Schechter (ed.), *Innovation in Multilateralism* (Tokyo, 1999), pp. 29–41.

[53] Compare Thomas M. Franck, *Nation against Nation: What Happened to the UN Dream and What the US Can Do about it* (Oxford, 1985), pp. 182–3.

By the same token, the unclarity of the law is no reason to lose faith in international organizations.[54] The more proper response is to accept and to live with the ambiguity of the law, and to accept and live with international organizations, if only because without them the world could easily become a far worse place. While there is no longer a reason to believe that they alone can guarantee the dream of instrumental reason, with more modest expectations about what they can achieve (or indeed about what they ought to aspire to) we might just be able to rescue what is valuable. But one thing is imperative, and that is that certain aspects of the law be developed in serious fashion: the weakness of the *ultra vires* doctrine, to name just one example, must be recognized for what it is and turned into a source of strength, for it is only the analysis of its weaknesses that can facilitate a different, more balanced use in the future.

In other words: while it is true that the law of international organizations is a volatile set of ideas (some more or less hard rules, others merely popular policy preferences), it is also clear that we can hardly imagine a world without international organizations anymore. Indeed, there is a distinct role for the organization: not as the *deus ex machina* of yesteryear, entering the scene to save the day or to save the world, but rather as the type of bounded political community which facilitates discussion and debate; no longer as a regulatory agency *par excellence*, but simply (and most importantly) as a place where international politics is conducted.

[54] See also Jan Klabbers, 'Introduction'. In Jan Klabbers (ed.), *International Organizations* (Aldershot, 2005), xi–xxv.

Bibliography

Aalders, Gerard, 'The Failure of the Scandinavian Defence Union, 1948–1949' (1990) 15 *Scandinavian Journal of History*, 125–53

Abbott, Kenneth W. and Snidal, Duncan, 'Why States Act through Formal International Organizations' (1998) 42 *Journal of Conflict Resolution*, 3–32

Abi-Saab, Georges, *The United Nations Operation in the Congo 1960–1964* (Oxford, 1978)

Acheson, Dean, *Present at the Creation: My Years in the State Department* (New York, 1969)

Adam, H. T., *Les organismes internationaux spécialisés* (Paris, several volumes)

Adede, A. O., 'Amendment Procedures for Conventions with Technical Annexes: The IMCO Experience' (1977) 17 *VaJIL*, 201–15

Ago, Roberto, ' "Binding" Advisory Opinions of the International Court of Justice' (1991) 85 *AJIL*, 439–51

Ahluwalia, Kuljit, *The Legal Status, Privileges and Immunities of the Specialized Agencies of the United Nations and Certain Other International Organizations* (The Hague, 1964)

Akehurst, Michael, *A Modern Introduction to International Law* (6th edn, London, 1987)

Allo, Alain-Pierre, 'Les accords administratifs entre l'Union Européenne et les organisations internationales'. In Daniel Dormoy (ed.), *L'Union Européenne et les organisations internationales* (Brussels, 1997), pp. 56–67

Allott, Philip, 'The Concept of International Law' (1999) 10 *EJIL*, 31–50

Al-Qahtani, Mutlaq, 'The Shanghai Cooperation Organization and the Law of International Organizations' (2006) 5 *Chinese JIL*, 129–47

Altman, Andrew, *Critical Legal Studies: A Liberal Critique* (Princeton, 1990)

Alvarez, José E., 'Financial Responsibility'. In Christopher C. Joyner (ed.), *The United Nations and International Law* (Cambridge, 1997), 409–31

'Institutionalised Legislation and the Asia-Pacific "Region" ' (2007) 5 *New Zealand Journal of Public and International Law*, 9–27

International Organizations as Law-makers (Oxford, 2005)

'Judging the Security Council' (1996) 90 *AJIL*, 1–39

'Legal Remedies and the United Nations' à la Carte Problem' (1991) 12 *Michigan JIL*, 229–311

'Multilateralism and its Discontents' (2000) 11 *EJIL*, 393–411

'Nuremberg Revisited: The *Tadic* Case' (1996) 7 *EJIL*, 245–64

Alzamora, Carlos, 'The UN Compensation Commission: An Overview'. In Richard B. Lillich (ed.), *The United Nations Compensation Commission* (Irvington, NY, 1995), pp. 3–14

d'Amato, Anthony, 'On Consensus' (1970) 8 *Can YIL*, 104–22

Amerasinghe, C. F., 'The Advisory Opinion of the International Court of Justice in the WHO Nuclear Weapons Case: A Critique' (1997) 10 *Leiden JIL*, 525–39

'Financing'. In René-Jean Dupuy (ed.), *Manuel sur les organisations Internationales* (2nd edn, The Hague, 1998), 313–37

Principles of the Institutional Law of International Organizations (Cambridge, 1996)

Angelet, Nicholas, 'Protest against Security Council Decisions'. In Karel Wellens (ed.), *International Law: Theory and Practice. Essays in Honour of Eric Suy* (The Hague, 1998), 277–85

Arangio-Ruiz, Gaetano, 'The "Federal Analogy" and UN Charter Interpretation: A Crucial Issue' (1997) 8 *EJIL*, 1–28

Archer, Clive, *International Organizations* (2nd edn, London, 1992)

Organizing Europe: The Institutions of Integration (2nd edn, London, 1994)

Archibugi, Daniele, 'Models of International Organization in Perpetual Peace Projects' (1992) 18 *Review of International Studies*, 295–317

Arendt, Hannah, *Between Past and Future* (1961; New York, 1993)

Eichmann in Jerusalem: A Report on the Banality of Evil (New York, 1963)

The Human Condition (Chicago, 1958)

Men in Dark Times (San Diego, 1968)

Arsanjani, Mahnoush H., 'Claims against International Organizations: *Quis Custodiet Ipsos Custodes*' (1981) 7 *Yale Journal of World Public Order*, 131–76

Asamoah, Obed Y., *The Legal Significance of the Declarations of the General Assembly of the United Nations* (The Hague, 1966)

Aufricht, Hans, 'Supersession of Treaties in International Law' (1951–2) 37 *Cornell Law Quarterly*, 655–700

Barkin, J. Samuel, *International Organization: Theories and Institutions* (New York, 2006)

Barnett, Michael N., 'Bringing in the New World Order: Liberalism, Legitimacy, and the United Nations' (1997) 49 *World Politics*, 526–51

Rules for the World: International Organizations in Global Politics (Princeton, 2004)

Barnett, Michael N. and Finnemore, Martha, 'The Politics, Power and Pathologies of International Organizations' (1999) 53 *International Organization*, 699–732

Barnett, Michael N. and Solingen, Etel, 'Designed to Fail or Failure of Design? The Origins and Legacy of the Arab League'. In Amitav Acharya and Alastair Iain Johnston (eds.), *Crafting Cooperation: Regional International Institutions in Comparative Perspective* (Cambridge, 2007), 180–220

Barton, John H., 'Two Ideas of International Organization' (1983–4) *Michigan Law Review*, 1520–32

Bauman, Zygmunt, *Modernity and Ambivalence* (Cambridge, 1991)

Beatty, David M., *The Ultimate Rule of Law* (Oxford, 2004)

Beck, Ulrich, *Was ist Globalisierung?* (Frankfurt am Main, 1997)

Becker, Joachim, *Die Anwendbarkeit der Theorie von den implied powers im Recht der Europäischen Gemeinschaften* (Münster, 1976)

Bederman, David J., 'The Souls of International Organizations: Legal Personality and the Lighthouse at Cape Spartel' (1996) 36 *VaJIL*, 275–377

'The Unique Legal Status of the Bank for International Settlements Comes into Focus' (2003) 16 *Leiden JIL*, 787–94

Bedjaoui, Mohammed, *The New World Order and the Security Council: Testing the Legality of its Acts* (Dordrecht, 1994)

Beetham, David, *Bureaucracy*, (2nd edn, Buckingham, 1996)

Behboodi, Rambod, 'Legal Reasoning and the International Law of Trade: The First Steps of the Appellate Body of the WTO' (1998/4) 32 *JWT*, 55–99

Bekker, Peter H. F., *The Legal Position of Intergovernmental Organizations: A Functional Necessity Analysis of their Legal Status and Immunities* (Dordrecht, 1994)

Bennett, Angela, *The Geneva Convention: The Hidden Origins of the Red Cross* (Stroud, 2005)

Berridge, G. R., *Diplomacy: Theory and Practice* (London, 1995)

Bertrand, Christine, 'La nature juridique de l'Organisation pour la Sécurité et de la Coopération en Europe (OSCE)' (1998) 98 *RGDIP*, 365–406

Bertrand, Maurice, 'The Historical Development of Efforts to Reform the UN'. In Adam Roberts and Benedict Kingsbury (eds.), *United Nations, Divided World* (2nd edn, Oxford, 1993), 420–36

Besselink, Leonard, 'Tussen supranationaliteit en soevereiniteit: over het niet-communautaire recht van de Europese Unie'. In Leonard Besselink *et al.*, *Europese Unie en nationale soevereiniteit* (Deventer, 1997), 125–58

Beyerlin, Ulrich, 'Pactum decontrahendo und pactum de negotiando im Völkerrecht?' (1976) 36 *ZaöRV*, 407–43

Bieber, Roland and Salomé, Isabelle, 'Hierarchy of Norms in European Law' (1996) 33 *CMLRev*, 907–30

Biersteker, Thomas J. and Weber, Cynthia (eds.), *State Sovereignty as Social Construct* (Cambridge, 1996)

Binder, Guyora, *Treaty Conflict and Political Contradiction: The Dialectic of Duplicity* (New York, 1988)

Björklund, Martin, 'Responsibility in the EC for Mixed Agreements – Should Non-member Parties Care?' (2001) 70 *Nordic JIL*, 373–402

Blix, Hans, 'The Role of the IAEA in the Development of International Law' (1989) 58 *Nordic JIL*, 231–42

Blokker, Niels M., 'Decisions of International Organizations: The Case of the European Union' (1999) 30 *Neth YIL*, 3–44

'International Organizations and their Members' (2004) 1 *IOLR*, 139–61

'Is the Authorization Authorized? Powers and Practice of the UN Security Council to Authorize the Use of Force by "Coalitions of the Able and Willing" ' (2000) 11 *EJIL*, 541–68

Blokker, Niels M. and Schermers, Henry G., 'Mission Impossible? On the Immunities of Staff Members of International Organizations on Mission'. In Gerhard Hafner *et al.* (eds.), *Liber Amicorum Professor Ignaz Seidl-Hohenveldern in Honour of his 80th Birthday* (The Hague, 1998), 37–54

Boak, A. E. R., 'Greek Interstate Associations and the League of Nations' (1921) 15 *AJIL*, 375–83

Bogdandy, Armin von and Bast, Jürgen (eds.), *Principles of European Constitutional Law* (Oxford, 2005)

Bogdandy, Armin von and Goldmann, Matthias, 'The Exercise of Public Authority through National Policy Assessment' (2008) 5 *IOLR* (forthcoming)

Bölingen, Stefan, *Die Transformation der NATO im Spiegel der Vertragsentwicklung: Zwischen sicherheitspolitischen Herausforderungen und völkerrechtlicher Legitimität* (Saarbrücken, 2007)

Bota, Liviu, 'The Capacity of International Organizations to Conclude Headquarters Agreements, and Some Features of Those Agreements'. In Karl Zemanek (ed.), *Agreements of International Organizations* (Vienna, 1971), 57–104

Bovens, Mark, *The Quest For Responsibility: Accountability and Citizenship in Complex Organisations* (Cambridge, 1998)

Bowett, Derek, 'The Impact of Security Council Decisions on Dispute Settlement Procedures' (1994) 5 *EJIL*, 89–101

The Law of International Institutions (4th edn, London, 1982)

Bowman, M. J., 'The Multilateral Treaty Amendment Process – A Case Study' (1995) 44 *ICLQ*, 540–59

Boyle, Alan E., 'Saving the World? Implementation and Enforcement of International Environmental Law through International Institutions', 3 *Journal of Environmental Law* (1991), 229–45

Boyle, Alan E. and Chinkin, Christine, *The Making of International Law* (Oxford, 2007)

Boyle, James, *Shamans, Software, and Spleens: Law and the Construction of the Information Society* (Cambridge, MA, 1996)

Bradlow, Daniel D. and Schlemmer-Schulte, Sabine, 'The World Bank's New Inspection Panel: A Constructive Step in the Transformation of the International Legal Order' (1994) 54 *ZaöRV*, 392–415

Brierly, J. L., 'The Covenant and the Charter' (1946) 23 *BYIL*, 83–94

Brölmann, Catherine M., *The Institutional Veil in Public International Law: International Organisations and the Law of Treaties* (Oxford, 2007)

'The 1986 Vienna Convention on the Law of Treaties: The History of Draft Article 36*bis*'. In Jan Klabbers and René Lefeber (eds.), *Essays on the Law of Treaties: A Collection of Essays in Honour of Bert Vierdag* (The Hague, 1998), 121–40

Broms, Bengt, *The Doctrine of Equality of States as Applied in International Organizations* (Helsinki, 1959)

'The Slow Renewal Process of the United Nations'. In K. Kiljunen (ed.), *Finns in the United Nations*, (Helsinki, 1996), 270–89

'Subjects: Entitlements in the International Legal System'. In R. St J. MacDonald and D. M. Johnston (eds.), *The Structure and Process of International Law* (The Hague, 1983), 383–423

United Nations (Helsinki, 1990)

Brower, Charles, 'The Hague as Leading Host of International Organizations'. In Agata Fijalkowski (ed.), *International Institutional Reform: 2005 Hague Joint Conference on Contemporary Issues of International Law* (The Hague, 2007), 344–6

Brown, Dan, *The Da Vinci Code* (New York, 2003)

Brownlie, Ian, *Principles of Public International Law* (4th edn, Oxford, 1990)

System of the Law of Nations Part I: State Responsibility (Oxford, 1983)

Buchanan, Ruth, 'Perpetual Peace or Perpetual Process: Global Civil Society and Cosmopolitan Legality at the World Trade Organization' (2003) 16 *Leiden JIL*, 673–99

Buergenthal, Thomas, *Law-making in the International Civil Aviation Organization* (New York, 1969)

Buffard, Isabelle and Zemanek, Karl, 'The "Object and Purpose" of a Treaty: An Enigma?' (1998) 3 *ARIEL*, 311–43

Bühler, Konrad G., *State Succession and Membership in International Organizations: Legal Theories versus Political Pragmatism* (The Hague, 2001)

Búrca, Gráinne de, 'The Drafting of the European Union Charter of Fundamental Rights' (2001) 26 *ELR*, 126–38

'Fundamental Human Rights and the Reach of EC Law' (1993) 13 *Oxford Journal of Legal Studies*, 283–319

Burci, Gian Luca, 'Institutional Adaptation without Reform: WHO and the Challenges of Globalization' (2005) 2 *IOLR*, 437–43

Byers, Michael, *Custom, Power, and the Power of Rules* (Cambridge, 1999)

Cain, Kenneth, Postlewait, Heidi and Thomson, Andrew, *Emergency Sex (and Other Desperate Measures)* (London, 2004)

Cameron, Iain, 'UN Targeted Sanctions, Legal Safeguards and the European Convention on Human Rights' (2003) 72 *Nordic JIL*, 159–214

Cannadine, David (ed.), *The Speeches of Winston Churchill* (London, 1990)

Caron, David D., 'The Legitimacy of the Collective Authority of the Security Council' (1993) 87 *AJIL*, 552–88

Carr, E. H., *The Twenty Years' Crisis 1919–1939* (1939; London, 1981)

Carver, Jeremy, 'Intervention'. In International Law Association, *Report of the Sixty-eighth Conference* (London, 1998), 614

Cass, Deborah Z., 'The "Constitutionalization" of International Trade Law: Judicial Norm-generation as the Engine of Constitutional Development in International Trade' (2001) 12 *EJIL*, 39–75

The Constitutionalization of the World Trade Organization: Legitimacy, Democracy, and Community in the International Trading System (Oxford, 2005)

Cassese, Antonio, 'Consensus and Some of its Pitfalls' (1975) 58 *Rivista di Diritto Internazionale*, 754–61

International Law in a Divided World (Oxford, 1986)

'Remarks on Scelle's Theory of "Role Splitting" *(dédoublement fonctionnel)* in International Law' (1990) 1 *EJIL*, 210–31

Castan, Melissa, 'APEC: International Institution? A Pacific Solution' (1996) 15 *University of Tasmania Law Review*, 52–76

Castaneda, Jorge, *Legal Effects of United Nations Resolutions* (New York, 1969)

Charlesworth, Hilary and Chinkin, Christine, *The Boundaries of International Law: A Feminist Analysis* (Manchester, 2000)

Charney, Jonathan, 'Universal International Law' (1993) 87 *AJIL*, 529–51

Chayes, Abram and Handler Chayes, Antonia, *The New Sovereignty: Compliance with International Regulatory Agreements* (Cambridge, MA, 1995)

Cheng, Bin, 'Introduction to Subjects of International Law'. In Mohammed Bedjaoui (ed.), *International Law: Achievements and Prospects* (Dordrecht, 1991)

'United Nations Resolutions on Outer Space: "Instant" International Customary Law?'. Reproduced in Bin Cheng (ed.), *International Law: Teaching and Practice* (London, 1982), 237–62

Chimni, B. S., 'Co-optation and Resistance: Two Faces of Global Administrative Law' (2005) 37 *New York University Journal of International Law and Politics*, 799–827

'International Institutions Today: An Imperial Global State in the Making' (2004) 15 *EJIL*, 1–37

International Law and World Order: A Critique of Contemporary Approaches (New Delhi, 1993)

Chiu, Hungdah, *The Capacity of International Organizations to Conclude Treaties, and the Special Legal Aspects of the Treaties So Concluded* (The Hague, 1966)

'Succession in International Organisations' (1965) 14 *ICLQ*, 83–120

Churchill, Robin R. and Ulfstein, Geir, 'Autonomous Institutional Arrangements in Multilateral Environmental Agreements: A Little-noticed Phenomenon in International Law' (2000) 94 *AJIL*, 623–59

Ciobanu, Dan, 'Credentials of Delegations and Representation of Member States at the United Nations' (1976) 25 *ICLQ*, 351–81

Clark, Alan, *Diaries* (1993; London, 1999)

Clark, Ian, *Globalization and Fragmentation: International Relations in the Twentieth Century* (Oxford, 1997)

Claude, Inis L., Jr, *Swords into Plowshares: The Problems and Progress of International Organization* (4th edn, New York, 1984)

Coicaud, Jean-Marc and Heiskanen, Veijo (eds.), *The Legitimacy of International Organizations* (Tokyo, 2001)

Commission Européenne, *Corps diplomatique accrédité auprès des Communautés européennes et représentations auprès de la Commission: Décembre 1995* (Luxembourg, 1995)

Conforti, Benedetto, *The Law and Practice of the United Nations* (The Hague, 1997)

Cooker, Chris de (ed.), *Accountability, Investigation and Due Process in International Organizations* (Leiden, 2005)

Cox, Robert W., *Production, Power, and World Order: Social Forces in the Making of History* (New York, 1987)

Craig, Paul, 'Constitutions, Constitutionalism, and the European Union' (2001) 7 *European Law Journal* 125–50

Craig, Paul and De Búrca, Gráinne (eds.), *The Evolution of EU Law* (Oxford, 1999)

Craven, Matthew C. R., 'The European Community Arbitration Commission on Yugoslavia' (1995) 66 *BYIL*, 333–413

Crisp, Roger and Slote, Michael (eds.), *Virtue Ethics* (Oxford, 1997)

Croce, Benedetto, *History of Europe in the Nineteenth Century* (New York, 1933, trans. Furst)

Cross, Eugene D., 'Pre-emption of Member State Law in the European Economic Community: A Framework for Analysis' (1992) 29 *CMLRev*, 447–72

Curtin, Deirdre, 'The Constitutional Structure of the Union: A Europe of Bits and Pieces' (1993) 30 *CMLRev*, 17–69

'EU Police Cooperation and Human Rights Protection: Building the Trellis and Training the Vine', in Ami Barav *et al.*, *Scritti in onore di Giuseppe Federico Mancini, volume II* (Milan, 1998)

Postnational Democracy: The European Union in Search of a Political Philosophy (The Hague, 1997)

Curtin, Deirdre and Dekker, Ige F., 'The EU as a "Layered" International Organization: Institutional Unity in Disguise'. In Paul Craig and Gráinne de Búrca (eds.), *The Evolution of EU Law* (Oxford, 1999), 83–136

Curtin, Deirdre and Nollkaemper, André, 'Conceptualizing Accountibility in International and European Law' (2005) 36 *Neth YIL*, 3–20

Dam, Kenneth W., *GATT: Law and International Economic Organization* (Chicago, 1970)

Danilenko, Gennady M., *Law-making in the International Community* (Dordrecht, 1994)

Dashwood, Alan, 'External Relations Provisions of the Amsterdam Treaty' (1998) 35 *CMLRev*, 1019–45

'Implied External Competence of the EC'. In Martti Koskenniemi (ed.), *International Law Aspects of the European Union* (The Hague, 1998), 113–23

'The Limits of European Community Powers' (1996) 21 *ELR*, 113–28

Dashwood, Alan and Heliskoski, Joni, 'The Classic Authorities Revisited'. In Alan Dashwood and Christophe Hillion (eds.), *The General Law of EC External Relations* (London, 2000), 3–19

Daum, Ulrich, 'INTERPOL – öffentliche Gewalt ohne Kontrolle' (1980) 35 *Juristenzeitung*, 798–801

Davies, Gareth, 'Subsidiarity: The Wrong Idea, in the Wrong Place, at the Wrong Time' (2006) 43 *CMLRev*, 63–84

Dekker, Ige and Wessel, Ramses, ' "Lowering the Corporate Veil": Het recht der internationale organisaties vanuit de institutionele rechtstheorie'. In M. A. Heldeweg *et al.* (eds.), *De regel meester: Opstellen voor Dick W. P. Ruiter* (Enschede, 2001)

Denys, Christine, *Impliciete bevoegdheden in de Europese Economische Gemeenschap: Een onderzoek naar de betekenis van 'implied powers'* (Antwerp, 1990)

Detter, Ingrid, *Law Making by International Organizations* (Stockholm, 1965)

Dickie, John, *Inside the Foreign Office* (London, 1992)

Diepen, Remco van, *Voor Volkenbond en vrede: Nederland en het streven naar een nieuwe wereldorde 1919–1946* (Amsterdam, 1999)

Doehring, Karl, 'Unlawful Resolutions of the Security Council and their Legal Consequences' (1997) 1 *Max Planck Yearbook of United Nations Law*, 91–109

Dormoy, Daniel, 'Aspects récents de la question du financement des opérations de maintien de la paix de l'Organisation des Nations Unies' (1993) 39 *AFDI*, 131–56

'Recent Developments Regarding the Law on Participation in International Organisations'. In Karel Wellens (ed.), *International Law, Theory and Practice. Essays in Honour of Eric Suy* (The Hague, 1998), 323–32

Dossal, Amir A., 'United Nations Partnerships: Working Together for a Better World'. In Roy S. Lee (ed.), *Swords into Plowshares: Building Peace Through the United Nations* (Leiden, 2006), 139–57

Dugard, John, *Recognition and the United Nations* (Cambridge, 1987)

Durch, William J., 'Paying the Tab: Financial Crises'. In William J. Durch (ed.), *The Evolution of UN Peacekeeping: Case Studies and Comparative Analysis* (New York, 1993), 39–58

Dworkin, Ronald, *Law's Empire* (London, 1986)

Eagleton, Clyde, 'International Organization and the Law of Responsibility' (1959/I) 76 *RdC*, 319–425

Economidès, Constantin P. and Kolliopoulos, Alexandros G., 'La clause de déconnexion en faveur du droit communautaire: une pratique critiquable' (2006) 110 *RGDIP*, 273–302

Ehlermann, C. D., 'The Financing of the Community: The Distinction between Financial Contributions and Own Resources' (1982) 19 *CMLRev*, 571–89

Eldar, Ofer, 'Vote-trading in International Institutions' (2008) 19 *EJIL*, 3–41

Eleftheriadis, Pavlos, 'The Direct Effect of Community Law: Conceptual Issues' (1996) 16 *YEL*, 205–21

El-Erian, Abdullah, 'Preliminary Report on the Second Part of the Topic of Relations between States and International Organizations' (1997/II, pt 1) *YbILC*, 139–55

Elias, T. O., 'Modern Sources of International Law'. In Wolfgang Friedmann *et al.* (eds.), *Transnational Law in a Changing Society: Essays in Honor of Philip C. Jessup* (New York, 1972), 34–69

Elliott, Mark, 'The Ultra Vires Doctrine in a Constitutional Setting: Still the Central Principle of Administrative Law' (1999) 58 *Cambridge Law Journal*, 129–58

Engström, Viljam, 'Implied Powers of International Organizations: On the Character of a Legal Doctrine' (2003) 14 *FYIL*, 129–57

Erskine, Toni (ed.), *Can Institutions Have Responsibilities? Collective Moral Agency and International Relations* (Basingstoke, 2003)

Esty, Daniel C., 'Good Governance at the Supranational Scale: Globalizing Administrative Law' (2006) 115 *Yale Law Journal*, 1490–1562

Everling, Ulrich, 'Reflections on the Structure of the European Union' (1992) 29 *CMLRev*, 1053–77

    'Sind die Mitgliedstaaten der Europäischen Gemeinschaft noch Herren der Verträge? Zum Verhältnis von Europäischem Gemeinschaftsrecht und Völkerrecht'. In Rudolf Bernhardt *et al.* (eds.), *Völkerrecht als Rechtsordnung, internationale Gerichtsbarkeit, Menschenrechte: Festschrift für Hermann Mosler* (Berlin, 1983), 173–91

    'Zur Stellung der Mitgliedstaaten der Europäischen Union als "Herren der Verträge"'. In Ulrich Beyerlin *et al.* (eds.), *Recht zwischen Umbruch und Bewahrung: Festschrift für Rudolf Bernhardt* (Berlin, 1995), 1161–76

Falk, Richard A., *Human Rights Horizons* (New York, 2000)

Farrall, Jeremy Matam, *United Nations Sanctions and the Rule of Law* (Cambridge, 2007)

Fassbender, Bardo, *Targeted Sanctions and Due Process* (New York, 2006)

    'The United Nations Charter as Constitution of the International Community' (1998) 36 *Columbia JTL*, 529–619

Fasulo, Linda, *An Insider's Guide to the UN* (New Haven CT, 2004)

Fennesy, J. G., 'The 1975 Vienna Convention on the Representation of States in their Relations with International Organizations of a Universal Character' (1976) 70 *AJIL*, 62–72

Feuerle, Loie, 'Informal Consultation: A Mechanism in Security Council Decisionmaking' (1985) 18 *New York University Journal of International Law & Politics*, 267–308

Fidler, David P., 'The Future of the World Health Organization: What Role for International Law?' (1998) 31 *Vanderbilt JTL*, 1079–126

Finger, Matthias and Magarinos-Ruchat, Bérangère, 'The Transformation of International Public Organizations: The Case of UNCTAD'. In Dennis Dijkzeul and Yves Beigbeder (eds.), *Rethinking International Organizations: Pathology and Promise* (New York, 2003), 140–65

Fischer-Lescano, Andreas and Teubner, Gunther, *Regime-Kollisionen: Zur Fragmentierung des globalen Rechts* (Frankfurt am Main, 2006)

Fischer Williams, John, *Chapters on Current International Law and the League of Nations* (London, 1929)

Fitzmaurice, Sir Gerald, 'Fourth Report on the Law of Treaties' (1959/II) YbILC

'Some Problems Regarding the Formal Sources of International Law'. In F. M. van Asbeck *et al.* (eds.), *Symbolae Verzijl* (The Hague, 1958), 153–76

Fleischhauer, Carl-August, 'The Constitutional Relationship between the Secretary-General of the United Nations and the International Court of Justice'. In Georges Abi-Saab *et al.*, *Paix, développement, démocratie: Boutros Boutros-Ghali Amicorum Discipulorumque* (Brussels, 1999), 451–74

Footer, Mary E., *An Institutional and Normative Analysis of the World Trade Organization* (Leiden, 2006)

Foster, Robert J., *Coca-Globalization: Following Soft Drinks from New York to New Guinea* (New York, 2008)

Fox, Hazel, 'The Advisory Opinion on the Difference Relating to Immunity from Legal Process of a Special Rapporteur of the Commission of Human Rights: Who has the Last Word on Judicial Independence?' (1999) 12 *Leiden JIL*, 889–918

'State Responsibility and Tort Proceedings against a Foreign State in Municipal Courts' (1989) 20 *Neth YIL*, 3–34

Francioni, Francesco, 'Multilateralism à la Carte: The Limits to Unilateral Withholdings of Assessed Contributions to the UN Budget' (2000) 11 *EJIL*, 43–59

Franck, Thomas M., *The Empowered Self: Law and Society in the Age of Individualism* (Oxford, 1999)

Fairness in International Law and Institutions (Oxford, 1995)

Nation against Nation: What Happened to the UN Dream and What the US Can Do about it (Oxford, 1985)

The Power of Legitimacy among Nations (Oxford, 1990)

'The "Powers of Appreciation": Who is the Ultimate Guardian of UN Legality?' (1992) 86 *AJIL*, 519–23

Franck, Thomas M. and Nolte, Georg, 'The Good Offices Function of the UN Secretary-General'. In Adam Roberts and Benedict Kingsbury (eds.), *United Nations, Divided World* (2nd edn, Oxford, 1993), 143–82

Frid, Rachel, 'The European Economic Community – A Member of a Specialized Agency of the United Nations' (1993) 4 *EJIL*, 239–55

The Relations Between the EC and International Organizations: Legal Theory and Practice (The Hague, 1995)

Friedmann, Wolfgang, *The Changing Structure of International Law* (New York, 1964)

Frost, Mervyn, *Ethics and International Relations: A Constitutive Theory* (Cambridge, 1996)

Frowein, Jochen A., 'Are there Limits to the Amendment Procedures in Treaties Constituting International Organisations?'. In Gerhard Hafner *et al.* (eds.), *Liber Amicorum Professor Ignaz Seidl-Hohenveldern in Honour of his 80th Birthday* (The Hague, 1998), 201–18

'Reactions by Not Directly Affected States to Breaches of Public International Law' (1994/IV) 248 *RdC*, 347–437

Fuller, Lon L., *The Morality of Law*, rev. edn (New Haven CT, 1969)

Gaeta, Paola, 'The Dayton Agreements and International Law' (1996) 7 *EJIL*, 147–63

Gaillard, Emmanuel and Pingel-Lenuzza, Isabelle, 'International Organisations and Immunity from Jurisdiction: To Restrict or to Bypass?' (2002) 51 *ICLQ*, 1–15

Galbreath, David, *The Organization for Security and Cooperation in Europe* (London, 2007)

Gardner, Lloyd C., *Architects of Illusion: Men and Ideas in American Foreign Policy 1941–1949* (Chicago, 1970)

Gauweiler, Marijke, *Die rechtliche Qualifikation interorganschaftlicher Absprachen im Europarecht* (Mainz, 1988)

Gerstenberg, Oliver, 'Denationalization and the Very Idea of Democratic Constitutionalism: The Case of the European Community' (2001) 14 *Ratio Juris*, 298–325

Giddens, Anthony and Hutton, Will, 'Fighting Back'. In Will Hutton and Anthony Giddens (eds.), *On the Edge: Living with Global Capitalism* (London, 2001), 213–23

Ginther, Konrad, *Die völkerrechtliche Verantwortlichkeit internationaler Organisationen gegenüber Drittstaaten* (Vienna, 1969)

Glennon, Michael J., *Constitutional Diplomacy* (Princeton, 1990)

Goldsmith, Jack L. and Posner, Eric A., *The Limits of International Law* (Oxford, 2005)

Gowa, Joanne, *Ballots and Bullets: The Elusive Democratic Peace* (Princeton, 1999)

Gowlland-Debbas, Vera, 'The Function of the United Nations Security Council in the International Legal System'. In Michael Byers (ed.), *The Role of Law in International Politics: Essays in International Relations and International Law* (Oxford, 2000), 277–313

Granvik, Lena, *The Treaty-making Competence of the European Community in the Field of International Environmental Conventions* (Helsinki, 1999)

Gras, Jutta, *The European Union and Human Rights Monitoring* (Helsinki, 2000) *Monitoring the Convention on the Rights of the Child* (Helsinki, 2001)

Gray, Christine, *Judicial Remedies in International Law* (Oxford, 1987)

Grieco, Joseph M., 'Anarchy and the Limits of Cooperation' (1988) 42 *International Organization*, 485–508

Griffiths, John, 'Is Law Important?' (1979) 54 *New York University Law Review*, 339–74

Gruber, Judith E., *Controlling Bureaucracies: Dilemmas in Bureaucratic Governance* (Berkeley, 1987)

Gruber, Lloyd, 'Power Politics and the Free Trade Bandwagon' (2001) 34 *Comparative Political Studies*, 703–41

Guzman, Andrew T., *How International Law Works: A Rational Choice Theory* (Oxford, 2008)

Haas, Ernst B., *Beyond the Nation-State* (Stanford, 1964)

Habermas, Jürgen, *The Divided West* (Cambridge, 2006, Cronin trans.)

Haggard, Stephan and Simmons, Beth A., 'Theories of International Regimes' (1987) 41 *International Organization* 491–517

Hahn, Hugo J., 'Continuity in the Law of International Organization' (1964) 13 *ÖZöR*, 167–239

Hailbronner, Kay, 'Die Immunität von Europol-Bediensteten' (1998) 53 *Juristenzeitung*, 283–9

Halpin, Andrew, 'The Concept of a Legal Power' (1996) 16 *Oxford Journal of Legal Studies*, 129–52

Hambro, Edvard, 'Permanent Representatives to International Organizations' (1976) 30 *Yearbook of World Affairs*, 30–41

Happold, Matthew, 'Security Council Resolution 1373 and the Constitution of the United Nations' (2003) 16 *Leiden JIL*, 593–610

Harlow, Carol, 'Global Administrative Law: The Quest for Principles and Values' (2006) 17 *EJIL*, 187–214

Harmon, Michael, *Responsibility as Paradox: A Critique of Rational Discourse on Government* (Thousand Oaks, CA, 1995)

Hart, H. L. A., *The Concept of Law* (Oxford, 1961)
  Punishment and Responsibility: Essays in the Philosophy of Law (Oxford, 1968)

Hartley, Trevor C., 'The Constitutional Foundations of the European Union' (2001) 117 *Law Quarterly Review*, 225–46
  The Foundations of European Community Law (3rd edn, Oxford, 1994)

Hartmann, Gunther, 'The Capacity of International Organizations to Conclude Treaties'. In Karl Zemanek (ed.), *Agreements of International Organizations* (Vienna, 1971), 127–63

Hartwig, Matthias, *Die Haftung der Mitgliedstaaten für internationale Organisationen* (Berlin, 1993)

Hatzopoulos, Vassilis, 'Why the Open Method of Coordination is Bad for You: A Letter to the EU' (2007) 13 *European Law Journal*, 309–42

Heiskanen, Veijo, 'The Rationality of the Use of Force and the Evolution of International Organization'. In Jean-Marc Coicaud and Veijo Heiskanen (eds.), *The Legitimacy of International Organizations* (Tokyo, 2001)
  International Legal Topics (Helsinki, 1992)

Heliskoski, Joni, 'The Jurisdiction of the European Court of Justice to Give Preliminary Rulings on the Interpretation of Mixed Agreements' (2000) 69 *Nordic JIL*, 395–412
  Mixed Agreements as a Technique for Organizing the International Relations of the European Community and its Member States (The Hague, 2001)

Siv Hellén, 'The Establishment and Development of the Nordic Investment Bank – An Institution Sui Generis'. In Sabine Schlemmer-Schulte and Ko-Yung Tung (eds.), *Liber Amicorum Ibrahim F.I. Shihata* (The Hague, 2001), 401–27

Henkin, Louis, *International Law: Politics and Values* (Dordrecht, 1995)
  'International Law: Politics, Values and Functions' (1989/ IV) 216 *RdC*, 9–416

Herbst, Jeffrey, 'Crafting Regional Cooperation in Africa'. In Amitav Acharya and Alastair Iain Johnston (eds.), *Crafting Cooperation: Regional International Institutions in Comparative Perspective* (Cambridge, 2007), 129–44

Heusel, Wolfgang, *'Weiches' Völkerrecht* (Baden Baden, 1991)

Hey, Ellen, 'The World Bank Inspection Panel: Towards the Recognition of a New Legally Relevant Relationship to International Law' (1997) 2 *Hofstra Law and Policy Symposium*, 61–74

Higgins, Rosalyn, *The Development of International Law through the Political Organs of the United Nations* (Oxford, 1963)

Hilf, Meinhard, 'The ECJ's Opinion 1/94 on the WTO – No Surprise, but Wise?' (1995) 6 *EJIL*, 245–59

Hirsch, Burkhard, 'Immunität für Europol – eine Polizei über dem Gesetz?' (1998) 31 *Zeitschrift für Rechtspolitik*, 10–13

Hirsch, Moshe, *The Responsibility of International Organizations toward Third Parties: Some Basic Principles* (Dordrecht, 1995)

Hirschman, Albert O., *Exit, Voice, and Loyalty: Responses to Decline in Firms, Organizations, and States* (Cambridge, MA, 1970)

Hodson, Dermot and Maher, Imelda, 'The Open Method as a New Mode of Governance: The Case of Soft Economic Policy Coordination' (2001) 39 *JCMS*, 719–46

Hoekman, Bernard and Kostecki, Michel, *The Political Economy of the World Trading System: From GATT to WTO* (Oxford, 1995)

Hoelscher, Christoph and Wolffgang, Hans-Michael, 'The Wassenaar-Arrangement between International Trade, Non-proliferation, and Export Controls' (1998/I) 32 *JWT*, 45–63

Hoffmann, Stanley, 'International Systems and International Law'. In Klaus Knorr and Sydney Verba (eds.), *The International System: Theoretical Essays* (Princeton, 1961), 205–37

Hofstadter, Richard and Hofstadter, Beatrice K. (eds.), *Great Issues in American History, Vol. III: From Reconstruction to the Present Day, 1864–1981* (rev. edn, New York, 1982)

Hohfeld, Wesley N., *Fundamental Legal Conceptions as Applied in Judicial Reasoning* (1919; Westport, CN, 1978)

Hoof, G. J. H. van, *Rethinking the Sources of International Law* (Deventer, 1983)

Horn, Frank, *Reservations and Interpretative Declarations to Multilateral Treaties* (Amsterdam, 1988)

Horwitz, Morton J., *The Transformation of American Law 1870–1960: The Crisis of Legal Orthodoxy* (Oxford, 1992)

Howard, Michael, *The Invention of Peace: Reflections on War and International Order* (London, 2000)

Howse, Robert, 'The Legitimacy of the World Trade Organization'. In Jean-Marc Coicaud and Veijo Heiskanen (eds.), *The Legitimacy of International Organizations* (Tokyo, 2001), 355–407

Hoyt, Edwin C., *The Unanimity Rule in the Revision of Treaties: A Re-examination* (The Hague, 1959)

Huber, Max, *Die soziologischen Grundlagen des Völkerrechts* (1910; Berlin, 1928)

Hudec, Robert E., *The GATT Legal System and World Trade Diplomacy* (New York, 1975)

Hüfner, Klaus, 'Financing the United Nations: The Role of the United States'. In Dennis Dijkzeul and Yves Beigbeder (eds.), *Rethinking International Organizations: Pathology and Promise* (New York, 2003), 29–53

Hurd, Ian, *After Anarchy: Legitimacy and Power in the United Nations Security Council* (Princeton, 2007)

Hutton, Will and Giddens, Anthony (eds.), *On the Edge: Living with Global Capitalism* (London, 2001)

Huxley, Julian, *Memories II* (Harmondsworth, 1973)

Hylton, Daniel N., 'Default Breakdown: The Vienna Convention on the Law of Treaties' Inadequate Framework on Reservations' (1994) 27 *Vanderbilt JTL*, 419–51

Ikenberry, G. John, 'Institutions, Strategic Restraint, and the Persistence of American Postwar Order' (1998–9) 23 *International Security*, 43–78

International Law Association, *Report of the Sixty-eighth Conference (The Taipei Conference)* (London, 1998)

Jackson, John H., 'Dispute Settlement and the WTO: Emerging Problems' (1998) 1 *JIEL*, 329–51

'The Jurisprudence of International Trade: The DISC Case in GATT' (1978) 72 *AJIL*, 747–81

World Trade and the Law of GATT (Indianapolis, 1969)

Jacobi, Susanne, 'The OSCE Court: An Overview' (1997) 10 *Leiden JIL*, 281–94

Jans, Jan H., 'Autonomie van de wetgever? Voorafgaande bemoeienis van Europese instellingen met nationale regelgeving'. In Leonard Besselink *et al.*, *Europese Unie en nationale soevereiniteit* (Deventer, 1997), 51–113

'National Legislative Autonomy? The Procedural Constraints of European Law' (1998/I) 25 *LIEI*, 25–58

Jansson, Kurt, 'The United Nations Before and Now'. In Kiljunen (ed.), *Finns in the United Nations*, 33–60

Jawara, Fatoumata and Kwa, Aileen, *Behind the Scenes at the WTO: The Real World of International Trade Negotiations* (updated edn, London, 2004)

Jenks, C. Wilfred, *International Immunities* (London, 1961)

Law in the World Community (London, 1967)

'The Revision of the Constitution of the International Labour Organization' (1946) 23 *BYIL*, 303–17

'Unanimity, the Veto, Weighted Voting, Special and Simple Majorities and Consensus as Modes of Decision in International Organisations'. In D. W. Bowett *et al.*, *Cambridge Essays in International Law: Essays in Honour of Lord McNair* (London, 1965) 48–63

Jennings, Sir Robert Y., 'General Course on Principles of International Law' (1967/II) 121 *RdC*, 323–606

'Law-making and Package Deal'. In Roberto Ago *et al.* (eds.), *Mélanges offerts à Paul Reuter. Le droit international: unité et diversité* (Paris, 1981), 347–55

'Nullity and Effectiveness in International Law'. In D. W. Bowett *et al.*, *Cambridge Essays in International Law: Essays in Honour of Lord McNair* (London, 1965), 64–87

Kaddous, Christine, 'L'Arrêt France c. Commission de 1994 (accord concurrence) et le contrôle de la légalité des accords externes en vertu de l'art. 173 CE: la difficile réconciliation de l'orthodoxie communautaire avec l'orthodoxie internationale' (1996) 32 *CDE*, 613–33

Kamminga, Menno T., 'State Succession in Respect of Human Rights Treaties' (1996) 7 *EJIL*, 469–84

Kaniel, Moshe, *The Exclusive Treaty-making Power of the European Community up to the Period of the Single European Act* (The Hague, 1996)

Kant, Immanuel, *Zum ewigen Frieden: Ein philosophischer Entwurf* (1795; Stuttgart, 1984)

Kapteyn, P. J. G. and VerLoren van Themaat, P., *Inleiding tot het recht van de Europese Gemeenschappen na Maastricht* (5th rev. edn, Deventer, 1995)

Introduction to the Law of the European Communities (3rd rev. edn, The Hague, 1998, ed. L. Gormley)

Kapteyn, P. J. G., *et al.* (eds.) *International Organization and Integration: Annotated Basic Documents and Descriptive Directory of International Organizations and Arrangements* (2nd rev. edn, The Hague, 1981–4)

Keith, Kenneth J., *The Extent of the Advisory Jurisdiction of the International Court of Justice* (Leiden, 1971)

Kelsen, Hans, *Introduction to the Problems of Legal Theory* (1934; Oxford, 1992, trans. Litschewski Paulson and Paulson)

Kennedy, David, 'Challenging Expert Rule: The Politics of Global Governance' (2005) 27 *Sydney Law Review*, 5–28

'A New World Order: Yesterday, Today, and Tomorrow' (1994) 4 *Transnational Law and Contemporary Problems*, 1–47

International Legal Structures (Baden Baden, 1987)

'Receiving the International' (1994) 10 *Conn JIL*, 1–26

'The Move to Institutions' (1987) 8 *Cardozo Law Review*, 841–988

Kennedy, Paul, *The Parliament of Man: The Past, Present, and Future of the United Nations* (New York, 2006)

Keohane, Robert O., *After Hegemony: Cooperation and Discord in the World Political Economy* (Princeton, 1984)

'International Relations and International Law: Two Optics' (1997) 38 *Harvard ILJ*, 487–502

Kiljunen, Kimmo (ed.), *Finns in the United Nations* (Helsinki, 1996)

Killmann, Bernd-Roland, 'Procurement Activities of International Organizations – An Attempt at a First Insight in Evolving Legal Principles' (2003) 8 *ARIEL*, 277–300

Kingsbury, Benedict, 'The Concept of Compliance as a Function of Competing Conceptions of International Law'. In Edith Brown Weiss (ed.), *International Compliance with Nonbinding Accords* (Washington, 1997), 49–80

Kingsbury, Benedict, Krisch, Nico and Stewart, Richard B., 'The Emergence of Global Administrative Law' (2005) 68 *Law and Contemporary Problems*, 15–61

Kirgis, Frederic L., Jr, *International Organizations in their Legal Setting* (2nd edn, St Paul, MN, 1993)

'The Security Council's First Fifty Years' (1995) 89 *AJIL*, 506–39

'Specialized Law-making Processes'. In Christopher C. Joyner (ed.), *The United Nations and International Law* (Cambridge, 1997), 65–94

Klabbers, Jan, book review of José E. Alvarez, *International Organizations as Law-makers* (2006) 3 *IOLR*, 153–7

Book review of C. F. Amerasinghe, *Principles of the Institutional Law of International Organizations* (1997) 66 *Nordic JIL*, 553–5

'The *Bustani* Case before the ILOAT: Constitutionalism in Disguise?' (2004) 53 *ICLQ*, 455–64

'The Changing Image of International Organizations'. In Jean-Marc Coicaud and Veijo Heiskanen (eds.), *The Legitimacy of International Organizations*, 221–55

'Checks and Balances in the Law of International Organizations'. In Mortimer Sellers (ed.), *Autonomy in the Law* (Dordrecht, 2007), 141–63

'Compliance Procedures'. In Daniel Bodansky, Jutta Brunnée and Ellen Hey (eds.), *The Oxford Handbook of International Environmental Law* (Oxford, 2007), 995–1009

'The Concept of Legal Personality' (2005) 11 *Ius Gentium*, 35–66

The Concept of Treaty in International Law (The Hague, 1996)

'Constitutionalism Lite' (2004) 1 *IOLR* 31–58

'The General, the Lords, and the Possible End of State Immunity' (1999) 68 *Nordic JIL*, 85–95

'(I Can't Get No) Recognition: Subjects Doctrine and the Emergence of Non-state Actors'. In Jarna Petman and Jan Klabbers (eds.), *Nordic Cosmopolitanism: Essays in International Law for Martti Koskenniemi* (Leiden, 2003), 351–69

'Informal Instruments before the European Court of Justice' (1994) 31 *CMLRev*, 997–1023

'Institutional Ambivalence by Design: Soft Organizations in International Law' (2001) 70 *Nordic JIL*, 403–21

'International Law in Community Law: The Law and Politics of Direct Effect' (2002) 21 *YEL*, 263–98

'International Organizations in the Formation of Customary International Law'. In Enzo Cannizzaro and Paolo Palchetti (eds.), *Customary International Law on the Use of Force* (Leiden, 2005), 197–95

'Introduction'. In Klabbers (ed.), *International Organizations*, xi–xxv

'Kadi Justice at the Security Council?' (2007) 4 *IOLR* 293–304

'The Life and Times of the Law of International Organizations' (2001) *Nordic JIL*, 287–317

'The New Dutch Law on the Approval of Treaties' (1995) 44 *ICLQ*, 629–43

'Off Limits? International Law and the Excessive Use of Force' (2006) 7 *Theoretical Inquiries in Law*, 59–80

'On Babies, Bathwater, and the Three Musketeers, or the Beginning of the End of European Integration'. In Veijo Heiskanen and Kati Kulovesi (eds.), *Function and Future of European Law* (Helsinki, 1999), 275–81

'On Rationalism in Politics: Interpretation of Treaties and the World Trade Organization' (2005) 74 *Nordic JIL* 405–28

'Over het leerstuk der impliciete bevoegdheden in het recht der internationale organisaties'. In Hanneke Steenbergen (ed.), *Ongebogen recht: Opstellen aangeboden aan prof. dr. H. Meijers* (The Hague, 1998), 1–11

'Presumptive Personality: The European Union in International Law'. In Martti Koskenniemi (ed.), *International Law Aspects of the European Union* (The Hague, 1998), 231–53

'The Redundancy of Soft Law' (1996) 65 *Nordic JIL*, 167–82

'Reflections on the Politics of Institutional Reform'. In Peter Danchin and Horst Fischer (eds.), *United Nations Reform and the New Collective Security* (Cambridge, 2009, forthcoming)

'Restraints on the Treaty-making Powers of Member States Deriving from EU Law'. In Enzo Cannizaro (ed.), *The European Union as an Actor in International Relations* (The Hague, 2002), 151–75

'Safeguarding the Organizational *Acquis*: The EU's External Practice' (2007) 4 *IOLR*, 57–89

'Some Problems regarding the Object and Purpose of Treaties' (1997) 8 *FYIL*, 138–60

'Straddling Law and Politics: Judicial Review in International Law'. In R. St J. MacDonald and D. M. Johnston (eds.), *Towards World Constitutionalism* (Leiden, 2005), 809–35

Treaty Conflict and the European Union (Cambridge, 2009)

'Two Concepts of International Organization' (2005) 2 *IOLR* 277–93

'The Undesirability of Soft Law' (1998) 67 *Nordic JIL*, 381–91

(ed.), *International Organizations* (Aldershot, 2005)

Klabbers, Jan and Koskenniemi, Martti, 'Succession in Respect of State Property, Archives and Debts, and Nationality'. In Klabbers *et al.* (eds.), *State Practice* (The Hague, 1999), 118–45

Klabbers, Jan and Vreugdenhil, Annerie, 'Dispute Settlement in GATT: DISC and its Successor' (1986/I) *LIEI*, 115–38

Klabbers, Jan, *et al.* (eds.), *State Practice regarding State Succession and Issues of Recognition* (The Hague, 1999)

Klein, Naomi, *The Shock Doctrine* (London, 2007)

Klein, Pierre, *La responsabilité des organisations internationales dans les ordres juridiques internes et en droit des gens* (Brussels, 1998)

'Quelques réflexions sur le principe de spécialité et la "politisation" des institutions spécialisées'. In Laurence Boisson de Chazournes and Philippe Sands (eds.), *International Law, the International Court of Justice and Nuclear Weapons* (Cambridge, 1999), 78–91

Köck, Heribert Franz, 'Die "implied powers" der Europäischen Gemeinschaften als Anwendungsfall der "implied powers" internationaler Organisationen überhaupt'. In Karl-Heinz Böckstiegel *et al.* (eds.), *Völkerrecht, Recht der internationalen Organisationen, Weltwirtschaftsrecht: Festschrift für Ignaz Seidl-Hohenveldern* (Cologne, 1988), 279–99

'Questions Related to the Recognition of the European Communities' (1997) 2 *ARIEL*, 49–68

Koh, Harold Hongju, 'Transnational Public Law Litigation' (1991) 100 *Yale Law Journal*, 2347–402

Koho, Lauri, 'Military Advisor in the Office of the Secretary-General'. In Kimmo Kiljunen (ed.), *Finns in the United Nations* (Helsinki, 1996), 105–33

Koivisto, Mauno, *Witness to History* (London, 1997)

Koivurova, Timo, 'The Legal Status of Arctic Cooperation'. In Lassi Heininen and Gunnar Lassinantti (eds.), *Security in the European North: From 'Hard' To 'Soft'* (Rovaniemi, 1999), 143–60

Koopmans, T., 'The Role of Law in the Next Stage of European Integration' (1986) 35 *ICLQ*, 925–31

Koremonos, Barbara, Lipson, Charles and Snidal, Duncan (eds.), *The Rational Design of International Institutions* (Cambridge, 2004)

Korhonen, Outi, Gras, Jutta and Creutz, Katja, *International Post-Conflict Situations: Challenges for Co-operative Governance* (2nd edn, Helsinki, 2001)

Koschorrek, Wilfried, 'Financial Crisis'. In Rüdiger Wolfrum (ed.), *United Nations: Law, Policies and Practice, Volume I* (Munich, 1995), 523–31

Koskenmäki, Riikka, 'Legal Implications Resulting from State Failure in Light of the Case of Somalia' (2004) 73 *Nordic JIL*, 1–36

Koskenniemi, Martti, 'Breach of Treaty or Non-compliance? Reflections on the Enforcement of the Montreal Protocol' (1992) 3 *Yearbook of International Environmental Law*, 123–62

'Constitutionalism as Mindset: Reflections on Kantian Themes about International Law and Globalization' (2007) 8 *Theoretical Inquiries in Law*, 9–36

'Faith, Identity, and the Killing of the Innocent: International Lawyers and Nuclear Weapons' (1997) 10 *Leiden JIL*, 137–62

'The Fate of Public International Law: Between Technique and Politics' (2007) 70 *Modern Law Review*, 1–30

Fragmentation of International Law: Difficulties Arising from the Diversification and Expansion of International Law. Report of the Study Group of the International Law Commission (Helsinki, 2007)

From Apology to Utopia: The Structure of International Legal Argument (Helsinki, 1989)

'The Future of Statehood' (1991) 32 *Harvard ILJ*, 397–410

The Gentle Civilizer of Nations: The Rise and Fall of International Law 1870–1960 (Cambridge, 2001)

'Hierarchy in International Law: A Sketch' (1997) 8 *EJIL*, 566–82

'International Law Aspects of the Common Foreign and Security Policy'. In Martti Koskenniemi (ed.), *International Law Aspects of the European Union*, 27–44

'Lauterpacht: The Victorian Tradition in International Law' (1997) 8 *EJIL*, 215–63

'Le Comité de Sanctions (créé par la résolution 661 (1990) du Conseil de Sécurité)' (1991) 37 *AFDI*, 119–37

'The Police in the Temple. Order, Justice and the UN: A Dialectical View' (1995) 6 *EJIL*, 325–48

'The Politics of International Law' (1990) 1 *EJIL*, 4–32

'The Preamble of the Universal Declaration of Human Rights'. In Gudmundur Alfredsson and Asbjorn Eide (eds.), *The Universal Declaration of Human Rights* (The Hague, 1999), 27–39

'The Wonderful Artificiality of States' (1994) 88 *Proceedings of the American Society of International Law*, 22–9

(ed.), *International Law Aspects of the European Union* (The Hague, 1998)

Koutrakos, Panos, *EU International Relations Law* (Oxford, 2006)

Krasner, Stephen D. (ed.), *International Regimes* (Ithaca, 1983)

Kratochwil, Friedrich, *Rules, Norms, and Decisions* (Cambridge, 1989)

Kufuor, Koti Ofeng, 'Securing Compliance with the Judgments of the ECOWAS Court of Justice' (1996) 8 *African Journal of International & Comparative Law*, 1–11

Kumm, Matthias, 'The Legitimacy of International Law: A Constitutionalist Framework for Analysis' (2004) 15 *EJIL*, 907–31

Kunz, Josef L., 'Privileges and Immunities of International Organizations' (1947) 41 *AJIL*, 828–62

Kuosmanen, Taru, *Bringing Justice Closer: Hybrid Courts in Post-conflict Societies* (Helsinki, 2007)

Kuyper, Pieter Jan, 'The Netherlands and International Organizations'. In H. F. van Panhuys *et al.* (eds.), *International Law in the Netherlands, Volume II* (Alphen aan den Rijn, 1979), 3–41

Kuyper, Pieter Jan and Paasivirta, Esa, 'Further Exploring International Responsibility: The European Community and the ILC's Project on Responsibility of International Organizations' (2004) 1 *IOLR*, 111–38

Lane, Jan-Erik, *Constitutions and Political Theory* (Manchester, 1996)

Lang Jr., Anthony, 'The United Nations and the Fall of Srebrenica: Meaningful Responsibility and International Society'. In Toni Erskine (ed.), *Can Institutions Have Responsibilities? Collective Moral Agency and International Relations* (Basingstoke, 2003), 183–203

Langhorne, Richard, 'Establishing International Organisations: The Concert and the League' (1990) 1 *Diplomacy and Statecraft*, 1–18

Lansing, Robert, *The Peace Negotiations: A Personal Narrative* (Boston, 1921)

Lasok, Dominie and Bridge, J. W., *Law and Institutions of the European Community* (5th edn, London, 1991)

Lauterpacht, Elihu, *Aspects of the Administration of International Justice* (Cambridge, 1991)

'The Development of the Law of International Organization by the Decisions of International Tribunals' (1976/IV) 152 *RdC*, 381–478

'Judicial Review of the Acts of International Organizations'. In Laurence Boisson de Chazournes and Philippe Sands (eds.), *International Law, the International Court of Justice and Nuclear Weapons* (Cambridge, 1999), 92–102

'The Legal Effect of Illegal Acts of International Organisations'. In D. W. Bowett *et al.*, *Cambridge Essays in International Law: Essays in Honour of Lord McNair* (London, 1965), 88–121

Lauterpacht, Hersch, *The Function of Law in the International Community* (Oxford, 1933)

Lauwaars, Richard H., *Lawfulness and Legal Force of Community Decisions* (Leiden, 1973)

Lauwaars, Richard H. and Timmermans, C. W. A., *Europees Gemeenschapsrecht in kort bestek* (3rd edn, Groningen, 1994)

Lavalle, Roberto, 'The "Inherent" Powers of the UN Secretary-General in the Political Sphere: A Legal Analysis' (1990) 37 *Neth ILR*, 22–36

Lawson, Rick, *Het EVRM en de Europese Gemeenschappen* (Deventer, 1999)

Lee, Lawrence L. C., 'The Basle Accords as Soft Law: Strengthening International Banking Supervision' (1998) 39 *VaJIL*, 1–40

Lee, Roy S., 'The Rwanda Tribunal' (1996) 9 *Leiden JIL*, 37–61

Lefeber, René, *Transboundary Environmental Interference and the Origin of State Liability* (The Hague, 1996)

Lenaerts, Koen and DeSomer, Marlies, 'Towards a Hierarchy of Legal Acts in the European Union? Simplification of Legal Instruments and Procedures' (2005) 11 *European Law Journal*, 744–65

Lijnzaad, Liesbeth, *Reservations to UN-Human Rights Treaties: Ratify and Ruin?* (Dordrecht, 1995)

Limburg, Gerard, 'The United Nations Conference on the Law of Treaties between States and International Organizations or between International Organizations' (1986) 33 *Neth ILR*, 195–203

Lindell, Ulf, *Modern Multilateral Negotiation: The Consensus Rule and its Implications in International Conferences* (Lund, 1988)

Linklater, Andrew, *The Transformation of Political Community* (Cambridge, 1998)

Lobel, Jules, 'Benign Hegemony? Kosovo and Article 2(4) of the UN Charter' (2000) 1 *Chicago JIL*, 19–36

Lowe, Vaughan, 'Can the European Community Bind the Member States on Questions of Customary International Law?'. In Martti Koskenniemi (ed.), *International Law Aspects of the European Union*, 149–68

Lowe, A. V. and Fitzmaurice, Malgosia (eds.), *Fifty Years of the International Court of Justice* (Cambridge, 1996)

Luck, Edward C., *The Security Council: Practice and Promise* (London, 2006)

Maas Geesteranus, G. W., 'Recht en praktijk in het verdragenrecht'. In E. W. Vierdag and G. W. Maas Geesteranus, *Spanningen tussen recht en praktijk in het verdragenrecht* (Deventer, 1989), 91–122

MacCormick, Neil, *Legal Reasoning and Legal Theory* (Oxford, 1978)

MacGibbon, Iain, 'General Assembly Resolutions: Custom, Practice and Mistaken Identity'. In Bin Cheng (ed.), *International Law: Teaching and Practice* (London, 1982), 10–26

MacLeod, I., Hendry, I. D. and Hyett, Stephen, *The External Relations of the European Communities* (Oxford, 1996)

MacMillan, Margaret, *Paris 1919: Six Months that Changed the World* (New York, 2001)

Magliveras, Konstantinos D., *Exclusion from Participation in International Organisations: The Law and Practice behind Member States' Expulsion and Suspension of Membership* (The Hague, 1999)

Magliveras, Konstantinos and Naldi, Gino, *The African Union and the Predecessor Organization of African Unity* (The Hague, 2004)

Majid, Amir A., *Legal Status of International Institutions: SITA, INMARSAT and EURO-CONTROL Examined* (Aldershot, 1996)

Makarczyk, Jerzy, 'The International Court of Justice on the Implied Powers of International Organizations'. In Jerzy Makarczyk (ed.), *Essays in International Law in Honour of Judge Manfred Lachs* (The Hague, 1984), 501–19

  'Legal Basis for Suspension and Expulsion of a State from an International Organization' (1982) 25 *GYIL*, 476–89

Maluwa, Tiyanjana, 'International Law-making in the Organisation of African Unity: An Overview' (2000) 12 *African Journal of International and Comparative Law*, 201–25

Mangone, Gerard J., *A Short History of International Organizations* (New York, 1954)

Manin, Philippe, 'The European Communities and the Vienna Convention on the Law of Treaties between States and International Organizations or between International Organizations' (1987) 24 *CMLRev*, 457–81

Manusama, Kenneth, *The United Nations Security Council in the Post-Cold War Era: Applying the Principle of Legality* (Leiden, 2006)

Marchisio, Sergio and Di Blase, Antonietta, *The Food and Agriculture Organization* (Dordrecht, 1991)

Marks, Susan, *The Riddle of All Constitutions: International Law, Democracy, and the Critique of Ideology* (Oxford, 2000)

Marston, Geoffrey, 'The Origin of the Personality of International Organisations in United Kingdom Law' (1991) 40 *ICLQ*, 403–24

  'The Personality of International Organisations in English Law' (1997) 2 *Hofstra Law and Policy Symposium*, 75–115

May, Christopher, *The World Intellectual Property Organization: Resurgence and the Development Agenda* (New York, 2007)

May, Larry, *Sharing Responsibility* (Chicago, 1992)

McClanahan, Grant V., *Diplomatic Immunity: Principles, Practices, Problems* (London, 1989)

McGinnis, John O. and Movsesian, Mark L., 'The World Trade Constitution' (2000) 114 *Harvard Law Review*, 511–605

McGoldrick, Dominic, *The Human Rights Committee: Its Role in the Development of the International Covenant on Civil and Political Rights* (Oxford, 1991)

McKinnon Wood, H., 'The Dissolution of the League of Nations' (1946) 23 *BYIL*, 317–23

McNair, Lord A. D., *The Law of Treaties* (Oxford, 1961)

Mendelson, Maurice, 'Reservations to the Constitutions of International Organizations' (1971) 45 *BYIL*, 137–71

Mendelson, Maurice and Hulton, Susan, 'The Iraq–Kuwait Boundary: Legal Aspects' (1990) 23 *RBDI*, 293–332

Mensah, Thomas A., 'The International Tribunal for the Law of the Sea' (1998) 11 *Leiden JIL*, 527–46

Meron, Theodor, 'Article 46 of the Vienna Convention on the Law of Treaties (*Ultra Vires* Treaties): Some Recent Cases' (1978) 49 *BYIL*, 175–99

Merrills, J. G., *The Development of International Law by the European Court of Human Rights* (2nd edn, Manchester, 1993)

International Dispute Settlement (2nd edn, Cambridge, 1991)

Miller, Anthony J., 'Privileges and Immunities of UN Officials' (2007) 4 *IOLR*, 169–257

'United Nations Experts on Mission and their Privileges and Immunities' (2007b) 4 *IOLR*, 11–56

Mills, Susan R., 'The Financing of UN Peacekeeping Operations: The Need for a Sound Financial Basis'. In Indar Jit Rikhye and Kjell Skjelsbaek (eds.), *The United Nations and Peacekeeping: Results, Limitations and Prospects* (Houndmills, 1990)

Monaco, Riccardo, 'Le caractère constitutionnel des actes institutifs d'organisations internationales'. In Suzanne Bastid *et al.* (eds.), *Mélanges offerts à Charles Rousseau* (Paris, 1974), 153–72

Monar, Jörg, 'Interinstitutional Agreements: The Phenomenon and its New Dynamics after Maastricht' (1994) 31 *CMLRev*, 693–719

Moravcsik, Andrew, 'The Origins of Human Rights Regimes: Democratic Delegation in Postwar Europe' (2000) 54 *International Organization*, 217–52

Morgenstern, Felice, 'Legality in International Organizations' (1976–7) 48 *BYIL*, 241–57

Legal Problems of International Organizations (Cambridge, 1986)

Morgenthau, Hans J., *Politics Among Nations: The Struggle for Power and Peace* (2nd edn, New York, 1955)

Morse, David A., *The Origin and Evolution of the ILO and Its Role in the World Community* (Ithaca, NY, 1969)

Muller, A. S., *International Organizations and their Host States* (The Hague, 1995)

'International Organizations and their Officials: To Tax or Not to Tax?' (1993) 6 *Leiden JIL*, 47–72

'Setting up the International Criminal Court' (2004) 1 *IOLR*, 189–96

Murphy, Robert, *Diplomat among Warriors* (London, 1964)

Mus, Jan, *Verdragsconflicten voor de Nederlandse rechter* (Zwolle, 1996)

Myers, Denys P., 'Liquidation of League of Nations Functions' (1948) 42 *AJIL*, 320–54

Myjer, Eric (ed.), *Issues of Arms Control Law and the Chemical Weapons Convention* (The Hague, 2001)

Nardin, Terry, *Law, Morality, and the Relations of States* (Princeton, 1983)

Nascimento e Silva, G. E. do, 'The 1986 Vienna Convention and the Treaty-making Power of International Organizations' (1986) 29 *GYIL*, 68–85

'Privileges and Immunities of Permanent Missions to International Organizations' (1978) 21 *GYIL*, 9–26

Nelson, Richard W., 'International Law and US Withholding of Payments to International Organizations' (1986) 80 *AJIL*, 973–83

Nicholas, H. G., *The United Nations as a Political Institution* (3rd edn, Oxford, 1967)

Nicolson, Harold, *Comments 1944–1948* (London, 1948)

Nussbaum, Arthur, *A Concise History of the Law of Nations* (rev. edn, New York, 1954)

Oakeshott, Michael, *Rationalism in Politics and Other Essays* (London, 1962)

Obradovic, Daniela, 'Repatriation of Powers in the European Community' (1997) 34 *CMLRev*, 59–88

Oeter, Stefan, 'German Unification and State Succession' (1991) 51 *ZaöRV*, 349–83

Offe, Claus, *Modernity and the State* (Cambridge, 1996)

Okeke, C. N., *Controversial Subjects of Contemporary International Law* (Rotterdam, 1974)

O'Neill, Onora, *Towards Justice and Virtue: A Constructive Account of Practical Reasoning* (Cambridge, 1996)

Onuf, Nicholas G., *World of Our Making* (Columbia SC, 1989)

Ooik, Ronald H. van, *De keuze der rechtsgrondslag voor besluiten van de Europese Unie* (Deventer, 1999)

Oparil, Richard J., 'Immunity of International Organizations in United States Courts: Absolute or Restrictive?' (1991) 24 *Vanderbilt JTL*, 689–710

Orford, Anne, *Reading Humanitarian Intervention* (Cambridge, 2003)

Orozco, Claudia, 'The WTO Solution: The Advisory Centre on WTO Law' (2001) 4 *Journal of World Intellectual Property*, 245–9

Orwell, George, *Collected Essays, Journalism and Letters, Volume I: An Age Like This 1920–1940* (1968; Harmondsworth, 1970)

    The Collected Essays, Journalism and Letters of George Orwell. Volume 4: In Front of your Nose 1945–1950 (1968; Harmondsworth, 1970)

Osieke, Ebere, *Constitutional Law and Practice in the International Labour Organisation* (Dordrecht, 1985)

    'The Legal Validity of Ultra Vires Decisions of International Organizations' (1983) 77 *AJIL*, 239–56

    'Ultra Vires Acts in International Organizations – The Experience of the International Labour Organization' (1976–7) 48 *BYIL*, 259–80

Österdahl, Inger, 'The EU and its Member States, Other States, and International Organizations – The Common European Security and Defence Policy after Nice' (2001) 70 *Nordic JIL*, 341–72

Owada, Hisashi, 'Japan's Constitutional Power to Participate in Peace-keeping' (1997) 27 *New York University Journal of International Law and Politics*, 271–84

Paasivirta, Esa, 'The European Union: From an Aggregate of States to a Legal Person?' (1997) 2 *Hofstra Law & Policy Symposium*, 37–59

Pallis, Mark, 'The Operation of UNHCR's Accountability Mechanisms' (2005) 37 *New York University Journal of International Law and Politics*, 869–918

Pauwelyn, Joost, *Conflict of Norms in Public International Law* (Cambridge, 2003)

    'Pay Up and Play the Game', *The Economist* (18 September 1999), 18

Pérez de Cuellar, Javier, 'The Role of the UN Secretary-General'. In Adam Roberts and Benedict Kingsbury (eds.), *United Nations, Divided World* (2nd edn, Oxford, 1993), 125–42

Pescatore, Pierre, 'The GATT Dispute Settlement Mechanism: Its Present Situation and its Prospects' (1993/2) 27 *JWT*, 5–20

Peters, Anne, 'Compensatory Constitutionalism: The Function and Potential of International Norms and Structures' (2006) 19 *Leiden JIL*, 579–610

Petersmann, Ernst-Ulrich, 'How to Constitutionalize International Law and Foreign Policy for the Benefit of Civil Society.' (1998) 20 *Michigan JIL*, 1–30

'How to Reform the UN System? Constitutionalism, International Law, and International Organizations' (1997) 10 *Leiden JIL*, 421–74

'The WTO Constitution and Human Rights' (2000) 3 *Journal of International Economic Law*, 19–25

Philpott, Daniel, 'Sovereignty: An Introduction and Brief History' (1995) 48 *Journal of International Affairs*, 353–68

Pliakos, Astéris, 'La nature juridique de l'Union européenne' (1993) 29 *RTDE*, 187–224

Poiares Maduro, Miguel, *We the Court: The European Court of Justice and the European Economic Constitution* (Oxford, 1998)

Politakis, G. P., 'Enforcing International Humanitarian Law: The Decision of the Appeals Chamber of the War Crimes Tribunal in the Dusko Tadic Case (Jurisdiction)' (1997) 52 *ZöR*, 283–329

Pollock, Sir Frederick, *League of Nations* (2nd edn, London, 1922)

Potter, Pitman B., 'Origin of the Term International Organization' (1945) 39 *AJIL*, 803–6

Power, Michael, The Audit Society: Rituals of Verification (Oxford, 1997)

Rajagopal, Balakrishnan, 'From Resistance to Renewal: The Third World, Social Movements, and the Expansion of International Institutions' (2000) 41 *Harvard ILJ*, 529–78

Rapisardi-Mirabelli, A., 'Théorie générate des unions internationales' (1925/II) 7 *RdC*, 345–93

Ratner, Steven R., *The New UN Peacekeeping: Building Peace in Lands of Conflict after the Cold War* (New York, 1995)

Reinisch, August, 'Accountability of International Organizations According to National Courts' (2005) 36 *NYIL*, 119–67

International Organizations before National Courts (Cambridge, 2000)

Reinisch, August and Weber, Ulf Andreas, 'In the Shadow of Waite and Kennedy' (2004) 1 *IOLR*, 59–110

Reisman, W. Michael, 'An International Farce: The Sad Case of the PLO Mission' (1989) 14 *Yale JIL*, 412–32

Reuter, Paul, *Institutions internationales* (Paris, 1967)

Reuterswärd, Reinhold, 'The Legal Nature of International Organizations' (1980) 49 *Nordisk TIR*, 14–30

Ribbelink, O. M., *Opvolging van internationale organisaties* (The Hague, 1988)

Righter, Rosemary, *Utopia Lost: The United Nations and World Order* (New York, 1995)

Rigo Sureda, Andres, 'The Law Applicable to the Activities of International Development Banks' (2004) 308 *RdC*, 9–252

Riles, Annelise, *The Network Inside Out* (Ann Arbor, 2000)

Ringmar, Erik, 'Re-imagining Sweden: The Rhetorical Battle over EU Membership' (1998) 23 *Scandinavian Journal of History*, 45–63

Rittich, Kerry, *Recharacterizing Restructuring: Law, Distribution and Gender in Market Reform* (The Hague, 2002)

Rochester, J. Martin, 'The Rise and Fall of International Organization as a Field of Study' (1986) 40 *International Organization*, 777–813

Roessler, Frieder, 'The Agreement Establishing the World Trade Organization'. In Jacques H. J. Bourgeois *et al.* (eds.), *The Uruguay Round Results: A European Lawyers' Perspective* (Brussels, 1995), 67–85

Roht-Arriaza, Naomi, 'Compliance with Private Voluntary Standards: The Example of the International Organization for Standardization's ISO 14000 Environmental Management and Related Standards'. In Edith Brown Weiss (ed.), *International Compliance with Nonbinding Accords* (Washington, 1997), 205–18

Roosevelt, Eleanor, *The Autobiography of Eleanor Roosevelt* (Boston, 1984)

Rorty, Richard, *Philosophy and Social Hope* (London, 1999)

Rosand, Eric, 'The Security Council as "Global Legislator": Ultra Vires or Ultra Innovative?' (2004–5) 28 *Fordham International Law Journal*, 542–90

Rosenne, Shabtai, *Developments in the Law of Treaties 1945–1986* (Cambridge, 1989)
'United Nations Treaty Practice' (1954/II) 86 *RdC*, 281–443

Rouyer-Hameray, Bernard, *Les compétences implicites des organisations internationales* (Paris, 1962)

Rubenfeld, Jed, 'Unilateralism and Constitutionalism' (2004) 79 *New York University Law Review*, 1971–2028

Ruggie, John Gerard, *Constructing the World Polity* (London, 1998)

Sack, Jörn, 'The European Community's Membership of International Organizations' (1995) 32 *CMLRev*, 1227–56

Sadurska, Romana and Chinkin, Christine M., 'The Collapse of the International Tin Council: A Case of State Responsibility?' (1990) 30 *VaJIL*, 845–90

Sands, Philippe, 'The Tin Council Litigation in the English Courts' (1987) 34 *Neth ILR*, 367–91

Sands, Philippe and Klein, Pierre, *Bowett's Law of International Institutions* (5th edn, London, 2001)

Sapiro, Miriam, 'Changing the CSCE into the OSCE: Legal Aspects of a Political Transformation' (1995) 89 *AJIL*, 631–7

Sarooshi, Danesh, *International Organizations and their Exercise of Sovereign Powers* (Oxford, 2005)
'The Legal Framework Governing United Nations Subsidiary Organs' (1996) 67 *BYIL*, 413–78
The United Nations and the Development of Collective Security: The Delegation by the UN Security Council of its Chapter VII Powers (Oxford, 1999)

Sato, Tetsuo, *Evolving Constitutions of International Organizations* (The Hague, 1996)

Schachter, Oscar, 'Alf Ross Memorial Lecture: The Crisis of Legitimation in the United Nations' (1981) 50 *Nordisk TIR*, 3–19
'The Invisible College of International Lawyers' (1977) 72 *Northwestern University Law Review*, 217–26

Scharf, Michael P., 'Dead Beat Dead End: A Critique of the New US Plan for Payment of UN Arrears' (2000) 6 *New England International and Comparative Law Annual*, 1–4
'Musical Chairs: The Dissolution of States and Membership in the United Nations' (1995) 28 *Cornell ILJ*, 29–69
'*The Prosecutor v. Slavko Dokmanovic:* Irregular Rendition and the ICTY' (1998) 11 *Leiden JIL*, 369–82

Scharf, Michael P. and Dorosin, Joshua L., 'Interpreting UN Sanctions: The Rulings and Role of the Yugoslavia Sanctions Committee' (1993) 19 *Brooklyn JIL*, 771–827

Scharf, Michael P. and Shaw, Tamara A., 'International Institutions' (1999) 33 *International Lawyer*, 567–86

Scharpf, Fritz W., 'The Joint-decision Trap: Lessons from German Federalism and European Integration' (1988) 66 *Public Administration*, 239–78
'The Joint-decision Trap Revisited' (2006) 44 *JCMS*, 845–64

Schauer, Frederick, *Playing by the Rules: A Philosophical Examination of Rule-based Decision-making in Law and in Life* (Oxford, 1991)

Schechter, Michael G., 'Leadership in International Organizations: Systemic, Organizational and Personality Factors' (1987) 13 *Review of International Studies*, 197–220

Schermers, H. G., *De gespecialiseerde organisaties: Hun bouw en inrichting* (Leiden, 1957)
Inleiding tot het internationale institutionele recht (2nd edn, Deventer, 1985)
'International Organizations and the Law of Treaties' (1999) 42 *GYIL*, 56–65

Schermers, Henry G. and Blokker, Niels M., *International Institutional Law* (4th edn, Leiden, 2003)

Schilling, Theodor, 'The Autonomy of the Community Legal Order: An Analysis of Possible Foundations' (1996) 37 *Harvard ILJ*, 389–409

Schlag, Pierre, 'Law as the Continuation of God by Other Means' (1997) 85 *California Law Review*, 427–40

Schlesinger, Stephen C., *Act of Creation: The Founding of the United Nations* (Boulder, CO, 2003)

Schmalenbach, Kirsten, *Die Haftung internationaler Organisationen* (Frankfurt am Main, 2004)

Schmidt, Susanne K., 'Only an Agenda Setter? The European Commission: Power over the Council of Ministers' (2000) 1 *European Union Politics*, 37–61

Schrijver, Nico, 'The Future of the Charter of the United Nations' (2006) 10 *Max Planck Yearbook of United Nations Law*, 1–34
'UNESCO's Role in the Development and Application of International Law: An Assessment'. In Abdulqawi A. Yusuf (ed.), *Standard-setting in UNESCO: Normative Action in Education, Science and Culture. Volume I* (Leiden, 2007), 365–84

Schulte Nordholt, Jan Willem, *Woodrow Wilson: Een leven voor de wereldvrede. Een biografie* (Amsterdam, 1990)

Schutte, Julian J. E., 'Legal and Practical Implications, from the Perspective of the Host Country, Relating to the Establishment of the International Tribunal for the Former Yugoslavia' (1994) 5 *Criminal Law Forum*, 423–50

Schwartz, Bryan and Leven, Elliot, 'International Organizations: What Makes Them Work?' (1992) 30 *Can YIL*, 165–94

Schwebel, Stephen M., *Justice in International Law* (Cambridge, 1994)

Searle, John R., *The Construction of Social Reality* (London, 1995)

Seidl-Hohenveldern, Ignaz, *Corporations in and under International Law* (Cambridge, 1987)
'Functional Immunity of International Organizations and Human Rights'. In Wolfgang Benedek *et al.* (eds.), *Development and Developing International and European Law: Essays in Honour of Konrad Ginther on the Occasion of his 65th Birthday* (Frankfurt am Main, 1999), 137–49
'International Economic "Soft Law" ' (1979/II) 163 *RdC*, 165–246
'Internationale Organisationen aufgrund von soft law'. In Ulrich Beyerlin *et al.* (eds.), *Recht zwischen Umbruch und Bewahrung: Festschrift für Rudolf Bernhardt* (Berlin, 1995), 229–39

'Piercing the Corporate Veil of International Organizations: The International Tin Council Case in the English Court of Appeals' (1989) 32 *GYIL*, 43–54

Seyersted, Finn, *Common Law of International Organizations* (Leiden, 2008)

  Objective International Personality of Intergovernmental Organizations: Do their Capacities Really Depend upon the Conventions Establishing Them? (Copenhagen, 1963)

  'Treaty-making Capacity of Intergovernmental Organizations: Article 6 of the International Law Commission's Draft Articles on the Law of Treaties between States and International Organizations or between International Organizations' (1983) 34 *ÖZöRV*, 261–7

Shanks, Cheryl, Jacobson, Harold K. and Kaplan, Jeffrey H., 'Inertia and Change in the Constellation of International Intergovernmental Organizations' (1996) 50 *International Organization*, 593–627

Shaw, Jo and More, Gillian (eds.), *New Legal Dynamics of the European Union* (Oxford, 1995)

Shihata, Ibrahim, *The European Bank for Reconstruction and Development* (London, 1990)

  'Human Rights, Development and International Financial Institutions' (1992) 8 *American University Journal of International Law and Policy*, 27–37

  'The Multilateral Investment Guarantee Agency (MIGA) and the Legal Treatment of Foreign Investment' (1987/III) 203 *RdC*, 95–320

Shraga, Daphna, 'The United Nations as an Actor Bound by International Humanitarian Law' (1998) 5 *International Peacekeeping*, 64–81

Shraga, Daphna and Zacklin, Ralph, 'The International Criminal Tribunal for the Former Yugoslavia' (1994) 5 *EJIL*, 360–80

Siedentop, Larry, *Democracy in Europe* (London, 2000)

Siekmann, Robert C. R., *National Contingents in United Nations Peace-keeping Forces* (Dordrecht, 1991)

Simma, Bruno and Alston, Philip, 'The Sources of Human Rights Law: Custom, Jus Cogens, and General Principles' (1992) 12 *Australian YIL*, 82–108

Simmonds, Kenneth R., 'The Community's Declaration upon Signature of the UN Convention on the Law of the Sea' (1986) 23 *CMLRev*, 521–44

Simpson, Gerry, *Great Powers and Outlaw States: Unequal Sovereigns in the International Legal Order* (Cambridge, 2004)

  'Two Liberalisms' (2001) 12 *EJIL*, 537–71

Singer, J. David, *Financing International Organization: The United Nations Budget Process* (The Hague, 1961)

Singer, Michael, 'Jurisdictional Immunity of International Organizations: Human Rights and Functional Necessity Concerns' (1995) 36 *VaJIL*, 53–165

Singh, Nagendra, *Termination of Membership of International Organisations* (London, 1958)

Skogly, Sigrun, *The Human Rights Obligations of the World Bank and the International Monetary Fund* (London, 2003)

Skubiszewski, Krzysztof, 'Implied Powers of International Organizations'. In Yoram Dinstein (ed.), *International Law at a Time of Perplexity: Essays in Honour of Shabtai Rosenne* (Dordrecht, 1989), 855–68

  'Recommendations of the United Nations and Municipal Courts' (1972–3) 46 *BYIL*, 353–64

Slaughter (Burley), Anne-Marie, 'International Law and International Relations: A Dual Agenda' (1993) 87 *AJIL*, 205–39

A New World Order (Princeton, 2004)

'The Real New World Order' (1997) 76 *Foreign Affairs*, 183–97

Sloan, Blaine, 'General Assembly Resolutions Revisited (Forty Years Later)' (1987) 58 *BYIL*, 39–150

Sluiter, Göran, 'To Cooperate or Not to Cooperate? The Case of the Failed Transfer of Ntakirutimana to the Rwanda Tribunal' (1998) 11 *Leiden JIL*, 383–95

Smouts, Marie-Claude, 'United Nations Reform: A Strategy of Avoidance'. In Michael G. Schechter (ed.), *Innovation in Multilateralism* (Tokyo, 2000), 29–41

Snyder, Francis, 'The Effectiveness of European Community Law: Institutions, Processes, Tools and Techniques' (1993) 56 *Modern Law Review*, 19–54

Sohn, Louis B. (ed.), *International Organisation and Integration: Student Edition* (Dordrecht, 1986)

Spruyt, Hendrik, *The Sovereign State and its Competitors* (Princeton, 1994)

Stein, Eric, 'Lawyers, Judges, and the Making of a Transnational Constitution' (1981) 75 *AJIL*, 1–27

Steiner, George, *Errata: An Examined Life* (London, 1997)

Steyger, Elies, *Europe and its Members: A Constitutional Approach* (Aldershot, 1995)

Stiglitz, Joseph, *Globalization and its Discontents* (London, 2002)

Stoessinger, John G., and associates, *Financing the United Nations System* (Washington, 1964)

Strang, Lord, *The Diplomatic Career* (London, 1962)

Strohl, Pierre, 'Les aspects internationaux de la liquidation de la société Eurochemic' (1990) 36 *AFDI*, 727–38

Suy, Eric, 'The Constitutional Character of Constituent Treaties of International Organizations and the Hierarchy of Norms'. In Ulrich Beyerlin *et al.* (eds.), *Recht zwischen Umbruch und Bewahrung: Festschrift für Rudolf Bernhardt* (Berlin, 1995), 267–77

'The Status of Observers in International Organizations' (1978/II) 160 *RdC*, 75–179

Sybesma-Knol, R. G., 'The New Law of Treaties: The Codification of the Law of Treaties Concluded between States and International Organizations or between Two or More International Organizations' (1985) 15 *Georgia Journal of International and Comparative Law*, 425–52

The Status of Observers in the United Nations (Brussels, 1981)

Szasz, Paul C., 'Adjudicating Staff Challenges to Legislative Decisions of International Organizations'. In Gerhard Hafner *et al.* (eds.), *Liber Amicorum Professor Ignaz Seidl-Hohenveldern in Honour of his 80th Birthday* (The Hague, 1998), 699–720

'General Law-making Processes'. In Christopher C. Joyner (ed.), *The United Nations and International Law* (Cambridge, 1997)

'Granting International Organizations *Ius Standi* in the International Court of Justice'. In A. S. Muller *et al.* (eds.), *The International Court of Justice: Its Future Role after Fifty Years* (The Hague, 1997), 169–88

'The Role of the UN Secretary-General: Some Legal Aspects' (1991) 24 *New York University Journal of International Law and Politics*, 161–98

'The Security Council Starts Legislating' (2002) 96 *AJIL*, 901–5

Takamaa, Kari T., 'Aspects of Procedure and Jurisprudence of the Asian Development Bank Administrative Tribunal 1991–1996' (1997) 8 *FYIL*, 70–137

Tallgren, Immi, 'Completing the "International Criminal Order": The Rhetoric of International Repression and the Notion of Complementarity in the Draft Statute for an International Criminal Court' (1998) 67 *Nordic JIL*, 107–37

Tammes, A. J. P., 'Decisions of International Organs as a Source of International Law' (1958/II) 94 *RdC*, 265–363

Hoofdstukken van internationale organisatie (The Hague, 1951)

Tasioulas, John, 'In Defence of Relative Normativity: Communitarian Values and the *Nicaragua* Case' (1996) 16 *Oxford Journal of Legal Studies*, 85–128

Taylor, Paul, 'The United Nations System under Stress: Financial Pressures and their Consequences' (1991) 17 *Review of International Studies*, 365–82

Teasdale, Anthony L., 'The Life and Death of the Luxembourg Compromise' (1993) 31 *JCMS*, 567–79

Temple Lang, John, 'Community Constitutional Law: Article 5 EEC Treaty' (1990) 27 *CMLRev*, 645–81

'The Ozone Layer Convention: A New Solution to the Question of Community Participation in "Mixed" International Agreements' (1986) 23 *CMLRev*, 157–76

Terry, Larry D., *Leadership of Public Bureaucracies: The Administrator as Conservator*, 2nd edn (Armonk, NY, 2003)

Tesón, Fernando, *A Philosophy of International Law* (Boulder, CO, 1999)

Teubner, Gunther, *Law as an Autopoietic System* (Oxford, 1993, trans. Adler and Bankowska)

Thirlway, H. W. A., 'The Law and Procedure of the International Court of Justice 1960–1989, Part 8' (1996) 67 *BYIL*, 1–73

Tiilikainen, Teija, 'To Be or Not to Be? An Analysis of the Legal and Political Elements of Statehood in the EU's External Identity' (2001) 6 *European Foreign Affairs Review*, 223–41

Tomuschat, Christian, 'Article 19'. In Bruno Simma (ed.), *The United Nations: A Commentary* (Oxford, 1994), 327–39

'Obligations Arising for States Without or Against their Will' (1993/IV) 241 *RdC*, 195–374

Toth, A. G., 'The Legal Status of the Declarations Annexed to the Single European Act' (1986) 23 *CMLRev*, 803–12

Toulmin, Stephen, *Cosmopolis: The Hidden Agenda of Modernity* (Chicago, 1990)

Trachtman, Joel P., 'Bananas, Direct Effect and Compliance' (1999) 10 *EJIL*, 655–78

Traub, James, *The Best Intentions: Kofi Annan and the UN in the Era of American World Power* (London, 2006)

Tunkin, Grigory I., 'The Legal Nature of the United Nations' (1966/II) 119 *RdC*, 1–67

Tuytschaever, Filip, *Differentiation in European Union Law* (Oxford, 2006)

Unger, Roberto Mangabeira, *The Critical Legal Studies Movement* (Cambridge, MA, 1986)

Law and Modern Society: Toward a Criticism of Social Theory (New York, 1976)

Urquhart, Brian, *A Life in Peace and War* (New York, 1987)

Uruena, René, 'The Underlying Question: The World Trade Organization and its Powers to Adopt a Competition Policy' (2006) 3 *IOLR*, 55–91

Vanhamme, Jan, *Volkenrechtelijke beginselen in het Europees recht* (Groningen, 2001)

Vattel, Emmerich de, *The Law of Nations* (1758; New York, n.d., trans. Chitty)

Verwey, Delano, *The European Community, the European Union and the International Law of Treaties* (The Hague, 2004)

Verzijl, J. H. W., *International Law in Historical Perspective. Part II: International Persons* (Leiden, 1969)

Vierdag, E. W., 'The ICJ and the Law of Treaties'. In A. V. Lowe and Malgosia Fitzmaurice (eds.), *Fifty Years of the International Court of Justice* (Cambridge, 1996), 145–66

    'Some Remarks on the Relationship between the 1969 and the 1986 Vienna Conventions on the Law of Treaties' (1987) 25 *Archiv des Völkerrechts*, 82–91

Vignes, Daniel, 'La participation aux organisations internationales'. In René-Jean Dupuy (ed.), *Manuel sur les organisations internationales* (2nd edn, The Hague, 1998), 61–87

Virally, Michel, 'La notion de fonction dans la theorie de l'organisation internationale'. In Suzanne Bastid *et al.*, *Mélanges offerts à Charles Rousseau: La communauté internationale* (Paris, 1974), 277–300

    L'organisation mondiale (Paris, 1972)

Vos, Ellen, 'EU Committees: The Evolution of Unforeseen Institutional Actors in European Product Regulation'. In Christian Joerges and Ellen Vos (eds.), *EU Committees: Social Regulation, Law and Politics* (Oxford, 1999), 19–47

Vree, J. K. de, *Political Integration: The Formation of Theory and its Problems* (The Hague, 1972)

Waltemathe, Arved, *Austritt aus der EU: Sind die Mitgliedstaaten noch souverän?* (Frankfurt am Main, 2000)

Waltz, Kenneth N., *Man, the State, and War* (New York, 1959)

Walzer, Michael, *Just and Unjust Wars* (3rd edn, New York, 2000)

Ward, Ian, *The Margins of European Law* (London, 1996)

Watson, Geoffrey R., 'Constitutionalism, Judicial Review, and the World Court' (1993) 34 *Harvard ILJ*, 1–45

Weatherill, Stephen, 'Beyond Preemption? Shared Competence and Institutional Change in the European Community'. In David O'Keeffe and Patrick Twomey (eds.), *Legal Issues of the Maastricht Treaty* (London, 1994), 13–33

Weil, Prosper, 'Towards Relative Normativity in International Law?' (1983) 77 *AJIL*, 413–42

Weiler, Joseph H. H., 'Alternatives to Withdrawal from an International Organization: The Case of the European Economic Community' (1985) 20 *Israel Law Review*, 282–98

    'The Community System: The Dual Character of Supranationalism' (1981) 1 *YEL*, 267–306

    The Constitution of Europe (Cambridge, 1999)

Weiler, Joseph H. H. and Haltern, Ulrich R., 'The Autonomy of the Community Legal Order – Through the Looking Glass' (1996) 37 *Harvard ILJ*, 411–48

Weiler, Joseph H. H., Slaughter, Anne-Marie and Stone Sweet, Alec, 'Prologue – The European Courts of Justice'. In Anne-Marie Slaughter, Alec Stone Sweet and Joseph H. H. Weiler (eds.), *The European Courts and National Courts: Doctrine and Jurisprudence* (Oxford, 1998), v–xiv

Weiler, Joseph H. H. and Wind, Marlene (eds.), *European Constitutionalism Beyond the State* (Cambridge, 2003)

Weiszäcker, Richard von, 'All Depends on Member States'. In Georges Abi-Saab *et al.*, *Paix, développement, démocratie. Boutros Boutros-Ghali Amicorum Discipulorumque Liber* (Brussels, 1999), 827–37

Wellens, Karel C., *Remedies against International Organisations* (Cambridge, 2002)

Wellens, K. C. and Borchardt, G. M., 'Soft Law in European Community Law' (1989) 14 *ELR*, 267–321

Wendt, Alexander, *Social Theory of International Politics* (Cambridge, 1999)

Wendt, Frantz, *The Nordic Council and Co-operation in Scandinavia* (Copenhagen, 1959)

Went, A. E. J., *Seventy Years Agrowing: A History of the International Council for the Exploration of the Sea 1902–1972* (Copenhagen, 1972)

Wessel, Ramses A., 'The EU as Black Widow: Devouring the WEU to Give Birth to a European Security and Defence Policy'. In Vincent Kronenberger (ed.), *The EU and the International Legal Order: Discord or Harmony?* (The Hague, 2001), 405–34

  'The International Legal Status of the European Union' (1997) 2 *European Foreign Affairs Review*, 109–29

Wet, Erika de, 'The International Constitutional Order' (2006) 55 *ICLQ*, 51–76

Wet, Erika de and Nollkaemper, André (eds.), *Review of the Security Council by Member States* (Antwerp, 2003)

Wheen, Francis, *Karl Marx* (London, 1999)

White, Alan R., *Grounds of Liability* (Oxford, 1985)

White, Nigel D., *The Law of International Organisations* (Manchester, 1996)

  'The UN Charter and Peacekeeping Forces: Constitutional Issues' (1996) 3 *International Peacekeeping*, 43–63

Wickremasinghe, Chanaka and Verdirame, Guglielmo, 'Responsibility and Liability for Violations of Human Rights in the Course of UN Field Operations'. In Craig Scott (ed.), *Torture as Tort* (Oxford, 2001), 465–89

Wight, Martin, 'Why is There No International Theory?'. In Herbert Butterfield and Martin Wight (eds.), *Diplomatic Investigations: Essays in the Theory of International Politics* (London, 1966), 17–34

Williams, Paul R., 'State Succession and the International Financial Institutions: Political Criteria v. Protection of Outstanding Financial Obligations' (1994) 43 *ICLQ*, 776–808

Wincott, Daniel, 'Political Theory, Law and European Union'. In Jo Shaw and Gillian More (eds.), *New Legal Dynamics of European Union* (Oxford, 1995), 293–311

Winter, J. A., 'Direct Applicability and Direct Effect: Two Distinct and Different Concepts in Community Law' (1972) 9 *CMLRev*, 425–38

Witte, Bruno de, 'Sovereignty and European Integration: The Weight of Tradition'. In Anne-Marie Slaughter *et al.* (eds.), *The European Court and National Courts: Doctrine and Jurisprudence* (Oxford, 1998), 277–304

Wittich, Stephan, 'Permissible Derogation from Mandatory Rules? The Problem of Party Status in the Genocide Case' (2007) 18 *EJIL*, 591–618

Wood, Michael C., 'Security Council Working Methods and Procedure: Recent Developments' (1996) 45 *ICLQ*, 150–61

Woods, Ngaire, *The Globalizers: The IMF, the World Bank, and their Borrowers* (Ithaca, NY, 2006)

Wouters, Jan, Hoffmeister, Frank and Ruys, Tom (eds.), *The United Nations and the European Union: An Ever Stronger Partnership* (The Hague, 2006)

Wyatt, Derrick and Dashwood, Alan, *The Substantive Law of the EEC* (3rd edn, London, 1993)

Yee, Sienho, 'The Time Limit for the Ratification of Proposed Amendments to the Constitutions of International Organizations' (2000) 4 *Max Planck Yearbook of United Nations Law*, 185–213

Yemin, Edward, *Legislative Powers in the United Nations and Specialized Agencies* (Leiden, 1969)

Young-Bruehl, Elisabeth, *Hannah Arendt: For Love of the World* (New Haven, 1982)

Zacklin, Ralph, *The Amendment of the Constitutive Instruments of the United Nations and Specialized Agencies* (Leyden, 1968)

    'The Role of the International Lawyer in an International Organisation'. In Chanaka Wickremasinghe (ed.), *The International Lawyer as Practitioner* (London, 2000), 57–68

Zemanek, Karl, *Das Vertragsrecht der internationalen Organisationen* (Vienna, 1957)

    'The United Nations Conference on the Law of Treaties Between States and International Organizations or Between International Organizations: The Unrecorded History of its "General Agreement"'. In Karl-Heinz Böckstiegel *et al.* (eds.), *Völkerrecht, Recht der internationalen Organisationen, Weltwirtschaftsrecht: Festschrift für Ignaz Seidl-Hohenveldern* (Cologne, 1988), 665–79

    (ed.), *Agreements of International Organizations and the Vienna Convention on the Law of Treaties* (Vienna, 1971)

Zilioli, Chiara and Selmayr, Martin, 'The External Relations of the Euro Area: Legal Aspects' (1999) 36 *CMLRev*, 273–349

Zoller, Elisabeth, 'The "Corporate Will" of the United Nations and the Rights of the Minority' (1987) 81 *AJIL*, 610–34

Index